GUIDE TO
MILITARY INSTALLATIONS

GUIDE TO MILITARY INSTALLATIONS

4th Edition

Dan Cragg

STACKPOLE
BOOKS

Published by
STACKPOLE BOOKS
5067 Ritter Road
Mechanicsburg, PA 17055

Cover design by Mark B. Olszewski

Printed in the United States of America

Fourth Edition

10 9 8 7 6 5 4 3 2 1

This guide was compiled from classified materials, most of which were obtained directly from the installations. The author and the publisher strive to make this guide as complete as possible; any installations not included here either have very small military populations or chose not to participate.

Library of Congress Cataloging-in-Publication Data

Cragg, Dan.
    Guide to military installations / Dan Cragg.—4th ed.
        p.   cm.
    Includes index.
    ISBN 0-8117-3023-9
    1. United States—Armed Forces—Facilities—Directories.
    I. Title.
    UC403.C7   1994
    355.7'023'73—dc20
                                             94-15253
                                                 CIP

To Sun and Tam,
faithful companions
in life's grand sojourn

Bell tower of the U.S. Cavalry Museum of Fort Riley, Kansas. (U.S. Army photo)

CONTENTS

COLORADO   73

MICHIGAN   181

MISSISSIPPI   184

MISSOURI   191

MONTANA   194

NEBRASKA   196

WASHINGTON — 307

WISCONSIN — 316

WYOMING — 318

PART TWO
OVERSEAS INSTALLATIONS

PART THREE
MAPS

PREFACE

Welcome to the fourth edition of *Guide to Military Installations*.

The furious round of base closings and force realignments both at home and overseas that was under way when we sent the third edition of the *Guide* to press in the fall of 1990 has continued well into 1993. Since January 1990, 160,000 troops stationed abroad, most of them in Germany, had been brought home. Further cuts were announced by the Department of Defense in 1993 that would reduce that number even further, to 65,000 personnel in Europe by 30 September 1996. As of July 1993, 840 overseas installations worldwide, 773 of them in Europe, had been identified for closing, reduction of operations, or reversion to standby status. These 840 installations represented 50 percent of the U.S. facilities that were active in 1990. Some of these sites were so small that they were never included in this *Guide*, but among them were some very old friends.

The jury is still out on some of the domestic installations designated for closing by the various commissions. Because of the potentially disastrous effect the recommended closures could have on local economies, Congress is looking very closely at those recommendations, and it is expected that some will be reversed or modified.

This edition reflects the actual base closures that had been effected by the fall of 1993. Where the ax remains poised, this fact has been duly noted, but the respective entries have been updated nevertheless.

• • •

Some installations, once backwater outposts, have actually benefited from the closings, picking up new units and missions and new life, and we are pleased to include them this time around. Also, we proudly welcome the Coast Guard to this fourth edition. Finally, all entries reflect the most up-to-date information available on the many changes that have occurred since the last editon in the deployment of our military forces worldwide.

• • •

The *Guide* is divided into two general sections, domestic and overseas, with a third section consisting of maps showing the location of each installation by service, both domestic and foreign. The respective states and countries are arranged alphabetically, and within these are the installations, arranged alphabetically by military service. At the end of each entry is the address of the official to contact for more information, and the domestic entries also offer a commercial telephone number.

Each entry contains information regarding the installation's history and mission; facts on housing, schools, personal and recreational services available there; and something about the local area. As with the previous editions, we have excluded details on topics such as transportation of household goods and automobiles, travel pay and allowances, and so on. Those who need such information should contact the appropriate service representatives.

While designed primarily for the use of active-duty and retired military personnel, Department of Defense civilian employees, and their families, the *Guide* is also intended to serve as a valuable tool for anyone who travels. Most military installations in the United States are to some degree open to the public, and a side trip to a military post or base can prove a worthwhile diversion for John and Jane Public on their annual family vacation. Besides, all these installations belong to the American taxpayers, and where security restrictions do not apply, they should feel free to stop by and see how their money is being spent.

Active-duty personnel are authorized access to morale and personal support services at any Department of Defense installation anywhere in the world. Retired military personnel are *generally* authorized the same access in the United States, depending on availability; overseas the rules may be different, so travelers should check with the overseas commands they will be visiting. Members of the general public visiting any military installation should always check with the security personnel at the main gate before proceeding onto the grounds.

• • •

To the many public affairs officers who made this *Guide* a reality, I offer my humble thanks. You may have considered responding to our importunate letters just another onerous detail that comes with the job, but to us at Harrisburg and Springfield, we could not have done this work without you. Indeed, some of you went far out of your way to help us; should we ever meet (hopefully not all at the same time!), the first drinks are on me.

I owe a special debt of thanks to those readers who were kind enough to take the time to write me with their criticisms and suggestions. Foremost among them must be Freeman R. Smith, CWO-4, USAF (Retired), of Carmichael, California. At age seventy-four, Mr. Smith is still "plugging away" at his IBM-clone computer, "humming 'til the wee hours." Others are Mari Clark of Alameda, California; Howard R. Downey, director of the City of Provo, Utah, library; and John D. Voss of Los Gatos, California. When I write that some place is north of another when actually it's *south* of there, you're the folks who'll let me know about it.

Finally, to those wild and wonderful people at Stackpole Books, especially Ann Wagoner, my editor: You have the patience of Job and the wisdom of Solomon, and your reward will be a large bowl of sausage soup.

PART ONE

United States Installations

ALABAMA

Air Force

MAXWELL AIR FORCE BASE

Education is their business at Maxwell Air Force Base, home of the Air University, the Air Force's largest complex of professional schools, including the Air War College, the Air Command and Staff College, the Squadron Officer School, and the Air Force Senior NCO Academy. In addition to its educational functions, Maxwell also has jurisdiction over Gunter Annex just across town, home for the Air Force Standard Systems Center.

History. First established in 1918 as Wright Field (because in 1910 Orville Wright chose the site to establish a flying school), the installation was renamed in 1922 to honor 2nd Lt. William C. Maxwell, a native of Atmore, Alabama. Maxwell was killed in an air crash in the Philippines. The Air University was established at Maxwell AFB in 1946, and today it provides educational services for more than 500,000 airmen annually.

Housing and Schools. More than 1,600 sets of family quarters are available between Maxwell and Gunter. Temporary housing is available to families moving in with permanent-change-of-station orders.

Maxwell operates an elementary school (kindergarten through sixth grade) on base, while older children are bused to Montgomery schools. Both Maxwell and Gunter operate child-care centers. Associate, bachelor's, and graduate degrees in eighteen majors are offered on base through Troy State University in Montgomery, and Auburn University offers three doctoral degree programs at Maxwell.

Personal Services. Medical care is provided by a four-floor, intermediate-sized referral facility at the USAF Regional Hospital, Maxwell. An excellent commissary and base exchange are available, with branches at Gunter Annex. Officers and NCO open messes are also available.

Recreation. Recreational facilities are plentiful. Maxwell offers two eighteen-hole golf courses and a sixteen-lane bowling center, as well as gymnasiums and a recreation center. For the outdoorsman, fishing is available at several places on the installation, particularly in the two lakes near the base picnic area and in the Alabama River, which borders the base on the northeast. The family camp on base is open year-round and offers six camper sites with hookups and three tent sites, as well as fishing, hiking, tennis, and appropriate equipment.

Maxwell operates the Lake Pippin and Lake Martin recreation areas. At the Lake Pippin site, located on Choctawhatchee Bay on Florida's northern Gulf coast near Niceville, there are thirty furnished trailers, a playground, picnic areas, swimming areas, and boat rentals. At Lake Martin, fifty miles northeast of the base, there are ten trailers and fifty camper spaces, a playground and a picnic area, fishing, camping, swimming, and boating. Both sites are open year-round.

The Local Area. Maxwell AFB is about two miles northwest of Montgomery's business district. Montgomery is the third largest city in Alabama and has a population of over 180,000. It was at Montgomery in February 1861 that the Confederate States of America were formed and Jefferson Davis took office as president of the CSA. Snow and ice are a rarity at Maxwell, which is situated in the famous Sun Belt of the Deep South. A tour at Maxwell is not only good for the mind, it's good for the body as well.

For more information write to: 502nd Air Base Wing Public Affairs Office, 50 LeMay Plaza South, Maxwell AFB, AL 36112-6334, or call (205) 953-1110.

Army

FORT McCLELLAN

The 1993 Base Realignment and Closure Commission recommended closing Fort McClellan, but at press time no firm date had yet been announced.

The visitor to Fort McClellan might think he's visiting a college instead of the "Military Showplace of the South," as Fort McClellan is a sprawling campus where some 18,000 soldiers train each year at the Military Police and Chemical Corps schools.

History. Named in honor of Maj. Gen. George B. McClellan, general-in-chief of the U.S. Army from 1861 to 1862, Camp McClellan began its existence as an infantry training center in July 1917. The post was redesignated Fort McClellan in July 1929. The Women's Army Corps School was established there in 1952, and in 1954 it became the home of the U.S. Women's Army Corps Center, until the corps was disestablished in October 1978. The Military Police School moved there in 1975, and in December 1979 the U.S. Army Chemical School returned. (It had been at Fort McClellan from 1951 to 1973.)

Today Fort McClellan occupies about 46,000 acres in the foothills of the Appalachian Mountains. The climate is mild throughout the year, a real bonus for military personnel because that enhances training and off-duty recreation. Fort McClellan is a beautiful, well-maintained installation that offers the most modern facilities along with classic, historical architecture and beautiful scenery.

Housing and Schools. There are 571 sets of family quarters at Fort McClellan. Enlisted families may expect to wait several months to a year after application for quarters. Guest housing is available on a reservation basis for personnel making a permanent-change-of-station move; it is also available for temporary-duty accommodations.

Fort McClellan operates an elementary school program for dependent children from kindergarten through sixth grade. The post education center offers schooling at all levels from elementary to graduate. College courses are offered through Jacksonville State University, Gadsden State Junior College, and Central Alabama Community College.

Personal Services and Recreation. The more than 2,700 permanent-party personnel and their 4,200 family members at Fort McClellan are well served by modern facilities of all kinds. More than 69,000 retirees are also served by these facilities, which include the Noble Army Hospital, a modern 100-bed facility providing inpatient and outpatient care for eligible personnel. The commissary contains over 57,000 square feet; the post exchange has over 67,000 square feet of floor space. Recreational activities of all kinds are also available on post, including an eighteen-hole golf course, one of the best in the area.

The Local Area. Fort McClellan is three miles north of Anniston, population 26,000. Atlanta is only ninety miles to the east and Birmingham is fifty-five miles west. The surrounding area offers a wide variety of attractions, including the Anniston Community Theater, the Knox Concert Series, and the fastest NASCAR track in nearby Talladega County. The deepest gorge east of the Rockies, Little River Canyon, is located just north of Gadsden. The area abounds with Civil War history. The Chickamauga and Chattanooga National Military Parks are nearby, across the Georgia state line. Talladega National Forest runs north and south, just east of Fort McClellan, and Alabama's many rivers, lakes, ponds, forests, and mountain areas offer visitors and residents alike many opportunities for camping, hunting, boating, fishing, and sightseeing.

For more information write to: U.S. Army Chemical and Military Police Centers and Fort McClellan, Attention: ATZN-PAO, Fort McClellan, AL 36205-5000, or call (205) 848-5575.

FORT RUCKER

The steady whop-whop-whop of helicopter rotor blades forms a backdrop to the normal cadence of life at Fort Rucker, the "Home of Army Aviation." Every soldier and every civilian who works there is in some way dedicated to the mission of keeping flying soldiers ready to fight with the ground troops as a part of the Army's modern combined-arms team.

History. Occupying over 63,000 acres in the southeastern Alabama countryside, Fort Rucker opened in 1942. Named after a Confederate general, Edmund W. Rucker, a Tennessee native, Fort Rucker became involved in Army aviation in August 1954, when the U.S. Army Aviation School moved there from Fort Sill, Oklahoma. The post's population today is approximately 18,000, with more than 6,500 active-duty personnel and 3,800 family members.

The rolling and wooded countryside around Fort Rucker is well watered by lakes and streams, and with its proximity to the Gulf of Mexico, military anglers find it a paradise of fresh- and saltwater fishing. The climate is mild, and snow and ice are rare. By early April, the noonday temperatures on post are usually in the low eighties, but breezes from the Gulf, ninety miles to the south, and frequent rainfall moderate the summer nights.

Professional child care is available at Fort Rucker. (U.S. Army photo)

Housing and Schools. There are over 1,500 sets of family quarters at Fort Rucker, and guest-house facilities are available. The post also has 50 mobile home lots. There are approximately 300 bachelor quarters and over 400 rooms for temporary-duty personnel.

Dependent children in kindergarten through sixth grade attend the on-post school. The school also offers services for mildly mentally handicapped, learning-disabled, speech-impaired, and gifted students. Services are also offered for students who speak English as a second language.

A child-development services staff provides special care for all age groups, while child-development services offers full-day, part-day, preschool, hourly care, and family child-care services for children from four weeks to twelve years old.

Military personnel interested in further educational opportunities are offered programs conducted on post by the University of Southern California, the University of Denver, Troy State University, and Embry-Riddle Aeronautical University. Enterprise State Junior College and George C. Wallace State Community College offer courses on post as well as in nearby communities. The Alabama Aviation and Technical College is located in nearby Ozark.

Personal Services. Medical care is provided by the modern, seventy-two-bed Lyster Army Community Hospital, which provides care to more than 50,000 people. Its various outpatient clinics average more than 17,000 visits a month. The commissary offers 27,000 square feet of sales space with a meat market and a deli. The exchange has a shopping mall complete with a one-hour photo shop, a flower shop, and various food emporia.

Recreation. For the self-confident and robust outdoorsman, the Lake Tholocco Outdoor Recreation Office offers military personnel and their dependents over 600 acres of water for fishing, swimming, and water skiing, with boats and canoes for rent at nominal fees. The Fort Rucker Florida Recreation Area, on Choctawatchee Bay between Freeport and Niceville on State Highway 20, contains fifteen two-bedroom house trailers and twenty campsites with electric hookups. In addition, the information, tour, and travel office at Fort Rucker provides information and makes reservations for military recreation areas, sells tickets to all types of popular events, and has discount tickets for such places as Walt Disney World.

For the retiring indoorsperson, Fort Rucker's NCO and officers club systems provide a full range of services including on-post catering, dining and banquet rooms, and party, conference, and seminar areas at the main officers club and the Lake Lodge. There is also an Olympic-size swimming pool at the main officers club.

The Local Area. Fort Rucker is situated approximately ninety miles south of Montgomery, the state capital, and thirty miles northwest of Dothan. The towns of Enterprise, Daleville, and Ozark are just west, south, and east, respectively. Fort Rucker is an hour-and-a-half's drive from the Gulf of Mexico and about three hours from Mount Cheaha State Park, the highest point in the state.

For more information write to: Headquarters, U.S. Army Aviation Center and Fort Rucker, Attention: Army Community Services, Fort Rucker, AL 36362-5033, or call (205) 255-3815/3735

REDSTONE ARSENAL

It's a long way from Peenemunde on the shores of the Baltic, where the Germans developed their V-1 and V-2 rockets during World War II, to Huntsville, Alabama, but over 100 German scientists made the trip—via Fort Bliss, Texas—in 1950. Among them was the noted Wernher von Braun, who later played a significant role in America's space program.

History. Created in 1941 to make conventional ammunition and toxic chemicals, Redstone's involvement in the space age began early in 1949 and continued in 1950 when the Army moved its missile experts there from Texas. Today the arsenal is home to the U.S. Army Missile Command (MICOM), which oversees the research, development, engineering, testing, procurement, production, and logistical support of the Army's missile and rocket systems. To do this job the installation supports a daily working population of nearly 14,000 people, 10,000 of them civilian workers. More than 1,000 military families live on the arsenal. At press time Redstone was awaiting the activation of the U.S. Army Missile, Armaments, and Chemical Command, which will combine the activities of MICOM and the Army Armaments, Munitions, and Chemical Command (AMCCOM) at Rock Island Arsenal, Illinois.

Housing and Schools. Redstone has over 1,100 sets of family quarters in two- and four-bedroom units. With a permanent military population of around 2,500, chances for getting on-post quarters are very good. Bachelor housing consists of air-conditioned brick barracks for enlisted soldiers in the lower grades and over 100 rooms for senior NCOs and officers. The installation also has guest lodging facilities.

Dependent children attend schools in Huntsville. There are a nursery and a preschool on post. The University of Alabama, Alabama A & M, and Oakwood College offer college courses for adult education.

Personal Services. Medical and dental care at Redstone are provided through the forty-bed Fox Army Community Hospital. There are a post exchange, a commissary, and the usual morale and support activities.

Recreation. The northern Alabama climate offers mild winters and humid summers with long spring and fall seasons, making outdoor recreation possible all through the year. The installation's 38,000 acres include many lakes, ponds, and streams open to fishing; Redstone also has excellent hunting for waterfowl, small game, and deer. Boating and camping are also available, and the Redstone Recreation Center offers programs that cover a wide range of interests from amateur photography to bowling.

The Local Area. Huntsville, situated on a northern bend of the Tennessee River, is a thriving modern city of 150,000 inhabitants and is keyed to the pulsating life of the space age. Located in the Alabama mountain lakes section, Huntsville is conveniently close to one of the foremost resort areas in the South. Chattanooga, Tennessee, is to the northeast, and Birmingham to the south, on Interstate 65.

For more information write to: U.S. Army Missile Command, Attention: AMSMI-IN, Redstone Arsenal, AL 35898, or call (205) 876-2151.

Coast Guard

MOBILE AVIATION TRAINING CENTER

History. In 1966 the vacant 232-acre Air Force Reserve facility located at Mobile's Bates Field was acquired by the Coast Guard for the purpose of establishing there a standardized pilot-training program. In December 1966 Air Station Mobile was officially commissioned with the transfer of HU-16E Albatross aircraft from Biloxi, Mississippi, and the establishment of fixed-wing and rotary-wing pilot training units.

In 1969 the Helicopter Icebreaker Support Unit (IBSU), now known as the Polar Operations Division, was established at Mobile and the installation became known as the Aviation Training Center. Today the 500 active-duty and civilian personnel of each of the eight divisions of the center—operations, training, polar operations, aviation engineering, medical, comptroller, services, and facilities engineering—work together to support Coast Guard missions worldwide. HU-25A Guardian aircraft stand on alert in support of 8th Coast Guard District missions such as search-and-rescue and enforcement of maritime laws. HU-25C Nightstalker air interceptor jets from Mobile are on the front line of defense in our nation's war against drug smuggling. HH-65A aircraft from the Polar Operations Division deploy on Coast Guard icebreakers to the ends of the earth, where they fly scientific, logistical, and occasionally search-and-rescue missions. The training division provides initial and recurrent training to Coast Guard pilots. The Aviation Training Center is the largest air unit in the Coast Guard.

Housing, Schools, and Personal Services. While there is no family housing onboard the center, temporary lodging is available in the form of visiting officer and enlisted units that are available by reservation. One-room off-base apartment rentals start at $200 per month; two-bedroom units range from as little as $375 a month to as much as $600. A security deposit plus first and last months' rent are usually required upon signing a lease. This can run as much as $700.

Dependent children attend one of the ninety-one public schools in Mobile County. College-level courses are available from Faulkner University, Alabama Aviation and Technical College, the University of South Alabama, and other institutions.

The center has a large grocery annex and a Coast Guard exchange with a service station and barber and beauty shops. A swimming pool is available, as are equipment and boat rentals and a base picnic area. A full-service medical clinic is also available.

The Local Area. The Aviation Training Center is located at Mobile Municipal Airport, six miles west of Interstate 65 along Airport Boulevard. Downtown Mobile and Mobile Bay are about eight miles east of the Center.

The modern city takes its name from a French trading post—Fort Louis de la

Mobile—established nearby in 1702. Today Mobile is the second largest city in the state of Alabama and a thriving seaport town on the Gulf of Mexico situated on the west bank of the Mobile River where it enters Mobile Bay. With a population of over 200,000, Mobile offers plenty of historical, cultural, and recreational activities for everyone, including the celebrated Azalea Trail, a thirty-seven-mile flower-lined drive.

For more information write to: Commanding Officer, USCG Aviation Training Center, Attention: Public Affairs Branch, Mobile, AL 36608-9682, or call (205) 639-6428.

ALASKA

Air Force

EARECKSON AIR FORCE STATION

Eareckson AFS is located on Shemya Island, in the Bering Sea, 1,500 miles southwest of Anchorage in a small cluster of rocks known as the Near Islands. The Near Islands are near the international date line: Travel a few miles south on a Sunday and you'll find yourself in Monday. Shemya's black volcanic sand inspired its traditional name, "Black Pearl of the Aleutians," but those who live there commonly call it "The Rock," for obvious reasons.

History. The U.S. military first came to Shemya in 1943 to build a runway to accommodate B-29 Stratofortresses, but the largest bombers that ever flew from there during World War II were B-24s. Even today you can still find many structures from those days—bunkers, 37mm antiaircraft gun emplacements, and the remains of a gun in the courtyard of Building 600, where the barber and beauty shops are now located.

Today, Eareckson is operated by the 673rd Air Base Group. The major tenant unit is the 16th Space Surveillance Squadron, which collects intelligence information on missile tests and orbiting earth satellite vehicles. Detachment 1 of the 55th Operations Group also collects sensitive intelligence data. About 550 active-duty personnel and 15 civilian employees are assigned to Eareckson.

Housing and Personal Services. Personnel assigned to Eareckson serve unaccompanied tours. The station has billets for about 660 personnel, 50 officer and 610 enlisted. There are also accommodations for approximately 45 visiting personnel.

The base exchange provides an extensive range of services, including a small snack bar, a check-cashing service, barber and beauty shops, and catalog sales. Personnel being assigned to Eareckson are advised to bring their own radios, stereos, TVs, and VCRs, as well as their own hobby and sports equipment, microwave cookware, cameras, and coffee makers. There are no commercial laundry or dry-cleaning services available at Eareckson, but free washers and dryers are available in the dormitories, and ironing boards are said to be plentiful there.

Medical and dental care are provided by small clinics on the island while more definitive care is available in Anchorage.

Recreation. Eareckson's premier recreation event is a thirty-day leave everyone assigned there is authorized to take about midway through his or her tour. Until that time, there is a four-lane bowling center and a new recreation center at Eareckson that offers basketball, racquetball, a weight room, and an indoor running track. The rec center also has several rooms for meetings and social functions as well as a multi-purpose theater, ceramics shop, and tailor shop. The station library contains over 4,000 volumes as well as newspapers and periodicals. Membership in Club 356 is open and free. The club provides a dining room on Friday and Saturday nights with weekly menu specials and lounge services.

Cable TV service is available in individual rooms at prices from $8 to $20 per month. This service includes HBO, Showtime, and a twenty-four-hour-a-day movie channel run by the communications center.

Off-duty employment is also available at Eareckson since most of the regular jobs on the station are held by military personnel, including licensed barber and beautician positions.

The Local Area. Shemya Island measures 4.5 miles long by 2.5 miles at its widest point. It rises from sea level to 240 feet on the northern side, where steep cliffs drop to a rocky shoreline. Temperatures range from an average high of 51° F. in August to a low of 28° F. in February. Generally it is cold and windy on Shemya, so off-duty wear should include jackets, flannel shirts or wool sweaters, and sturdy jeans and boots. During the summer months days are long, with up to seventeen hours of daylight; during the winter, daylight only lasts about eight hours.

The only land animals on Shemya are small blue foxes, although in season sea lions and seals can be found along the island's shoreline. Two of the twelve lakes on Shemya are stocked with Dolly Varden trout and landlocked salmon. Flounder, halibut, and Japanese perch can be caught off the base dock. Beachcombing is a frequent pastime on Shemya.

For more information, write to: Public Affairs Representative, 673 ABG, Unit 12514, APO AP 96512-2514, or call (907) 392-3401.

EIELSON AIR FORCE BASE

What do oil, Dr. Henry Kissinger, and Gen. "Chappie" James all have in common? Eielson Air Force Base, for one thing. They were all drawn together in 1975 when President Gerald Ford stopped at Eielson and delivered a speech on the merits of the newly begun Alaskan Oil Pipeline. Pump Station No. 8 of that line is only ten miles south of the base. Add to that the fact that Eielson has the only combat-ready forward-air-control squadron in Alaska, and you have quite a combination.

History. Eielson was known simply as "Mile 26" when it opened in 1943, because it was the site of a U.S. Army Signal Corps telegraph station exactly twenty-six miles from Fairbanks that provided a link with Valdez, Alaska. During World War II, Eielson served as a storage area for excess Lend-Lease aircraft on their way to Russia, and Russian airmen were stationed there to take their possession. On 4 February 1948, Mile 26 was redesignated Eielson Air Force Base in honor of Carl Ben Eielson, a famed arctic pioneer and aviator. Today the base is home for the 343rd Wing, whose pilots fly the F-16 Fighting Falcon and the OA-10 Thunderbolt II. The wing's primary mission is to provide close-air support and forward air control for Army ground forces in Alaska. Approximately 3,000 active-duty personnel and their 4,300 dependents call Eielson home.

Housing and Schools. There are 1,367 sets of family quarters at Eielson, but space is usually very limited from May to September. The base also has accommodations for 735 single and unaccompanied military personnel. Local housing is expensive. One-bedroom apartments average $500 a month; efficiencies about $395, plus utilities. The average rent for a two-bedroom apartment is $1,500 to $2,000 the first month, including utilities. Variable housing allowance is available to personnel living off base, and a cost-of-living allowance is paid to all personnel to offset the high cost of housing in Alaska.

The Fairbanks North Star Borough School District operates three elementary schools, one junior high school, and one senior high school on base for children residing on Eielson. A preschool and a child-care center are also available. The University of Alaska-Anchorage, University of Alaska-Southeast, and Wayland Baptist University offer many undergraduate courses on base, and La Verne University offers classes leading to a master's degree in business management.

Personal Services. Medical care at Eielson is provided by the 343rd Medical Group clinic staff with referrals to Bassett Army Hospital at Fort Wainwright for care beyond the clinic's capability. The base exchange stocks over 15,000 items, and the commissary offers shoppers a complete selection of groceries.

Recreation. Recreational facilities include a twenty-lane bowling center, gymnasium, three tennis courts, auto and wood hobby shops, and a recreation center. A ski lodge is located four miles southeast of the base. The Birch Lake Recreation Area, about thirty-five miles south of Eielson, offers cabins, trailer pads with or without electric hookups, tent sites, a marina, a lodge, and a picnic area. The site offers camping, boating, hiking, and picnicking from Memorial Day through Labor Day.

The Local Area. Fairbanks is located twenty-six miles north of Eielson and sits 110 miles south of the Arctic Circle. The greater Fairbanks North Star borough boasts a population of more than 79,000 permanent residents. In June, the sunlight shines a maximum of twenty-one hours and forty minutes, and in December a bright day sees the sun shining three hours and forty-seven minutes. The average low temperature in January is minus 19° F., and the average high in July is a balmy 70° F.

For more information write to: 343rd Wing Public Affairs Office, 3112 Broadway Ave., Ste. 5, Eielson AFB, AK 99702-1870, or call (907) 377-2116.

ELMENDORF AIR FORCE BASE

Elmendorf Air Force Base lies farther north than Helsinki, Finland, and is almost as far west as Hawaii, but it lies in the northern suburbs of Alaska's largest city, some 1,400 air miles from Seattle. With a population over 222,000, Anchorage has almost 50 percent of the total population of the state of Alaska.

History. Elmendorf began as an airfield called Fort Richardson. In November 1940 the field was designated Elmendorf Field, after Hugh M. Elmendorf. In March 1951, the Army relocated its garrison to the new Fort Richardson, on the southeast side of Anchorage, and the installation came under the authority of the Air Force. Today the base's 13,000-square-acre expanse is home for the 3rd Wing, whose pilots fly two squadrons of the F-15C/D Eagle, and one squadron each of F-15E Strike Eagles, E-3A AWACs, and C-130s/C-12s. Approximately 7,000 active-duty personnel and 10,900 dependents and 2,400 civilian employees call Elmendorf home.

Housing and Schools. There are more than 1,600 sets of family quarters at Elmendorf. Bachelor housing consists of 68 bachelor-officer quarters, 40 units for senior NCOs, and spaces for 1,100 billets in organizational housing (better known as barracks).

The base has three elementary schools, kindergarten through sixth grade, and a special-education school. High school programs are available off base. A main child-care center and four auxiliary centers as well as numerous family-day-care providers are located on the installation. Education services for adults include a number of college programs from Chapman College, University of La Verne, the University of Alaska, Alaska Pacific University, Wayland Baptist University, and Embry-Riddle Aeronautical University.

Personal Services. Medical care is available from the 3rd Wing medical center, a modern, seven-story medical facility offering sixteen specialty clinics.

Services and facilities available on base include a commissary with 7,000 line items, a complete exchange complex with numerous concessions, a package liquor store, a 60,000-volume library, enlisted and officers clubs, and the Galaxy Cafeteria, located in the base passenger terminal, which is open twenty-four hours a day.

Recreation. Recreational facilities include an eighteen-hole golf course, a forty-lane bowling center, hobby shops, a base theater, and many athletic programs.

The base also has several lakes where boating, fishing, and other water sports are available.

For more information write to: Public Affairs Office, 3rd Wing, Elmendorf AFB, AK 99506-2530, or call (907) 552-1110.

Army

FORT GREELY

"We battle cold and conquer mountains" is a fitting motto for the Army's Northern Warfare Training Center at Fort Greely, Alaska. Located about 107 miles southeast of Fairbanks, Fort Greely covers some 650,000 acres and has been the site for the testing of a wide variety of military items since the Cold Regions Test Center was established there in 1949.

History. Named after Maj. Gen. Adolphus Washington Greely, arctic explorer, Fort Greely was established in June 1942 under the Lend-Lease program as a transfer point for American and Russian pilots. In August 1955, the post was designated Fort Greely. It is a small post in terms of population: approximately 450 military personnel and their 300 dependents, and 700 civilian employees. This figure fluctuates with influxes of temporary-duty personnel.

Housing and Schools. There are 361 sets of family quarters at Fort Greely. Waiting time for these units was running at approximately two weeks as of January 1993. Off-post rentals early in 1993 were available starting at about $400 per month for a furnished one-bedroom apartment to as much as $550 for a three-bedroom furnished house. Monthly utility rates during the winter were running at $160. Guest housing is available at reasonable rates, however.

Fort Greely operates an on-post school for children in kindergarten through eighth grade. Students in grades nine through twelve attend the Delta Junction School, about six miles from the post. The Army Education Center provides a broad variety of courses and services, including extension courses offered by the University of La Verne and Central Texas College.

Personal Services and Recreation. Medical services are provided by a staff of two doctors, a clinical nurse, and a staff of thirty paraprofessionals. Patients requiring specialty clinics, inpatient care, or surgery are sent to Bassett Army Hospital at Fort Wainwright.

The post exchange offers shoppers more than 10,000 line items, and the commissary, situated in a completely new facility, offers military personnel and their dependents 5,700 line items—supermarket-type shopping a long way from any supermarket. The post also offers many other morale support facilities such as officers and NCO open messes, a theater, an eight-lane bowling alley, auto and crafts hobby shops, skeet and trap ranges, and a gymnasium with a complete physical fitness center, including a six-lane indoor pool. The post library is stocked with over 17,000 volumes.

The Local Area. Winters are dark, cold, and windy at Fort Greely. Winds in excess of sixty miles per hour are common. The average winter temperature there is minus 20° F., and the average summer temperature is 60° F. The average annual snowfall is thirty-eight inches. On-post hunting is excellent for moose, bear, and small game, and the area has many streams, creeks, and lakes that are known for good fishing. Bolio Lake, twelve miles from the main post, is a favorite fishing and boating spot. Skiing is permitted on post, and there is also good skiing at Black Rapids twenty-five miles away. A ski shop, a boat shop, and a rod and gun club are located on post.

For further information write to: Public Affairs Office, Fort Greely, AK 96508, or call (907) 873-4706.

FORT RICHARDSON

Fort Richardson is truly in the Alaska millions of Americans dream of visiting—a wilderness that begins right on post, where moose freely roam. Only a brief drive from the post is the center of the port city of Anchorage (population 240,000). Fort Richardson occupies 62,000 acres and is situated on the northeast side of town, adjacent to Elmendorf Air Force Base. Rimming the city to the east are the Chugach Mountains.

History. Named in honor of Brig. Gen. Wilds P. Richardson, a pioneer explorer in Alaska, Fort Richardson was originally located on the site of Elmendorf AFB from 1940 to 1941 and moved to its present location in 1950. The post is home to the U.S. Army Garrison, Alaska, headquarters and to elements of the 6th Infantry Division (Light), which has forces at both Fort Richardson and Fort Wainwright. The post supports a population of approximately 4,400 military personnel, 5,600 family members, and 1,540 civilian employees.

The 6th Infantry Division is scheduled to be reorganized into a light infantry brigade task force by October 1994, with a loss of about 2,800 soldiers. Some of that force will remain at Fort Richardson, but at press time it was not known exactly what impact this restructuring would have on the post.

Housing and Schools. There are about 1,600 sets of family quarters, ranging in size from detached houses for colonels and higher-ranking officers to duplexes for field-grade officers and eight-plex housing for other grades.

The 6th Infantry has an excellent education-services plan through the Fort Richardson Education Office that includes a basic-skills education program, a high school completion program, and college programs on post and at local college campuses. Three on-post elementary school facilities are available for dependent children through the Anchorage School District. Child-care facilities, including certified home-care providers and centers for infants, toddlers, and preschoolers, are available on post. Before- and after-school care are available for children through sixth grade. A diverse youth-services program is also offered for school-age children and teens. Child-care facilities are available on post.

Personal Services. On-post medical care is provided through outpatient facilities only; inpatient hospital care is available at nearby Elmendorf AFB. A large commissary and post exchange are also located on post.

Recreation. Fort Richardson offers an excellent outdoor recreation program. The largest activity is the Seward Army Recreation Camp located on Resurrection Bay, 129 miles south of Anchorage, where people enjoy mountain climbing, hiking, boating, and fishing. The Black Spruce Army Travel Camp for recreational vehicles located near Otter Lake offers electrical and water hookups, dump facilities, showers, a washer and dryer, and a children's playground. Otter Lake Recreation Area is five miles from the main post and covers a total of 2,900 acres (the lake covers 99 acres). The on-post outdoor recreation center offers a skeet and trap range as well as an archery range.

The Local Area. The Anchorage area has a mild climate with its summers comparable to those in Seattle or San Francisco. On the shortest day of the year there are a little more than five hours of sunlight, and on the longest day the sun shines for more than nineteen hours. During the summer months it is possible to enjoy a wide variety of outdoor activities such as flying, camping, hunting, fishing, and rock collecting. In the winter, activities include skiing, snowmobiling, and ice fishing.

For more information write to: Public Affairs Office, 6th Infantry Division (Light), Attention: APVR-PR-PO, Fort Richardson, AK 99505-5900, or call (907) 384-2113/2072.

FORT WAINWRIGHT

"Above all, keep your chin down, eyes in the pan, knees bent, and dig-shake, dig-shake, dig-shake," advises a prospector's guide to gold panning in Alaska. There is gold in Alaska, in more ways than one, and for some soldiers an assignment to the 6th Infantry Division (Light) at Fort Wainwright may be a golden opportunity to participate in a challenging and exciting experience in one of the world's most spectacular natural wonderlands.

History. Fort Wainwright is located just to the east of Fairbanks along the Chena River, some 350 miles by road north of Anchorage and 1,500 miles northwest of Dawson Creek, British Columbia, Canada, along the Alaska Highway. Named after Gen. Jonathan M. Wainwright, defender of Bataan against the Japanese in the Philippines in World War II, the post began its existence in January 1961, when Ladd Air Force Base was transferred to the Army and renamed Fort Wainwright.

Housing and Schools. Approximately 2,100 units of family housing are available for all grades. The cost of living is high in the Fairbanks area, comparable to such cities as Boston, New York, and Washington, D.C.

Dependent schooling is conducted through the Fairbanks North Star School District and includes four elementary schools and a special-education school on post.

Fort Wainwright offers many ways for both soldiers and their dependents to broaden their formal education. Off-duty courses are offered through the University of Alaska, the Tanana Valley Community College, and the Hutchinson Career Development Center in Fairbanks.

Personal Services and Recreation. Fort Wainwright offers a complete range of community services, from the fifty-bed Bassett Army Community Hospital and large commissary and post exchange to a 23,000-volume library and a nine-hole golf course. Recreational facilities also include a bowling alley, a movie theater, hobby shops, tennis courts, an indoor pool, and two gymnasiums.

Brown, grizzly, and black bears as well as moose may be hunted in season on designated areas on post, and fishing is excellent throughout the state. (The limit on post is fifteen fish per angler per day.)

The Local Area. At Fort Wainwright, the temperature may dip to minus 65°F. in December when the days are mostly dark with only brief periods of light, and the ground does not begin to thaw until April.

In summer months, when temperatures often reach into the 90s, the post's Golden North Service Club schedules many interesting trips for military personnel and their dependents at very reasonable prices. These include excursions into the Klondike at Dawson Creek and Mount McKinley National Park, via the Alaskan Railroad. Birch Lake, on the Richardson Highway, is run by the Recreation Services Office at Eielson Air Force Base and offers swimming, fishing, waterskiing, camping, picnicking, and boating.

Personnel planning to drive to Fort Wainwright from the "Lower Forty-eight" may do so on the Alaska Highway, which is 1,520 miles long between Dawson Creek, British Columbia, and Fairbanks. Depending on road conditions and weather, the drive may take up to seven days, so persons making this trip should be prepared.

For more information write to: Public Affairs Office, Fort Wainwright, AK 99703-5000, or call (907) 353-6701.

Navy

ADAK NAVAL AIR STATION

Adak boasts many of the comforts of home: You can sit in the local ice cream shop and enjoy a scoop of strawberry ripple while the wind screams by outside at eighty miles per hour and the earth trembles gently under your feet.

History. The U.S. Navy established a Naval Operating Base on Adak Island in 1942, and today it is the site of several command and tenant activities, including the Adak Search and Rescue Coordination and a Naval Security Group Activity. Adak is home to over 4,200 active-duty personnel, their dependents, and civilian employees.

Housing and Schools. There are 954 units of government family quarters available on Adak. Depending on the priority of each servicemember's orders, there is a two- to six-month waiting period for government housing on Adak. There are no guest facilities. Only active-duty personnel, Department of Defense employees, and their dependents are authorized entry to Adak, and that requires a minimum thirty-day advance notice.

Schools are available for children and adults. The state of Alaska finances Ann C. Stevens Elementary, Mount Moffett Middle School, and Bob Reeve High School, which has a current enrollment of about 200 students. The University of Alaska offers courses leading to an associate degree. Additionally, the Adak Community

Education Program provides GED, SAT, and ACT exams and other certificate and degree programs. A day-care center and a preschool are also available on Adak.

Personal Services. The medical care available on Adak consists of flight and general surgery, obstetrics and gynecological services, pediatrics, and family practice. No other clinical specialties are routinely available on the island. Personnel requiring specialty care are flown to Elmendorf Air Force Base, Alaska, or Naval Station Bremerton, Washington. Limited dental care is available on the island.

The Adak commissary carries a complete line of foodstuffs: Milk and fresh fruits and vegetables are flown in twice weekly from Seattle, and a full line of canned and frozen vegetables is always available. A bakery offers fresh bread, rolls, cookies, and pastries. The Navy exchange offers a retail store carrying most items generally sold in exchanges in the continental United States. The exchange also operates a barber and beauty shop, a sporting goods store, a garage and service station, a mini mart, a credit union, a post office, and a delicatessen. The service station offers car rentals at the rate of twenty-five dollars per day plus optional insurance for another two dollars per day. A Baskin Robbins and a McDonald's are also available.

Recreation. Recreational facilities include a ten-lane bowling alley, craft shops, indoor swimming, racquetball, tennis, weight-training facilities, a sauna, and clubs open seven days a week with menu selections from short-order to full-service dining.

The Local Area. Adak Island is located in the center of the Aleutian chain in a group of small specks of land known as the Andreanof Islands, of which Adak is one of the larger. Adak is 2,062 miles west of Seattle, 1,200 miles southwest of Anchorage, and 2,070 miles northeast of Tokyo. Siberia is about 700 miles to the northwest. No animals or trees are native to the island, and there is no civilian community.

The area frequently experiences earth tremors. The most severe of these occurred in 1957 and reached 8.0 on the Richter scale. Buildings on Adak are specially constructed to withstand damage from earthquakes and high winds, which sometimes exceed 120 knots. The tsunami, or tidal wave caused by earthquakes far beneath the sea, is rare at Adak. The last one occurred in 1958 and caused only minor damage. Williwas are sometimes a hazard on Adak. These are intensely fierce gusts of wind resulting from the damming of air on the windward slopes of mountain peaks that overflow suddenly down the leeward slopes at a velocity that often reaches 100 miles per hour.

The average high temperature on Adak in August is 52° F., and the average January high is 34° F., but the wind-chill factor often drives the air temperatures even lower. Average rainfall is forty-seven inches with an average annual snowfall of seventy-nine inches; cloud overcast covers the island 87 percent of the year. Because of the proximity of active volcanoes (Great Sitkin is twenty-three miles northeast of Adak), the island is covered with ash. Adak is far enough south that it does not experience the extended seasonal periods of light and darkness that make life so peculiar in other parts of Alaska.

Fishing is a very popular sport on Adak. Many species, including salmon, may be caught in the freshwater lakes on the island and in the surrounding sea. Shrimp can be caught on the docks during August, September, and October, and king crab can be caught in season. Keeping an eye out for tsunamis and williwas, the fishermen and hikers have plenty of opportunity to enjoy themselves on Adak.

For further information write to: Public Affairs Office, NAVSTA, Box 2, FPO Seattle, WA 98791, or call (907) 592-8251.

ARIZONA

Air Force

DAVIS-MONTHAN AIR FORCE BASE

The first Europeans to come to Tucson were lost. That was back about the year 1535, and they were the survivors of the ill-fated Navarez expedition to Florida. With Davis-Monthan Air Force Base now firmly anchored in the city of Tucson, airmen looking for an assignment (or just visiting) should have no trouble finding the place.

History. Davis-Monthan is named after two Air Corps officers who died in separate aircraft crashes. Lt. Samuel H. Davis died in a crash at Carlstrom Field, Florida, in 1921; Lt. Oscar Monthan died in a crash near Honolulu, Hawaii, in 1924. The Army Air Corps established an airfield at Davis-Monthan in 1927. Today Davis-Monthan is home for the 355th Wing, 12th Air Operations Group, 71st Special Operations Squadron, and the Aerospace Maintenance and Regeneration Center. The 355th's mission is to provide worldwide deployable combat-ready OA-10 forward-air-controller support and EC-130 command, control, and communications countermeasures capability.

Housing and Schools. More than 1,200 units of family housing are available at Davis-Monthan. Temporary lodging for families is provided for permanent-change-of-station personnel on a space-available, day-to-day basis. Guest housing is also available with a ninety-day reservation.

Elementary schooling is available on the base for children from kindergarten to sixth grade, and a child-care center is also maintained on base. The base education office offers college courses through the University of Arizona, Arizona State University, the University of Phoenix, and other institutions.

Personal Services. Medical care is provided by the thirty-five-bed Davis-Monthan Hospital. This facility has a staff of over 475 and serves a community of 60,000 people. The base exchange carries over 30,000 items on display in a 29,000-square-foot sales area. The base commissary serves approximately 55,000 customers a month.

Recreation. Recreational facilities available on base include an eighteen-hole golf course, a twenty-lane bowling center, eight tennis courts, and a base swimming pool. Also available are a gymnasium, hobby shops (wood, auto, and ceramic), and both NCO and officers clubs. Davis-Monthan has two picnic areas and a skeet range.

The Local Area. With over 300 days of sunshine a year and clear, unpolluted air, Tucson is a fine place for outdoor activities. The city's residents own thousands of swimming pools, and there are seventeen golf courses open year-round. Tucson, with a population of nearly 650,000 people, has eighty parks, all of them with some kind of recreational facilities.

Tucson is surrounded by mountains. The Tortolitas and Santa Catalinas are to the north, the Tucsons to the west, the Rincons to the east, and the Santa Ritas to the south. Mount Lemmon, in the Santa Catalinas, is more than 9,100 feet high.

Phoenix is about 105 miles north of Davis-Monthan and Nogales, and the U.S.-Mexican border is about 60 miles south of the base.

For more information write to: Public Affairs Office, Davis-Monthan AFB, AZ 85707, or call (602) 750-3204.

LUKE AIR FORCE BASE

Luke Air Force Base is named after the first airman to earn the Medal of Honor—Lt. Frank Luke, Jr., a native of Phoenix. In action over France in 1918, he destroyed eighteen enemy aircraft in just seventeen days. Forced to make an emergency landing behind enemy lines, he defended himself from capture until he was gunned down by German soldiers. It is entirely fitting that this base, known as the "Home of the Fighter Pilot," is named after this hero.

History. Opened in 1941, Luke today occupies 4,197 acres twenty miles west of Phoenix. There are over 20,000 people at Luke, 6,000 active-duty and reserve personnel, 1,500 civilian employees, and over 12,000 dependents. The base is now home for the 58th Fighter Wing, which trains aircrews in the F-16 Fighting Falcon and the F-15E Strike Eagle. About 2.7 million acres at the Barry M. Goldwater Air Force Range are available to Luke pilots for aerial maneuvers.

Housing and Schools. There are approximately 900 base quarters for married personnel at Luke and 40 transient living quarters that may be reserved by families traveling on official change-of-station orders.

There is one civilian elementary school adjacent to the base (kindergarten to sixth grade) and numerous elementary, junior high, and senior high schools close by. College courses are available on base from a variety of institutions. These include Golden Gate University, Grand Canyon College, Arizona State University, and Embry-Riddle Aeronautical University.

Personal Services. The 58th Medical Group hospital is a complete medical-care facility that maintains forty beds for inpatients. Located on base are a large exchange store, a commissary, a number of concessions and snack bars, and officers and NCO clubs.

Recreation. Recreational facilities include a bowling center, a gymnasium, hobby and craft shops, three swimming pools, a recreational center, a skeet and trap range, a riding stable, and tennis courts.

The Local Area. The city of Phoenix offers much in the way of culture and recreation for personnel stationed at Luke. The 150-acre Papago Park Desert Botanical Garden and the Phoenix Zoo, located in the Botanical Garden park, are major visitor attractions in the city. The city also offers many museums and galleries as well as horse and dog races, horse shows, and professional sports. The community boasts many fine parks, especially South Mountain Park with 15,000 acres affording picnicking, horseback riding, and hiking.

For more information write to: 58th Fighter Wing/PA, 7383 N. Litchfield Rd., Luke AFB, AZ 85309-1534, or call (602) 856-6011.

WILLIAMS AIR FORCE BASE

Affectionately known as "Willie," Williams Air Force Base, located twenty-five miles southeast of Phoenix, was selected by the 1991 Base Closure Commission to close in September 1993 after more than fifty years of service to the nation.

Army

FORT HUACHUCA

A proud Buffalo Soldier greets you as you enter the main gate at Fort Huachuca, and this is fitting; of more than seventy frontier cavalry posts established by the U.S. government in Arizona during the 1800s, Huachuca is the last one to host active Army troops. "Buffalo Soldier" was a nickname given to black cavalrymen by the Plains Indians, and the veterans of the 9th and 10th Cavalry Regiments brought the name with them when they were assigned to Fort Huachuca in the early 1900s. Huachuca's Buffalo Soldier is nine feet tall and made of bronze, a fitting monument to this group of American soldiers.

History. Fort Huachuca (the name comes from an Indian word that means "place of thunder") was established in March 1877, when Capt. Samuel Marmaduke Whitside and two companies of the 6th Cavalry were ordered to build a post in the foothills of the Huachuca Mountains. In 1886 the fort was Gen. Nelson A. Miles's headquarters and forward supply base for his campaign against Geronimo and his Apache warriors. It was men from Huachuca's B Troop, 4th Cavalry, who chased

Geronimo in 1886 and finally brought him to bay after five months and a 3,000-mile pursuit throughout southeast Arizona. Today, Fort Huachuca's 73,000 acres are home for the U.S. Army Intelligence Center and School, the U.S. Army Information Systems Command, the Joint Interoperability Test Center, the 11th Signal Brigade, and other specialized units. The post has a permanent population of almost 6,000 military personnel, 5,500 civilian employees, and over 4,700 dependents.

Housing and Schools. Fort Huachuca boasts 1,955 family quarters that are considered adequate by Army standards. Fort Huachuca also has 274 bachelor housing units, 169 visiting-officer quarters and enlisted rooms, and 33 guest rooms that provide temporary lodging for military personnel on permanent-change-of-station status. Additionally, there are eight distinguished visitors' suites.

The post operates three elementary schools, as well as a child-care center. Besides the full range of testing and MOS-related skill programs, the Army Education Center offers college-level courses on post from Cochise College, the University of Arizona, and the University of Northern Colorado.

Personal Services. On-post facilities include a modern and well-stocked commissary and post exchange and Raymond W. Bliss Army Community Hospital, a 110-bed facility offering a full range of inpatient and outpatient medical care.

Recreation. The post offers an extensive outdoor recreation and equipment-loan facility, including four campgrounds. Hunting and fishing are permitted on post in season. The area's moderate climate (snow falls only occasionally in winter, and the average annual rainfall is only twenty inches) is conducive to outdoor activities year-round.

The Local Area. Fort Huachuca is bordered on the east and north by the town of Sierra Vista (population 32,000). Surrounded by beautiful mountains (*sierra*), the view (*vista*) is entirely unobstructed by the smog that often plagues cities in other places. Sierra Vista is situated on the broad and level plain of the San Pedro Valley at an altitude of over 4,600 feet. The town is 75 miles southeast of Tucson and 180 miles from Phoenix. Tombstone is a twenty-five-minute drive east of Sierra Vista, and Nogales, Arizona, and the Mexican border are 65 miles to the southwest. A bit farther away is the Grand Canyon, 79 miles north of Flagstaff.

Fort Huachuca is sometimes called the "best-kept secret in the Army," because the area combines the best of small-town and metropolitan living plus southwestern informality along with a moderate cost of living.

For more information write to: Army Community Services Office, Attention: ATZS-PAM, U.S. Army Intelligence Center and Fort Huachuca, AZ 85613-6000, or call (602) 533-5972.

YUMA PROVING GROUND

History. The U.S. Army has been at Yuma since 1850, when it established a hilltop fort across the Colorado River from the present site of Yuma Proving Ground, in what is now Imperial County, California. The present Yuma Proving Ground (YPG) began as Yuma Test Branch in 1943. Today it covers nearly 1 million acres, or 200 square miles, in the southwestern portion of Arizona, consisting of twenty-six ranges and test facilities where experts test weapons and aircraft armament systems as well as all sorts of military equipment for desert warfare.

Housing and Schools. There are 289 sets of family quarters at YPG, and a ten-room guest facility is operated there for transients.

An elementary school is operated on post, as is a day-care center. Adult education is offered through the YPG Education Center.

Personal Services. The U.S. Army Health Clinic, YPG, provides emergency and routine medical service to soldiers, their families, and retired personnel. Persons requiring hospitalization are referred to the Yuma Regional Medical Center or to Fort Huachuca, Balboa Naval Hospital in San Diego, or William Beaumont Hospital at Fort Bliss, Texas. Space-available dental care is offered for dependents and retired military personnel.

YPG has a commissary and a post exchange. The exchange operates several concessions, including a service station. The facilities at YPG are complemented somewhat by those at the Marine Corps Air Station, Yuma, on the south edge of town adjacent to the Yuma International Airport. At YPG are a delicatessen, a pizza shop, an arts and crafts center, a library, a leisure-travel office, a thrift shop, a gas station, and a credit union.

Recreation. Recreational facilities include a swimming pool, a six-lane bowling center, a post theater, a gymnasium, and a recreation services boat dock at Imperial Dam, three miles from the main post on the Colorado River. Sporting equipment such as trailers and camping equipment is available for rent at the Morale Support Supply Office on post.

The Local Area. Although the climate in this part of Arizona is very dry, with less than three inches of rain per year, fishing is great in the Colorado River. There are a number of excellent camping and fishing sites within thirty-five miles of town, including Laguna Dam, Mittry Lake, Imperial Dam, Senator's Wash (not named after a political scandal!), Squaw Lake, and Martinez Lake, where bass, catfish, and bluegill are abundant.

Yuma, with a metropolitan population of more than 60,000, has one of the finest winter climates in the country, with the average temperatures in the seventies and sunshine an average of 93 percent of the time. There are numerous historical points of interest in and around the city, including the old Territorial Prison, Fort Yuma, and the border towns of San Luis (twenty-three miles south) and Mexicali (fifty-five miles south). In Old Mexico, seventy-five miles south of San Luis, is the Sea of Cortez or Gulf of Lower California, with a wide expanse of clean, white beach offering fishing, surf casting, clam digging, and swimming. Europeans first came to the site of present-day Yuma with the Spanish explorer Hernando de Alarcon in

1540. The name Yuma is said to derive from the Spanish *umo*, meaning "smoke," after the huge fires once built by local Indians attempting to induce rain.

For more information write to: Commander, U.S. Army Yuma Proving Ground, Attention: STEYP-PA, Yuma, AZ 85365, or call (602) 653-6189.

Marine Corps

YUMA MARINE CORPS AIR STATION

History. Marine Harrier, Skyhawk, and Phantom jets have been a familiar sight streaking over the bombing and gunnery ranges adjacent to Yuma Marine Corps Air Station in the southwestern Arizona skies since the Marine Corps took over the former Vincent Air Force Base in 1959. One can only speculate what Hernando de Alarcon, the first white man to see the area, would make of the changes that have occurred there since he visited in 1540.

Today the station occupies over five square miles and is home and workplace for approximately 5,000 permanently assigned military personnel. During the course of an average year, units deploying to Yuma for training account for another 10,000 personnel and 900 aircraft accommodated at the station. Aircraft flying from Yuma MCAS use 2.8 million acres (an area equal to the state of New Jersey) of training ranges, all within ten minutes' flying time of the station's 13,300-foot main runway. Today Yuma MCAS is home to Marine Air Group (MAG) 13, a tactical air-combat unit flying the AV-8B Harrier II fighter aircraft.

Housing and Schools. There are more than 800 sets of family quarters at Yuma. The waiting period for quarters depends on the rank of the sponsor and can stretch from as few as four months for an enlisted person to eight months for some officers. There are, however, about 100 mobile home parks available in the civilian community, and the station also operates a thirteen-unit hostess house for transients and visiting active-duty and retired personnel and their dependents.

Dependent children attend local schools. A child-care center is operated on the station, and on-base educational facilities cover the full range of opportunities for improvement in vocational military skills, as well as off-duty pursuit of college courses. Instruction is available from Arizona Western College, Northern Arizona University, Cochise College, Southern Illinois University, and Webster College.

Personal Services. The quality of life onboard the station is enhanced by a full range of commissary and Marine Corps exchange operations. Medical and dental care are provided by on-base clinics. Inpatient and specialty medical care are available through civilian sources or the Naval Regional Medical Center in San Diego.

Recreation. The special-services office operates a vigorous recreational activities program for the personnel at Yuma. These include a twelve-lane bowling alley, a gym, tennis courts, swimming pools, a stables area, athletic and camping gear issue, hobby shops, a skeet club, and officers, staff NCO, and enlisted clubs.

The Local Area. Yuma, a city of 70,000 people, is a beautiful town with a dry and delightful climate, especially during the winter months. Annual rainfall is less than three inches, but the town is surrounded by water in the form of canals and small lakes formed by the Colorado River. This gives the angler and water sports enthusiast much opportunity to engage in these pastimes most of the year. The sun shines at Yuma an estimated 93 percent of the time.

The surrounding area has many interesting places to see, and there are many activities to participate in, from greyhound racing to gun shows and rodeos. Every summer, one may enter the annual inner-tube race on the Colorado, or just stand on the riverbank and watch the courageous contenders float by. Historic Fort Yuma and the notorious Yuma Territorial Prison and Museum are favorite tourist attractions, as are the state parks and many recreational lakes in the immediate vicinity. And of course, Mexico is only twenty-three miles south of Yuma.

For more information write to: Public Affairs Office, P.O. Box 99113, Yuma, AZ 85369-9113, or call (602) 341-2275.

ARKANSAS

Air Force

EAKER AIR FORCE BASE

After fifty years of service to America, Eaker Air Force Base, situated about four miles northwest of the town of Blytheville, was closed in 1992.

LITTLE ROCK AIR FORCE BASE

History. When the first airmen came to Jacksonville, Arkansas, in 1955, there were no quarters ready for them at the air base, so the local people put them up. In 1952, a Little Rock citizens' committee began raising the money needed to purchase the first 6,000 acres of land required for the base's construction, and eventually this land was donated to the U.S. government by the citizens. Arkansas congressman Brooks Hays personally turned the first shovel to begin construction on base housing. Military personnel have always been cordially welcomed at Little Rock.

Today the base is home to 5,200 military personnel, and it employs a civilian workforce of 700. The host unit is the 314th Airlift Wing, which has the dual mission of worldwide airlift and airlift crew training to conduct tactical air operations globally. It is responsible for all C-130 training for the Department of Defense, the Coast Guard, and many allied nations.

Housing and Schools. There are over 1,500 units of family housing on the base. The average waiting time for quarters is from eight to fifteen months for two- and three-bedroom units to eight to twelve months for four-bedroom units. Off-base rentals range from $250 to $400 per month, plus utilities. Home rentals range from $350 to $750 per month. Transient quarters are very limited, and first priority goes to personnel on temporary duty.

The children of military families stationed at Little Rock attend two on-base elementary schools. Students in grades seven through twelve attend North Pulaski High School off base. A child-care center is operated on the base, and the base child-development center provides care of children ages six weeks to ten years. The education office offers off-duty college-level courses from such institutions as Arkansas State University, Park College, Southern Illinois University, the University of Arkansas, and Webster College.

Personal Services. The USAF Hospital, Little Rock, is a twenty-bed health-care facility that was completely renovated and updated in 1979. The commissary at Little Rock is one of the fifteen largest in the Air Force, with 10,000 line items for sale. The base exchange offers a complete line of retail goods as well as many concessions. There is also a family service center that provides assistance through various programs including information, referral, financial management, relocation, and volunteer resource program services.

Recreation. Recreational facilities at Little Rock are excellent. Among the many offered are a gymnasium, an eighteen-hole golf course, and a twenty-four-lane bowling center. Besides the officers and enlisted clubs, there are various arts and crafts and hobby shops, and a saddle club. The Base Lake, a thirty-seven-acre body of water, offers good fishing and two picnic areas.

The Local Area. Jacksonville, the town just outside the base, has a population of over 28,000 people, and much of its recent growth is directly attributable to the opening of the air base there in 1955. Little Rock, the Arkansas state capital, has a population of 167,000. The base is about twenty miles northeast of the city. Metropolitan Little Rock owns nineteen municipal parks and a 200-acre zoo. The climate is temperate, with an average mean temperature of 61° F. Snow is rare and precipitation is usually in the form of rain, which averages approximately forty-eight inches a year.

Hunting is permitted on base in prescribed areas, and Little Rock itself is situated in the middle of the state's magnificent hunting and fishing areas. The great Ouachita National Forest begins just a little to the west of the base, and the Greers Ferry Area, forty-five miles from Jacksonville, offers 40,000 acres for fishing, swimming, and water sports.

For more information write to: 314th Airlift Wing Public Affairs Office, Little Rock AFB, AR 72099-5000, or call (501) 988-3601.

CALIFORNIA

Air Force

BEALE AIR FORCE BASE

What do the Army Camel Corps and Beale Air Force Base have in common? Gen. Edward Fitzgerald Beale. During the administration of Franklin Pierce, Beale, then an Army officer, suggested to Secretary of War Jefferson Davis that the Army's transportation problems in the Southwest could be alleviated by importing camels from North Africa to act as beasts of burden. The idea was tried, but the Army lost interest and Beale went on to a successful career in business.

History. Opened in 1942, Camp Beale was home to the Army's 13th Armored Division, which trained infantry and tank crews on its 86,000 acres. Although reduced to 23,000 acres when acquired by the Air Force, today Beale is one of the largest bases in the Air Combat Command. The base is home to the 9th Wing, which flies the U-2 Dragon Lady, and to more than 3,400 military personnel, their 4,000 family members, and a civilian workforce of more than 1,300 people.

Housing and Schools. There are over 1,700 units of family housing available at Beale, plus a mobile home park that can accommodate 176 trailers. The housing area is situated about ten miles from the flight line, in the foothills of the Sierra Nevada. Temporary lodging is available for visitors and newly assigned personnel.

Two elementary schools, for children in kindergarten through sixth grade, are operated on the base, and a child-care center is available there as well. Educational opportunities for adults are offered through California State University, the University of Southern California, and Chapman College, all of which conduct on-base classes.

Personal Services. On-base services include an excellent, twenty-five-bed USAF hospital, a base exchange, a commissary, and complete banking facilities.

Recreation. Recreational facilities at Beale range from hunting preserves to family garden plots. The sports-minded will find a gymnasium, a sixteen-lane bowling center, swimming pools, a nine-hole golf course, and a fine intramural sports program. A recreation center, arts and crafts and hobby shops, and an on-base picnic area are also offered. The base has many lakes and streams well stocked with fish, and small-game hunting on the base is very good for pheasant, duck, quail, rabbit, and dove.

The Local Area. Beale lies just ten miles west of the twin cities of Marysville and Yuba City, which have a combined population of 50,000. Lake Tahoe and Reno are not far to the east, and the Oroville State Recreation Area is less than forty miles north of Marysville. The climate in this area offers long, hot summers with little humidity, and the winters are relatively mild. In the summer months, striped bass weighing up to fifty pounds may be caught in the local rivers.

For more information write to: Public Affairs Office, Beale AFB, CA 95903-5300, or call (916) 634-8889.

CASTLE AIR FORCE BASE

In 1991 the Base Closure Commission recommended that Castle Air Force Base be closed in September 1995.

Castle Air Force Base is located in the famous San Joaquin Valley, one of the most fertile regions in California. Because the area is situated between the Sierra Nevada to the west and California's coastal mountains to the east, the climate there is generally desertlike, with dry summers and fairly mild winters. But in the winter the fog becomes so thick that sometimes the California Highway Patrol has to guide drivers along the five-mile Sante Fe Road that runs between the town of Merced and the base, and flight operations are delayed because of poor visibility.

History. Castle AFB was opened in September 1941 as Merced Army Air Field. In January 1946 it was renamed in honor of Brig. Gen. Frederick Walter Castle, who was killed while leading a formation of 2,000 bombers in a raid against a target in Germany. For his heroism Castle was awarded the Medal of Honor. Today, Castle AFB is home to the 93rd Bomb Wing, the 34th Bomb Squadron, and other activities. The base has an active-duty population of about 4,500 personnel plus more than 11,000 military dependents and 1,200 civilian employees.

Housing and Schools. More than 900 units of family housing are available at Castle, situated in two off-base housing areas: Castle Gardens, one-half mile from the base; and Castle Vista, one and one-half miles away and within the city limits of Atwater.

A nursery school and a child-care center are operated on the base for dependent children. Public and parochial schools are located in nearby Atwater and Merced. On-base college programs are available to military personnel from Merced College, Chapman College, and Golden Gate University. Correspondence courses are also offered.

Personal Services. Medical care is provided by a twenty-five-bed USAF hospital. Conditions that are beyond the capability of the Castle medical facility are referred to Travis AFB, Oakland Naval Medical Center, or Letterman Army Medical Center at the Presidio of San Francisco. Other services available on base include a main base exchange, a clothing sales store, many base exchange concessions, a commissary, officers and enlisted clubs, and banking facilities.

Recreation. Recreational facilities at Castle are excellent and include a sixteen-lane bowling center, wood and automotive hobby shops, a crafts center, a recreation center, a skeet and trap facility, and many athletic facilities.

The Local Area. Castle is located adjacent to the city of Atwater, population 20,000, and seven miles northeast of Merced, population 50,000. Fresno, with 220,000 people, is sixty-five miles south of the base, and Modesto, with 150,000 residents, is thirty-five miles north. Yosemite National Park is only eighty miles to the east of the base. Sequoia and Kings Canyon National Parks are situated only fifty miles east of Fresno. San Francisco lies about one hundred road miles to the northwest of the base.

California is one of the most geographically diverse states in the Union, with mountains, deserts, a 1,000-mile coastline, and over 10,000 campsites situated in some of the most magnificent and scenic parks and national forests to be found anywhere in the country.

For more information write to: 93rd BMW Public Affairs Office, Castle AFB, CA 95342-5000, or call (209) 726-4636.

EDWARDS AIR FORCE BASE

With a wooden propeller attached to its nose to disguise its real propulsion system, the Bell XP-59A, America's first jet aircraft, arrived at Edwards Air Force Base in September 1942 and made its first test flight there on 1 October 1942. On 14 April 1981, the space shuttle *Columbia* landed there, another important first in the base's long and exciting history.

History. Edwards began its official existence in 1933, when it was used as a bombing range for the Army Air Corps, and in 1937 Air Corps gunnery and bombing maneuvers were held there. Known initially as Muroc Army Air Field and later as Muroc Air Force Base, in 1949 the installation was named in honor of Capt. Glen W. Edwards, a native of California who was killed in a test flight of the "flying wing" experimental bomber in June 1948. Today Edwards's 301,000 acres are home to Headquarters, 412th Test Wing; Headquarters, 650th Air Base Wing; the USAF Test Pilot School; the Phillips Laboratory; the U.S. Army Aviation Technical Test Center; and other tenant units. Edwards is also responsible for the management of the 1.7 million acres of the Utah Test and Training Range. Today Edwards is home to about 4,500 military personnel, their 6,000 family members, and 8,000 civilian employees.

Housing and Schools. Edwards has over 1,900 sets of government quarters, spread throughout nine separate housing areas. There is also a mobile home park that can accommodate more than 180 trailers. Unaccompanied personnel are housed in one-bedroom, apartment-style units for officers and two- and three-story dorms for enlisted people. The base has a preschool, three elementary schools, and a junior-senior high school. The education services center offers college courses from Cerro Coso Community College, Chapman College, the University of Southern California, California State College, and California State University.

Personal Services. The personal services and facilities available at Edwards include the fifteen-bed Air Force Systems Command hospital, a commissary, a base exchange with many concessions such the Colonial Inn cafeteria located near the flight line and a service station, and family support and child-development centers.

Recreation. Recreational facilities include a twenty-lane bowling alley, a gym with an enclosed swimming pool open year-round, and an eighteen-hole, par seventy-two golf course. A variety of hobby shops (auto, ceramics, and wood), stables, aero and rod and gun clubs, and a community center are available. Officers and NCO clubs are located on base, as are a library, a theater, a skating rink, and a thirty-five-channel cable TV package.

The Local Area. Edwards AFB is located about twenty miles east of Mojave and eight miles west of Boron, sandwiched between the small communities of Lancaster, thirty-five miles to the south, and California City, twenty miles to the north. In the bigger picture, Edwards is one hundred miles northeast of Los Angeles, ninety miles northwest of San Bernardino, and eighty miles southeast of Bakersfield. The climate there is dry and the weather generally clear. Temperatures average around 100° F. in the summer, 40° F. in winter, but the humidity is low; about four inches of rain fall there in the average year. The base is situated in the Antelope Valley, one of many such valleys in the Mojave Desert area, and is at an elevation of 2,300 feet.

For more information write to: Public Affairs Office, 2 S. Rosamond Blvd., Edwards AFB, CA 93523-1225, or call (805) 277-3510.

GEORGE AIR FORCE BASE

After more than fifty years of service to the U.S. Air Force, George Air Force Base was closed in December 1992.

LOS ANGELES AIR FORCE BASE

Los Angeles Air Force Base is located in El Segundo, three miles south of Los Angeles International Airport. It is not like a conventional air base, because little of a conventional nature goes on there. Los Angeles AFB is a key installation in the space-development program.

History. The base was dedicated in July 1964 and today is home for Air Force Materiel Command's Space and Missile Systems Center with the mission of strengthening our national defense through the full exploitation of space. LAAFB occupies about 100 acres of urban-industrial real estate and employs 2,600 military and 1,100 civilian personnel. The adjacent Aerospace Corporation employs another 3,500 people.

Housing and Schools. Housing is located nineteen miles south of the base at the Fort MacArthur Annex. The 570 officer and enlisted townhouses and renovated field-grade homes are in high demand, with a waiting time of about nine to twelve months. Temporary living facilities and visiting quarters are available at Fort MacArthur. Housing off base is very expensive: Two-bedroom apartment rentals begin at $750 per month.

Dependent children attend schools off base. Adult education is offered on base by several colleges, and more than 100 colleges and universities are situated in the greater Los Angeles area, giving servicemembers a wide variety of choices.

Personal Services. Medical care at the base is provided by a USAF clinic, but patients are seen there by appointment only (except for emergencies). Definitive medical care is provided by local civilian hospitals or the Naval Regional Medical Center in Long Beach, the Naval Hospital in San Diego, or March Air Force Base, about sixty miles away. A large commissary is located on base, and a base exchange operates there with a main store, a flower shop, a laundry and dry cleaner, a service station, and other concessions. Officers and NCO club facilities are also offered.

Recreation. Recreational facilities include a gymnasium, hobby shops (auto and arts and crafts), and a recreational supply checkout facility where camping, athletic, and water sport equipment are available.

It should be remembered that Los Angeles AFB is divided into two areas. Area A is restricted to access, while Area B, where most of the base morale and support facilities are situated, is open to the public.

The Local Area. Although there is little to see at the base itself, the local area abounds with sights and attractions. Fort MacArthur provides a pool, a picnic area, and an unparalleled view of the Pacific Ocean. Tourist draws in the area range from skiing in the local mountains to sunning on the beaches. Disneyland and Universal Studios tours are prime attractions. The weather is very nice during the early spring months, but from June to September the smog associated with the Los Angeles area can be very unpleasant, as can the traffic, which sometimes transforms the freeways into parking lots.

For more information write to: Space and Missile System Center Public Affairs Officer, Los Angeles AFB, Los Angeles, CA 90009-2960, or call (310) 363-1110.

MARCH AIR FORCE BASE

Every day of the year aircrews of the 22nd Air Refueling Wing roar into the California skies in their KC-10A Extender refueling aircraft to perform their part in the Strategic Command's mission to be combat ready at all times and deployable to anywhere in the world.

History. Named in honor of Lt. Peyton C. March, who died in an air crash in 1918, March Field officially opened on 1 March 1918, which makes it the oldest West Coast Air Force base. Today it comprises 8,000 acres astride Interstate 215 near the cities of Moreno Valley and Riverside. The more than 3,800 military personnel, their 5,000 family members, 3,500 reserve components personnel, and 1,700 civilian employees who live and work at the base belong to various units such as Headquarters, Fifteenth Air Force, and the 452nd Air Refueling Wing (Air Force Reserve).

Housing and Schools. There are 910 sets of family quarters at March Air Force Base, situated in two housing areas: Green Acres, on the main base; and Arnold Heights, across Interstate 215 in West March. Arnold Heights offers residents a swimming pool, a chapel, and a branch of the main exchange. Although a temporary living facility is available at March, space is limited and incoming families are encouraged to make reservations up to sixty days in advance. Personnel on leave or retired personnel may find accommodations at March, but on a space-available basis only.

School-age children attend the public schools in the local area. An elementary school is located in the Arnold Heights housing area on the base. The base also offers parents a child-care center and a preschool facility. The base education services office offers college courses from Riverside City College, Chapman College, Embry-Riddle University, Southern Illinois University, the University of Redlands, and the University of Southern California.

Personal Services. Medical care at March is provided by an eight-bed hospital facility that is also the referral facility for a number of other bases in Southern California, Nevada, and Arizona. An excellent, well-stocked commissary and base exchange, located in the base exchange complex, offer patrons the convenience of on-base shopping, including watch repair, a florist, dry cleaning, videocassette rental, a fast-food restaurant serving deli sandwiches and pizza, and a Burger King. Also in the complex is a 500-seat theater. There is a banking facility a block from the complex and a credit union just outside the main gate.

Recreation. Facilities at March include an eighteen-hole golf course as well as a sixteen-lane bowling alley. Three swimming pools, several tennis courts, a riding club, various types of craft facilities, and a well-equipped gymnasium are available.

The Local Area. March AFB is located in the city of Moreno Valley approximately ten miles from Riverside and about fifty-eight miles from Los Angeles. The climate in the Riverside area is very mild, with an annual average temperature of around 73° F. The winters there are characterized by fog and frost, but the sun usually manages to shine 70 to 80 percent of the time. The Riverside-Moreno Valley area is one of the fastest-growing sections of Southern California.

Only a few miles from the base is Lake Perris, which offers swimming, boating, and camping. The San Bernardino National Forest is nearby, and the attractions of the Los Angeles area, such as Disneyland, Knott's Berry Farm, *Queen Mary/Spruce Goose*, and Universal Studios are only an hour away.

For more information, write to HQ Fifteenth Air Force, Public Affairs Division, March AFB, CA 92518-5000, or call (714) 655-1110.

MATHER AIR FORCE BASE

Mather AFB was closed in September 1993.

McCLELLAN AIR FORCE BASE

McClellan Air Force Base occupies 3,700 acres of land ten miles northeast of Sacramento and is home to more than 2,700 active-duty personnel, their 7,000 family members, and more than 12,600 civilian employees. The key words at McClellan are *maintenance* and *logistics*. The Air Logistics Center has responsibility as system manager for aircraft such as the A-10, the F/EF-111, and the F-117A (Stealth fighter).

History. The base began life in 1937 as the Sacramento Air Depot but was renamed later that year in honor of Maj. Hezekiah McClellan, a pioneer in the charting of Alaskan air routes, who was killed while flight testing an aircraft near Centerville, Ohio.

Housing and Schools. There are over 620 family housing units at McClellan located in three separate housing areas situated around the base. Transient billeting and guest housing are available to both officers and enlisted personnel for short-term occupancy.

The base operates a child-care center, but dependent school-age children attend classes in one of the seventeen school districts operated in Sacramento County. The base offers a child-care center with the capacity for 140 children. The education services office offers on-base college courses from such institutions as Embry-Riddle Aeronautical University and the University of Idaho.

Personal Services. The USAF clinic at McClellan offers outpatient services to active-duty personnel, retirees, and dependents, with referrals to the David Grant USAF Medical Center at Travis Air Force Base. Other facilities include a base exchange, a commissary, and a package store. Excellent officers and NCO clubs are also available.

Recreation. Recreational facilities include a nine-hole golf course, three swimming pools, a gymnasium, a twenty-lane bowling center, hobby shops, numerous clubs and associations, and a two-story recreational center.

The Local Area. McClellan AFB is situated at the intersection of Interstate 80 and Business 80, in the northeast section of Sacramento. The climate in this part of California is temperate, with low humidity most of the year. Annual rainfall averages less than eighteen inches, with most of it falling from December through February. About 1.5 million people live in the Sacramento area, 320,000 in the city of Sacramento itself. San Francisco is 90 miles to the west; Lake Tahoe, Reno, and the Sierras are approximately 120 miles to the east of the base; and Napa and Sonoma Counties are within easy driving distance.

For more information write to: Public Affairs Office, 5241 Arnold Avenue, Ste. 3, McClellan AFB, CA 95652-1089, or call (916) 643-2111.

NORTON AIR FORCE BASE

After more than fifty years of service, Norton AFB was closed in March 1994.

ONIZUKA AIR FORCE BASE

Onizuka Air Force Base occupies twenty-three acres at Sunnyvale, thirty-seven miles south of San Francisco and half a mile north of Moffett Field Naval Air Station. At Onizuka, the Air Force monitors and controls on-orbit military spacecraft from sites all over the world.

History. Onizuka, named for Lt. Col. Ellison S. Onizuka, who died aboard the *Challenger* space shuttle in 1986, has been in the space business since 1960, when it was the Satellite Test Annex. In 1971, it was renamed Sunnyvale Air Force Station. It became Onizuka Air Force Base in August 1987.

Onizuka is home to the 750th Space Group and Detachments 2 and 6 of the Air Force Space Missile Systems Center. The 750th Space Group controls all Defense Department space shuttle missions from launch through landing. There are about 900 military personnel, 200 civilian employees, and approximately 2,000 contractor personnel at Onizuka.

Housing and Schools. Onizuka has control of 600 units of family housing located at Moffett NAS. Children attend schools in the Bay Area.

Personal and Recreational Services. Onizuka has a small convenience store and a consolidated open mess. A small weight room is available for use by personnel stationed at Onizuka. The facilities at nearby Moffett Field are open to Onizuka personnel. Beaches, mountain resorts, and Yosemite National Park, as well as the city of San Francisco, are within comfortable driving distance of the base.

For more information write to: Public Affairs, 750SGP, 1080 Lockheed Way Box #53, Sunnyvale, CA 94089-1236, or call (408) 752-3110.

TRAVIS AIR FORCE BASE

Travis Air Force Base has earned its name as the "Gateway to the Pacific." Until fairly recently, most troops deploying to the Far East and returning home from there processed through Travis. In 1973 Travis welcomed 143 American POWs from North Vietnamese prison camps, and in 1975 the base hosted thousands of South Vietnamese refugees fleeing their country after the Communist conquest.

History. Named in honor of Brig. Gen. Robert F. Travis, who was killed in a B-29 crash at the end of the local runway in August 1950, Travis AFB was activated as Fairfield-Suisun Army Air Field in 1942 and renamed in 1951. Today it occupies over 6,000 acres fifty miles northeast of San Francisco and is home to the men and women of the 60th Airlift Wing, which is responsible for four squadrons that fly the C-141 Starlifter and C-5 Galaxy aircraft. Travis is home to 7,300 active-duty personnel, their 9,100 family members, 5,200 reserve components personnel, and more than 2,000 civilian employees.

Housing and Schools. There are over 2,400 units of family housing available at Travis, as well as fifty spaces in the on-base mobile home park. Temporary living quarters are available to families traveling on permanent-change-of-station orders.

Travis operates a child-care center and three elementary schools (kindergarten through fifth grade). A junior high and a high school are located just off base. The base education center provides assistance in enrolling in several undergraduate and graduate-level courses offered on base through Golden Gate University, Southern Illinois University, Chapman University, and Embry-Riddle Aeronautical University.

Personal Services. Medical care is provided by the 300-bed David Grant USAF Medical Center. The commissary at Travis stocks more than 12,000 line items and serves 70,000 patrons each month. The base exchange complex offers a wide variety of concessions. Food concessions available include a Baskin Robbins ice cream shop, a Burger King, Anthony's Pizza, and snack bars. The base club system includes officers and all-ranks enlisted clubs.

Recreation. Athletic and recreational facilities include two swimming pools, an eighteen-hole golf course, a thirty-two-lane bowling alley, a gym, an equestrian center, two physical fitness centers, an arts and crafts center, and several jogging courses. Two parks are located on the base, North Gate and Eucalyptus. Both offer picnicking and games, and the latter features many eucalyptus trees. The base family camp is open year-round and has twenty-four camper spaces with hookups and twelve without, restrooms, a playground, and two pavilions with barbecue pits. Camping, volleyball, hiking, and softball, as well as camping- and fishing-gear rentals, are also available.

The Local Area. Travis is immediately adjacent to the twin cities of Fairfield and Suisun. Fairfield has a population of over 80,000, while Suisun City is home to more than 19,000 people. Nearby Vacaville, seven miles north of Travis, has a population of more than 66,000. Sacramento is about forty-five miles to the east and San Francisco about fifty miles to the west.

For more information write to: Public Affairs Office, 527 Waldron St., Travis AFB, CA 94535-2127, or call (707) 424-1110.

VANDENBERG AIR FORCE BASE

Vandenberg Air Force Base is one of the few places where you can sit in the ice cream parlor in the main exchange complex and savor a dish of chocolate chip while ICBMs roar overhead to targets 4,200 miles downrange in the Pacific Ocean. Since 1958, Vandenberg has launched about 1,600 missiles. Rocketry is the central feature of all activity on the base.

History. Named after Gen. Hoyt S. Vandenberg, the second Air Force Chief of Staff, the base was chosen as the Air Force's first missile installation in 1956. Today it is the third largest base of the Air Force, covering more than 98,000 acres (that's 154 square miles!). The host organization at Vandenberg is the 30th Space Wing.

Housing and Schools. There are 2,080 sets of family quarters at Vandenberg and 172 mobile home–park spaces. Transient families traveling on official orders may obtain temporary quarters on a reserved basis. Off-base rentals run from $575 to $950 per month.

The base offers a child-care center, two elementary schools, and a middle school; high school students attend classes off base. The education center is the focal point for college course enrollments.

Personal Services. The forty-five-bed USAF hospital at Vandenberg provides complete medical care for all active-duty and retired personnel and their families. Among the other service facilities are the three-million-dollar main exchange complex, a commissary, and complete banking facilities.

Recreation. Recreational facilities include a swimming pool, an eighteen-hole golf course, and a twenty-lane bowling center. Also available are officers and NCO clubs, an arts and crafts complex, a rod and gun club, and a gymnasium. Vandenberg also offers an excellent tour program to such places as Las Vegas, Reno, San Francisco, and Los Angeles.

The Local Area. Nearby communities include Vandenberg Village, Mission Hills, and Lompoc. These three towns have a total combined population of 36,000 people, and all are located within ten miles of the base. Santa Maria, the largest local community, has 50,000 residents. Santa Barbara, an hour's drive southeast of Vandenberg, is a city of 75,000 inhabitants.

For most of the year, Vandenberg's average high temperature stays between 60° F. and 65° F., with lows ranging between 40° F. and 50° F. With its proximity to the ocean, the base experiences considerable periods of heavy fog, especially in the summer months.

Just a few miles west of the base lie the Sierra Madre and Los Padres National Forest. Los Padres covers over 1.7 million acres and offers more than 300 campsites and picnic areas and two major ski areas. Deer, boar, and wildfowl may be hunted in its reserves.

For more information write to: Public Affairs Division, Vandenberg AFB, CA 93437-5000, or call (805) 866-3595

Army

FORT IRWIN NATIONAL TRAINING CENTER

When you leave Barstow
To go to Fort Irwin,
There is nothing to show
That the post is there,
The closer you get
The more you wonder
Is there really a post,
WHERE?

—Barbara Parker, Fort Irwin ACS Volunteer

Fort Irwin is there, all right, thirty-seven miles northeast of Barstow, California, midway between Las Vegas and Los Angeles—1,000 square miles of some of the most rugged terrain in the United States. As the poet will testify, however, isolated and harsh as the post is, the Army community there has a big heart and offers everyone a warm welcome.

History. The land that now constitutes Fort Irwin was first set aside for military training in August 1940. Originally a subpost of Camp Haan, which was adjacent to what is now March Air Force Base in Riverside, Fort Irwin was named after Maj. Gen. George Leroy Irwin, commander of the 57th Field Artillery Brigade in World War I. The installation has had a checkered history of deactivations and activations, the most recent in October 1980 when it was activated as the National Training Center (NTC). Since then 472,833 soldiers have trained there on unit maneuvers in the desert environment.

The NTC is home to the 177th Armored Brigade, known as "Opposing Force," because their mission is to replicate a Russian-style motorized rifle regiment and employ Russian-style tactics using U.S. armor, aircraft, and other combat vehicles visually modified to resemble Russian equipment. Other tenant units include the Foreign Military Intelligence Battalion, the USAF's 4445th Tactical Training Squadron, and others. The post has a permanent military population of more than 4,900, plus 7,500 family members and 2,900 civilian employees.

Housing and Schools. There are 1,636 units of government housing available at Fort Irwin, including 75 mobile home pads. Ten mobile homes serve as temporary-housing facilities. Dependent schooling is provided by the Silver Valley Unified School District: On-post schooling consists of an elementary and middle school; high school students attend Silver Valley High in Daggett, thirty-four miles south of Fort Irwin. Child care is available through several centers on post. Adult education is provided through the post education office and consists of college courses offered by Barstow College and California Baptist College.

Personal Services. Weed Army Community Hospital, a twenty-five-bed facility, is the primary health care provider for personnel at Fort Irwin; dental care is available for dependents on a space-available basis.

A new post exchange and commissary, the Leaders Club, an arts and crafts center, the soldiers club, a Burger King, a laundry and dry-cleaning service, a pizza parlor and delivery service, a flower shop, a barber shop, a beauty salon, a package beverage store, a Baskin Robbins ice cream parlor, and a shopette are all located on base.

Recreation. As befits an isolated post, Fort Irwin offers lots in the way of recreation for those living there. The NTC offers a twenty-lane bowling center, an eighteen-hole miniature golf course, and riding stables. Soldiers Park, located near the family swimming pool, offers barbecue facilities, picnic tables, and plenty of shade trees. A modern fitness center offers all types of indoor sports, and the Ingalls Recreation Center has a big-screen TV, pool tables, video games, and a 640-seat auditorium for special events. The rod and gun club promotes hunting, fishing, archery, and recreational shooting.

There are two swimming pools at Fort Irwin—the family pool and the troop pool—both open year-round. The information, tours, and travel office arranges tours to many California amusement centers, including Disneyland and Universal Studios. And for those who enjoy the pleasures of the mind, the Fort Irwin Post Library offers 20,000 books, 100 magazines, and 12 major newspapers from which to choose.

The Local Area. The weather in this area is hot and dry. The average high summer temperature at Fort Irwin is around 100° F., with an average low in the winter of 37° F. The average annual rainfall there is only two and a half inches.

Remote as it may seem to be, the Barstow–Fort Irwin area is rich in natural wonders and California history and is still a haven for tourists. Barstow itself is the site of the largest silver strike in California's history and mining still goes on there today. The San Bernardino National Forest is only sixty miles south of Barstow, San Diego is a four-hour drive away, and world-famous attractions such as Death Valley, Palm Springs, and the Colorado River are all within easy driving range.

For more information write to: Public Affairs Officer, HQ, National Training Center and Fort Irwin, Fort Irwin, CA 92310-5000, or call (619) 386-4511.

FORT ORD

The 1991 Base Closure Commission recommended that Fort Ord be closed by July 1996.

"The greatest meeting of land and water in the world," wrote author Robert Louis Stevenson of the Monterey Peninsula in 1879. So impressed was he by the area's breathtaking beauty that he used it as the setting for his novel, *Treasure Island.* Few spots anywhere, in real life or in fiction, can match its year-round moderate climate and its rugged coastlines, and few other places can boast its graceful combination of a sense of history and Spanish-Mexican-American tradition.

History. Fort Ord itself occupies about 28,000 acres (not including another 42,000 at Camp Roberts and 164,000 at Fort Hunter Liggett) of rolling plains and rugged hills on the north shore of the Monterey Peninsula, extending eastward into the fertile Salinas Valley, its western border nudging the sand dunes and the water of Monterey Bay. Named in honor of Maj. Gen. Edward Ord, who served at the Presidio of Monterey and later commanded Union troops in the Civil War, the post was originally established as a maneuver area and a field artillery range. Today it is home to the 7th Infantry Division (Light), which was scheduled to move to Fort Lewis, Washington, in 1993. At press time Fort Ord's population comprised 5,000 military personnel and 3,000 family members.

Housing and Schools. More than 4,700 sets of family quarters are available, and the Brostrom Mobile Home Park has 215 units for lease or purchase from the local contractor who operates the facility. Another 83 apartments are leased by the post housing office for junior enlisted personnel. Guest housing consists of a 30-room unit, the Light Fighter Lodge; 55 self-contained cottages and apartments; and 150 "sleeping rooms." Reservations should be made up to sixty days in advance. Troop housing consists of modern, dormitory-type buildings with two to four soldiers sharing individual rooms.

The post education center offers programs to assist military personnel in career development and college-level courses. Classes are available on the post as well as at local institutions such as Monterey Peninsula College, Golden Gate University, Hartnell College, Embry-Riddle Aeronautical University, the University of California–Santa Cruz, and San Jose State University. For dependent children, there are four elementary schools and a junior high school on post. Child care is also available for children ages six weeks to twelve years.

Personal Services. Fort Ord has a fifty-bed hospital, a large commissary with two small convenience stores, and a post exchange with twelve branches.

Recreation. The post's recreational facilities cater to a wide variety of tastes, from chess clubs to scuba diving. The outdoor recreation office offers many programs for sportsmen, from hunting and fishing to athletic facilities.

The Local Area. Fort Ord is located 105 miles south of San Francisco and some 320 miles north of Los Angeles. More than a million people each year visit the area's many parks, beaches, and recreational areas, where boating, fishing, camping, and excursions through majestic scenery form the major attractions. Somewhat farther away are such attractions as the Los Padres National Forest and the Pfeiffer Redwoods State Park, which contains 1,000-year-old trees that stand as high as 240 feet. The Fort Ord Tour Office offers complete tourist information and arranges ticket sales for local, San Francisco Bay Area, and Los Angeles events, as well as discount tickets for major commercial attractions, including tours to Disneyland, Lake Tahoe, Yosemite, and Tijuana, Mexico.

For more information write to: Army Community Services Office, Fort Ord, CA 92941-5000, or call (408) 242-5713.

PRESIDIO OF MONTEREY

For most of the more than 2,000 years human beings are known to have lived on the site of the Presidio of Monterey, English has not been the primary language. Today, if the shades of any of the Rumsen Indians or Spanish settlers who lived there in former times still linger on the site, the place must seem to them a veritable Babel of languages, with everything from Albanian to Vietnamese spoken there.

History. The Presidio is actually a subpost of Fort Ord, which is only a few miles to the north and shares in the great natural beauty of the Monterey Peninsula. Originally claimed by the Spanish in 1602, the area was not permanently settled by them until 1770. The original presidio, or fort, was built in 1792. It was taken over by the United States in 1846. In 1946, the Army established a language school there that became the Defense Language Institute in 1963. Today the Presidio is home to about 2,800 active-duty personnel, 1,500 family members, and 1,100 civilian employees.

Housing and Schools. Because the Presidio's basic mission is to support a school population, housing for married personnel assigned there permanently is limited, with only ninety-six sets of family units, ninety-three bachelor officer quarters, and 2,500 enlisted quarters available. Housing is available off post and at Fort Ord, as is schooling for dependent children. There is a day-care center at the Presidio with a capacity of eighty children.

As of summer 1993, the average monthly rental for a two-bedroom furnished apartment off post was $845; furnished two-bedroom houses were renting for around $1,200 a month; and utility rates were ranging from $80 to as much as $300 per month.

Servicemembers assigned to the Defense Language Institute as students or permanent-party personnel may pursue off-duty education. Currently, thirty different language courses are taught there to about 5,000 resident and 100,000 nonresident Department of Defense personnel each year. These courses are taught by a faculty of 750 foreign-born instructors and a military and civilian staff of 900. The Institute uses 450 classrooms, 1,270 language lab positions, the latest audiovisual training aids, a library of over 100,000 foreign-language texts and periodicals, and an electronic media center complete with computer-assisted learning aids. The Institute has been accredited by the Accrediting Commission for Community and Junior Colleges of the Western Association of Schools and Colleges. The courses taught vary in length from twenty-four to forty-seven weeks, depending upon the difficulty of the language being taught.

The Fort Ord Education Center regularly provides counselors who visit the Institute to assist personnel who wish to attend colleges and universities in the immediate area.

Personal Services. The installation offers the basic facilities found on any military post, including a bank, a credit union, clubs, and an exchange store. Commissary facilities are available at nearby Fort Ord, and personnel stationed at the Presidio are eligible to take advantage of all the other facilities offered there.

The Local Area. The climate at the Presidio is one of the most attractive features there because it has no extremes. The lows average 56° F. and the highs, 75° F. year-round. Most rain falls between the months of November and February and averages about seventeen inches per year.

For more information write to: Public Affairs Office, Attention: ATFL-PAO, DLIFC, Presidio of Monterey, CA 93944-5006, or call (408) 647-5119.

PRESIDIO OF SAN FRANCISCO

At press time the Presidio of San Francisco was scheduled to close in September 1994.

The Presidio of San Francisco is unique in that it is not only one of the most beautiful military installations in the world, but it is one of the few located entirely within a major metropolitan area. Sitting in the shadow of the Golden Gate Bridge (literally!), the Presidio is home and workplace for 2,000 military personnel and civilian employees. Additionally, 4,000 dependents live on the installation and within its subposts around the Bay Area.

History. First established by the Spanish in 1776, the Presidio has been an active U.S. Army installation since 1846. Today it is not only an important link in the Army's command structure but is the site for thirty-two tenant commands including Headquarters, 6th U.S. Army; Letterman Army Medical Center; and elements of the Defense Language Institute.

Housing and Schools. The Presidio operates over 1,300 units of family housing in the Bay Area and also three guest facilities. While dependent children attend local schools, there are a day-care center on the post and an in-home program that can accommodate over 200 children.

Personal Services and Recreation. Medical care at the Presidio is provided by the fifty-bed Letterman Army Medical Center. A large commissary and post exchange are also available. Recreational facilities consist of a bowling alley, two movie theaters, a pool, a golf course, and a yacht club, as well as tennis courts, riding stables, auto and hobby craft shops, and two gymnasiums.

The Local Area. The high cost of living in the Bay Area is somewhat offset by the many choices for recreational and sporting activities available there. Located on the tip of the San Francisco Peninsula bordered by the Pacific Ocean and San Francisco Bay, the Presidio offers all forms of water sports except swimming—the Pacific currents keep the water chilly.

The weather in the San Francisco area is temperate, with the warmest months in early to mid fall. Summers are cool and winters are moderate. The area does have a rainy season that runs from November through April, followed by a dry season the rest of the year.

"The City," as her residents refer to San Francisco, is regarded as the most "European" American metropolis. New Presidians will find many opportunities to sample and enjoy the cosmopolitan lifestyle and the cuisines of many diverse cultures. They will also discover they are not very far from other California attractions, the ski resorts and casinos of the Sierra Nevada, the wine country of Northern California, and the beaches of Southern California, none more than a day's drive from the Presidio.

For more information write to: Public Affairs Office, Bldg. 38, Presidio of San Francisco, CA 94129-7000, or call (415) 561-2211.

SIERRA ARMY DEPOT

Located in sparsely populated Lassen County in northeast California, Sierra Army Depot is forty miles southeast of Susanville and fifty-five miles northwest of Reno, Nevada. Its high-desert location (the average elevation in Lassen County is 4,200 feet above sea level) is ideal for the storage of munitions and other stocks.

The mission of the depot is to receive, store, issue, and renovate munitions as well as demilitarize surplus ammunition. It also provides storage and maintenance of operational stocks and tactical support systems. Its facilities consist of 1,253 buildings, which provide 2.3 million square feet of covered storage. Sierra has a total of 36,000 acres available for open controlled storage as well: These facilities can hold up to 200,000 tons of munitions. Amedee Army Airfield at Sierra provides a 7,100-foot runway that can accommodate all kinds of aircraft.

Sierra Army Depot has an active-duty population of 400 ordnance and security personnel, plus about 350 family members.

Housing and Schools. There are 25 sets of officer family quarters (three- and four-bedroom units) plus 140 enlisted family quarters (two-, three-, and four-bedroom units). There is usually no waiting for these quarters for officers and senior NCOs; junior NCOs can expect to wait one to eight months. Off-post housing is very limited. Rentals start at around $200 per month for one-bedroom, unfurnished apartments and can run as high as $400 per month for three-bedroom units. Utility bills can average another $200 per month.

Housing for unaccompanied personnel consists of 12 units for officers and 386 for enlisted personnel. Sixteen units of temporary lodging are available at the rate of $8 per night.

On-post dependent schooling is provided by the Fort Sage Unified School District in Herlong. Sierra Primary School hosts all students in kindergarten through fifth grade; Fort Sage Middle School accommodates grades seven and eight; and children in grades nine through twelve attend Herlong High. A preschool for about fifty children is also available on post. Adult education is available at Lassen Community College in Susanville and the University of Nevada and Truckee Meadows Community College in Reno.

Personal Services. Primary medical and dental care are provided by on-post clinics. Emergency, specialist, and long-term care are offered at Letterman Army Medical Center and local hospitals.

A commissary and exchange are available at Sierra. The latter offers a full range of retail services, including a barber and beauty shop, a service station, a snack bar, a laundromat, a beverage store, and a convenience store.

Recreation. Recreation facilities include a bowling alley, a theater, lighted tennis courts, two baseball fields, and a gym. Racquetball courts and a photo lab are available at the Dotson Center, while the post library is housed in the community center. Also available are auto, wood, and ceramics hobby shops, a riding stable, and trap and skeet ranges.

The Local Area. Herlong is a small community of about 1,800 located in the Honey Lake Valley Basin of the Sierra Nevada. Precipitation is rare throughout Lassen County, averaging only about fourteen inches per year, most of that in the form of snow. Compensating for the dryness, the sun shines in this part of the world on about 275 days out of the year.

For more information write to: Commander, Sierra Army Depot, Attention: ACS, Herlong, CA 96113-5000, or call (916) 827-4425.

Coast Guard

ALAMEDA COAST GUARD SUPPORT CENTER

Located in the Oakland Estuary between Oakland and Alameda, the Coast Guard Support Center is situated on a 500-acre artificial island formed in 1913. Built originally by the federal government to contain office buildings, it has been a Coast Guard station since 1926.

Today the island is home to the Pacific Area Command of the Coast Guard. Other commands sharing the island include the Pacific Maintenance and Logistics Command; Support Center Alameda; Marine Safety Office, San Francisco; Joint Task Force (JTF) 5; and four 378-foot high-endurance cutters—the *Sherman*, the *Morganthau*, the *Munro*, and the *Boutwell*. JTF 5 is a Department of Defense Command, headed by a Coast Guard admiral but representing each military service, with the mission of supporting the war on drugs. Approximately 1,600 active-duty and reserve personnel work on the island.

Family housing and schools for the children of active-duty personnel assigned to the island are available in the surrounding community and at a number of other military installations in the Bay Area such as Treasure Island and the Presidio of San Francisco. Bachelor quarters for officers and enlisted personnel are available on the station. Medical care is provided on an appointment basis by an outpatient clinic, with referrals to the Oakland Naval Medical Center.

Other facilities include a small Coast Guard exchange with a gas station, a fully equipped gym, a swimming pool, and a galley.

For more information write to: Commander (DPA-NR), 11th Coast Guard District, Coast Guard Island, Bldg. 42, Alameda, CA 94501-5100, or call (510) 437-3325.

PETALUMA COAST GUARD TRAINING CENTER

Situated forty miles north of San Francisco and only ten miles from the Pacific Ocean, Petaluma Coast Guard Training Center occupies an 800-acre tract of land in Northern California's rolling pastoral countryside on the Sonoma-Marin County line. The site of six sheep ranches before it was purchased by the Army in 1942, the land was acquired by the Coast Guard as a training command in 1971. Two of the original ranch houses are still standing: One has the proud distinction of serving as the office of the command's enlisted advisor, and the other is the commanding officer's quarters.

Today the center is the Coast Guard's West Coast resident training facility for petty officers, graduating approximately 7,000 students a year from some fifty courses in subjects such as health services, electronics, leadership and management, and maritime law enforcement. It is also home to the Coast Guard's Chief Petty Officer Academy. The center's resident population averages 500 students plus a faculty and staff of about 400 active-duty personnel and their 500 family members.

Housing and Schools. Petaluma has 127 units of two-, three-, and four-bedroom family quarters available, 115 of them for enlisted personnel. Waiting time for occupancy varies from three weeks to three months. A 44-unit visiting enlisted quarters and an eight-room guest house are available with reservations. A day-care center is available on the base, and dependent schooling is provided in Petaluma.

Personal Services and Recreation. Medical care is provided by a clinic that has its own pharmacy, dental care, x-ray, and lab facilities. More definitive care is available at Travis Air Force Base. Although Petaluma has no commissary, it does boast a mini mart, a delicatessen, and an exchange. There is also a tailor/dry cleaner, a credit union, a barber shop, a post office, and a gas station. Recreational facilities include an auto hobby shop, a bowling alley, a gym and fitness center, a swimming pool, a movie theater, a library, and a consolidated club facility.

The Local Area. By far one of the most popular attractions at Petaluma is the wonderful rolling countryside that surrounds the center and provides it with the tranquil environment so necessary to the learning process. Petaluma, a small community of about 33,000, is situated thirty miles west of the Napa Valley, a few miles east of the Point Reyes National Seashore, and within easy driving distance of San Francisco.

For more information write to: Public Affairs Office, USCG Training Center, Petaluma, CA 94952-5000, or call (707) 765-7373.

Marine Corps

BARSTOW MARINE CORPS LOGISTICS BASE

Barstow Marine Corps Logistics Base is situated a few miles east of Barstow, in the Mojave Desert. To the north is Fort Irwin and the China Lake Naval Weapons Center; Edwards Air Force Base lies immediately to the west along Interstate 15; and Twentynine Palms Marine Corps Base is to the east. The gateway to Death Valley National Monument lies about 100 miles from the base. The area is warm and dry.

History. The first Marines landed at Barstow in December 1942. The base actually consists of two sites—the headquarters at Nebo, near Interstate 40 two miles east of Barstow; and Yermo, an annex, eleven miles from Barstow (eight miles northeast of Nebo). Both sites are 2,100 feet above sea level and in the heart of the Mojave Desert. Today the base's mission is to procure, maintain, repair, store, and issue all classes of supplies and equipment needed by Marines stationed west of the Mississippi, and that includes those stationed in the Far East as well. MCLB Barstow has the largest rail operation in the Department of Defense and has the only container consolidation point for the Marine Corps. There are approximately 600 Marines and 2,000 civilian workers at the base to do the job.

Housing and Schools. There are 364 sets of family quarters at Barstow, three junior enlisted barracks, three staff NCO barracks, and seven single rooms for bachelor officers. A transient facility, known as the Oasis, is available to incoming personnel on a limited-stay (seven days) basis.

A child-care center is operated on the base with a capacity for 125 children ranging in age from six weeks to twelve years. Nearby Barstow, population 20,000, has a good public school system and is used by the military dependents living on the base. On base, Marines and their dependents may pursue college courses offered through Park College of Missouri. They may also pursue courses at Barstow Community College.

Personal Services. Medical and dental care are provided to active-duty and retired personnel and their families by branch clinics. Two branches of Marine Corps West Federal Credit Union are available on base. A commissary, a seven-day store, a Marine Corps exchange, and other activities are offered at Barstow.

Recreation. Barstow is an isolated station. Therefore, recreation services and facilities and morale and support programs are very important there. Recreation opportunities include a club system, two swimming pools, a nine-hole golf course, three tennis courts, a gym, a bowling alley, a skeet and trap range, stables (boarding only), two indoor racquetball courts, two lighted outdoor handball courts, one lighted football field, two lighted baseball fields, an auto/crafts hobby shop, and a 30,000-volume library open seven days a week.

The Local Area. The city of Barstow lies on the banks of the Mojave River and has many recreational attractions, including ten parks, swimming, and municipal golf. Nearby places of interest include Calico Ghost Town, ten miles north of Barstow, and the San Bernardino Mountains, an hour's drive away, which afford skiing, fishing, hunting, and boating. Las Vegas is only three hours north of Barstow. The Afton and Rainbow Basin/Owl Canyons are also interesting places to visit. The Calico Dig, fifteen miles north of Barstow and six miles east of Calico Ghost Town, is an unusual park site arranged around an archaeological excavation developed by the National Geographic Society and the San Bernardino County Museum.

For more information write to: Public Affairs Office, USMC Logistics Base, Barstow, CA 92311-5000, or call (619) 577-6430 or (800) THE-USMC.

CAMP PENDLETON

Within its 125,000-acre area, Camp Pendleton has two mountain ranges and seventeen miles of coastline along the Pacific Ocean. All of this is within an hour's drive of the San Diego city limits.

History. First commissioned in September 1942, Camp Pendleton is now a vast military complex where the daytime population exceeds 75,000. Camp Pendleton, named after Maj. Gen. Joseph H. Pendleton, is now home to the 1st Marine Expeditionary Force, 1st Marine Division ("The Old Breed"), 1st Force Service Support Group, and Marine Aircraft Group 39, 1st Surveillance, Reconnaissance and Intelligence Group.

Housing and Schools. More than 5,100 units of family housing are available at Camp Pendleton. Sixty-four temporary accommodations (thirty-five with kitchens) are also available at Ward Lodge, the hostess house. Priority is given to Marines and Navy personnel permanently stationed at Camp Pendleton. An on-base mobile home park has 248 spaces that are rented by the base housing office. The base offers bachelor accommodations for over 26,000 enlisted and officer personnel.

On-base dependent schooling, from prekindergarten through sixth grade, is available. While there is one junior high school on base, most junior high and high school students attend classes off base. A number of colleges offer courses on base for personnel interested in obtaining academic credits or completing degrees. These institutions include Chapman, Miracosta, and Palomar Colleges, as well as National University of San Diego and the University of Southern California.

Personal Services. As befits a community the size of Camp Pendleton, a variety of services and support facilities are available there, including a Marine Corps exchange with a central exchange complex and satellite facilities located at other places on the base. A main commissary and a commissary annex are also handy. The 156-bed hospital treats an average of 21,000 outpatients monthly. The hospital is located on Lake O'Neill, about ten miles inland from Camp Pendleton's main gate. There is also an outpatient clinic located in Vista.

Recreation. Recreation facilities at Camp Pendleton are excellent. Chief among them is the Lake O'Neill Recreation Center with facilities for fishing, boating, and picnicking. But many other facilities are also available, including an archery range; swimming pools; an on-base lake; tennis, basketball, racquetball, and volleyball courts; weight-training facilities; and a skeet and trap range. Because of Camp Pendleton's proximity to the sea, it is ideal for the surfer or beachgoer. Beach parking for RVs is also available.

The Local Area. The surrounding communities offer military personnel much in the way of recreation and the best in gracious living. Oceanside, which lies just to the southeast of the main gate, is in reality a second home for many of the military personnel in the area. Camp Pendleton is bordered on the northwest by San Clemente. The town of Vista, about three miles to the south and seven miles inland from the ocean, is believed to have the most uniformly balanced climate of any spot in the whole country. Generally, the area abounds in state parks and recreational areas, and the mild climate permits year-round enjoyment of the outdoors.

For more information write to: Joint Public Affairs Office, Camp Pendleton, CA 92055-5001, or call (619) 725-5566.

EL TORO MARINE CORPS AIR STATION

The 1993 Base Realignment and Closure Commission recommended that El Toro MCAS be closed. At press time the final date for closing was not known.

El Toro is home for Marine Corps aviation on the West Coast. Together with Tustin, seven miles away, El Toro occupies 6,200 acres astride the Santa Ana Freeway, about forty miles south of Los Angeles and seventy miles north of San Diego, just a few miles north of Camp Pendleton. Today more than 5,100 active-duty military personnel, 3,000 family members, and 1,000 civilians live and work at El Toro.

History. Commissioned in March 1943, the station today is home for the 3rd Marine Aircraft Wing, which has been at El Toro since September 1955. The men of the 3rd fly the F/A-18 Hornet. Marine Aircraft Group 16 at Tustin, seven miles northwest of El Toro, flies the CH-53 "Super Stallion" helicopter.

Housing and Schools. More than 1,100 units of family housing are available at El Toro. A temporary lodging facility is available with twenty-four rooms at thirty-three dollars per night.

Dependent education is available in the Capistrano and Saddleback Unified School Districts, which offer twenty-four elementary schools, five junior high schools, one special-education school, and a community college. A child-care center is available on the station for children up to nine years old. The joint education office offers a wide variety of programs for military personnel and their dependents, including college-level courses from Webster University, the University of Southern California, Irvine Valley College, National University, Chapman College, Northrop University, and Southern Illinois University.

Personal Services. Medical care is provided by a branch clinic of Long Beach Naval Hospital. The El Toro Marine Corps exchange is the third largest in the Corps and offers snack bars, an automotive service center, barber and beauty shops, dry cleaning, watch and jewelry repair, optical offices, and radio and TV repair shops to its patrons. The commissary is a completely self-service facility located next door to the main exchange.

Recreation. In addition to NCO and officers clubs, El Toro offers a sixteen-lane bowling center, a gymnasium, an eighteen-hole golf course, an aero club, an auto hobby shop, stables, tennis and racquetball courts, and a library with 45,000 volumes.

El Toro also offers residents the use of a picnic area, a campground with four campsites available for recreational vehicles, and an Olympic-size swimming pool that is open from May to October. The station also operates Big Bear Lake Recreational Facility, about 100 miles northeast of El Toro in the San Bernardino Mountains. Eight chalets and five camper spaces are available there, and the facility is open year-round. Skiing, hiking, fishing, and outdoor sports can all be enjoyed in the area.

The Local Area. The equitable climate that makes Southern California renowned throughout the world permits outdoor activities year-round. Immediately to the east of the station are the Santa Ana Mountains and the Cleveland National Forest with plenty of opportunity for camping, hiking, and other outdoor recreation. Nearby Disneyland offers four weekends in April designated as a special salute to the armed forces personnel stationed in the area. Tickets and information are available at the special services office.

El Toro is only a few miles north of Mission Viejo, located in the coastal foothills of the Santa Ana Mountains; San Juan Capistrano is about nine miles south of the station. Santa Ana is eight miles north of the station and offers military personnel stationed there all the amenities of a modern city of over 200,000 inhabitants. Just a few miles beyond Santa Ana is Anaheim, one of the fastest-growing communities in California.

For more information write to: Joint Public Affairs Office, 3rd Marine Aircraft Wing and Marine Corps Air Station, El Toro, CA 92709-5010, or call (714) 726-2920/2932.

SAN DIEGO MARINE CORPS RECRUIT DEPOT

The San Diego Marine Corps Recruit Depot consists of 388 acres located in metropolitan San Diego, adjacent to the international airport (Lindbergh Field) and two major interstate highways serving Southern California.

History. The Marine Corps' association with San Diego goes back to July 1846, when a landing party of Marines and sailors from the USS *Cyanne* seized the town from Mexico. The MCRD was acquired from the city of San Diego in 1919. Its recruit training mission dates to 1923. During World War II, more than 223,000 men were trained there. Currently, more than 19,000 young men complete the rigorous twelve-week training cycle annually. Approximately 2,000 Marines are permanently assigned to the depot to receive, process, and train male enlisted personnel and supervise the 1,200 recruiters operating out of 450 offices west of the Mississippi River.

Housing and Schools. Other than for senior officers, there are neither government quarters nor guest housing at the depot. Approximately 7,900 units of Navy family housing and 108 mobile home sites spread out over thirty-three locations in the San Diego area are available to depot personnel. As of May 1993, waiting lists varied from four months in the Cabrillo, Bay View, and Ramona housing areas, to forty-two months at the Strand. Navy Lodges are available in three locations: Naval Station, San Diego; North Island; and Miramar Naval Air Station. Permanent-change-of-station personnel have priority at these facilities.

There is no dependent schooling at any Navy or Marine Corps installation in the San Diego area. The state of California administers a free school system, which military families utilize. The depot education office offers many services to active-duty personnel and their dependents, including counseling for high school, vocational, college, and university educational programs. The San Diego area has six accredited four-year universities. There are also three regular community college campuses within the city and four others in the county, all of them offering Associate of Science and Associate of Arts degrees.

Personal Services. The depot medical clinic sees dependents and retired personnel on an emergency basis only. There is no commissary at the depot, but commissary stores are available at San Diego Naval Station, North Island and Miramar Naval Air Stations, San Diego Naval Training Center, and Imperial Beach Outlying Landing Field, all of which are convenient to one or more of the housing areas. A self-service store at the depot, operated by the Marine Corps exchange, offers basic items such as milk and eggs.

Recreation. There is unlimited recreation both on and off the base: skiing, fishing, sailing, power boating, skin diving, surfing, camping, picnicking, and swimming, just for starters. At the depot are many facilities for sports, including a bowling alley and tennis and racquetball courts. The special services office offers many recreational trips to places such as Disneyland, Las Vegas, and Big Bear Ski Resort.

The Local Area. The city of San Diego (population 1,171,200) offers one of the most equitable climates in the world, with an average yearly temperature of 63° F. To the west is the Pacific Ocean, and to the east the land rises gradually to mountains that stand over 6,500 feet high; beyond the mountains is desert. The area is rich in parks and forests and is ideal for camping, fishing, and hunting.

For more information write to: Public Affairs Office, Marine Corps Recruit Depot, 1600 Henderson Ave., Ste. 120, San Diego, CA 92140-5093, or call (619) 524-1365.

TUSTIN MARINE CORPS AIR STATION

Tustin MCAS is scheduled to close by the summer of 1997.

Established in 1942, Tustin Marine Corps Air Station is located about seven miles northwest of El Toro MCAS. The host unit at Tustin is Marine Aircraft Group 16, which consists of one logistics and two training squadrons, six heavy helicopter squadrons, and five medium helicopter squadrons. There are about 4,000 active-duty personnel with 2,700 family members currently assigned to Tustin.

Housing, Schools, and Personal Services. There are about 1,300 units of family housing at Tustin plus 16 bachelor officer facilities and 1,300 units for unaccompanied enlisted personnel.

Children attend schools in the local area, but a child-care center at Tustin can accommodate seventy-five children. On-base courses are offered for adults from Chapman College and National University.

Medical and dental care are provided by branch clinics, with definitive care available locally or at San Diego Naval Hospital. There is a Marine Corps exchange at Tustin, and personnel assigned there can use the commissary at El Toro. The exchange offers merchandise sales, a service station, a snack bar, barber and beauty shops, a floral shop, and a dry-cleaning and laundry facility.

Recreation. Tustin offers a complete club system for officers, staff NCOs, and enlisted personnel. There are also a fitness center, athletic fields, tennis and racquetball courts, and a swimming pool.

For more information write to: Director, JPAO, Attention: Admin., H&HS, MCAS El Toro, P.O. Box 95002, Santa Ana, CA 92709-5002, or call (714) 726-2100.

Recruits tackle an obstacle on the confidence course at San Diego Marine Corps Depot. (USMC photo)

TWENTYNINE PALMS MARINE CORPS AIR-GROUND COMBAT CENTER

Twentynine Palms Marine Corps Air-Ground Combat Center (MCAGCC or "mick-AG-see") is situated six miles north of the community of Twentynine Palms. The town was supposedly named after the twenty-nine palm trees that once grew at the oasis there, but a survey conducted in 1885 was able to locate only twenty-six of the twenty-nine. Nevertheless, the name stuck.

History. The Marine Corps came to Twentynine Palms in 1953 when a Marine Corps base was established there. In 1979 the installation was redesignated the Air Ground Combat Center. Today it occupies more than 900 square miles of land (three-quarters the size of Rhode Island) in the southern reaches of the Mojave Desert. The vast area is used to evaluate the Marine Corps combined-arms training program. The base is home for the HQ Battalion Regimental Combat Team 7 and the Marine Corps Communications-Electronics School. The center also hosts combined-arms (i.e., infantry, artillery, and armor) exercises in brigade- and battalion-sized combat operations designed to evaluate the units' capabilities to fight a Soviet-type threat.

Today the base is home to some 11,000 military personnel and their 8,500 dependents and employs a civilian workforce of about 1,400.

Housing and Schools. More than 1,800 public quarters are available at the MCAGCC, situated in seven housing areas, and there are seventy-five mobile home parks. A twenty-four-room temporary lodging facility is also available.

Dependent children attend schools in Twentynine Palms. Day-care facilities are available that can accommodate more than 300 children. Adult education is provided through the education office from the base through the College of the Desert's Twentynine Palms Campus, Chapman College, National University, and the United Training Institute.

Personal Services. Medical care is provided by Naval Hospital Twentynine Palms. This is a twenty-nine-bed facility; specialty care is available at Camp Pendleton and in San Diego. The center has an excellent Marine Corps exchange facility that offers a wide variety of concessions, including an ice cream shop, a Burger King, a Domino's Pizza, a snack shop, an auto rental service, and four snack bars. A commissary store and a package store as well as a credit union and officers and NCO clubs are also available.

Recreation. Recreational facilities include three swimming pools, a nine-hole golf course, a twenty-lane bowling center, hobby shops, a theater, a riding stable, a gym, a skeet range, and hobby and crafts centers.

The Local Area. The climate at the MCAGCC is arid, with the relative humidity ranging between 29 and 69 percent. The average temperature there is 67° F., but it has been known to drop as low as 15° F. and soar as high as 130° F.

About 14,500 people live in the city of Twentynine Palms. Less than an hour's drive to the southwest is Palm Springs, with about 39,000 people. The town of Joshua Tree (population 6,500) is only fifteen miles southwest of the base. Both Joshua Tree and Twentynine Palms are gateways to the 500,000-acre Joshua Tree National Monument.

For more information write to: Joint Public Affairs Office, MCAGCC, Box 78801, Twentynine Palms, CA 92278-8101, or call (619) 368-6000.

Navy

ALAMEDA NAVAL AIR STATION

The 1993 Base Realignment and Closure Commission recommended that Alameda NAS be closed. At press time the date for closing was not known.

Two big things about Alameda Naval Air Station are the aircraft carriers USS *Abraham Lincoln* and USS *Carl Vinson*, which are both homeported there. To accommodate the aircraft that fly from these titans, Alameda has runways that vary in length from 7,200 to 8,000 feet. A 1,000-foot-wide ship channel connects the station's piers to the waters of San Francisco Bay. To keep the channel open, more than one million cubic yards of silt are dredged out of it each year.

History. Alameda NAS came to life in June 1936, when the city presented to the federal government the land on which the station was to be built. Today it covers a total of 2,842 acres, 1,108 of which are underwater, and it is home to the Naval Aviation Depot, which employs about 3,500 civilian personnel. Approximately 13,000 military personnel and 5,000 dependents call the station their home. The station is also home port for over 2,000 naval air reservists living throughout the area encompassed by Northern California, Nevada, and Utah.

Housing and Schools. A total of 1,513 units of family housing are available at Alameda, as well as 70 units, forming a Navy Lodge, for transients on an overnight, short-term basis. There are no on-station dependent schools. A child-care center is operated at the station for the convenience of families with preschool children. On-base educational opportunities are offered through Chapman College, Embry-Riddle Aeronautical University, and Central Texas College.

Personal Services. Medical care is provided by the Alameda Branch Clinic, Naval Medical Command, Oakland. Other facilities include a commissary store with a wide variety of fruits and vegetables, fresh meats, and other foodstuffs, and a Navy exchange with a full range of concessions. For those who prefer fast-food cuisine, a McDonald's, the Flight Deck Pizza shop, and the Strike Zone deli are located on the station.

Recreation. Recreational facilities are excellent and include a twenty-four-lane bowling center, a boathouse and marina, an auto hobby shop, and a gymnasium. Outdoor recreation is provided by a six-hole, par-eighteen golf course, and a picnic area that will accommodate up to 300 people at a time. Also available are a newly completed RV center, sailboat rentals, wet slips for rent, an Olympic-size swimming pool, and an indoor swimming pool. A tour and travel center offers military personnel and their families a variety of opportunities for trips and excursions throughout the area.

The Local Area. Alameda NAS is located on an island in the eastern part of San Francisco Bay, between San Francisco on the west and Oakland on the east. Treasure Island is directly to the northwest of the station, in the middle of the bay channel. Local attractions include beautiful views of San Francisco, tours of Alcatraz Island, Fisherman's Wharf, Pier 39, Chinatown, and the Napa Valley.

For more information write to: Public Affairs Office, Bldg. 1, Room 161, NAS Alameda, CA 94501-5000, or call (510) 263-3079.

CHINA LAKE NAVAL AIR WEAPONS STATION

The China Lake site of the Naval Air Warfare Center Weapons Division and the Naval Air Weapons Station China Lake are located adjacent to the city of Ridgecrest, about 150 miles north of Los Angeles in Southern California's Mojave Desert. The station covers more than a million acres of land and is situated under restricted military airspace of nearly 17,000 square miles, making it the Navy's largest land activity.

History. The Navy came to China Lake in November 1943, when the Naval Ordnance Test Station (NOTS) was established there. In 1967 NOTS became the Naval Weapons Center. The NAWCWPNS and NAWS China Lake were established in January 1992. Today the NAWCWPNS is the Navy's full-spectrum research, development, test, evaluation, and in-service engineering center for air warfare weapon systems. China Lake takes its name from a huge, dry lakebed in the area, which is said to have taken its name from the Chinese laborers who worked the mines in the area during the 1880s.

Housing and Schools. The China Lake military community has 787 units of family housing at its disposal and supports 2,200 residents. There are also three elementary schools and one junior high school on the station.

Personal Services and Recreation. Personal support facilities include the NWC Federal Credit Union, a branch medical clinic, officers and enlisted clubs, a commissary, and a small exchange. Recreational facilities include a golf course with snack bar, a gym and indoor swimming pool, a bowling alley, and tennis courts. Escorted tours to the Little Petroglyph Canyon are available on weekends.

The Local Area. Ridgecrest, with a population of 30,000, supports a variety of schools, churches, shopping areas, and restaurants. Hiking, fishing, and camping opportunities are abundant in the nearby Sierra Nevada, while winter recreation sports can be enjoyed at Mammoth Mountain and June Lake. Historic Randsburg, site of the Yellow Astor gold mine, is located approximately twenty-five miles south of Ridgecrest. Ninety miles to the northeast is Death Valley National Monument.

For more information write to: Public Affairs Office, Naval Air Weapons Station, China Lake, CA 93555-6001, or call (619) 939-3511.

CONCORD NAVAL WEAPONS STATION

The Concord Naval Weapons Station occupies approximately 12,000 acres some thirty-five miles northeast of San Francisco and seventy miles southeast of Sacramento. It is a wildlife preserve, with much of its acreage leased for grazing. Some of its acres are devoted to a U.S. Agricultural Department experimental tree farm. Wild deer, Tule elk, foxes, quail, pheasants, and golden eagles, as well as many other kinds of birds and animals, live in its forests.

History. Established in 1942 as an annex to the Naval Ammunition Depot, Mare Island, the Concord station today is a trans-shipment point for ammunition and other hazardous cargo; provides support for ammunition, weapons, and weapons systems; and is home port and logistic support facility for Pacific Fleet auxiliary ammunition ships. The station is divided into the Inland area and the Tidal area. The Inland area contains weapons maintenance buildings and the Marine barracks. The Tidal area extends to Suisun Bay and contains three modern deep-water piers capable of berthing and working six ships at once.

There are about 550 active-duty personnel onboard the station.

Housing and Schools. There are 362 units of family housing onboard the station and no guest facilities.

Dependent children attend local schools. Off-duty educational opportunities for adults are available at Diablo Valley Junior College at Concord and Los Medanos College at Pittsburg.

Personal Services. Although there is a Navy exchange onboard the station, there is no commissary. Major commissaries and exchanges are located throughout the area, at Oakland Army Base, Treasure Island, Travis Air Force Base, Mare Island, and Alameda Naval Air Station. The Naval Regional Medical Center's branch clinic and branch dental clinic are adequate for routine medical care only, 7:30 A.M. to 4:00 P.M., Monday through Friday. Inpatient care is available from the Naval Regional Medical Center at Oakland.

Recreation. Recreational facilities available at the station include a gym, tennis courts, a swimming pool, a picnic area, a library, a community center, and officers and enlisted clubs.

The Local Area. Concord is a "commuter city" of 103,000 residents. This population makes it the largest city in Contra Costa County. The Diablo Valley, where Concord is situated, is one of the more beautiful regions of the San Francisco Bay Area, with all the amenities of modern urban living but few of the inconveniences, such as smog and slums. A tour of duty at the station provides an excellent chance to explore the San Francisco Bay Area as well as all of Northern California. The Sierra Nevada are only a four-hour drive from the station. There one may find year-round recreational activities plus the spectacular beauty of Lake Tahoe and Yosemite National Park. Napa Valley and San Francisco are only an hour's drive from the station. The coastal Redwood Area is a three-hour drive, and the beautiful Monterey Peninsula and Carmel are only a two-hour drive away.

For more information write to: Public Affairs Office, WPNSTA, Concord, CA 94520-5000, or call (510) 246-5450.

CORONADO NAVAL AMPHIBIOUS BASE

Coronado Naval Amphibious Base is located on San Diego Bay, adjacent to State Highway 75, about one mile south of the business center of the city of Coronado. The base occupies more than 1,000 acres and is host to more than two dozen commands, among them Commander Naval Surface Force, U.S. Pacific Fleet; Naval Beach Group 1; Naval Special Warfare Command; Tactical Air Control Group 1; and the Naval Amphibious School.

History. Established in June 1943, the base today has the mission of training thousands of regular and reserve personnel of the U.S. Navy as well as allied forces in the highly specialized art of amphibious warfare. Approximately 4,500 active-duty personnel are assigned to the base.

Housing and Schools. There are a number of family housing projects for Navy and Marine Corps personnel in the San Diego area, but housing is still in short supply throughout the area. Housing for personnel assigned to Coronado is handled through the naval base housing office in San Diego. Navy Lodge accommodations for transient personnel are available at Miramar Naval Air Station, North Island Naval Air Station, and the San Diego Naval Station. The base provides more than 400 bachelor officer units and more than 2,800 dormitory spaces for enlisted personnel. There are forty-three family units on the base for officers only.

Dependent children of sponsors assigned to the Naval Amphibious Base attend schools throughout the California public school system. The base has a child-development center that can accommodate 135 children from six weeks to five years old. Adults assigned to the base may attend college courses through the Navy Campus from Southwestern College, Chapman College, Southern Illinois University, and National University. Off-base programs are offered at San Diego State University, University of California, Point Loma College, Grossuont College, LaVerne University, and San Diego Community College.

Personal Services. Dental and medical care are available on base. Cases that cannot be handled at the Naval Medical Branch Clinic are referred to the San Diego Naval Hospital. There is a Navy exchange at the base and commissary stores at San Diego Naval Station, Miramar NAS, North Island NAS, San Diego Naval Training Center, and in Imperial Beach. Officers and enlisted mess facilities are available at Coronado as is an all-hands restaurant.

Recreation. Recreational facilities at the base include a bowling alley, a gym, outdoor tennis and basketball courts, a recreation gear locker, a theater, and a marina and RV park one mile south of the base on Highway 75. The Gator Beach Recreation Area beside the ocean offers cabañas, a snack bar, showers and changing facilities, barbecue pits, and fire rings and is open year-round for private parties.

For more information write to: Public Affairs Officer, Naval Amphibious Base, Coronado, San Diego, CA 92155-5000, or call (619) 437-3024.

EL CENTRO NAVAL AIR FACILITY

Like enormous and beautiful migratory birds, the Navy's precision aerobatics team, the Blue Angels, migrates to El Centro for three months every winter to train and prepare for their summer exhibition schedule. Because of its superb flying weather year-round, the "birds" of the fleet squadrons also come to this part of the Imperial Valley to train.

History. Commissioned in May 1946, the El Centro Air Facility occupies about 2,300 acres seven miles west of El Centro, and has a complement of 250 officers and enlisted personnel. The facility's mission is to support the operational fleet units that come there for bombing and gunnery practice and to use its simulated carrier deck landing area. In 1977, a permanent unit of Attack Squadron 174 was assigned there to provide maintenance support for A-7 pilots who use the facility's bombing ranges.

Housing and Schools. There are 170 units of family housing available at El Centro for married personnel. A Navy Lodge consisting of four two-bedroom mobile homes is available for rent by transients and visitors.

School-age dependent children attend public schools in Imperial Valley communities. Adults may take advantage of Imperial Valley College and San Diego State University, which have programs in Imperial and Calexico.

Personal Services. Medical care at El Centro is provided by a dispensary that is equipped to handle all routine and many emergency situations. The referral hospital is San Diego Naval Hospital, approximately 125 miles west of El Centro; civilian medical care is also available in the nearby communities in case of emergency.

The Navy exchange and commissary store are housed in a shopping complex that also has a barber shop and a theater.

Recreation. Recreational facilities at El Centro include two swimming pools, tennis courts, a bowling alley, a golf driving range, softball and football fields, a go-cart track, and auto, wood, and hobby shops. A wide variety of recreational equipment is available for rent from the special services office, including camping trailers, outboard motors, and fishing and camping gear.

The Local Area. The Imperial Valley climate offers a decidedly hot summer with maximum temperatures over 100° F. during June through September, but temperatures during the winter are ideal, between 75° F. and 90° F.—shirtsleeve weather year-round. Rainfall averages less than three inches per year.

The Mexican border at Mexicali is only a few miles south of the facility. To the west, along U.S. Highway 8, lies the Anza-Borrego Desert State Park, the Petrified Forest, and the many recreational areas of the Cleveland National Forest.

For more information write to: Public Affairs Office, NAF, El Centro, CA 92243, or call (619) 339-2519.

FLEET ANTI-SUBMARINE WARFARE TRAINING CENTER, PACIFIC

The Fleet Anti-Submarine Warfare Training Center (ASWTC), Pacific, is located three miles west of San Diego, one mile west of Lindburg Field in Point Loma, and just to the south of the San Diego Naval Training Center.

History. The Fleet ASWTC was established in 1939 when the West Coast Sound School was commissioned at the San Diego Destroyer Base. Initially this school offered one course in underwater sound tactics and sonar equipment operation, and its first graduating class consisted of 70 personnel. The curriculum was expanded in World War II, and during the war a total of 4,000 officers and 10,800 enlisted men were graduated. Today the ASWTC's mission is to provide skilled ASW tacticians, operators, and technicians capable of supporting the ASW requirements of the U.S. Navy. The current population onboard the center is 42 officers, 718 enlisted personnel, 78 civilian employees, and 680 student personnel.

Housing and Schools. Housing for permanent-party personnel is available throughout the San Diego area. Bachelor enlisted housing at the center can accommodate over 1,000 soldiers. Dependent children attend schools in the Oakland/San Diego area.

Personal Services and Recreation. The center has a small Navy exchange and a deli. Recreational facilities include a gym, a swimming pool, a softball field, two volleyball courts, a racquetball court, two tennis courts, and a picnic area.

For more information write to: Commanding Officer, FLEASWTRACENPAC, 32444 Echo Ln., Ste. 100, San Diego, CA 92147-5199, or call (619) 524-1685.

LEMOORE NAVAL AIR STATION

Located just to the southwest of Fresno in the beautiful San Joaquin Valley, Lemoore Naval Air Station is just about at the center of the state of California. It is also at the heart of training readiness for the pilots who fly carrier-based aircraft from the Pacific Fleet. As such, the station plays a very important role in the national defense.

History. Lemoore is one of the newer Navy facilities in California, having been commissioned in July 1961. Its 18,000 acres contain two 13,500-foot runways officially known as Reeves Field, after Adm. Joseph M. Reeves. The station is headquarters for Commander, Strike Fighter Wing, U.S. Pacific Fleet; eleven strikefighter squadrons; and one carrier air wing.

Housing and Schools. There are 1,590 family dwellings onboard Lemoore, and a 46-unit Navy Lodge for transient personnel and guests. Two grammar schools and a child-care center are onboard the station, and West Hills College, Chapman College, and Embry-Riddle Aeronautical University offer on-base college-level courses. The Navy Campus for Achievement assists in making arrangements for eligible personnel to attend these courses as well as others at California State University-Fresno or Fresno Pacific College.

Personal Services. Medical care is provided by the Naval Hospital, Lemoore, a twenty-bed facility.

A commissary store, a Navy exchange, a library, a theater, a cafeteria, a bowling alley, a service station, a post office, a credit union, and personalized services are all contained in a well-laid-out, beautifully landscaped mall within easy distance of bachelor and family housing and the station administration area.

Recreation. On-base recreational facilities are abundant and incude a gym; tennis courts; swimming pools; archery, pistol, skeet, and trap ranges; and photo, electronics, and hobby shops.

The Local Area. The San Joaquin Valley region offers much in the way of outdoor recreation and sightseeing. For the boatman and water sports enthusiast, the Pacific Ocean lies only two hours from Lemoore, and the "high lakes" of the Sierras are easily accessible.

Birds and small game can be hunted in the vicinity of the station, and deer and wild boar may be taken in the hills around nearby Avenal and Coalinga, while the Sierras are available for bear hunting. Winter sports are available at resorts such as Sierra Summit, Badger Pass, Dodge Ridge, and Wolverton, all of which are accessible from Lemoore. Yosemite, Kings Canyon, and Sequoia National Parks, as well as other scenic wonders, are in the surrounding area.

Lemoore itself is a small town of about 13,200 inhabitants and boasts a healthy, arid climate. Fresno, about forty miles to the north, is the largest city in the vicinity.

For more information write to: Public Affairs Office, NAS, Lemoore, CA 93246-5001, or call (209) 998-3394.

LONG BEACH NAVAL HOSPITAL

In 1991 the Defense Base Closure and Realignment Commission recommended that Long Beach Naval Station and Long Beach Naval Hospital be closed by October 1996.

Long Beach Naval Hospital is located on a sixty-five-acre tract of land just southeast of the Los Angeles metropolitan area. It lies approximately seventeen miles from Long Beach Naval Station and thirty-five miles from El Toro Marine Corps Air Station.

History. Commissioned in 1967, the 114-bed hospital today supports a population of 35,000 active-duty personnel and 250,000 dependents, retirees, and their dependents. The hospital operates six outlying branch medical clinics located at Long Beach Naval Station, Seal Beach Naval Weapons Station, and China Lake Naval Air Weapons Station.

Education and Personal Services. Educational opportunities abound in the Long Beach area. Within a short driving distance are several major universities such as the University of California-Los Angeles and Pepperdine University. Several junior and community colleges are also located throughout the area. A Navy Campus office is located at Long Beach Naval Station for educational information and assistance.

Commissary, exchange, and recreational services are available at Long Beach Naval Station and El Toro Marine Corps Air Station.

The Local Area. Long Beach is situated in the center of Southern California, 25 miles from Los Angeles, 110 miles from San Diego, and 450 miles from San Francisco. The area is noted for its extensive beaches, tourist attractions, entertainment, and never-ending sunshine. The weather is normally mild to warm with average temperatures ranging from 54° F. in January to 82° F. in July.

For more information write to: Commanding Officer, Naval Hospital, 7500 Carson St., Code 901, Long Beach, CA 90822-5199, or call (213) 420-5445/5203.

MARE ISLAND NAVAL SHIPYARD

The 1993 Base Realignment and Closure Commission recommended that Mare Island Naval Shipyard be closed. At press time the date for closing was not yet known.

Isla de la Yegua—Mare Island—got its name in 1830 when a mare belonging to the leader of a Mexican mapping expedition was carried away by the current of the Sacramento River as the party forded Carquinez Straits. Eventually, the horse managed to reach the island and safety.

History. Mare Island has been the site of U.S. Naval activity since David G. Farragut took command there in September 1854. Its area today covers more than 2,600 acres of land and 1,800 additional acres of tideland. It is home to a number of commands: the Mare Island Naval Shipyard, the Combat Systems Technical Schools Command, the Engineering Duty Officer School, and twenty-four others.

Housing and Schools. There are over 480 sets of family quarters on the base, which are available to personnel of all ranks on a first-come, first-served basis from the date of application. Personnel from ships homeported at the base or vessels undergoing overhaul there are eligible for these quarters on an equal basis with permanently assigned personnel. Voluntary housing is available in Vallejo for all enlisted grades. An additional 1,400 units of family housing are available at Novato, twenty-three miles north of the Golden Gate Bridge. There are no guest-house facilities at Mare Island, but 216 units of transient family housing are available for ship personnel. Rents for furnished, two-bedroom apartments off base ranged from $520 to $725 a month in 1989.

A dependents elementary school is operated by the Vallejo Unified School District, and a day-care center and a preschool are on the station. The Navy Campus office provides vocational and educational counseling and assistance for personnel seeking college credits through examination and off-duty courses. Southern Illinois University and Chapman College participate in these programs and offer advanced degrees.

Personal Services. The station supplies only outpatient medical care; comprehensive medical care is available locally or at Oakland Naval Hospital. A large commissary and main exchange with three mini marts and a country store are provided.

Recreation. Recreational facilities include an officers and enlisted club system, a movie theater, a nine-hole golf course, a bowling alley, a swimming pool, tennis and racquetball courts, a saddle club, and equipment rentals.

The Local Area. Mare Island, on the eastern shore of San Pablo Bay, a northern extension of San Francisco Bay, is actually part of the city of Vallejo, the second largest city in Northern California. The climate there is thoroughly enjoyable year-round, permitting all kinds of outdoor activities all the time.

Fishing is permitted on the island, within certain restrictions, and although hunting or taking of game is prohibited, duck, geese, pheasant, and rabbit hunting are allowed at the Skaggs Island facility at nearby Sonoma. Vallejo offers many recreational sites, dozens of them in the immediate vicinity, including parks and historical attractions. Route 29 north of the city runs through the famous Napa Valley vineyard region.

For more information write to: Public Affairs Officer, Mare Island Naval Shipyard, Vallejo, CA 94592-5100, or call (707) 646-3537.

MIRAMAR NAVAL AIR STATION

Miramar Naval Air Station is a 23,400-acre installation located in the northern suburbs of San Diego and, as such, is one of the largest military bases in the area. The station averages 250 aircraft onboard on any given day of the month, with up to 265,000 operations per year.

History. Known as Camp Kearney before World War II, the station became an auxiliary airfield to the North Island Naval Air Station after the war began. Today it is an all-weather master jet station and home for all the Pacific Fleet fighter and early warning squadrons. The total population includes about 12,000 military and 3,000 civilian personnel.

Housing and Schools. There are 375 housing units and a 108-space mobile home park onboard the station, so the availability of family quarters could be described as tight. The station does have a ninety-unit Navy Lodge for the use of all personnel.

A child-care center is also located on the station. Older children attend school off base, while adults may pursue educational programs during their off-duty time through the Navy Campus.

Personal Services and Recreation. A Navy exchange and commissary store are onboard the station, as is a complete club system. A bowling center, an eighteen-hole golf course, and a five-acre stocked pond with picnic facilities, as well as swimming, a stable and riding area, and the Mills Park picnic area round out the outdoor recreational facilities offered at Miramar.

For more information write to: Public Affairs Officer, NAS, Miramar, San Diego, CA 92145, or call (619) 537-NAVY.

MOFFETT FIELD NAVAL AIR STATION

In 1991 the Base Closure and Realignment Commission recommended that Moffett Field be closed by September 1997.

Hangar One at Moffett Field is today a naval historical monument and dominates the skyline of the northwestern section of the Santa Clara Valley. Built in 1933 to house the Navy's biggest lighter-than-air craft, the USS *Macon*, it covers eight acres and stands 198 feet high. Its two "orange peel" doors weigh 600 tons each.

History. Commissioned as the Sunnyvale Naval Air Station in April 1933, in 1942 the station was renamed in honor of Rear Adm. William A. Moffett, who perished in the crash of the dirigible *Akron* in 1933. Today, Moffett Field's men and women perform a key role in the Navy's antisubmarine warfare mission encompassing 83 million square miles of ocean extending from Alaska down the U.S. West Coast and out to Hawaii, and across the Pacific to Okinawa, the Philippines, and Japan.

Housing and Schools. There are over 700 sets of family quarters at Moffett Field. The station also has a 46-unit Navy Lodge available for personnel of all ranks. Dependent schooling is conducted off base. The educational services office offers advice and counseling to military personnel in professional programs leading to a Navy commission, and the Navy Campus manages and directs all civilian-related educational programs, from high school completion to college degree completion.

Personal Services. A Navy exchange and commissary store are available at Moffett. There is also a branch medical clinic, but nonemergency cases are seen by appointment only. Serious or specialist cases are referred to the Oakland Naval Regional Medical Center.

Recreation. The recreational facilities at Moffett Field are superb. They include clubs as well as hobby shops, a sixteen-lane bowling alley, extensive picnic and barbecue facilities, a golf course, a gym, and handball courts. Tennis and swimming are also available on the station.

The Local Area. The entire Bay Area abounds with recreational and educational opportunities. The huge metropolis of San Francisco is just to the north; San Jose, to the south, is a thriving city of 750,000 people; and the fifteen other communities in the area are growing rapidly. For those who prefer nature, Yosemite National Park is about two and a half hours' drive away; Lake Tahoe, four hours; and the Sierra Foothills, only two hours from Moffett Field.

For more information write to: Public Affairs Office, NAS, Moffett Field, CA 94035, or call (415) 404-4029.

NAVAL POSTGRADUATE SCHOOL

In June 1880 the "Big Four"—Leland Stanford, Charles Crocker, Collis Huntington, and Mark Hopkins—founded the Hotel Del Monte, overlooking Monterey Bay, which they billed as being the "most elegant seaside resort in the world." During the sixty-three years between its founding and the property's acquisition by the Navy as a preflight school, the Hotel Del Monte hosted some of the richest and most flamboyant characters of the day. The Barbara McNitt Ballroom of the old hotel is still used today by the postgraduate school.

History. The school was originally established at Annapolis, Maryland, in June 1909 and moved to Monterey in 1951. It is now a 615-acre campus offering thirty-some different curricula, and since 1945 the school has awarded over 18,000 academic degrees to Navy personnel in science, engineering, management, and other fields. The school has a complement of 1,000 personnel assigned as staff and faculty serving 1,800 students from all services.

Housing and Schools. There are 877 units of family quarters for officer personnel of the school, located at Mesa Village, about two miles from the campus. An additional 130 sets for enlisted personnel are located at Fort Ord, five miles from the school. Although there is no Navy Lodge at Monterey, guest housing is sometimes available at Fort Ord or the Presidio of Monterey. The cost of living is high in Monterey. One-bedroom apartments rent for $550 and up.

Civilian educational opportunities are accessible to all military personnel stationed in the Monterey area. The Monterey Institute of International Studies, located in downtown Monterey, warmly welcomes military students, and Chapman University operates a resident education center at Fort Ord with on-post evening school programs leading to bachelor's and advanced degrees in the liberal arts.

Personal Services. A Navy exchange at the school offers a wide variety of personal services, including snack bars, a service station, and many others. Although there is no commissary there, the commissary at Fort Ord is available, as is the Fort Ord Main Post Exchange.

With an ideal climate in a state where ideal climate is the rule, the Monterey Peninsula offers recreational activities of all sorts year-round. The school owns three Shields-class sailing sloops, which may be used by personnel stationed there. Also on the campus are an eighteen-hole golf course, picnic grounds that can accommodate 200 people, and a gym. In addition, tennis and swimming are available, and bottom-fishing trips can be arranged through the recreation department for the weekends and holidays.

The Local Area. Monterey's chief industries are fishing, tourism, and the military. In nearby Pacific Grove, the fine for disturbing the butterflies that migrate there each year is $1,000, and the flowers never stop blooming in Carmel-by-the-Sea, only a ten-minute drive from the school.

For more information write to: Public Affairs Officer, 1 University Circle, NPS, Monterey, CA 93943, or call (404) 656-2023.

NORTH ISLAND NAVAL AIR STATION

North Island Naval Air Station has been the site of many aviation firsts. The first parachute jump at San Diego was made there in 1914, and in 1923 the first nonstop cross-country flight ended there. Also in 1923, Col. Charles A. Lindbergh took off from North Island for St. Louis on the first leg of his flight from New York to Paris.

History. Commissioned in November 1917, North Island's 2,500 acres today comprise one of the most important naval air and sea bases in California. Its primary mission is to provide support to the Pacific Fleet, and in this role it serves as the home base for over 10,000 personnel assigned to fifty commands and activities, as well as aircraft carriers, cruisers, and supply ships.

Housing and Schools. Housing is very tight at North Island, with only about fifty units, and personnel reporting there are encouraged to check with the housing office in San Diego for quarters elsewhere in the area. There is a ninety-room Navy Lodge on the beach at North Island.

The California public school system supplies dependent schooling; child-care centers are operated at both North Island and nearby Imperial Beach. Programs for adults are offered through the Navy Campus onboard the station. These range from high school studies to doctorates offered by a number of institutions of higher learning.

Personal Services. Medical care at North Island is provided by an outpatient branch medical clinic; comprehensive care facilities are at San Diego. A commissary and Navy exchange with a convenience store, cafeterias, snack bars, and other facilities are also offered.

Recreation. Recreational opportunities abound at North Island. There are an eighteen-hole golf course; handball, racquetball, tennis, and squash courts; and a twenty-four-lane bowling center. The gym has a complete physical fitness center including a seven-mile jogging course that winds its way through the station. Skeet, trap, and pistol ranges are situated in the area just north of the beaches.

Fishing is permitted from Piers Foxtrot, Juliet, and Kilo as well as from the seawall between piers Juliet and Kilo. The beach and picnic areas are open year-round.

The Local Area. North Island forms the south side of San Diego Bay, opposite the Marine Corps Recruit Depot and San Diego International Airport. The island today is actually a peninsula. To the south of the station is Coronado Naval Amphibious Base, which is connected to Imperial Beach by a narrow isthmus known appropriately as Silver Strand Beach. To the west is the Pacific Ocean. The ideal moderation of the climate in the San Diego area makes for year-round comfort.

For more information write to: Commanding Officer, Attention: Public Affairs Office, P.O. Box 357033, San Diego, CA 92135-7033, or call (619) 545-8167.

OAKLAND FLEET INDUSTRIAL SUPPLY CENTER

Established 15 December 1941, the Oakland Fleet Industrial Supply Center is today a 541-acre complex, including 120 acres of prime waterfront real estate, adjacent to the port of Oakland. It also operates facilities at Point Molate and Alameda. Its mission is to supply support services to fleet units and shore activities and maintain a storage capability for use in times of national emergency.

To perform this mission, the center has a complement of over 800 active-duty personnel and 2,400 civilian employees who operate fifty-one storage buildings comprising 10 million square feet of covered storage space plus 1 million square feet of open storage, another million square feet of office space, and a 44-million-gallon fuel storage facility at Point Molate, a 419-acre complex about sixteen miles away. On an average workday, 4,500 personnel pass through the center's gates. Berthing facilities at Oakland include four piers with berthing for eleven vessels. This facility services thirty vessels home ported there as well as another fifty vessels assigned throughout the Bay Area. These include the USS *Abraham Lincoln*, the USS *Samuel Gompers*, the USS *Carl Vinson*, and the USS *Kansas City*.

The center is home to over thirty tenant activities, including the Defense Reutilization and Marketing Office; Fleet Hospital Support Office; Military Sealift Command, Pacific; Navy Public Works Center, San Francisco Bay; the Defense Logistics Agency; and units of the California National Guard and U.S. Coast Guard.

Personal Services and Recreation. While personal and recreational services are available to center personnel throughout the Oakland–San Francisco Bay area, the center does have a small Navy exchange, a gym, a softball field, a horseshoe pit, and basketball, racquetball, and tennis courts.

For more information write to: Commander, Oakland Fleet and Industrial Supply Center and Naval Supply Center, Oakland, CA 94625-5000, or call (510) 302-4967.

OAKLAND NAVAL HOSPITAL

The 1993 Base Realignment and Closure Commission recommended Naval Hospital Oakland be closed. At press time the date for closing was not yet known.
Oakland Naval Hospital, known locally as Oak Knoll, occupies a 195-acre tract on the site of the former Oak Knoll Golf and Country Club in the East Oakland foothills, between San Leandro and Oakland. The hub of the center is the main hospital building, a 225-bed, nine-story structure, one of four naval teaching hospitals. The hospital also has seven subordinate branch medical clinics and provides residency training in six specialties and operates three advanced hospital corpsman schools. About 12,000 patients are admitted each year; more than 288,000 inpatients are seen in an average year. The staff numbers 2,200 personnel, which includes 550 civilians.

History. Established in 1942 as a temporary facility, the Oakland Naval Hospital today services a total military and retired population of 125,000 personnel throughout more than 10,000 square miles of Northern California.

Housing and Schools. There are only eighty-one family housing units at Oak Knoll, but eligible personnel may apply for quarters at several nearby military installations. Temporary lodgings, including a Navy Lodge, are available at Naval Supply Center Oakland, Oakland Army Base, and Alameda Naval Air Station. There are neither dependent schooling nor child-care facilities at Oakland.

Personal Services. Military personnel at Oak Knoll use the commissary facilities at Alameda, Moffett Field, Treasure Island, Mare Island, and Oakland Army Base. There is a small Navy exchange at the base as well as a package store. An officers and enlisted open mess is located in the original clubhouse of the Oak Knoll Golf and Country Club.

Recreation. Recreational opportunities at the hospital include basketball, volleyball, bowling, swimming, tennis, racquetball, and handball.

San Francisco offers a wide variety of dining, shopping, and sightseeing opportunities including Alcatraz, Union Square, Fisherman's Wharf, and Chinatown. San Francisco Bay provides ample boating and fishing, while Napa Valley's world-famous wineries are only a short drive away. Also only a few hours away by car, Reno and Lake Tahoe provide year-round indoor and outdoor entertainment.

The Local Area. Oak Knoll is a beautiful spot, perched above the city of Oakland, wooded and grassy, with a brook that meanders across the compound, and deer often graze there in the early morning hours. With a year-round ideal climate and rustic quiet, Oak Knoll is one of the most pleasant military installations stateside.

Knowland State Park, home of the Oakland Zoo, is within easy walking distance of the center. Lake Merritt, in downtown Oakland, is a 160-acre natural body of salt water surrounded by beautiful drives and parks. The annual mean temperature in the Bay Area is 57° F., and the sun shines there most of the year, making all kinds of outdoor sports and recreational activities possible at all times.

For more information write to: Public Affairs Office, Naval Hospital, Oakland, CA 94627-5000, or call (510) 633-5918.

POINT MUGU NAVAL AIR WARFARE CENTER

The Point Mugu Naval Air Warfare Center Weapons Division comprises four separate locations: the Point Mugu site, primarily responsible for test and evaluation; the China Lake site; the Naval Weapons Evaluation Facility at Albuquerque, New Mexico, handing nuclear weapons training; and the Naval Ordnance Missile Test Station, White Sands, New Mexico, testing surface missile systems. The Point Mugu site is home to approximately 3,000 active-duty personnel and their 2,000 family members, and 4,000 civilian employees.

History. From its beginning in 1946 as Naval Air Missile Test Center to its 1992 consolidation with the China Lake installation and the two New Mexico facilities, Point Mugu remains the Navy's full-spectrum research, development, test, evaluation, and in-service engineering center for air warfare weapons. It also maintains and operates the air, land, and sea Naval Western Test Range Complex, including 35,000 square miles of sea test range area along the Southern California coast.

Housing and Schools. There are two family housing areas at Point Mugu with more than 600 sets of quarters: One is at the center and the other in Camarillo, eight miles away. The Mugu Lagoon Beach Motel offers a 24-unit modern temporary lodging facility.

Although there is no dependent schooling on station at Point Mugu, children are bused to local schools in the Oceanview and Oxnard Unified School Districts. Children residing in family housing in Camarillo attend schools in the Pleasant Valley School District. The Navy Campus for Achievement Office offers advanced schooling through Oxnard and Ventura Colleges and extension courses.

Personal Services. Medical and dental care are provided by branch clinics for active-duty personnel only; dependents and retired personnel and personnel with problems of a specialized nature are referred to the Naval Regional Medical Clinic at Port Hueneme. There are a Navy exchange and a commissary store at Point Mugu, but the larger facilities at Port Hueneme are also used by Point Mugu shoppers.

Recreation. Point Mugu has an eight-lane, ABC-sanctioned bowling alley, a gym and adjacent fitness center, a nine-hole golf course, indoor squash and handball courts, and an outdoor tennis court. The base also features several lighted playing fields for softball, baseball, T-ball, and other sports. A large, recently renovated outdoor swimming pool is adjoined by a shaded picnic area.

For more information write to: Public Affairs Office, Code PO703, NAWS, Point Mugu, CA 93042-5001, or call (805) 989-8094.

PORT HUENEME NAVAL CONSTRUCTION BATTALION CENTER

People have been dropping in on the Port Hueneme area since 1542 and liking it. "Endless summer" is the way one early Spaniard described the climate of Ventura County. Hueneme (pronounced "y-nee-mee") is from a Chumash Indian word meaning "resting place" or "halfway."

History. First opened in May 1942, the center is only a few weeks younger than the Seabees it was built to support. Today it is home to five U.S. Naval Mobile Construction Battalions: 3, 4, 5, 40, and 17. Its 1,600 acres are a bustling complex that supports the activities of 4,200 active-duty personnel and their 1,700 family members. The center has more than forty miles of roads and streets and twenty-five miles of railroad track.

Housing and Schools. About 800 family quarters are available for eligible personnel in two-, three-, and four-bedroom units at both the center itself and at Camarillo, about ten miles from the center. Guest quarters are in the form of a twenty-two-unit Navy Lodge; maximum length of stay is thirty days, depending on availability of space. Although there is no dependent schooling on the center, there is a prekindergarten program as well as a child-care center that can accommodate more than 150 children.

The Navy Campus for Achievement Office provides assistance in planning educational programs that enable service personnel to advance according to their individual backgrounds and interests.

Personal Services and Recreation. A Navy exchange and commissary store offer a full range of patron services for military personnel and their families. Recreational activities include a bowling center, a golf course, a gym, a swimming pool, tennis courts, and other facilities.

The Local Area. Ventura County is a region rich in the lore of early California, with a wealth of natural beauty and resources that have made it famous. About the size of the state of Delaware, Ventura County includes mountains, farms, cities, seacoast, villages, and ranches. Average year-round temperatures are between 50° F. and 80° F. Metropolitan Los Angeles is only an hour's drive away, close enough for convenience but far enough away to avoid the congestion and inconvenience of urban living.

For more information write to: Public Affairs Office, NCBC, Port Hueneme, CA 93043-5000, or call (805) 982-4711.

SAN DIEGO NAVAL MEDICAL CENTER

Originally established as a temporary facility in 1917, the San Diego Naval Medical Center (SDNMC) is today one of the largest and most modern medical treatment facilities of the Department of Defense. SDNMC includes branch medical clinics at San Diego Naval Station; Coronado Naval Amphibious Base; North Island Naval Air Station; San Diego Naval Training Center; San Diego Marine Corps Recruit Depot; Miramar Naval Air Station; and El Centro Naval Air Station.

SDNMC performs its vital mission with a staff of 3,000 active-duty personnel supplemented by 1,300 civilian employees, who maintain a 560-bed acute-care and a 200-bed light-care facility tending to the needs of nearly 500,000 military personnel and their families in the San Diego area.

Housing, Schools, and Personal Services. Family housing at SDNMC is very tight, consisting of only four units for officers, but government family and local rental housing are available throughout the San Diego area. Bachelor accommodations for about 1,300 unaccompanied enlisted personnel are available. Sixteen spaces are available for the families of critically ill patients at Fisher House, but temporary lodging for other visitors is not offered. School-age children attend local schools, and a day-care center at the hospital can accommodate eighty children.

A small Navy exchange operates a retail sales store, barber and beauty shops, a gift shop, a laundry and dry-cleaning facility, an optical shop, a mini mart, and a pizza parlor. Although there is no commissary at the hospital, commissary facilities are available at other military bases throughout the San Diego area.

Recreation. A base swimming pool and gym and fitness facilities are available at the hospital complex, as are movies, various games, and the Liberty Port Cafe, which offers fast food. A leisure travel service as well as an information, ticket, and tours office are operated by the morale, welfare, and recreation office.

For more information write to: Commander, Naval Hospital, Attention: ALA, San Diego, CA 92134, or call (619) 532-6400.

SAN DIEGO NAVAL STATION

The San Diego Naval Station is one of more than a dozen naval installations in the San Diego area. It occupies approximately 1,100 land and sea acres between San Diego and National City along the eastern shore of San Diego Bay, opposite Silver Strand Bay.

History. The station was commissioned in 1922 as the U.S. Destroyer Base, San Diego. It became the San Diego Naval Station in 1946. Today it is home to over 7,000 military personnel and supports a civilian workforce of about 5,900. More than 40,000 officers and enlisted personnel are attached to the station's permanent strength from the seventy-four surface warfare ships berthed there. The station is the Navy's major West Coast logistics base for surface operations, dependent activities, and tenant activities, of which there are forty-nine, including elements of Commander, Surface Force, U.S. Pacific Fleet, and Fleet Training Center.

Housing and Schools. Thirteen military family housing areas are located throughout the San Diego area, housing about 15 percent of the active-duty personnel and families assigned there. Temporary lodging is available at the station's Navy Lodge.

Although there is no dependent schooling onboard the station itself, the San Diego area has a variety of private and public schools for children. The area also has a good selection of community colleges and universities for adult education.

Personal Services and Recreation. The station has a large variety of recreational services as well as a commissary store, the main Navy exchange, and a smaller fleet store. The facilities include swimming pools, tennis courts, racquetball courts, and one nine-hole and two eighteen-hole golf courses at an off-station site called the Admiral Baker Recreation Center. The station also operates three child-care centers.

The Local Area. The station is only seven miles from downtown San Diego, and residential communities are within five blocks of the main gate, although the area is industrially and commercially zoned. The station is fifteen miles from the United States–Mexico border. Shipbuilders National Steel and Shipbuilding and Southwest Marine are on the north and south borders of the station respectively.

For more information write to: Commander, Naval Station, Attention: Code 01, San Diego, CA 92136-5084, or call (619) 556-1246.

SAN DIEGO NAVAL SUBMARINE BASE

Located on the tip of Ballast Point in the Point Loma area, San Diego Naval Submarine Base is home to a combined force of fifteen submarines, two sub tenders, two dry docks, four deep-submergence vehicles, and a major training activity.

History. Named Ballast Point because the stones from this place were once used for ballast in sailing ships, the first European to visit here was Juan Rodriguez Cabrillo, in September 1542. About 160 years later the first Roman Catholic mass celebrated in what is today the state of California took place at Ballast Point, and a monument to that event stands today at the entrance to the sub base chapel. The U.S. military came here in 1852 and for many years the installation that is now the submarine base was known as Fort Rosecrans, after Union Army Maj. Gen. William Rosecrans. In 1959 Fort Rosecrans was turned over to the Navy and in 1981 it was designated a naval submarine base.

Today the base is a 330-acre complex that has a complement of 6,300 active-duty personnel, 300 reservists, a civilian workforce of 400 personnel, and 6,000 family members. Its tenant commands include Commander, Submarine Force, U.S. Pacific Fleet Representative West Coast; submarine squadrons 3 and 11; and the Submarine Training Facility.

Personal Services. Family housing is available at other installations in the San Diego area and in the local community, as are schools for dependent children. The sub base operates a child-care center that can accommodate 100 children. Medical care is available at San Diego Naval Center. There is no commissary at the base but it does have a small Navy exchange. A full range of recreational activities is also provided, including a recreation center, hobby facilities, a gym, a swimming pool, and outdoor sports such as volleyball and tennis.

For more information write to: Commander, Naval Submarine Base, Attention: Public Affairs, 140 Sylvester Rd., San Diego, CA 92106-3521, or call (691) 553-1011.

SAN DIEGO NAVAL TRAINING CENTER

Although the 1993 Base Realignment and Closure Commission recommended that the Naval Training Center be closed, this is not expected to be fully implemented until 1998.

The San Diego Naval Training Center occupies a total of 550 acres along the north shore of North San Diego Bay, just to the west of the Marine Corps Recruit

Depot and San Diego International Airport, along Harbor Drive and opposite Coronado, the site of North Island Naval Air Station.

History. The center was commissioned in 1923. At that time the site was manned by only ten officers and fifty enlisted personnel and was capable of training a recruit population of only 1,500. Today, the center graduates 40,000 personnel annually from the Recruit Training Command and Service School Command; over 1 million sailors have trained there since 1923. The average population is that of a small city—about 10,000 people.

Housing and Schools. Housing for personnel permanently assigned to the center is available throughout the San Diego area, the closest project being the Gateway Village for enlisted personnel on Rosecrans Street, immediately adjacent to the center. These are multi-unit, one- to four-bedroom dwellings. Dependent schooling is available locally through the California public school system. An on-base child-development center offers services for children ages six weeks to five years. Home day care is also available from more than 200 certified providers who are military spouses living in the fifteen off-base military family housing areas around San Diego. The Navy Campus at the center provides active-duty personnel a wide variety of services from basic-skill training and high school completion programs to graduate degree programs, many of them conducted at the center itself during off-duty hours.

Personal Services and Recreation. The center has a full range of morale and support services, including a Navy exchange, a commissary, clubs and messes, and recreational facilities. The latter include two gyms, a bowling center, a golf course, and a sailing and motor boat marina.

For further information write to: Public Affairs Office (Code PAO)1, Naval Training Center, San Diego, CA 92133-5000, or call (619) 524-4210.

Recruit graduation at San Diego Naval Training Center. (U.S. Navy photo)

SKAGGS ISLAND NAVAL SECURITY GROUP ACTIVITY

Skaggs Island Naval Security Group Activity was closed on 30 September 1993.

TREASURE ISLAND NAVAL STATION

Treasure Island (TI) is situated in the middle of San Francisco Bay and is connected to the land on both sides by the San Francisco–Oakland Bay Bridge (Interstate 80). It is only one of several naval installations in the area, but it is probably the most uniquely situated of them all.

History. Treasure Island was originally constructed in the 1930s as a site for the Golden Gate International Exposition. Today it is home for about fifty tenant commands, including Headquarters, 12th Marine Corps District, and the Coast Guard Station on Yerba Buena Island, just to the south of the station and connected to it by a narrow isthmus. Treasure Island has a military population of 2,000 personnel and about 700 civilian workers and 1,600 dependents.

Housing and Schools. Family housing onboard TI is limited to 1,000 units of quarters. No guest lodging is available at TI, but accommodations are available at Alameda NAS and the Naval Supply Center in Oakland.

There are a child-care facility and an elementary school at TI. Children are bused to junior and senior high schools in San Francisco.

Personal Services. Medical care at TI is provided by the branch clinic of the Naval Regional Medical Center, Oakland. The NRMC is the inpatient referral facility for TI personnel or for those patients requiring extensive medical treatment that cannot be provided by the branch clinic. Other service facilities include a credit union, a commissary, and a Navy exchange.

Recreation. Recreational facilities at TI are excellent and include the marina at the main gate and a gymnasium. Also available are the Basilone Theater (capacity 982); a twelve-lane bowling center; auto and craft hobby shops; and a ticket and tours office that provides discount tickets and arrangements for trips and activities in the Bay Area and elsewhere (including trips to Hawaii). The tours office will also assist in planning for ski trips to such places as Oregon, Utah, Wyoming, and the Canadian Rockies.

For more information write to: Family Services Center, Naval Station, Treasure Island, San Francisco, CA 94130-5014, or call (415) 395-5176.

COLORADO

Air Force

FALCON AIR FORCE BASE

Located ten miles east of Peterson AFB, groundbreaking for the facilities at Falcon took place in May 1983, and operations began there on 1 October 1985. The installation was granted base status by the Air Force in 1988. The major unit at Falcon is the 50th Space Wing, which has the mission of controlling the Department of Defense satellite system and operating the Air Force Satellite Control Network. To accomplish this mission, the 50th Wing operates satellite centers at Falcon and tracking stations around the world. Currently, there are 2,000 military personnel and 300 civilians assigned duty at Falcon.

Services and Recreation. Housing, schooling, exchange services, and medical care are available to Falcon personnel at Peterson AFB. Peterson does have a small aid station and dental clinic as well as a country store, The Falcon's Nest.

Recreational facilities include the Satellite Dish dining facility, an à la carte establishment that is open to all personnel; a weight room; racquetball courts; a par course; outdoor basketball and volleyball courts; and a softball field.

For more information write to: Office of Public Affairs, 50th Space Wing, Falcon AFB, CO 80912-5000, or call (719) 550-5040.

LOWRY AIR FORCE BASE

Located on the border of the cities of Denver and Aurora, and just a short distance from the grounds of Fitzsimons Army Hospital, Lowry Air Force Base is an air base without any planes. Lowry's flying mission ended in 1966, but in earlier years the base saw B-29 crews and President Eisenhower's summer White House, and it was the home of the Air Force Academy until its permanent site was completed at Colorado Springs in 1958.

History. Named in honor of 1st Lt. Francis Brown Lowry, a Colorado aerial observer who was killed in World War II, Lowry AFB was first established in February 1938. Today its Technical Training Center, a part of the Air Training Command, graduates over 25,000 students from all services and thirty-five foreign nations each year from more than 440 courses ranging from avionics and undergraduate space training to logistics and meteorology. Lowry is home to more than 3,450 active-duty military personnel, 4,500 civilian employees, and more than 5,400 dependents.

Housing and Schools. Lowry has 95 family housing units for officers and 772 for enlisted personnel. Temporary quarters are available to families coming in and departing from the base on permanent-change-of-station orders. Living off base in the Denver metropolitan area can be expensive. Average apartment rental rates, without utilities, are about $250 for a one-bedroom furnished unit and $350 for a two-bedroom furnished unit. Local sales taxes average 5 to 7 percent.

Public and private schools are available for dependent children in the surrounding communities. Two child-care facilities at Lowry provide care for children ages six weeks to ten years. The base education center offers a full range of counseling and assistance to adults who wish to pursue civilian educational programs.

Personal Services. Primary medical care for active-duty personnel is provided by the USAF clinic. Dependents receive health services at nearby Fitzsimons Army Medical Center. Lowry has a dental clinic for military personnel and a family dental plan; dependents not enrolled may be seen on a space-available basis.

The base offers an exchange with various concessions and has a commissary store, as well as four banking institutions for the convenience of military personnel and their families. Officers, NCO, and airmen's clubs are also available. Similar facilities are available at Fitzsimons.

Recreation. Excellent outdoor recreation facilities are available to personnel stationed at Lowry. The Dillon Recreation Area, about eighty-six miles west of the base, is a sixty-eight-acre wooded campground offering thirty-three camper spaces with picnic tables, grills, comfort stations, and drinking water; hookups are available at twenty-three of the sites. Camping and fishing are offered there as well as equipment rentals. The base family camp, open year-round, has twenty-seven camper spaces with all hookups, barbecue grills, and picnic tables. The site offers camping, hiking, picnicking, recreation and youth centers, and a ticket and tours office. Other on-base recreational facilities include three gyms, two movie theaters, an auto hobby shop, a sixteen-lane bowling center, an eighteen-hole golf course, and one indoor and two outdoor swimming pools.

The Local Area. About 1.8 million people live in the Denver metropolitan area, 250,000 of them in the suburb of Aurora alone. The area's altitude (over a mile) makes for light, clean air. Aurora itself has over 3,000 acres of parkland and sixty-three miles of bicycle trails. Denver is a rapidly growing city that will have an estimated 2.35 million inhabitants by the year 2000 if growth rates continue at their present pace.

The climate in the Denver area is generally very mild, and the natural wonders and outdoor playgrounds of the Rocky Mountains are readily accessible to people living in this region.

For more information write to: Public Affairs Office, Technical Training Center, Lowry AFB, CO 80230-5000, or call (303) 370-2161.

PETERSON AIR FORCE BASE

Pike's Peak, at over 14,000 feet high, dominates the skyline of Colorado Springs to the west. With between 300 and 350 days of sunshine in the year, it's a wonder any of our military personnel stationed at Colorado Springs can stand by their posts. And there are a lot of military people around town: The U.S. Air Force Academy is on the northwest side of town, the Army's Fort Carson is situated on the southwest border of the city, Cheyenne Mountain AFB is just southwest of the city, and Falcon AFB is just to the east.

History. The base opened in 1941 and was later named in honor of 1st Lt. Edward J. Peterson, a Colorado native who died in the crash of an F-4 Lockheed aircraft in 1942. Today its 1,176 acres are home to the 3rd Space Support Wing. The wing supports the North American Defense Command, the U.S. Space Command, the Army and Air Force Space Commands, Cheyenne Mountain AFB, and many other Air Force activities throughout the world. Approximately 6,000 military personnel and 11,000 dependents live and work at Peterson.

Housing and Schools. There are 490 units of family housing at Peterson and a mobile home park; temporary lodging is also available. Personnel and their families traveling on permanent-change-of-station orders may reserve accommodations.

A child-care center is maintained at the base, but school-age children attend classes in Colorado Springs, for which busing is provided. Adults may pursue college courses at the base education center. Degree programs are offered by a number of colleges, including the University of Colorado, Regis and Webster Colleges, the University of Southern Colorado, and the University of Denver.

Personal Services. A base exchange, a commissary, a package store, and many other personal service facilities are available on the base. Medical services are provided by a USAF clinic, with referrals to the Air Force Academy Hospital, Evans Army Community Hospital, Fort Carson, and Fitzsimons Army Medical Center in Aurora.

Recreation. Recreational facilities include an eighteen-hole golf course, a twenty-lane bowling center, craft and hobby shops, and a swimming pool. Peterson also has a complete athletic program, but newcomers should acclimate themselves to the elevation (over 6,000 feet) before engaging in any strenuous exercise. If you shoot or ski, a good way to start is by firing off a few rounds at the skeet and trap range or renting equipment at the base ski shop. For hunters and fishermen, Colorado has a hunting season that runs from late September to late November and has a total of more than 11,000 miles of streams and over 2,400 lakes, most of which are open to public fishing. There is also a fishing program at Peterson, with two stocked ponds available. A Colorado fishing license and a Peterson pond permit are required.

For more information write to: 3SSW Public Affairs, Peterson AFB, CO 80914-5000, or call (303) 554-4698.

U.S. AIR FORCE ACADEMY

History. Established in 1954, the U.S. Air Force Academy is the newest of the three service academies and one of the newest and most beautiful of all Air Force installations.

The academy grounds cover approximately 18,000 acres in a beautiful natural setting just eight miles north of Colorado Springs. The site is at the foot of the Rampart Range of the Rockies, and Pike's Peak towers in the distance. The altitude at the academy varies from 6,340 to 8,040 feet above sea level; the area where the cadets live averages 7,300 feet.

The academy has a population of about 12,000 people: 1,200 officers and 1,600 enlisted personnel, plus 2,400 civilian employees and about 2,000 dependents. The cadets number 4,700. With 800,000 visitors per year, it can get downright crowded there. The academy grounds are divided into four areas to separate the cadets, support functions, families of active-duty personnel, and the flying areas.

Housing and Schools. There are 1,200 sets of family quarters at the academy. About twenty-eight units are available for transient families, and those traveling on official orders may reserve space in them; visitors are accommodated on a space-available basis only. There are two elementary schools and one high school on base, as well as other schools adjacent to the academy.

Personal Services. The academy hospital is an ultramodern, 126-bed, fully staffed medical facility that serves the cadets, assigned military personnel, and their dependents, as well as other active-duty and retired people and their families. Located in the housing area is a community center that includes recreational and shopping facilities for assigned military personnel and their families.

Recreation. Among the academy's more notable recreational facilities are the eighteen-hole Eisenhower Golf Course and the 52,150-seat Falcon Stadium. The Academy is a national wildlife preserve and has as many as 1,500 deer on its grounds during the winter. Bear and elk are occasionally seen there, as well as wildcats, antelope, mountain lions, and other types of wildlife.

One of the most attractive places on the grounds is the Cadet Chapel, considered one of the leading attractions in Colorado. Its seventeen spires rise 150 feet into the air. All regular services held there are open to the general public.

For more information write to: Directorate of Public Affairs, USAF Academy, CO 80840-5151, or call (303) 472-1818.

Army

FITZSIMONS ARMY MEDICAL CENTER

Situated on the western edge of the Great Plains, Aurora, Colorado, is appropriately known as the "Gateway to the Rockies." Its name, from the Roman goddess of the dawn, is also appropriate, because at an altitude of over a mile (5,342 feet), Aurora catches the first glimpse of "rosy-fingered dawn" as the sun rises in the east.

History. Named in honor of 1st Lt. William Thomas Fitzsimons, a doctor who was the first American officer to be killed in action in World War I, ground was broken for what is today Fitzsimons Army Medical Center (FAMC) on 19 April 1918. It received its present name in ceremonies on 1 July 1920. Today the hospital complex occupies 576 acres. Its 504 beds serve a population of more than 63,000 people in the Aurora–East Denver area, including all members of the armed forces in the area (Lowry Air Force Base is nearby). More than 57,000 patients visit the hospital's clinics each month; more than 16,000 people are admitted annually. Served by a staff of more than 250 physicians and 265 nurses, the complex is supported by 1,000 civilian employees and 1,500 military personnel. FAMC is regional hospital for a fifteen-state area from Utah to Michigan, providing medical care to one million beneficiaries.

Housing and Schools. There are a total of 289 family housing units at Fitzsimons. A guest house is available for the use of incoming families of personnel assigned to the hospital as well as the families of patients and other visitors. Other personnel may use the facility on a space-available basis.

Dependent children attend excellent schools in the local community. A nursery for preschool children is available at FAMC, and child care is provided for over 170 children. The FAMC Education Center provides counseling and educational assistance to personnel interested in taking courses from pre-high school to the master's degree level.

Personal Services. The FAMC commissary and post exchange, combined with those available at nearby Lowry AFB, offer shoppers an excellent line of goods. The post exchange concessions at FAMC include beauty and barber shops, an auto repair concession, dry cleaners, tailors, and laundry facilities as well as an optical concession, a Burger King, and a liquor store.

Recreation. Recreational facilities include an eighteen-hole golf course, a twenty-lane bowling center, an arts and crafts center, an auto hobby shop, a post gym, and officers and NCO clubs.

The Local Area. Fitzsimons is located in Aurora, Colorado's third largest city, and is about seven miles east of downtown Denver (metropolitan population 800,000). The average annual temperature is about 50° F. with low humidity. Rarely is the area struck by heavy snow or extremely cold weather.

For more information write to: Public Affairs Office, FAMC, Aurora, CO 80045-5000, or call (303) 361-8241.

FORT CARSON

Known as the "Mountain Post," Fort Carson is located five miles south of Colorado Springs in the "state closest to heaven" in more ways than one. "The air is fraught with health and vigor. Life is poetry, an idyll of blue sky, clear atmosphere and distant view of the kind that gives wing to the imagination," wrote Gen. William J. Palmer, founder of Colorado Springs. Those who visit Fort Carson should be forewarned: They may want to remain there.

History. Named after the famous frontiersman Kit Carson, Fort Carson opened in May 1942 as an infantry training center. Today its 137,000 acres are home for the 4th Infantry Division (Mechanized) and the 43rd Support Group. Fort Carson houses 17,000 military personnel and over 36,000 family members, 3,300 civilian employees, and 5,000 reserve components personnel.

Housing and Schools. There are over 1,800 sets of family housing available at Fort Carson. Transient enlisted accommodations are also available at the Ivy Inn's 135 units, which may accept personnel with families, but on a space-available basis only.

There are on-post schools for children in kindergarten through eighth grade. High school students are bused to nearby Fountain. A day-care center that can accommodate 380 children is also available on post. The Army Education Center offers every form of self-improvement through education, including on-post college courses sponsored by such institutions as the University of Colorado and the University of Southern California.

Personal Services. Fort Carson's medical needs are served by ultramodern, 195-bed Evans U.S. Army Community Hospital. A large commissary is located on post, and the post exchange offers a large main store and five troop stores. The main post shopping mall has an Anthony's Pizza shop, a Baskin Robbins ice cream parlor, a Dunkin' Donuts, a Frank's Franks stand, a Burger King, and a Popeye's chicken restaurant.

Recreation. Fort Carson is a gold mine of recreational activities of all kinds. The morale support activities office offers everything from a sauna bath and racquetball/handball and squash courts to tennis courts and an eighteen-hole golf course. The outdoor recreation branch offers such classes as fishing, gold panning, and rock hunting. Fishing trips are conducted throughout the year, with hunting, white-water rafting, and cross-country skiing in season. Five lakes on post are stocked with trout and other kinds of game fish. Guns, ammunition, and recreation equipment may be purchased on post. Fort Carson operates Turkey Creek Ranch, a 1,235-acre recreational area located on the reservation only eleven miles south of the main gate. Picnic areas and other activities are available on the site.

The Local Area. The surrounding area abounds with some of the grand scenic wonders of the United States. Colorado Springs, with 300 days of sunshine a year, is called the Sunshine Capital of the Rockies. The city maintains 3,400 acres of mountain trails, canyons, swimming pools, tennis, and golfing facilities. Pike's Peak, a few miles west of the Springs (as Colorado Springs is known), rises almost three miles above sea level, and it was there that Katharine Lee Bates was inspired to write the words of "America the Beautiful."

Just to the north of Colorado Springs is the U.S. Air Force Academy, a spot that draws more tourists than any other spot in the state. Denver, a modern metropolis of over one million people, is only sixty miles to the north, and Pueblo, with 120,000 inhabitants, lies about forty miles south of the post.

For more information write to: Public Affairs Office, Fort Carson and 4th Infantry Division (Mechanized), Fort Carson, CO 80913-5000, or call (719) 579-5811.

CONNECTICUT

Coast Guard

U.S. COAST GUARD ACADEMY

An answer on the TV game show *Jeopardy!* pertaining to the Coast Guard Academy might be "A U.S. square-rigger named originally after a Nazi party hero." The question is "What is the *Eagle?*" Built in 1936 in Hamburg, Germany, and originally commissioned the *Horst Wessel*, the *Eagle* was renamed after being taken as a prize following World War II. Today the *Eagle* is a training barque for Coast Guard cadets and sails the seven seas representing the U.S. Coast Guard's proud traditions.

History. The U.S. Coast Guard Academy was created in 1876 as the Revenue Cutter School of Instruction. Originally based in New Bedford, Massachusetts, the academy came to New London in 1932, when the city gave the Coast Guard ground along the Thames River. Today the academy commissions 160 to 170 ensigns annually. At any given time the corps of cadets averages 900 members, of whom 16 to 18 percent are women. The academy offers six technical academic majors (civil, electrical, and marine engineering and marine, mathematical, and computer sciences) and two nontechnical academic majors (government and management).

Besides cadets, the working-day population at the academy includes approximately 400 active-duty personnel and 300 civilian employees.

Housing and Schools. Except for the superintendent, the assistant superintendent, the commandant of cadets, the commanding officer of the *Eagle*, and single enlisted members, all personnel live in the local community. The children of Coast Guard families stationed at the academy attend schools in the local area, although a child-development center was opened on the academy grounds in 1993.

Personal Services and Recreation. The academy has a small exchange and mini mart but no commissary. An outpatient medical clinic is available for cadets and active-duty servicemembers. Commissary services, as well as inpatient medical facilities, are available at the New London Submarine Base. Recreational facilities as well as intramural sports programs are offered at the academy.

The Local Area. The academy is located just off Interstate 95, a two-and-a-half-hour drive from New York City (south) and Boston (north). Points of interest in the local area include Ocean Beach Park, the Thames Science Center, and Lyman Allyn Art Museum in New London. The Nautilus Memorial Submarine Museum in Groton and the Mystic Marinelife Aquarium and Seaport located in Mystic are just five and twelve minutes respectively from the Academy grounds by car.

For more information write to: Commandant, U.S. Coast Guard Academy, Attention: Public Affairs, 15 Mohegan Ave., New London, CT 06320-4195, or call (203) 444-8444.

An aerial view of the U.S. Coast Guard Academy. (U.S. Coast Guard photo)

Navy

NEW LONDON NAVAL SUBMARINE BASE

New London's association with the "silent service" commenced one day in 1915 when the monitor *Ozark* escorted four subs—the whole U.S. submarine service at that time—into the yard. Today the 500 acres and 400 buildings that constitute the base support a population of 70,000 military and civilian personnel (22,500 family members and 1,800 civilian employees) and are home for the vessels and crews of Submarine Group 2, one of the most powerful naval flotillas in the world.

Housing and Schools. Despite the fact that New London is the largest base of its kind in the free world, family housing is at a premium. There are over 3,100 sets of family quarters and 105 rental mobile home spaces. The waiting list varies from immediate occupancy to as long as a year, depending on the grade of the sponsor and the size of the quarters needed. A Navy Lodge located two miles from the base offers sixty-eight efficiency units, with priority for reservations going to transient personnel on permanent-change-of-station orders.

The rental market off base is aggressive. An unfurnished one-bedroom apartment without utilities will cost from $400 to $600 a month; a two-bedroom home, from $500 to $750 a month. Older single-family homes with basements may be bought starting around $120,000; newer homes in good locations begin at around $160,000.

Dependent schooling is conducted off-base in the nearby area. A child-care center with a capacity for seventy-eight children ages six weeks to six years is available. The educational services office assists military personnel in various career-enhancement programs, while the Navy Campus program offers a full range of educational services designed to improve off-duty educational opportunities for Navy personnel. College courses are available from the University of Connecticut, Southern Illinois University, the University of New Haven, Mitchell College, and Mohegan Community College.

Personal Services and Recreation. Medical care is provided by a twenty-five-bed hospital facility. A commissary store and Navy exchange offering many service facilities are available on the base, as well as two bowling alleys, one twenty-four- and one ten-lane. There are also a nine-hole golf course; a marina operated by the Navy Yacht Club, Groton; a gym; ice skating in the winter at North Lake; and a pool hall and game room. The base also has an indoor twenty-five-meter swimming pool; hobby, carpentry, and auto shops; and a Nautilus fitness center.

The Local Area. New London Submarine Base is located along the east bank of the Thames River, five miles north of Groton. The climate in this area is known for moderately cold winters with occasional storms, while the summers are cool along the coast, hot inland; gentle winds prevail most of the time. The local area is rich in history. Most of the towns in the vicinity have been there for more than 300 years: New London was laid out in 1646; Groton was settled around 1650; Waterford in

1663; Ledyard about 1635; Montville in 1670; Stonington in 1649; and East Lyme about 1660.

Many parks, beaches, and hunting and fishing areas can be found throughout the region and are open year-round. Boating is also a very popular pastime in this part of New England.

For more information write to: Public Affairs Office, Box 44, Naval Submarine Base New London, Groton, CT 06349, or call (203) 449-4636.

DELAWARE

Air Force

DOVER AIR FORCE BASE

Dover Air Force Base is both an aerial port that provides efficient movement of cargo, mail, and passengers and the site of the USAF Port Mortuary.

History. Dover Air Force Base was opened in 1941, and since it is situated only three miles east of Dover, took its name from the state capital. Its 3,908 acres are home for the 436th Airlift Wing and the 512th Airlift Wing (Reserve Associate) and its thirty-eight C-5 Galaxies, the largest cargo aircraft in the U.S. Air Force Inventory. More than 7,000 military and 1,300 civilian personnel are assigned to Dover.

Housing and Schools. More than 1,500 sets of family quarters are located on the base and in nearby Lebanon, about four miles southwest of the installation. Transient family accommodations are available on the base, but reservations are accepted only for families traveling on permanent-change-of-station orders.

A child-care center and two on-base elementary schools are operated at Dover. The base education office offers a number of college courses for interested adults. Participating institutions include Southern Illinois University, the University of Delaware, Delaware State College, Wilmington College, and Wesley College.

Personal Services. Medical care for military personnel and their families is provided by a well-equipped base hospital with referrals to either the U.S. Navy Medical Center at Philadelphia or the Malcolm Grow U.S. Air Force Medical Center at Andrews Air Force Base, Maryland. The base exchange offers a wide variety of shopping in the main store and at the many concessions it operates on the base. The commissary provides a complete line of food items for a population of approximately 20,000 eligible personnel.

Recreation. Recreational facilities offered at Dover include an eighteen-hole golf course, three swimming pools, a base picnic area, and a twenty-lane bowling alley. Also available are officers and NCO clubs and a gymnasium.

The Local Area. The weather at Dover can be disagreeable at times. Ice and snow are common in the winter, and the summers are hot and humid. Therefore, the fall and the spring are about the most pleasant times of the year for this area. But weather permitting, there is much to do and see in the Dover area.

Dover has been Delaware's capital since 1777, and the old state house, built originally in 1722, is still standing. Since Delaware was the first state to ratify the Constitution on 7 December 1787, it has the nickname of the "First Star State."

The Atlantic beaches along the Delaware coast are famous. Rehoboth Beach is only about fifty miles south of the base; and Ocean City, Maryland, one of the East Coast's more well-known resort areas, is about seventy-five miles south of Dover.

For more information write to: Public Affairs Office, Dover AFB, DE 19902, or call (302) 677-3379.

DISTRICT OF COLUMBIA

THE PENTAGON BUILDING

There is hardly an American who does not know at least something about the Pentagon Building. In fact, so prominent is the defense establishment in this country's news that often the Defense Department and even the military services themselves are referred to simply as "the Pentagon." But one thing many people do not know is that the Pentagon Building is the only defense headquarters in the world that regularly conducts free guided tours, open to the public, or that since 1976, when the tour program started, over one million tourists of all nationalities have taken tours.

These Pentagon tours are something of which we Americans can be justly proud, because their very existence is a concrete expression of the openness that truly characterizes most of our government's operations and proof that the U.S. government, created to serve its people, really belongs to those people.

Construction began on the Pentagon Building on 11 August 1941, the first occupants moved in on 29 April 1942, and the building was completed on 15 January 1943, at a total cost of eighty-three million dollars. Built on the site of an old swamp along the Virginia side of the Potomac River, just to the east of Arlington National Cemetery, the original building site required more than five million cubic yards of earth fill and 41,492 concrete piles in the construction of its foundation. The engineers processed 680,000 tons of sand and gravel, dredged from the nearby river, into 435,000 cubic yards of concrete, which was then used to mold the Pentagon's unique form.

The five-sided building stands five floors (more than 77 feet) high and occupies 29 of the 583 acres that comprise the Pentagon Building and its grounds. Each of the building's five sides (hence its name) is 921 feet long, and within those walls are 6.6 million square feet of floor space containing 17.5 miles of corridors, 131 stairways, 284 rest rooms, 691 drinking fountains, and 7,754 windows filled with 309,276 square feet of glass.

To visualize what the Pentagon looks like and how it is organized, think of five five-sided wheels, one set within the other. These "wheels" are the *rings*, and they are labeled A through E, E ring being the outer and biggest wheel and A ring the innermost and smallest in circumference of the five. Now picture ten "spokes" radiating from the "hub" of the concentric five-wheel arrangement. These spokes are *corridors*, and they are numbered 1 through 10. If a given room number in the building is, say, 5C315, then it is on the fifth floor, C ring, third corridor, bay 15. Once a person masters this simple floor plan, it is possible to walk between any two points inside the building in seven minutes or less.

Approximately 23,000 military personnel and civilian employees work within the gray, unadorned walls of the Pentagon Building. Each day they consume more than 4,500 cups of coffee, 1,700 pints of milk, and 6,800 soft drinks prepared or served by a restaurant staff of 230 persons dispensed in one dining room, two cafeterias, six snack bars and, during spring and summer, an outdoor snack bar in the center courtyard of the building (known jokingly as "ground zero"). Those thousands of people log over 200,000 telephone calls each day via 100,000 miles of telephone cable strung throughout the building.

When the Pentagon workers end their day they wind their way home over more than thirty miles of access highways, including express bus lanes and a subway system that links the Pentagon with the outlying areas of Virginia and Maryland and the District of Columbia. Those who carpool try to locate their automobiles among the 8,770 chariots crammed into the Pentagon's sixteen parking lots spread over a total of sixty-seven acres surrounding the building.

Guided tours of the Pentagon are conducted Monday through Friday, except federal holidays, beginning at 9:30 A.M. and every half hour thereafter until 3:30 P.M. Visitors must present a valid picture ID to go on the tour. The tour consists of a short film and a walk through the hallways of the building. The tour covers approximately a mile and lasts about one hour. Included along the walk are various historical and artistic exhibits, which are regularly featured along the building corridors: the Commander in Chief's Corridor; Army, Air Force, and Navy Executive Corridors; the Air Force Art Collection; the Time-Life Art Collection; the Hall of Heroes; the Military Women's Corridor; the Flag Corridor; and several corridors dedicated to famous generals.

The tour guides are specially selected young men and women of the armed forces—superbly trained and qualified in their military specialties—who volunteer for temporary tour guide duty.

Individual visitors are welcome any time. Public transportation to the Pentagon via the Blue and Yellow Metrorail lines and Metrobus is the easiest way to reach the building. Limited pay parking (minimal fee) is available after 9:00 A.M. at the visitor's parking area located off Boundary Channel Drive. Signs direct visitors to the tour windows.

Special arrangements are necessary for the handicapped and require ten days' notice. Groups of twenty or more must make reservations ten days in advance.

Access to the Pentagon Building is strictly controlled. Persons holding valid Department of Defense building passes or military identification cards are authorized entry upon display of those documents; all others must pass through a metal detector and be escorted while they are inside the building.

To make reservations or for more information write to: Director, Pentagon Tours, Room 1E776, The Pentagon, Washington, DC 20301, or call (202) 695-1776.

U.S. SOLDIERS' AND AIRMEN'S HOME, ARMED FORCES RETIREMENT HOME

The U.S. Soldiers' and Airmen's Home (USSAH) and the U.S. Naval Home (USNH—see the appropriate entry under Mississippi) make up the Armed Forces Retirement Home (AFRH). Although members of all services (including the Coast Guard, when those personnel serve under Navy command) are eligible for admission to either home, each maintains the character and traditions of its parent service and gives priority in admission to former members of the Army and Air Force at USSAH and Navy and Marine Corps at USNH.

Neither home requires any support from U.S. taxpayers. Both rely solely on income provided by law from the men and women who are eligible for admission. These contributions take the form of a monthly donation of fifty cents deducted from the pay of all active-duty enlisted personnel, warrant officers, and limited-duty officers, and fines and forfeitures imposed by courts-martial and nonjudicial punishment. Other funds come from the interest paid by the U.S. treasury on the home's trust fund, a monthly user fee paid by each resident, and money donated or bequeathed by estates.

To be eligible for admission, a person must be at least sixty years of age and have been discharged or released from service in the armed forces under honorable conditions after twenty or more years of active service. He or she cannot have been convicted of a felony and must be free of drug, alcohol, or psychiatric problems.

Each facility of the home is managed by a director appointed by the Secretary of Defense in coordination with the Armed Forces Retirement Home Board. In addition, each home is overseen by a local board of trustees.

U.S. Soldiers' and Airmen's Home. Located two and a half miles north of the U.S. Capitol building, the Soldiers' and Airmen's Home has overlooked the nation's capital since it was founded in 1851. Four presidents, including Abraham Lincoln, have had the summer White House on the grounds of the home. Today its 300 acres boast four structures designated as national historic landmarks.

The home's parklike grounds, with trees and plants of many varieties, spreading lawns, and well-tended, quiet roadways and paths, are more like a college campus than the "old soldiers' home." These grounds include a nine-hole golf course, garden plots for the residents, two fishing lakes with cookout equipment, and four hotel-size dormitories that house 1,600 men and women.

The home offers a spacious guest house, its own laundry facility, a variety of arts and crafts shops, a bank, a post office, a large gym, and a bowling alley. There is a 300-bed long-term medical care facility available on the grounds for the exclusive care of the residents. A new 200-bed facility was completed in April 1992 and is one of the most modern facilities of its kind on the East Coast.

The home's director summarizes its mission like this: "Providing the best possible care and service to our Distinguished Veterans, for they deserve nothing less."

Inquiries about admission may be made by writing to: Admissions Office, USSAH, 3700 N. Capitol St. NW, Washington, DC 20317, or by calling (800) 422-9988 or (202) 722-3337.

Air Force

BOLLING AIR FORCE BASE

The primary focus of life at Bolling Air Force Base is the city of Washington, D.C., which lies just to the north, within jogging distance, of the base.

History. Named in honor of Col. Raynal C. Bolling, who was killed in World War I, the base was established as Bolling Field in 1918. Today it occupies 604 acres along the east shore of the Potomac River, opposite Washington National Airport. Its 1100th Air Base Group provides administrative and logistical support to Air Force units and more than 35,000 active-duty and retired Air Force personnel and civilians stationed in the National Capital Area. The USAF Band and the Air Force Presidential Honor Guard are also stationed at Bolling.

Housing and Schools. Government family quarters available on the base consist of 1,100 units for enlisted personnel (405 for the Navy and the Marines) plus 295 reserved for officers. Waiting times for quarters vary: Airmen can expect a twenty-four-month wait; junior NCOs, twelve to eighteen months; senior NCOs, two to four months; junior officers, twenty-four to thirty months; and senior officers, twelve months. Off-base housing is very expensive: An unfurnished one-bedroom apartment costs from $350 to $600 a month. A three-bedroom house rents from $700 to $1,300. Security deposits consisting of one month's rent in advance are normally required.

Guest housing is available for transient personnel on a reserved basis if they are traveling on permanent-change-of-station orders.

A child-development center is operated on the base, but schooling for dependent children is available only in the surrounding community. On-base college courses are offered by the University of Maryland, Central Texas College, and Webster University.

Personal Services. A dispensary is maintained at Bolling as a satellite facility of the Malcolm Grow Medical Center at nearby Andrews Air Force Base, Maryland. Although excellent commissary and base exchange facilities are available at Bolling, nearby Fort McNair, Fort Myer, Cameron Station, and Andrews AFB also offer similar outlets.

Recreation. Recreational facilities include a base marina with its own dry dock and berthing for 130 boats. A ten-lane bowling center, an arts and crafts center, a hobby shop for auto enthusiasts, softball and soccer fields, a miniature golf course, a golf driving range, and batting cages are also available.

For more information write to: Public Affairs Office, HQ AFDW, Bolling AFB, DC 20332-5000, or call (202) 767-4783.

Army

FORT LESLEY J. McNAIR

Located where the Anacostia River empties into the Potomac, Fort McNair is not only rich in U.S. history, its proximity to the seat of the federal government guarantees it a ringside seat on the future.

History. When Maj. Pierre C. L'Enfant drew up the plans for the federal city of Washington, he intended the land on which Fort McNair now stands to be used for a military garrison. Established in 1794, the post is one of the oldest military installations in the country. It was blown up to prevent the British from occupying it in the War of 1812, and the conspirators in President Abraham Lincoln's assassination were executed there in 1865. Maj. Walter Reed conducted much of his research into the causes of yellow fever at the post, where he died in 1902.

Named in honor of Lt. Gen. Lesley J. McNair, Army Ground Forces commander who was killed in Normandy in 1944, Fort McNair today is headquarters for the Military District of Washington, the National War College, the Industrial College of the Armed Forces, and the Inter-American Defense College. Approximately 1,000 military personnel work within the post's ninety-eight acres.

Housing and Schools. Housing is very limited at Fort McNair, with most of the units available reserved for general officers. There are 22 units for officers and a dozen for enlisted personnel. Most married soldiers assigned to duty at Fort McNair live either at Forts Myer and Belvoir in Virginia or elsewhere in the National Capital Region. There are 188 units for single enlisted personnel at the post but there is no temporary lodging.

There are no dependent schools at Fort McNair, nor is there a day-care program on post. A small education center is located in Building 41, and adult education is provided through programs at Fort Myer and the many local colleges and universities throughout the Washington area.

Personal Services. Medical care for personnel stationed at Fort McNair is provided by a small health clinic, which provides normal sick-call support. A commissary and a post exchange are located on the installation, and the exchange operates a service station, a barber shop, a beauty shop, and a dry-cleaning facility.

Recreation on post consists of a small, nine-hole golf course, a bowling alley, a small gym with weight-room facilities, a swimming pool, four tennis courts, an outdoor basketball court, a small picnic area, two softball fields, an arts and crafts center, and a movie theater.

The Local Area. Fort McNair is located in the southwestern portion of the District of Columbia, very convenient to the National Airport and the Pentagon, and is regularly serviced by Department of Defense shuttle buses and local commercial buses. The Bureau of Printing and Engraving, Jefferson Memorial, the Tidal Basin, the Mall, the Lincoln Memorial, the Washington Monument, and the Smithsonian's museums are all within walking distance of the post; other local attractions are accessible by public transportation, which services Fort McNair on a regular basis.

For more information write to: Public Affairs Office, HQ, U.S. Army Military District of Washington, Fort Lesley J. McNair, Washington, DC 20319-5050, or call (202) 475-0535.

WALTER REED ARMY MEDICAL CENTER

"The spread of yellow fever can be most effectively controlled by measures directed to the destruction of the mosquitoes and the protection of the sick against these insects," wrote Maj. Walter Reed in 1901. With that simple statement—it seems so obvious to us today—he passed sentence on the scourge of yellow fever and made medical history. In 1902, at the age of fifty-one, he died in the post hospital at Fort McNair, Washington, D.C., from complications following a routine appendectomy.

History. Walter Reed General Hospital opened 1 May 1909 and was named in honor of Maj. Walter Reed. It is founded on principles that integrate patient care, teaching, and research so that patients may no longer die from insect-borne diseases like yellow fever or from surgical complications. Today the main hospital, an ultramodern medical facility, rises 125 feet high in the northeast corner of the main post area, providing accommodations for 22,000 inpatients a year; its outpatient facilities service thousands of people daily. The Walter Reed Army Medical Center is also home for the Walter Reed Army Institute of Research, the Armed Forces Institute of Pathology, and the Army Institute of Dental Research.

Housing and Schools. On-post housing is severely limited. A few officers quarters are available in the main post area and the Forest Glen facility, but most families live off post. Some 211 enlisted families are housed at the nearby Glen Haven facility. There are no bachelor officer quarters on post or mobile home facilities in the vicinity. The Walter Reed Inn, located across from the Georgia Avenue gate, is a visiting officer quarters. The guest house is available to accommodate incoming families, but priority for reservations goes to families of seriously ill patients. A modern enlisted troop billet provides spaces for over 700 personnel.

Dependent children attend schools throughout the Washington metropolitan area. There is limited day-care on post. The Army education center at Walter Reed offers a complete program of counseling and educational planning and testing as well as both on- and off-duty college courses from a number of institutions.

Personal Services. Officers club facilities are available at the Walter Reed Inn and an NCO club is located on the main post, and while there are a commissary and post exchange at nearby Forest Glen (ample parking is available there with bus service to main post approximately every thirty minutes during normal duty hours), there is also a small exchange at Walter Reed itself.

Recreation. There are a bowling alley, a pool, a movie theater, auto and craft shops, tennis courts, and a picnic area for personnel stationed at Walter Reed.

The Local Area. Walter Reed is very near a number of large military installations in the Washington metropolitan area such as Fort Myer, Bolling Air Force Base, and Andrews Air Force Base. Facilities not available at Walter Reed are therefore accessible within easy commuting distances.

Walter Reed is located in the northern reaches of the District of Columbia and conveniently close to Maryland and Virginia; downtown Washington with all the attractions of the nation's capital is only a few minutes away via a well-developed public transportation network.

The center is adjacent to scenic Rock Creek Park, an entrance to which is located opposite the 16th Street gate. The park offers hiking, picnicking, and riding areas.

For more information write to: Walter Reed Army Medical Center, Attention: HSWS-PACS, Washington, DC 20307, or call (202) 576-3501.

Marine Corps

MARINE BARRACKS, WASHINGTON, D.C.

History. Established in 1801, the Marine Barracks, Washington, D.C., is the oldest post of the Corps and has been the residence of every commandant of the Marine Corps since 1806. The barracks occupies one square block in southeast Washington at the corner of Eighth and I streets, only nine blocks from the Capitol. In 1976, the home of the commandant and the barracks were placed on the National Register of Historic Landmarks.

The primary mission of the barracks is to provide a light infantry battalion for ceremonial duties in and around the Washington area. These include Friday evening parades at the barracks and sunset parades at the Marine Corps War Memorial in nearby Arlington, Virginia. The command consists of two infantry companies, a guard detachment, a headquarters and service company, and the Marine Corps Institute. Special units include the Silent Drill Platoon, U.S. Marine Drum and Bugle Corps, the U.S. Marine Band ("The President's Own"), and the U.S. Marine

Color Guard. The barracks has a complement of about 1,200 active-duty personnel and 40 civilian employees.

Housing, Schools, and Personal Services. There are five officer family quarters at the barracks. All others are accommodated in several government-owned housing complexes located nearby. Dependent children attend the local public schools. Off-duty education is available from a variety of local institutions such as George Washington, Georgetown, Catholic, and American Universities in the District of Columbia; George Mason University in Fairfax County, Virginia; and the University of Maryland in nearby College Park.

Comprehensive medical, commissary, exchange, and other services are available throughout the local area. At the barracks there are a barber shop, a small exchange, a mess hall, and a gym and fitness center.

For more information write to: Public Affairs Office, Marine Barracks, 8th and I Streets, SE, Washington, DC 20390-5000, or call (202) 433-4173.

Navy

WASHINGTON NAVY YARD

The Washington Navy Yard (WNY) is headquarters for Naval District Washington (NDW). The commandant and his staff of military and civilian personnel serve over 15,000 military and 25,000 civilian personnel in the military units and facilities under the District's control. The WNY was first established in 1799, and today it is a national historic landmark under the protection of the National Park Service. Over 200,000 tourists visit the yard every year. The yard is the workplace for over 2,000 active-duty personnel and 5,300 civilian employees.

Housing and Schools. NDW administers several hundred family housing units in the Washington area, at Naval Housing Bellevue, at Bolling Air Force Base, and in Waldorf, Maryland. Temporary lodgings are available at the fifty-unit Navy Lodge in southeast Washington, as well as at Andrews Air Force Base.

Numerous excellent public and private schools are available for dependent children in the Washington area, as well as colleges and universities for adults.

Personal Services. Military health care facilities are also excellent—Malcolm Grow U.S. Air Force Hospital at Andrews AFB, Walter Reed Medical Center in the District of Columbia, and the Naval Hospital at Bethesda, Maryland. A dispensary and dental clinic are also available at the Navy Yard for the treatment of acute illnesses and emergencies. The Navy Yard also offers a small Navy exchange and a mini mart for shopping, as well as a service station, a bank, and a barber shop. More extensive military shopping facilities (an exchange and a commissary) are available at nearby Fort Myer, Virginia; Fort McNair, District of Columbia; and Andrews AFB, Maryland.

Recreation. The recreational facilities situated at installations throughout the metropolitan area are also available to naval personnel. The Navy Yard itself has an outdoor swimming pool, a gymnasium, five tennis courts, a recreational services lending center, a picnic grounds, and trailer and recreational vehicle parking.

The Local Area. The Navy Yard itself is a tourist attraction. Latrobe Gate was built in 1805 and is the oldest continuously staffed Marine sentry post in the nation. Also housed there are the Marine Corps Museum, the Navy Memorial Museum, the Navy Art Gallery, and the Willard Park Naval Weapons Collection.

For more information write to: Public Affairs Division, NDW, Washington, DC 20374-2002, or call (202) 433-2670.

FLORIDA

Air Force

EGLIN AIR FORCE BASE

Located on Choctawatchee Bay, just a few miles from the open waters of the Gulf of Mexico, the summertime temperatures at Eglin Air Force Base can sometimes dip to minus 65° F. and snow can accumulate up to fifteen inches; at other times the weather here can change from junglelike heat and humidity to a desert aridity with temperatures as high as 165° F. and winds at over 100 miles per hour. This is not on the Gulf beaches, of course, but in the McKinley Climatic Laboratory, where weather conditions are simulated in order to test the capabilities of military equipment. Eglin normally has long, hot summers and short, mild winters.

History. Named in honor of Lt. Col. Frederick Eglin, who was killed in 1937 in an air crash near Anniston, Alabama, Eglin AFB became an autonomous installation in 1940. Today it is home for the Munitions Division of the Air Force Systems Command. It comprises an area of some 720 square miles, or two-thirds the size of the state of Rhode Island. The Eglin Gulf Test Range covers over 44,000 square miles of Gulf water. With a population of nearly 61,000 people (military and civilian personnel and their dependents), the base is in reality a small, self-contained city.

Housing and Schools. Eglin has more than 2,700 family quarters. The base also has two elementary schools for dependent children, a day-care center for 218 children, and an in-home day-care program. College-level courses are offered through the base education center by several universities, including Okaloosa-Walton Community College, the University of West Florida, Troy State University, Saint Leo College, and the University of Florida.

Personal Services. Medical care is provided at the 150-bed Eglin USAF Regional Hospital, which treats an average of 1,000 outpatients every day. The base also has a large commissary and base exchange, each of which operates satellite outlets (shoppettes) for the convenience of Eglin shoppers.

Recreation. Recreational facilities at Eglin include a bowling alley, beaches, swimming pools, a gym, two golf courses, boat rentals, beach clubs, and a well-rounded athletics and sports program. The Eglin Family Camp, which is open year-round, has seventeen camper spaces with electricity; camping sites; picnic areas; and facilities for picnicking, fishing, and water skiing.

Some 380,000 acres are available for camping, canoeing, fishing, and hunting. Some of the best hunting in the Southeast is available on the installation, with game animals including deer, quail, turkey, and squirrel.

The Local Area. The area of the Gulf Coast where Eglin is located is known as the Emerald Coast; the natural beauty and bounty of the area centered on Fort Walton Beach and Destin, with Okaloosa Island to the south and Choctawatchee Bay to the east, make it one of the nation's finest playgrounds. Temperatures range from 70° F. to 95° F. in the summer and from 50° F. to 75° F. in the winter, making outdoor activities possible an average of 340 days a year. During the summer, the Gulf waters reach temperatures in the eighties, and all types of water sports can be enjoyed there.

Eglin is located about forty miles east of Pensacola, six miles northeast of Fort Walton Beach, and just a bit west of the twin communities of Niceville and Valparaiso.

For more information write to: Air Force Development Test Center, Public Affairs Office, Eglin AFB, FL 32542-5000, or call (904) 882-3931.

HOMESTEAD AIR FORCE BASE

Homestead AFB was almost completely destroyed by Hurricane Andrew in 1992, and the 1993 Base Realignment and Closure Commission recommended that it be closed.

HURLBURT FIELD

"Any time, any place" is the motto of the 1st Special Operations Wing, the host unit at Hurlburt Field. And as key players in such military contingencies as the capture of Manuel Noriega in Panama in 1989 and Operation Desert Storm in 1991, the airmen of the 1st SOW have lived up to their motto.

History. Named in honor of 1st Lt. Donald W. Hurlburt, who was killed in a crash at nearby Eglin Air Force Base in 1943, the present-day home of the Air Commandos began its life in 1948 as a gunnery and training field, part of the Eglin complex. Today Hurlburt Field covers some 6,600 acres of land and is home and workplace to almost 6,000 military personnel, 9,000 dependents, and over 900 civilian personnel. Hurlburt is also home to the 823rd Red Horse Civil Engineering Squadron, USAF Special Operations School, Special Missions Operational Test and

Evaluation Center, the Joint Warfare Center, and the 41st Training Group (Blue Flag).

Housing and Schools. There are 380 sets of family quarters at Hurlburt plus 300 more off base. The waiting list is from one to two years for most families.

Preschool and child-care programs are available at Hurlburt. The base education office provides the full range of adult educational programs, including on-base college courses from leading universities.

Personal Services. Personal support services include a USAF medical and dental clinic, a base exchange, a commissary, a child-care center, and banking facilities. The medical clinic is a satellite facility of the Eglin regional hospital, the seventh largest of its kind in the Air Force.

Recreation. Recreational facilities available at Hurlburt Field include a base marina, a swimming pool, an arts and crafts center, an eighteen-hole golf course, a bowling alley, a theater, a library, and officers and NCO clubs.

The Local Area. Hurlburt is located near Fort Walton Beach on Florida's Emerald Coast, which sparkles in the heart of northern Florida's Panhandle region. Fort Walton is about forty miles east of Pensacola and about seventy miles west of Panama City. This is an area where fishing, tennis, golf, the beaches, and the dining are without question superb.

For more information on Hurlburt Field and environs, see the entry on Eglin Air Force Base or write to: Dept. of the Air Force, 1st SOWA/PA, 131 Bartley St., Ste. 326, Hurlburt Field, FL 32544-5271, or call (904) 884-7464.

MacDILL AIR FORCE BASE

MacDill Air Force Base is located at the tip of a peninsula that juts into Tampa Bay. Tampa is to the north of the base, and Clearwater and Pinellas Park are to the west, across Old Tampa Bay. The climate is warm, and Tampa remains green year-round.

History. Opened in 1941 and named in honor of Col. Leslie MacDill, today the base is home for the 56th Tactical Training Wing, which trains combat aircrews and maintenance personnel in the F-16 fighter aircraft. The base is also home to the headquarters of the U.S. Central Command, which has the mission of responding to crises anywhere in the world. MacDill is also the host for the U.S. Special Operations Command, which is responsible for all operations involving U.S. special forces units.

In addition to the training mission and supporting several tenant units on base, MacDill is responsible for the Avon Park Air Force Range, a 106,000-acre bombing range ninety-five miles east of Tampa. It is one of the largest ranges of its kind in the United States.

Housing and Schools. About 800 units of family housing, a mobile home park, and temporary lodging are all available at MacDill.

A child-care center and an elementary school are maintained on base, while the base education center offers college courses for adults through St. Leo College, Golden Gate University, and Hillsborough Community College.

Personal Services. On-base personal service facilities include a USAF regional hospital as well as a base exchange mall and a commissary.

Recreation. Recreational facilities include two eighteen-hole golf courses, a sixteen-lane bowling center, two outdoor swimming pools, a gymnasium, hobby shops, a beach, and a marina. The base family camp, located at the south end of the installation near the beach, offers forty-four trailer pads with electric and water hookups, a snack bar, a playground, and swimming, boating, and fishing. Avon Park also offers much in the way of outdoor recreation for MacDill personnel. This includes hunting, fishing, and camping. The annual mean temperature in the Avon Park region is 73° F., as one might expect in a place situated between the town of Frostproof to the north and Lake June in Winter Haven to the south.

The Local Area. Tampa is a handsome metropolis set among beautiful natural surroundings, with a pleasant subtropical climate all year. It offers about everything a modern American could wish for, except snow. Tampa is the site for the Cincinnati Reds' spring training, as well as home for the NFL's Tampa Bay Buccaneers, and just about every kind of sport is played there, from dog races to golf.

Orlando—and Disney World—is only a ninety-minute drive from Tampa, and even the Florida Keys and the whole expanse of the Atlantic coast are not too much farther removed, easily accessible in the course of a weekend trip.

For more information write to: Community Relations Office, MacDill AFB, FL 33608-5000, or call (813) 830-2215.

PATRICK AIR FORCE BASE

Patrick Air Force Base is not only situated on Florida's Space Coast but is also an integral part of the aerospace programs that have made this part of the United States world famous. Cape Canaveral and the Kennedy Space Center are only a few miles to the north of the base. Patrick itself is the headquarters of the USAF 45th Space Wing, which is responsible for the Eastern Range, extending more than 10,000 miles downrange from Cape Canaveral.

History. Opened in 1940 as the Banana River Naval Air Station, the Air Force acquired the base in 1948 and renamed it in honor of Maj. Gen. Mason M. Patrick, Chief of the Army Air Service from 1921 to 1927. Tenant units at the base include Headquarters, Air Force Technical Applications Center; the Defense Equal Opportunity Management Institute; 41st, 71st, and 301st Air Rescue Squadrons; and others. About 3,400 military personnel and 5,000 dependents call Patrick AFB home.

Housing and Schools. There are 1,350 units of family housing at Patrick, some of which are located right beside the ocean, just a short walk from the beaches.

Good public schools are available for dependent children in the local area, and the Air Force operates a child-care center on base for preschoolers. College courses are offered on base in both day and evening formats from Brevard Community College, Rollins College, the University of Central Florida, Florida Institute of Technology, and Embry-Riddle Aeronautical University.

Personal Services. Patrick has an excellent medical facility in the fifteen-bed

45th Medical Group hospital. The commissary at the base was opened just newly renovated and expanded and offers over 86,000 square feet of sales and warehouse space. The base exchange offers over 25,000 items and many concessions besides its normal retail sales outlets.

Recreation. With Florida's year-round subtropical climate, recreational facilities are plentiful and heavily utilized at Patrick. On-base facilities include two swimming pools, an eighteen-hole golf course, a marina, boat charters, and a yacht club. Indeed, any spot in the state of Florida is heaven to those who like the outdoors.

The Local Area. Patrick is located right on Florida's Atlantic coast, just a short distance south of Cocoa Beach. Orlando and Disney World are within an easy drive inland, and Daytona Beach is not far north of Patrick. Hunting, fishing, camping, hiking, swimming, and golf—just about every outdoor recreational activity except mountain climbing and winter sports—are available to the people fortunate enough to live at Patrick AFB.

But by far, the most interesting and thrilling outdoor activity at Patrick is "bird watching." The Atlas-Centaur, Delta, Trident, and Titan space-vehicle launches are familiar sights along the Space Coast, not to mention the spectacular launches from the Kennedy Space Center that speed astronauts into space. It is a familiar sight to all Americans, but one that never fails to awe the most jaded space watcher.

For more information write to: Public Affairs Office, Patrick AFB, FL 32925, or call (407) 494-5933.

TYNDALL AIR FORCE BASE

Every two years something extraordinary occurs at Tyndall Air Force Base: William Tell. William Tell is a fighter-weapons meet held to provide realistic training and evaluation of aircrews, weapons systems, and support personnel. The competition provides a realistic test of each team's capability to perform its mission under the pressure of simulated combat. Tyndall has been host to the show for the past twenty-two years. The meet has been interrupted only twice: an intermission from 1966 to 1970 during the Vietnam War and again in 1990, when the competition was canceled because of Desert Storm.

History. Named in honor of Lt. Frank B. Tyndall, who was killed in a crash near Mooresville, North Carolina, in July 1930, the base was activated in 1941. Tyndall is an Air Combat Command asset and the 325th Fighter Wing, under the 1st Air Force, is the installation host. Tyndall covers 29,000 acres between the Gulf of Mexico to the south and Saint Andrew Bay to the north and west. It boasts many miles of white, sandy beaches.

Housing and Schools. There are 1,171 family housing units at Tyndall. A facility for transient families, which consists of 40 suites, is available through the base billeting office.

A Bay County elementary school is operated on the base for children in kindergarten through sixth grade. Students in seventh through twelfth grades attend other Bay County schools in the vicinity. A child-care center is also located on the base.

On-base college courses are offered by Gulf Coast Community College, Troy State University, the University of West Florida, and Embry-Riddle Aeronautical University.

Personal Services. Medical facilities at Tyndall are provided by the 325th Medical Group, which operates a thirty-five-bed complex consisting of an eighteen-chair dental clinic as well as a family practice and other clinics. The community mall includes a commissary, a main base exchange, a snack bar, barber and beauty shops, a flower shop, an optical shop, and a watch repair facility. Also available are three shoppettes, a service station, a theater, a beverage store, and an auto repair shop.

Recreation. Recreational facilities at Tyndall are excellent. The family camp there offers three fully furnished cottages, seventeen RV sites with full hookups, fourteen RV sites with electric and water hookups, and eight primitive tent sites. The camp also offers a bathhouse, playground, mail service, horseshoes, shuffleboard, miniature golf, and RV accessory and TV rentals.

Indoor recreational facilities consist of an arts and crafts complex, a sixteen-lane bowling center, youth and community activities centers, and a fitness center with complete exercise and weight-lifting equipment. Swimming pools and an excellent beach area (with bathhouse facilities and a snack bar) are also available at Tyndall. Golfers will be delighted with the Tyndall eighteen-hole, championship golf course, which is open all year.

The Local Area. The weather in the Panama City–Tyndall area is generally very comfortable. During January and February the temperatures sometimes drop to freezing, but a raincoat with a removable liner is usually all the Tyndall resident needs to bring with him from the north.

The Bay County area of the Florida Panhandle offers miles and miles of sugar-white beaches; scores of freshwater lakes; and acres and acres of forest that make the location a paradise for hunters, fishermen, and water-sports enthusiasts. The area boasts a population of around 130,000, with the largest cities being Panama City and Panama City Beach (20 miles west of the base). Pensacola is about 100 miles to the west and Tallahassee is 100 miles to the east; Disney World at Orlando is about 350 miles south of Tyndall.

For more information write to: Public Affairs Office, 325th Fighter Wing, 500 Minnesota Ave., Ste. 3, Tyndall AFB, FL 32403-5425, or call (904) 283-2983.

Coast Guard

MIAMI COAST GUARD AIR STATION

Originally commissioned at Dinner Key on Biscayne Bay in June 1932, Miami Coast Guard Air Station was moved to its present location at Opa Locka Airport, just a few miles north of Hialeah, in 1965.

The station's missions include search and rescue, maritime law enforcement, environmental protection, and logistics. To carry out these missions, the station operates nine HH-65A "Dolphin" helicopters, ten HU-25 "Falcon" jets, and several other special-purpose aircraft. CGAS Miami personnel carry out over 800 search-and-rescue operations each year. During the period 1991–92, station personnel flew over 1,700 search-and-rescue missions, saving 3,000 lives, and assisted 6,500 people in saving over $450 million in property. Law-enforcement efforts resulted in the confiscation of hundreds of tons of marijuana and cocaine.

CGAS Miami has a complement of 80 officers and 300 enlisted personnel plus 15 reservists and 2 civilian employees.

Housing, Schools, and Personal Services. CGAS Miami controls about 100 units of family quarters. Schools are available in the local area. Health care is provided by a small medical and dental clinic. There are a small commissary and exchange at the station.

For more information write to: Public Affairs Office, CGAS Miami, Opa Locka Airport, Opa Locka, FL 33054-2397, or call (305) 923-2100.

Navy

CECIL FIELD NAVAL AIR STATION

The 1993 Base Realignment and Closure Commission recommended that Cecil Field be closed, but at press time the date for closing had not yet been determined.

Cecil Field is one of three major naval bases located in the Jacksonville area. Jacksonville Naval Air Station, about fourteen miles east of Cecil Field on the west bank of the Saint Johns River, and Mayport Naval Station, approximately forty miles to the northeast of Cecil Field, are the others.

History. Cecil Field was first established in 1941 and named after Cmdr. Henry B. Cecil, who died in the crash of the dirigible *Akron* in 1933. Today Cecil Field covers more than 25,000 acres occupied with runways that handle an annual average of 400,000 takeoffs and landings. It is home to over 9,000 military and civilian personnel who support the operations of twenty FA-18 and S-3 squadrons.

Housing and Schools. There are over 290 units of family housing at Cecil Field, in addition to forty-eight mobile home spaces. Waiting periods vary from more than two years for enlisted two-bedroom units to only thirty days for four-bedroom units; officers may expect to wait from nine months for four-bedroom units for commanders and above to as little as sixty days for lieutenants requiring three-bedroom units.

Dependent schooling is conducted in the Florida public and private schools located off base, although child care is available onboard the station. The Navy Campus office offers testing and counseling for college programs in the Jacksonville area.

Personal Services. A commissary store and Navy exchange are among the many personal services facilities at Cecil Field. A branch dispensary of the

Jacksonville Naval Hospital offers pediatric and dependent outpatient care, as well as a full range of emergency room facilities and a number of specialty clinics. Dental treatment is available from a new and modern facility.

Recreation. Recreational facilities include an officers and enlisted club system, an eighteen-hole golf course, fishing in two small lakes at the station, and six picnic areas. Swimming is also available in two community pools.

For more information write to: Public Affairs Office, P.O. Box 111, Cecil Field NAS, Jacksonville, FL 32215-5000, or call (904) 778-6055.

CORRY STATION NAVAL TECHNICAL TRAINING CENTER

Corry Station Naval Technical Training Center lies three miles north of Pensacola Naval Air Station in West Pensacola, its southern border formed by Interstate 98.

History. The training center was named in honor of Medal of Honor winner William M. Corry, Jr., and the Navy first came to this location in 1928. Originally called Corry Field, the installation was used to train fighter pilots. In 1973 the station was redesignated a naval technical training center. Today it trains Navy personnel in cryptology, electronic warfare, and optical instrumentation (repair and calibration of optical instruments such as compasses, binoculars, and sextants). The center graduates about 6,000 students a year. The average daily complement at the center is 3,400 active-duty personnel.

Housing and Schools. Family housing at Corry Station consists of about 200 enlisted units situated in the family housing area in the southeast section of the installation. Officer housing is available at Pensacola Naval Air Station. Unaccompanied enlisted personnel live in barracks (bachelor enlisted facilities) that accommodate about 2,800 personnel. Rentals in the area as of the winter of 1993–94 were starting at about $300 to $350 per month for a one-bedroom apartment, not including utilities or security deposit.

A small child-care facility is available on the station, but dependent children attend local public schools. Adult education courses can be arranged through the Navy Campus located in Building 506 at the center.

Personal Services. There are a medical and a dental clinic at Corry Station, and definitive medical care is available from the Naval Aerospace Regional Medical Center just west of the station, off Interstate 98. A very large Navy exchange–commissary complex is situated next to the family housing area.

Recreation. Corry Station has an officers and enlisted club for those who prefer to relax indoors. There are also a bowling center, a theater, an amusement center, craft and hobby shops, a library, and a gymnasium. Outdoor recreation facilities include a running track, a swimming pool, and tennis and handball courts.

For more information write to: Commanding Officer, Attention: Public Affairs, Code 03, Naval Technical Training Center, 640 Roberts Ave., Rm. 112, Pensacola, FL 32511-5138, or call (904) 452-2000.

JACKSONVILLE NAVAL AIR STATION

Jacksonville Naval Air Station is situated on the banks of the Saint Johns River, just ten miles to the south of the heart of Jacksonville. Cecil Field Naval Air Station is a few miles directly west of the station.

Jacksonville is home for Commander, Naval Aviation Activities Jacksonville; the 2,500 individuals of Patrol Wing 11; 1,500 personnel of Helicopter Antisubmarine Wing 1; and supporting units. In all, there are over 9,000 military personnel and 7,000 civilians at the base.

Housing and Schools. More than 650 sets of family quarters are located at Jacksonville NAS. The waiting period for occupancy is from three to twenty-four months, depending on the sponsor's rank and bedroom entitlement. There are also thirty-six mobile home spaces at the station. Navy Lodge facilities consist of twenty-eight two-bedroom units.

Dependent schooling is conducted off base, in the various public and private schools located about Duval County. There is a day-care facility on the station. Higher education is available through a variety of institutions in the Jacksonville area, including the University of North Florida, Jacksonville University, and Florida Community at Jacksonville.

Personal Services. Jacksonville has a commissary and Navy exchange complex. The exchange at Jacksonville offers services ranging from garden supplies to an ice cream shop and several cafeterias and snack bars.

Medical care for military personnel and their dependents is provided by the 310-bed Naval Regional Medical Center onboard the Jacksonville station.

Recreation. Recreational facilities abound at Jacksonville: an eighteen-hole golf course at the station; four swimming pools, tennis courts, and fishing at Lake Casa Linda, Scotlis Lake, and in the Saint Johns River; a marina; and picnic grounds furnished with playgrounds, barbecue grills, ball fields, restrooms, and shelters.

For more information write to: Public Affairs Office, Box 2, NAS, Jacksonville, FL 32212, or call (904) 772-2415.

KEY WEST NAVAL AIR STATION

Dubbed the southernmost city in the continental United States, the two-by-four-mile island city of Key West derives its name from the corruption of the Spanish *Cayo Hueso* (pronounced ky-o wes-o), which means "island of bones." This grim name is supposed to have originated when an early Spanish visitor discovered a pile of bones there, remains from an Indian battleground. A place that has never known frost, Key West draws thousands of Americans who go there every year to warm their bones in its semitropical climate.

History. Naval air came to Key West in July 1917 when ground was broken for construction of a small coastal air patrol station at Trumbo Island. Key West's strategic importance to our defense in the Caribbean has increased steadily ever since. In 1943, planes from Boca Field virtually eliminated the German U-boat threat off the Keys. Today Key West NAS is home for Tactical Electronic Warfare Squadron 33 and Fighter Squadron 45. It is also home for the U.S. Navy's only hydrofoil squadron, Patrol Combatant Missile Hydrofoil Squadron 2. It well deserves its nickname, "Gibraltar of the Gulf."

Housing and Schools. There are 1,479 sets of family quarters at Key West, including a twenty-six-space mobile home park. As a general rule, the waiting period for Navy family housing in Key West is from six to nine months. Rental housing in the city of Key West is expensive and scarce. Rates range from $700 a month for a small, two-bedroom apartment to $1,000 a month or more for a three-bedroom unit. The Navy Lodge, completed in 1993, offers twenty-six rooms at forty dollars per night. There is no guest house at Key West.

A child-care day center is located on base, with a maximum occupancy of ninety children between the ages of two months and seven years; family home day care is also available. School-age children attend schools in the city of Key West. In addition, the Florida Keys Community College is open to military personnel from the station.

Personal Services and Recreation. A commissary store, Navy exchange, and other service facilities onboard the station enhance the quality of life there. Anyone on a normal tour of duty at the station would have a hard time *not* being served by the special services office, which offers boating, swimming pools and beaches, tennis, fishing, and a wide variety of indoor programs such as bowling, movies, hobby shops, and gymnasiums.

The Local Area. With an annual mean temperature of 77.7° F., outdoor activities are the rule year-round in the Keys. And of course, fishing and water sports are the area's recreational mainstays. Key West itself is one of the fishing capitals of the world, with 600 varieties of fish to be caught in the warm, clear waters that surround the island city. Special military rates are offered for some deep-sea fishing excursions. No license is required for saltwater fishing. Skin diving in the crystal-clear waters offshore is a very popular pastime.

The Key West nightlife is another unique feature of the area since most of the clubs and restaurants are open-air, due to the mild year-round climate. The nearest shopping available is in the Miami area, approximately 160 miles from the station.

For more information write to: Public Affairs Office, NAS, Key West, FL 33040-6300, or call (305) 293-9976.

MAYPORT NAVAL STATION

Mayport Naval Station provides logistical support for the operating forces of the Navy and other commands. Eighteen ships are currently homeported at Mayport. Ships can put to sea from Mayport more quickly than from any other naval complex in the United States. A two-mile channel permits vessels to be in deep water in less than forty-five minutes under emergency conditions.

History. Commissioned in December 1942, Mayport today occupies 3,400 acres at the mouth of the Saint Johns River, east of Jacksonville, and as of 1 July 1992, now includes the Naval Air Station and fifty-eight tenant commands.

Housing and Schools. Mayport has nearly 1,300 units of family housing, both on and off base. A new oceanfront Navy Lodge will be open for the summer 1994 season, to replace the nineteen two-bedroom trailers currently being operated there as a Navy Lodge.

Although there is no dependent schooling onboard the station, elementary and junior high schools are located in the immediate vicinity and high school students are bused into Jacksonville. The Navy Campus at Mayport sponsors a full range of programs designed to assist Navy personnel in advancing their professional and academic education. Several colleges offer courses on the base, and both Florida Community College and the University of North Florida are within easy driving distance.

Personal Services. Mayport has a full range of support services and facilities, including Navy exchange and commissary store facilities. The branch medical clinic provides care for active-duty personnel and very limited services for dependents. Dependents and retirees are eligible to use the NAVCARE clinic just one mile outside the station's main gate along Mayport Road.

Recreation. Recreational facilities of all kinds abound for Navy personnel at Mayport. Hunting and fishing on the station are controlled by the commanding officer. The base features an eighteen-hole golf course, oceanfront beaches, and several lighted ball fields and tennis courts. There is also a gymnasium complex with a full range of indoor sports and exercise facilities. The base also offers a club system, an auto hobby shop, and its own deep-sea fishing boat, the *Golden Anchor II*.

The Local Area. Interesting things to see and do are offered within easy traveling distance of Mayport. The city of Jacksonville is a modern metropolis of over 700,000 inhabitants, and today it is the largest city in land area in the United States, with over 841 square miles within its boundaries.

Saint Augustine, North America's oldest city, is only thirty-eight miles south along the Atlantic coast from Mayport, and Daytona Beach is only an hour-and-a-half drive away. A weekend outing is sufficient to take in Disney World at Orlando or the Cocoa Beach resort area.

For more information write to: Public Affairs Office, P.O. Box 280032, Naval Station, Mayport, FL 32228-0032, or call (904) 270-5226.

ORLANDO NAVAL TRAINING CENTER

The 1991 Base Realignment and Closure Commission recommended closing Orlando Naval Training Center, but at press time it was expected this would not be done until sometime in 1995.

Welcome to Navy World—Orlando Naval Training Center—which is not far from Disney World. The big difference between the two places is that at Disney World you're encouraged to lounge and linger and have a leisurely meal; at Orlando

NTC, the two enlisted dining facilities can feed 9,500 sailors in only ninety minutes. That's 105 people a minute. But there are other, not-so-subtle differences.

History. Orlando NTC was officially commissioned on 1 July 1968. Originally it began life as an Army Air Corps base, in December 1940. Today the NTC's mission is to provide basic, primary, advanced, and specialist training for officers and enlisted personnel of the regular Navy and the Navy Reserve, which it has done for over 90,000 men and women since 1969. The NTC consists of the Naval Training Station, Recruit Training Command, Service School Command, Construction Battalion Unit 419, and various tenant activities. The center is home to approximately 15,000 military and civilian personnel. Its 1,827 acres of land are divided into two areas, the NTC itself on the north side of Orlando, and the Annex on the south side of the city.

Housing and Schools. More than 960 units of government family housing are available for NTC personnel, all located at the Annex (formerly McCoy Air Force Base). There is also a Navy Lodge available at NTC for active-duty and retired personnel and their families.

Dependent children attend the local public schools. Child-care facilities are available at both the NTC and the Annex. Courses are available on base for adults from the Florida Institute of Technology, Southern Illinois University, Columbia College, and the University of Central Florida.

Personal Services. Medical care at Orlando NTC is provided by the Orlando Naval Hospital, which operates a 153-bed Main Hospital and branch medical clinics.

A Navy exchange retail store is available at both the NTC and the Annex; the NTC has a convenience store, and the Annex offers a commissary, a consolidated package store, and a Navy exchange food service facility. An ice cream shop, a leisure living center, and a package store are also located at the NTC, as are officers, CPO, and enlisted clubs.

Recreation. Recreational facilities include a twenty-four-lane bowling center, a nine-hole golf course, a gymnasium, a marina on Lake Baldwin, a ceramics shop, and a picnic area, also at the lake. A swimming pool and beach area on Lake Baldwin, a movie theater, and a wood hobby shop round out the recreational picture at the NTC. At the Annex there are an automotive hobby shop, a twelve-lane bowling center, a gym, a swimming pool, a nine-hole golf course, and a family camp with trailer facilities.

The Local Area. Orlando is located in central Florida, approximately sixty miles from the Atlantic Coast and some ninety miles from the Gulf of Mexico to the west. The city has a population of approximately 830,000. The annual average temperature in Orlando is 72° F. Approximately fifty inches of rain fall there each year, but the area is seldom battered by hurricanes or violent storms, as are the seacoast regions of Florida. In August the humidity averages 80 percent.

Eight lakes are located in the city of Orlando, all of which contribute to the natural beauty of the city and its suburbs. An estimated twenty million people visit the area annually, many of them attracted to nearby Disney World, Sea World, Stars Hall of Fame, and Gatorland Zoo.

For more information write to: Public Affairs Division, NTC, Orlando, FL 32813-5005, or call (407) 646-4501.

PANAMA CITY COASTAL SYSTEMS STATION

Established originally in 1942 as a naval amphibious training base, the Panama City Coastal Systems Station (CSS) has been involved with surface warfare research and development since it became a mine countermeasures station in 1945. Today it is a major activity under the Naval Surface Warfare Center with an active-duty complement of 670 personnel, a civilian workforce of over 1,400, and 1,200 family members.

Housing, Schools, and Personal Services. There are only sixty-five units of family housing at the CSS. Dependent children attend schools in the local community. On-base medical care is provided by a dispensary, while referral and inpatient care are available at nearby Tyndall Air Force Base. Likewise, commissary facilities are available at Tyndall, but CSS does have a small Navy exchange complex consisting of a retail store with personalized services.

Recreation. CSS has a ten-lane bowling center, a fitness center, a swimming pool, hobby shops, a library that boasts 6,000 volumes, and an outdoor recreation center with a marina, campsites, and other facilities.

For more information write to: Commander, Coastal Systems Station, Attention: Public Affairs, Panama City, FL 32407-7001, or call (904) 234-4011.

PENSACOLA NAVAL AIR STATION

Pensacola is quite literally the "Cradle of Naval Aviation." In 1913 it was selected as the site for the first naval aeronautic station, and in 1914 nine pilots and twenty-three mechanics arrived to fulfill its mission; by 1944 the installation was training 12,000 aviators a year.

History. The Navy first came to Pensacola in November 1825, when several officers wrote to President John Quincy Adams recommending a spot on Pensacola Bay for a Navy yard. Today the base occupies over 16,500 acres and has a population of over 22,000—13,000 military personnel and 9,000 civilians. Pensacola Naval Air Station is home to the Chief of Naval Education and Training and a number of other commands, including the Blue Angels Flight Demonstration Squadron and the USS *Forrestall* (AVT-59).

Housing and Schools. There are over 780 units of family housing at Pensacola, situated on 125 acres throughout the area. The Navy Lodge offers thirty-eight guest units for active-duty personnel and their dependents.

Dependent children of Navy families at Pensacola attend school in Escambia and Santa Rosa counties, where there are a total of sixty elementary, fifteen middle, and thirteen senior high schools. There is a child-care center on base as well. The Navy Campus offers assistance in taking courses from Pensacola Junior College, George Stone Vocational Technical School, Troy State University, Embry-Riddle Aeronautical University, and the University of West Florida, whose campus is only ten miles northeast of downtown Pensacola.

Personal Services. Medical care is provided by the 342-bed, eight-story Naval Hospital Pensacola. Other services include a commissary store and a Navy exchange with a full range of concessions from an ice cream shop to a flower shop.

Recreation. Recreational facilities at Pensacola NAS are excellent. There are two golf courses, one twenty-seven-hole and an eighteen-holer; a twenty-one-lane bowling center; outdoor and indoor swimming pools; clubs (officers and consolidated); and an active athletic program that includes a well-equipped gym. Oak Grove Park, a recreation area located on the station and open year-round, offers a magnificent opportunity to relax on the Gulf of Mexico. Facilities available there include twelve beach condos, forty-two RV lots, seventeen picnic areas, and two group picnic areas. The park stretches one and one-half miles along the beach. Sherman Cove, near the west gate of the station, offers boats and motors and other equipment for rent, as well as storage facilities for privately owned boats. Pier fuel, bait, and tackle are also available there.

Pensacola NAS is located on Pensacola Bay, opposite Fort Pickens and the Gulf Islands National Seashore. The city of Pensacola (population 60,000) is just to the north of the station. Opposite Pensacola, on East Bay, is Eglin Air Force Base. Pensacola is 50 miles east of Mobile, Alabama, and 200 miles west of Tallahassee, Florida.

For more information write to: Public Affairs Office, NAS, Pensacola, FL 32508-5000, or call (904) 452-2311.

WHITING FIELD NAVAL AIR STATION

Welcome to "Scratch Ankle," a nickname the town of Milton, Florida, acquired during the days when smugglers used to experience some difficulty climbing the briar-covered steps of the local trading post. Today Milton is seven miles south of Whiting Field and nobody scratches his ankles around there much anymore.

History. Whiting Field Naval Air Station was commissioned in July 1943 and named in honor of Capt. Kenneth Whiting, a pioneer military aviator who was taught to fly by Orville Wright himself. Today Whiting Field is home to Training Air Wing 5, which includes 3,635 personnel and the aircraft of Training Squadrons 2, 3, and 6 and Helicopter Training Squadrons 8 and 18. Property holdings of the station total 3,973 acres at the main complex and thirteen outlying landing fields in a five-county region.

Housing and Schools. Whiting Field has over 400 units of family housing available in two housing areas—329 at Whiting Pines and 82 units in Magda Village. Bachelor officers and enlisted personnel live in two-room bedroom suites with a shared lounge area. There are 72 transient rooms for officers and enlisted personnel, and reservations for these accommodations can be made up to ninety days in advance.

Although no dependent schooling is conducted at Whiting, the local schools are rated very highly. One facet of the adult education program available at Whiting Field is the Pensacola Junior College, which offers service personnel a college prep program and a variety of practical and academic credit courses at the station. Troy State University and the University of West Florida also offer courses on base.

Personal Services and Recreation. Whiting Field offers a complete spectrum of Navy exchange and commissary services, as well as clubs, messes, and medical and dental care. The special services facilities include a twelve-lane bowling center, three swimming pools, tennis courts, an eighteen-hole golf course, skeet and archery ranges, and Whiting Park, located on Blackwater River in Milton. The recreation area includes facilities for refueling boats, a pier facility, a picnic area, and swimming and beach areas. Equipment is also available for rent.

The Local Area. The West Florida Panhandle is noted for its pleasant overall quality of life and relaxed atmosphere; the climate there is ideal, with sunshine more than 340 days of the year. There are national parks, national seashore areas, beautiful beaches, and historic sites within just a few miles of the station. Whiting Field is thirty-five miles northeast of Pensacola and only a few miles to the northwest of Eglin Air Force Base. The Gulf of Mexico lies directly to the south, as does the Gulf Islands National Seashore.

For more information write to: Public Affairs Office, NAS, Whiting Field, 7550 USS Essex St., Ste. 101, Milton, FL 32570-6155, or call (904) 623-7011.

GEORGIA

Air Force

MOODY AIR FORCE BASE

History. The idea for an air base in the Lowndes County, Georgia, area began when a group of public-spirited citizens interested the War Department in a 9,300-acre tract called the Lakeland Flatwoods Project northeast of Valdosta. In May 1941, the Agriculture Department granted the War Department exclusive use of the land and on 19 February 1942 the Moody Field Advanced Pilot Training School opened its doors there. Today Moody is responsible for over 11,000 acres of land, including two 8,000-foot runways, and during fiscal year 1992 the base had a total estimated economic impact of $173 million on the local economy.

Named after Maj. George Putnam Moody, who was killed in an aircraft accident in Wichita, Kansas, in April 1941, the base today is home to the 347th Fighter Wing's 68th, 69th, 70th, 307th and 308th squadrons flying the F-16C/D Fighting Falcon. Approximately 3,700 military personnel and 8,350 dependents call Moody home these days. The base employs over 750 civilian personnel, and more than 7,100 military retirees in the area use its facilities.

Housing and Schools. There are 304 units of family housing available at Moody, 268 for enlisted personnel and 36 for officers. Off-base rentals are reasonable and range from as little as $250 a month for some apartments to as much as $500 a month for duplexes and town houses; a detached house in this area can cost up to $700 a month to rent. Temporary housing on base is available, but reservations should be made at least thirty days in advance. Twelve two-room family living units compose Moody's temporary lodging facility for incoming families.

There are no on-base schools for dependent children at Moody, although a child-development center is operated on base. Adult education is conducted through the Education Services Office and consists of both graduate and undergraduate programs through Georgia Military and Valdosta State Colleges.

Personal Services. Medical care at Moody is provided by a twenty-four-bed hospital. The base dental clinic provides care in all the basic dental specialties. This care is extended to retired personnel and dependents on a space-available basis. The commissary at Moody is large and well stocked. The base exchange, besides operating a "tank and tote" (convenience store and service station), also offers barber and beauty shops, a garden shop, an optical center, florist shops, a laundry, and a snack bar.

Recreation. Besides officers and enlisted clubs, Moody offers the full range of outdoor recreational activities. Picnicking and fishing are available at Mission Lake on base and at Grassy Pond, about twenty-two miles south of the base. Grassy Pond is a 489-acre site composed of two ponds covering a total of 261 acres. Back on base there is a nine-hole golf course, plus two swimming pools, a physical fitness center, arts and crafts programs, a base library with 29,000 volumes, a movie theater, and a fourteen-lane bowling center.

The Local Area. Moody Air Force Base is located ten miles northeast of Valdosta, a city of 40,000. Valdosta boasts an original name, from Val D'Aosta, "the Vale of Beauty," after Georgia ex-governor George M. Troupe's estate. Valdosta is the county seat of Lowndes County and is situated only twenty miles from the Florida-Georgia border. Today the area is an important producer of naval stores such as turpentine and resin, which come from area pine forests.

The proximity of both the Atlantic Ocean and the Gulf of Mexico give the Valdosta area a mild, almost subtropical climate with an average annual rainfall of forty-seven inches. May through September are the hottest months in this part of Georgia with temperatures averaging 80° F. in the afternoons with 60 percent humidity. The winters are mild, with lows in the forties, and wet, with three to four inches of rain per month, November through March. Snow is rare in this area.

For more information write to: 347th Wing Public Affairs Office, 5251 Berget St., Ste. 3, Moody AFB, GA 31699-1795, or call (912) 333-3395.

ROBINS AIR FORCE BASE

Robins Air Force Base, specifically the Air Logistics Center there, is the largest single industrial complex in the state of Georgia. It employs 18,900 military and civilian personnel and extends over more than 8,790 acres, within which there are ninety-two miles of paved roads and thirteen miles of railroad. The base has an economic impact in the surrounding communities of more than $2 billion.

History. Robins AFB is named after Brig. Gen. Augustine Warner Robins, ex-chief of the Air Corps Materiel Division. The adjacent city of Warner Robins, a town of 50,000 people, also takes its name from the general. The base was opened in March 1942 as Wellston Depot, after the original name of the hamlet that later became the town of Warner Robins. In September 1942, the depot was renamed Warner Robins Air Depot and the base was redesignated Warner Robins Army Air Field.

Housing and Schools. There are 1,396 units of family housing on the base. Completely furnished temporary housing is available for families near Luna Lake. These units—forty of them, sleeping five persons each—are assigned on a space-available basis only for periods of seven to thirty days.

A child-care center and two elementary schools, Robins and Linwood, are operated on the base. High schools are available in the town of Warner Robins. The Robins Resident Center offers undergraduate and graduate-level college courses for adults. These courses are conducted by the University of Georgia, Macon Junior College, and Georgia College; Georgia College offers advanced-degree programs through the Robins Graduate Center. The Mercer University also offers undergraduate and postgraduate courses on the base.

Personal Services. Medical care is provided by a twenty-bed USAF hospital staffed by approximately 390 personnel. A commissary and base exchange complex are also available.

Recreation. Recreational facilities include an officers and enlisted club system, hobby shops, a recreation center, picnic areas, five swimming pools, a riding stable, a skeet range, a 6,100-yard golf course, a sixteen-lane bowling facility, and a completely equipped gym. Robins Park, a 200-acre recreational area located in the southern sector of the base, offers a family camp, lakes, and family garden plots. The family camp has trailer pads and tent sites and is open year-round. Three lakes—Duck, Luna, and Scout—are available for fishing and boating.

Adjacent to Robins AFB is the Museum of Aviation, which more than 200,000 people visit each year to see the aircraft and missile exhibits, static displays, and films on aviation history shown daily in the theater.

The Local Area. Warner Robins is located in approximately the geographical center of the state of Georgia, about sixteen miles south of Macon. Macon, a city of 106,000, offers much in the way of cultural activities and recreation, with 600 acres of parkland and playgrounds within the city limits. Lake Tobesofkee, two miles from the city, offers boating and fishing, and Lake Sinclair, thirty-five miles north of town, offers fishing, picnicking, and camping. The state of Georgia has more than 300,000 acres of man-made lakes and hundreds of miles of coastline along the Atlantic Ocean. The mild climate permits outdoor recreation year-round.

For more information write to: WR-ALC/PA, 215 Page Rd., Ste. 106, Robins AFB, GA 31098-1662, or call (912) 926-2137.

Army

FORT BENNING

"For two centuries I have kept your Nation safe, purchasing freedom with my blood. To tyrants, I am the day of reckoning; to the suppressed, the hope for the future. Where the fighting is thick, there am I . . . I am the Infantry! FOLLOW ME!" Thus proclaim the opening lines of the poem "I Am the Infantry." Those are fitting words for the "Home of the Infantry," Fort Benning, Georgia.

History. Named in honor of Maj. Gen. Henry Lewis Benning, a distinguished Confederate soldier, Fort Benning came to life in October 1918, when the first troops arrived there to begin training for the battlefields of France in World War I. In October 1918, the Infantry School of Arms was established at Fort Benning. Today, the post's 182,000 acres provide training and maneuver areas for soldiers preparing to become infantrymen through twenty-three different courses, including Infantry Officer Basic and Advanced Courses, the Airborne and Ranger courses, and others. In addition, basic infantry training is conducted there, and Fort Benning is also home for the 3rd Brigade, 24th Infantry Division; the 36th Engineer Group; and the 3rd Ranger Battalion, 75th Ranger Regiment, and its regimental headquarters.

Housing and Schools. Fort Benning has over 4,000 units of family housing. The Fort Benning Guest House offers accommodations for military personnel, their guests, and dependents.

Dependent schools are operated on post for students in kindergarten through grade eight, as well as prekindergarten and nursery school. The post education center offers opportunities ranging from basic-skills review through job-skills education and post-secondary and graduate degrees. Participating institutions include Chattahoochie Valley State Community College, Columbus College, and Troy State University. Professional educational counseling services are offered as well as military and civilian academic testing.

Personal Services. Martin Army Hospital is a completely renovated, nine-story building with a 500-bed capacity that provides medical care to an eligible patient population of more than 100,000.

Fort Benning has a large main exchange with various specialty shops and twenty-seven branch exchanges. The commissary offers all the conveniences of a modern urban grocery store complex.

Recreation. Fort Benning also has a complete range of recreational services and activities, including two bowling alleys, five swimming pools, two eighteen-hole golf courses, four movie theaters, arts and crafts centers, tennis courts, gymnasiums, and two camping and fishing areas.

The Local Area. Fort Benning is located on the south side of Columbus (population 171,000). Phenix City, Alabama, is just across the Chattahoochee River from Columbus. The Columbus area's mean annual temperature is 65° F., making outdoor activities a year-round possibility. A wealth of recreational opportunities exist in and around the cities, including 2,000 acres of parks as well as hunting and fishing and water sports. The Destin Recreation Center, on Florida's Gulf Coast between Pensacola and Panama City, is operated by Fort Benning. During heavy usage (Memorial Day through Labor Day), personnel stationed at Fort Benning have priority for cabins; in other seasons other active-duty and retired personnel may reserve these facilities. Trailer pads and camper spaces are available all the time on a first-come, first-served basis.

For more information write to: Army Community Services Officer, U.S. Army Infantry Center, Fort Benning, GA 31905-5065, or call (706) 545-3512.

FORT GORDON

Located on 55,000 acres of farmland and woodlands nine miles southwest of Augusta, Fort Gordon covers portions of four Georgia counties. During its more-than-forty-year history, Fort Gordon has hosted infantry, armor, and military police training. Today it is the home of the Signal Corps and is dedicated to training soldier-technicians in the installation, operation, and maintenance of the Army's modern communications-electronics equipment. Fort Gordon's workforce consists of 12,000 soldiers, 5,100 civilian employees, and 18,000 dependents.

History. Named in honor of Confederate Lt. Gen. John Brown Gordon, Fort Gordon was activated in December 1941 and trained the men of two infantry divisions and an armored division for combat on the battlefields of World War II. The Signal Corps Training Center was established there in September 1948, and Fort Gordon's history has been associated with the communicators ever since. With the projected construction of the National Science Center for the Communications and Electronics Foundation, Fort Gordon will enter the twenty-first century and become the "Professional Home of the Signal Corps."

Housing and Schools. More than 800 sets of family quarters are situated on the post, as well as modern guest-house facilities. Although no dependent schools are operated on the post, many fine schools are nearby. The post offers four child-care facilities. The Fort Gordon Education Center offers a program that includes courses leading to a high school diploma, and college-level courses for both undergraduate and postgraduate degrees are offered by Southern Illinois University, Georgia Southern University, Ohio University, Central Michigan University, and other institutions of higher learning.

Personal Services. Every convenience for graceful living is available at Fort Gordon. The fourteen-story, 400-bed Dwight David Eisenhower Army Medical Center provides up-to-date patient care to a population of some 89,000 active and retired military and to their families.

Recreation. The mild climate that prevails in the area permits outdoor activities year-round. Outdoor recreation facilities include the Fort Gordon Recreation area, an 865-acre lake reservoir located twenty-six miles from post featuring camping, water skiing, a beach, and picnic areas. Mirror Lake and Wilkerson Pond, on post, also provide recreation facilities. The post boasts two golf courses, one eighteen-hole and one nine-hole; a stable; five gyms; two swimming pools; two bowling alleys; auto and craft hobby shops; officers and enlisted club systems; and an FM radio station.

The Local Area. Augusta is a rapidly growing community on the banks of the Savannah River on the Georgia–South Carolina border, 125 miles northwest of Savannah. The Augusta metropolitan area boasts a population of over 396,000. Augusta offers Fort Gordon residents and visitors many cultural advantages and a number of large and attractive parks and playgrounds. Sumter National Forest is just to the north over the South Carolina border, and numerous state parks in the area offer swimming, boating, hunting, and fishing.

The cost of living in the greater Augusta area is very close to the national average and just a little over for utility costs.

For more information write to: Army Community Services Office, U.S. Army Signal Center, Fort Gordon, GA 30905-5000, or call (706) 791-6001.

FORT McPHERSON

Known affectionately as "Fort Mac" to Atlantans and Fort McPherson personnel, Fort McPherson occupies 487 acres of well-landscaped ground four miles southwest of downtown Atlanta. Fort McPherson also operates two subposts: Fort Gillem, a 1,500-acre site located in Forest Park, ten miles from Atlanta, and Fort Buchanan, Puerto Rico.

History. Named after Maj. Gen. James Birdseye McPherson, a Union Army general killed during the battle for Atlanta in 1864, Fort McPherson came into existence in the summer of 1885 and received its first garrison, nine batteries of the 4th Artillery Regiment, in 1889. Today, it is home for Headquarters, Forces Command, which has the mission of maintaining the readiness of active Army and reserve units throughout the United States and its territories. It also serves as headquarters for the 3rd U.S. Army and Army Reserve Command. Fort Gillem is home for the 2nd U.S. Army, the U.S. Army Southeast Region Recruiting Command, and other activities.

Housing and Schools. Fort McPherson is a very small post, with only 112 sets of family quarters, so most military personnel live off the installation. There are, however, guest accommodations available for all ranks. Temporary-duty and permanent-change-of-station personnel have priority; all others may be accommodated on a space-available basis only.

Although there are no on-post schools for dependents at Fort McPherson, there is a small day-care center for children. The post education center provides counseling and testing services as well as college-level courses at both undergraduate and postgraduate levels.

Personal Services and Recreation. Fort McPherson provides welfare and morale services for assigned active-duty personnel plus an estimated 10,000 retired personnel and their families in the Atlanta area. These include a U.S. Army Health and Dental Clinic, an eighteen-hole golf course, a swimming pool, a gymnasium, bowling lanes, picnic areas, an automotive shop, officers and NCO clubs, and sports facilities.

There are commissary and post exchange services at both Fort McPherson and Fort Gillem. Fort McPherson operates an excellent recreation area at Lake Allatoona, one hour north of Atlanta, with motel, cabin, boating, beach, and picnicking facilities.

The Local Area. Fort McPherson is practically in Atlanta and surrounded by suburbia. The climate is mild to hot almost the whole year, permitting outdoor activities most of the time. The Atlanta area is rich in Civil War history as well as state parks and recreation areas. Fort McClellan, Alabama, and Fort Benning, Georgia, are within easy driving distance. Fort Gordon, near Augusta, and Fort Stewart, near Savannah, are a bit farther removed but still accessible to military personnel desiring to use the many facilities at these places.

For more information write to: Headquarters, Fort McPherson, Attention: AFZK-PO, Bldg. 65, Fort McPherson, GA 30330-5000, or call (404) 752-2204.

FORT STEWART

Fort Stewart is a "growing post." In 1975, it was a stagnant backwater community comprising mostly World War II facilities with a dim and uncertain future. Then, with the announcement of plans for the reactivation of the 24th Infantry Division at Fort Stewart, a tremendous construction program began to upgrade the post's facilities. Fort Stewart is the largest installation east of the Mississippi River, covering an area of more than 279,000 acres and measuring thirty-nine miles east to west and nineteen miles north to south. Hunter Army Airfield, on the southwest side of Savannah, covers 5,400 acres.

History. Named in honor of Brig. Gen. Daniel Stewart, Revolutionary War hero, great-grandfather of Theodore Roosevelt, and great-great-grandfather of Eleanor Roosevelt, Fort Stewart was activated in June 1940 as an Antiaircraft Artillery Center. The post reached its peak strength of 55,000 men in August 1943, and then declined steadily until 1 July 1974, when the 1st Battalion (Ranger), 75th Infantry, parachuted into the area to mark a new beginning for the post as a home for infantry units. The 24th Division was activated there in September 1975. Today Fort Stewart's units are an important element of this nation's Rapid Deployment Force.

Housing and Schools. Fort Stewart has over 2,300 family housing units and eighty-six mobile home spaces. Guest facilities are limited at Fort Stewart, with personnel being accommodated at the seventy-room guest house on a space-available basis only.

Two elementary schools provide educational facilities on post from kindergarten through sixth grade; children in grades seven through twelve attend schools in nearby Hinesville. The Army education center offers a full array of educational services, including innovative master's degree programs enabling personnel to obtain degrees in eleven to fifteen months.

Personal Services. Complete post exchange and commissary facilities are available at Fort Stewart and Hunter Army Airfield. The 121-bed Winn Army Community Hospital offers a full range of health-care services.

Recreation. The morale support activities office provides a wide range of programs and facilities, from modern air-conditioned multipurpose craft shops to outdoor recreation; the Stewart-Hunter Sports Program is one of the most comprehensive in the Army Forces Command. The installation also provides shooting, hunting, fishing, and picnic areas, and sporting equipment rentals for nominal fees.

The Local Area. Fort Stewart is located about forty-one miles southwest of Savannah, a bustling modern city with a population of about 141,000, and it is located in one of the most spectacular recreational and sporting areas along the whole Atlantic coast. The winters are mild and the summers are semitropical—hot and humid—providing opportunity for outdoor activities almost the whole year. Savannah Beach, about thirty minutes from Hunter Army Air Field, is a summer resort offering swimming, fishing, boating, and other outdoor activities. Hilton Head, South Carolina, a forty-five-minute drive across the Talmadge Memorial Bridge, is another major tourist center.

For more information write to: Headquarters, 24th Infantry Division and Fort Stewart, Attention: AFZP-PO, Fort Stewart, Georgia 31314-5000, or call (912) 767-8666.

Marine Corps

ALBANY MARINE CORPS LOGISTICS BASE

Although the Marine Corps Logistics Base Drum and Bugle Corps is renowned for blatting out such traditional military airs as "No Slum Today," it's the job of the people at the logistics base, through the stores distribution system, to see that Marines do have their "slum"—an old word for meat stew, not garbage, although Marines who have to subsist on the field rations proffered by today's logisticians might prefer yesteryear's "slum" instead.

History. The Marine Corps Logistics Base (MCLB) was commissioned in March 1952. Today it has the overall mission of acquiring, repairing, storing, issuing, rebuilding, and distributing supplies and equipment, as well as conducting formal schooling and providing a central quality assurance program for the Marine Corps. The base is home to 1,100 active-duty personnel and their 2,000 family members and has a civilian workforce of more than 5,900.

Housing and Schools. There are more than 680 sets of government family quarters at the MCLB. Waiting times for these units range from five to thirty days. While there are no temporary or guest quarters at the base, there are nineteen trailer spaces for privately owned house trailers.

Dependent children of personnel assigned duty at the base attend the local public schools. Three child-development centers and one preschool are available on base. The base education center offers college courses through Darton College, Albany State College, and Albany Technical Institute.

Personal Services. Medical care is provided by a branch clinic of the Naval Regional Medical Center, Jacksonville, Florida. The dental clinic is operated under the auspices of the Naval Dental Clinic, Jacksonville. Retired military personnel and dependents not covered under the Delta Dental Plan are seen there on a space-available basis.

An excellent commissary store and a Marine Corps exchange are available at the base. The exchange operates a service station, a beauty shop, a barber shop, a snack bar, a laundry and dry-cleaning shop, and a seven-day store.

Recreation. Recreational facilities at MCLB include a nine-hole golf course, four swimming pools, a base theater, a six-lane bowling alley, a skeet range, a gymnasium, an auto hobby shop, and a base library.

The base rod and gun club (which also operates the skeet range) offers members assistance in obtaining Georgia state hunting and fishing licenses. Both hunting and fishing are permitted on the base and permits are obtained through the natural resources and environmental affairs office.

Officers and enlisted clubs are also located at the MCLB.

The Local Area. Albany lies upon the banks of the Flint River, approximately 175 miles south of Atlanta, in the southwestern corner of Georgia. Fort Benning and Columbus are about eighty miles to the northwest of Albany. Robins Air Force Base is about eighty miles due north of the MCLB, with Macon twenty miles beyond. Tallahassee, Florida, is about 100 miles south of Albany.

For more information write to: Public Affairs Office, MCLB, Albany, GA 31704-5000, or call (912) 439-5215.

Navy

ATLANTA NAVAL AIR STATION

Atlanta Naval Air Station and Dobbins Air Force Base are like love and marriage: You can't have one without the other. Situated in northwestern Georgia at Marietta, the two bases are only fifteen miles northwest of Atlanta, and they share the same runways. Dobbins, however, is strictly an Air Force Reserve installation with a very small active-duty complement.

History. Atlanta NAS consists of 181 acres just outside the town of Marietta. The facility began operations there in 1959, after moving from its original location at Fort Gordon. Today NAS Atlanta is home for Light Attack Squadron 205, flying the A6E/KA-6D Intruder; Fleet Logistics Squadron 46, flying the McDonnell Douglas C-9 "Skytrain"; and Marine Aircraft Group 42, flying the OV-10D Bronco and the AH-1J Cobra helicopter. The station is home to approximately 1,100 active-duty military personnel, 180 civilian employees, and some 3,100 dependents. Its primary mission is the training of reserve personnel, about 1,400 of whom train there on a regular basis.

Housing and Schools. Housing is very tight at Atlanta NAS, with about fourteen sets of government quarters available on the station. The housing referral office assists newcomers in finding accommodations in Marietta or Atlanta.

There are no dependent schools at Atlanta NAS, either, but the station does operate a small day-care facility.

Personal Services. Medical care is provided by a small dispensary, and there is no commissary at Atlanta NAS. The station does have a small exchange and a package store; Dobbins has a small exchange as well as a shopette. Commissary facilities are available at Fort McPherson, in Atlanta.

Recreation. Recreational facilities on the station include a consolidated mess, an outdoor swimming pool, a racquetball/handball court, and a six-lane bowling alley. A new fitness center and auto hobby shop are also available. Camping and athletic equipment can be obtained from the special services office. At Dobbins there are a consolidated open mess, a gymnasium, and sixteen slots for recreational vehicles. The Lake Allatoona Recreational Area, about twenty miles from Marietta, has a wide variety of outdoor recreational facilities, including two cabins, three trailers, and nine campsites. Camping, fishing, swimming, hiking, and boating are available, as are equipment rentals.

The Local Area. The climate in the Atlanta area is generally mild with average temperatures of 43° F. and about fifty inches of rainfall per year. The Civil War history buff will find this a fascinating area. The symbol of Atlanta, the Phoenix, represents the city's rise from its ashes after it was burned by the Union troops.

The surrounding countryside offers a large and diversified selection of recreational activities available year-round, from county and state parks to Kennesaw Mountain National Battlefield Park. The city of Atlanta itself offers all the conveniences and advantages of a large metropolitan area.

For more information write to: Public Affairs Office, NAS, Atlanta, GA 30060-5099, or call (404) 421-5406.

KINGS BAY NAVAL SUBMARINE BASE

History. Kings Bay Naval Submarine Base was constructed beginning in 1978 on the site of a former U.S. Army Ocean Terminal. Today it covers an area of approximately 16,000 acres. The base provides support to the submarine-launched ballistic missile system (SLBM) and operates facilities providing that support. Currently, Kings Bay supports a squadron of fleet nine Poseidon-class ballistic missile (FBM) subs of Submarine Squadron 16 and five Ohio-class FBM submarines—the USS *Tennessee*, the USS *Pennsylvania*, the USS *West Virginia*, the USS *Kentucky*, and the USS *Maryland* of Submarine Squadron 20.

The base population consists of approximately 5,600 active-duty personnel and their 7,700 family members, and over 2,500 civilian employees.

Housing and Schools. A total of 665 government family housing units are available on the base: one- to four-bedroom units for enlisted personnel and two- to four-bedroom dwellings for officers. There are 461 enlisted and 126 officer quarters for single and unaccompanied personnel. Temporary lodging is available in the twenty-six-room Navy Lodge. The lodge permits guests to stay up to fourteen days.

Schools in the area include the Crooked River Elementary School (one mile from the family housing area) and other elementary, middle, and high schools. The base has a day-care center that can accommodate 185 children ages four weeks to twelve years. Adult education is available from the Navy Campus through Valdosta State College and other institutions.

Personal Services. Kings Bay has an outpatient medical clinic and a dental clinic. The nearest naval hospital is at Jacksonville Naval Air Station, sixty miles south of Kings Bay. Both commissary and Navy exchange facilities are available on the base. Also available are the base personalized services center, a beauty shop, a barber shop, the Navy Federal Credit Union, a cafeteria, a pizzeria, a Baskin Robbins ice cream parlor, a package store, a laundromat, a convenience store, and a service station.

Recreation. Recreational facilities include a gymnasium with racquetball and handball courts, lighted outdoor basketball courts, lighted softball fields, lighted tennis courts, a lighted football/soccer field, an eighteen-hole golf course, an outdoor swimming pool, a sixteen-lane bowling center, an auto hobby shop, fishing lakes, and an outdoor recreation checkout facility with campers, boats, and other equipment.

The Local Area. This part of Georgia enjoys a temperate climate with mild, short winters and long, comparatively warm summers. The year-round temperature averages 67° F., with winter averages of 54° F. and summer averages of 80° F. Normal rainfall in the Kings Bay area amounts to fifty-one inches, with most of it occurring during the afternoon hours in the summer months.

Kings Bay is located in Camden County, the southeasternmost county in Georgia. The base is about five miles east of Interstate 95 from exits 1, 2, or 2A. The closest major cities are Jacksonville, Florida, and Brunswick, Georgia, about forty miles south and north of the base, respectively.

For more information write to: Public Affairs Officer, 1063 USS Tennessee Avenue, Naval Submarine Base Kings Bay, GA 31547-2606, or call (912) 673-2000.

HAWAII

Air Force

HICKAM AIR FORCE BASE

Hickam Air Force Base lies about nine miles west of downtown Honolulu, between Pearl Harbor and Honolulu International Airport. It is home for Headquarters, Pacific Air Forces, the Air Force component of the Pacific Command; the host unit at the base is the 15th Air Base Wing. The base is located in some of the most beautiful country in the United States.

History. Named in honor of Lt. Col. Horace M. Hickam, who died in an air crash in 1934, the base was completed in 1938. Today it is a 2,700-acre work site for nearly 5,000 active-duty military and 2,400 civilian personnel. With dependents, the base population is over 12,000. The 15th Air Base Wing provides support for Air Force units stationed in Hawaii and other places in the Pacific area.

Housing and Schools. There are over 2,200 units of family housing at Hickam. There is usually a waiting list for all ranks.

Excellent public and private schools are available for dependent children throughout Hawaii, and a child-care center and a day-care preschool are operated at Hickam. The Hickam Education Center provides undergraduate and evening classes on base under the auspices of Chaminade University, Embry-Riddle Aeronautical University, Wayland Baptist University, Troy State University, the University of Oklahoma, and Hawaii Pacific University.

Personal Services. A USAF clinic at Hickam provides routine medical care for active-duty and retired personnel and their families. Nearby Tripler Army Medical

Center, a 550-bed complex, offers definitive inpatient care for all eligible personnel. Hickam also offers a commissary, a base exchange, a credit union, and a bank.

Recreation. Recreational facilities for personnel stationed at Hickam are excellent. The base has two golf courses, one eighteen-holer by the ocean and a par-three course in the Ohana Nui Housing Area. Hickam Harbor offers swimming, boating, sailing, fishing, and picnicking. Small boats may be rented. In addition, an excellent recreation center and a fully equipped arts and crafts center are available, as well as two freshwater swimming pools and a thirty-lane bowling center.

There are excellent recreational areas for military personnel and their families assigned to Hickam. One is the Bellows Air Force Station, twenty-five miles from the base. The station sits on about 1,500 acres of land and has a 12,000-foot beach-front with 102 furnished beach cottages available year-round. Approximately 220,000 personnel take advantage of the site each year. Kilauea Military Camp, located on the big island of Hawaii, is situated 4,000 feet up the side of Kilauea Volcano and is operated as a joint-service recreational facility. It is open year-round and offers cabins, apartments, dormitories, an exchange, a dining hall, bowling, hiking, tennis, golf, and guided tours of Volcano National Park and other local points of interest.

For more information write to: 15th Air Base Wing, Public Affairs Division, Hickam AFB, HI 96853-5000, or call (808) 449-6367.

The 171-foot Freedom Tower is one of Hickam's most well-known landmarks. (USAF photo)

WHEELER AIR FORCE BASE

See Schofield Barracks. As of November 1, 1991, control of Wheeler reverted to the U.S. Army and it was renamed Wheeler Army Airfield.

Army

FORT SHAFTER

Named after Maj. Gen. William R. Shafter, who led troops in Cuba during the Spanish-American War in 1898, Fort Shafter was the first permanent U.S. military installation established in the Hawaiian Islands when it was built in 1907.

The major activity at Fort Shafter today is Headquarters, U.S. Army, Pacific (USARPAC), the Army component of U.S. Commander in Chief, Pacific (USCINCPAC). USARPAC is responsible for providing Army ground combat forces throughout the Pacific region (except Korea), support for those forces administratively and logistically, and reserves and contingency plans to meet any ground threat to U.S. interests in the Pacific. USARPAC's area of responsibility embraces over 100 million square miles in fifty countries, which have a total population of 2.5 billion. The USARPAC general staff is situated in Richardson Hall, named in honor of Lt. Gen. Robert C. Richardson, Jr., a veteran of both world wars. Built in 1944, Richardson Hall is known as the "Pineapple Pentagon."

Located next door to Tripler Army Hospital, Fort Shafter's population consists of 1,200 active-duty personnel, 500 civilian employees, and over 1,200 family members.

Housing and Schools. In general, personnel assigned duty at Fort Shafter who are eligible to occupy family housing will be assigned to one of the 20,000 sets of family quarters the Army administers in Hawaii. At Fort Shafter itself are bachelor officer and senior enlisted quarters as well as guest-house units. The Hawaiian public school system operates an elementary school on post; older children attend school in Honolulu. College courses available through the Army Education Service include on-post courses from the University of Honolulu, Central Michigan University, Chaminade University, and Hawaii Pacific University.

Personal Services. There is a dental clinic on post; full medical services are provided by Tripler Army Medical Center next door. Fort Shafter has both a commissary and a post exchange. Also available are barber and beauty shops, a gas station, snack bars, a tailor shop, a watch repair shop, a car care center, a tailor shop, a shoe repair shop, and other retail outlets.

Recreation. In addition to the unlimited variety of recreational opportunities available everywhere in the Hawaiian Islands, Fort Shafter has a par-sixty-eight, 5,661-yard, nine-hole golf course; a twenty-two-lane bowling alley; a swimming pool; a gym; volleyball, tennis, and basketball courts; and a baseball field. For the more sedentary, there are officers and NCO clubs, a craft shop, a theater, and a community center.

For more information write to: Public Affairs Office, U.S. Army, Pacific, Fort Shafter, HI 96858-5100, or call (808) 471-7110.

HALE KOA HOTEL

The words *hale koa* in Hawaiian mean "house of the warrior," and for armed forces personnel, their dependents, and guests looking for first-class accommodations on Honolulu's world-famous Waikiki Beach at Fort DeRussy, that means the Hale Koa Hotel.

The Hale Koa was built with nonappropriated funds generated by profits from military clubs and exchanges around the world. Reserved exclusively for the use of armed forces personnel, it enjoys a well-earned reputation as the military's most attractive and most popular recreation facility. Active-duty military personnel of all services, including National Guard and reserve members, cadets and midshipmen from the service academies, personnel on active duty for training, and individuals classified by the Department of Veterans Affairs as 100 percent disabled are eligible to use Hale Koa.

The Hale Koa has 419 guest rooms, each offering a private bath, air-conditioning, color TV, and balconies with panoramic views of the Pacific Ocean or the verdant Koolau Mountains. Room rates vary, depending on active-duty or retired status as well as room location and the amount of ocean view afforded. The 1992–93 room rates based on double occupancy ranged from $42 to $109 per night. Reservations can be made up to a year in advance.

The Hale Koa occupies several acres right on Waikiki Beach. Guests may enjoy one-third of a mile of white-sand beach for sunbathing, swimming, snorkeling, and surfing. A freshwater swimming pool, tennis courts, and sand volleyball courts are located on the grounds. Indoors is a complete range of conveniences, including an activities desk, a fitness center, self-service laundry facilities on each floor, a post exchange, a car rental desk, a barber and beauty shop, a discount tour and travel office, and a jewelry shop.

The superb dining and entertainment facilities offered by the Hale Koa are available not only to hotel guests but to all military personnel and their guests. Weekly dinner shows include Tuesday Night Magic, Tama's Polynesian Revue, and even a Hale Koa Hawaiian Luau on the beach, all at affordable prices. Live entertainment is featured nightly in the Warriors Lounge. For quick snacks and meals, there are two outdoor snack bars with ready-to-go items like hamburgers, fried chicken, and local-style favorites. The modestly priced Territorial Coffee House serves breakfast, lunch, and dinner every day of the week. The pride of the hotel is its signature restaurant, the Hale Koa Room, renowned for its distinctive menu, beverages, and service. On Sundays the Hale Koa Room features a champagne brunch buffet.

It is estimated that over one million military personnel and their dependents use the Hale Koa's facilities each year. A new pool complex was recently completed and a new luau grounds opened in the spring of 1993. Future expansion plans include building an additional hotel tower and extensive landscaping of Fort DeRussy Park.

For more information write to: Hale Koa Hotel, 2055 Kalia Rd., Honolulu, HI 96815-1998, or call (808) 955-0555. For reservations call toll free from the continental United States, (800) 367-6027.

SCHOFIELD BARRACKS / WHEELER ARMY AIRFIELD

Anyone who has seen the movie classic *From Here to Eternity* has seen Schofield Barracks, because the picture was filmed there. Bullet holes from the Japanese attack on the morning of 7 December 1941 can still be seen in some of the buildings.

History. Named in 1909 in honor of Lt. Gen. John M. Schofield, a Civil War veteran, Schofield Barracks' 14,000 acres today are home to the 25th Infantry Division (Light), "Tropic Lightning." After distinguished service in three wars—World War II, Korea, and Vietnam—the division is back at Schofield, which has been its permanent home since it was established there in October 1941. Schofield's population today includes about 15,600 military personnel, their 11,000 dependents, and 4,600 civilian employees.

As of 1 November 1991, Wheeler Army Airfield (formerly Wheeler Air Force Base) came under the control of Schofield Barracks. The landing strip at Wheeler was first cleared in 1922 and that same year named Wheeler Field in honor of Maj. Gen. Sheldon H. Wheeler. Today its 1,300 acres are home to the men and women of the 25th Infantry Division's aviation brigade and other units. Fort Shafter is also under the control of Schofield Barracks.

Housing and Schools. There are 4,674 units of family housing (693 officer, 3,981 enlisted) available to personnel stationed at Schofield and Wheeler. As of January 1993, there was a waiting period of three to twenty-three months for most grades and bedroom categories. Guest housing is available at rates from $15 to $29 per person plus $5 for each additional person. Off-post housing is very expensive in Hawaii. Average first-month rental fees as of January 1993, including security deposit (one month's rent paid in advance), range from $1,500 to $2,600. Utilities are not included in these figures.

Four elementary schools and an intermediate school are available on post for Schofield/Wheeler's children. Another elementary school is located at Fort Shafter. Three child-care facilities with capacities from 32 to 210 children are also available. The post education center offers courses from Chaminade University, Embry-Riddle Aeronautical University, Hawaii Pacific, and the University of Hawaii at the undergraduate level; graduate programs are available from Pepperdine and Central Michigan Universities, the University of Southern California, and Oklahoma State University.

Personal Services. Medical care at Schofield is provided by a U.S. Army health clinic. Extensive care is available at Tripler Army Hospital, about fifteen miles south of the post. A commissary is located on the post, and commissaries are also located at Hickam Air Force Base and Pearl Harbor Naval Complex. The post exchange at

Schofield offers a wide variety of concessions, including four snack bars, a Burger King, a Frank's Franks stand, a Pizza Pub, a service station and garage, an optical shop, banking facilities, a car rental service, barber and beauty shops, and a Baskin Robbins ice cream parlor.

Recreation. Recreational services at Schofield Barracks are excellent and include an arts and crafts shop, two bowling centers, two eighteen-hole golf courses, and a gym. Officers and enlisted clubs as well as a movie theater are also available, as is an auto repair shop. Recreational equipment rentals are available, as are camping, fishing, and diving equipment. Bicycles may be rented at very reasonable fees as well.

The Local Area. Schofield Barracks is twenty-five miles north of Honolulu on the island of Oahu, the most heavily populated island in the chain (three-quarters of the state's population of about one million people). In size, Oahu is the third largest of the Hawaiian Islands. In addition to being the cultural and social center of the state, Oahu is the site of famous Waikiki Beach and the USS *Arizona* Monument at Pearl Harbor. The main campus of the University of Hawaii is in Honolulu, in Manoa Valley.

For more information write to: Public Affairs Office, 25th Infantry Division, Schofield Barracks, HI 96857, or call (808) 655-8729.

TRIPLER ARMY MEDICAL CENTER

Located eight miles from Waikiki, Tripler Army Medical Center is the largest military treatment facility in the Pacific and is the only Army medical center not located on the U.S. mainland.

The role of the 537-bed hospital is as unique as its geographic location. True to its motto, "Concern, care, and service," Tripler routinely provides out- and inpatient care to 62,000 active-duty personnel of all services, 93,000 dependents and retirees, 152,000 Pacific Islands beneficiaries, and 110,000 veterans, which includes the forty-five beds provided at Tripler under the auspices of the Department of Veterans Affairs. Tripler is also a major teaching center.

History. Named in 1920 honor of Brevet Brig. Gen. Charles Stuart Tripler, the first medical director of the Army of the Potomac during the Civil War, Tripler originally opened in 1907 as a post hospital at Fort Shafter. The center was moved to its present location on Monalua Ridge in 1948.

Wings A through E, completed in 1948, contain 1.6 million square feet and 537 beds (with room to expand to 1,100 in an emergency). Three new wings, F, G, and H, were begun in 1982 and opened in 1985 at a cost of $106 million. These wings have 433,000 square feet and house the emergency room, pathology unit, lab, surgical units, and specialty inpatient care units.

Housing. Approximately 200 units of family housing are available at the center itself; additional housing is located at Fort Shafter. Guest housing consisting of forty-one units is also available. The center also administers thirty-five units of bachelor officer and twenty-eight units of bachelor enlisted housing.

Personal Services and Recreation. There is no commissary and there is only a small post exchange at Tripler. Dependents schools and day-care facilities are also unavailable there; these services are offered at various nearby military installations. The center does have a bowling alley, a swimming pool, a gymnasium, a library, a driving range, and racquetball and tennis courts. Tripler Army Medical Center is located only eight miles from Honolulu and offers an excellent view of the city from its elevation. Waikiki is a twenty-five-minute drive from Tripler.

For more information write to: HQ, Tripler Army Medical Center, Attention: HSHK-IO, Tripler AMC, HI 96859-5000, or call (808) 433-6661.

Tripler Army Medical Center is the regional medical center in the Pacific area. (U.S. Army photo)

Marine Corps

CAMP H. M. SMITH

Named after Lt. Gen. Holland M. "Howlin' Mad" Smith—who ironically is best known for the incident in World War II when he got howling mad at Army Gen. Robert C. Richardson, after whom Richardson Hall at Fort Shafter is named—Camp Smith began life as the site of a Navy hospital in 1942 and was acquired by the Marine Corps in 1955.

Today Camp Smith is headquarters for Commander in Chief, Pacific; Marine Forces, Pacific; and other commands. The installation is home to 1,600 active-duty personnel, more than 500 civilian employees, and 1,500 family members.

Housing and Schools. Camp Smith has a few family housing units for officers and quarters for about 120 single enlisted personnel. Children of sponsors assigned duty at Camp Smith attend local schools. There are no child-care facilities at Camp Smith.

Personal Services. There is a medical clinic at Camp Smith for active-duty personnel, but definitive medical care is provided by Tripler Army Hospital. No commissary is available, but there is a small Marine Corps exchange as well as a gas station, a laundry/dry-cleaning facility, a beverage store, a tailor shop, and a snack bar.

Recreation. Camp Smith offers a spectrum of recreational facilities that ranges from horseback riding to a library. This includes a campground, an auto hobby shop, racquetball and handball courts, a swimming pool, tennis and volleyball courts, and a weight room. Officers, staff duty, and enlisted clubs are also available.

For more information write to: Commanding General, Fleet Marine Force Pacific, Attention: Force PAO, Box 64124, Camp H. M. Smith, HI 96861-4124, or call (808) 477-6331.

KANEOHE BAY MARINE CORPS AIR STATION

History. From its rather obscure beginnings in 1939 as a small seaplane base, Kaneohe Bay Marine Corps Air Station ("K-Bay," as it is known) has grown into home for over 15,000 Marines, sailors, and their dependents. The 1st Marine Expeditionary Brigade is the largest tenant unit aboard the station.

Kaneohe Bay lies on the north side (the windward side) of the island of Oahu, opposite Honolulu and across the Koolau Mountains, which rise to a height of 4,000 feet. Kaneohe Bay MCAS is situated on the Mokapu Peninsula, which forms the eastern shore of the bay and is the site of the University of Hawaii's Marine Lab and the Kaneohe Bay Park.

Housing and Schools. There are over 1,800 units of family housing at the station and a temporary lodging facility with guest accommodations. The station offers living facilities for over 5,800 unaccompanied personnel.

Aside from a preschool facility, dependent schoolchildren at Kaneohe attend the Hawaii public school system, the ninth largest in the United States. The base education office provides complete information and assistance to all personnel on a full range of educational programs, from high school equivalency to college degrees in a variety of subjects.

Personal Services. Medical and dental facilities are available at Kaneohe. Tripler Army Medical Center provides a full range of medical specialties to all armed forces personnel stationed in the Hawaiian Islands, and personnel requiring these services are referred there from Kaneohe when necessary.

Other services include the main Marine Corps exchange, a commissary, a banking facility, and a complete club system for all ranks. The base morale, welfare, and recreation office performs a variety of services, including assisting in the purchase of discount tickets for local attractions and events and making arrangements for recreational activities such as deep-sea fishing trips and cottage rentals at a number of beaches in the area.

Recreation. In the immediate vicinity of Kaneohe Bay there are a number of recreational sites: Waimanalo Bay State Recreational Area a few miles to the east, along the coast; Waiahole Beach Park near Waikane; Kahana Valley State Park to the west, along the coast; and various other scenic and cultural attractions.

For more information write to: Joint Public Affairs Office, MCAS, Kaneohe Bay, HI 96863-5001, or call (808) 257-5743.

Navy

BARBERS POINT NAVAL AIR STATION

Although the 1993 Base Realignment and Closure Commission recommended closing Barbers Point NAS, no date had been fixed for closing at press time.

Barbers Point occupies about 3,600 acres of land to the west of Pearl Harbor and Ewa Beach, Oahu, and is just south of the Farrington Highway. It is home to about 5,500 military personnel and employs approximately 1,500 civilian workers. Commissioned in April 1942, the station is also home port today for twenty-eight tenant commands, including Commander, Patrol Wing 2; six patrol squadrons; a helicopter antisubmarine squadron; and the Army's 214th Aviation Company.

Housing and Schools. There are a limited number of family quarters onboard the station, about 850, and another 1,500 at Iroquois Point, but as everywhere else in the Hawaiian command, assignments require long waits and, once received, may not be at the installation itself. In addition to two public elementary schools, there are two child-care centers and a preschool. The Navy Campus provides guidance and assistance for adults interested in furthering their formal education.

Personal Services. A commissary store, a mini mart, and a Navy exchange that includes the main store, a garden shop, a cashier facility, a bakery, a beauty shop, a barber shop, an ice cream parlor, dry cleaners, a uniform center, a tailor shop, a laundromat, an optical shop, a florist, a personalized services facility, a delicatessen, a Pizza Hut, and a McDonald's. Medical care is provided through an outpatient clinic only, with definitive medical care available at Tripler Army Medical Center in Honolulu.

Recreation. The station's most attractive features are its fine recreational facilities. These include officers and enlisted clubs. Also available are a bowling alley, a fitness center, hobby shops, and other facilities. For outdoor recreation there are an eighteen-hole golf course, ten tennis courts, and five squash and racquetball courts. In addition, beach cottages large enough to accommodate six persons per unit are available, fourteen for enlisted personnel and eight for officers.

Location. Barbers Point is about thirty-five minutes from Honolulu by car. The nearest bus stop is a mile from the main gate. A car is essential for getting around off base.

For more information write to: Public Affairs Office, NAS, Barbers Point, HI 96862-5050, or call (808) 684-6266.

The Aloha Tower is one of Honolulu's most famous landmarks. This structure used to be the area's tallest building, but now it is dwarfed by modern high rises. (U.S. Army photo)

PEARL HARBOR NAVAL COMPLEX

Pearl Harbor takes its name from the Polynesian *wai momi*, which means "water of pearl," the name the ancient Hawaiians bestowed on the location after the pearl oysters that once grew in the water there.

History. At 7:55 A.M. on 7 December 1941, Pearl Harbor earned an unsought place in history, and today the sunken hulk of the USS *Arizona*, the tomb of more than 1,100 sailors and Marines who died when the Japanese bombs sunk her, lies under thirty-eight feet of water at the bottom of the harbor.

Established as a coaling station in 1902, Pearl Harbor today is the U.S. Navy's most important island base in the Pacific. More than seventy naval commands are based there, including the Naval Station, the Submarine Base, the Navy Shipyard, the Naval Supply Industrial Center, and other commands, making it the hub of activities for the thousands of Navy personnel and their dependents in Hawaii. Valued at more than $1.5 billion, the base occupies over 12,500 acres of prime real estate just to the west of downtown Honolulu.

Housing and Schools. Aside from a few sets of quarters reserved for senior officers, family housing is not available on base at Pearl Harbor. However, the Navy operates about 11,000 family housing units in the Hawaii area, most of them off base in scattered housing areas on the island of Oahu. Waiting periods vary according to the season, there being a greater turnover in the summer months than at other times of the year.

Preschool and child-care centers are located at Pearl Harbor, but dependent schooling for personnel stationed there is available off base in the Hawaii public school system. Opportunity for adult education is excellent everywhere in Hawaii. The University of Hawaii, Chaminade University, Hawaii Pacific College, and other institutions are used by personnel who desire to finish high school or obtain advanced academic degrees. Arrangements to participate may be made through the Navy Campus for Achievement, of which there are two at Pearl Harbor—one at the naval station and the other at the submarine base.

Personal Services. The Navy exchange at Pearl Harbor offers eighty-seven facilities and sixty-six sales outlets. Medical care is provided by various outpatient clinics, with major treatment available at nearby Tripler Army Medical Center.

Recreation. Recreational facilities abound, with two bowling centers, six swimming pools, twelve tennis courts, five indoor and three outdoor squash and racquetball courts, deep-sea fishing trips, an eighteen-hole golf course, a marina, and a sports arena.

The Local Area. The Hawaiian Islands are a tropical paradise, and off-base outdoor recreational activities are available throughout the year. While very mild temperatures prevail at sea level, temperatures can become quite cool at higher elevations inland. Rainfall varies from very wet in some areas to very dry in others, so that the islands offer contrasts of tropical rain forests and desertlike areas within just a few miles of each other.

It should be remembered that Hawaii is really a chain of eight principal islands, and when a mainlander refers to them as Hawaii, he is usually thinking of Oahu, the site of Honolulu. The island of Hawaii lies farther to the east and is several times larger and much less densely populated than Oahu. All the Hawaiian islands offer many attractions, including the 13,000-foot peak of Mauna Loa Volcano on Hawaii.

For more information write to: Public Affairs Office, Naval Base, Pearl Harbor, Box 110 (Code 013), Pearl Harbor, HI 96860-5020, or call (808) 471-0281.

IDAHO

Air Force

MOUNTAIN HOME AIR FORCE BASE

Although its name sounds like the title of a folk ballad, Mountain Home Air Force Base is appropriately named. It sits on a plateau nearly 3,000 feet above sea level and is surrounded by the Sawtooth Mountains to the northeast and the Owyhee Mountains to the southwest. Some of the peaks to the north rise as high as 9,500 feet. The Snake River, which flows by about three miles south of the base, has carved a 600-foot deep canyon for itself there.

History. Opened in 1943, the base today is home for the 366th Wing, which flies the F-15C Eagle air-superiority fighter, F-15E Strike Eagle air-to-ground/air-superiority fighter, F-16C Fighting Falcon multirole fighter, B-52G Stratofortress heavy bomber, and the KC-135 Stratotanker air refueler. About 3,400 active-duty personnel and approximately 5,000 family members call Mountain Home home. The 366th Wing is the Air Force's first and only air intervention composite wing.

Housing and Schools. More than 1,500 units of family housing are on base, situated in six housing areas. They range from row-type houses to duplex and town-house dwellings. Temporary lodging is available at the Sagebrush Hotel, and guests may be accommodated there when space is available. Elementary and junior high school students attend on-base schools; there is a senior high school in the city of Mountain Home. A child-care center is operated on base. Adult education can be obtained on base from Boise State University, Park College, and Embry-Riddle Aeronautical University.

Personal Services. Medical and dental care are provided by a new thirty-one-bed USAF hospital. A commissary, a base exchange, a service station, a shopette/package store, and an open mess system are available.

Recreation. Recreational facilities include a sixteen-lane bowling center, arts and crafts and auto hobby shops, and a nine-hole golf course. The base Outdoor Adventure Program sponsors organized skiing, white-water rafting, hiking tours, and other outdoor events, while the recreation center sponsors a variety of trips to nearby cultural areas. Also available are a rod and gun club, an indoor twenty-five-meter swimming pool, and a riding stable with twenty acres of fenced pasture. The base also operates its own private marina facility at the nearby Strike Dam Recreation Area.

The Local Area. The climate in southern Idaho is dry, with hot summers and cold winters. The average annual snowfall in the Mountain Home area is only eleven inches. This means, of course, that some kind of outdoor activity is possible all year.

The base is located ten miles southwest of the friendly little town of Mountain Home and fifty miles southeast of Boise, the capital city of Idaho and home to about 135,000 people. Hunting, fishing, many outdoor attractions, and lots of sightseeing are Idaho's special features. The state operates twenty-one parks, and there are over two dozen ski resorts there, as well as more than 3,000 miles of snowmobile trails. Deer, elk, moose, antelope, bighorn sheep, mountain goat, and black bear are hunted in the state, and many varieties of freshwater fish can be caught in its many lakes, rivers, streams, and ponds.

For more information write to: Public Affairs Office, 366 WG, 366 Gunfighter Ave., Ste. 190, Mountain Home AFB, ID 83648-5392, or call (208) 828-2110.

ILLINOIS

Air Force

CHANUTE AIR FORCE BASE

Chanute Air Force Base is now closed.

SCOTT AIR FORCE BASE

History. Unlike all other U.S. Air Force installations, Scott AFB is named after an enlisted man, Army Cpl. Frank S. Scott, who was killed in the crash of his Wright biplane at College Park, Maryland, on 28 September 1912.

Scott AFB opened in 1917 as a training field for World War I pilots. Today the base extends over 3,000 acres and hosts a population of 23,000 military personnel, civilian employees, and dependents. Scott is home for the Air Mobility Command, the Military Airlift Command, the Air Force Communications Command, the 375th Aeromedical Airlift Wing, and more than forty other units.

Housing and Schools. Scott has more than 1,700 family quarters, as well as spaces for 105 private mobile homes. Thirty-six units of temporary housing are available for military families in transit. The cost of living in southern Illinois is moderate compared to other parts of the country.

While there are no dependent schools on base, good schools are located in the nearby community. There is a child-development center on base. The base educational service office offers many educational opportunities for military personnel, civilians, and their dependents at Scott. A full range of counseling and testing are available, plus college courses from such institutions as Belleville Area College, McKendree College, Park College, Webster University, and Southern Illinois University at Carbondale and Edwardsville.

Personal Services. Medical care is provided at the 115-bed USAF medical center. Other services at Scott include a commissary with 25,000 square feet of sales space, a main exchange with many concessions, a banking facility, and a credit union. The family support center offers a variety of programs and assistance.

Recreation. Recreational facilities at Scott include an eighteen-hole golf course, two gymnasiums, a twenty-four-lane bowling alley, swimming pools, and a stable. A rod and gun club offers three skeet and two trap ranges and a small-bore rifle and pistol range. An arts and crafts center, an aero club, and officers and enlisted clubs are also available. A recreation area at Scott Lake is used for picnicking, hiking, biking, and other activities.

The Local Area. Scott AFB is seven miles northeast of the community of Belleville, which has a population of over 44,000. The biggest attraction in the area is Saint Louis, Gateway to the West, which is twenty miles to the west of the base. Saint Louis has a population of 2.5 million and is a thriving cultural and economic center on the Missouri side of the Mississippi River.

For more information write to: Public Affairs Office, Scott AFB, IL 62225-5154, or call (618) 256-4241

Army

CHARLES MELVIN PRICE SUPPORT CENTER

Located in Granite City just across the Mississippi River from Saint Louis, the Charles Melvin Price Support Center is home to the U.S. Army Aviation and Troop Command (ATCOM).

ATCOM's mission is to equip Army aviation with modern warfighting aircraft, fixed- and rotary-wing, and soldiers with clothing, food, water, and facilities. For instance, ATCOM's weapon system manager for clothing and services exercises oversight of 30 Army laundries and 10 dry-cleaning facilities as well as 127 military clothing stores and 81 central issue facilities throughout the Army. ATCOM's aviation programs include management and research and development, which includes thirty models of fixed-wing aircraft such as the C-20J Gulfstream Jet; rotary-wing models such as the attack helicopters AH1 Cobra, AG 64 Apache, UH60 Blackhawk, and RAH 66 Comanche; and utility models such as the UH1 Iroquois ("Hueys") and CH47 Chinook.

Tenant units at the center include the 2nd Battalion, 334th Infantry, 84th Division (Training); 226th Transportation Company, Railway Engineer; 376th Transportation Company; 624th Engineer Platoon; Naval Construction Force Unit 4; and U.S. Coast Guard Naval Engineer Support Unit.

There are 2,100 active-duty personnel assigned to the center along with 4,000 reserve component personnel, 8,000 civilian employees, and 3,500 family members.

Housing and Personal Services. There are 164 units of family housing at the center, 58 for officers and 106 for enlisted personnel. As of February 1994, waiting times for these quarters was averaging twelve months for all grades for two-bedroom units. Local apartment rentals were averaging from $320 a month for unfurnished one-bedroom units up to $600 a month for three-bedroom apartments, not counting the required $200 security deposit.

Children attend local schools, but a day-care center is available on post.

Health care is provided by an Army clinic located in Saint Louis, at Scott Air Force Base, about twenty-five miles southeast of Granite City, or by local institutions. A commissary and post exchange are located at the center.

Recreation. Recreational facilities include tennis, softball and soccer fields, a swimming pool, a bowling alley, auto and arts and crafts shops, a golf course, a library, and a gym. For those who prefer to recreate sitting down with a potent beverage or delectable comestibles, there is also the Depot Junction Club.

For more information write to: HQ, U.S. Army Aviation and Troop Command, Attention: AMSAT-B-P, 4300 Goodfellow Blvd., Saint Louis, MO 63120-1798, or call (618) 452-1164.

FORT SHERIDAN

After 106 years of service to the U.S. Army, Fort Sheridan was closed in the spring of 1993.

ROCK ISLAND ARSENAL

Rock Island Arsenal is a 946-acre island situated in the Mississippi River and bordered on the south by Rock Island and Moline, Illinois, and on the north by Davenport and Bettendorf, Iowa. The island is about three miles long and three-quarters of a mile wide at its widest point.

History. The island was acquired by the U.S. government through treaty with the Indians in 1804, and Fort Armstrong was built there in 1816. The arsenal was first established in 1862, and in 1863 a prison was built there to accommodate 12,000 Confederate prisoners of war.

The total island population today is 8,000 military and civilian personnel. Home of the U.S. Army Armament, Munitions, and Chemical Command, the arsenal is responsible for the production of carriages, recoil mechanisms for towed and self-propelled artillery, and tank armament.

Housing and Schools. Fifty-eight sets of government family quarters are located at Rock Island. One guest transient facility is also available.

Dependent children attend local public schools. A child-development center on post can accommodate 160 children, and certified child-care homes are also available.

Personal Services. Medical care is provided by the U.S. Army Health Clinic. Dependents and retired personnel are seen there by appointment. A post exchange and a commissary are also available, as are a club, a cafeteria, and a barber shop.

Recreation. The Quad Cities offer recreational opportunities and facilities for every member of the family. The area boasts more than eighty parks and playgrounds, a forest preserve, and ten public and seven private country clubs. Other facilities include archery ranges, baseball and softball diamonds, bowling alleys, bridle paths, driving ranges, horseshoe courts, movie theaters, swimming pools, trap shooting ranges, and a zoo. Arsenal Island itself contains many interesting attractions including pre-Columbian Indian mounds and the Rock Island National Cemetery. The cemetery was established in 1865 and contains the remains of about 10,000 veterans and some of their dependents from all the services. The Confederate Cemetery contains the bodies of about 2,000 prisoners who died at Rock Island while interned there during the Civil War. On the western tip of the island is the Fort Armstrong Blockhouse replica, which was erected in 1916 on the centennial of the fort's founding. Not far from there is Pioneer Cemetery, where soldiers and early settlers of the area lie. Fort Armstrong was a focal point in the Black Hawk War of 1832, and such American greats as Zachary Taylor, Jefferson Davis, and Abraham Lincoln gathered there with the expedition that fought the Indians.

The Local Area. About 385,000 people live in the vicinity of the arsenal. Davenport has about 100,000 inhabitants, followed by Rock Island with about 50,000 and Moline with 47,000, while Bettendorf follows up with around 30,000 and East Moline with 22,000.

For more information write to: Public Affairs Office, HQ, USAMCCOM, Rock Island, IL 61299-6000, or call (309) 782-5421.

A casting is poured at the Rock Island foundry. (U.S. Army photo)

Navy

GLENVIEW NAVAL AIR STATION

The 1993 Base Realignment and Closure Commission recommended closing Glenview, but at press time no firm date had yet been announced for its closing.

Located five miles west of Lake Michigan and about eighteen miles north of downtown Chicago, Glenview Naval Air Station is possibly one of the easiest places to get to in the United States. O'Hare International Airport, only ten miles away, is the busiest airport in the world, served by every major domestic airline and most foreign ones. In a pinch you can get there by boat, along the Saint Lawrence Seaway.

History. Glenview NAS began as the Curtiss-Reynolds Airport in 1937. In 1942 construction began on the Naval Reserve Aviation Base, which conducted primary flight training for naval and Marine Corps aviators throughout World War II. The station takes its name from the village of Glenview, which annexed the station's 1,200 acres in 1971. Today approximately 1,500 active-duty personnel, 1,200 dependents, and 175 civilian employees live and work at the station, which supports 3,600 drilling reservists from all services.

Housing and Schools. Approximately 280 units of family housing are available at Glenview, supplemented by seventy-six mobile home spaces; additional housing is available at the nearby Great Lakes Naval Base.

Children living on the station attend local schools. There is a small day-care center at the station. Adult education is available through the station's Navy Campus or in the local community.

Personal Services. Medical care at Glenview is provided by a branch clinic of the Great Lakes Hospital. Both the commissary and exchange facilities at Glenview are small, and personnel onboard the station do their serious shopping at Great Lakes or Fort Sheridan.

Recreation. Recreation facilities at the station consist of a bowling alley, a golf course, a movie theater, a picnic area, a pool, a gymnasium, a hobby shop, and handball and tennis courts. The local area, however, abounds with cultural and recreational opportunities. Within easy driving distance are a great variety of state parks and recreation areas. With Lake Michigan so close, water sports are staple recreational activities.

The Local Area. The Chicago metropolitan area extends approximately seventy-five miles from the downtown environs and is home to over 11 million people. Chicago proper has a population of 3.2 million. At Glenview NAS itself the mean average temperature is 50.8° F. and very humid: Average rainfall is over thirty-three inches with thirty-eight inches of snow during an average winter.

For more information write to: Public Affairs Office, Glenview NAS, Glenview, IL 60026-5000, or call (708) 657-1000.

GREAT LAKES NAVAL TRAINING CENTER

From the day in 1911 when Great Lakes Naval Training Center received its first trainee, Seaman Recruit Joseph W. Gregg, the Naval Training Center's Recruit Command has been turning landsmen into sailors—approximately 3 million to date. Each year, the Recruit Training Command graduates more than 40,000 new recruits.

The total average population at Great Lakes, including the Naval Training Center, tenant commands, active-duty and civilian personnel, and their dependents, is about 30,000 people. This includes approximately 20,000 military personnel, 3,400 civilian employees, and 6,000 family members, making Great Lakes the Navy's largest training center and fifth largest naval installation in the United States. Great Lakes is a small city, and as such it has all the facilities and services required to keep a metropolis going.

Housing and Schools. More than 2,200 sets of government quarters are available for married personnel at Great Lakes. An attractive, modern, sixty-room Navy Lodge is also on base.

Children of Great Lakes personnel attend off-base schools in the North Chicago public school system, although a large child-care facility is operated on the base. The Navy Campus offers college-level programs through local institutions as well as night classes on base and in local schools for those who wish to complete high school graduation requirements.

Personal Services. Medical care is provided to the community at the fifteen-floor, 173-bed naval hospital, which has sixteen clinics and eleven operating rooms.

A commissary store and a Navy exchange with several branches and numerous services are available, including two automotive service stations, cafeterias, three beverage convenience stores, and a flower shop.

Recreation. Located as it is on the shores of Lake Michigan, Great Lakes Naval Training Center offers diverse recreational opportunities year-round. Winter sports include skiing, sledding, and ice skating. There is a marina on base, too. During the summer, swimming is available at two beaches on base or at the outdoor pool. A comprehensive recreation program offers something for everyone, including tennis and racquetball courts, a physical fitness center, an eighteen-hole golf course, and fishing areas. The recreational services department runs an excellent intramural sports program.

The Local Area. By far the biggest attractions in the area are the cities of Chicago and Milwaukee. Chicago offers a wide variety of sightseeing and recreation opportunities, from museums to the architectural wonders of the world's tallest office building. There are also Six Flags Great America amusement park and shopping in some of America's largest malls. But if the big city is not to your liking, you can always try your lungs calling hogs at the Illinois State Fair, show your prize petunias in Dixon, or just relax and visit one of the state's sixty-two parks.

The area averages thirty-six inches of snow in winter and thirty-two inches of rain annually. The coldest month is January, with an average temperature of 24°; July is the warmest month, with an average temperature of 72°.

For more information write to: Public Affairs Office, Naval Training Center, Great Lakes, IL 60088-5000, or call (708) 688-2201.

INDIANA

Air Force

GRISSOM AIR FORCE BASE

At press time Grissom AFB was scheduled to close in September 1994.

History. Military airpower first came to the Tri-City area in January 1943 when Bunker Hill Naval Station, named after the nearby hamlet of Bunker Hill, opened. The Air Force took over the facility in June 1954 and renamed it the Bunker Hill Air Force Base. In May 1968, the base was renamed in honor of Lt. Col. Virgil I. Grissom, an Indiana native and one of three astronauts who died when their Apollo spacecraft burned at Cape Kennedy, Florida, in January 1967.

Today Grissom is home to the 305th Air Refueling Wing, which flies KC-135 Stratotankers in support of the Strategic Air Command's B-52 bomber force. Approximately 2,300 active-duty personnel and their 3,500 dependents live at Grissom today.

Housing and Schools. There are over 1,100 units of family housing at Grissom. Temporary lodging for families on the move is available at the Grissom Inn. Other persons may be accommodated there as well, but only on a space-available basis.

A child-care center is operated on base, right outside the housing area. Dependent schools are available in the nearby civilian community. The base education office offers several off-duty college degree programs through Ball State University and Indiana Vocational/Technical College.

Personal Services. The base exchange at Grissom offers a number of concessions in addition to its normal retail outlet. The base commissary carries 6,000 line items displayed in 17,000 square feet of sales area. Those with a taste for fast food can take the edge off their appetites at the newly opened Burger King. Banking facilities are also available on base. Medical care is provided by an eighteen-bed hospital.

Grissom also has a nine-hole golf course, a 700,000-gallon swimming pool, a ten-lane bowling center, a gymnasium, and auto and ceramics hobby shops. Boating and fishing equipment rental is available through recreational supply for those who wish to enjoy the several large lakes located near the base.

The Local Area. Grissom is located in north-central Indiana, at about the center of a triangle formed by Logansport to the west, Peru to the east, and Kokomo to the south (thus the nickname "Tri-City" area). Indianapolis, state capital and major population center of the state, is about fifty miles to the south of Kokomo, easily reached from Grissom on a weekend jaunt.

For more information write to: Public Affairs Office, 305th AREFW, Grissom AFB, IN 46971-5000, or call (317) 688-5211.

Army

FORT BENJAMIN HARRISON

Fort Benjamin Harrison is scheduled to be deactivated on 10 July 1997, with major functions beginning to relocate in October 1994: the AG, Finance, and Recruiting schools to Fort Jackson, South Carolina; the Defense Information School to Fort Meade, Maryland; and the Enlisted Records and Evaluation Center to Alexandria, Virginia.

History. Fort Benjamin Harrison was established by an act of Congress in March 1903, but the fort remained nameless until 1906. In that year, President Theodore Roosevelt named the installation after his predecessor and friend. After serving as an officer training camp during World War I and an infantry post until World War II, the fort was placed on the inactive list in 1947.

In 1950, following a two-year period in which the post was an Air Force base, ground was broken for the Army's largest administration building, the Finance Center, now known as the Maj. Gen. Emmett J. Bean Center. Fort Benjamin Harrison is also home to the Adjutant Generals Corps, the Finance Corps, the Soldier Support Center, the Defense Information School, the Enlisted Records and Evaluation Center, the Recruiting and Retention School, and the Defense Finance and Accounting Service, Indianapolis Center.

Housing and Schools. Limited government housing is offered on post, but guest-house accommodations are available. The Indianapolis metropolitan area has a wide variety of housing choices, however, and the cost of living is moderate.

Children attend Indianapolis area schools, but there is a day-care center on post. The education center offers many programs for adult family members. Several universities offer undergraduate and graduate college extension courses on post. College courses may also be taken off post at nearby universities.

Personal Services and Recreation. Commissary, post exchange, banking facilities, medical facilities, and other personal services are offered. A full range of recreation facilities includes an eighteen-hole golf course, a bowling alley, a movie theater, a pool, a gymnasium, craft shops, tennis courts, and three recreation lakes.

The Local Area. The post is located east of Indianapolis. The home of President Benjamin Harrison in the city is a national historic landmark. Northeast of the city is a restored 1836 village, the Conner Prairie Pioneer Settlement. Prices are in the average range for U.S. cities and below those for most major metropolitan areas.

For more information write to: Public Affairs Office, Soldier Support Center, Fort Benjamin Harrison, IN 46216-5040, or call (317) 542-4198.

Students from all five branches of the Department of Defense train at Fort Harrison's Defense Information School. (U.S. Army photo)

KANSAS

Air Force

McCONNELL AIR FORCE BASE

McConnell Air Force Base lies in the southeastern quadrant of Wichita, which in the 1920s was the home of many of aviation's pioneers, such as Clyde V. Cessna, Walter H. Beech, and J. H. Engstrom. The base was established at Wichita primarily so that training in the B-47 jet bomber could take place near the aircraft factory where it was being produced. Since that time the city has expanded out to the vicinity of the base.

History. Established in June 1951 as Wichita Air Force Base, the facility was renamed McConnell Air Force Base in 1952 in honor of two of the three "Flying McConnell Brothers" from Wichita who enlisted in the Army Air Corps during World War II. Today the base is home to the 384th Bombardment Wing and several tenant units and boasts a permanent population of over 3,500 military personnel and 6,000 dependents.

Housing and Schools. There are 587 units of family housing at McConnell. Waiting periods average from as little as thirty days for field-grade officers to as many as thirty months for junior NCOs. Limited guest-house facilities are available with reservations taken only for temporary-duty personnel.

A child-care center and an elementary school for dependent children are located on base. Older children attend junior high and senior high schools off base. Off-duty educational opportunities for adults are excellent. College-level courses are offered on base by Butler County Community College, Kansas Newman College, Embry-Riddle Aeronautical University, and Webster College.

Personal Services and Recreation. Commissary, base exchange facilities, a service station, officers and NCO open mess systems, banking facilities, and other personal services are available on base. Recreational facilities include a wood craft shop, an automotive center, an arts and crafts center, one outdoor swimming pool, a gymnasium, and a nine-hole golf course. A base park with an all-weather pavilion and an outdoor multipurpose recreation court are also provided.

The Local Area. Wichita is a bustling metropolis of more than 270,000 people. The city operates over 2,000 acres of parks and playgrounds and a 210-acre zoo. There are also a symphony orchestra, a ballet, and eighty private and three municipal golf courses.

For more information write to: Public Affairs Office, McConnell Air Force Base, KS 67221-5000, or call (316) 652-3141.

Army

FORT LEAVENWORTH

Fort Leavenworth is a post of many firsts. It was the first fort established west of the Missouri River, the first continuously occupied settlement in Kansas, and the site of the oldest continuously occupied house in Kansas (the Rookery, built in 1832 as a post headquarters).

History. Named after Col. Henry Leavenworth, who founded the post in 1827, Fort Leavenworth has been witness to much of the history of the American West. The Oregon and Sante Fe Trails crossed the Missouri River, and ox teams pulled loaded wagons through Fort Leavenworth on their way west. The post was an important Army headquarters in the West during the Mexican War of 1846, the Civil War, and the Indian Wars. Since 1881 it has been the home of the Army's Command and General Staff College, the oldest in the Army's advanced educational system. Since 1873 it has also been the site of the U.S. Disciplinary Barracks (the "Fort Leavenworth Long Course"). Today Fort Leavenworth is home to the U.S. Army Combined Arms Command.

Housing and Schools. Fort Leavenworth is a completely self-contained military post. It has 1,586 units of family housing and twelve guest-house units available to personnel of all ranks. (Reservations are required thirty days in advance.)

The post has three elementary schools and a junior high school as well as daycare and preschool programs; complete educational services are also available for military personnel on the post.

Personal Services and Recreation. Fort Leavenworth hosts a post exchange and commissary and a twenty-five-bed hospital. The full range of support and morale services available on post include a bowling alley; an eighteen-hole golf course; squash, handball, and tennis courts; a movie theater; swimming pools; a gymnasium; craft shops; and a riding stable.

The Local Area. Fort Leavenworth is adjacent to the city of Leavenworth (population 36,700), about thirty-five miles northwest of Kansas City, Missouri, on the Missouri River. The average temperatures range from a low of 21° F. in January to a high of 92° F. in July. Normal annual rainfall is thirty inches.

For more information write to: Headquarters, Combined Arms Command and Fort Leavenworth, Attention: Public Affairs Office, Fort Leavenworth, KS 66027-5050, or call (913) 684-5604.

FORT RILEY

Fort Riley may be the only post in the history of the U.S. Army to have been commanded by an enlisted man. When the senior officer at the post, Maj. E. A. Ogden, died in a cholera epidemic on 3 August 1855, the installation was left temporarily without a commander. Into the gap strode ex-sergeant of dragoons Percival Lowe, Ogden's supervisor of transportation. He put down an attempted mutiny and restored order to the garrison. One hundred people died during the epidemic, and their unmarked graves occupy a corner of the Fort Riley Cemetery.

History. Fort Riley was named after Maj. Gen. Bennett Riley, a Mexican War hero. Construction began on Fort Riley in May 1853. During the Indian Wars the post played an important role. The famed 7th Cavalry Regiment formed there in 1866; in 1890, the 7th was back at Riley, and it moved out from there to participate in the last campaign of the Indian Wars, which culminated at the Battle of Wounded Knee on 29 December 1890. Today Fort Riley's 101,000 acres are home for the 1st Infantry Division ("Big Red One").

Housing and Schools. More than 3,000 sets of family quarters are available at Fort Riley, and the waiting list ranges from only a few weeks to several months, depending on the sponsor's rank and the size of his or her family. Guest-house accommodations are available in the order confirmed reservations are received. Bachelor officer and NCO housing is also available.

Fort Riley has five elementary schools and one junior high school in addition to a preschool, and a child-care center is operated to accommodate children between the ages of six weeks and twelve years. The Fort Riley Army Education Center provides a full range of educational services, from a high school completion program to graduate studies. Because these courses are offered on the post, they may be started and completed during a soldier's tour there. Classes are also available from Kansas State University, Central Michigan University, Upper Iowa University, Central Texas College, and Barton Community College.

Personal Services. Irwin Army Medical Community Hospital, a multistory, 200-bed facility, offers complete patient care services to the military personnel and their families stationed at Fort Riley. Six dental clinics are operated on post. A post exchange, a commissary, and other facilities are also available.

Recreation. A full range of athletic and recreation programs are available at Fort Riley. The Outdoor Recreation Center has fishing boats and water skis for the 16,000-acre Milford Reservoir Area. There are four picnic parks on post, as well as the Camp Moon Lake picnic and playground area. A new skateboard park opened in the spring of 1993.

The Local Area. Fort Riley is located about 2 miles east of Junction City and 14 miles west of Manhattan, home of Kansas State University. From the post to Abilene is 25 miles; Kansas City, 130; Lawrence, 91; Topeka, 64; and Wichita, 114. Because of its location, the weather at Fort Riley is subject to frequent and often sharp changes. The winters are generally dry and cold, and the summers are hot, windy, and sometimes very humid. Just to the west of the post is Milford Lake, and immediately to the northeast is Tuttle Creek Lake and Tuttle Creek Pottawatomie State Fishing Lake, both ideal for fishing and water sports.

For more information write to: Public Affairs Officer, Fort Riley, KS 66442-5016, or call (913) 239-2022.

KENTUCKY

Army

FORT CAMPBELL

Fort Campbell is situated between Hopkinsville, Kentucky, to the north and Clarksville, Tennessee, to the south, astride the Kentucky-Tennessee border with most of its acreage in Tennessee. It not only is beautiful country but also is country rich in history.

History. Named after Gen. William Bowen Campbell, a hero of the Mexican War and former governor of Tennessee, Fort Campbell came into being in February 1942 as an armor and infantry training center. In 1956, the famous 101st Airborne Division ("Screaming Eagles") was reactivated at Fort Campbell under the command of Maj. Gen. Thomas Sherburne, Jr. Known today as the 101st Airborne Division (Air Assault), the Screaming Eagles still call Fort Campbell home.

Housing and Schools. There are more than 4,200 units of family quarters at Fort Campbell, situated in nine separate family housing areas. Transient family quarters are also available, as well as a seventy-five-room guest house, with first priority going to incoming personnel on permanent-change-of-station orders.

Fort Campbell operates its own school system consisting of four elementary schools, two junior high schools, and a high school; prekindergarten and nursery services are also available. The Army education center offers a full range of educational services and benefits available for military personnel, including on-post college courses provided by local institutions as well as out-of-state colleges.

Personal Services. Fort Campbell boasts a modern, 243-bed hospital, one of the finest facilities of its kind in the Kentucky-Tennessee area. The post exchange and

A soldier rappels from a UH-1 helicopter at the Air Assault School, Fort Campbell.
(U.S. Army photo)

commissary complex at Fort Campbell afford residents and eligible visitors the convenience of modern shopping. The PX mall and liquor store activities are open seven days a week. A large number of post exchange concessions, such as a Burger King, Baskin Robbins, Pier 101 seafood restaurant, a barbecue and pizza shop, a cafeteria, an optical shop, a radio-TV repair shop, and beauty shops, are located within the new modern mall.

Recreation. Entertainment and recreational activities, both indoors and outdoors, are also available on post. These range from a cabaret dinner theater to parks and picnic areas. With moderately hot summers and long and mild autumns, outdoor activities of all kinds are possible in the Fort Campbell area year-round.

The Local Area. Hopkinsville, a town of about 30,000, lies about 15 miles to the north of Fort Campbell; Louisville is 161 miles northeast. Clarksville, Tennessee (population 55,000), is 5 miles to the south; Nashville is 70 miles south. The area is rich in Civil War history. The Henry and Donelson Campaign took place in the area in February 1862, and Fort Donelson National Military Park and Cemetery may be seen just across Lake Barkley from Fort Campbell. North of Fort Donelson and about an hour's drive from the post is the Land Between the Lakes—170,000 acres of public land developed for outdoor recreation. Lake Barkley on the east and Kentucky Lake on the west were formed when Kentucky and Barkley Dams were constructed as part of a Tennessee Valley Authority program. They offer 220,000 surface acres of water and more than 3,500 miles of shoreline.

For more information write to: Headquarters, 101st Airborne Division and Fort Campbell, Attention: AFZB-PO, Fort Campbell, KY 42223, or call (502) 798-2151.

FORT KNOX

Most people think of Fort Knox only as the site of the Bullion Depository, the structure that houses most of the gold stocks of the United States; sorry, no visitors are permitted! Less well known, yet just as important in many ways, is Fort Knox, home of the U.S. Army Armor Center; visitors are always welcome here.

History. Named after Maj. Gen. Henry Knox, George Washington's Chief of Artillery, Fort Knox was established in June 1918 as an artillery training center. In July 1940, a small armor school was created there, and since that time the installation's role has been inextricably associated with tanks. The mission of the Armor Center today is to train officers and enlisted soldiers for mounted combat and to develop weapons and tactics for their use. The Armor Center also conducts basic training, and is the home of the U.S. Army Recruiting Command.

Today Fort Knox, a "Kentucky Certified City," is a post of 110,000 acres with a daytime population of over 32,000 military and civilian personnel, which makes it one of the largest communities in the commonwealth of Kentucky.

Housing and Schools. Five thousand family and 1,000 bachelor transient housing units are available, as well as family housing and bachelor transient housing. The Wickham Guest House offers hotel accommodations at considerable savings to the military traveler on a first-come, first-served basis.

Duty at Fort Knox offers soldiers and their families the advantages of gracious living to be found at all major military installations, and a few that are not found at other places. The post operates ten dependent schools for children in kindergarten through high school. Preschool and child-care centers are also available. The continuing education branch offers college courses from such institutions as the University of Southern California, the University of Kentucky, the University of Louisville, and Western Kentucky University.

Personal Services. Military personnel and their dependents are provided with the best possible medical care at the 170-bed Ireland Army Community Hospital, which has approximately two dozen general medical, surgical, and specialty clinics; in addition, five dental clinics are located on post.

A large commissary and a large post exchange offering a four-seasons store and several annexes are located at Fort Knox.

Recreation. The morale support division operates a complete range of arts and crafts and automotive craft shops, six swimming pools, two golf courses, twenty-five tennis courts, six gyms and fitness centers, and other attractions.

The private organizations at Fort Knox catering to the morale and welfare of the military families located there are too numerous to mention, but they range in scope and activity from Alcoholics Anonymous to the Tank Town Twirlers Round and Square Dance Club.

Fort Knox is located on the Indiana-Kentucky border, approximately twenty-five miles south of Louisville, on U.S. Route 31W. The Fort Knox area is a scenic and historical locale that offers a wide variety of outdoor activities from parks and picnic areas to hunting and fishing. The Camp Carlson Outdoor Recreation Area at Fort Knox features an Army Travel Camp with a lodge and family cabins for rent. Hunting and fishing licenses, firearms instruction, and shooting ranges are all available on post.

For further information write to: Public Affairs Office, U.S. Army Armor Center and Fort Knox, Attention: P.O. Box 995, ATZK-PAO, Fort Knox, KY 40121-5000, or call (502) 624-4413.

LOUISIANA

Air Force

BARKSDALE AIR FORCE BASE

Barksdale Air Force Base occupies over 22,000 acres near Shreveport and Bossier City, and is an integral part of those communities. With a workforce numbering almost 10,000 military and civilian personnel, the economic impact of the base on the local area exceeds $798 million annually.

History. Dedicated in February 1933, the base is named after Lt. Eugene Hoy Barksdale, a World War I airman who died while flight testing an observation airplane in 1926. Today Barksdale is home for Headquarters, 8th Air Force, and the 2nd Wing. The wing operates the B-52 Stratofortress bomber and the versatile KC-135 Stratotanker. The Air Mobility Command's 458th Operations Group flies the KC-10. Barksdale is also home for the 917th Fighter Group, which flies the A-10 Thunderbolt II.

Housing and Schools. There are 429 units of family housing at the base and 24 units of guest housing. Guest housing is reserved only for military families traveling on official orders; all others are accommodated on a space-available basis only. Although no dependent schools are operated on the base, the base education center provides a wealth of professional, academic, and vocational opportunities for adults. Louisiana Tech University, Georgia Military College, Southern Illinois University, and many others offer undergraduate and graduate programs there.

Personal Services and Recreation. The usual spectrum of personal services and facilities such as a sixty-five-bed USAF hospital, a base exchange, a commissary, and recreational facilities are available at Barksdale. The latter include an eighteen-hole golf course; a bowling alley; a gymnasium; two pools; a movie theater; auto, wood, and arts and crafts shops; a riding club; two picnic areas; and hunting and fishing.

The Barksdale Family Camp, located on the installation, offers twelve camper spaces with water and electricity hookups, a picnic area, a softball field, and a playground, as well as areas for picnicking and camping. Equipment for rent includes tents, stoves, lanterns, and other camping supplies. The camp is situated in both open and wooded areas and has many shade trees such as oaks and hickories.

The Local Area. Barksdale AFB is situated four miles east of Shreveport, within the city limits of Bossier City in the northwestern portion of Louisiana. Summer months there are consistently warm, with maximum temperatures exceeding 100° F. about ten days of the year and 95° F. about forty-five days of the year. The humidity is high in all seasons. Spring and fall are the most pleasant times of the year, and autumn is generally the best time for outdoor activities.

Toledo Bend, Caddo, Cross, Bodcau L'Erling, and Bistineau Reservoir Lakes are nearby and offer a wide variety of water recreation from fishing to skiing, boating, and swimming.

For more information write to: Public Affairs Division, 841 Fairchild Ave., Ste. 103, Barksdale AFB, LA 71110-2270, or call (318) 456-3065.

ENGLAND AIR FORCE BASE

England Air Force Base closed in December 1992.

Army

FORT POLK

Fort Polk has suffered from a "Camp Swampy" image through the years. As troops passed through there for training, the word got out that if you loved swamps, mosquitoes, and boredom, Polk was the place. But this image changed forever in 1974 when the 5th Infantry Division (Mechanized) moved there. Redesignated the 2nd Armored Division in 1992, the division moved to Fort Hood, Texas, to be replaced by the 2nd Armored Cavalry Regiment, the 108th Air Defense Artillery Brigade, the 42nd Field Artillery Brigade, and the Joint Readiness Training Center.

History. Named after Confederate Gen. Leonidas Polk, Fort Polk was built in 1941 to support the famous Louisiana Maneuvers. Fort Polk has always been one of the Army's best training facilities. The reservation covers some 198,000 acres of varying terrain from dense, jungle-type environment to broad, rolling plains.

Housing and Schools. Fort Polk has over 4,000 sets of family quarters. The seventy-unit Magnolia House, built in 1988, offers accommodations for transient personnel. Bachelor officers may be assigned quarters in a new 150-suite high-rise, and senior enlisted personnel have a modern 68-suite billet. There are accommodations for 398 mobile homes on the post; spaces are available on a first-come, first-served basis. Ultramodern barracks complexes resembling college dorms have replaced the old wooden facilities. Each complex includes a post exchange branch store, a snack bar, a gymnasium, a chapel, and a dining facility.

On-post schooling is conducted through the local school system for dependent children in kindergarten through fourth grade. Other children attend schools in Pickering and Leesville. The Army education center offers programs of instruction ranging from remedial training through graduate studies. Language training and testing programs of various kinds are also available. The Fort Polk campus of Northwestern University offers a four-year curriculum.

Personal Services. In 1977, a $2.5 million commissary offering 51,000 square feet of shopping space was opened, and in 1978, a large, solar-powered shopping mall was completed. The commissary was enlarged and renovated in 1989. A new 169-bed hospital opened in 1983.

Recreation. On-post recreational facilities include a bowling alley, three swimming pools, an eighteen-hole golf course, an auto hobby shop, a skeet and trap range, over a dozen tennis courts, a lake, a dinner theater, a new athletic complex, and a youth activities center.

The Local Area. The rolling hills of western Louisiana are a sportsman's paradise. The year-round mild climate permits constant outdoor activity. Fort Polk maintains the Toledo Bend Recreation Facility with mobile homes for rent. The facility is located to the northwest of the post on the Toledo Bend Reservoir on the Texas-Louisiana border. The Lake Charles area, noted as a water sports center for the entire Gulf Coast region, is located sixty miles south of Fort Polk; the country south of Lake Charles is composed of deep marshes providing the finest duck and goose hunting in the country. The Gulf of Mexico lies a little less than 100 miles south of the reservation.

Fort Polk is adjacent to the small communities of DeRidder (population 13,700) and Leesville (population 10,500). The city of Alexandria to the northeast of the post has excellent shopping centers, recreational activities, and historical attractions. Just a few miles south of the Alexandria-Pineville area begins the Cajun country, with its French heritage. Baton Rouge is about 100 miles to the southeast of Alexandria, and New Orleans is 150 miles southeast. Houston is 195 miles southwest.

For more information write to: Headquarters, Fort Polk, Fort Polk, LA 71459-5000, or call (318) 531-2911.

Navy

NEW ORLEANS NAVAL AIR STATION

Nestled among 3,200 acres along the west bank of the Mississippi River twelve miles southeast of New Orleans, New Orleans Naval Air Station is home to about 1,500 full-time active-duty personnel and almost 3,700 reservists. It is the first military installation in the nation to be designed, built, and commissioned as a joint-use facility (Navy, Air Force, Marines, and Coast Guard).

History. The station was commissioned in December 1957, and in January 1958 the first aircraft were flown from the new runways. In April 1958, the installation was dedicated to Alvin Andrew Callender, a native of New Orleans who lost his life in World War II. Therefore, the station is sometimes referred to as Callender Field. Today the station is home to two naval reserve squadrons and five tenant commands, including a U.S. Coast Guard air station and the U.S. Customs Service, Air Support Branch.

Housing and Schools. There are 216 units of family housing available at New Orleans NAS, as well as a twenty-two-unit Navy Lodge at the Naval Support Activity, just off General de Gaulle Avenue not far from the Superdome.

Schools for dependent children are available in the surrounding area, but a day-care center is operated on the station. The Navy Campus offers classes toward bachelor's and master's degrees on the air station and at the Naval Support Activity. In addition, the city of New Orleans offers many educational opportunities for military personnel in their off-duty time.

Personal Services and Recreation. There is a branch of the Navy exchange at the station, but commissary and main exchange facilities are located at the Naval Support Activity nearby. A dispensary provides medical care for personnel onboard the station. The special services department operates recreation equipment rental, a swimming pool, picnic grounds, athletic courts and fields, boat and camper rentals, an auto hobby shop, a bowling center, and a gym. Also available is an eighteen-hole golf course and an ongoing intramural sports program.

For further information write to: Commanding Officer, ATTN: Code 005, NAS, New Orleans, LA 70143-5000, or call (504) 393-3260.

NEW ORLEANS NAVAL SUPPORT ACTIVITY

Situated on both banks of the Mississippi River, the New Orleans Naval Support Activity (NSA) has a complement of over 3,000 active-duty personnel, more than 300 reserve components personnel, 1,990 civilian employees, and 430 family members.

History. The west bank portion of the NSA has been of interest to the Navy since 1849, when the site was originally purchased for a Navy yard, which was never developed. Today the west bank facility is home to the NSA and other activities such as the Medical Clinic New Orleans, Special Boat Unit 22, and HQ Eighth Marine Corps District.

The east bank facility was acquired in 1919 and today houses the operations of a number of active-duty and reserve component commands, including Commander Naval Reserve Force, Commander Naval Air Reserve Force, Enlisted Personnel Management Center, Fast Sealift Squadron 1, Military Sealift Command Unit New Orleans, and Navy Recruiting District New Orleans.

Shuttle boat service across the Mississippi is available on a scheduled basis throughout the day during the week.

Housing and Schools. The NSA manages 286 units of family housing situated in the Gilmore Park family housing complex within easy walking distance of the base. Bachelor officer and enlisted accommodations are available in a twenty-two-unit Navy Lodge. Children attend the Orleans Parish public schools. A child-care facility for forty-two children is available at the west bank facility. College courses available through the Navy Campus are provided by Northwood Institute and Troy State University.

Personal Services. Outpatient medical care is provided by the Naval Medical Clinic New Orleans. A clinic is also available at the naval air station in Belle Chasse. Definitive medical care is available from local hospitals or at Keesler Air Force Base, Mississippi. A commissary store and Navy exchange are available as well as a mini mart and package store, a service station, an optical shop, barber and beauty shops, a cafeteria, and other retail outlets.

Recreation. For those who enjoy relaxing over food and drink, the NSA offers the Fairwinds officers/CPO club, the Port-O-Call all-hands dining facility, and the Big Easy West enlisted club. There is also a McDonald's in the Navy exchange.

More strenuous recreational activities are available at the swimming pool; an eight-lane bowling center; fitness centers on both banks of the Mississippi; tennis, racquetball, and basketball courts; and softball and football/soccer fields. A picnic grounds and a recreational trailer park with sixteen hookups are also available. And for those who wish to read about life on the Mississippi, there is a 13,000-volume library open to all.

For more information write to: Public Affairs Office, Naval Support Activity, 2300 General Meyer Ave., New Orleans, LA 70142-5007 or call (504) 948-5011.

MAINE

Air Force

LORING AIR FORCE BASE

The 1991 Base Realignment and Closure Commission recommended the Loring AFB be closed by 30 September 1994.

Loring Air Force Base is located about as far as you can go on U.S. Highway 1 without leaving the country. Although speaking the French-Canadian dialect is not a prerequisite for an assignment at Loring, the base is very close to Canada's border with the United States at New Brunswick, and Quebec Province is not much farther north.

History. Loring AFB was under construction for seven years, from 1946 until 1953, when it opened. Known first as Limestone Air Force Base, after the nearby town of Limestone, its name was changed in October 1954 to honor Maj. Charles J. Loring, Jr., a Korean War Medal of Honor recipient. Today the base occupies more than 9,000 acres of land in the northeasternmost corner of Maine. It is home to the 42nd Bomb Wing's 2,200 military personnel and their 3,000 family members.

Housing and Schools. More than 1,800 units of family housing are available for personnel assigned to Loring. Guest quarters consisting of twenty-eight units are available at the base, as are transient airmen's quarters.

Dependent children in kindergarten through sixth grade attend on-base schools; all others attend Limestone High School. Most of the Limestone student body is composed of children from the base. A child-care facility is also available on base. Adult education on base offers college courses from New Hampshire College, the

University of Maine at Presque Isle, and Northern Maine Vocational-Technical Institute.

Personal Services. Medical care at Loring is available from the two-story, fifteen-bed USAF hospital. Limited dependent dental care is also offered. Other support facilities include a main exchange, a new commissary store with over 8,500 line items in stock, and a shopette.

Recreation. There's plenty of recreation at Loring. The base has an Olympic-size indoor swimming pool, open six days a week year-round. The bowling center offers a sixteen-lane alley, and the gymnasium has two full-sized basketball courts, five racquetball courts, a weight room, and a universal gym. The base recreation center offers an arts and crafts shop, and there is also an auto/wood hobby shop. Officers and NCO club facilities are located on base.

Loring has a nine-hole, par-seventy-two golf course and a ski slope, located behind the NCO housing area. A ski chalet offers rentals and a snack bar. Skiers will find Maine a paradise, with fifty-three courses available as soon as the snow falls.

Campers and outdoors persons will find the Dow Pines Recreation Area and Farm-Camp a paradise also. Located 38 miles northeast of Bangor, near Aurora, some 200 miles from Loring, the trip is worth the trouble. Five cabins (each sleeping six people), a guest lodge that sleeps six, and a main lodge that sleeps eight are available, plus seventeen trailer pads (with water and electricity), tent sites, a recreation hall, and a boat launch facility. Dow Pines offers boating, canoeing, swimming, hiking, cycling, fishing, picnicking, and backpacking. Bicycles, boats, motors, fishing equipment, and even pool tables can be rented there.

The Local Area. Winters are cold in this part of Maine, with temperatures frequently dropping to minus 20° F. Summers are mild, with temperatures in the seventies, but fall is the most beautiful season of all, offering weather unequaled anywhere else in the country.

Loring is located near Limestone, a small community of 3,000. Fort Fairfield, about twelve miles from the base, is a town of about 6,000 residents.

Canada is only a short drive from Loring to the east. Montreal at 400 miles and Quebec City at about 200 miles are somewhat farther afield, but both New Brunswick and Quebec provinces may be entered at the nearby borders. Grand Falls and Edmundston, New Brunswick, are within easy driving distances of Loring. Boston and New York are about 400 miles and 600 miles, respectively, south of the base.

For more information write to: 42nd Wing PA, Loring AFB, ME 04751-5000, or call (207) 999-1110.

Navy

BRUNSWICK NAVAL AIR STATION

History. Brunswick was first settled in 1628 by Thomas Purchase, who fled to Boston in 1675 after his settlement was attacked by Indians during King Philip's War. Built on land that for two centuries had been used exclusively for growing blueberries, Brunswick NAS was commissioned in April 1943 to train Royal Canadian Air Force pilots in formation flying, gunnery, and carrier landings. Today, the station has two 8,000-foot runways and is home and workplace for over 5,000 active-duty and civilian personnel who support the antisubmarine operations of the six squadrons of Patrol Wing 5.

Housing and Schools. There are 756 sets of family quarters on the station: 168 officer and 588 enlisted. The on-base housing shortage is critical. Local rentals vary from $300 to $500 for one-bedroom apartments to $600 to $1,200 for four-bedroom houses. Utilities are often extra and, because of the severity of the winters in Maine, can add up to $200 per month to those costs. There are twenty rental mobile home spaces available. The station also has a sixteen-unit Navy Lodge motel. Personnel not on permanent-change-of-station orders are accommodated on a space-available basis.

School-age children attend schools off base, but a nursery and a preschool are operated on the station. The Navy Campus offers programs from high school completion to undergraduate and postgraduate college courses, as well as vocational courses and educational testing. College-degree programs are offered by New Hampshire College.

Personal Services and Recreation. Medical service at Brunswick is provided by a branch clinic. There is no inpatient medical care, and outpatients are seen by appointment only, except for emergencies. Martin's Point Medical Facilities also provide a range of medical services to uniformed personnel and dependents.

A commissary and a Navy exchange with many customer services are available at Brunswick. The morale, welfare, and recreational services office operates a well-equipped fitness center, a nine-hole golf course, a hobby complex, picnic grounds, a twelve-lane bowling alley, tennis courts, an indoor swimming pool, and other recreational facilities and programs.

The Local Area. Hunting, fishing, hiking, and skiing are among the outdoor attractions either on the station or nearby. In 1978, a ski slope and over five kilometers of cross-country ski trails were completed on the base. Good hunting and fishing can be enjoyed within a short drive of the base. Outdoor recreational equipment, from skis to motorized canoes, can be rented through the station recreational services office. Outdoorsmen especially should remember that the weather in Maine is unpredictable, with warm and humid summers and lots of snow and cold in the winter.

The average snowfall is about seventy-seven inches annually. But with 3,500 miles of coastline, 6,000 lakes, and 5,100 rivers, Maine is one of the most beautiful states in the Union.

The town of Brunswick has about 20,000 people, and Topsham, across the Androscoggin River, has 7,000 more. Bath, a few miles east of the station on the Kennebec River, is a thriving little community, best known for its marine museum and the Bath Iron Works, a prime contractor for the Navy in that area. Brunswick itself lies about halfway between Portland to the south and Augusta, the state capital, to the north, and is accessible by Interstate 95.

For more information write to: Public Affairs Officer, NAS, Brunswick, ME 04011-5000, or call (207) 921-2527.

CUTLER NAVAL COMMUNICATIONS UNIT

Welcome to "Downeast" Maine!

Rock-bound coastline, remote beaches, scenic views, offshore islands, mountains, lakes, ponds, rivers, dense forest wilderness as far as you can see—this is the natural beauty of the state of Maine. What is not available right on the station—and most of these natural features are—is just a bit farther inland.

History. Cutler Naval Communications Unit was commissioned in June 1961 and today is home for about 300 personnel. The primary mission of the station is to operate and maintain the most powerful very-low-frequency (VLF) radio transmitter in the world. It has an output of 2 million watts, twenty times the power of any major commercial radio broadcasting station. The base actually consists of three separate areas comprising over 3,000 acres on a peninsula jutting into the Atlantic between the towns of Cutler to the east and Machias to the west.

Housing and Schools. Family housing at Cutler consists of sixty-one units located on the station. Housing is normally available when reporting in, but because of limited commercial rentals, personnel are not encouraged to bring their families until on-base housing is obtained. There are no guest facilities at Cutler.

Dependent schooling is conducted either at a newly opened elementary school, Bay Ridge Elementary in Cutler, or for high school students, at Washington Academy, a semiprivate school located in East Machias. The University of Maine offers a wide variety of two- and four-year degree programs. Classes are scheduled for both day and evening.

Personal Services. The station is self-contained. There is a Navy exchange and commissary store, and, although these facilities are small, they carry a full range of necessary items. Routine medical care is provided at the base medical clinic, and specialist care is arranged off base.

Recreation. Summers in this part of the world are warm during the day and cold at night. Winters are severe, with an average snowfall of up to sixty inches. Considerable fog is normal during June and July. Although the ocean does not warm up enough for enjoyable swimming, the many lakes in the area do provide swimming. Fishing and hunting are permitted on the base. Each year the station reservoir is stocked with brook trout, while the VLF peninsula has deer, rabbit, grouse, and pheasant.

The Local Area. This section of Maine is small-town country. The nearest major shopping mall is in Bangor, nearly 100 miles southwest of Cutler. The people who live at Cutler are friendly and helpful, which goes a long way to offset the inconvenience of the isolation.

For more information write to: Public Affairs Office, NAVCOMMU Cutler, East Machias, ME 04630-1000, or call (207) 259-8203.

WINTER HARBOR NAVAL SECURITY GROUP ACTIVITY

History. The Navy first came to this area in August 1917 when a radio station was commissioned at Otter Cliffs, about five miles across Frenchman Bay from the current main base on the tip of the Schoodic Peninsula. The main site was opened in 1935 and in 1958 its name was changed to Winter Harbor, after the town north of the site on the other side of the eastern extension of Acadia National Park.

Today the Naval Security Group Activity (NSGA) plays a vital role in the Navy's Tactical Ocean Surveillance system, training people who maintain and operate its Classic Wizard System worldwide. The NSGA operates from three sites: main base, at the tip of the Scoodic Peninsula; the operations site near Corea, ten miles from the main base; and Detachment Alfa, in Prospect Harbor. The NSGA has a complement of 380 active-duty personnel and 66 civilian employees. About 250 dependents also call Winter Harbor home.

Housing and Schools. NSGA operates three housing areas consisting of a total of 124 family housing units. The waiting time for these quarters is from three to six months. There are accommodations at the main site for about 195 unaccompanied personnel. Local rental housing is in short supply and short-term to accommodate the tourist season (May through September). Utilities during the winter can run as much as $200 per month.

Dependent children attend schools in Winter Harbor and East Sullivan. There is a child-development center at the main site that can accommodate twenty-eight children ages six weeks to six years.

Personal Services. Medical and dental care are provided by branch clinics at the main site. Definitive medical care is available in Newport, Rhode Island, and Ellsworth, Maine. There is a Navy exchange at Winter Harbor as well as a package store, a barber shop, a gas station, and a galley/mess hall. At the main site is also a small but well-stocked commissary store.

Recreation. The NSGA operates five house trailers and six recreation cabins, fully furnished and open year-round. Reservations are recommended, especially during the summer months. There is also a campground with seven camper sites and three tent sites that is open April 15 through October 15. For those who enjoy outdoor sports, there are two miles of hiking trails on base through wooded and shorefront areas, tennis and racquetball/handball courts, and a multi-use recreation area that includes a ball field, a playground, and barbecue pits. Indoor recreation facilities include a community center, a gym and fitness room, a four-lane bowling alley, and an auto hobby shop.

The Local Area. Maine has three distinct seasons with variable weather. Summers are mild with temperatures averaging in the seventies. Fog is common along the coast. Winter sees subfreezing temperatures, snow, wind, and frequent storms. Winter driving can be very hazardous. Overall, however, Maine is one of the most beautiful states in the nation, with more than seventeen million acres of forestland, 3,500 miles of coastline, 6,000 lakes, and 5,100 rivers.

For more information write to: Commanding Officer, Attention: 10, Naval Security Group Activity, Winter Harbor, ME 04693, or call (207) 963-5534.

MARYLAND

Air Force

ANDREWS AIR FORCE BASE

Almost everybody who is anybody has landed at Andrews Air Force Base at one time or another since it was opened in 1942; the base serves as the aerial port of entry for visiting foreign heads of state and other official U.S. government visitors. It is also the home base for the president's plane, *Air Force One*. But there are many other activities at the base—none quite so glamorous as receiving kings and presidents, but important nonetheless.

History. Known as Camp Springs Army Air Field when it first opened in 1942, the installation's name was changed in 1945 to honor Lt. Frank M. Andrews, who was killed in an air crash in 1943. Today the base covers over 4,300 acres ten miles southeast of Washington, D.C., and is both home and workplace for 25,000 active-duty personnel, their dependents, and civilian employees. The major unit is the 89th Airlift Wing.

Housing and Schools. There are over 2,000 units of family housing at Andrews, plus 210 mobile home spaces. Waiting periods vary, but enlisted personnel through grade E-6 generally stay on the housing list at least twelve months before being assigned quarters. Sixty units of temporary housing are available on a reservation basis for families on official orders, but all others are considered on a space-available basis only. Andrews has over 2,200 dormitory spaces for single enlisted personnel.

Schooling is available in Prince George's County. Adult education programs at the base are excellent. Undergraduate courses are offered by Prince George's

Community College, the University of Maryland, and others. George Washington and Central Michigan Universities, among others, offer graduate programs on the base. Sixty colleges and universities are located within commuting distance of the base, making it one of the finest spots in the Air Force for higher education.

Personal Services. Other services are also excellent. Malcolm Grow USAF Medical Center, a 285-bed multispecialty hospital and dental facility, offers definitive medical care. A complete commissary and base exchange system are also available, as are excellent recreational opportunities.

Recreation. The base has two eighteen-hole golf courses, a skeet range, a twenty-four-lane bowling center, tennis courts, three outdoor swimming pools, auto and wood hobby shops, a ski and camping shop, a frame shop, a 1,000-seat base theater, officers and NCO clubs, and a family camping area. The latter contains twelve spaces for campers with hookups and tenting spaces as well.

The Local Area. The recreational activities available to Air Force personnel stationed in the Washington, D.C., area are too numerous to mention here. The nation's capital offers almost unlimited attractions, from touring government buildings to visiting museums and attending concerts. A great variety of restaurants and nightclubs abound in the District of Columbia, and major points of interest in both Virginia and Maryland are within easy driving distance of the base. A family cannot see all the things there are to see or do all the things there are to do in this remarkable part of the United States on just one tour at the base.

For more information write to: Public Affairs, Andrews AFB, DC 20331-5000, or call (301) 981-9111.

Army

ABERDEEN PROVING GROUND

Aberdeen Proving Ground, the Army's oldest active proving ground, was established on December 14, 1917. Located on a 72,000-acre tract extending along and into the Chesapeake Bay, APG provides installation support services to more than fifty tenant activities. Today Aberdeen is home to the U.S. Army Test and Evaluation Command and fifty tenant activities with a daytime population of more than 14,000 people: 5,800 military personnel, 9,300 civilian employees, and 9,800 family members. Nearly 2,800 members of the civilian workforce are engineers, scientists, and mathematicians whose work encompasses basic research and test and evaluation.

Housing and Schools. More than 1,400 sets of family quarters are located at Aberdeen, including 70 trailer spaces. Transient accommodations include a guest house and over 300 temporary lodging facilities. Children attend schools in Harford County. The two child-development centers available on post have a capacity of over 340 children.

Personal Services. Health care at Aberdeen is provided by an outpatient health clinic that provides optometry, pediatric, internal medicine, gynecology, physical therapy, general medicine, surgery, and dental treatment. Inpatient care is available at Fort Meade and Walter Reed Army Medical Center.

A large commissary and a large exchange are located at Aberdeen itself, with small exchange and commissary annexes at nearby Edgewood.

Recreation. Two physical fitness centers, three gyms, two recreation centers, six arts and crafts centers, two golf courses, a theater, two libraries, fishing, hunting, camping, and picnicking can all be enjoyed at Aberdeen.

For more information write to: Public Affairs Office, USA Test and Evaluation Command, Attention: AMSTE-PA, Aberdeen Proving Ground, MD 21005-5055, or call (410) 278-1142.

FORT DETRICK

Massive dish antennas punctuate the skyline at Maryland's Fort Detrick, marking the home of the 1110th U.S. Army Signal Battalion, a key station in the defense communications system. Communications facilities located at Fort Detrick connect the president and his military authorities with our defense establishments throughout the world. Twenty-five other major activities are located at the 1,200-acre site operated by the U.S. Army Health Services Command. These include the U.S. Army Medical Research and Development Command, the U.S. Army Medical Research Institute of Infectious Diseases, the U.S. Army Biomedical Research and Development Command, the Defense Medical Standardization Board, the Naval Medical Materiel Support Command, and the U.S. Army Space Command, CONUS.

Housing and Schools. Housing is tight at Fort Detrick with only 155 units, 40 for officers, and 115 for enlisted personnel. There is usually a waiting period of six to nine months before on-post housing becomes available. Adequate housing can be obtained in Frederick, and new arrivals normally locate off-post housing within two weeks; the housing referral office assists newcomers in the home-hunting process.

Dependent children of military personnel stationed at Fort Detrick attend local schools in Frederick County, but a child-care and development center is located on post for children from six weeks to twelve years of age. Also available is an in-home family child-care program provided by adults living in government quarters who are certified by Fort Detrick's child-development services office. Adult educational services are provided by the post education center, which arranges tuition assistance for eligible personnel to attend college courses at local campuses such as Hood College and Frederick Community College in Frederick or Mount Saint Mary's College, located nearby.

Personal Services. A new commissary opened at Fort Detrick in the spring of 1992. Shoppers can also use the commissary at Fort Ritchie, twenty-three miles away, or the one at Fort Meade, thirty-five miles away. The post exchange complex at Fort Detrick is a modern self-service store. Near the PX are laundry and dry-cleaning services and a hair-care facility. A military clothing sales store opened in January 1993. A three-pump gas station is also operated by the exchange service.

Routine health care is provided by a health clinic and a dental clinic. The latter offers care to retired personnel and family members on a space-available basis. Referral hospitals for specialized or emergency inpatient care are located in Frederick or the Washington, D.C., area.

Recreation. A variety of recreational activities are available on post, including the post field house, which provides basketball, racquetball, squash, handball, weight-training facilities, and a sauna. The post also has six surfaced tennis courts, a four-lane bowling center, family garden plots, an outdoor swimming pool, a well-stocked library, and picnicking and fishing at the Nallin Farm Recreational Area. The information, ticketing, and registration office offers discount tickets to amusement parks in Maryland, Virginia, and Pennsylvania, and tickets and transportation to various sporting and cultural events available throughout the area.

The Local Area. Frederick is a community of 50,000 that was laid out in 1745. It was in the Frederick County Courthouse that on 23 November 1765 twelve judges proclaimed the first repudiation of the British Stamp Act, an act of defiance that led eventually to the American Revolution. Hessian prisoners from various Revolutionary War battles were once quartered in the stone barracks, which is still standing on the grounds of the Maryland School for the Deaf. Frederick is also famous as the last resting place of Francis Scott Key, composer of the "Star-Spangled Banner."

Despite its proximity to Washington and Baltimore and its own gradual expansion over the years, Frederick remains essentially an agricultural community with a quiet charm characteristic of small-town America. Nevertheless, many high-tech research firms have moved into the area so that Frederick today is considered a part of the Washington-Baltimore metropolitan area, with a corresponding rise in housing costs. But the city abounds with parks and playgrounds, and the downtown area, complete with shops and restaurants of every kind, has been dubbed "Georgetown North," after the exclusive Georgetown area of the District of Columbia.

For more information write to: Public Affairs Office, Fort Detrick, MD 21702-5000, or call (301) 663-2018.

FORT MEADE

History. Established in May 1917 and named in honor of Maj. Gen. George G. Meade, who commanded the Union Army at the Battle of Gettysburg, today Fort Meade comprises over 6,000 acres between Baltimore and Washington, D.C., just a few miles south of the Baltimore International Airport. It is home for the 10,000 active-duty personnel and their 10,500 family members, and more 27,000 civilian employees of the First U.S. Army, the National Security Agency, and many other units and activities.

Housing and Schools. There are more than 2,000 sets of family quarters on the post, allocated into several different housing areas. A guest house with fifty-four units is also available there.

Fort Meade has four elementary schools, a middle school, and a high school. There are also two new child-care facilities, each capable of handling up to 300 children. Adult education is available through the Army education center. College courses are offered from the University of Maryland, Bowie State University, George Washington University, American University, and Central Michigan University.

Personal Services. Medical care at Fort Meade is provided by the eighty-bed Kimbrough Army Community Hospital. A commissary and main post exchange shopping complex are also available. Post exchange concessions range from a beauty shop to tailor service, and several branch exchanges operate throughout the post.

Recreation. Excellent recreational facilities are offered at Fort Meade. For the person who enjoys indoor activities, the McGill Recreation Center has a ballroom, a stage and dressing rooms, a lounge, and classroom and game areas. The Gaffney Sports Arena offers basketball, squash, handball courts, a sauna, weight rooms, and a twenty-five-meter Olympic swimming pool. And naturally, the club system on post allows sportsters to relax over a cup of decaf after a hard session of toning up the muscles. Also on post are a thirty-six-lane bowling center, a large post theater, and an arts and crafts center.

Outdoor recreation facilities at Fort Meade include Burba Park, a recreation area with a lake, four picnic pavilions, and a cottage. In addition, there are two eighteen-hole golf courses, a bowling center, a rod and gun club, a riding stable, seventeen tennis courts, two outdoor swimming pools, and an equipment issue facility.

The Local Area. Fort Meade is centrally located for the serious sightseer. Baltimore, suburban Maryland, Washington, D.C., and northern Virginia are all accessible by bus or subway. Historic Annapolis, the majestic Chesapeake Bay, and the Eastern Shore of Maryland are all less than a thirty-minute drive from Fort Meade.

For more information write to: Garrison Public Affairs Office, AFKA-ZI-PAO-CR, Fort George G. Meade, MD 20755-5025, or call (410) 677-6361/5301.

FORT RITCHIE

Although Fort Ritchie is a young installation, the vicinity has been at the heart of the nation's history since cannons for George Washington's army were forged in nearby Waynesboro. Two of the bloodiest battles of the American Civil War were fought nearby as well—Antietam and Gettysburg. Situated in the Catoctin Mountains of northwestern Maryland just south of the Pennsylvania border, the post is rightfully considered as one of the most beautiful military installations in the country by those who know it.

History. Fort Ritchie was named Camp Albert C. Ritchie after the governor of Maryland in 1926; construction began in May of that year. The installation's name was changed to Fort Ritchie in 1951, and today it is home for the 1,100 military personnel, their 1,400 dependents, and the 1,100 civilian employees of the U.S. Army's 7th Signal Command.

Housing and Schools. Fort Ritchie is a small post, covering only 648 acres of rolling mountain slopes. There are 341 sets of family quarters there; the waiting list for junior-enlisted homes is approximately six months. The wait for senior-enlisted quarters is four months, while the wait for company-grade units averages two months. Guest housing is available for use by military families awaiting quarters. Troop and bachelor housing is modern and comfortable.

No dependent schooling is available at Fort Ritchie, although the post does operate a nice child-care facility. The education center offers a variety of courses from pre-high school to college level. On-post college courses are available from the University of Maryland, Frostburg State College, and Hagerstown Junior College, and off-post classes can be taken at Mount Saint Mary College and Penn State University.

Personal Services. The Fort Ritchie health clinic is small and provides only limited services, but complete and comprehensive medical care facilities are available at Fort Meade, Maryland, and Walter Reed General Hospital, Washington,

Headquarters, U.S. Army Garrison at Fort Ritchie, was built by the U.S. Army Maryland National Guard in the 1920s. (U.S. Army photo)

D.C. There is a dental clinic at Fort Ritchie, but no regular dental care is offered there for family members.

Available on post are banking facilities and a newly built post exchange and commissary.

Recreation. On-post recreational facilities include a bowling alley, a theater, a nine-hole golf course, a swimming pool, tennis courts, a fitness center, and craft shops. Fort Ritchie's man-made lakes, Upper and Lower Royer, cover twenty acres and are the focus of summer and winter fun, which include boating, fishing, and swimming. The post is adjacent to the Appalachian Trail, America's premier hiking trail, and there are a number of state parks and forests nearby for camping, fishing, hunting, and hiking.

The Local Area. Waynesboro, Pennsylvania (population 26,000), is located only six miles from post; Hagerstown, Maryland, twelve miles; Gettysburg, Pennsylvania, twenty-five miles; and Frederick, Maryland, a shopping Mecca, twenty-eight miles. Baltimore and Washington, D.C., are within seventy-five miles of the post. Historic spots nearby include Gettysburg National Military Park; Antietam National Military Park; Harper's Ferry, West Virginia; Mercersburg, Pennsylvania, the birthplace of James Buchanan; and the historic areas of York and Lancaster, Pennsylvania, home of the Pennsylvania Dutch.

For more information write to: Fort Ritchie Public Affairs Office, Fort Ritchie, MD 21719-5010, or call (717) 878-5874/5306.

Navy

ANNAPOLIS NAVAL STATION

Situated just across the Severn River from the U.S. Naval Academy, the Annapolis Naval Station's existence has been inextricably entwined with that of the naval academy for nearly 150 years.

History. The U.S. Navy first came to this part of Maryland in 1851, six years after the founding of the naval academy, when the first midshipmen training ship, USS *Preble*, arrived at what was then Fort Severn. The academy was officially commissioned 15 May 1947. Today the 850 active-duty personnel and 120 civilian employees at the station provide service support for the professional development of the midshipmen through small-craft operations, the Robert Crown Sailing Center, the Naval Construction Battalion Unit 403, and the Marine barracks.

Housing and Schools. There are 420 units of family housing—including 146 three-bedroom, thirty-nine four-bedroom, eighteen two-bedroom enlisted units, and sixteen mobile home pads—available to personnel assigned to the station, but they are shared by naval academy faculty and staff and personnel assigned to the Naval Surface Warfare Center (adjacent to the station). Unaccompanied enlisted personnel are billeted at the station: About 170 beds are available.

The Naval Academy Primary School, located on the station golf course, accommodates children from prekindergarten through the fifth grade. A child-development center with a capacity of 100 children is located on the station.

Personal Services. A commissary–Navy exchange complex is located just outside the naval station's main gate. This includes barber and beauty shops, car rental, a flower shop, a gift wrap and package delivery service, a garden shop, laundry and dry-cleaning services, an optical shop, and a tailor shop. There are also a gas station, a mini mart, and a beverage store. A McDonald's is located just outside the main gate.

Primary medical care is available at the naval medical clinic at the academy complex. There is a branch dental clinic onboard the station. Emergency and specialized medical care are available at the National Naval Medical Center in Bethesda, outside Washington, D.C., or at Anne Arundel General Hospital and Medical Center in Annapolis.

Recreation. Aside from the Naval Academy Golf Course that borders the north side of the naval station itself, onboard are a marina, auto and wood hobby shops, a swimming pool, a tennis court, picnic grounds, and Little League, hardball, and softball fields. Just adjacent to the picnic grounds is the Retelle Recreation Area, with a fishing pier, fourteen RV campsites, tenting, and a party room. The marina can accommodate boats up to thirty feet. Two sailboats, one twenty-seven feet and the other twenty-eight feet long, are available for rental, as are smaller boats and windsurfing boards.

The Clipper Club, an all-hands facility featuring family dinners, special events, and other activities, is located just inside the main gate. The officers club is located at the naval academy.

For more information write to: Commanding Officer, Naval Station, 58 Bennion Rd., Annapolis, MD 21402-5054, or call (410) 267-2385.

BETHESDA NATIONAL NAVAL MEDICAL CENTER

Located just across Wisconsin Avenue from the National Institutes of Health and one mile inside the Capital Beltway (Interstate 495), the National Naval Medical Center (NNMC) in Bethesda is certainly one of the most important, well-known, and attractive military installations in the entire Washington-Baltimore metropolitan area.

History. The site for the NNMC was personally selected by President Franklin D. Roosevelt in 1938. The year before, using a piece of White House stationery, he sketched the design for the center's main hospital building. Ground breaking took place on 29 June 1939, and the center was officially commissioned on 5 February 1942.

Today the center is staffed by more than 6,000 personnel, 4,800 military and 2,100 civilian. As the referral medical facility for cases worldwide, NNMC admits over 17,000 patients each year and, with an operating capacity of more than 400 beds, is in the top ten of the largest medical facilities in the United States. The center itself comprises ten adjoining buildings. Building 1, which rises more than eighteen stories above the center grounds, is the original hospital building. Today it houses the NNMC headquarters, outpatient clinics, and offices. Other activities onboard the center include the Uniformed Services University of the Health Sciences, a fully accredited medical school operated by the Assistant Secretary of Defense for Health Affairs, the Armed Forces Radiobiology Research Institute, the Naval School of Health Sciences, the Naval Medical Research Institute, and others.

Housing and Schools. At the center itself are only eight sets of family quarters, all for officers. Enlisted housing is available nearby in the form of fifty rental units for personnel in pay grades E-4 and above. Eligible military personnel are authorized housing at nearby installations operated by the Naval District Washington and other services. Bachelor officer and enlisted accommodations are available at the center. The Navy Lodge at the center has twenty-two units available at the rate of thirty-five dollars per day for families on permanent-change-of-station orders and the relatives of inpatients at the NNMC. The Zachary and Elizabeth Fisher House offers accommodations for military families undergoing life-threatening medical crises. It can accommodate up to sixteen people in its seven units.

The children of personnel assigned to the NNMC attend local public schools. A child-care center at the NNMC has a capacity of eighty-two children. Adult education is available from colleges and schools throughout the area.

Personal Services. Although the NNMC has no commissary, a small Navy exchange is available as well as a mini mart, a package store, a restaurant, a Baskin Robbins ice cream shop, and a service station. Commissary facilities are available at nearby military installations such as Fort Myer and Fort Meade.

Recreation. Both officers and enlisted clubs are available at the center, as well as a gym with an indoor swimming pool, a spa, a sauna, and a weight and Nautilus room; five tennis courts; a twenty-lane bowling center; and an intramural sports program.

For more information write to: Public Affairs, National Naval Medical Center, Bethesda, MD 20814-5000 or call (301) 295-5727.

PATUXENT RIVER NAVAL AIR STATION

History. The present quarters of the Naval Air Warfare Center Aircraft Division commander—part of the Mattapany Estate—are built upon the site of a Jesuit mission that was established there shortly after 1634. This was the same year local Indians saw property values skyrocket when the first white settlers landed at Saint Mary's, about seven miles from the station's main gate. The mission property was confiscated by Lord Baltimore, and some of the original structure of a brick home built on the site in 1666 was incorporated into the existing structure, which may date from as early as 1722. Quarters "W," the official residence of the Naval Air Station commander, the Somerville House, was built by Dr. George Somerville around 1780–90.

Today the major activity at Patuxent River NAS is the Naval Air Warfare

Center Aircraft Division, which has as its mission the full spectrum of research, development, test and evaluation, engineering, and fleet support for air platforms. Station population includes 3,100 active-duty personnel and over 6,000 dependents.

Housing and Schools. Although there are 857 sets of family quarters onboard the station, there is a ninety-day to two-year waiting period for them. A new temporary Navy lodging facility opened in 1991.

Public and private schools are available in Saint Mary's County for dependent children, but there are a day school and child-care center onboard the station. Active-duty personnel and dependents may take courses from a number of colleges, including George Washington and Embry-Riddle Aeronautical Universities, the University of Maryland, the University of Southern California, and Florida Institute of Technology.

Personal Services. Personal services available at the station include a beautiful, modern, thirteen-bed naval hospital with a full range of outpatient clinical services. The Navy exchange provides a complete line of merchandise, as does a large new commissary store.

Recreation. Recreation facilities include an officers and enlisted club system, a community center, a bowling center, an eighteen-hole golf course, and indoor and outdoor swimming pools.

Outdoor facilities include the West Basin Marina, a three-barn stable, and numerous campgrounds. Several of these have water and electrical hookups, while others are primitive tent or self-contained trailer sites; a large number of fifteen- and twenty-three-foot camper trailers may be rented through the auto hobby shop at the station.

The Local Area. Saint Mary's County, located at the southernmost tip of the state of Maryland, is surrounded by water, the Potomac River to the west and the Patuxent River to the east. The southernmost portion of the land juts into the Chesapeake Bay. Washington, D.C., is sixty-five miles to the northwest of Lexington Park, a small community situated just outside the station's main gate; Baltimore is seventy-nine miles to the north.

For more information write to: Family Services Center, NAS, Patuxent River, MD 20670-5409, or call (301) 863-3000.

U.S. NAVAL ACADEMY

The U.S. Naval Academy's mission, quite simply stated, is to develop midshipmen morally, mentally, and physically and to imbue them with the highest ideals of duty, honor, and loyalty in order to provide graduates who are dedicated to a career of naval service and have potential for future development in mind and character to assume the highest responsibilities of command, citizenship, and government.

History. The naval academy was originally founded at Fort Severn as the Naval School in October 1845. The Naval School was redesignated the U.S. Naval Academy in 1850.

Today, the academy accomplishes its mission on a beautiful 338-acre site located on the south shore of the Severn River at Annapolis, the capital of Maryland and one of the oldest communities in the East. The commandant of midshipmen commands a 4,300-member brigade of midshipmen, the academic direction of whose education is toward a bachelor of science degree and a commission in the Navy or Marine Corps.

The academy is supported by the personnel of Annapolis Naval Station, a subordinate command of the academy, located across the river.

Housing and Schools. There are over 400 units of family housing at the station for officers and enlisted personnel assigned there, but no guest or temporary housing.

A dependents school for children through the fifth grade is operated at the station, and a child-care center is operated by the special services office in the community center building; dependent children may attend advanced schools, public and private, in the Annapolis area.

Personal Services. A commissary and Navy exchange are located on the naval station. The latter provides a number of outlets, including a gas station, auto parts/service, a garden shop, and a mini mart.

Recreation. The special services office at the naval station offers recreational programs and facilities ranging from golf tournaments to intramural sports. Sailing facilities and qualified instructors are also available, as is a marina for the use of all personnel who own boats. There are also a swimming pool, an ice rink, a movie theater, a bowling alley, and a gymnasium onboard the naval station.

Midshipman march on parade at Tecumseh Court at the U.S. Naval Academy. (U.S. Navy photo)

The Local Area. Founded originally in 1649 as Providence, Annapolis today is a picturesque community of 33,000 inhabitants. It is situated about midway between Washington, D.C., and Baltimore in what is primarily farming country. Many original eighteenth-century buildings are preserved within the city's boundaries. The waterfront section of the city, as an example, is a registered national historic landmark. Annapolis is a two-hour drive from the Civil War battlefield at Antietam. Baltimore, one of the most important seaports on the Atlantic Coast, is thirty miles north of Annapolis and contains many historic and cultural attractions, including the Fort McHenry National Shrine and Museum.

Across the Chesapeake Bay from Annapolis is the famed Maryland Eastern Shore, and beyond is the Delaware-Maryland-Virginia Atlantic coastline.

For more information write to: Public Affairs Officer, U.S. Naval Academy, Annapolis, MD 21402-5000, or call (410) 267-2291.

MASSACHUSETTS

Air Force

HANSCOM AIR FORCE BASE

Hanscom Air Force Base owns neither runways nor aircraft. No military aircraft have been stationed there since 1973. Neither does Hanscom handle weapons systems or munitions. Hanscom Air Force Base handles information, and as all military personnel know, *information is power*.

History. Named in honor of Laurence G. Hanscom, who died in an aircraft crash in 1941, the base opened in May 1941 as a training installation. Today it is home for the Electronic System Center (ESC) of the U.S. Air Force. ESC develops electronic systems that enable Air Force commanders to make the most effective use of their forces. Were it an industrial corporation it would rank in the upper half of *Fortune*'s listing of the 500 largest American corporations. Over 2,100 civilian professionals—engineers, computer specialists, business managers, logisticians, and contracting specialists—assist in the ESC mission in company with 2,500 active-duty personnel and their dependents.

Housing and Schools. Hanscom has 858 units of family housing plus 42 temporary lodging units for transient families. The Hartwell Mobile Home Park has 96 trailer sites as well.

A child-care center and a preschool are operated on the base, as is an elementary school for children in kindergarten through eighth grade. Educational opportunities for adults are available on the base from such institutions as Western New England College.

Personal Services. A USAF clinic provides outpatient medical care for active-duty personnel and their dependents at Hanscom. Fort Devens Army Hospital, twenty miles to the west, and the U.S. Public Health Service Hospital at Brighton are used for referrals. A base exchange and commissary are available on the installation, as well as officers and NCO open messes.

Recreation. Recreational facilities and programs include a twelve-lane bowling center; an Olympic-size swimming pool; a fitness center; tennis courts; and an auto shop. The base shares a nine-hole golf course about four miles from the base with the Veteran's Hospital in Bedford, and an eighteen-hole course at Fort Devens is about twenty miles away. Base personnel also have access to the Fourth Cliff Recreational Area located on the tip of a small peninsula south of Boston. The site offers eighteen chalets, eleven camper spaces, and twenty tent sites. Swimming, fishing, and picnicking are permitted there.

The Local Area. Hanscom is located about eighteen miles northwest of Boston, within the boundaries of four of the most historic towns in the United States—Lexington, Concord, Bedford, and Lincoln—placing it in the center of American Revolution country. Bedford produced the only flag carried in the initial combat against the British, and south of the base lies Walden Pond, made famous by Henry David Thoreau. Nearby are also the homes of Ralph Waldo Emerson, Louisa May Alcott, and Nathaniel Hawthorne.

Massachusetts offers a great variety of cultural and recreational opportunities. The state has 1,500 miles of Atlantic coastline, 270 golf courses, 29 state forests, and 40 skiing areas.

For more information write to: Public Affairs Office, Hanscom AFB, MA 01731-5000, or call (617) 377-4469.

Army

FORT DEVENS

The 1991 Base Closure and Realignment Commission selected Fort Devens for closure by October 1995.

Fort Devens is located in Middlesex and Worcester Counties, thirty-five miles northwest of Boston, twelve miles south of the New Hampshire border, and adjacent to the town of Ayer. It is in the heart of some of the most famous ski country in the eastern United States.

History. Named in honor of Maj. Gen. Charles Devens, a Union Army general and later attorney general of the United States during the presidency of Rutherford B. Hayes, Fort Devens came into existence in September 1917 as an infantry training center. Today it is home for the 46th Combat Support Hospital, the 10th Special Forces Group (Airborne), the U.S. Army Intelligence School, and other units.

Housing and Schools. There are over 1,700 sets of family quarters at Fort Devens. The post also has a fifteen-space mobile home park. Guest housing is available for permanent-change-of-station and transient military personnel and their families on a limited basis. Waiting time for quarters varies according to the number of bedrooms required, rank, and time of year.

Children attend local schools.

Personal Services. Medical care is provided by Cutler Army Hospital. There is a dental clinic on the post. The post has a modern, 22,000-square-foot, self-service, supermarket-style commissary; a post exchange that offers a wide range of concessions; and officers and NCO club facilities. Fort Devens also offers a modern child-care facility that is the prototype for the entire Department of Defense.

Recreation. A varied recreational services program is offered at Fort Devens, including athletic fields, a bowling alley, an eighteen-hole golf course, three gymnasiums, an auto crafts shop, a movie theater, two Nautilus facilities, and, during the winter, an ice skating area. In addition, there are nine tennis courts; two swimming pools; and swimming at Mirror Lake, a natural swimming area located on the installation. The Robbins Pond Travel Camp, located on Robbins Pond within the installation, offers a number of outdoor activities in season (April to October), with trailer and tenting sites as well as picnic facilities.

The Local Area. Fort Devens lies at the heart of some of the nation's finest ski country, and ski equipment is available for rent on the post. Immediately adjacent to the post are the Benjamin Hill and the Hartwell Hill ski areas.

The area of New England where Fort Devens is situated is rich in history. Within an easy drive of the post are the Minuteman National Historical Park near Concord and Boston itself, which not only offers all the attractions of a major city but also is rich in American Colonial and Revolutionary history.

For more information write to: Public Affairs Office, Fort Devens, MA 01433-5030, or call (508) 796-3307/2159.

Coast Guard

CAPE COD COAST GUARD AIR STATION

The Cape Cod Air Station is located in one of the most famous tourist areas of the country, and the thousands of people who visit Cape Cod each season give the men and women of the air station plenty of business—more than 400 search-and-rescue missions per year.

History. Established in 1970 as a tenant command at Otis Air Force Base when Air Station Salem, Massachusetts, and Air Detachment Quonset Point, Rhode Island, were consolidated, Cape Cod Air Station became the largest active-duty military command in the area when the Air Force departed in 1973. Today it is home to more than 500 military and civilian personnel. Air station crews fly both helicopters and fixed-wing aircraft in the performance of a variety of Coast Guard missions in the offshore areas from the Canadian border to central New Jersey.

Housing and Schools. There are 631 sets of family quarters on base. They are single, ranch-type units; single, flat-top units; and multiplex units. Due to the high cost of housing locally, the waiting list for these homes varies from one to nine months from arrival date. Off-base rentals vary with the season, but weekly summer rentals may cost as much as monthly rates during the winter. The average year-round rates range from $300 to $500 for a one-bedroom apartment to $600 to $900 for a three-bedroom house.

Children of personnel assigned to the station attend three elementary schools on base that are operated under the Bourne Public School Department. A day-care center on base can accommodate up to 100 children. The station education office is a full-service center offering courses from Cape Cod Community and Western New England Colleges.

Personal Services and Recreation. Medical service is provided at a Coast Guard combined medical and dental outpatient clinic. A commissary and Coast Guard exchange offer a wide variety of customer services. The morale, welfare, and recreation department provides a large selection of recreational equipment including boats, camping gear, lawn mowers, and sporting equipment. Discount tickets to theater productions, concerts, museums, and sporting events are available. MWR also operates a nine-hole golf course, an auto hobby shop, and a library.

The Local Area. Cape Cod, curling seventy miles out into the Atlantic, is one of the most scenic and historic regions of New England, best known for its beaches, quaint towns, and outdoor attractions. To the south are such famous attractions as Nantucket, Martha's Vineyard, and the Elizabethan Islands. The Cape has fifteen townships constituting Barnstable County. Many of the townships, established two or three centuries ago, are divided into villages that offer a lifestyle and atmosphere uniquely their own.

Cape Cod National Seashore occupies almost the entire shore of the Lower and Outer Cape and offers ideal access to dunes, woods, marshlands, and beaches. Fishing, boating, and hunting opportunities abound on Cape Cod. Fishermen can choose from game, bottom, freshwater, and surf fishing. There are several harbors where boats can be moored, but most people use one of the many town or public ramps on both sides of the Cape's shores. An abundance of migratory birds and wildfowl can be shot in season. Deer can also be hunted, including during a short season on Otis in the more remote parts of the base.

For more information write to: Public Affairs Officer, USCG Air Station Cape Cod, Otis ANGB, MA 02542 or call (508) 968-6316.

Navy

SOUTH WEYMOUTH NAVAL AIR STATION

The 1993 Base Realignment and Closure Commission recommended closing South Weymouth, but at press time a firm date had not yet been announced.

Known as New England's home of the Naval Air Reserve, South Weymouth NAS serves as the host command for three reserve force squadrons, eleven tenant activities, and twenty-six reinforcing/sustaining units. The active-duty force is made up of about 1,000 personnel. More than 2,000 reservists drill there monthly. The station covers 1,400 acres in the towns of Weymouth, Abington, and Rockland. Much of the land remains undeveloped and in its natural state of wetlands and forest. Two runways are located aboard the facility—a 7,000-foot strip running north-south, and a 6,000-foot strip running east-west.

History. NAS South Weymouth was established in 1941 as a lighter-than-air (blimp) facility to guard against German subs in the North Atlantic. The original hangar covered eight acres, could hold six airships, and stood 191 feet high and 956 feet wide. It was replaced in the sixties by a pair of modern buildings that now house three aviation squadrons. Decommissioned after World War II, the station was put back into active service in 1953 and today is home to Navy squadrons VP-92 and HSL-74, and Marine squadron HML-771.

Housing and Schools. There are 365 sets of family quarters available to personnel stationed at South Weymouth, 165 of them on the installation. The remainder are in two complexes, one in Quincy, ten miles north, and the other at Otis Air National Guard base, fifty miles south. There is no Navy Lodge at South Weymouth.

Dependents attend the Weymouth school system. A small child-development center is operated on the station. Many opportunities for off-duty education are available through major universities in Boston and junior and community colleges throughout the area.

Personal Services. Limited medical care is offered by the station's branch medical/dental clinic. Advanced care is available at Naval Hospital Newport, Rhode Island, sixty miles south. The station has a small main exchange and a convenience store annex with a package store. A snack bar and the Captain's Table All-Hands Restaurant are inexpensive on-base alternatives to normal galley dining. There are also an officers club and an enlisted club for after-hours entertainment. The Navy Federal Credit Union has a branch at the station.

Recreation. NAS South Weymouth's Shea Fitness Center complex is among the most modern and complete in the Navy, despite the relatively small size of the command. It features a Nautilus-cardiovascular room, a free-weight room, two racquetball courts, and a basketball court. Also available are a pair of softball fields, four tennis courts, an auto hobby shop, and an Olympic-size outdoor swimming pool. The morale, welfare, and recreation department operates an intramural sports program year-round. Numerous group excursions such as ski trips and golf tournaments and discount tickets to local events are offered through the special services office in the Shea Center.

The Local Area. The station is located on eastern Massachusetts's South Shore, only twenty miles south of Boston and forty-five miles north of Providence, Rhode Island. The region has four distinct seasons, with snowfall normally occurring from December to March and summer temperatures in the seventies from May to September.

For more information write to: Family Service Center, Naval Air Station, South Weymouth, MA 02190-5000 or call (617) 786-2581.

MICHIGAN

Air Force

K. I. SAWYER AIR FORCE BASE

The 1993 Base Realignment and Closure Commission recommended closing K. I. Sawyer AFB, but at press time no firm date had yet been announced.

Welcome to the North Pole. The average annual snowfall at K. I. Sawyer Air Force Base is 137.6 inches; during the winter of 1970–71, 221.4 inches of the white stuff fell. Snow remains on the ground in this part of Michigan from late autumn until early spring. About 130 days out of the year at K. I. Sawyer there is either snow or sleet, and in the winter the temperatures (figuring the wind-chill factor) sometimes dip to a chilly minus 30° F. The monthly average temperatures for winter are 31° in November, 19° in December, 12° in January, and 25° in February.

History. Named after Kenneth I. Sawyer, a Marquette County road commissioner, the base first opened in 1956. Today it is home for the 46th Air Refueling Squadron, the 410th Communications Squadron, and the 410th Medical Group. Sawyer's 5,200 acres are home to 3,200 military personnel, 600 civilian employees, and over 4,700 family members.

Housing and Schools. The base has nearly 1,900 units of family housing, all comfortably insulated. There are also spaces for 199 house trailers. In addition, a 36-unit temporary-lodging facility is available to transient families.

The base operates a child-care center as well as two elementary schools. Older children attend high school in the town of Gwinn, six miles from the base, and college courses are available for adults from the Northern Michigan University of

Marquette, which offers more than 100 undergraduate courses. Base personnel can work toward a master of science degree in business administration from Michigan Technological University.

Personal Services. K. I. Sawyer has a fifteen-bed USAF hospital that offers full medical care for active-duty and retired personnel and their families. Family dental care is available on a space-available basis only. The base also offers a base exchange and concessions, a commissary, a service station, banking facilities, and officers and NCO club systems.

Recreation. Recreation facilities include an eighteen-hole golf course; a bowling alley; auto, woodworking, ceramics, and photography hobby shops; a recreation center; and a fitness center. The base also operates a ski hill with two tows and Little Trout Lake, which is a well-stocked body of water that offers not only fishing but also swimming and picnicking.

The Local Area. K. I. Sawyer is located twenty-three miles southeast of Marquette, a city of more than 22,000 people. Marquette is situated in Michigan's Upper Peninsula area, that part of the state bordered on the north by Lake Superior and by Lake Michigan on the south and Lake Huron on the east. Only a few miles to the east of the base is the Hiawatha National Forest, which stretches entirely across the peninsula. There are more than 165,000 acres of parkland in the Upper Peninsula's eighteen state and three national parks.

For more information write to: Public Affairs Office, K. I. Sawyer AFB, MI 49843-5000, or call (906) 372-2828.

SELFRIDGE AIR NATIONAL GUARD BASE

Located twenty-one miles north of Detroit on the shores of Lake Saint Clair, Selfridge ANGB is one of the most active and diverse military installations in the country, supporting the needs of the Army, Navy, Marine Corps, Air Force, and Coast Guard.

History. Selfridge was officially activated as a military installation on 1 July 1917 as Selfridge Field, named in honor of 1st Lt. Thomas E. Selfridge, the first person to die in an aircraft accident. It was designated Selfridge Air Force Base in 1947, and Selfridge Air National Guard Base on 1 July 1971. Today Selfridge hosts units of the Michigan Air National Guard; the Army's Tank Automotive Command; the Navy's Naval Air Facility, Detroit; a Marine wing support group; and Coast Guard Air Station, Detroit. The base has an active-duty population of 1,000 personnel from all services, 2,100 civilian workers, and 2,300 family members. In addition, approximately 5,500 reservists and guardsmen train at Selfridge.

Housing and Schools. Base housing is located in two areas: Main Base, which has a total of 477 units for senior officers and junior enlisted personnel; and Sebille Manor, three miles from the base, which has quarters for 162 officers and 218 NCOs and warrant officers. Off-base housing is expensive. A one-bedroom unfurnished apartment rents for about $400 per month with $40 to $120 a month for utilities, depending on the season.

Selfridge also has a twenty-seven-room facility for transient personnel that costs $32 a night for personnel on leave, $23 a night for VIPs, and $21.50 a night for all others. The base guest house offers sixteen units for $16 to $19 per night. Bachelor quarters consist of seventeen rooms for officers at $5.40 to $6.00 per day, and twenty-one rooms for NCOs, at $4.50 per day. Unaccompanied enlisted personnel are accommodated in a barracks that has facilities for fifty-two Army personnel and another that has ninety-five rooms for Navy personnel.

Children attend schools in the local area. An on-base child-care facility can accommodate 123 children ages six weeks to twelve years. Adult off-duty college courses are available at the base education center through Northwood Institute.

Personal Services. Outpatient medical care is provided by a U.S. Army health clinic and a dental clinic. Emergency and specialized care are available at local community hospitals.

The Selfridge base exchange system consists of a main store and three branches. The main store includes barber and beauty shops, a dry cleaner and laundry, a snack bar, and an Anthony's Pizza. Banking facilities and a beverage store are also available. Selfridge has a large, well-stocked commissary, and there is a gas and service station on the base.

Recreation. Selfridge ANGB has an officer and NCO/enlisted club system offering dining, cocktail lounges, and special events. The Navy operates the Mole Hole enlisted mess, which offers a bar and lounge, cafeteria service, party and catering services, and entertainment.

Indoor recreation includes auto and wood hobby shops, a multicraft center, a photo lab, a bowling center, a fitness center, a library, a large pool, and a theater. For outdoor recreation, there are five tennis courts, two baseball fields, three softball fields, a soccer field, and an eighteen-hole golf course. There are also a rod and gun club with skeet and trap ranges, and an archery club. The outdoor recreation center schedules camping, hiking, and fishing trips as well as equipment rental, boat slip rental reservations, and recreational vehicle storage.

The Local Area. Selfridge sits on Anchor Bay, the northern extension of Lake Saint Clair, which is fed by the Saint Clair River from Lake Huron to the north and flows by the Detroit River into Lake Erie to the south. Ontario province, Canada, is just across the bay from Selfridge. The average temperature in this region is 80° F. in the summer and down to minus 5° F. in the winter. Camping, hiking, fishing, skiing, and hunting opportunities, as well as resorts and historical sites, abound throughout the state.

For more information write to: Commander, USA TACOMSA-Selfridge, Attention: AMSTA-CYAF, Bldg. 780, Selfridge ANGB, MI 48045-5016, or call (313) 466-5903.

WURTSMITH AIR FORCE BASE

Wurtsmith AFB was closed in June 1993.

MISSISSIPPI

Air Force

COLUMBUS AIR FORCE BASE

Columbus Air Force Base opened in 1941 as Kaye Field, an advanced twin-engine flying school that trained 8,000 pilots for the Army Air Corps during World War II. It was closed in 1946 and then reactivated in 1951. Today it is home for the 14th Flying Training Wing (ATC) and 1,800 military personnel, as well as approximately 2,700 military dependents and 1,500 civilian employees.

Housing and Schools. There are over 800 units of family housing at Columbus, mostly duplexes. The area has an affordable cost of living. Off-base housing and rentals are reasonable.

There is a child-development center on the base. Dependent children are bused to Columbus City schools; several parochial and private schools can also be found in the city. Educational opportunities for adults consist of college courses offered by East Mississippi Community College, Mississippi University for Women, Mississippi State University, and the East Mississippi Community College's Vocational-Technical Center.

Personal Services and Recreation. Services available include a seven-bed USAF hospital, a commissary and base exchange, banking facilities, a club system for enlisted personnel and officers, and snack bars. Recreation facilities include two swimming pools; a gymnasium; a nine-hole golf course; a bowling center; a youth activities center; a community center; auto, wood, and ceramics hobby shops; several playground areas; picnic facilities; horse stables; a skeet range; and fishing and sea-sonal hunting areas.

The Local Area. As northeastern Mississippi's largest city, Columbus offers entertainment, shopping, and cultural attractions. Also nearby are two premier schools of the Southeastern Conference: Mississippi State University, a pacesetter in college baseball and basketball; and the University of Alabama and its football tradi-tion of the Crimson Tide. Only hours away are the Atlanta Braves, Falcons and Hawks, and the New Orleans Saints. Memphis, Nashville, Birmingham, New Orleans, and the Florida Panhandle are all popular weekend getaways. Bass fishing, boating and water skiing are popular on the Tennessee-Tombigbee Waterway. Hunting is among the best in the country. A state park and several U.S. Army Corps of Engineers–managed campgrounds are nearby.

For more information write to: Public Affairs Office, 14th Flying Training Wing, 555 Seventh St., Ste. 203, Columbus AFB, MS 39710-1009, or call (601) 434-7068.

KEESLER AIR FORCE BASE

History. During the more than forty-five years Keesler Air Force Base has exist-ed, its mission has been training. During World War II, more than 336,000 men went through the Army Air Forces Technical School and Basic Training Center located there, at the rate of about 17,000 a month. During the Korean War, more than 30,000 technicians were graduated from Keesler's courses every year, and today around 25,000 men and women attend its 250 different courses in such fields as com-puters, avionics, communications, intelligence, personnel, and administration.

Named in honor of 2nd Lt. Samuel Reeves Keesler, Jr., a native Mississippian who gave his life in France during World War I, Keesler's 3,600-acre tract, which is fully inside the city limits of Biloxi, houses the Air Education and Training Command, the 81st Training Wing, and other units. It is home to over 9,000 mili-tary personnel and their 13,000 dependents and a civilian workforce of over 4,000; the average daily student population is another 4,000 military personnel.

Housing and Schools. Keesler has 1,953 family housing units. In addition, the base offers over 1,300 transient units and a fifty-one-space mobile home park.

A child-care center and kindergarten are available at Keesler, and there are parochial and public schools in Biloxi. In addition, a summer day camp is held on base each year for children ages six to thirteen. Biloxi offers adult education courses at Jefferson Davis Junior College and the University of Southern Mississippi.

Personal Services. The Keesler Medical Center is a 350-bed inpatient hospital staffed by more than 1,800 medical personnel, making it the second largest medical facility in the U.S. Air Force. The base also has a complete commissary and exchange system, a club system, and banking facilities.

Recreation. Recreational facilities include two gymnasiums; two recreation cen-ters; two bowling centers, one with twenty-four lanes and the other with twelve; four swimming pools; an eighteen-hole golf course; hobby shops; a marina and picnic park; and two playgrounds for children.

The Local Area. Keesler AFB is located in the city of Biloxi, a historic community on the Gulf of Mexico that has seen many flags in its day: French, English, Spanish, the Republic of West Florida, the United States, Magnolia State, and the state of Mississippi. Jefferson Davis, president of the short-lived Confederacy, lived at Biloxi in his Beauvoir estate for a dozen years, and today the property has been restored to its original condition.

Recreational activities abound in the Biloxi area, from fishing in the Gulf and surrounding bays, bayous, and rivers to hunting. Small game and wildfowl are available in the surrounding woodlands. For sightseeing, New Orleans is not far to the west nor is Mobile, Alabama, to the east. North of Biloxi is the DeSoto National Forest, which offers much in the way of camping, hiking, and fishing. To the south is the Gulf Islands National Seashore Park.

For more information write to: Public Affairs Office, 720 Chappie James, Ste. 101, Keesler AFB, MS 39534-2603, or call (601) 377-2783.

Navy

GULFPORT NAVAL CONSTRUCTION BATTALION CENTER

Gulfport Naval Construction Battalion Center plays an important role in the Seabees' global mission. The Naval Construction Training Center, one of the Seabee Center's major tenant commands, trains over 6,000 students per year in a total of nineteen formal courses and 164 special training courses. Naval mobile construction battalions deploy throughout the world, while individual Seabees may be called upon any time to undertake specialized assignments anywhere in the world.

History. The Navy first occupied the Gulfport site in June 1942 as an advanced base depot. The Naval Construction Battalion Center was established there in 1952. Today the center is home for the 20th Naval Construction Regiment (Naval Mobile Construction Battalions 1, 7, 74, and 133), the Marine and Naval Reserve Centers, and the Training Center.

Housing and Schools. One hundred sets of enlisted family quarters are available at Gulfport. These quarters consist of sixteen five-bedroom and eighty-four four-bedroom units. There are also seven sets of officer quarters consisting of single houses and duplexes. In addition, the center provides spaces for twenty-five mobile homes.

Although there is no dependent schooling at the center, a child-care facility is provided. The Navy Campus offers advice and assistance to active-duty personnel and their dependents who desire to pursue college courses during their off-duty hours.

Personal Services. Medical care is provided by the Naval Aerospace and Regional Medical Center branch clinic located at the center. Personnel who require care beyond the scope of that provided at the branch clinic are referred to the USAF medical center at Keesler AFB, a 340-bed facility, or to the NRMC itself, at Pensacola, Florida.

The Navy exchange provides a retail store with 16,000 feet of display space, while the commissary store carries more than 3,500 line items.

Recreation. An enlisted sports club is available, as are a nine-hole golf course, a twelve-lane bowling center, a gymnasium, automotive and hobby shops, two swimming pools, and a recreation park and fishing lake.

The Local Area. The city of Gulfport lies about ten miles west of Biloxi and some sixty miles east of New Orleans, along the Gulf of Mexico. The entire Gulf coast area is famous for its fishing and the easy and gracious style of life the people there enjoy. With a generally mild climate, residents enjoy outdoor activities year-round. The nearby communities of Long Beach, Bay Saint Louis, Pass Christian, and Ocean Springs provide many opportunities for recreation and sightseeing.

For more information write to: Public Affairs Office, NCBC, Gulfport, MS 39501, or call (601) 871-2393.

Gulfport Naval Construction Center Headquarters is important to the mission of the Seabees. (U.S. Navy photo)

MERIDIAN NAVAL AIR STATION

The 1993 Base Realignment and Closure Commission recommended closing Meridian NAS, but at press time no firm date had yet been announced.

Meridian Naval Air Station is situated fifteen miles northeast of downtown Meridian, a community that considers itself a part of the Navy "family" and whose citizens freely admit their town is a better place to live because of the men and women of the U.S. Navy.

History. Meridian NAS was commissioned as a naval auxiliary air station on 14 July 1961 and later redesignated as a naval air station in July 1968. The main base occupies more than 8,000 acres with an additional 4,000 under its control at the outlying field, Joe Williams, and the Sea Ray target facility. Meridian is home for Commander, Training Air Wing One; the Naval Technical Training Center; two training squadrons; various tenant commands; and over 4,000 military personnel, civilian employees, and dependents.

Housing and Schools. There are 520 military family housing units onboard Meridian. Assignments are made according to the applicant's rank, family composition, and category of quarters needed. While the station does not offer a Navy Lodge, the billeting office complex is capable of housing over 700 male and female personnel.

Dependent schooling is conducted off base in the various public and private schools situated in Lauderdale County. Higher education is available at the Meridian Junior College campus, which offers both day and night courses. In addition, a degree-granting branch of Mississippi State University, located on the Meridian campus, enables military personnel to obtain college credits leading to master's degrees. College courses are also offered on station.

Personal Services. Medical care is provided by a modern, well-equipped branch medical clinic. Specialty care and hospitalization are available at Pensacola, Florida, or through civilian sources locally.

The Navy exchange and commissary mall is a unique feature of life onboard Meridian Naval Air Station. It provides all the conveniences of a small shopping center and is centrally located. The mall houses a commissary store, a bank, a Navy exchange, a bowling alley, a beauty shop, a laundry and dry-cleaning facility, a tailor, a uniform shop, a McDonald's, a country store, and a service station.

Recreation. Mississippi is famous as an "outdoor" state, because of its mild climate year-round. At Meridian there are an eighteen-hole golf course; two swimming pools; tennis and racquetball/handball courts; a riding stable with many backwoods trails; boating, hunting, and fishing in season; and the boisterous camaraderie of the Sportsmen's Association. For those who enjoy indoor activities as well, the station offers a library stocked with 12,000 books and subscriptions to over 60 newspapers and magazines, a new gymnasium, all-hands and enlisted clubs, an auto hobby shop, and a wood shop.

The Local Area. The city of Meridian is home to about 47,000 people and boasts a fine public school system, a sixty-five-piece symphony orchestra and symphony chorus, and 104 churches representing twenty-five different denominations.

The Meridian area Navy League supports the military community in many ways, two of which are the Military Citizen of the Year award and Flight Instructor of the Year award.

Meridian is 155 miles southwest of Birmingham, Alabama, 90 miles east of Jackson, Mississippi, 247 miles north of New Orleans, and 180 miles north of Pensacola, Florida. Vicksburg, about 120 miles west of the station, is the site of one of the most important sieges and battles of the Civil War, and nearer by is the Lake Okatibbee Reservoir, 4,000 acres licensed to the Mississippi Game and Fish Commission for public hunting.

For more information write to: Public Affairs Officer, Box 23, Naval Air Station Meridian, MS 39309, or call (601) 679-2211.

PASCAGOULA NAVAL STATION

One of our newest naval installations, Pascagoula Naval Station is located on Singing River Island, ten miles from the Gulf of Mexico, thirty-five miles east of Gulfport, Mississippi, and thirty-five miles west of Mobile, Alabama. Ground-breaking ceremonies for construction of the installation took place on 28 May 1988. Personnel moved onto the installation in January 1991, and it was officially opened 4 July 1992.

Today Pascagoula is home port for four Perry-class guided missile frigates of the Atlantic Fleet: the *Gallery*, the *Stephen W. Groves*, the *Jack Williams*, and the *John L. Hall*. In the late fall of 1993 its complement was 1,000 active-duty personnel, 200 civilian employees, and about 1,000 family members. At press time, the population was expected to increase significantly, to about 2,300 personnel, as vessels ported at Mobile Naval Station were transferred to Pascagoula when their base closed in June 1994.

Housing, Schools, and Personal Services. There are no family quarters at Pascagoula Naval Station. Navy families live in Pascagoula, a town of about 29,000, and in the surrounding communities, and their children attend local public schools. On the station itself are accommodations for 140 unaccompanied sailors. Medical care is provided by branch medical and dental clinics, with inpatient care available at nearby Keesler Air Force Base or local community hospitals. There is a small exchange but no commissary at Pascagoula. Recreation is offered in the form of a sports and fitness center, and all the facilities of Keesler Air Force Base and Gulfport Naval Construction Battalion Center, about thirty miles west of Pascagoula, are open to Pascagoula personnel.

The Local Area. Pascagoula Naval Station is a model for environmental quality. It was constructed with no asbestos or lead and has modern in-ground tanks and an ongoing recycling program. The pier, connected by a 2.8-mile causeway to the mainland, is a state-of-the-art double-deck structure, one of only six such facilities in the Navy today.

For more information write to: Commanding Officer, Naval Station Pascagoula, Attention: Public Affairs, Pascagoula, MS 39567-5000, or call (601) 761-2002.

U.S. NAVAL HOME, ARMED FORCES RETIREMENT HOME

The U.S. Naval Home (USNH) facility of the Armed Forces Retirement Home, located on the Mississippi Beach in Gulfport, has a long and distinguished history as "a comfortable harbor" for sailors, Marines, and Coast Guard members. (For details on the overall policies pertaining to the operation of the Armed Forces Retirement Home, see the entry for the U.S. Soldiers' and Airmen's Home, Washington, D.C.)

Sanctioned on 10 July 1832 by Congress "to provide an honorable and comfortable home for old and disabled personnel of the Navy and Marine Corps, and the Coast Guard while operating as a part of the Navy, who are entitled to benefits of the institution," the original home was established in 1833 on land once owned by the William Penn family in Philadelphia, where it remained until August 1976.

The present-day home stands on the grounds that were once those of the Gulf Coast Military Academy, a military preparatory school for boys founded in the early years of this century.

The home is ideally situated about 75 miles east of New Orleans NAS and 100 miles west of Pensacola NAS, which offer many attractions and services. Locally there is ample shopping and entertainment. Both Gulfport and nearby Biloxi are resort-oriented communities offering a wide variety of outdoor activities. The weather is generally mild, almost tropical.

The home now welcomes retired soldiers and airmen, although most of the members are from the sea services. In addition to medical care, the home provides residents with private rooms, complete dining and food services, a barber/beauty shop, a movie theater, an exercise room, a swimming pool, chapel services, a greenhouse, a post office, banking services, a bowling alley, and an overpass to the beach.

The single rooms are furnished with a bed, a built-in desk, a nightstand, a lamp, and a chair. Each room has a half bath with lavatory and toilet. Communal showers and baths are located on each floor. The home provides an ideal setting in a thriving resort community. Members can participate in home volunteer activities, community activities, recreation, entertainment, arts, and pure relaxation. A user fee is charged each resident equal to 25 percent of any federal payments he or she receives each month.

All in all, the U.S. Naval Home is today what it always was intended to be: "A home . . . for the faithful tar who has been either worn out or maimed in fighting the battles of his country. A comfortable harbor . . . where he may safely moor and ride out the ebb of life, free from the cares and storms by which he has been previously surrounded."

For more information write to: Director, U.S. Naval Home, 1800 Beach Dr., Gulfport, MS 39507-1597, or call (800) 332-3527.

MISSOURI

Air Force

WHITEMAN AIR FORCE BASE

Whiteman Air Force Base is located two miles south of Knob Noster, a community of 2,300 souls. One might well ask how the town and the base derived their interesting names. Early settlers named the town after the Latin *noster*, which means "our," and two knobs or hills that overlook the original townsite. The base got its name in honor of 2nd Lt. George A. Whiteman, the first aviator to die in combat in World War II. Lt. Whiteman was a native of Sedalia, nineteen miles to the east of the base.

History. Whiteman AFB opened in 1942 as the Sedalia Army Air Field and was renamed in 1951. Today it is home to the 351st Strategic Missile Wing. The wing is responsible for 150 Minuteman II ICBMs based within a 10,000-square-mile area of Missouri countryside. The 509th Bomb Wing, home of the B-2 bomber, was activated there in 1993. Approximately 8,600 people—military personnel and their families, and civilian employees—live and work at Whiteman.

Housing and Schools. There are 978 units of government housing available at Whiteman.

The Whiteman Elementary School provides educational services for children in kindergarten through fourth grade; older children attend schools off base in the communities of Knob Noster, Warrensburg, and Sedalia. A child-care center for 150 children is operated on base. On-base college courses are available from Central Missouri State University, Park College, and Georgia Military College.

Personal Services. Personal services available at Whiteman include a twenty-five-bed USAF hospital, an eight-million-dollar complex that provides both inpatient and outpatient services. Banking facilities, a commissary with over 17,000 square feet of space, a base exchange, a community center, and officers and NCO clubs are also part of the scene at Whiteman. Plans are being made for a new service station, following completion of the commissary expansion now under way.

Recreation. Recreational facilities include an eighteen-hole, 6,525-yard golf course; a recreation center; a sixteen-lane bowling center; a gymnasium; two large outdoor swimming pools; and Peace Park, where static aircraft displays are set up. There are also an outdoor picnic area, two base lakes for fishing, a library, and a 350-seat base theater that offers a Cinemascope screen.

The Local Area. Whiteman is located about sixty-five miles east of Kansas City and Independence. Jefferson City, the state capital, is approximately eighty miles to the east of the base. About fifty miles southeast of the base is the Lake of the Ozarks Recreation Area, Grand Arm. The facility is operated by the Army at Fort Leonard Wood and contains forty trailers, eight camper spaces, and twenty tent sites, and provides camping, fishing, boating, hiking, and water skiing, as well as sporting equipment rentals.

Not quite so far away is Knob Noster State Park, a wooded recreational area covering 3,400 acres where fishing, camping, picnicking, and swimming are available. The state of Missouri affords a wide variety of outdoor activities and points of interest. There are, for instance, more than 4,000 caves in the state, twenty-three of them commercially operated with guided tours.

For more information write to: Public Affairs Division, 351st Strategic Missile Wing, Whiteman AFB, MO 65305-5000, or call (816) 687-3727.

Army

FORT LEONARD WOOD

Spread over 63,000 acres in the south-central Missouri Ozarks, Fort Leonard Wood (called Fort Wood locally) is one of the larger Army training centers in the United States. Surrounded on three sides by the Mark Twain National Forest, Fort Wood is a clean, fresh, and unspoiled location where the military has managed to blend its activities with nature.

History. Named after Maj. Gen. Leonard Wood, Medal of Honor winner in the Geronimo Campaign of 1886, the post was established as a basic-training center in 1940. Since then, Fort Wood has introduced more than one million men and women to the Army. With the transfer of the U.S. Army Engineer Center and School from

Fort Belvoir, Virginia, to Fort Leonard Wood in May 1988, Fort Wood became the home of the Army Engineers, and its name was officially changed to the U.S. Army Engineer Center and Fort Leonard Wood.

Housing and Schools. Fort Wood is a completely self-contained installation providing every service and facility required by a community of well over 30,000. Fort Leonard Wood has two main housing areas for military families, consisting of more than 2,800 sets of quarters that range in size from two- to four-bedroom units. Waiting lists are established by a date of eligibility based on the date of departure from the previous duty station. Seventy guest-house units are also available for the use of authorized personnel and their families and guests. These facilities cannot be reserved. In addition, there are 340 units of bachelor officer and NCO housing on post.

On-post schools provide dependent children with educational facilities from kindergarten through the eighth grade. The Army education center provides educational opportunities ranging from the basic skills education program to graduate-level courses offered by Drury and Webster Colleges and the University of Missouri. In addition, Columbia and Central Texas Colleges offer on-post undergraduate courses.

Personal Services. General Leonard Wood Army Community Hospital is an extremely modern, 500-bed facility that provides the military community with excellent medical care. The post has a main exchange and five branch exchanges, a garden shop, and a toy store. There is also a very large main commissary plus two convenience stores.

Recreation. Fort Wood has a vigorous recreation services program ranging from libraries to golfing, swimming, bowling, and intramural sports. Outdoor recreation facilities and activities are also available on post. A twenty-five-mount riding academy is maintained by the morale support activities division on the post, and the Big Piney hiking and riding trail is located only six miles south of the post. The trail winds seventeen miles through a variety of Ozark terrain.

The Fort Leonard Wood Lake of the Ozarks Recreation Area, a 360-acre tract bounded on one side by the Lake of the Ozarks, is located fifteen miles northeast of Camdenton, a sixty-minute drive from the post. In addition to a post exchange snack bar and a warm-weather pavilion with a dance floor, the site offers forty air-conditioned trailers, a swimming area, picnic grounds, campsites, and a marina.

The Local Area. Fort Leonard Wood's central location provides convenient access to major cities and tourist attractions of the Midwest. Saint Louis is 135 miles northeast; Springfield, 85 miles southwest; and Rolla, 28 miles northeast. Saint Robert (population 1,400) is immediately outside Fort Wood's main gate, and Waynesville (population 3,500) is seven miles northwest.

For more information write to: Headquarters, U.S. Army Engineer Center and Fort Leonard Wood, Attention: Community Services Office, Fort Leonard Wood, MO 65473-5000, or call (314) 596-1126.

MONTANA

Air Force

MALMSTROM AIR FORCE BASE

Malmstrom Air Force Base is located two miles east of Great Falls in "Big Sky country," prairie land 3,300 feet above sea level. The area was visited by the Lewis and Clark expedition in 1805, which duly noted the "great falls" of the Missouri River located there.

History. Known as Great Falls Army Air Force Base when it opened in 1945, the installation was renamed in 1955 in honor of Col. Einar Axel Malmstrom, who was killed nearby in the crash of a T-33 jet. Today its host unit is the 43rd Air Refueling Wing, which flies the KC-135 Stratotankers. The major tenant unit is the 341st Missile Wing, which is responsible for 50 Minuteman III and 150 Minuteman II missiles spread out over 23,000 square miles of Montana countryside.

Housing and Schools. Malmstrom has over 1,400 units of government housing. While there are no dependent schools on the base, there is a child-care center, and public and parochial schools are available off base in Great Falls. The base education center offers on-base courses from the College of Great Falls, Embry-Riddle Aeronautical University, Park College, and Northern Montana University.

Personal Services and Recreation. Services available at Malmstrom include a new Air Force clinic, a new commissary, a base exchange, banking facilities, and officers and NCO clubs. Recreational facilities include a swimming pool, a sixteen-lane bowling center, an arts and crafts center, and auto, welding, and wood crafts shops. A sports arena provides various facilities for sports and physical fitness. The base also operates a family camp open from 1 May to 31 October that offers ten camper spaces with all hookups.

The Local Area. More than 1,500 lakes are to be found in the state of Montana, many of them excellent fishing spots. Game that can be hunted includes moose, elk, deer, antelope, grizzly and black bear, fur-bearing animals, varmints, and game birds.

Two major national parks, Yellowstone and Glacier, are located in the state, and the area around Great Falls is dotted with thousands of acres of woodland comprising the Lewis and Clark and Helena National Forests. Helena, the capital of Montana, is about 70 miles south of Great Falls. The Canadian border is about 120 miles north of the base. Modern travelers to Montana are as impressed by the state's vast natural beauty as were the men of the Lewis and Clark expedition of 1805.

For more information write to: 43rd ARW Public Affairs Office, 7015 Goddard Dr., Malmstrom AFB, MT 59402-6863, or call (406) 731-4044.

NEBRASKA

Air Force

OFFUTT AIR FORCE BASE

The earth has turned many times since the men of the 22nd U.S. Infantry established Fort Crook in 1896. Today what used to be called Fort Crook, a post that was home to the foot-slogging infantry, is the control center for one of the most awesome fleets of modern weapons ever assembled.

The first landing strip was built at Offutt in 1921, and in 1924 it was named Offutt Field in honor of 1st Lt. Jarvis Jennes Offutt, a native of Omaha who was killed in an air crash during World War I. Offutt is the home of Headquarters, U.S. Strategic Command, and more than 10,000 active-duty personnel and civilian employees. The host unit at Offutt is the 55th Wing, which has the mission of conducting global electronic and scientific reconnaissance missions. U.S. Strategic Command is a unified command combining Air Force and Navy strategic forces. From its Offutt headquarters, it exercises operational control of all strategic weapons through various task-force commanders.

Housing and Schools. There are 484 officer and 2,169 enlisted housing units at Offutt. Sixty-two units of temporary housing, and visiting and bachelor officer quarters are also available; single enlisted personnel live in dormitory housing clustered near the base exchange, commissary, and recreation area. Apartment rental prices in the area vary greatly. A two-bedroom apartment ranges from $300 to $400 per month. New homes in Plattsmouth start at around $60,000; in Papillion, the range is from $80,000 to $120,000.

Three elementary schools, a preschool, and a child-care center are operated on the base. Junior and senior high school students attend local schools. For adults wishing to extend their education, the base education office offers on-base programs leading to bachelor's degrees from such institutions as the University of Nebraska, Southern Illinois University, and Embry-Riddle Aeronautical University. Graduate programs are offered from the University of Nebraska, the University of Oklahoma, Creighton University, and Embry-Riddle.

Personal Services. The Ehrling Bergquist USAF Regional Hospital at Offutt offers excellent medical care to military personnel and their families. A base exchange and three mini exchanges provide military shoppers with numerous retail bargains, and the base commissary is a completely modern facility offering over 10,000 items stocked in 32,000 square feet of sales space.

Recreation. Recreational facilities at Offutt extend from hobby and arts and crafts shops to an eighteen-hole golf course, a twenty-lane bowling center, and a complete gymnasium. There are also four swimming pools, a movie theater, a recreation center, and officers and NCO clubs. The base family camp, located on the shores of a well-landscaped, man-made lake, offers ten camper spaces with electricity and other facilities. Picnicking and fishing can be enjoyed there, and camping and fishing equipment may be rented on the site.

The Local Area. Offutt is located about ten miles south of Omaha on the outskirts of the city of Bellevue, a community of over 32,000 people situated on the banks of the Missouri River. Omaha, a city of over 600,000, dominates the immediate vicinity and offers many recreational opportunities to the personnel stationed at Offutt, from live theater and excellent dining to ballet and football.

The weather in the Omaha area is diverse. Summer temperatures usually average below 90° F. In winter the average temperature is 33° F. Depending on whether you're an optimist or a pessimist, the sun shines about half the time or it's overcast half the time.

For more information write to: Public Affairs Division, Offutt AFB, NB 68113-3206, or call (402) 294-3663.

NEVADA

Air Force

NELLIS AIR FORCE BASE

If a military installation can be said to have a personality, that of Nellis Air Force Base is clearly split between the sparkle and glitter of Las Vegas, 8 miles to the southwest, and the Department of Energy's Nuclear Testing Site, located in the 1,350-square-mile Nellis Range that begins some 65 miles northwest of the city. Frenchman Flat and Yucca Flat are the primary weapons testing sites, although only Yucca and Pahute Mesa are used for atomic-weapons testing these days, and the "bangers" are all set off underground anyway.

History. Named in honor of Lt. William Nellis, a Nevadan who was killed in combat over Europe in 1944, Nellis was established as an Army Air Corps gunnery school in 1941. Today it is home of the USAF Tactical Fighter Weapons Center, which is charged with the mission of developing fighter tactics, training, and testing.

Nellis also controls the Indian Springs Desert Warfare Training Center situated on the southern edge of the bombing and gunnery range, about forty-five miles northwest of the main base. The only one of its kind in the Air Force, the center trains active-duty, Air National Guard, and Air Force Reserve security police personnel in desert ground combat tactics.

Housing and Schools. There are over 1,400 sets of government family quarters at Nellis and 100 transient facilities for short-term occupancy, principally for incoming and departing personnel on permanent-change-of-station orders.

Child-care and preschool programs are available on base. Community College of Southern Nevada, Embry-Riddle Aeronautical University, the University of

Phoenix, and the University of Nevada–Las Vegas all offer undergraduate college courses as well as programs leading to associate and graduate degrees.

Personal Services. Medical care is provided by a thirty-five-bed hospital. A joint Air Force–Department of Veterans Affairs medical center is scheduled to open near the base in the spring of 1994. Base commissary and exchange facilities, including annexes at Indian Springs, are offered, along with numerous base exchange concessions.

Recreation. Recreational facilities include a recreation center, a gymnasium, swimming pools, bowling lanes, a golf course, hobby and craft shops, an open mess system, and two youth centers.

The Nellis Rod and Gun Club provides information concerning local hunting and fishing sites and licensing procedures. Trout and bass are plentiful in local streams and lakes, and dove, pheasant, quail, and other game birds (as well as big game) may be hunted in the surrounding countryside.

The Local Area. Las Vegas, with a population of more than 310,000, deserves its title of "Entertainment Capital of the World." Not only do its world-famous casinos and hotels cater to the millions of tourists who come here each year to gamble, but they offer shows that regularly feature some of the world's greatest stars.

If you fancy the priceless treasures of the outdoors, Hoover Dam and the Lake Mead Recreation Area are only a few miles from the base. A dry climate makes for comfortable living year-round. Three national parks, Bryce, Zion, and Grand Canyon North Rim, are situated within easy driving distance of the base, and the Nellis Community Center offers special rates to service personnel and their families at nearby ski resorts.

For more information write to: Public Affairs Office, Ste. 221, 4370 N. Washington Blvd., Nellis AFB, NV 89191-7078, or call (702) 652-2750.

Navy

FALLON NAVAL AIR STATION

If your children grow up to become swaggering, carousing old salts, they won't have learned their bad habits at Fallon Naval Air Station. A state famous for its legalized gambling, Nevada frowns upon minors participating, and anyone under the age of twenty-one caught gambling is subject to the full power and majesty of Nevada's legal system.

History. The station was commissioned in 1944 as an auxiliary station under the control of Alameda Naval Air Station, California, and redesignated a naval air station in January 1972. Today it is home to approximately 2,300 naval personnel and civilian employees who provide services for the Navy squadrons that deploy there for weapons delivery training carried out among the thousands of acres of four impact areas situated in the surrounding desert.

Housing and Schools. There are 301 sets of family quarters available at Fallon, including 70 two-bedroom units adjacent to the main gate. A Navy Lodge offers 5 three-bedroom and 1 two-bedroom cottage-type units for transients and visitors, with permanent-change-of-station personnel getting priority.

Dependents schooling is available for grades one through twelve in the nearby Churchill County School System. Child care is also available. High school completion programs are available at Fallon, and Western Nevada Community College at Fallon offers various associate's degree programs.

Personal Services. A new commissary store, a Navy exchange, an enlisted and officers club system, and a dispensary are located at Fallon. Most specialty and inpatient care required by dependents is handled under the CHAMPUS program with local physicians; the nearest military medical facility capable of handling these situations is the Naval Regional Medical Center at Oakland, California.

Recreation. Because the sun shines over Fallon an average of ten months out of the year, outdoor recreation of all kinds can be enjoyed there. The station offers a go-cart speedway, two lighted tennis courts, horseshoe pits, three picnic areas, a basketball court, three softball fields, and a fitness trail. Indoor recreation in the form of a gymnasium, a hobby shop and auto shop complex, and an indoor swimming pool are also offered. Hunting and fishing are permitted on the station, and boating can be enjoyed at Lake Lahontan just west of Fallon. Skiing is available at twenty-five resorts located within a 150-mile radius of the station. There are numerous clubs and social organizations in Fallon, such as the Fallon Footlighters Community Theater Group and the Churchill County Arts Association. Charter bus tours to various point of interest are frequently arranged through the special services office. Some casinos at Reno even provide bus service to and from the base.

The Local Area. The city of Fallon has a population of 4,500 and is the principal city in Churchill County. Reno is approximately seventy miles to the west. The area boasts several ghost towns, including Fairview, Wonder, and Rawhide.

One of the most interesting natural features of the area is Sand Mountain, twenty-four miles east of Fallon, where strange vibrating moans and roars greet you as you climb the mountain. Scientists believe the noises are caused by heat, friction, and possibly electrical forces. Others think they are the echoes of the poor souls who have lost their money in Reno's casinos.

For more information write to: Public Affairs Office, NAS, Fallon, NV 89406, or call (702) 426-2880.

NEW HAMPSHIRE

Air Force

PEASE AIR FORCE BASE

After more than thirty-four years of service to the nation, Pease Air Force Base was deactivated on 1 October 1990. Today the facilities there are being looked after by a small caretaker force of civilian personnel.

Navy

PORTSMOUTH NAVAL SHIPYARD

History. The Portsmouth Naval Shipyard was authorized in 1799. The first vessel built there was the USS *Washington*, a seventy-four-gun ship, but the first ship built along the Piscataqua was HMS *Falkland* in 1690, perhaps the first warship ever built in North America. During the Revolution, several ships were constructed in this area for the Continental Navy, including John Paul Jones's flagship, USS *Ranger*.

As the only naval shipyard solely responsible for the repair and overhaul of nuclear submarines, Portsmouth is not open to visits by the general public, but active-duty or retired personnel and their dependents are authorized the use of all personnel support, morale, and welfare facilities located on the base. The base population consists of 104 active-duty personnel, their 1,300 family members, 5,700 civilian employees, and an average of about 1,000 active-duty sailors in port at any given time.

Housing and Schools. There are 234 sets of family quarters at the shipyard—34 officer and 200 enlisted. Enlisted housing is very new and consists of units with two, three, and four bedrooms. Temporary lodging is available for officers and enlisted personnel, but reservations are required.

Dependent schooling is available in the local area, and a child-development center is operated on the base. The University of New Hampshire at Durham, a few miles to the west of Portsmouth, offers programs to active-duty personnel, as do other small colleges in the area.

Personal Services. There is a small Navy exchange at Portsmouth. An officers, CPO, and enlisted club system is operated at Portsmouth. Outpatient medical care is available at the Navy Medical Clinic.

Recreation. Recreational facilities and activities offered include bowling, a hobby shop, a library, a gymnasium, billiard tables, and tennis, squash, and handball courts. Outdoor activities include ice skating, a marina and boat launch area, and swimming and picnicking on Jamaica Island at the far end of the base during the summer months. Licensed freshwater fishing is permitted at Meade Pond; saltwater fishing off Pier 15 is authorized in the back channel with no license required. Hunting and fishing licenses may be purchased at the morale, welfare, and recreation office, where complete information may also be obtained concerning base activities as well as events in the surrounding area. The MWR office also assists in purchasing tickets for events as far away as Boston.

The Local Area. Portsmouth Naval Shipyard is located on Seavey's Island, across the mouth of the Piscataqua River from the city of Portsmouth. The town of Kittery, Maine (population 10,000), is just to the north across the back channel, via the causeway. Kittery was the home port for John Paul Jones's *Ranger;* the first U.S. submarine, L-8, was built at Kittery in 1917.

The Portsmouth area has an average annual temperature of 45° F., with minimums as low as minus 12° F. and highs of 95° F. Snowfall averages about seventy-two inches per year and rainfall, forty-two inches annually. Moose and White Mountains lie just to the north of Portsmouth, and the immediate area has many good camping sites and opportunities for outdoor recreational activities for all seasons, including sightseeing.

For more information write to: Public Affairs, Portsmouth Naval Shipyard, Portsmouth, NH 03804-5000, or call (207) 438-1260.

NEW JERSEY

Air Force

McGUIRE AIR FORCE BASE

As the Air Mobility Command's largest aerial port of embarkation on the East Coast, McGuire Air Force Base has earned its title as the "Gateway to NATO." The AMC terminal at McGuire is a familiar sight to countless numbers of military personnel and their families who have embarked there for flights to Europe and come back into the country again through the same facility.

History. Opened in 1937 as an Army Air Corps facility under the control of nearby Camp Dix, the base was renamed in honor of Maj. Thomas B. McGuire, Jr., a native of Ridgewood, New Jersey, who won the Medal of Honor in World War II. McGuire AFB today covers 4,000 acres of land some eighteen miles south of Trenton, the state capital. It is home to 4,400 military and 1,800 civilian personnel and 9,800 dependents as well as 5,600 Air National Guard and Air Force Reserve personnel. The 438th Airlift Wing is the host unit and flies the C-141B Starlifter.

Housing and Schools. More than 1,700 sets of family quarters are available at McGuire in addition to 176 mobile home spaces. Temporary lodging for families consists of 30 units and is restricted to families traveling on permanent-change-of-station orders. Transient housing is available for about 1,100 personnel. Local housing is both scarce and expensive. A one-bedroom, unfurnished apartment may rent for $350 to $525. Because local landlords require one month's rent in advance and a security deposit equal to one-half the first month's rent, figure on between $1,500 and $2,275 to cover move-in costs.

A child-development center with the capacity of 144 children is operated on base with home care available for another 300 children. School-age children attend public schools in the community of North Burlington, and private and parochial schools are also located in the immediate vicinity. The base education office offers excellent opportunities for service personnel and their families to obtain college credits. Courses are offered by such institutions as Southern Illinois University, Embry-Riddle Aeronautical University, and the University of Southern Colorado.

Personal Services. Medical care is offered by the 438th Medical Group, which has assumed responsibility for the 250-bed Walson Air Force Hospital due to the downsizing of neighboring Fort Dix. The Fort Dix–McGuire AFB base exchange/post exchange complex and Dix/McGuire commissary offer a full range of convenience shopping, including barber and beauty shops, a specialty shop, an optical shop, a photo shop, a car-care center, and a Burger King.

Recreation. Recreational facilities on base include a twenty-four-lane bowling alley; an eighteen-hole, par-seventy-two golf course; a complete gymnasium; a recreation center; auto and craft shops; tennis courts; three swimming pools; and a base movie theater. In addition, the McGuire Aero Club provides the military community the opportunity to learn to fly and to acquire advanced pilot certificates.

The Local Area. The base is only about forty-five miles from Philadelphia, and both Newark and New York City are easily accessible from McGuire. The climate is moderate with warm summers and winter temperatures averaging from 22° F. to 36° F. in January. The summers are modified somewhat by the state's proximity to the Atlantic Ocean. New Jersey boasts 127 miles of excellent beaches.

Recreational activities available in the state range from horse racing at Monmouth Park and other places to fishing, hunting, sailing, and surfing.

For more information write to: Public Affairs Officer, 438th AW/PA, 2901 Falcon Ln., McGuire AFB, NJ 08641-5002, or call (609) 724-1100.

Army

BAYONNE MILITARY OCEAN TERMINAL

Jutting some two and one half miles into New York Harbor, the Military Ocean Terminal, Bayonne (MOTBY), is situated at the very heart of one of the world's greatest metropolitan areas. The terminal is located on a 432-acre, man-made peninsula in Bayonne. Immediately to the west, just across Newark Bay, is the city of Newark. Brooklyn lies less than three miles away to the east across the Hudson River's Upper Bay, and south of Bayonne across the Kill Van Kull is Staten Island. The Statue of Liberty National Monument stands off Jersey City, which is only a five-minute drive north of the terminal.

The basic mission of MOTBY is to accomplish the expeditious movement of Department of Defense–sponsored cargo and privately owned vehicles through installation facilities at the terminal and commercial terminals and piers within its assigned area of responsibility.

MOTBY's headquarters is the Military Traffic Management Command, Eastern Area, which is co-located on the terminal. Sixteen other federal agencies also call MOTBY home, the largest tenant being the Navy's Military Sealift Command, Atlantic.

Housing and Schools. The Bayonne Terminal is limited in some respects. Family housing is restricted to approximately 125 sets of quarters. There are no schools on post for dependent children, but more-than-adequate public schooling is available in the surrounding area. A child-care facility is located on the terminal as well as a youth services center.

Liberty Lodge, a forty-room guest house, is located at the terminal and provides reasonably priced temporary lodging for active-duty and retired military personnel, civilian personnel on temporary duty at MOTBY, and military family members using the Privately Owned Vehicle Processing Center.

Personal Services. Through the U.S. Army Garrison, Bayonne, the installation offers a post exchange, a community club, a library, a movie theater, a bowling alley, an auto repair shop, woodworking and ceramics craft shops, a fitness center, and other morale support facilities. A diner, a bank, a dry cleaner, and a travel office are also available.

The Local Area. The surroundings abound with points of interest. The highly developed New Jersey highway system permits access to a wide variety of shopping centers and vacation spots, including the seashore, professional sports facilities, skiing and boating areas, and cultural attractions simply too numerous to mention. New York City is only fifteen miles to the northwest. Liberty State Park, Jersey City, New Jersey, where a ferry can be boarded to Ellis Island and the Statue of Liberty, is only fifteen minutes from MOTBY. The cost of living is high in the New York City area.

For more information write to: Public Affairs Office, Military Traffic Management Command, Eastern Area, Bayonne, NJ 07002-5302, or call (201) 823-6351.

FORT DIX

From its earliest days, Fort Dix has been dedicated to the development of the "ultimate weapon"—the infantryman. Training is still the major military activity at Fort Dix today, in support of the reserve component now—750,000 man-days in fiscal year 1993 alone.

History. Named after Maj. Gen. John Adams Dix, a nineteenth-century soldier-statesman, Camp Dix was originally established in 1917 as a training post for troops who would fight in Europe during World War I. In 1939, the post was designated a permanent Army installation and renamed Fort Dix. The post was earmarked for semiretirement in 1988, but the 1991 Base Closure and Realignment Commission recommended transition to reserve components training instead, and this was completed in 1993.

Covering more than 30,000 acres of wooded New Jersey countryside—4,000 for maneuvers and training, 13,000 for ranges and impact areas—Fort Dix's ranges can accommodate all weapons from pistols to tanks and eight-inch howitzers. It shares common boundaries with McGuire Air Force Base and Lakehurst Naval Air Station. Major tenants today include the Kelly U.S. Army Reserve Center, the National Guard High Technology Training Center, Walson Air Force Hospital, the Federal Bureau of Prisons, the FBI, the U.S. Coast Guard's Atlantic Strike Team, and the New Jersey Department of Corrections.

Approximately 1,300 active-duty personnel of all services are stationed at Fort Dix along with a civilian employee population of 12,000. The average reserve component training strength at Fort Dix is 23,000 personnel.

Housing and Services. Fort Dix has retained 1,197 sets of family quarters available in one- to four-bedroom units. Guest-house facilities are also offered.

Medical care at Fort Dix is provided by the 464-bed Walson Air Force (formerly Army) Community Hospital. The post exchange and commissary at Fort Dix are both large and well stocked. Recreational facilities include a bowling alley, an eighteen-hole golf course, a sports arena, tennis and handball courts, two swimming pools, a skeet and trap range, and two movie theaters. Picnicking and camping are permitted around the Brindle Lake Recreation Area.

The Local Area. Fort Dix is situated approximately in the center of New Jersey, seventeen miles southeast of Trenton, seventy-two miles south of New York City, and forty-five miles east of Philadelphia. Its climate is generally moderate. Snowfall averages twenty inches per year, and the annual average rainfall is twenty-nine inches. Outdoor recreation—hunting, fishing, camping, and tourism—are available year-round to military personnel stationed at Fort Dix. The installation commander annually designates authorized hunting and trapping areas on the reservation, and permits are sold at the Fort Dix Outdoor Recreation Center.

New Jersey is a state with so much to see and do that the visitor is well advised to "expect the unexpected." Attractions from American Revolution sites to luxurious resorts are available throughout the year. A wide variety of winter sports can be enjoyed at many locations throughout the state.

For more information write to: Public Affairs Office, Fort Dix, NJ 08640-5000, or call (609) 562-4034.

FORT MONMOUTH

Some little-known facts about Fort Monmouth are that it has seventy-nine miles of electric power lines, fifty miles of water lines, forty-one miles of sewage lines, did *not* figure in the Revolutionary War Battle of Monmouth (so Molly Pitcher never slept there), and is right smack dab in the middle of one of the most beautiful resort areas in the northeast.

History. The U.S. Army came to Fort Monmouth on 4 June 1917, and shortly thereafter the site was designated Signal Corps Camp, Little Silver. Later that same year the installation's name was changed to Camp Alfred Vail, in honor of the New Jersey inventor. In 1925, the post was officially designated Fort Monmouth, after the men who died on the Revolutionary War battlefield nearby.

Today the post's 1,560 acres are home to the U.S. Army Communications-Electronics Command, the Army Information Systems Management Activity, Army Chaplain Center and School, U.S. Military Academy Preparatory School, and Joint Interoperability Engineering Organization. Fort Monmouth's population is made up of 2,140 military personnel, 7,600 civilian employees, and about 3,500 military dependents.

Housing and Schools. There are 1,164 units of family housing at Fort Monmouth, situated in three housing areas, one on the main post and two located nearby. The post has a guest house consisting of sixteen rooms and three suites, which are normally available to active-duty and retired personnel and their guests for up to a week at a time. Off post, a one-bedroom apartment rents for $575 during the off season and up to $1,025 during the summer, plus utilities.

The post operates a preschool for dependent children and latch-key and certified child-care home programs. Adult education is available through the education center, which offers college classes from Brookdale Community College, Fairleigh Dickinson University, Kean College, Temple University, and Monmouth College.

Personal Services. Medical care is provided to Fort Monmouth residents by Patterson Army Community Hospital, a thirty-five-bed acute-care health facility. A ten-chair dental clinic provides comprehensive dental care for assigned military personnel and routine care for dependents on a space-available basis.

The post commissary offers 65,000 square feet of shopping space adjacent to a 200-car parking lot. The post exchange is located in the same complex as the commissary. This complex offers one-stop shopping and includes a cafeteria, a barber shop, an optical shop, a watch repair shop, a tailor shop, laundry and dry-cleaning facilities, a credit union and bank, a military clothing sales store, and a four-seasons store. The center has parking for 600 cars.

Recreation. A unique recreational feature at Fort Monmouth is the Army Communications-Electronics Museum, which offers a significant collection of historical equipment and documents that trace the development of Army communications from 1860 to the present day. The newly refurbished Army Chaplains Museum reflects the history of the army chaplaincy back to before the Revolution.

The post also offers a field house with an Olympic-size swimming pool; a twenty-lane bowling center; craft shops; a 1,000-seat movie theater; a library containing 100,000 books, magazines, and newspapers; and an outdoor recreation program that includes an eighteen-hole golf course, tennis courts, garden plots, a marina on Oceanport Creek, and year-round fishing on Husky Brook Pond. There is also a swimming pool at the Charles Wood Housing Area.

The Local Area. Fort Monmouth is located fifty miles south of New York City and forty miles south of Newark International Airport. The post is within easy driving distance of such notable sights and recreation spots as the Monmouth Battlefield and Freehold Raceway to the west, the Atlantic coast to the east,

Gateway National Recreation Area to the northeast, and the megalopolis of New York City to the north. Monmouth Park Racetrack is only five minutes from the post's east gate.

For more information write to: Public Affairs Office, Attention: AMSEL-EA-PA, HQ, U.S. Army Communications-Electronics Command, Fort Monmouth, Fort Monmouth, NJ 07703-5016, or call (908) 532-1409.

Coast Guard

CAPE MAY TRAINING CENTER

Located on a 450-acre point of land between the Atlantic Ocean and Cape May Harbor, a large portion of Cape May Training Center is preserved in its natural state as protected wetlands. In fact, Cape May is the nesting grounds for two species of endangered birds. The Coast Guard began operations on this property in 1948.

The center's mission is to "graduate motivated entry-level enlisted men and women ready and able to serve with a sense of pride and commitment in the nation's finest seagoing service." The training center itself is staffed by 350 active-duty men and women and civilian employees. Also onboard are approximately 500 other personnel assigned to the Cape May Coast Guard Station, Cape May Group and Air Station, and the cutters *Alert, Hornbeam, Matinicus, Point Batan,* and *Point Franklin.*

Housing and Schools. The center maintains 174 family housing units just outside the front gate and leases another 120 along the New Jersey shore. An additional twenty-four two-bedroom family housing units are scheduled for completion during fiscal year 1994. The permanent-party barracks consist of sixty-five rooms. A small transient-lodging facility is available for personnel on orders.

There are no schools on base, but a small child-care facility is available.

Personal Services. Although there is no commissary at Cape May, the exchange does 5 million dollars worth of business a year. Besides a 10,000-square-foot retail store, there are officers and enlisted clubs, a package store, a laundry/tailor shop, a barber/beauty shop, and a uniform shop. The contractor-operated dining facility onboard the center seats 550 on the recruit side, 80 on the permanent-party side, and another 24 in the CPO dining room.

Medical care at Cape May is provided by a twenty-two-bed dispensary staffed by seven Public Health Service medical doctors, seven PHS dentists, and seven civilian nurses. The facility has its own pharmacist and an enlisted staff of fifty-eight hospitalmen. Contract services include a pediatrician, a gynecologist, an optometrist, a psychiatrist, and a dental hygienist. Military retirees and dependents of active-duty personnel are eligible for care on a space-available basis.

Recreation. The center provides two gyms; an Olympic-size swimming pool; two racquetball courts; indoor and outdoor tennis courts; two softball fields; indoor and outdoor volleyball courts; an aerobic, therapy, and weight room; and a steam room with a hot tub. There are also a picnic pavilion and equipment rental of campers, power- and sailboats, canoes, camping equipment, and a fifteen-passenger van for excursions.

The Local Area. Located about ninety miles southeast of Philadelphia at the end of the Garden State Parkway, Cape May is situated in one of the most scenic parts of New Jersey. Atlantic City, about forty-five miles north of the base, is famed for its nightlife and casinos. The nearby resort towns of Wildwood Crest, Wildwood, and North Wildwood have a population of about 5,000 each.

For more information write to: Public Affairs Office, U.S. Coast Guard Training Center, Cape May, NJ 08204-5000, or call (609) 898-6900, ext. 6914.

Navy

EARLE NAVAL WEAPONS STATION

Earle Naval Weapons Station is located in Colts Neck, New Jersey, fifty-four miles south of New York City and seventy-nine miles north of Philadelphia. Founded 13 December 1943, it is named for Rear Adm. Ralph Earle, Chief of the Bureau of Ordnance during World War I.

Earle NWS provides support and home-port services to Atlantic Fleet ammunition ships and is home to Mobile Mine Assembly Group 3, Shore Intermediate Maintenance Activity, Combat Logistics Squadron 2, and the ammunition ships *Seattle*, *Detroit*, *Suribachi*, *Nitro*, and *Butte*. The station's complement is about 400 active-duty personnel and 700 civilian employees.

Housing and Schools. Earle NWS operates 565 units of family housing—37 quarters for officers and 528 for enlisted personnel. There are also 24 DoD homes and 8 mobile home spaces available. There is no dependents schooling on the station, but there is a child-development center that can accommodate 104 children from six weeks to five years of age.

Personal Services. Outpatient medical care is provided by the branch medical clinic and its waterfront annex clinic with referrals to local civilian hospitals or Patterson Army Community Hospital at Fort Monmouth. Among its other services, the clinic offers smoking cessation programs. Although there is no commissary at the station, one is available at Fort Monmouth and McGuire Air Force Base. There are a small Navy exchange and a convenience store at Earle.

Recreation. Earle NWS offers two gyms, three outdoor pools, outdoor tennis courts, ball fields, a fitness center, a youth center, a picnic pavilion, and a bowling center. There are also two all-hands clubs at the station as well as auto and ceramics hobby shops. Hunting is authorized in certain areas onboard the station where rabbit, squirrel, quail, and grouse may be taken in season.

For more information write to: Commander, Naval Weapons Station Earle, Attention: Public Affairs Office, 201 Highway 34 South, Colts Neck, NJ 07722-5000, or call (908) 866-2171.

LAKEHURST NAVAL AIR WARFARE CENTER

Lakehurst is remembered chiefly as the site of the *Hindenburg* disaster that occurred there on 6 May 1937, when the dirigible was destroyed by a fire of undetermined origin during mooring operations. The crash site is just to the front of where the Navy exchange stands today. From 1921 to 1961 Lakehurst was the United States' lighter-than-air airship center, and today Hangar Number One still stands, a remainder of the days when it housed the *Graf Zeppelin*, the *Hindenburg*, and every rigid airship in the U.S. Navy at one time or another. Today it houses the world's largest training aid, a 400-foot aircraft carrier flight deck.

History. Established originally as an ammunition proving ground for the Russian Imperial government in 1915, Lakehurst became a U.S. Army ammunition proving ground in 1917 and was named Camp Kendrick. Camp Kendrick was taken over by the Navy as an air station in 1921. It was redesignated the Naval Air Warfare Center Aircraft Division (NAWCAD), Lakehurst, in 1977. Today the center occupies 7,400 wooded acres approximately sixty miles east of Philadelphia and only ten miles from New Jersey's famed seashore resorts. The total military and civilian population at Lakehurst is over 3,500; NAWCAD has a staff of more than 2,500 personnel, two-thirds of whom are engineers, scientists, and technicians.These people are dedicated to providing quality products and services to the fleet in support of naval aviation.

Housing and Schools. Approximately 220 units of government housing are available at the center, as well as 52 mobile home sites. The Navy exchange operates a Navy Lodge for transients and visitors. Permanent-change-of-station personnel may obtain spaces on a reserved basis at this facility. Although there are no schools for dependent children at the center, there is a day-care facility there and a new one is under construction that will accommodate up to 250 children.

Personal Services and Recreation. NAWCAD lies just to the east of the Fort Dix Military Reservation, so military families stationed there may enjoy the many facilities available at both Fort Dix and McGuire Air Force Base.

The NAEC has both medical and dental facilities, a commissary and exchange, and a consolidated club. The Navy exchange also operates a package store.

Recreational facilities include a bowling center, a golf course, tennis and racquetball courts, a swimming pool, a gymnasium, and a conservation area where hunting and fishing are permitted in season.

The Local Area. Philadelphia is one hour to the west of the center, and New York is about an hour's drive to the north. The northern New Jersey and Catskill ski regions are also nearby, and New Jersey's famous shore resorts are only minutes to the east of the center. NAWCAD is located in the state's famous Pine Barrens, a national reserve, which is studded with beautiful lakes, rivers, and forests offering camping, hunting, hiking, swimming, boating, and fishing.

For more information write to: Public Affairs Office, Code O1P, NAWCAD, Lakehurst, NJ 08753-5041, or call (908) 323-2620.

NEW MEXICO

Air Force

CANNON AIR FORCE BASE

The lowest point in the state of New Mexico is 3,000 feet above sea level. The highest spot is more than 13,000 feet, and Cannon Air Force Base is four-fifths of a mile high at 4,295 feet. This puts Cannon squarely in the high plains country of eastern New Mexico and the Texas Panhandle.

History. Named in honor of Gen. John K. Cannon, one of the nation's outstanding leaders in the development of airpower, Cannon AFB traces its existence back to 1942, when the Army Air Corps took control of the civilian airfield at Clovis and named the site Clovis Army Air Base. Today the base is home to the Air Force's 27th Fighter Wing, which operates the swing-wing F/EF-111 aircraft. The base now covers a land area of almost 4,500 acres and boasts a population of almost 12,000 people: 5,200 military, 460 civilian employees, and 6,800 dependents.

Housing and Schools. There are over 1,200 units of family housing at Cannon with an additional 361 units scheduled to be ready in 1994. The base also has a mobile home park with 56 spaces. There are 42 temporary living units at Cannon, which may be used by families traveling on official orders.

Cannon AFB operates a day-care center and preschool for dependent children. Clovis has several elementary and junior high schools and one high school to which military children living at Cannon are sent. Adult education available at the base includes courses offered by Clovis Community College, Eastern New Mexico University, Chapman College, and other institutions.

Personal Services. Base facilities include a modern and well-equipped twenty-five-bed USAF hospital and a commissary that stocks more than 7,500 line items in its 18,000-square-foot sales area. The base exchange and its concessions as well as a base shopette and several food facilities offer much to the quality of life at Cannon AFB.

Recreation. Recreational facilities include a sixteen-lane bowling alley, an eighteen-hole golf course, and a completely equipped gymnasium. There are also two swimming pools at the base, a skeet and trap range, officers and enlisted clubs, and a recreation center. The outdoor recreation program offers trips and tours throughout the year.

The Local Area. Cannon AFB is situated 7 miles west of Clovis, a town of about 32,000, and is 105 miles west of Lubbock, Texas. Albuquerque, population 285,000, is about 260 miles west of Clovis. The climate in this part of the state is dry, with little rainfall or snowfall during an average year. Although winter temperatures are sometimes low and summers are hot, the low humidity makes them bearable.

Clovis, established in 1906 by the Santa Fe Railway, takes its name from Clovis I, King of the Franks from 461 to 511 A.D. There are eight public parks in Clovis totaling 240 acres and offering recreational activities from bowling to a zoo. Portales, 15 miles south of Cannon, is a city of museums: the Roosevelt County Museum, the Paleo-Indian Institute, the Miles Museum, and the National History Museum are all on the main campus of Eastern New Mexico University; the Backwater Draw Early Man Museum is just a few miles north of town on U.S. Highway 70. All these museums are fitting for a place that has been populated for at least 12,000 years, although the town has been there only since the 1880s.

For more information write to: 27 FW Public Affairs, 100 S DL Ingram Blvd., Ste. 102, Cannon AFB, NM 88103-5216, or call (505) 784-4131.

HOLLOMAN AIR FORCE BASE

Six miles southwest of Alamogordo is Holloman Air Force Base. Nestled between the Sacramento and the San Andreas mountains, the base is home to the 49th Fighter Wing. Holloman's aircraft include the AT-38B, F-4E, and the F-117A stealth fighter.

History. The history of Holloman began in February 1942 when Alamogordo Army Airfield was established on the site. On 16 July 1945, the atomic age was ushered in with the explosion of the first atomic bomb. This took place in the northwest corner of the airfield's bombing range, now known as Trinity Site. In February 1948, the base was renamed after Col. George V. Holloman, a pioneer in the guided-missile-research field.

The 6,000 military and civilian personnel at Holloman are responsible for the base's 55,000 acres, which are spread throughout south-central New Mexico.

Housing and Schools. More than 1,500 units of family housing are available at Holloman, and there is a ten-unit temporary-living facility for families on official orders, who may reserve lodging on a space-available basis only.

Holloman operates a child-care center as well as a school complex that includes kindergarten through grade eight. Middle and senior high schools are available in nearby Alamogordo. The education center offers adults college courses from a variety of institutions including New Mexico State University–Alamogordo, Park College, Troy State, and Central Texas College.

Personal Services. Excellent medical facilities are offered at Holloman in the form of a twenty-bed USAF hospital. William Beaumont Army Medical Center is available in El Paso, Texas, about ninety miles south of the base. Holloman has a commissary stocked with 10,000 line items and a base exchange that features numerous concessions.

Recreation. Recreation facilities at Holloman are also outstanding. The base offers a twenty-four-lane bowling center, a nine-hole golf course, and two swimming pools. A physical fitness center, a consolidated hobby shop, a skeet and trap club, a boarding stable, and a community center are also offered. The Holloman Family Camp, which is open year-round, has twelve camper spaces with all hookups and picnicking as well as fishing and camping equipment rentals.

The Local Area. Holloman AFB is located ten minutes from the White Sands National Monument, which is open year-round. Alamogordo has a population of about 31,000, just large enough to offer the advantages of a modern metropolis and none of the disadvantages such as crowding and pollution.

The climate in this part of New Mexico is dry and hot. Summer temperatures average from the mid-eighties to the mid-nineties, but low humidity, about 35 percent year-round, makes the heat bearable. The winters are fairly mild, with little or no snowfall.

For more information write to: Public Affairs Office, 490 First St., Ste. 2800, Holloman AFB, NM 88330-8277, or call (505) 479-5406.

KIRTLAND AIR FORCE BASE

Kirtland Air Force Base is located on the southeast side of Albuquerque, beside the Albuquerque International Airport. The elevation of the airport is 5,312 feet above sea level. The sun shines there 76 percent of the time, and the humidity averages 30 percent in summer and only 44 percent in the winter.

History. Kirtland AFB was named in honor of Col. Roy C. Kirtland, an early military aviator. Military aviation first came to Albuquerque in 1939. Today the base is home to approximately 150 tenant organizations that comprise a total workforce of 20,200 people. The largest organization at Kirtland is Sandia National Labs, which employs over 7,200 people. Air Force units include the host unit, the 377th Air Base Wing, the 542nd Crew Training Wing, the Air Force Phillips Laboratory, and the Air Force Operational Test and Evaluation Center.

Housing and Schools. There are 2,100 sets of family quarters at Kirtland. The base also offers fifty-eight units in its temporary-living facility, which may be obtained by families traveling on official orders; visitors may be accommodated on a space-available basis only.

A child-care center is operated on the base, and there are three Albuquerque elementary schools located there as well. Junior and senior high school students attend schools in Albuquerque. On-base college programs are offered by Chapman College, Embry-Riddle Aeronautical University, Southern Illinois University, the College of Santa Fe, New Mexico Highlands University, and Webster College. The University of New Mexico is also located in Albuquerque.

Personal Services. The Air Force–VA hospital provides both inpatient and outpatient medical services. The commissary at Kirtland is one of the largest in the Air Force. The base exchange service operates a wide variety of retail stores and concessions; the main exchange building was constructed in 1977 and extended and renovated in 1989.

Recreation. Recreation facilities at the base are quite excellent and include two gymnasiums, four swimming pools, an eighteen-hole golf course, bowling lanes, and many other facilities and programs designed to permit base personnel to make the most of their leisure time. The National Atomic Museum, open seven days a week, is a major tourist attraction. Its displays chronicle the development of nuclear weapons as well as the peaceful development of atomic energy. Films and lecture demonstrations are also offered.

The Local Area. Albuquerque, a city of 400,000 people, was founded by the Spanish in 1706 and takes its name from La Villa de San Francisco de Albuquerque, after the king of Spain's patron saint and the duke of Albuquerque. The city offers residents and visitors over 100 parks, and the Albuquerque Zoo is one of the best in the country.

For more information write to: Public Affairs Division, 377th Air Base Wing, 2000 Wyoming, SE, Kirtland AFB, NM 87117-5606, or call (505) 844-0011.

Army

WHITE SANDS MISSILE RANGE

White Sands Missile Range is a national test range designed to support research, development, testing, and evaluation for the Army, Navy, Air Force, National Aeronautics and Space Administration, and other approved U.S. government agencies and foreign governments. The range also plans and conducts development testing and evaluation of Army missiles, rockets, and materiel systems.

History. White Sands Missile Range is located in south-central New Mexico in a region known as the Tularosa Basin between the Sacramento Mountains on the east and the San Andres and Organ Mountains on the west. The range opened on 9 July 1945 as White Sands Proving Ground. One week later the first atomic bomb was exploded on the range at an area now known as Trinity Site. Missile testing began in September 1945 with Tiny Tim firings and "took off" with captured

German V-2 rockets in 1946. More recently, White Sands served as the landing site for the space shuttle *Columbia* on 30 March 1982, at the Range's Northrup Strip.

Housing and Schools. White Sands has over 840 sets of family quarters. Temporary quarters are usually available for new families. Civilian personnel are authorized on-base housing, on a space-available basis. Sixty-four units are available for unaccompanied military personnel as well.

Dependent children attend school on post from kindergarten through grade eight; high school is available at Onate High in Las Cruces, about a forty-five-minute bus ride from the base. The education center offers college courses from New Mexico State University, Dona Ana Branch of New Mexico State, Troy State University, and Florida Institute of Technology.

Personal Services and Recreation. Medical care is provided by the McAfee U.S. Army Health Clinic, an ultra-modern outpatient medical facility. There is also a dental clinic at White Sands, and as a designated remote facility, the clinic offers comprehensive dental care for military personnel and their families.

The post offers a commissary with 10,000 line items and a post exchange with

Missiles have been tested at White Sands Missile Range, New Mexico, since 1945. (U.S. Army photo)

many concessions such as an optical shop, a flower shop, a cafe, a service station, a video arcade, and a full line of convenience foods.

Recreational facilities include a swimming pool, a golf course, tennis courts, a gymnasium, hobby and craft shops, a park with RV hookups, and camping and hiking areas.

The Local Area. At an elevation of almost 4,000 feet with an average rainfall of only ten inches, White Sands is a dry area with temperatures averaging a high of 92° F. in summer and a low of 36° F. in winter.

Las Cruces, a few miles from the main post, is a community that reflects the blending of three cultures—Indian, Spanish-Mexican, and American. The Pan-American Fiesta brings alive the history of the area, as do other pageants and programs throughout the year; the Indians of Tortugas hold an annual Christmas pageant as they have for centuries. The town also benefits from a wide variety of cultural activities sponsored by New Mexico State University. El Paso, Texas, just to the south, is called the "Gateway to the West," and along with other attractions in the area, Fort Bliss is located there with its many splendid facilities. Within a day's driving, one can see a range of natural features from mountains and Indian ruins to lava beds formed by ancient volcanoes.

For more information write to: Public Affairs Office, Bldg. 122, White Sands Missile Range, NM 88002-5047, or call (505) 678-1134.

NEW YORK

Air Force

GRIFFISS AIR FORCE BASE

It was in the heart of present-day Rome, New York, that the Stars and Stripes first flew in battle, at the siege of Fort Stanwix. The siege lasted from 3 August to 23 August 1777, when the 750-man garrison was finally relieved by forces under the command of Gen. Benedict Arnold. The whole exciting story is admirably told in Walter D. Edmonds's classic, *Drums along the Mohawk.*

History. In 1942, when America was again besieged by its enemies, the Rome Air Depot was established. In 1948, it was renamed in honor of Lt. Col. Townsend E. Griffiss, a Buffalo, New York, pilot who died in an aerial accident in England during the war. Today Griffiss occupies 4,000 acres within the northeastern section of the city of Rome and is home to the Air Force's 416th Bomb Wing. The 416th's mission is to keep its cruise-missile-equipped B-52G bombers flying. A total force of 8,000 military and civilian personnel work around the clock at Griffiss to fulfill that mission.

Housing and Schools. Griffiss has approximately 730 sets of family quarters plus fifty rental lots for mobile homes for the use of military personnel. The waiting time for housing ranges from as little as two months for a three-bedroom unit for junior NCOs to as much as two years for a two-bedroom unit; officers can wait from as little as one month up to as much as fourteen months for quarters. About thirty-five units are available for personnel reporting in or checking out of the base; other transients are accepted in these units on a space-available basis only.

Apartment rents off base range from $350 a month for two-bedroom units up to as much as $550 a month for three-bedroom suites. Two- and three-bedroom homes rent starting at around $450 a month. These figures do not include deposits, usually one month's rent in advance.

While Griffiss does not operate any dependent schools on base, Bellamy Elementary School is within walking distance of the mobile home park, and child care for 230 children is available on the base, including family day care in quarters. The base education center provides on- and off-base educational opportunities for adults in the form of college courses from Mohawk Valley Community College, the State University of New York, Rensselaer Polytechnic Institute, Syracuse University, Utica College, Embry-Riddle Aeronautical University, and the New School for Social Research.

Personal Services. On-base facilities include the twenty-five-bed Griffiss Hospital, which provides inpatient medical care as well as general dental service. The commissary at Griffiss stocks 8,500 line items and also offers shoppers a delicatessen section. The base exchange stocks 22,500 items. Both the commissary and base exchange are housed in a shopping complex that also contains a military clothing sales store; a beverage shop; a grill and hot dog stand; barber, beauty, flower, and optical shops; tailor, laundry, and dry-cleaning shops; and a video-rental concession.

Recreation. Recreational opportunities available at Griffiss include a brand-new co-located club that incorporates officers, enlisted, and golf-course clubhouse facilities; a twenty-lane bowling alley; an Olympic-size swimming pool; a movie theater; a gymnasium; a library with more than 30,000 volumes and approximately 200 periodicals and newspapers; and various craft and hobby shops. Outdoor facilities consist of a ski chalet located on the base and a family camp with hookups for ten self-contained trailers or campers, a thirty-six-par, and a nine-hole golf course.

The Local Area. The city of Rome has a population of about 30,000 and is situated in some of the most scenic country of the northeastern United States. Oneida Lake is fifteen miles to the west. Its twenty-mile length makes it an ideal recreation spot for boating and fishing. The famous Mohawk River flows right through the center of Rome and connects with the Barge Canal on the south side of the city. Syracuse to the west and Utica, Schenectady, Albany, and the Hudson Valley to the east are easily accessible via the New York State Thruway, which lies only a few miles south of Rome. The Adirondack Park begins only a few miles north and east of the base, and Watertown, the Thousand Islands, Canada, and Fort Drum are about sixty-five miles to the north.

For more information write to: 416th Bomb Wing Public Affairs Office, 325 Brooks Rd., Ste. 201, Griffiss Air Force Base, Rome, NY 13441-5401, or call (315) 330-1110.

PLATTSBURGH AIR FORCE BASE

Plattsburgh Air Force Base is unique in that it symbolizes almost every aspect of our national heritage. It is the second oldest military installation in the United States, having been established in 1814. (West Point is a few years older.) Some of the most famous figures in American military history have been stationed there, including Gen. Ulysses S. Grant.

History. The Air Force has been at Plattsburgh only since 1954, although some of the first permanent buildings at the base, built in 1838, are still in use. Today the base is home for the 380th Air Refueling Wing, whose 2,600 people keep the wing's KC-135 air refueling tankers flying. Plattsburgh is today actually two bases in one. The "Old Base" is composed of what was once Plattsburgh Barracks, where the oldest buildings are situated. The base population consists of approximately 2,600 active-duty personnel and 3,700 dependents.

Housing and Schools. There are 1,639 sets of family quarters available at Plattsburgh, and 23 rooms in the temporary living facility for military personnel on permanent-change-of-station orders. (Others are accommodated on a space-available basis.)

The Air Force operates a child-development center on the base. Plattsburgh AFB also hosts two elementary schools accommodating more than 700 students. The base education office offers one of the most extensive on-base adult education programs in the Air Mobility Command. Plattsburgh State University College, Clinton

The "Old Stone Barracks" is one of the historic buildings at Plattsburg Air Force Base. (USAF photo)

Community College, the University of Southern California, and Southern Illinois University are some of the participating institutions.

Personal Services. The new commissary at Plattsburgh is co-located with the base exchange. Nine concessions are available for the convenience of military shoppers and their families. A package store and officers and enlisted clubs are also available. Medical care is provided by a twenty-bed Air Force medical group facility.

Recreation. Recreational facilities at the base include a twelve-lane bowling center, a nine-hole golf course, and two gymnasiums, one with an indoor swimming pool. Also available are wood and hobby shops and a modern recreation center.

The Local Area. Plattsburgh AFB is located just a few miles south of the city of Plattsburgh, virtually on the shores of Lake Champlain. The Canadian border is a few miles north of the city; Montreal is 65 miles north; Burlington, Vermont, is 50 miles to the east; and New York City is 306 miles to the south. Immediately to the west is New York's famed Adirondack Park, but the dominating geographic feature of the area is Lake Champlain itself. This is the land of James Fenimore Cooper's *Leatherstocking Tales* and Kenneth Roberts's *Rabble in Arms*. The last naval battle between the British and American people was fought on the lake near Plattsburgh in September 1814.

For more information write to: 380 ARW Public Affairs Division, 100 U.S. Oval, Ste. B, Plattsburgh AFB, NY 12903-3318, or call (518) 565-5000.

Army

FORT DRUM

A few miles to the east of Fort Drum begins the Adirondack Park, some 6,000 square miles of lakes, forests, mountains, and streams that form one of the most famous tourist attractions in the northeastern United States. Just to the northeast of the post is the Saint Lawrence River's Thousand Islands and Thousand Islands State Park. Across the river is Ontario, Canada, and to the west of Fort Drum and Watertown is Lake Ontario, the easternmost of the Great Lakes.

History. Named after Lt. Gen. Hugh A. Drum, a commander of the 1st U.S. Army during the early years of World War II, Fort Drum is now the home of the 10th Mountain Division (Light Infantry) and also a training facility for U.S. Army National Guard and Reserve units. The post is situated nine miles northeast of Watertown (population 29,000). Fort Drum is currently home to 10,000 active-duty personnel. Syracuse is eighty miles to the south via Interstate 81, and Kingston, Ontario, is seventy miles to the north. Lake Placid, site of the 1932 and 1980 Olympics, is one hundred miles to the east. Toronto and Montreal are only five hours away by car.

Housing and Schools. There are presently 4,272 sets of family quarters at Fort Drum. No dependent schooling is available on post, but Fort Drum's education office offers a wide range of programs, including college courses up to graduate level. Most courses are affiliated with Jefferson Community College in Watertown, Syracuse University in Oswego and Potsdam, and Empire State College.

Personal Services and Recreation. Fort Drum has a post exchange, a commissary, and a health clinic. There is a swimming and picnic beach on the installation as well as an outdoor equipment rental facility. The newly opened physical fitness center and soldiers gym include indoor pools. The post also has a bowling alley, a movie theater, craft and hobby shops, tennis and racquetball courts, and numerous outdoor sports fields.

The summers at Fort Drum are mild and short, and the winters are long and cold. Snow falls from November to April, with heavy accumulation from December through February.

For more information write to: Public Affairs Office, Bldg. P10000, Rm. 121, Fort Drum, NY 13602-5028, or call (315) 772-5461.

FORT HAMILTON

History. The military presence at Fort Hamilton stretches back to the very birth of the American Republic when on 4 July 1776 a small American battery on the site of the present-day installation fired into one of the British men-of-war convoying troops to suppress the Revolution. The cornerstone of Fort Hamilton was put into place in June 1825, although at the time it was known as Fort Lewis. The installation was not officially named Fort Hamilton—after our first secretary of the treasury, Alexander Hamilton—until the twentieth century. During its long history, such notables as Robert E. Lee and Thomas "Stonewall" Jackson served there.

Today Fort Hamilton is home of the New York City Recruiting Battalion Long Island and the Military Entrance Processing Station for New York City. It also supports more than 300 reserve and National Guard units. It is the only active Army post in the New York metropolitan area.

Housing and Schools. Fort Hamilton controls over 700 units of family housing. On the post itself are 118 town-house units and Hamilton Manor, a high-rise consisting of 324 apartments. Another 188 units are located at Fort Totten. The Adams Guest House is available for incoming permanent-change-of-station personnel for up to thirty days; others may use the facility on a space-available basis with a seven-day-maximum-stay rule.

Although a child-development center is operated on the post, schooling for dependent children is available only in the local community. Adult educational services are available from the post education center and include a full range of academic testing as well as tuition assistance for those who wish to attend off-duty college courses.

Personal Services. Personal support facilities include the Ainsworth U.S. Army Health Clinic, an outpatient health care facility. Referrals are made there to local hospitals or military hospitals at installations elsewhere along the East Coast. The U.S. Army dental clinic provides space-available dental care for military dependents.

The post exchange offers a full range of shopping possibilities as well as numerous concessions, including a snack bar, a service station, a package beverage store, and branch post exchange outlets at Fort Totten. There is also a commissary at the post that is open six days a week.

Recreation. Morale and welfare facilities include a community club, a bowling center, an arts and crafts shop, a recreation center, a gymnasium, a post theater, and a library containing 28,000 volumes and over 50 magazines and newspapers. Located in the best-preserved portion of the original fort is the Harbor Defense Museum, which houses a collection of artifacts that tell the fascinating story of the discovery and fortification of New York Harbor.

The Local Area. The neighborhood around Fort Hamilton offers a tremendous variety of shops and other attractions and conveniences. Adequate public transportation is available for trips to Manhattan (via subway and bus) and Governor's Island and the Statue of Liberty.

For more information write to: Public Affairs Office, NYAC, Fort Hamilton, NY 11252-5700, or call (718) 630-4820.

SENECA ARMY DEPOT ACTIVITY

Construction was begun on Seneca Army Depot Activity in July 1941 as a munitions project covering more than 10,000 acres along the eastern shore of Seneca Lake, some fifteen miles south of the town of Geneva. Ever since then the depot has been primarily involved in the storage and handling of conventional weapons and ammunition. Seneca Lake is to the west and Cayuga Lake is to the east; today the reservation also includes the 7,000-foot airstrip of what was once Sampson Air Force Base. The post population is small, consisting of a garrison of only 3 military personnel and 300 civilian employees.

Seneca Army Depot is not an "open post." All visitors must sign in at the main gate and are required to wear temporary identification badges at all times while on the installation.

The depot provides a recreation area and travel camp on Seneca Lake that is open to active-duty and retired military personnel and their dependents.

For more information write to: Public Affairs Office, Seneca Army Depot Activity, Romulus, NY 14541, or call (607) 869-1110.

U.S. MILITARY ACADEMY

The U.S. Military Academy is our nation's oldest military academy. Steeped in tradition and history, its purpose is to provide the nation with leaders of character who serve the common defense. The West Point community includes approximately

2,000 officers and enlisted staff and faculty members whose primary duty is the education and training of the more than 4,000 cadets at the USMA.

History. Located on the Hudson River some sixty miles north of New York City, West Point is situated in some of the most beautiful and historic countryside of the Northeast. It was Benedict Arnold's attempt to deliver the plans of the fortress at West Point to the British in 1780 that revealed him as a traitor. In 1802, the fort at West Point was designated a training school for officers by an act of Congress. Famous generals such as Grant, Lee, Pershing, MacArthur, Eisenhower, Patton, Westmoreland, and Schwarzkopf are among West Point's graduates.

Housing and Schools. About 1,500 units of government quarters are available at West Point. They range in size from two to four bedrooms, while bachelor quarters range from efficiency apartments to two-bedroom units. The oldest quarters were built in 1894 and the newest in the 1970s. Some are located at West Point proper and some at Stewart Army Subpost, approximately seventeen miles northwest of the reservation. Guest quarters ranging from single rooms with shared bathrooms to three-bedroom apartments are available only at Stewart and must be reserved thirty days before occupancy.

Assignment to family quarters is mandatory: Approval must be obtained from the housing office before moving off post.

There are on-post schools for children in kindergarten through grade eight; high school students are bused to schools in nearby Highland Falls. The post education center assists active-duty personnel with a variety of educational programs from basic skills enhancement through graduate-level college courses.

Personal Services and Recreation. Keller Army Community Hospital is a sixty-five-bed modern health-care facility that provides complete health services to the Corps of Cadets, and active-duty and retired military personnel and their dependents. West Point also has a post exchange, a commissary, and other facilities and services for military personnel and their families, including a wide variety of both indoor and outdoor recreation activities from swimming and bowling to golf and ice skating. Outdoor recreation equipment can be obtained from the Community Recreation Division, including backpacks, sleeping bags, camping equipment, fishing boats with motors, and trailers.

The Local Area. The West Point military reservation is only a ten-minute drive north of the Palisades Interstate Park, which offers visitors outdoor recreation year-round. The Hudson River Valley is full of beautiful scenic and interesting historic landmarks, including Washington's Revolutionary War headquarters in Newburgh. The famous resort area of the Catskill Mountains is only a little more than one hour north of West Point via good roads, and New Hampshire, Vermont, Massachusetts, Connecticut, and Upstate New York are within easy driving distances for longer trips. In addition, the cultural and historic attractions of New York City are only an hour away.

For more information write to: U.S. Military Academy West Point, NY 10996, or call (914) 938-4011.

Coast Guard

GOVERNORS ISLAND SUPPORT CENTER

If Giovanni da Verrazano, the first European to see Governors Island when he sailed by there in the year 1524, could see the changes time has wrought upon the neighborhood since then, they'd knock the old boy stiff.

History. The Manahatas Indians called the place "Pagganck," and when the Dutch bought it from them in 1637 for a sum that may have amounted to no more than two ax heads, a string of beads, and a handful of nails, they named it "Nooten Eylandt," or "Nutten Island," after the groves of oak, hickory, and chestnut trees that grew there. The English took possession of the island in 1674. The oldest standing structure on the island today is the home of Governors Island Support Center's commanding officer, built in 1708 as the residence for the royal governor of the colony of New York.

The Coast Guard came to Governors Island in 1966. Today its 175 acres are home to the support center's 38 officers, 185 enlisted personnel, 13 Public Health Service officers, 4 Navy chaplains, and 645 civilian workers. The center supports the personnel assigned to duty with Commander, Atlantic Area; Maintenance and Logistics Command Atlantic; USCG Group New York/Captain of the Port; USCG Marine Inspection Office New York; and the U.S. Coast Guard Station New York.

The more than fifty men and women assigned to the station operate nine vessels and handle an average of 560 cases a year. Other vessels assigned to the island are the cutters *Dallas* and *Gallatin*, the ice-breaking tugs *Penobscot Bay* and *Sturgeon Bay*, and the buoy tenders *Sorrel* and *Red Beech*.

The island is home to more than 3,500 Coast Guard personnel, their 2,300 family members, and a civilian workforce of more than 700.

Housing and Schools. More than 800 family housing units are available at Governors Island, some on the site of historic Fort Jay. Accommodations for more than 500 unaccompanied officers and enlisted personnel are available, as are limited guest facilities. An elementary school for children in kindergarten through sixth grade is operated on the island, and schooling is also available in New York City. A child-care facility is also provided.

Personal Services. Medical and dental care are available on the island as are a commissary, an exchange, a country store, a deli, a service station, barber and beauty shops, a Burger King, a cafeteria, a package store, and officers, CPO, and enlisted clubs.

Recreation. Governors Island provides a complete array of recreational and athletic facilities including an arts and crafts shop, an auto craft shop, a movie theater, and a library. For the sports-minded there are handball, racquetball, and tennis courts, a gym, a nine-hole golf course, softball fields, swimming pools, and picnic grounds.

The Local Area. Of the more than 225 buildings on Governors Island, thirty-eight were built before 1900. These include the structures at Fort Jay, completed in 1798 and now being used as a family housing area; the Admiral's House, built in 1840 and now home of the Atlantic Area Commander; and Castle Williams, completed in 1811 and used as a prison from the Civil War until 1966.

Troops first came to Governors Island in 1755 when the Royal Americans, under the command of Sir William Pepperell, camped there. During the Revolution, American troops erected defenses on the island against the British fleet, but the British occupied the place on 15 September 1776 anyway. The British left there in 1783. The U.S. Army garrisoned the island in 1794 and remained there for the next 172 years, until relieved by the U.S. Coast Guard on 30 June 1966.

For more information write to: Governors Island Gazette, Bldg. 110, Governors Island, NY 10004, or call (212) 668-7320.

Navy

SCOTIA NAVAL ADMINISTRATIVE UNIT

The Scotia Naval Administrative Unit provides logistical support and services to the Naval Nuclear Power Training Unit (NPTU) in West Milton, New York, and personal property and administrative services in the West Milton, Saratoga, Schenectady, and Scotia areas of New York for approximately 1,900 resident active-duty Navy personnel and their 3,000 dependents. Most of these personnel are assigned to the NPTU, but Scotia supports about twenty Navy commands in the area, including Navy Recruiting Area 1, and Naval Reserve Recruiting Command Detachment 6.

Housing, Schools, and Personal Services. Scotia operates 200 units of family housing in Saratoga Springs, about seven miles from NPTU and twenty from Scotia: 100 fully furnished, modern two-bedroom apartments for students; and 100 two-bedroom townhouse units for resident enlisted personnel grade E-6 and below. Local rentals for families average between $500 and $900 per month; bachelors can expect to pay between $175 and $300 per month as long as they are willing to share their accommodations.

Dependent children attend school in the Saratoga Springs City School District. There are several colleges in the area, public and private, including Skidmore College, Rensselaer Polytechnic Institute, Russell Sage College, and State University of New York at Albany.

Medical care is provided by an outpatient medical clinic located in the Benedict Community Health Center at Ballston Spa. Referral and emergency care are provided by Saratoga Hospital or Plattsburgh Air Force Base. There are a commissary and Navy exchange store at Scotia as well as a mini mart at the Saratoga Springs housing complex. Recreational facilities available at Scotia include outdoor sports areas, a playground, and a picnic area; equipment rental is available at both Scotia and Ballston Spa.

The Local Area. Scotia is three miles west of downtown Schenectady; NPTU, Ballston Spa, is about twenty-five miles north. Nestled among the Adirondacks, Catskills, and Berkshire Mountains, the area offers plenty of outdoor recreational opportunities including fishing, boating, camping, hiking, and winter sports. The world-famous spa at Saratoga Springs (population 25,000) is a major attraction, as are the horse races held there every August. The Revolutionary War's Saratoga Battlefield is another attraction. Boston, New York City, and Canada are all within only a few hours' drive. The summers in this part of the state are mild, with daytime temperatures in the eighties, dropping into the fifties at night; winters can be harsh with as much as 100 inches of snow and temperatures that can dip to minus 20° F.

For more information write to: Public Affairs Office, Naval Administrative Unit, Scotia, NY 12302-9460, or call (518) 370-0352.

NORTH CAROLINA

Air Force

POPE AIR FORCE BASE

The airmen at Pope are fond of pointing out that it is they who put the "air" in "airborne" for the Army paratroopers stationed at nearby Fort Bragg, North Carolina. This is a fact, because the C-130E Hercules aircraft based at Pope airlift Army paratroopers and special forces personnel daily in the performance of their training missions. In addition, Pope's aviators are trained and ready to deliver personnel and equipment to just about any place in the world where they might be needed—with or without parachutes and at a moment's notice. Also newly assigned to Pope is the 75th Fighter Squadron whose A-10s conduct close air support for the Army troopers.

History. Pope Air Force Base is one of the oldest Air Force installations. Named after 1st Lt. Harley Halbert Pope, who was killed in 1917 when his aircraft crashed into the Cape Fear River near Fayetteville, the base was commissioned in March 1919. Today Pope is home for the 23rd Wing, the first composite wing formed under the Air Force's restructuring program, and various tenant units such as the 317th Airlift Wing and the USAF Mobility Center. Under the composite wing concept, the unique strengths of different types of aircraft are used for specific missions flown out of a single base under one commander. Thus the 4,500 men and women of 23rd Wing can drop paratroopers and kill tanks.

Housing and Schools. An important fact of life at Pope is Fort Bragg, where airmen and soldiers enjoy the joint use of the many facilities and programs there for military personnel and their families. Pope has 459 sets of family quarters for Air

Force personnel. The waiting list for these quarters varies from two to twenty months, depending on the sponsor's date of arrival at the base and the size of his family; the average waiting time is about twenty months. But Pope personnel also share some of the 1,500 quarters situated on Fort Bragg. Temporary lodging is available on base for transient personnel, with reservations going only to incoming and outgoing permanently assigned airmen and their families.

Many rental properties are available off base. A family can expect to pay about $325 to $450 a month for a three-bedroom, two-bath home in the Fayetteville area.

A child-care center is operated at Pope. Dependent children go to school in Fayetteville, where there are nineteen public schools. The education center on base offers college courses for adults from Embry-Riddle Aeronautical, Golden Gate, and Southern Illinois Universities, as well as Webster, Central Texas, and Methodist Colleges.

Personal Services. A small base exchange and commissary are available at Pope with larger facilities at Fort Bragg. Officers and NCO club systems and many other personal services are offered at Pope. Medical care is provided at a USAF clinic, with consultation and inpatient care provided at nearby Womack Army Hospital.

Recreation. Recreational services include an eighteen-hole golf course, a sixteen-lane bowling alley, two swimming pools, a gymnasium, hobby shops, tennis courts, and a picnic area overlooking the base. There is also a wonderful variety of recreational activities at Fort Bragg.

The Local Area. Recreation and sightseeing are available almost everywhere in North Carolina, in over one million acres of national forests and thirteen state parks that are open to residents and visitors. The Atlantic coast to the east and the Blue Ridge and Great Smoky mountains to the west are near enough to Pope to be accessible for weekend trips.

For more information write to: Public Affairs Office, 23rd Wing (ACC), 259 Maynard St., Pope AFB, NC 28308-2391, or call (919) 394-4183.

SEYMOUR JOHNSON AIR FORCE BASE

Seymour Johnson Air Force Base is located within the city limits of Goldsboro, which lies about fifty miles southeast of Raleigh, the state capital.

History. The base was named after Lt. Seymour Johnson, a native of Goldsboro who was killed in an aircraft accident near Norbeck, Maryland, in 1941. The host unit at the base is the 4th Wing, which flies the F-15E Strike Eagle and the KC-10 Extender. The major tenant unit is the 916th Air Refueling Group, a reserve unit that shares the maintenance responsibilities for the KC-10s and about one-third of the aircrews. The base's military population consists of 4,600 active military personnel, 675 reservists, and almost 1,200 civilians.

Housing and Schools. There are currently 1,698 units of family housing on base, in addition to 45 mobile home spaces, but there is a critical shortage of temporary lodging off base. Temporary lodging on base, with or without dependents, may be obtained on a space-available basis. Local rentals range from $300 to $450 a month for two-bedroom apartments to as much as $550 a month for a three-bedroom unit. Two- and three-bedroom homes rent for $550 and up. Average cost for a two-bedroom mobile home is $250 per month.

A child-development center and before- and after-school programs operate on the base. Local public and private schools offer a variety of curricula for military family members. The base education center provides assistance and guidance to adults wishing to continue their educational development.

Personal Services and Recreation. A modern twenty-bed USAF hospital provides most of the medical and dental services for military personnel and their dependents at the base. Seymour Johnson AFB also offers commissary and exchange facilities and enlisted and officers club systems. A family camp, open year-round, is available with hookups for eight campers. A gymnasium, a golf course, a theater, and many other recreational facilities are also on base.

For more information write to: Family Services, 1255 Andrews St., Ste. 100, Seymour Johnson AFB, NC 27531-2404, or call (919) 736-5400.

Army

FORT BRAGG

The "jumpingist" post in the Army, Fort Bragg is the "Home of the Airborne." It has earned this reputation over the years as troopers from the 18th Airborne Corps, the 82nd Airborne Division, the 1st Special Operations Command (Airborne), and the Army Parachute Team (Golden Knights) continually parachute out of "perfectly good" airplanes.

History. Named after a Confederate general, Gen. Braxton Bragg, a former artilleryman and North Carolinian, Camp Bragg emerged as a field artillery post in August 1918. It was redesignated Fort Bragg in September 1922, and the first military parachute jump was made there in 1923 from an artillery observation balloon. The first airborne units trained there in 1942, and during World War II all five airborne divisions used in the war—the 82nd, the 101st, the 11th, the 13th, and the 17th—trained there. Today the post's 149,000 acres provide homes and maneuver areas for the over 41,000 active-duty personnel and their 11,000 dependents. Over 9,000 civilian employees work at Fort Bragg. A subinstallation, Fort Pickett, Virginia, consists of 45,000 acres with an active-duty population of 100 personnel. Fort Pickett is a training site for more than 21,000 reserve component personnel annually.

Housing and Schools. There are more than 4,800 sets of family quarters at Fort Bragg, ranging from two- to four-bedroom multiple apartments to single houses in nine separate housing areas. Three transient or guest facilities are operated on the post, and reservations may be made for up to thirty days.

Six elementary schools, a middle school, and a junior high are operated on post with a student enrollment of over 4,900, and the Army education center offers programs that include an individual learning center and MOS library, a language school, and college courses offering degrees up to the masters level.

Personal Services. Fort Bragg is an entirely self-contained installation that offers soldiers and their families the complete range of facilities and services available to the modern military community, from commissary and post exchange facilities to complete medical and dental care.

Recreation. Fort Bragg's morale support activities division offers an outstanding leisure-time program, which includes over seventy different facilities. They include nineteen tennis courts, three twenty-four-lane bowling centers, three movie theaters, a riding stable, an eighteen-hole golf course, a skeet range, a rod and gun club, an ice-skating rink, and nine physical fitness centers offering everything from weight lifting to swimming. The outdoor program includes Smith Lake, with picnic areas, a beach, and an Army travel camp with twenty-four sites for recreational vehicles.

The Local Area. Fayetteville, a city of more than 75,000, is just off post on Bragg Boulevard. The community offers many cultural opportunities and interesting historical sites. A one-hour drive in any direction will take the traveler to some feature of North Carolina's "Variety Vacationland." Fayetteville is a two-hour drive from the state's famed Atlantic beaches, and within a 200-mile radius are some of the nation's most unspoiled parks and campgrounds and the Blue Ridge Mountains.

For further information write to: Public Affairs Office, XVIII Airborne Corps and Fort Bragg, Fort Bragg, NC 28307, or call (919) 396-0011.

Marines take part in training exercises at Camp Lejeune. (USMC photo)

Marine Corps

CAMP LEJEUNE

Camp Lejeune occupies 151,000 acres consisting of sandy beaches and swamps along the North Carolina coast between Wilmington to the south and Cherry Point Marine Corps Air Station a few miles to the north. Camp Lejeune has an actual perimeter of some eighty-five miles, with fourteen miles fronting the ocean paralleled by the famous Intercostal Waterway. The New River divides the installation roughly in half.

History. Construction began on the installation, named in honor of Gen. John Archer Lejeune, in April 1941. Today it is home to more than 41,000 military personnel, 12,000 dependents, and a civilian workforce of over 4,700. The three major commands aboard are the 2nd Marine Division, the 2nd Force Service Support Group, and the Marine Corps Base. Marine Aircraft Groups 26 and 29 are based at the New River Marine Corps Air Station (Helicopter), which comprises an installation of 2,600 acres immediately adjacent to Lejeune.

Housing and Schools. Camp Lejeune offers every facility and service available on a major military installation, including about 4,500 units of family housing, ranging in size from one-bedroom dwellings to four-bedroom town houses. Camp Lejeune also has a ninety-unit hostess house for personnel in transit, their families, and authorized guests.

The Camp Lejeune Dependents School System includes all grades, kindergarten through high school. The base education office offers adult education programs that range from mere "fun" classes to college-level courses.

Personal Services. The three commissaries at Camp Lejeune offer excellent shopping; the ones at Hadnot Point and Tarawa Terrace offer 7,000 line items; the New River facility, 4,000 line items. The Marine Exchange offers over 100 activities at Camp Lejeune and New River; indeed, the Lejeune exchange is one of the largest in the corps. Medical service is provided by the U.S. Naval Hospital, a 265-bed facility, one of the largest and best-equipped military hospitals in the South.

Recreation. Recreational activities abound at Camp Lejeune, from horseback-riding facilities, swimming pools, and skeet and trap shooting to beach cabañas; New River has several picnic recreation areas and a marina. The base also operates Onslow Beach, a year-round seashore recreational facility with seventy-four camp sites. Reservations are required thirty days in advance for stays of not more than seven days. Campsites are on the beach and in heavily wooded areas on the inland waterway. The coastal regions of the Carolinas are good places for hunting and fishing. Animals available for hunting include turkey, bear, deer, and duck; both freshwater and saltwater fishing can also be enjoyed.

Camp Lejeune is 116 miles southeast of Raleigh, the capital of North Carolina and a city of 500,000. Wilmington, North Carolina, is about 40 miles south of Camp Lejeune. The small town of Jacksonville is 5 miles east.

For more information write to: Community Relations Chief, Joint Public Affairs Office, P.O. Box 8438, Camp Lejeune, NC 28542-5000, or call (919) 451-1113.

CHERRY POINT MARINE CORPS AIR STATION

Cherry Point Marine Corps Air Station occupies about 12,000 acres of land at its primary complex, approximately midway between New Bern and Morehead City, adjacent to the town of Havelock just off U.S. 70 along the Neuse River. Croatan National Forest borders the station, and to the southwest is Camp Lejeune. Not far to the north are Pamlico and Albemarle Sounds and the Cape Hatteras National Seashore area. Altogether, this is fascinating country, rich in history and an outdoorsman's paradise.

The air station was commissioned in May 1942, and today it is home for 11,000 Marines and sailors and approximately 5,000 civilian employees of the Marine Corps air station and the naval aviation depot. Cherry Point MCAS is one of the best all-weather jet bases anywhere, and it is the largest Marine Corps air station.

Ground crews launch an AV-8B Harrier on a bombing training mission at Cherry Point MCAS. (USMC photo)

Housing and Schools. The MCAS controls over 2,800 units of family housing. Depending on the availability of these quarters, waiting periods of a few weeks to a few months are not uncommon.

Cherry Point has no on-base schooling, but a child-care center is open from September through May. Hourly care is provided Monday through Friday and Sunday morning for church services. The education–extension school offices offer a testing section, counseling on all subjects related to adult education, and enrollment in a large number of college programs consisting of undergraduate and postgraduate degree work offered by Boston and Southern Illinois Universities, Park College, and Craven Community College, among others.

Personal Services and Recreation. A Marine Corps exchange, a commissary, and a wide range of athletic and recreational facilities and programs are provided at Cherry Point. Medical care at the station is provided by a forty-three-bed naval hospital. On-station recreation includes a bowling alley; three swimming pools; a movie theater; handball, racquetball, and tennis courts; an eighteen-hole golf course; a riding stable; a gymnasium; and an archery range. Picnic and camping areas on the station may be used year-round. Hunting and fishing are permitted on the station, providing state and local licensing requirements are met.

The Local Area. The region of North Carolina in which Cherry Point MCAS is situated offers a great diversity of recreational opportunities, from the pine forests inland to the Atlantic Ocean seashore just a few miles east of the station. Cape Hatteras is only ninety miles to the northeast.

Just outside the main gate is the town of Havelock. New Bern is situated seventeen miles northwest of the air station. Founded in 1710 by Swiss and German colonists, it is North Carolina's second oldest city. Eighteen miles southeast of Cherry Point is Morehead City, home to the largest fleet of charter fishing boats in the central Atlantic Coast area. The generally mild climate permits some form of outdoor activity year-round.

For more information write to: Joint Public Affairs Office, Marine Corps Air Station, Cherry Point, NC 28533-5001, or call (919) 466-4241.

NEW RIVER MARINE CORPS AIR STATION

Originally established in April 1944, the New River Marine Corps Air Station (MCAS) today comprises over 2,600 acres just south of the city of Jacksonville, across the New River from Camp Lejeune. It is home to Marine Aircraft Groups 26 and 29 and more than 5,000 active-duty personnel, 200 civilian employees, and 2,200 family members.

Housing, Schools, and Personal Services. The station operates 435 sets of family quarters as well as more than 1,800 units for unaccompanied officer and enlisted personnel. There is an elementary school at New River as well as a child-care center. Routine health care is provided by a branch clinic with referral and inpatient care available at Camp Lejeune. Both commissary and exchange services are available at New River. A full range of recreational facilities is also provided at the station, but station personnel and their families may also take advantage of the Onslow Beach recreation area operated by Camp Lejeune.

For more information write to: Joint Public Affairs Office, H&HS, PSC Box 21002, MCAS New River, Jacksonville, NC 28545-1002, or call (910) 451-6196/6197.

NORTH DAKOTA

Air Force

GRAND FORKS AIR FORCE BASE

Dakota comes from an American Indian word meaning "friend." Grand Forks Air Force Base, with its Minuteman silos and B-1B bombers poised to soar into flight in the event of provocation, is a great reassurance to those who are our friends and an equally great deterrent to those who are not.

Construction began at Grand Forks AFB in 1956, and the first SAC weapons system, a KC-135 Stratotanker, arrived there in 1960. Today the base occupies over 5,000 acres fifteen miles west of the city of Grand Forks and is home and workplace for 5,200 military personnel, 7,000 dependents, and 700 civilians of the 319th Bomb Wing, 321st Strategic Missile Wing, and various other commands.

Housing and Schools. There are over 2,200 sets of family dwellings at the base. Temporary lodging is also available, with first priority going to permanent-change-of-station personnel, although personnel on leave and guests of airmen assigned to Grand Forks are also welcome when space limitations permit.

Dependent schooling, kindergarten through eighth grade, is provided on base. High schools are available in downtown Grand Forks. Higher education is provided through the base education office and includes programs offered by the University of North Dakota, Park College, Central Michigan University, Lake Region Community College, and Embry-Riddle Aeronautical University. All these institutions offer on-base courses.

Personal Services. Medical care at Grand Forks is provided by a thirty-five-bed USAF hospital. Dental care for dependents is limited to emergency procedures and preventive dental care. A well-stocked (8,500 line items) commissary and base exchange, banking facilities, NCO and officers clubs, and on-base taxi service on call twenty-four hours a day add to the overall convenience of life at Grand Forks.

Recreation. Recreational activities include an indoor swimming pool; a modern, air-conditioned recreation center; a sixteen-lane bowling center; a nine-hole golf course; hobby shops; and other activities.

The Local Area. Grand Forks is a modern city of over 40,000 people. The surrounding area abounds with things to do. Larimore, fifteen miles west of the base, offers golf, fishing, and swimming; boating, swimming, and camping are available at Park River, two miles west of Grand Forks. At Mayville, thirty-five miles south of the base, the Golden Lake Game Management Area offers camping, swimming, boating, and fishing. The Canadian border is about seventy-five miles north of Grand Forks, and the major Canadian city of Winnipeg, with many historic and scenic attractions, is about sixty-five miles north of the border, a border that requires no passport to cross.

For more information write to: Community Relations Office, Grand Forks AFB, ND 58205-5000, or call (701) 747-5017.

MINOT AIR FORCE BASE

Minot Air Force Base occupies about 5,000 acres thirteen miles north of the city of Minot in land that is flat and treeless; where it gets very cold in the winter and hot in the summer; where agriculture is the main business in the surrounding countryside; and where you can listen to a symphony orchestra or attend art exhibits among the various shopping malls located in Minot.

History. The Air Force first came to Minot in 1957, and today it is a major ACC base for the Minuteman III ICBM and the B-52H bomber. The base is headquarters for the 5th Bomb Wing, which is responsible for the control of the 91st Strategic Missile Wing and the 5th Bombardment Wing, as well as other units scattered throughout the state.

Housing and Schools. There are over 2,460 sets of family quarters at Minot. Also on base are a hotel for transient officers and enlisted personnel and 40 units of temporary quarters for families awaiting permanent housing.

A child-care center is operated on the base, as are the North Plains Elementary School, Dakota Elementary School, and Memorial Junior High School. High schools are available in Minot. The base education services center provides high school equivalency programs and continuing-education programs offering degrees from Minot State University, North Dakota School of Science, and Central Michigan University.

Personal Services. Medical care is provided by the 5th Medical Group. Personal services include a commissary, a base exchange with numerous concessions, officers and NCO club facilities, banking, a credit union, and a theater.

Recreation. Recreational activities include a twenty-two-lane bowling center, two full gymnasiums, a nine-hole golf course, snowmobiling, stables, and the base's very own theater troupe.

The Local Area. Minot is a thriving little metropolis of 35,000 people that boasts many fine recreational facilities for all seasons: gardens, swimming pools, and tennis in the summer; skiing, hockey, curling, and even ice sculpturing in the winter. The state of North Dakota is well watered and contains many excellent fishing spots. Hunters will also find lots of game there, and the state offers many excellent recreational sites.

For more information write to: Public Affairs Representative, 201 Summit Dr. Unit 4, Minot AFB, ND 58705-5000, or call (701) 723-6212.

OHIO

Air Force

WRIGHT-PATTERSON AIR FORCE BASE

Wright-Patterson Air Force Base is one of the nation's most important military installations. It employs more people than any other Air Force base in the world, approximately 32,000 military and civilian personnel. It is the headquarters for a vast worldwide logistics system and is also the foremost research and development center in the U.S. Air Force. This is particularly fitting because nearby Dayton, home of the Wright brothers, is the "Birthplace of Aviation."

History. Known as McCook Field when it was established in 1917, renamed Wilbur Wright Field in 1924 and then Patterson Field in 1931 (after Lt. Frank Patterson, who died there in an airplane crash), Wright-Patterson got its present name in 1948. Today the base occupies 8,174 acres a few miles east-northeast of Dayton. The host organization is the Aeronautical Systems Center.

Housing and Schools. There are more than 2,300 units of family housing at Wright-Patterson and 80 mobile homes in the base trailer park. Forty units of temporary lodging are also available on a reserved basis for incoming or outgoing permanently assigned personnel; temporary housing is on a space-available basis for all others.

A preschool and six child-care centers are operated on the base, but dependents schooling is available only off base, in the surrounding communities. The base education office assists adults in furthering their education, from evening high school classes to participation in the Dayton Miami Valley Consortium, an association of

238

local universities and colleges offering various degrees. These include Urbana, Clark Technical, Antioch, Wilmington, Southern State, Sinclair Community, and Edison State Colleges; Wright State, Wilberforce, and Central State Universities; United Theological Seminary; and the Air Force Institute of Technology.

Personal Services. Medical care at Wright-Patterson is provided by the base's 301-bed hospital complex, which extends its services to over 60,000 active-duty and retired military personnel and their families residing in the area. The base commissary stocks over 5,000 items and is the fifth largest in the Air Force. The commissary is part of a shopping complex covering four acres, all under one roof.

Recreation. Recreation facilities on base include one nine-hole and two eighteen-hole golf courses, three gymnasiums, five swimming pools, four indoor and sixteen outdoor tennis courts, a twenty-lane bowling alley, four lakes, a recreation center, an arts and crafts shop, an auto hobby shop, two health clubs, picnic areas, and a family camp with trailer pads and tent sites. The base has 60 acres of man-made lakes with good fishing and about 1,000 more acres where hunting is permitted. Hadden Park Recreation Area consists of 60 acres of woodland.

The Local Area. Over four million people live in the greater Dayton area, within ninety minutes' commuting distance of the city. Cincinnati is due south of Dayton; Springfield and Columbus are a bit to the northeast.

For more information write to: Public Affairs Office, Wright-Patterson AFB, OH 45433, or call (513) 255-3334.

OKLAHOMA

Air Force

ALTUS AIR FORCE BASE

Altus Air Force Base is home for some of the largest and most powerful aircraft in the world—five C-5 Galaxies, fifteen C-141 Starlifters, and twenty-two KC-135R Stratotankers. The C-5, one of the world's largest aircraft, is so huge that only 17 of them would have been needed to complete the whole Berlin Airlift, an operation that needed 308 conventional aircraft. The C-141s are big airplanes too, but the C-5's cargo floor area is triple that of the C-141A and double that of the C-141B models. With four engines that can develop 38,000 pounds of thrust apiece, the Galaxy's engines roar at Altus.

History. Altus had a modest beginning in 1942 when it was opened as a flight training school during World War II. Today its 4,694 acres are home to the 97th Air Mobility Wing, which provides aircrews with transition training on the C-141s and C-5s, and worldwide air-refueling support.

Housing and Schools. There are 800 units of family housing at Altus. Also available are two three-bedroom units and an eight-family transient lodging facility used as guest housing, primarily for incoming and outgoing airmen permanently assigned to the base; others are permitted on a space-available basis only. A child-care center is offered on the base, but the town of Altus has an excellent public school system consisting of eight elementary schools, one junior high school, and a seventy-acre senior high campus.

The base education office arranges for off-duty college-level courses at both the undergraduate and graduate levels. Western Oklahoma State College in the Altus community offers a curriculum divided into seven divisions covering business, communications, math and science, humanities and fine arts, social science, physical education, and military science.

Personal Services and Recreation. A commissary, a base exchange, a relatively new fifteen-bed USAF hospital, a dental clinic, and banking facilities are only a few of the services offered on the base. Recreational facilities include a golf course, a rod and gun club, swimming pools, officers and NCO clubs, a gymnasium with a variety of fitness machines, a ten-lane bowling alley, hobby and craft shops, and a vigorous intramural sports program.

The Local Area. Altus is a thriving community of 25,000. The weather there is excellent, with approximately 340 flying days out of the year and an average rainfall of twenty-two inches. The base is only 2 miles from the town, 149 miles from Oklahoma City, and about a dozen miles to the nearest bend of the Red River and the Texas-Oklahoma border.

Outdoor recreational facilities abound in this region of the state. The Quartz Mountain State Park, with fishing, boating, and skiing, is 18 miles north of Altus. Hunting areas are located at the upper end of the Altus Reservoir and on the shores of the Steed Reservoir, 30 miles from the base, in the Mountain Park Public Hunting Area. The Great Plains Recreation Area is 20 miles northeast of Altus, and buffalo, elk, deer, and longhorn steers may be observed, but not hunted, in the Wichita Mountain Wildlife Refuge.

For more information write to: 97th AMW Public Affairs Office, 100 Inez Blvd., Altus AFB, OK 73523-5047, or call (405) 481-7700.

TINKER AIR FORCE BASE

Tinker Air Force Base occupies over 4,800 acres of land nine miles southeast of Oklahoma City. Much of that acreage was donated to the government by the community, and Tinker has become so integral a part of the economy of the city that its citizens have acquired control of large acreages in the vicinity to assure the compatibility of their community development to base operations.

History. Established in 1941 as an industrial plant geared for the repair of long-range bombers, the base is named in honor of Maj. Gen. Clarence L. Tinker, a native of Pawhuska, Oklahoma, who was killed leading a bomber attack against Wake Island during World War II. Today approximately 21,000 military and civilian personnel live and work at the base at the Oklahoma City Air Logistics Command, 654th Support Group, 552nd Air Control Wing, and associate units.

Housing and Schools. Air Force personnel have 730 family housing units for their use, and temporary lodging is available on a reserved basis for permanent-change-of-station personnel. All others are accepted on a space-available basis only.

An elementary school on base provides education for children in kindergarten through sixth grade. The Air Force operates two on-base child-care centers and one preschool for dependent children. There are several colleges and university campuses in the city. The education services center of the base education office provides assistance to personnel desiring to participate in courses offered by these institutions, as well as a highly developed work-skill and vocational-training program.

Personal Services. The fifteen-bed USAF hospital at Tinker provides excellent medical care for active-duty and retired personnel and their families. The base exchange offers excellent shopping opportunities, and through its large number of concessions, it offers a full range of dining and service facilities. Tinker also has a very large main commissary and two shopettes.

Recreation. A wide range of recreational activities are offered at Tinker, including a twenty-two-lane bowling center, an eighteen-hole, par-seventy-two golf course, a gun club, tennis courts, a twenty-five-meter swimming pool, enlisted and officers clubs, hobby and craft shops, and a riding stable. Outdoor facilities include a base picnic area and a family camp with twenty-nine camper pads and other facilities.

The Local Area. The climate in the Oklahoma City area is mild, with hot summers and cold winters. Annual average snowfall is less than ten inches, and rainfall averages about thirty-two inches per year. Severe thunderstorms and tornadoes do sometimes occur in the area, generally from March through early June.

Oklahoma City is home to over 444,000 people, with more than 958,000 people living in the metropolitan area. The city is bordered by two famous rivers: the Cimarron to the north and the Canadian, which forms the southwestern border of the town. The many lakes, reservoirs, and streams in the vicinity afford plenty of opportunities for water sports and fishing. Many spots nearby are rich in the history of the American West, such as the American Indian Hall of Fame State Memorial at Anadarko, Fort Sill, and the Chisholm Trail Museum near Kingfisher.

For more information write to: Public Affairs, 3001 Staff Dr. 1AG78A, Tinker AFB, OK 73145-3010, or call (405) 739-2026.

VANCE AIR FORCE BASE

History. The U.S. government bought the land on which Vance Air Force Base is now situated from the city of Enid for one dollar. That was back in 1941, and the base was used then as a flying school. In July 1949 it was named in honor of Lt. Col. Leon R. Vance, a former resident of Enid who won the Medal of Honor posthumously for action in World War II. Today Vance is home for the 71st Flying Training Wing of the Air Training Command. The 71st graduates about 250 pilots from its undergraduate pilot training program each year. Vance's population consists of about 850 active-duty personnel, 1,100 Air Force family members, and about 1,400 civilian employees.

Housing and Schools. About 230 units of military family housing are available at Vance.

There are no dependent schools on base, but an elementary school is located just outside the main gate. Older children attend local schools in Enid and Waukomis. A child-development center is operated on base. Graduate, undergraduate, and vocational classes are available in the local area. Phillips University, Enid

Higher Education Program, and O. T. Autry Vocational School are the three main institutions serving base personnel. The Enid Higher Education Program consists of Northern Oklahoma College and Oklahoma State, Northwestern Oklahoma State, and Phillips Universities.

Personal Services. Inpatient medical care for airmen and their families is not available at Vance. Persons requiring care beyond the capabilities of the USAF clinic are sent to the regional hospital at Sheppard Air Force Base, Texas, or to a civilian hospital in Enid. Dependent dental care is limited to x rays and emergency care. A new commissary with 32,000 square feet of sales space, a new base exchange, a club system, a clothing store, and a banking facility are among the personal services available at Vance.

Recreation. The Vance morale, welfare, and recreation office provides hobby shops, four tennis courts, an eight-lane bowling alley, two swimming pools, a gymnasium, a golf driving range, and a picnic area. The picnic area offers playground equipment, barbecue facilities, and a pavilion that is open year-round.

The Local Area. Vance is located about three miles south of Enid, a city of 45,000. It is considered the retail trade center for northwestern Oklahoma, and a variety of stores (including Oakwood Mall on the west side of town) are stocked with the latest merchandise. Enid is also the major medical center in northwest Oklahoma and serves as the principal referral center for physicians throughout this area of the state. Farming is the primary business in the countryside surrounding the city. With a generally temperate climate, the area around Vance experiences four distinct seasons in the year, with no extremes. Snow does not stay long on the ground when it does fall, and annual rainfall averages less than thirty inches. Oklahoma City, the state capital, lies approximately eighty miles to the southeast. The city is famous for its many museums, including the National Cowboy Hall of Fame and Western Heritage Center, the Air and Space Museum, and the Kirkpatrick Center Science and Arts Museum. Oklahoma City is also home of Tinker AFB and the Oklahoma City Zoo. With many amusement parks, malls, theaters, movies, and fine eating establishments, Oklahoma City can provide an enjoyable weekend.

For more information write to: 71st Flying Training Wing, Public Affairs Office, 246 Brown Parkway, Ste. 225, Vance AFB, OK 73702-5016, or call (405) 249-7476.

Army

FORT SILL

Many sites in the old Southwest can claim "Geronimo slept here," because the famous Indian warrior actually stopped in many places en route to his captivity in Florida. Not only did Geronimo once sleep in the Old Post Guardhouse at Fort Sill, he also sleeps nearby, in his grave near Quinettte Road and Dodge Hill Road.

History. Named after Brig. Gen. Joshua Sill, a Union officer killed in action during the Civil War, Fort Sill was established in January 1869 as a post for cavalry and infantry units charged with the mission of pacifying the Plains Indians. The first artillery units came to Fort Sill in 1876. Today it is known as the "Home of the Field Artillery," and its more than 94,000 acres provide ranges and training areas for 20,000 personnel attending courses at the U.S. Army Field Artillery School and Field Artillery Center each year. Its 9,000 permanent-party personnel are assigned to three artillery brigades and an aviation battalion.

Housing and Schools. Fort Sill has over 1,400 units of family housing. Fort Sill also has guest accommodations. Visitors may occupy them no more than seven days at a time, based on space availability; personnel awaiting assignment to family quarters may stay in them up to thirty days.

The Fort Sill Army Education Center provides military personnel with a complete program of educational activities. Courses are available from area colleges and universities, including Cameron University at Lawton and the University of Oklahoma at Norman.

Personal Services. Medical care at Fort Sill is provided by the 194-bed Reynolds Army Community Hospital. The post commissary covers more than 105,000 square feet. A main post exchange and various concessions are also available, including a four-seasons store, a toy store, a shopette, and a cafeteria.

Recreation. On-post recreational facilities consist of a thirty-six-lane bowling alley; four seasonal swimming pools, with one open year-round; two eighteen-hole golf courses; two recreation centers; and thirty-six intramural sports programs.

The Local Area. With an average annual temperature of 63° F. and average yearly precipitation of thirty-eight inches (including seven inches of snow), the Fort Sill area is well suited for all sorts of outdoor activities. Fort Sill's community and family activities office operates camping facilities on the Lake Elmer Thomas Recreation Area located on the post's West Range. Fort Sill also operates a recreational equipment rental facility. The Fish and Wildlife Branch sells Oklahoma and Fort Sill hunting and fishing permits.

Fort Sill and Lawton lie about sixty miles southwest of Oklahoma City. The Wichita Mountain Wildlife Refuge, just northwest of Fort Sill, is a 59,000-acre outdoor wonderland that provides the visitor with a spectacular glimpse of unspoiled nature.

Lawton (named after Maj. Gen. Henry W. Lawton, who served at the post during the Indian Wars) plays an important role in the community life of Fort Sill. A city of 88,700 inhabitants, its schools and commercial and cultural activities are utilized by the military personnel stationed at Fort Sill.

For more information write to: Public Affairs Office, Headquarters, U.S. Army Field Artillery Center and Fort Sill, Fort Sill, OK 73503-5100, or call (405) 351-2521.

PENNSYLVANIA

Army

CARLISLE BARRACKS

History. History and scholarship are the most distinguishing features of Carlisle Barracks. Home today for the U.S. Army War College and the U.S. Army Military History Institute, the post traces its founding back to May 1757 when the site served as a supply base for British expeditions against the French and their Indian allies in the West. During the Revolution it was used as an arsenal and also as the first American artillery school for the Continental Army. Known then as Washingtonburg, Carlisle Barracks picked up its present name around 1807. The post was burned by Confederate cavalry in July 1863 during the Gettysburg Campaign. From 1879 to 1918, it served as the famous Carlisle Indian School. The War College moved there in 1951.

Carlisle Barracks is a small post, four-fifths of a mile long and half a mile wide, containing 217 total acres. The resident student body is composed of approximately 290 personnel, all of whom are fairly senior officers. The remaining 1,200 personnel, of whom 839 are civilians, constitute the post's actual garrison; about 770 family members live at Carlisle while another 800 live off post.

Housing and Schools. There are 321 units of family housing at or nearby Carlisle Barracks for the use of permanent-party and student officer personnel. Assignments are made upon arrival. Limited guest quarters are available for personnel awaiting assignment to family quarters. A post nursery school provides day care for children six months to ten years of age, and there is preschooling on the post. A new child-development center that provides day care to approximately 100 children opened in 1993.

Personal Services and Recreation. Medical and dental care are provided by the Dunham U.S. Army Health Clinic, a modern medical outpatient treatment facility. A commissary and post exchange with a garden shop, a candy and ice cream shop, a convenience store, and a service station are also available.

Recreational facilities include an automotive craft shop; an eighteen-hole golf course; a gymnasium; a six-lane bowling alley; officers and NCO clubs; a track; a movie theater; an archery range; squash, racquetball, and tennis courts; a swimming pool; stables; soccer and football fields; an outdoor recreation facility; and a variety of arts and crafts shops.

The Local Area. Carlisle Barracks is located in the Cumberland Valley of Pennsylvania, about eighteen miles west of Harrisburg, the state capital, on U.S. 11. The city of Carlisle is one mile southwest of the post and twenty-seven miles north of Gettysburg. The driving time from Washington, D.C., to Carlisle is approximately two and one-half hours.

Although hunting is prohibited on the post, wild game is plentiful in the surrounding countryside. Military personnel become eligible for resident hunting and fishing licenses after living sixty days in Pennsylvania. The morale support activities office provides military personnel the loan of campers, tents, fishing equipment, ski equipment, and other recreational gear. The Carlisle Barracks Ski Club offers memberships to military personnel and their families, and offers special rates on equipment and season ski passes. There are about ninety-five "ski days" each winter on the slopes near the post.

For more information write to: U.S. Army War College, Attention: AWCCI, Carlisle Barracks, PA 17013-5050, or call (717) 245-3131.

FORT INDIANTOWN GAP

Fort Indiantown Gap (FTIG) is a large installation with a small permanent population situated in a scenic and historic part of rural Pennsylvania. It is twenty-three miles east of Harrisburg, easily accessible from Interstate 81 and Pennsylvania 72.

History. Fort Indiantown Gap draws its name from the many Indian villages that once flourished in the vicinity during the seventeenth and eighteenth centuries. During the French and Indian War the British settlements in this area of Pennsylvania were fiercely attacked by Indian war parties, necessitating the construction of many forts and blockhouses. One of the forts was named Swatara Fort, and today a large boulder and a bronze tablet mark its site along Range Road, one-half mile west of Inwood.

In 1930 the Pennsylvania National Guard conducted horse cavalry maneuvers at Fort Indiantown Gap, and between 1933 and 1940 the Commonwealth of Pennsylvania acquired the land there and erected buildings for a National Guard campsite. The federal government leased the site from the state in 1941.

Today Fort Indiantown Gap consists of 19,600 acres of land under federal lease from Pennsylvania. The reservation is approximately eleven miles long by five miles wide. It is bordered on the north by the Blue Mountains and on the east, south, and west by gently rolling farmland. On 1 October 1983, Fort Indiantown Gap became a subinstallation of Fort Meade, Maryland.

The major tenant units at Fort Indiantown Gap include Headquarters, FTIG, which is responsible for the physical maintenance of the installation as well as provision of logistical and technical service support to reserve components and finance support for Guardsmen and reservists in twenty-two states; the Pennsylvania Department of Military Affairs; the U.S. Army Readiness Group; Headquarters of the Senior Army Advisor to the Pennsylvania Army National Guard; and the 56th Ordnance Detachment (EOD), which has the two-fold mission of disposing of unexploded ordnance and training military and civilian personnel in explosives recognition, bomb search techniques, and general safety. Approximately 1,500 military and civilian personnel staff these tenant activities; about 200 active-duty personnel are stationed at the installation.

Housing and Schools. Housing at Fort Indiantown Gap is very limited. The waiting period for on-post quarters is eighteen to twenty-four months for all ranks. There is one mobile home park at FTIG, but sites are available only to personnel who own their own trailers. Additional government quarters are available at New Cumberland Army Depot, about twenty miles southwest of FTIG. Most accompanied personnel find accommodations in the surrounding communities, where a two-bedroom unfurnished apartment rents for about $400 a month plus from $80 to $140 a month for utilities, depending on the season. Bachelor enlisted personnel are housed in modern, fully air-conditioned two-room barracks complexes; there are approximately 1,200 rooms available on post for officers, but these are not considered adequate for permanent occupancy.

Dependent children attend various public and parochial schools in the school districts adjacent to FTIG. Day-care and preschool facilities are available in the local communities. The Army education center provides counseling Monday through Friday; CLEP and DANTES testing and school catalogs are available.

Personal Services. Hours of operation for most services at FTIG are "seasonal," or extended during the training season (May through September) and somewhat shorter during the rest of the year.

Medical care at FTIG is provided by a small health clinic. Dependents of active-duty personnel are seen by appointment; retired personnel and their dependents are supported by the Dunham Clinic at Carlisle Barracks.

There is no commissary at FTIG, but the commissaries at New Cumberland Army Depot and Carlisle Barracks are available to FTIG personnel. The post exchange is a modern, self-service facility open to eligible National Guard, reserve, active-duty, and retired personnel and their dependents. The post exchange offers a snack bar, a barber shop, a service station, and an alterations shop. Hours vary according to the training season.

Recreation. Athletic facilities available at FTIG include four lighted tennis courts; eight softball fields (two lighted); two racquetball courts; a putting green with sand trap, finesse iron range, and driving range; two volleyball courts; two lighted outdoor multipurpose hard-surface courts; a sauna; and a bowling alley. In addition, there is a library with 12,500 cloth-bound volumes, an auto craft shop, and a physical conditioning center. Hunting and fishing are permitted on the installation in designated areas during season. The Appalachian Trail runs about one mile north of FTIG's border. There is excellent hunting and fishing throughout this area, which is also near the Poconos resorts that are noted for their fine skiing in season.

The Local Area. FTIG is located twenty-three miles east of Harrisburg, the capital of Pennsylvania; forty-six miles west of Reading; and fourteen miles north of Lebanon. Hershey is only fifteen miles southwest of the installation. Other attractions include the fabulous and delectable bolognas processed in nearby Lebanon; the Tulpehocken Manor Inn and Plantation, a restored colonial farmhouse and Victorian manor; Cornwall Iron Furnace, which began operation in 1742; Indian Echo Caverns near Harrisburg; the Middle Creek Wildlife Area, a 5,000-acre wildlife management area; and Penn National Race Track, twelve miles east of Harrisburg, offering Thoroughbred racing at its finest.

Philadelphia, Baltimore, Washington, D.C., Gettysburg and Antietam National Battlefield Parks, Valley Forge, and New York City are all within easy driving distance from FTIG.

For more information write to: Public Affairs Office, Headquarters, Fort Indiantown Gap, Annville, PA 17003-5011, or call (717) 865-5444.

Navy

PHILADELPHIA NAVAL BASE

The 1991 Base Realignment and Closure Commission designated Philadelphia Naval Base to close in 1996.

History. The U.S. Navy was born in Philadelphia in 1775, when the Continental Congress provided for the outfitting of two small wooden ships. Coincidentally, so was the United States of America born here the following July, and as they say, the rest is history. Oh, yes, and in 1982, the city of Philadelphia celebrated its 300th anniversary.

The U.S. Navy first established a shipyard at Philadelphia in 1801. It was moved to its present location on the Delaware River in 1875. Today the base is a small city with fifty-two miles of streets and four miles of waterfront and is home for the Naval Shipyard, Ship Systems Engineering Station, 4th Marine Corps District and Recruiting Station, Navy Damage Control Training Center, and other commands. About 4,000 active-duty personnel are assigned to the base along with over 2,400 of their family members. In 1993 the commands there employed more than 11,000 civilian personnel.

Housing and Schools. The base has over 900 units of family housing; the newest of these were constructed in 1975 and consist of two-story brick town houses located at Mustin Field. A Navy Lodge was completed there in 1987.

Day-care and preschool facilities are provided on the base, and the Naval Support Activity Educational Services Office offers information and assistance regarding registration in local civilian schools and college programs as well as facilities and assistance for a variety of career-development programs, including a library of Navy training manuals and textbooks. There are also over ninety colleges and universities in the Philadelphia area that service personnel may attend.

Personal Services. The Philadelphia Naval Hospital, located one-half mile north of the base on Pattison Avenue, operates a small clinic on the base itself, while the main complex offers a full range of medical care, some of the best available to military personnel and their families on the entire East Coast. The base offers a large commissary and Navy exchange; the exchange also operates a variety of concessions offering services, including a convenience store, a tire center, a tailor shop, and a service station. Officers, CPO, and enlisted mess facilities are also operated on the base.

Recreation. The recreation center offers personnel an indoor sports complex consisting of an indoor swimming pool, a gymnasium, and a sauna. The center also provides equipment issue and rental services, as well as assistance in making reservations at nearby recreation areas such as Long Beach Island, New Jersey.

The Local Area. By far, the biggest off-base attraction is the city of Philadelphia itself. This is one of the major cultural, historical, and recreational attractions on the entire East Coast. Everything is available there, from professional sporting events to historic tours and excellent shopping in Center City. The Pocono Mountains, just a short drive to the north, offer hiking, camping, and skiing in season; and miles of beaches offer swimming along the New Jersey coast.

For more information write to: Commander, Naval Base Philadelphia, Attention: Public Affairs Officer, Philadelphia, PA 19112-5098, or call (215) 897-5120.

WILLOW GROVE NAVAL AIR STATION

The "Minutemen" of Willow Grove Naval Air Station—the naval reservists who train there—come from as far away as California and work hard to master the science of antisubmarine warfare. They are assisted in day-to-day squadron operations by a small cadre of Navy professionals who make up the active-duty complement onboard the station.

History. Commissioned in 1943, Willow Grove NAS takes its name from the nearest post office, the traditional method for naming naval air stations. Willow Grove's 1,100 acres are the weekend home to the more than 5,000 reservists who train there each month as well as a contingent of 1,400 active-duty Navy personnel, their 2,800 dependents, and civilian employees.

Housing and Schools. Housing for enlisted personnel assigned to Willow Grove consists of about 200 town houses located at Shenandoah Woods, about eight miles from the station, in Warminster. Eligibility requirements are strict. There are no guest facilities at Willow Grove. Bachelor housing consists of 78 quarters (suites and single- and double-occupancy rooms) for officers and spaces for 200 enlisted personnel in 5 bachelor enlisted quarters.

Although no dependent schooling is offered on the station, adequate public schooling is available nearby, and there is a child-development center at the station. Opportunities for off-duty adult education abound in this area as well. Numerous colleges offering many different programs are located in the suburban area around Willow Grove, and many others in Philadelphia can be utilized by Navy personnel.

Personal Services and Recreation. Medical care is provided by a branch clinic located at Warminster; more comprehensive care is available at the Army hospital at Fort Dix, New Jersey. Willow Grove NAS offers many personal services, including a Navy exchange and a mini mart open seven days a week. A commissary store is available at the Philadelphia Navy Yard complex.

The station has an outdoor Olympic-size swimming pool and other physical fitness facilities, including tennis and racquetball courts, a gym, weight-lifting equipment, a bowling center, an auto hobby shop, and a library. The station also operates three chalets in the Poconos, each sleeping six to eight persons, and three twenty-four-foot and two nineteen-foot campers at Cape May, New Jersey. These campers are available from Memorial Day through September.

The Local Area. Located in suburban Philadelphia, Willow Grove participates in the best of both possible worlds: the exciting life of one of the world's great cities and the natural beauty of eastern Pennsylvania, with its wide variety of geographical and historical attractions.

Willow Grove (population 20,000) is located only twenty miles from downtown Philadelphia. The city itself offers every attraction from professional sports to historical events and other activities. National and state parks and water-recreation activities are available throughout the area. Both the Pocono Mountains and the South Jersey shore are reasonable drives from Willow Grove and are popular vacation sites.

For more information write to: Public Affairs Office, Naval Air Station, Willow Grove, PA 19090-5010, or call (215) 443-1776/1777.

RHODE ISLAND

Navy

NAVAL EDUCATION AND TRAINING CENTER

History. The Naval Education and Training Center (NETC) sits along the eastern shore of Narragansett Bay, just north of Newport and west of Middleton. The Navy first came to the Narragansett Bay area in 1869 when an experimental torpedo station was established on Goat Island. (Goat Island was transferred to the city of Newport in 1951.) In 1881 the Navy acquired Coasters Harbor Island from the city of Newport, and it was there, a few years later, that the U.S. Naval War College and the Navy's first recruit-training station were established. Luce Hall, Pringle Hall, and Mahan Hall—the original buildings—are still in use at the war college complex on the island.

Today there are thirty-two separate commands in Newport that are devoted to the mission of officer training and education. The officer candidate school there, for instance, has commissioned more officers since its inception only a few years ago than the Naval Academy at Annapolis has commissioned in the past 125 years. Today the NETC has a permanent population of over 1,800 military and civilian personnel with a daily student population of over 500. The Navy is the single largest employer in Newport.

Housing and Schools. About 1,900 units of government housing are available for personnel assigned to the NETC in several housing areas throughout Rhode Island (the island where Newport and the NETC are located, not the state in general). In addition, a 50-unit mobile home park is available, as is a 67-unit Navy Lodge.

Dependent children attend local public and parochial schools. Nursery, child-care, and preschool facilities are also available. The Navy Campus offers associate degree programs from Roger Williams and Johnson and Wales Colleges on base, but off-base college programs are available from Salve Regina College, the University of Rhode Island, Bryant College, Rhode Island College, and Brown University, in Providence.

Personal Services. Medical and dental care are provided by the naval dental clinic and the 128-bed naval hospital. Other support facilities include Navy exchange retail stores, a commissary store, a package beverage store, and a gas station that offers car rentals and repairs. There are also snack bars, a cafeteria, beauty and barber shops, officers and enlisted clubs, and other facilities.

Recreation. Recreational facilities include the Katy Field Picnic Area and Carr Point Recreational Area on Coasters Harbor Island with excellent outdoor facilities as well as the Feature Point Picnic Area on Coddington Point. There is also a Navy beach at Sachuset Point, Middleton, where swimming and private parties may be enjoyed during the summer months.

On base are an indoor swimming pool, tennis courts, and a gymnasium. The auto hobby shop has fifteen repair stalls.

The Local Area. Newport is a fine old town, replete with magnificent mansions and museums. It was at Newport that French General Rochambeau landed in 1780 with men and materiel for the American Army that proved so decisive in winning the Revolution. In nearby Portsmouth is the site of Rhode Island's only major Revolutionary War land battle, at Butts Hill Fort. Such greats as Lafayette, Hancock, Greene, and Sullivan participated in the fighting on 2 August 1778. This battle also saw the first black regiment to fight for the American flag.

In Newport is the sloop *Providence*, first built in 1768 and now fully restored. The sloop had the added distinction of being naval hero John Paul Jones's first command. In Touro Park, at the corner of Bellevue Avenue and Mill Street, is the Old Stone Mill, a mysterious edifice that some people swear must have been built by the Vikings, hundreds of years before Columbus discovered America. There is not a shred of proof for this claim, but it is true that the tower was once owned by a colonist named Benedict Arnold, who used it as a windmill.

Another interesting place to visit is Newport's famous Cliff Walk and Ocean Drive, where you can take in the breathtaking scenery along the rocky seacoast and visit some of the stately mansions that grace the neighborhood.

For more information write to: Personal Services Center, Bldg. 1260, NETC, Newport, RI 02841, or call (401) 841-2383.

SOUTH CAROLINA

Air Force

CHARLESTON AIR FORCE BASE

If you have ever dreamed of living in a town by the sea that is steeped in history but as up-to-date as the C-141 Starlifter aircraft *and* where the climate is mild and pleasant all year, look no farther, because Charleston is the place.

History. Charleston Air Force Base is actually located ten miles north of the city and is part of North Charleston, a community of around 79,000 people. Although an airfield existed on the present site of the base long before World War II, the Army Air Corps did not take full control of the facility until 1941. Today the base contains more than 3,500 acres under the jurisdiction of the 437th Airlift Wing, and it serves as one of three aerial ports on the Atlantic coast. The base is home for about 4,000 active-duty military personnel and their 6,000 family members plus 1,900 civilian workers and 3,500 reservists.

Housing and Schools. Charleston offers 977 family housing units, all of them built between 1959 and 1961. Waiting periods vary from thirty days to ten months. The longest wait is for two-bedroom homes; six months is the average maximum. Charleston also has a seventy-five-unit trailer park. Although no temporary family lodging is available on the base, accommodations on a space-available basis may be had at Charleston House, a one-hundred-room guest facility.

Dependent children attend school off base. On-base educational opportunities for adults are offered through the education center and include programs from Central Michigan University, Webster College, Southern Illinois University,

Trident Technical College, and Baptist College at Charleston. Off-base programs are offered by the Citadel, the College of Charleston, and other institutions.

Personal Services. Outpatient medical care is provided by the USAF medical clinic, but inpatient care is available from the naval regional medical center in the city of Charleston. This is a modern, 207-bed facility ten miles from the base.

The base commissary has a sales area of over 32,000 square feet, carries 16,000 items, and is visited by over 37,000 customers each month; base exchange facilities offer over a dozen concessions for military shoppers. Other services include a day and night nursery open six days a week, a club system for officers and enlisted personnel, and banking facilities.

Recreation. With its subtropical climate and four distinct but mild seasons, recreation is a key aspect of life in the Charleston area. The Air Force provides a wide variety of sport and hobby facilities. There are three swimming pools; an eighteen-hole golf course; rod and gun, aero, and saddle clubs; a sixteen-lane bowling alley; a fully equipped gymnasium; and a family campground with sites for all types of recreational vehicles, adjacent to the picnic grounds.

The Local Area. Charleston itself abounds with historical attractions, not the least of which is Fort Sumter, the site of the bombardment that started the Civil War. Many other attractions are free to the general public. Parks and camping facilities abound, and the Atlantic coast affords access to public beaches with swimming, sailing, water skiing, pleasure boating, and deep-sea fishing.

For more information write to: Public Affairs Office, 437th AW/PA, Charleston AFB, SC 29404-5154, or call (803) 566-5582.

MYRTLE BEACH AIR FORCE BASE

Myrtle Beach AFB was deactivated in 1993.

SHAW AIR FORCE BASE

The four F-16 Fighting Falcon squadrons and the OA-10 Thunderbolt II squadron of the 363rd Fighter Wing are the heart of operations at Shaw Air Force Base. Shaw is also home to the 9th Air Force Headquarters, which is responsible for all fighter units east of the Mississippi and command of the Central Command Air Forces.

History. Named after 1st Lt. Ervin Davis Shaw, a Sumter County native who was shot down while flying a long-range reconnaissance mission over France during World War I, today the base is a small city of over 16,000 people: 5,800 military personnel, 560 civilian employees, and over 13,000 dependents. The base occupies 3,336 acres seven miles west of Sumter and has custodial responsibility for an additional 8,000 leased acres at Poinsett Bombing Range, southwest of Sumter.

Housing and Schools. On-base housing consists of 1,704 units. The longest waiting period for two- and three-bedroom on-base housing averages about a year.

The wait for other units is from three to six months. Guest housing is also available for transients and guests. The cost of living in the Shaw-Sumter area is reasonable.

Dependent children of service families stationed at Shaw attend primary schools in the immediate vicinity of the base. Educational opportunities for adults wishing to further their education are excellent. The base education center assists personnel in taking courses offered by the University of South Carolina, Saint Leo College, Central Carolina Technical College, Florence-Darlington Technical College, and Troy State University.

Personal Services. Medical care at Shaw is provided by the 363rd Fighter Wing Hospital, a thirty-bed facility. A commissary and base exchange with many concessions are among the many personal services available at Shaw.

Recreation. Shaw is not short on recreational facilities, either. The base offers an eighteen-hole golf course, three swimming pools, an excellent fitness center, a bowling alley, a rod and gun club, a picnic area, tennis courts, officers and enlisted open messes, and Wateree Lake Recreation Area. Wateree Lake is located thirty-five miles from the base, north of Camden. Fishing, sailing, and ski boats may be rented there, as well as cabins. Three small lakes on base are stocked with fish.

The Local Area. The city of Sumter has a population of 42,000 and boasts eight playgrounds and parks. The summers last from May through September, and the winters are mild, with some snow, but generally the snow does not remain long on the ground. The state of South Carolina in general is a recreational paradise, with fifty properties comprising 80,000 acres. There are also 400,000 acres of fishing lakes, and over 290 species of saltwater and freshwater fish. With a 281-mile coastline, water sports are available year-round.

Shaw is 41 miles west of Columbus, 94 miles southeast of Charleston, and 106 miles south of Charlotte, North Carolina.

For more information write to: 363rd Fighter Wing Public Affairs, Attention: Community Relations, 517 Lance Ave., Shaw AFB, SC 29152-5041, or call (803) 668-3621.

Army

FORT JACKSON

History. "Victory starts here," proudly proclaims Fort Jackson's motto, and to underscore this fact, the statue of Gen. Andrew Jackson, for whom the post was named, stands at the main entrance. The "Smokey Bear Hat" drill sergeants counting cadence in the early morning mist and soldiers marching to the lyrics of "Jody" songs have been part of Fort Jackson's hallmark since 2 June 1917, when the installation was established as an infantry training center.

Fort Jackson is located in Columbia, the capital city of South Carolina, and about 100 miles from Augusta, Georgia, to the west; Charlotte, North Carolina, to the north; and Charleston, South Carolina, to the south. Fort Jackson is a community of over 97,000: 14,000 soldiers and their 11,000 family members; a civilian workforce of more than 3,800; and 67,000 retirees and their families. Annually, more than 40,000 trainees pass through the basic and advanced individual courses at Jackson; another 380 personnel graduate from the Drill Sergeant School each year.

Housing and Schools. With 1,270 sets of family quarters, Fort Jackson offers soldiers and their families all the amenities of modern military living. Guest accommodations are also available on the post.

Dependent children living on post attend one of three elementary schools at Fort Jackson. There is also a child-development center on post. The University of South Carolina conducts undergraduate courses on post, while Midlands Technical, Coker, and Park Colleges, and Webster University offer courses, also on post, leading to degrees in business administration, social sciences, management, and health care.

Personal Services and Recreation. Moncrief Army Community Hospital, a modern 410-bed facility, provides a comprehensive array of medical and dental services. The post has a large commissary as well as three convenience stores and a large post exchange.

Recreation facilities consist of two movie theaters; two bowling alleys; five swimming pools; two golf courses; hobby shops; tennis courts; and Weston Lake Recreation Area, a 240-acre picnic area that also includes fishing, camping, and miniature golf.

The Local Area. South Carolina is a state filled with 400 years of history preserved in museums, churches, battlefields, forts, and plantation houses. Its mild climate encourages visitors and residents to participate in some form of outdoor recreation nearly year-round. This state offers 400,000 acres of lakes among its many natural attractions. The largest recreational area on the post is 240-acre Lake Weston, which is set among 1,200 rolling acres of woodland where soldiers and their families may camp, swim, fish, and golf.

For more information write to: Army Community Service, Fort Jackson, SC 29207-5060, or call (803) 751-5256.

Marine Corps

BEAUFORT MARINE CORPS AIR STATION

Beaufort Marine Corps Air Station comprises more than 6,700 acres at the airfield complex itself, on the northern side of Port Royal Sound, just off Highway 21, and another 1,100 acres three miles to the west, where the Laurel Bay family housing area is located.

The station was commissioned in June 1943. Today Beaufort is home to the ultrasophisticated F/A-18 "Hornet" fighter bombers of Marine Aircraft Group 31.

MCAS Beaufort is currently home and workplace for approximately 3,100 military personnel and their 5,500 dependents, and 600 civilian employees.

Housing and Schools. There are 176 units of family housing at the main airfield complex and another 1,100 quarters at Laurel Bay. There are also 157 spaces available in a mobile home park. The Detreville House offers temporary lodging at a reasonable price for those reporting in for duty or just staying a night or two. This hotel-like facility offers cable TV, a picnic and playground area, kitchenettes, laundry facilities, and other conveniences.

Two elementary schools are operated at Laurel Bay; high schools are available in nearby Beaufort. The Joint Education Office offers on-base classes that range from high school completion to postgraduate studies. In addition, the University of South Carolina, Beaufort Campus, and the Technical College of the Lowcountry are available for off-post attendance.

Personal Services and Recreation. Medical care for personnel and their families at MCAS Beaufort is available from the Beaufort Naval Hospital in nearby Port Royal. There are a small dispensary and a dental clinic located at the station. While there is no commissary at the station itself, there is a large one at Parris Island Recruit Depot, only eight miles away; an exchange and convenience store are located onboard the station as are a service station and other concessions.

Recreational facilities include a twelve-lane bowling alley, three swimming pools, auto and craft hobby shops, tennis courts, a gymnasium and physical fitness center, a skeet range, five fishing piers, two boat ramps, fifteen wildlife management areas, stables, and rentals for boating, camping, and sports equipment at moderate prices. Officers, staff NCO, and enlisted club facilities are also available at the station, and there is a full range of recreational activities at the Parris Island Recruit Depot.

The Local Area. Beaufort MCAS is located about seventy miles south of the city of Charleston, one of the most historic and beautiful places anywhere along the Atlantic coast. The nearest towns to the station are Beaufort, population 25,000, and Port Royal, population 3,000. These are beautiful, rustic towns whose major industry is tourism. Hundreds of thousands of people visit Hunting Island State Park on the Atlantic, about twenty miles due east of Beaufort, each season.

For more information write to: Joint Public Affairs Office, Marine Corps Air Station, Beaufort, SC 29904-5000, or call (803) 522-7201.

PARRIS ISLAND MARINE CORPS RECRUIT DEPOT

History. The earliest people to suffer the ordeal of initiation into a new world on Parris Island might have been French Huguenots who came there in 1562. Since 1941, thousands of young Americans have endured the ordeal of boot camp at the Parris Island Marine Corps Depot, passing initiation into the world of the U.S. Marines. "We don't train recruits . . . we make Marines" is the Parris Island motto.

The first Marine Corps post established at Parris Island was commissioned in 1891 and consisted of a very small garrison under the command of a first sergeant.

The depot's mission today is to administer recruiting and training for all the states east of the Mississippi (and training for female recruits nationwide). Parris Island itself consists of marsh and land area composed of several islands and extending over about 7,000 acres, 3,200 of which are habitable; recruits spend most of their time in the uninhabitable portion. Parris Island derives its name from Alexander Parris, who secured the title to the land in 1715.

Housing and Schools. There are 584 family housing units available to Marines stationed at the depot. Onboard the depot itself are 232 quarters for all grades; another 352 sets are maintained at the Laurel Bay Housing Area, three miles from Beaufort Marine Corps Air Station. At the depot are also 125 mobile home spaces, in the Argonne Trailer Park. An officers guest house and a hostess house provide inexpensive temporary lodging; the latter may not be used for longer than seven days, however.

Two elementary schools are open to military dependents at the Laurel Bay housing area. There are three high schools, three junior high schools, and twelve elementary schools in Beaufort. A day-care center is located at the depot. Adult educational services are provided by the education office at the depot and include testing and counseling as well as college courses on and off the base.

Personal Services. A commissary and a Marine Corps exchange with a variety of concessions are available at the depot. There are also a bank and Navy Federal Credit Union, a Burger King (now part of the Low Country Food Festival), a hot dog shop (in the bowling alley), a Baskin Robbins ice cream shop, and a Dunkin' Donuts.

Although there are branch medical and dental clinics at Parris Island, dependents are seen there only on an emergency basis. Definitive medical care is provided by Beaufort Naval Hospital, located on 127 acres along the Beaufort River on Ribaut Road, about halfway between Beaufort Marine Corps Air Station and Parris Island.

Recreation. Recreational activities include an eighteen-hole golf course; a twenty-lane bowling center; four swimming pools; officers, NCO, and enlisted clubs; a library; a theater; a fitness center; ceramics, woodworking, and auto hobby shops; a marina; and a museum.

The Local Area. The countryside around Parris Island is rich in history. Port Royal, across Battery Creek, between the depot main gate and the town of Beaufort, was first visited by the Spanish in the year 1525 and permanently settled by English immigrants in 1670. It was the site of an American Revolution battle in February 1779 and eventually became a Royalist stronghold after British occupation in 1782.

The town of Beaufort, five miles north of the depot, combines the graceful architecture of prerevolutionary and Civil War America with the convenience of modern living. Beaufort is not a particularly rich town in a material sense, but it is a place where family pride runs deep. Before the Civil War it was a cultured and affluent place and a seething cauldron of radical anti-Union sentiment; the Ordinance of Secession was drawn up there, and the town was one of the first in the South to be seized and occupied by Union forces.

Savannah, Georgia, is only forty-six miles to the south of the depot, and Charleston is a seventy-mile drive to the north. Hunting and fishing are varied in this area, and the mild climate permits outdoor activities year-round.

For more information write to: Public Affairs Office, P.O. Box 5059, Marine Corps Recruit Depot, Parris Island, SC 29905-0059, or call (803) 525-2943.

Navy

BEAUFORT NAVAL HOSPITAL

As the primary military health-care facility servicing both Parris Island Marine Corps Recruit Depot and the Beaufort Marine Corps Air Station, Beaufort Naval Hospital treats about 300,000 outpatients per year out of a total military population of 27,000 active-duty and retired personnel and their family members. The hospital is an ultra-modern, forty-nine-bed facility staffed by 420 active-duty personnel and 186 civilian employees.

Housing, Schools, and Personal Services. The hospital operates a total of sixty-one family quarters, eight for officers and fifty-three for enlisted personnel. Bachelor accommodations are provided on the installation for enlisted personnel. Children attend area schools. While there is no commissary at the hospital, there are a mini mart, a service station, an optical shop, a snack bar, a library, a branch of the Navy Federal Credit Union, and a barber/beauty shop. Located halfway between the air station and the recruit depot, hospital personnel may take full advantage of all the facilities provided by those sprawling installations.

Recreation. Recreational facilities include a swimming pool, tennis courts, and the Shipwreck Recreation Club, with its lounge, snack bar, catering service, and ticket/tour office. The morale and recreation department also operates a fitness trail, ball fields, and an equipment rental service.

For more information write to: Commanding Officer, Naval Hospital, Attention: Public Affairs, 1 Pinckney Blvd., Beaufort, SC 29902-6148, or call (803) 525-5600.

CHARLESTON NAVAL BASE

"Oh, to be in Charleston, now that April's here! But alas, no Charleston for Grandpa!" the Rhode Islander Howard Phillips Lovecraft wrote in the spring of 1935. Visitors have been enthusiastic about Charleston since the first English settlers arrived in 1670. In fact, the only visitors not known to have been exactly pleased with the Charlestonians were the Union soldiers at Fort Sumter when the opening shots of the Civil War were fired at them on 12 April 1861.

History. The present site of the Charleston Naval Base, the Navy's third largest home port, was acquired in 1901, and today its 20,500 acres are home and workplace for 22,000 military personnel and more than 11,000 civilians belonging to more than fifty-nine naval commands and fifty-seven ships and submarines.

Housing and Schools. More than 2,600 family quarters are available to Navy personnel in the Charleston area. There is a Navy Lodge onboard the base, with advance reservations accepted on a first-come, first-served basis. Trailers are also available at the Short Stay Recreation Area on a day-to-day basis.

Although there is no dependent schooling onboard any Navy installation in the area, three child-care centers are operated in the area. The Navy Campus also operates an off-duty education program that offers opportunities for active-duty personnel to complete high school and college-level programs.

Personal Services. There are three commissaries in the Charleston area: one at the base, one at the naval weapons station, and one at Charleston Air Force Base. Likewise, a large Navy exchange complex as well as the base exchange at Charleston Air Force Base are available to all military personnel and their families. The Beaufort Naval Regional Hospital is a modern hospital that provides a wide range of medical, surgical, and outpatient services; it is also available to personnel stationed in the Charleston area.

Recreation. Because of Charleston's average year-round temperature of 65° F. and the 65 percent probability of sunshine year-round, outdoor activities of all kinds are available to military personnel stationed in the area. These include camping, swimming, sailing, deep-sea fishing, and a host of other pursuits. The Short Stay Recreation Area is operated year-round. Located near the Atlantic coast on Lake Moultrie, about forty miles north of the base, the area consists of fifty-five acres with eighty camper sites, swimming areas, a marina, and picnic areas.

Indoor recreation facilities include a bowling alley, a gymnasium, wood and auto hobby shops, and squash and handball courts.

The Local Area. To the north of Charleston, bordered by the Atlantic on the east and by Lake Moultrie on the west, is the Francis Marion National Forest; beyond is Lake Moultrie, with many camping and fishing sites open to the public. The city of Charleston itself is a beautiful place that affords many contrasts between the old and the new. It abounds with relics and monuments commemorating events in American history since the Revolution. The city's preserved buildings reflect its development over the past three centuries; more than 1,000 buildings are protected in the city as historic landmarks.

For more information write to: Public Affairs Office, Naval Base, Charleston, SC 29408-5100, or call (803) 743-4111.

SOUTH DAKOTA

Air Force

ELLSWORTH AIR FORCE BASE

The name "Black Hills of South Dakota" conjures up an image in the minds of most Americans of gold, Sioux Indians, enormous buffalo herds, and the Dakota prairie. The fact is, not too long ago all those images would have been typical of the region where today the Minuteman II missiles share their holes with the prairie dogs, and the aircraft of the 28th Bomb Wing roam the skies above the ranges where buffalo still graze.

History. Named in honor of Brig. Gen. Richard Ellsworth, who died in the crash of an RB-36 aircraft in Newfoundland in 1953, the base began its existence as an Army Air Field in September 1942. Today it is home of the 28th Bomb Wing, 99th Tactics and Training Wing, and 28th Support Group. Ellsworth's population of over 22,000 includes over 6,000 military personnel and their 10,000 family members.

Housing and Schools. There are over 2,800 units of family housing at Ellsworth. Guest accommodations for incoming families are also available on a reserved basis; all others are accepted on a space-available basis only. The family quarters are located in seven separate housing developments. There are two child-care centers at the base, and school-age dependent children attend the Douglas School System.

The base education office offers a number of college programs for adults. These courses are available from the Black Hills State University, Embry-Riddle

Aeronautical University, National College, the University of South Dakota, and South Dakota State University.

Personal Services and Recreation. The thirty-five-bed USAF Hospital at Ellsworth is an excellent inpatient and outpatient facility. Other personal support facilities at the base include a well-stocked commissary and base exchange complex, officers and NCO clubs, and a consolidated beverage store.

Recreational facilities include a sixteen-lane bowling center, a nine-hole golf course, an eighteen-hole miniature golf course, a recreation center, a base theater, a riding club, and auto and wood hobby shops. Outdoor recreation facilities include large pavilions for picnicking, equipment rentals, a trap and skeet range, and a family camp with water and electricity hookups.

The Local Area. Ellsworth AFB is located twelve miles east of Rapid City, a metropolis of over 51,000 people. Just to the southeast of Rapid City are Buffalo Gap National Grassland and Badlands National Monument. Due south of the city are Mount Rushmore National Monument, Custer State Park, and Wind Cave National Park; to the west is the famous Black Hills National Forest. This area offers camping and magnificent sightseeing.

For more information write to: Public Affairs Officer, 28th BW, Ellsworth AFB, SD 57706-5000, or call (605) 385-5056.

TENNESSEE

Air Force

ARNOLD AIR FORCE BASE

Arnold Air Force Base is home for the Air Force Material Command's Arnold Engineering Development Center. The center conducts aerospace testing in its wind tunnels, jet and rocket engine altitude test cells, space chambers, and ballistic ranges for the Department of Defense, NASA, other federal agencies, civilian educational institutions, and commercial aerospace companies. Both full-size hardware and scale models are tested there under conditions simulating altitudes up to 1,000 miles and velocities up to twenty-three times the speed of sound (17,500 m.p.h.).

History. Named after pioneer aviator and five-star general of the Air Force Henry H. ("Hap") Arnold, the base occupies 40,000 acres in the middle of the state of Tennessee, about halfway between Nashville and Chattanooga. Testing began there in 1953.

Arnold Air Force Base is a small, tightly knit community that supports approximately 120 active-duty Air Force personnel, 200 Air Force civilian employees, and 3,500 civilian contract personnel. Due to the type of work done at the station, entry into the work areas is strictly controlled.

Housing and Schools. Arnold operates only forty housing units: twenty-three for officers and seventeen for enlisted personnel. Guest housing consists of forty-five rooms.

Dependent schooling is available off base. Motlow State Community College is located nearby at Tullahoma. Middle Tennessee State University is situated at

Murfreesboro and the University of the South is at Sewanee; both are less than an hour's drive from the base. The University of Tennessee Space Institute is located about six miles from the industrial area of the base, on the shore of Woods Reservoir.

Personal Services. A commissary and exchange offer a wide choice of items to personnel at the base. There is a medical aid station there too, but a full-time physician is not assigned to it. A civilian doctor comes in once a week to treat assigned active-duty personnel and their dependents only. Most of the services normally furnished active-duty personnel are available only at Redstone Arsenal, Alabama, approximately sixty miles to the south. No child-care facilities are available at Arnold AFB.

Recreation. Recreation facilities on the base include a nine-hole golf course, a skeet range, a rifle range, ball and tennis courts, and miles of nature trails. A family camp with twenty-two trailer spaces is available also. A consolidated hobby shop is situated in Arnold Village, the family housing area. There are waterfront picnic areas, two beaches, and boat ramps located at points along the Woods Reservoir shore, a 4,000-acre body of water offering water sports and fishing. The Arnold special services office maintains a fleet of two fishing boats, three ski boats plus two pontoon boats, and a sailboat, all of which are rented to service personnel at a minimal fee. Arnold also has a combined-ranks club.

The Local Area. Hunting is a popular activity on the base. Under the control of the Tennessee Wildlife Resources Agency, the Arnold game management area offers deer, duck, turkey, and small-game hunting.

Arnold Air Force Base is situated approximately sixty-five miles south of Nashville and sixty-five miles northwest of Chattanooga, on Interstate 24 at Exit 117, among the cities of Tullahoma, Manchester, and Winchester. The countryside there is beautiful, well wooded and well watered, and dotted with many fine state parks. The famous Jack Daniels Distillery is located nearby, near Lynchburg.

For more information write to: Public Affairs Office, Arnold AFB, TN 37389-2213, or call (615) 454-5586.

Navy

MEMPHIS NAVAL AIR STATION

History. Memphis Naval Air Station sprawls over more than 3,400 acres near the town of Millington, Tennessee. The station complement is approximately 14,000 active-duty and civilian personnel. The Naval Air Technical Training Center, one of the station's most important commands, is 5,000 strong and graduates approximately 19,000 Navy and Marine students annually. The Chief of Naval Technical Training is responsible for conducting over 4,000 Navy courses throughout the command's system of fifty-nine training facilities located at twenty-eight installations extending to locations all over the continental United States and Hawaii. It is safe to say the Memphis NAS has come a long way since it was originally commissioned as a Naval Reserve base in September 1942.

Housing and Schools. The station has over 1,000 family housing units for eligible personnel as well as a Navy Lodge. Lodge reservations are accepted only from personnel arriving or departing the station on permanent-change-of-station orders. A limited number of mobile home spaces are available onboard, on a first-come, first-served basis.

While there are no schools onboard the station for dependent children, a large day-care center is available. The Navy Campus for Achievement offers a number of on-base programs during off-duty hours with the cooperation of Memphis State University, the University of Arkansas, Embry-Riddle Aeronautical University, Southern Illinois University, and others. Professional guidance and counseling and assistance in course enrollment are available through the Navy Campus for active-duty, dependent, and civilian personnel.

Personal Services and Recreation. A commissary store and a Navy exchange with a number of concessions are located at the station. Medical care is provided by the 230-bed naval hospital.

A full range of indoor and outdoor recreational activities are available at Memphis NAS, including a golf course, a riding stable, and a lakes and picnics area comprising about thirty acres of water and fourteen separate picnic areas where fishing is permitted.

The Local Area. Memphis NAS, in Millington, is located approximately twenty miles north of Memphis, along U.S. Highway 51. Seven miles west of Millington are the Mississippi River Bluffs and Shelby Forest State Park, containing thousands of acres of woodlands, walking and riding trails, picnic areas, and boat and cottage rentals. Memphis is a bustling city with all the conveniences of modern life. The city is situated on Chickasaw Bluffs in the southwest corner of the state, and borders Mississippi and Arkansas. Winters in this area can be quite cold, and the summers are hot and humid.

For more information write to: Public Affairs Office, NAS Memphis, Millington, TN 38054-5000, or call (901) 873-5509.

TEXAS

Air Force

BERGSTROM AIR FORCE BASE

Bergstrom Air Force Base closed in September 1993.

BROOKS AIR FORCE BASE

History. Since originally opening seventy-five years ago, Brooks Air Force Base has gone from a base for the crude flying machines of World War I to a sophisticated aerospace medical research and training facility.

Named after Cadet Sidney Brooks, Jr., the first native San Antonian to die in World War I, Brooks AFB lies in the southeastern area of the city of San Antonio. The base's 3,000 military and civilian employees work at Brooks organizations such as the Armstrong Laboratory, the U.S. Air Force School of Aerospace Medicine, the Human Systems Program Office, and the Air Force Center for Environmental Excellence.

These organizations ensure that Air Force systems and operations are designed with human capabilities in mind; that weapon systems and the people operating them are compatible; that medical personnel are trained in aerospace medicine; and that the Air Force has the capability to handle all aspects of environmental cleanup, planning, and compliance.

Housing and Schools. There are only 170 units of family housing at Brooks.

The waiting periods for these quarters vary from sixteen to eighteen months, depending on the size of the sponsor's family and category of housing required. Temporary quarters are provided at the guest house for newcomers and visitors, where eight units are available, and reservations are accepted on a first-come, first-served basis only.

Dependent children attend local schools. There is a day-care center at the base, however, and the base education office offers a wide range of programs for military and civilian personnel and their dependents.

Personal Services. Services at Brooks include a base exchange, a commissary, a bank and credit union, and a medical clinic for treatment of routine medical problems; definitive care is available at Lackland Air Force Base or Brooke Army Medical Center, both conveniently nearby.

Recreation. Recreational facilities include officers and NCO clubs, a sports and fitness center, a rod and gun club, garden plots for airmen and their families, a riding stable, softball fields, swimming and wading pools, a nine-hole golf course, a picnic area, and a family camping area. A variety of youth programs are also available at Brooks.

Personnel stationed at Brooks may also use the fifty-one-acre Randolph Recreation Area at Canyon Lake, on the Guadalupe River, about seventeen miles west of New Braunfels; the Fort Sam Houston Recreation Area, near Canyon City; and the Kelly Air Force Base site on Lake Lyndon B. Johnson, in Llano County, about one hundred miles north of San Antonio.

For more information write to: Public Affairs Office, 2510 Kennedy Dr., Ste. 1, Brooks AFB, TX 78235-5120, or call (210) 536-3234.

CARSWELL AIR FORCE BASE

Carswell Air Force Base was closed in September 1993.

DYESS AIR FORCE BASE

Set in the middle of Texas Big Country, the very name Abilene elicits reminiscences of the Old West, cowboys, cattle drives, and gunfights. All that is gone now, if indeed it ever existed in quite the way we have come to think of it, and today the countryside surrounding Dyess Air Force Base is well integrated into the twentieth century—home of the B-1B, it is also the home of twenty-seven vintage aircraft located around the base.

History. The base is named in honor of Lt. Col. William Edwin Dyess, an extraordinary hero of World War II fame who died in a crash in California in 1943, after surviving some of the most harrowing experiences in combat. The base was first established in 1956 and today occupies over 6,400 acres about six miles southwest of Abilene. It is the home of more than 5,100 military personnel assigned to the 96th Wing, the 463rd Airlift Wing, and various tenant units.

Housing and Schools. There are 997 units of family housing at Dyess in one of the finest housing areas to be found on any Air Force base. Waiting periods for junior enlisted housing currently range from twenty-two to twenty-four months. Waiting periods vary for senior enlisted and company-grade quarters. Company- and field-grade officers may wait up to one year for housing. Guest facilities are available in the Dyess Inn.

Educational opportunities for children and adults living in Dyess are excellent. The Abilene Independent School District has two high schools, five junior high schools, and nineteen elementary schools, as well as excellent parochial and private schools. Adult education is offered by Abilene Christian University, Hardin-Simmons University, and McMurry College.

Personal Services. Base services include a base exchange complex and a 51,000-square-foot commissary with over 18,000 feet of sales space. Medical care is provided by a forty-bed hospital center.

Recreation. A recreation center, a ten-lane bowling center, an eighteen-hole golf course, tennis courts, a gymnasium, three swimming pools, and arts and crafts and auto hobby shops are available on the base. The Air Force family camp is located at Possum Kingdom, a beautiful resort area nearby.

The Local Area. The climate at Dyess is temperate, with annual temperature averages of around 64° F. The relative humidity stays at around 40 percent in the summer, which keeps the heat from becoming too oppressive. Average rainfall is about twenty-five inches.

Abilene is approximately 250 miles north of San Antonio and 175 miles west of Dallas. Much culture and outdoor recreation can be enjoyed in Abilene, from the Philharmonic Orchestra, Community Band, and Fine Arts Museum to the Abilene State Park, 19 miles south of town. Fort Phantom Hill, Nelson Park Zoo, Lake Fort Phantom, Lake Hubbard, Lake Abilene, and Lake Kirby are also attractions. The city boasts many fine shops and restaurants, a sixty-nine-acre city park, three eighteen-hole golf courses, hunting and fishing, and outdoor sports in the outlying areas.

For more information write to: Community Relations Office, 650 2nd St., Dyess AFB, TX 79607-1960, or call (915) 696-2863.

GOODFELLOW AIR FORCE BASE

Goodfellow Air Force Base is home of the Air Force's intelligence training mission. Each year thousands of Air Force, Army, Navy, and Marine students come there to learn the secrets and complexities of the latest intelligence skills. In today's fast-moving and technological world, every graduate is assured of a job after completing training.

History. Named after Lt. John J. Goodfellow, Jr., a resident of the nearby town of San Angelo who was killed when his plane crashed in France in 1918, the base opened in February 1941. Throughout World War II and for more than a decade afterward, Goodfellow's mission consisted of training pilots. Its flying mission ended in October 1958, when the Air Training Command transferred the base to the Security Service (now the Electronic Security Command). The base reverted to the Air Training Command in 1978. Today Goodfellow is home to 1,700 active-duty personnel, their 3,000 family members, a civilian workforce of over 600, and an average student population of about 1,000 personnel.

Housing and Schools. There are 296 sets of family quarters at Goodfellow: 96 government-controlled on base and another 200 leased units off base, near Lake Nasworthy. The first 134 sets of these leased quarters were opened in October 1987. New dormitories for enlisted and officer personnel, and a new transient family quarters complex are available for newly assigned personnel and their guests, on a space-available basis.

Dependent children attend schools in the San Angelo Independent School District. A child-care center is operated on base, and the base education services center provides counseling and information pertaining to local programs conducted on the base and at the campus of Angelo State University.

Personal Services. A 52,000-square-foot commissary offers over 6,000 items to shoppers, and the base exchange, with a number of concessions in its mini mall, offers a wide variety of shopping bargains. Medical care at Goodfellow is provided by a USAF clinic, with most services dispensed on an appointment basis. Referrals are made to a regional medical center in San Angelo as well as several smaller hospitals. Some military patients are referred to Wilford Hall Medical Center at Lackland Air Force Base in San Antonio or Dyess Air Force Base in Abilene.

Recreation. Recreational facilities include a new arts and crafts center, a woodworking center, an auto hobby shop, a recreation center, two gymnasiums, two swimming pools, an eight-lane bowling center, and Lake Nasworthy Recreation Camp, about ten miles southwest of the base. The area has fishing, boating, sailing, and outdoor sports. A spacious NCO club and a newly constructed officers club serve as the hub of Goodfellow's social life. Of special note to gourmets of Texas cooking, each September Goodfellow hosts the annual Armed Forces International Chili Cook-Off at the Lake Nasworthy Recreation Camp. The winner receives an invitation to the prestigious chili championship at Terlingua, Texas. Unreconstructed Yankees and other dudes must bring their own bicarbonate of soda.

The Local Area. Goodfellow AFB is adjacent to the town of San Angelo. The climate in this part of Texas is semi-arid, with average temperatures ranging between 46° F. and 88° F. throughout the year. Rain averages about seventeen inches a year and snowfall is very light.

San Angelo grew up around Fort Concho, which was established there in 1867 to protect settlers from the Indians. Today the Fort Concho Museum is a tourist spot.

The Concho River flows through the town of San Angelo, so water sports abound in the vicinity. There are also three lakes within a thirty-minute drive of the town: O. C. Fisher Reservoir; Twin Buttes Reservoir (with over 180,000 acre-feet of water); and Lake Nasworthy. Local celebrations worth the visitor's attention are the Lamblast, a World's Championship Lamb Cookoff, and the Fiesta del Concho in June, which includes a river parade, street dancing, and other activities. Angelo State University is an attraction to those who can stay long enough to take courses there in one of its thirty-seven undergraduate or twenty graduate programs. The San Angelo Coliseum, capable of seating over 5,000 people, hosts many public activities from rodeos and stock shows to symphony concerts.

For more information write to: Public Affairs Office, Goodfellow AFB, TX 76908-5000, or call (915) 654-3876.

KELLY AIR FORCE BASE

Logistics is the primary concern of the San Antonio Air Logistics Center at Kelly Air Force Base. To the more than 16,000 personnel of the ALC, logistics is very big business indeed. The center provides worldwide logistics support for a number of different weapon systems, including the C-5, the T-37, the T-38, and the new C-17 aircraft. It also manages more than 35,000 aircraft engines and nearly 55,000 nonaircraft engines, more than half of all the engines owned by the U.S. Air Force.

History. Named in honor of 2nd Lt. George E. M. Kelly, the first person to be killed in a mishap involving a military aircraft, Kelly welcomed the first planes on 9 April 1917. Kelly today occupies 4,000 acres in the southwest sector of San Antonio. Besides the Air Logistics Center, Kelly also hosts numerous tenant commands. Today Kelly's population consists of 4,400 active-duty personnel and more than 2,700 dependents.

Housing and Schools. There are 432 units of military family housing at Kelly, located in Billy Mitchell Village, near the main gate. (Forty-five units are on the base proper.) Temporary lodging for families and guests is very limited; sometimes temporary accommodations are available at Lackland Air Force Base, adjacent to the base on its southwest perimeter. Local homes rent for $500 and up. Unfurnished efficiency apartments start at about $250; rents for unfurnished one- and two-bedroom units start at $275 and $375 respectively.

Two child-development centers are operated on the base. Off-base education for both children and adults is excellent at San Antonio. College courses may be taken through the Southwest Texas State University, the University of Texas at San Antonio, Saint Mary's University, and Incarnate Word College.

Personal Services. Exchange and commissary facilities are provided throughout the San Antonio area, at Lackland, Kelly, Randolph, and Brooks Air Force Bases and Fort Sam Houston; medical and dental facilities are also available at these locations. The base restaurant system at Kelly operates thirteen cafeterias, and there are excellent officers and NCO clubs.

Recreation. Family campground accommodations are available on base on a first-come, first-served basis and consist of thirty-two paved pads with water, electric, and sewer hookups for RVs. The camp is open year-round. The maximum stay is fifteen days. Daily rates as of the summer of 1993 were eight dollars for RVs and three dollars for tent campers. Other facilities include a sixteen-lane bowling center, hobby shops, a gym, an eighteen-hole championship golf course, tennis courts, softball fields, and three swimming pools.

For more information write to: Director of Public Affairs, Kelly AFB, TX 78241, or call (210) 925-7951.

LACKLAND AIR FORCE BASE

The key word at Lackland Air Force Base is *training*. Lackland provides basic training for airmen and also conducts technical training and advanced technical training and hosts the Inter-American Air Forces Academy and Defense Language Institute English Language Center. Wilford Hall Medical Center, the Air Force's largest medical facility with 1,000 beds, conducts medical education and clinical research.

History. Lackland was named in honor of Brig. Gen. Frank D. Lackland, early commandant of Kelly Field Flying School, who died in 1943. Lackland covers 6,726 acres, including 3,973 acres at the Lackland Training Annex. The base employs over 3,400 civilians and is home for 7,000 permanent-party personnel, their 2,000 family members, and 6,900 students.

Housing and Schools. More than 700 units of family housing are available at Lackland, plus a wide variety of other lodging. Approximately 1,700 rooms and nearly 2,300 bed spaces are available for visiting personnel. The rooms accommodate two to five people and have a refrigerator, a TV in the lounge, a community bath, free washers and dryers, free cribs, and ice machines, as well as maid service.

Lackland has its own independent school district for children on base in kindergarten through grade twelve. Colleges in the area include the University of Texas at San Antonio, Saint Mary's University, Trinity University, Our Lady of the Lake University, Webster University, Southwest Texas State University at San Marcos, Incarnate Word College, San Antonio College, Saint Philips College, and Palo Alto College.

Personal Services and Recreation. Lackland's facilities include a commissary, a main exchange, four mini malls, a shopette/package store, a garden/toy shop, a club system, a child-development center, and two gas stations. Recreational facilities include two picnic areas, two theaters, three recreational centers, an arts and crafts

Visitors are welcomed at Lackland's basic military graduation parades. (USAF photo)

shop, an auto craft center, a rod and gun club, fourteen tennis courts, four swimming pools, three fitness centers, a bowling alley, an eighteen-hole golf course, and Medina Lake outdoor recreation area.

The Local Area. Lackland lies about eight miles southwest of downtown San Antonio. The area has many other military installations: Randolph, Kelly, and Brooks Air Force Bases and the Army's Fort Sam Houston.

For more information write to: Public Affairs Office, 2000 Bong Ave., Ste. 2, Lackland AFB, TX 78236-5110, or call (210) 671-2907.

LAUGHLIN AIR FORCE BASE

Laughlin Air Force Base is one of several "undergraduate" pilot training bases operated by the Air Force's Air Training Command. It sits seven miles east of the border town of Del Rio, Texas, adjacent to U.S. 90.

History. Named after 1st Lt. Jack Thomas Laughlin, the first Del Rioan pilot casualty of World War II, the base became operational in July 1942 under the Army Air Corps as part of the Central Flying Training Command. Today Laughlin's 47th Flying Training Wing (ATC) trains approximately thirty USAF students in each class, plus a small number of foreign students. The base has a military population of over 1,500 military personnel and 1,300 civilian employees, and supports over 7,000 dependents.

Housing and Schools. The USAF maintains 603 units of family housing and a fifty-four-space mobile home park. Laughlin has twenty-two temporary living facilities for the families of personnel on permanent-change-of-station orders. Others may be accommodated, but on a space-available basis only.

The base offers a child-care center, but children attend public schools in the surrounding community.

Personal Services and Recreation. Medical services are available at Laughlin's twenty-bed hospital with referrals to San Antonio for patients with conditions beyond the base hospital's capabilities. Other services include a commissary, a base exchange with numerous concessions, banking and credit facilities, a base theater, and an officers and NCO open mess system.

Recreation facilities include a skeet and trap range, picnic areas with playground facilities, a nine-hole golf course, a gymnasium, a ten-lane bowling center, a riding stable, tennis courts, three swimming pools, and a marina. The latter is located twenty-three miles northwest of the base. Many different types of watercraft, as well as campers and water skis, are available for rent there.

The Local Area. The climate around Del Rio, a town of about 30,000 people, is semiarid, with average winter temperatures of 50° F. and summer averages near 90°F. Del Rio sits just to the southeast of the Amistad National Recreation Area. Amistad is formed by Amistad Lake, one of the cleanest lakes in the nation and the largest in the state for water storage—5,660,000 acre-feet. The lake is eighty-five miles long. Striped bass weighing as much as sixty pounds can be caught in its waters. Hunting is also a popular sport in the area, and three hunting sites are located on base.

One of the major attractions in the Del Rio area is Ciudad Acuna, across the border in Coahuila, Mexico. Acuna is the sister city of Del Rio, and its quaint charms attract many tourists every year. One noted visitor was Pancho Villa. Twenty-five miles east of Laughlin, along U.S. 90, is Alamo Village, a reproduction of San Antonio's famous Alamo, constructed for the purpose of filming John Wayne's epic movie, *The Alamo*. It is one of the most authentic motion picture sets ever built.

The town of San Angelo lies 150 miles north of Del Rio, along Highway 277. Uvalde is 70 miles east of Del Rio, and San Antonio lies another 80 miles east of there, along U.S. 90.

For more information write to: Public Affairs Division, 47th Flying Training Wing (ATC), 561 Liberty Dr., Ste. 3, Laughlin AFB, TX 78843-5227, or call (210) 298-5988.

RANDOLPH AIR FORCE BASE

The "Taj Mahal" soars 147 feet into the air over Randolph, its intricate white spires pointing to a small blue and gold mosaic tile dome. The structure is covered with ornamental precast concrete, and the elegantly landscaped grounds surrounding its octagonal form lend to it an exotic Eastern atmosphere that reminded someone years ago of Shah Jahan's monument of Agra, and so it was named the Taj Mahal. The building's tower houses a 500,000-gallon water tank.

History. Named in honor of Capt. William M. Randolph, who was killed taking off from Gorham Field, Texas, Randolph Air Force Base was dedicated on 20 June 1930. Today the base is home to the 4,900 active-duty personnel of the Air Force's Training Command; Headquarters, Air Force Military Personnel Center; Headquarters, Air Force Recruiting Service; 12th Flying Training Wing; and more than twenty tenant commands. More than 11,000 family members and 5,000 civilians live and work at Randolph.

Housing and Schools. Randolph operates over 1,000 units of family housing, consisting of Wherry units and permanent Spanish-style structures. The Wherry quarters are two- and three-bedroom units restricted to enlisted personnel. Other enlisted quarters consist of two- and three-bedroom town houses and four-bedroom NCO duplexes. Officer quarters come in four-bedroom duplexes and two- and three-bedroom town-house units. Waiting periods last from 90 to 120 days. Some guest housing is available, but reservations are taken only for personnel on official orders.

A child-care center is operated on the base as well as dependent schools accommodating students from kindergarten through twelfth grade. The education services center offers more than 250 courses each year leading to associate, bachelor's, and master's degrees. Undergraduate institutions operating on base include Texas Lutheran College, Southwest Texas State University, San Antonio College, Saint Philip's College, Incarnate Word College, and Embry-Riddle Aeronautical University. Graduate degrees are offered by Saint Mary's and Southwest Texas State Universities.

Personal Services. The commissary at Randolph is a modern facility offering a variety of grocery, meat, and produce items, with seventeen checkout lanes for shoppers' convenience. The base exchange is also a modern facility, a solar-powered department store that offers a full range of personal and household needs.

Recreation. Recreational facilities include Eberle Park picnic area, a hunt and saddle club, an aero club, an eighteen-hole golf course, and a twenty-four-lane bowling center. Also available are an arts and crafts center, two gymnasiums, many ball parks, and nine soccer fields.

Randolph Recreation Area at Canyon Lake, seventeen miles west of New Braunfels offers more than 51 acres of heavily forested beachfront. The lake itself has eighty miles of shoreline and 8,240 acres of water area, permitting water sports and boat rentals.

For more information write to: 12th FTW Public Affairs, 1 Washington Circle, Ste. 4, Randolph AFB, TX 78150-4562, or call (210) 652-4410.

REESE AIR FORCE BASE

History. With an elevation of over 3,200 feet and more than 3,500 hours of sunshine a year, Lubbock was a natural choice as a site for pilot training. Known originally as Lubbock Army Air Field, the base opened in June 1941. In 1949 it was named in honor of Lt. Augustus F. Reese, Jr., who was killed in action at Cagliari, Sardinia, in May 1943. Lt. Reese had lived in Shallowater, six miles north of the base that now bears his name.

Today the base is home for the Air Training Command's 64th Flying Training Wing, which conducts Air Force officer specialized undergraduate pilot training. Each student pilot logs a total of 175 flying hours, approximately 500 hours of ground training, and 72 hours in the flight simulators and cockpit familiarization trainers. The training classes last fifty-two weeks.

Housing and Schools. There are over 400 units of family housing at Reese, plus a temporary-lodging facility consisting of 25 units that can accommodate incoming families for up to thirty days.

Dependent schoolchildren attend the Reese Elementary School just east of the base, and the junior and senior high schools that are part of the Friendship School District. The base education office, aside from providing counseling and testing services, assists with arrangements for adults to attend colleges both on and off base. On-base programs are offered by South Plains College, Wayland Baptist University, and Park College.

Personal Services. One of the finer attractions at Reese is the Family Shopping Center Mall, which includes the Army and Air Force Exchange Service and a new commissary. The USAF hospital on the base is a fourteen-bed composite medical facility fully capable of handling acute and minor illnesses and routine procedures. A children's preventive dentistry program is available; routine dental care for dependents is offered on a space-available basis.

Recreation. Recreational facilities and programs at Reese include officers and NCO open messes, recreation and youth centers, a picnic area, an arts and crafts center, and an auto hobby shop. Also provided are two outdoor swimming pools, a nine-hole golf course, tennis courts, a gymnasium, a ten-lane bowling center, and intramural and varsity sports.

The Local Area. Reese is located twelve miles west of Lubbock, a modern and progressive metropolis of over 185,000 people. It is eighth among Texas cities in population, thirteenth in median family income, with representatives of seventy-five of *Fortune* magazine's top 500 American corporations. The city is a major cultural and recreational center of western Texas.

Attractions include the Lubbock Symphony Orchestra, the Ranching Heritage Center exhibit of the museum of Texas Tech University, and the Lubbock County Museum. The Lubbock Cultural Affairs Council coordinates activities throughout the city. Lubbock is also a sports and recreation center. MacKenzie State Park, a garden spot, attracts more visitors than any other state park. Another recreational attraction is Buffalo Springs Lake, five miles southeast of the city, which provides areas for water skiing, fishing, boating, picnicking, hiking, and camping. Spectator sports such as the Southwest Conference football and basketball games at Texas Tech and rodeo and drag racing attract many people to the area.

For more information write to: Public Affairs Officer, 111 First St., Ste. 6, Reese AFB, TX 79489-5301, or call (806) 885-3410.

SHEPPARD AIR FORCE BASE

Great monuments do not exist only in museums. At Sheppard some of the famous aircraft in the history of U.S. aviation are on display, restored and mounted as if caught in actual flight and set to rest against the backdrop of the limitless Texas sky. The display includes the F-100 Super Sabre, the F-105 Thunderchief, the F-104 Starfighter, and many others.

History. Named in 1948 after U.S. Senator Morris Sheppard, a former chairman of the Senate Military Affairs Committee, the base was first established in 1941 as an Army Air Corps training school. Today its 5,400 acres are home for the 6,500 military and 3,200 civilian employees of the Sheppard Technical Training Center, one of six such centers under the control of the Air Training Command. The center comprises the 80th Flying Training Wing, the 396th Technical Training Group, and the 396th Medical, Field Training, Support, and Logistics Group.

Housing and Schools. Sheppard has over 1,200 units of family housing and 50 units of transient lodging. Only families of personnel on permanent-change-of-station orders or families of hospital patients may obtain lodging on a reserved basis; all others are taken on a space-available basis only. Sheppard also has over 1,500 rooms for visiting officers and enlisted personnel.

Children attend schools in the Burkburnett and Wichita Falls Independent School Districts. Schooling for adults interested in continuing their education is available on base from Midwestern State University, Vernon Regional Junior College, and Wayland Baptist College.

Personal Services. Services available at Sheppard include the base exchange complex and concessions, a commissary with 81,000 square feet of sales space, two service stations, several snack bars, and banking facilities. Medical care is provided by a 105-bed USAF regional hospital.

Recreation. Recreational facilities include a 40,000-volume library, an eighteen-hole golf course, two picnic areas, an aero club, a saddle club, officers and NCO clubs, two bowling lanes, three swimming pools, a recreation center, a 1,000-seat theater, auto and hobby shops, a skeet and trap range, and a gun club. The base also operates the Lake Texoma Recreation Annex, an 89,000-acre site located about 120 miles east of the base. Fishing, boating, water skiing, camping, and picnicking are offered there, plus forty-five cabins, each accommodating four to six people and twelve camper spaces with hookups. A small exchange is operated in the main lodge, and equipment rental is provided there.

The Local Area. Sheppard is located approximately 5 miles north-northeast of the town of Wichita Falls, a community of approximately 100,000 people. Wichita Falls is about 130 miles south of Oklahoma City and 130 miles northwest of Dallas–Fort Worth. The Oklahoma border town of Burkburnett, on the Red River, is 15 miles north of Wichita Falls.

The temperature in this part of Texas averages 98° F. in July and 58° F. in February, with an average annual rainfall of a little over twenty-seven inches, making outdoor activities possible year-round. Water skiing, fishing, camping, and hunting can be enjoyed within an easy drive of the base. Lake Waurika and Lake Wichita are close by; Lake Arrowhead, Lake Kemp, and Lake Nocona are located within a few dozen miles of the base. Historic Fort Sill is about fifty miles to the north of Sheppard, and the Wichita Mountain National Recreation Area is about fifty-five miles north.

For more information write to: Public Affairs Office, HQ Sheppard Technical Training Command, Sheppard AFB, TX 76311-5000, or call (817) 676-2511.

Army

FORT BLISS

In the 145 years since it was founded, Fort Bliss has witnessed almost the entire history of the U.S. Army in the Southwest, from Indian-fighting cavalry to sophisticated courses for missilemen and budding sergeants major.

History. Fort Bliss was first established in November 1848 as the Post of El Paso. In March 1854, it was renamed Fort Bliss in honor of William Wallace Smith Bliss, a veteran of the Florida Seminole and Mexican Wars and later adjutant general of the Army's Western Division. Today Fort Bliss is home to the Army's Air Defense School, whose Range Command controls over 1.1 million acres of ranges and maneuver areas. The installation is also home to the 11th Air Defense Artillery Brigade, the 3rd Armored Cavalry Regiment, and the U.S. Army Sergeants Major

Academy, the "capstone" school in the Army's Noncommissioned Officer Education System.

Housing and Schools. Fort Bliss offers every possible facility to today's soldier and his family. The post operates nearly 3,500 sets of family quarters for enlisted and officer personnel. Ordinarily these units are available from three to nine months after making application for them. Also, the inn at Fort Bliss is the official on-post, 103-room guest facility. It is available to active-duty and retired military service families and their guests.

There is an elementary school on post as well as a day-care center and an in-home day-care program; high schools are available in El Paso. The education center provides an ever-expanding program of academic, technical, and vocational subjects, from improvement of basic skills to graduate degrees, without the student having to leave the post.

Personal Services and Recreation. Excellent medical and health-care services are provided by William Beaumont Army Medical Center, a twelve-story, 500-bed ultramodern facility serving a population estimated at more than 130,000 active-duty servicemembers, retired personnel, and their families. A large commissary and a main exchange with twenty concessions are also available.

The post offers varied forms of outdoor and indoor recreation programs and facilities, from museums, music, and theater to camping equipment rental facilities and saddle, flying, and rod and gun clubs. With a dry and sunny climate (average rainfall is only 7.7 inches annually), outdoor activities are possible year-round.

The Local Area. El Paso, situated at the tip of West Texas on the borders of Mexico and New Mexico, is the fourth largest city in Texas, with a population of approximately 600,000. El Paso is a city of contrasts in culture, design, geography, and climate. At an elevation of over 3,600 feet, the air is dry and humidity is virtually nonexistent. Just across the border is Ciudad Juarez, the largest Mexican city on the United States–Mexico border. El Paso is a very convenient starting place for many exciting and interesting trips to the natural wonders and historical sites that abound throughout western Texas and New Mexico.

For more information write to: Army Community Services Office, Headquarters, U.S. Army Air Defense Center and Fort Bliss, Fort Bliss, TX 79916-6200, or call (915) 568-4505.

FORT HOOD

Fort Hood's "Hell on Wheels" does not mean that the post is hard on automobile tires. It's simply our largest armored post, occupying 339 square miles of Central Texas real estate. It is capable of supporting two full armored divisions and is home to the 32,000 men and women of the III Corps, the 1st Cavalry Division ("First Team"), and the 2nd Armored Division ("Hell on Wheels").

History. Named for Confederate Gen. John Bell Hood, Fort Hood was constructed in 1942 and served as the Army's Tank Destroyer Center throughout World

War II. Today the post has earned its reputation as the being "The Great Place."

Housing and Schools. There are twelve separate on-post housing areas containing a total of 5,500 sets of family quarters at Fort Hood. The post also has two guesthouse facilities, including the 75-room Poxon House, open to all military personnel and their family members.

Elementary schools are provided on post for dependent children, and the Fort Hood education centers provide complete education services for military personnel, from enhancement of basic military skills to preseparation counseling. College-level courses are available from local institutions such as Central Texas College, the University of Central Texas, the University of Mary Hardin-Baylor, and Temple Junior College.

Personal Services. Fort Hood, which supports 200,000 active-duty and retired personnel and their families, has every type of service facility used by soldiers in the modern Army.

Recreation. Fort Hood offers all types of indoor and outdoor recreation, including hunting and fishing in designated areas on the reservation. The morale support activities division maintains a fishing dock on Belton Lake year-round, and boats and motors are available for rent for a nominal fee. There are 127 ponds on the post, all suitable for fishing. In addition, Fort Hood has seventeen lakes of its own.

The Local Area. Located in the beautiful "hill and lake" country of Central Texas, Fort Hood's main post is about sixty miles north of the capital city of Austin and fifty miles south of Waco. With average temperatures ranging from 94° F. to 38° F. year-round, Fort Hood is particularly suited to all types of outdoor recreational activities.

Fort Hood is bordered on the north by the community of Gatesville and on the south by Killeen. To the southeast are Copperas Cove and Lampasas.

For more information write to: Army Community Service, Headquarters, III Corps and Fort Hood, Fort Hood, TX 76544-5056, or call (817) 287-4936.

FORT SAM HOUSTON

History. In its 114-year history, Fort Sam Houston has been host to notable winners and losers. The great Apache warrior Geronimo, en route to prison in Florida, stayed there for a month in 1886. And at 9:30 A.M. on 2 March 1910, Lt. Benjamin D. Foulois became this country's first military aviator by making a solo flight in a Wright Type-A biplane at Arthur MacArthur Field. He soared to a height of 100 feet, and his aircraft attained a speed of fifty miles per hour.

Named after the great Texas soldier and first president of the Republic of Texas, Samuel Houston, Fort Sam Houston began life as the Military Post of San Antonio in 1876; its name was officially changed to Fort Sam Houston in 1890. Today the post is home to Headquarters, 5th U.S. Army; the Army Health Services Command; Brooke Army Medical Center; and the Academy of Health Sciences. It comprises some 3,200 acres on main post and another 28,000 acres of maneuver areas and firing ranges at Camp Bullis (a training area twenty miles to the northwest of San Antonio). The post is home to over 11,000 active-duty personnel, their 15,000 family members, 14,000 reserve components personnel, and more than 5,800 civilian employees.

Housing and Schools. Over 1,100 units of family housing are available, but due to a massive renovation project that will take several years, the waiting period for quarters, beginning in 1994, will be two to three years for most grades. Guest-house facilities are available on a reserved basis.

In 1993, two-bedroom apartments rented for about $475 per month, plus utilities. Real estate prices ranged from as low as $45,000 for an older house to more than $90,000 for a newly built home; condominiums were selling in about the same range.

Dependent children on the post may attend school in grades from kindergarten to twelfth grade. A child-development center with a capacity for over 300 children ages six weeks to eight years is available. The Army education center offers a full range of courses and classes for military personnel, off and on duty, from MOS proficiency improvement to advanced academic degree completion programs.

Personal Services. Medical care is provided by the 500-bed Brooke Army Medical Center, one of the largest military health-care facilities in the world. The hospital is noted as one of the country's leading centers for the treatment of burn victims. Fort Sam has a commissary, two convenience food stores, a large main exchange, a four-seasons store, a toy store, and a shopette. A new commissary with over 102,000 square feet of sales space is expected to open early in 1994.

Recreation. Fort Sam offers a thirty-six-hole golf course; a twenty-four-lane bowling alley; two swimming pools; a riding stable; a movie theater; craft and hobby shops; handball, racquetball and squash courts; and even a dinner theater and playhouse. The post also offers various athletic and recreational facilities and programs. Fort Sam Houston operates the Canyon Lake Recreation Area fifty miles north of the post. The area offers thirty-two three-bedroom house trailers, thirty-two water and electric hookups for recreational vehicles, and numerous camping and picnicking sites. Personnel assigned to Fort Sam Houston may make reservations up to thirty days in advance; others, seven days in advance. Camp Bullis, approximately twenty miles northwest of Fort Sam Houston, offers a variety of programs geared toward the shooting sports such as hunting in season and archery and rifle ranges. Sand volleyball areas, horseshoe pits, and softball fields are also available.

The Local Area. The city of San Antonio, which was first settled by the Spanish in 1718, offers a delightful combination of the old and the new. The Alamo—the shrine to Texas liberty—and the Paseo del Rio, a beautiful riverfront promenade set in the heart of the city, offer pleasant contrasts to the city's modern skyline punctuated by the ultramodern HemisFair Tower and other impressive buildings. During the annual four-day "Night in Old San Antonio," a festival celebrating the city's Spanish-Mexican-American heritage, visitors have been known to consume up to 45,000 *miles* of tamales!

For more information write to: Public Affairs Office, Attention: AFZG-PO, Fort Sam Houston, TX 78234-5000, or call (512) 221-2080/5151.

Navy

CHASE FIELD NAVAL AIR STATION

After fifty years of service, Chase Field NAS was closed in 1993.

CORPUS CHRISTI NAVAL AIR STATION

History. Corpus Christi Naval Air Station lies along the south shore of Corpus Christi Bay, not far from the Gulf of Mexico, on land that was once acrawl with snakes among the mesquite brush. That was back in 1941. Today the station is head-quarters for the Navy's Chief of Naval Air Training, Training Air Wing 4, and various support and tenant commands, including the Corpus Christi Army Depot, which occupies over 120 acres of land leased from the station.

Housing and Schools. The station has 437 units of family housing and twenty-eight mobile home sites. The Navy exchange also operates an eighteen-unit Navy Lodge for transients as well as active-duty and retired visitors and their families. A preschool and child-care center are operated on the station, but dependent schooling is conducted in the Independent School District of Flour Bluff. The Navy Campus for Achievement assists active-duty personnel and their dependents in the pursuit of off-duty higher education. Courses are available from Corpus Christi State University and Del Mar College as well as Embry-Riddle Aeronautical University.

Personal Services. The station offers a full range of morale and welfare support activities, including a Navy exchange, a commissary store, and a fifty-bed naval hospital that provides medical and surgical services to nearly 40,000 eligible personnel in the vicinity of Corpus Christi.

Recreation. Recreational activities are more than adequate and include three swimming pools, six lighted tennis courts, a skeet and trap range, a fourteen-lane bowling alley, an eighteen-hole golf course, a gymnasium, and a hobby craft center. There is also a picnic ground with camper hookups and sailboat rentals at Sunfish Beach during the summer months. The warm and sunny climate permits year-round enjoyment of outdoor activities.

The Local Area. Corpus Christi is a sparkling jewel of a city of 260,000 people. It is one of the cleanest cities in the nation and one of the fastest growing. The port there is the eighth largest in the United States. The community also offers much to do in the way of sightseeing and recreation, from the Corpus Christi Symphony to the Bayfront Plaza and Ocean Drive, a very scenic route that runs right up to the naval air station.

Corpus Christi lies about 210 miles southwest of Houston, on the same parallel as Tampa, Florida, and about 160 miles north of Brownsville, Texas, and Matamoros, Mexico. The Gulf Coast of Texas offers many attractions, from hunting and fishing to sailing, bird watching, and various local celebrations. The latter include Corpus

Christi's Buccaneer Days in April, Bayfest in September, and the Airshow/Open House Festival held at the air station in May for the benefit of the Navy Relief Society. The Shrimporee held in nearby Aransas Pass in October is a must for seafood lovers.

For more information write to: Public Affairs Office, Bldg. 2, Rm. 120, Corpus Christi NAS, Corpus Christi, TX 78419-5000, or call (512) 939-2674.

DALLAS NAVAL AIR STATION

The 1993 Base Realignment and Closure Commission recommended that Dallas NAS be closed, but at press time a firm date had not yet been announced.

Located in the southwest corner of Dallas on Mountain Creek Lake, Dallas NAS is surrounded by the suburban cities of Grand Prairie, Duncanville, and Irving.

History. NAS Dallas was commissioned in May 1941. With the outbreak of World War II, it became a major site of aviation training for Navy and Marine Corps pilots as well as the acceptance point for aircraft built by the North American Aviation Plant (now LTV Aircraft Products Group). Today the station hosts fourteen major and twenty-nine smaller tenant commands representing all branches of the military service. Among these are fighter squadrons 201 and 202 and Marine Air Group 41. Dallas has an active-duty population of 2,000 personnel plus their 3,500 family members.

Housing and Schools. Housing, whether apartment or home hunting, is abundant in the Dallas–Fort Worth area. The station housing referral office assists in locating permanent or temporary quarters. Although there are no dependents schools onboard the station itself, the morale, welfare, and recreation department operates a child-care center that can accommodate 100 youngsters. Local communities provide schooling for older children. The Navy Campus at the station offers continuing-education programs for adults through Northwood Institute and Columbia University.

Personal Services. NAS Dallas has a small Navy exchange, a package store, and a small convenience store. Limited medical care is provided by a branch medical clinic, with most dependent or extensive care cases being referred to hospitals and physicians off station. The station has both enlisted and officers clubs.

Recreation. A top-notch weight room is available at the station along with basketball, racquetball, and tennis courts; a softball field; and an aerobics area. High on the list of recreational facilities is the marina on Mountain Creek Lake that has a boat ramp, camp gear rentals, auto-repair facilities, a picnic area, and boats ranging from canoes to power craft. The station also offers a bowling alley and a small swimming pool.

The Local Area. The Dallas–Fort Worth metroplex abounds with activities ranging from fine dining to zoos, museums, theme parks, major league baseball, football, fishing, boating, sport flying, and ballooning.

For more information write to: Public Affairs Office, Naval Air Station, Dallas, TX 75211-9501, or call (214) 266-6140.

INGLESIDE NAVAL STATION

Dedicated on 6 July 1992, Ingleside Naval Station is one of our newest naval facilities. Home port for training frigates, mine countermeasures ships, and coastal mine-hunters, the station and its tenant commands are responsible for meeting the operational, logistical, and administrative needs of the U.S. Atlantic Fleet.

History. Groundbreaking for Ingleside began on 20 February 1988. The South Texas Coastal Bend area was chosen as the location for the station because of its quick access to the deep waters of the Gulf of Mexico, the well-protected waters inside the barrier island, the existence of sufficient land, and the area's great potential for growth. The first vessel to arrive at Ingleside, in June 1992, was the mine countermeasures ship USS *Scout*—the first U.S. Navy ship to be home-ported in Texas since World War II. As of the fall of 1993, Ingleside had a complement of 2,000 active-duty personnel and 190 civilians. These personnel bring with them about 4,500 family members.

Housing, Schools, and Personal Services. As of the fall of 1993, Ingleside families were living in Corpus Christi and other communities situated in San Patricio and Nueces Counties. Likewise, Ingleside children were attending schools off base. The station has a bachelor enlisted facility that can accommodate 116 personnel. Health care is provided by small medical and dental clinics with referrals to local hospitals or the naval hospital located at the Corpus Christi Naval Air Station. Although there is no commissary at Ingleside, there are a Navy exchange, a galley, a full fitness center with swimming pool, tennis courts, and outdoor athletic fields.

For more information write to: Public Affairs Office, Naval Station Ingleside, Ingleside, TX 78362-5000, or call (512) 776-4200.

KINGSVILLE NAVAL AIR STATION

Kingsville Naval Air Station occupies 4,000 acres virtually on the doorstep of the King Ranch, one of the larger ranches in the world. It is home and workplace for approximately 930 active-duty personnel and 1,300 civilians belonging to the Training Air Wing 2. The wing performs the primary mission of training Navy aviators and turns out approximately 200 pilots every year. The station was commissioned on 4 July 1942 and was officially designated Naval Air Station, Kingsville, in 1968.

Housing and Schools. Family housing is tight at Kingsville, with accommodations for only 243 families. Housing is situated at Texas Terrace, about two miles from the station. Nineteen units of transient housing are available on the station at a cost of two dollars per night per adult and one dollar per child.

Although there is no dependent schooling at the station, a child-care facility is available. Many of the personnel stationed at Kingsville attend courses at Texas A & I University on the west side of town, eight miles from the station. With a student enrollment of 7,000 and a faculty of 250 members, the university offers bachelor's and master's degrees in many areas.

Personal Services. A Navy exchange and a commissary store are located on base. A medical clinic is also available, with referrals to Corpus Christi Naval Hospital (fifty-one miles from the station) and San Antonio. The station also has a consolidated package store, a service station, barber and beauty shops, and a mini mart.

Recreation. Recreational facilities include a boat barn with equipment check-out, a bowling center, a gymnasium, a swimming pool, a racquetball court, a skeet and trap range, and boarding for privately owned horses.

The Local Area. The climate in this part of Texas is hot and humid with the temperature averaging 84° F. during the summer months; yearly rainfall is about twenty-four inches.

The town of Kingsville has a population of over 25,000. The major attraction there is the vast King Ranch, which covers an expanse of 860,000 acres. The ranch begins only three miles from downtown Kingsville. The town itself is situated along U.S. 77 a few miles inland from the Gulf of Mexico and Padre Island National Seashore. Corpus Christi is forty miles to the north of Kingsville, and Brownsville/Matamoros is on the Gulf Coast, ninety-four miles south of Kingsville.

For more information write to: Public Affairs Officer, Naval Air Station, Kingsville, TX 78363, or call (512) 595-6146.

UTAH

Air Force

HILL AIR FORCE BASE

A few miles to the west of Hill Air Force Base is the Great Salt Lake, a vast inland body of water that sits 4,200 feet above sea level. Several miles to the east are the Wasatch Mountains and Wasatch National Forest. The base sits at the heart of Utah's population center, with Salt Lake City about thirty miles to the south and Ogden about eight miles to the north. And the skies belong to the U.S. Air Force.

History. Named in honor of Maj. Ployer P. Hill, who died in the crash of the first B-17 aircraft at Wright-Patterson AFB in 1935, the base was activated in 1940. During World War II Hill AFB provided rehabilitation, repair, and maintenance services for fighter and bomber aircraft. Today it occupies 6,698 acres and manages the 692,000 acres of the nearby Utah Test and Training Range. Its 17,000 military and civilian personnel staff the Ogden Air Logistics Center and tenant units. The ALC provides support for a number of Air Force weapons systems, including the F-16, the F-4, and all of the intercontinental ballistic missile fleet. The base is also home to active-duty and reserve F-16 wings.

Housing and Schools. Hill AFB has over 1,100 units of family housing and 45 rooms for guests. Guest-house facilities are provided for Department of Defense personnel on temporary-duty and permanent-change-of-station orders. Advance reservations are required.

Plenty of excellent elementary, secondary, and high schools as well as colleges and universities are available in the area. A child-development center is located on the base.

Personal Services. The USAF hospital provides a thirty-five-bed composite medical facility for active-duty and retired personnel and their families. Personal services include a commissary and base exchange with a wide variety of concessions, such as a service station, a barber shop, and base bus service.

Recreation. Recreational activities include an eighteen-hole golf course, a modern gymnasium, a twenty-lane bowling center, a theater, a library, a recreation center, hobby shops, two outdoor and one indoor swimming pools, indoor and outdoor tennis courts, a rod and gun club, and a total of fifteen restaurants and snack bars. Hill also offers two elegant clubs for those sophisticates who enjoy, as a break from Arnold Schwarzenegger movies over warm beer and day-old pizza in the barracks TV room, an occasional evening discussing the writings of Albert Camus over gourmet food in the company of delightful and charming conversationalists.

Hill operates a family camp featuring fourteen trailer pads with hookups, camping, swimming, picnicking, and playground facilities.

Off-base Air Force–operated recreation facilities are the Hillhaus Mountain Lodge and a site at Carter Creek. Hillhaus, about thirty miles east of the base, is part of the Ogden Recreation Area. Carter Creek, 120 miles east of Hill in the Uinta Mountains, is used in the summer for camping and in the winter for cross-country skiing and snowmobiling. It has six cabins and eight trailer spaces plus camping, hunting, fishing, hiking, and equipment rentals.

The Local Area. Salt Lake City, a metropolis of over 720,000, is a center of culture as well as the international headquarters of the Church of Jesus Christ of Latter Day Saints (Mormons). Ogden is also a thriving city with many excellent cultural

An F-16 fighter jet takes off at Hill AFB. (USAF photo)

attractions and historical sites. The Great Salt Lake dominates the area, stretching seventy-five miles north to south and twenty-five miles wide. It is salty enough to allow swimmers to float on its waters.

For more information write to: Public Affairs Office, Hill AFB, UT 84056-5990, or call (801) 777-7221.

Army

DUGWAY PROVING GROUND

Larger than the state of Rhode Island (802,000 acres), Dugway Proving Ground is located in the west-central part of Utah, about sixty-seven air miles southwest of Salt Lake City. The name Dugway is taken from the method used by the early pioneers to move their prairie schooners and Conestoga wagons through the mountains, by digging a trench or grade through the passes and then using oxen to haul the wagons up by the "dug way."

History. Dugway Proving Ground was officially established on 12 February 1942. Some of the buildings still in use date from this period, but considerable expansion and renovation have taken place since then. Today Dugway's mission is to test Army equipment in order to provide physical protection for military personnel in the field against chemical and biological agents. DPG also tests battlefield smoke and obscurants and conducts production qualification testing for mortar and artillery munitions. Dugway is home to approximately 130 permanent-party military personnel. The civilian workforce numbers about 1,300 employees.

Housing and Schools. DPG has over 600 units of family housing available, 104 newly constructed and the rest recently renovated. Accommodations are available for soldiers and families arriving or departing, and for their guests. Modern, well-equipped elementary and high schools are located on post for the children of military and civilian personnel assigned there. The schools are operated as part of the Tooele County School System. Dugway also offers a three-million-dollar day-care center built in 1990. Adult education is available through the education center, which offers high school courses and academic college courses at Utah state universities.

Personal Services. Although there is a health clinic on the installation, the nearest military hospital is at Hill Air Force Base, 110 miles northeast of Dugway. The nearest civilian hospital is in Tooele, about 40 miles northeast of the post.

A commissary, a post exchange, a bank, a credit union, a video-rental service, a snack bar at the bowling center, a beauty and barber shop, a laundry and dry cleaner, a gas station, and a community club are available at Dugway.

Recreation. Recreational facilities include an arts and crafts shop, an auto craft shop, a gymnasium, a post library, a post theater, a rod and gun club, a nine-hole golf course, a swimming pool, and a twelve-lane bowling center.

Outdoor recreation includes an annual ski program that offers lessons for beginners and bus transportation to nearby ski resorts during the season. A variety of recreational equipment is available for rent through the outdoor recreation office.

The Local Area. Summers at Dugway are moderately hot and very dry. Spring and fall are cool, and the winters are moderately cold, with short storms and some snow. About seven inches of precipitation fall in the area annually. The surrounding country is high in elevation: Dugway itself is 4,300 feet above sea level.

There are only two urban areas in the vicinity: Tooele, with a 1990 census of 14,000, and Grantsville, with a 1990 population of 4,500. The population density in Tooele County has an average of fifteen people to the square kilometer. The road connecting Dugway with Tooele passes over the Onaqui Mountain Range where, passing through 105 curves, it reaches an elevation of over 6,000 feet.

For more information write to: Public Affairs Office, Dugway Proving Ground, Dugway, UT 84022-5000, or call (801) 831-2116.

VIRGINIA

Air Force

LANGLEY AIR FORCE BASE

History. Langley Air Force Base is the one of the oldest continuously used bases in the U.S. Air Force. This is particularly fitting because Langley is situated in a part of the United States that is intimately associated with American history.

Langley Field, named in honor of Samuel Pierpont Langley, a pioneer of American aviation and former secretary of the Smithsonian Institution, was first opened in June 1917, when the 5th Aviation School, Army Signal Corps, was formed there. Today Langley hosts the Air Combat Command's headquarters, the 1st Fighter Wing, the 5th Weather Wing, and a number of other tenant commands. It is home to more than 8,000 active-duty personnel and their 12,000 family members, and has a civilian workforce of over 1,700.

Housing and Schools. Langley has more than 1,600 units of family housing, some located on the base itself and some in Bethel Manor, about five miles from the installation. Personnel in grades E-4 through E-9 can expect a six- to twelve-month wait for three- and four-bedroom units. Officers, depending on grade and size of quarters desired, may wait from two to twelve months for base housing. The longest waiting period is for two-bedroom units, which for lower-ranking enlisted personnel can last up to three years. Temporary-lodging facilities at Langley are always tight. Living off base can be expensive. Unfurnished apartments rent from as low as $295 a month for one bedroom to as high as $550 to $600 a month for four bedrooms. Houses rent from $400 to $600 a month. For those interested in buying a house in the area, prices range from $54,000 to $110,000.

A child-care center is operated on the base. Dependent schoolchildren attend public schools operated by the city of Hampton and York County. For adults wishing to pursue higher education, on-base courses are conducted by Christopher Newport College, the College of Hampton Roads, the College of William and Mary, George Washington University, Hampton Institute, Peninsula Business College, Virginia Peninsula Vocational-Technical Education Center, Thomas Nelson Community College, Golden Gate University, Embry-Riddle Aeronautical University, and Old Dominion University.

Personal Services. The USAF Regional Hospital at Langley is an eighty-bed medical facility that serves a local population of 184,000 active-duty and retired personnel and their families. Other services include a base exchange with a 38,500-square-foot shopping area and eight concessions and a commissary that serves approximately 63,000 customers a month.

Recreation. Recreational facilities include a thirty-six-hole, 6,200-yard golf course; a twenty-four-lane bowling center; auto and wood hobby shops; a marina with slips (both dry and wet) for over 120 private boats; and yacht, scuba, aero, saddle, and skeet clubs. In addition, there are four swimming pools, a gym, and a recreation center. Big Bethel Recreation Area, adjacent to Bethel Manor housing area, is available for picnicking and fishing.

The Local Area. Langley is located three miles north of Hampton in an area that has many major military installations: Fort Monroe, Fort Eustis, Oceana Naval Air Station, Norfolk Naval Base, and Yorktown Naval Weapons Station.

The Hampton–Norfolk–Newport News–Virginia Beach area is rich in things to do and interesting places to see. The area is a fisherman's paradise with plenty of freshwater and deep-sea fishing. Historic Fort Monroe, Hampton Roads, Williamsburg, Yorktown, Petersburg, and Richmond are within easy commuting distance.

For more information write to: 1st FW Public Affairs, 159 Sweeney Blvd., Ste. 100, Langley AFB, VA 23655-2292, or call (804) 764-2018.

Army

FORT BELVOIR

When Col. George William Fairfax erected his manor house in 1741, he called it *Belvoir*, meaning "beautiful to see." In later years, George William Fairfax, the colonel's eldest son, and his good friend and neighbor, George Washington, frequently rode over the acres of the Belvoir estate together. The manor was partially burned in 1783, and in 1814 the British demolished the remaining walls. But George Washington's graceful home, Mount Vernon, still stands above the banks of the Potomac a few miles from Belvoir, and the area is still very "beautiful to see." The ruins of Belvoir and the Fairfax family graves may still be seen on a bluff overlooking the Potomac, behind the officer housing area.

History. What is now Fort Belvoir was originally part of the old Fairfax estate. The post was designated Camp A. A. Humphreys in 1917 but renamed Fort Belvoir in 1935. Today Fort Belvoir's 8,600 acres are an installation of the Military District of Washington and home to more than seventy tenants. Among these are the Defense Mapping School, the Defense Systems Management College, the Intelligence Security Command, and the Belvoir Research, Development, and Engineering Center. The post has a daytime population of more than 12,000 people—3,000 active-duty military personnel and 9,000 civilian workers.

Housing and Schools. Fort Belvoir is a completely modern installation that possesses all the benefits, services, and facilities available to military personnel. There are over 1,600 sets of family quarters on post, ranging from detached housing for senior officers and NCOs to two-story, row-type housing for junior officers and enlisted personnel. The waiting list varies, depending on grade and family requirements. Limited guest accommodations are available for all ranks. Single life on post is excellent, too. Over 1,200 enlisted soldiers live in McCree Barracks in two-person rooms with wall-to-wall carpeting and private baths.

Dependent children may attend on-post school from kindergarten through grade six; grades seven through twelve are available at the nearby Hayfield Intermediate and High School. Two child-care facilities are operated on the post. The post education center operates a program offering many opportunities. Both on- and off-post college-level courses are available from Catholic University, the University of Virginia, the University of Maryland, and George Washington, Howard, and George Mason Universities.

Personal Services. With its large post exchange, well-stocked commissary, and a full range of medical care services available at the 129-bed DeWitt Army Hospital, military personnel at Fort Belvoir are assured gracious and healthy living.

Recreation. Fort Belvoir has a marina, indoor shooting ranges, and NCO and officers clubs. Licensed fishing is permitted in its ponds and on the Potomac River. There is a wildlife and wetlands refuge providing more than seven miles of hiking trails, and bow hunting is permitted during deer season. The Sosa Recreation Center provides a wide variety of social activities for all ages.

The Local Area. Fort Belvoir is located in historic Northern Virginia, the site of many of the most famous events that have occurred in this nation's development. Washington, D.C., is only twelve miles away, and two major Civil War battlefields, Manassas and Fredericksburg, are within easy driving distance. Gettysburg, Pennsylvania, is somewhat farther away but still close enough for a weekend's touring pleasure. Richmond, Colonial Williamsburg, and Yorktown are all located within easy driving distance.

For more information write to: Public Affairs Office, Bldg. 269, Fort Belvoir, VA 22060-5196, or call (703) 805-5001.

CAMERON STATION

The 1988 Base Closure and Realignment Commission recommended that Cameron Station be closed by the fourth quarter of fiscal year 1995.

Cameron Station is one of those rare military installations where thousands of people ply the business of defense during the daylight hours, but after dark the streets are rolled up. You can picnic, camp, shop, and even work at Cameron, but you can't live there.

History. There has been a military installation on the site of present-day Cameron Station since 1819, when the Washington General Depot was located there. In 1941 the post was expanded and became known as the Washington Quartermaster Depot. Legend has it that in 1949 it was named Cameron Station after the Right Honorable Thomas Lord Fairfax, Baron Cameron, who once owned the land on which the station is now situated. Nearby Fairfax County, which was founded in 1742, is named after Lord Fairfax who, along with George Washington and George Mason, was one of its most prominent residents in the years before the American Revolution. On the other hand, the post may be named after Cameron Run, a small stream that flows by the installation and empties into the Potomac River. But Cameron Run may have taken its name from the Right Honorable Thomas Lord Fairfax, so who's to say?

Today Cameron Station's 164 acres are home to the Deputy Chief of Staff for Logistics of the Military District of Washington, the headquarters for the Defense Logistics Agency, and the Defense Contract Audit Agency. About 300 military personnel are assigned duty at Cameron Station, and more than 4,000 civilian personnel work there as well.

Personal Services and Recreation. Because nobody lives at Cameron Station, there are no schools or educational activities there. The families of military personnel working at Cameron obtain housing and educational support services from nearby military installations or in the local communities. There is an austere overnight campground at Cameron Station.

By far the biggest attractions at Cameron are the commissary and the post exchange. The commissary is one of the largest in the United States. It regularly services an estimated 62,000 military families living in the Washington area. The post exchange is very large and among the various concessions it operates is a very large four-seasons store. The post also has a small dispensary and a credit union.

Persons who plan to use the Cameron Station facilities while stopping in the Washington area are warned that they are heavily used. While there is plenty of parking on the installation, finding a convenient spot is sometimes difficult, especially during the workday and often on weekends near the end of the month. Unless you have plenty of time, plan to arrive early to shop at the post exchange and commissary.

Recreational facilities include three picnic areas, a tennis court, and a fish-stocked lake. The lake also boasts a large number of geese and ducks raised for the enjoyment of children and picnickers, not hunters. Cameron Station also has a small officers club across the street from the credit union.

The Local Area. Cameron Station is located within the city limits of Alexandria, about one mile east of Interstate 395 on Duke Street in a neighborhood of high-rises and shopping centers.

The city of Alexandria was founded in 1749 and during much of its history was an important seaport serving the farmers and merchants in the Northern Virginia area. George Washington was prominent in the city's affairs both before and after the Revolution. About two miles east of Cameron Station, where Duke Street runs past the Amtrak station, is the 330-foot George Washington Masonic National Memorial. The memorial contains a fascinating collection of possessions and artifacts associated with our first president and Masonry in general, and free tours are conducted regularly. The view from the top of the tower, which takes in the District of Columbia and parts of Maryland and Virginia, is more breathtaking than from the Washington Monument.

Alexandria is a bustling tourist attraction with many exclusive shops, fine restaurants, and quaint old town houses along quiet, cobblestone streets. The city is convenient to the District of Columbia, Virginia, and Maryland.

For more information write to: Public Affairs Office, HQ, Military District of Washington, Fort Lesley J. McNair, Washington, DC 20319-5050, or call (703) 274-6059.

FORT EUSTIS

Fort Eustis is a site of contrasts. Capt. John Smith, famous as the savior of Jamestown (and the last English husband of Pocahontas), visited there in 1610, and its first prominent settler, John Rolfe (first English husband of Pocahontas), built his home there, near the site of the present-day golf course. Fort Eustis is also the home of the only flying saucer in captivity and a ship that is in use all the time but never goes anywhere.

History. Named in honor of Brevet Brig. Gen. Abraham Eustis, a distinguished artillery officer who served from 1808 to 1843, Fort Eustis was established in 1918 as an artillery training area. In 1946 it became the principal training post for the Army Transportation Corps, and today it is home to the Army Transportation Center and School, the Army Aviation Logistics School, the 7th Transportation Group, and other commands. The "ship that never sails" is a land ship, built into a pier and used to conduct classes in cargo-handling operations. Personnel assigned to the post train thousands of officers and enlisted soldiers every year in aviation maintenance, harbor-craft operations and maintenance, and rail and line haul motor transport. The post is also responsible for an over-the-shore training subinstallation near Virginia Beach, where Army personnel learn about amphibious logistical operations.

Today Fort Eustis is home to more than 5,800 active-duty personnel, their 16,000 family members, and a civilian workforce of more than 2,700.

Housing and Schools. Fort Eustis has over 2,300 sets of family quarters of many different basic designs, from two-story multiple units to detached homes for senior officers. Fort Eustis has 64 mobile home spaces and also offers guest accommodations for personnel on temporary-duty or permanent-change-of-station orders.

The education center hosts a variety of on-post college courses run by fully accredited institutions offering associate to postgraduate degrees in many subjects; off-post college courses are available at the College of William and Mary at Williamsburg.

There are no on-post schools at Eustis for dependent children, but plenty of excellent schooling is available in the local community. There is a day-care center on post as well as an in-home day-care program.

Personal Services and Recreation. Fort Eustis has both a large post exchange and a commissary. Medical care is provided by a sixty-five-bed hospital, and additional medical care is available at nearby Langley Air Force Base.

Recreational facilities include a bowling alley; a swimming pool; handball, racquetball, and tennis courts; an eighteen-hole golf course; auto and craft hobby shops; a post movie theater; a roller skating rink; a skeet range; and boating, hunting, and fishing areas.

The Local Area. Fort Eustis is situated on the western neck of a peninsula formed on the west by the James River and Hampton Roads, and on the east by the York River and the Chesapeake Bay. It is one of the most significant historical sites in the United States: Jamestown and Williamsburg are only a few miles to the north; Yorktown is just across the peninsula on the York River; and Fort Monroe is at the tip of the peninsula, at Hampton. Across from Hampton, via the Hampton Roads Bridge and Tunnel, are Norfolk and Virginia Beach, a famous resort area. North of Virginia Beach, along the Atlantic coast, is the Cape Henry Memorial, marking the first landing place of the Jamestown settlers in 1607. And from Norfolk, one may take the famous Chesapeake Bay Bridge and Tunnel some twenty miles north across the bay to Virginia's famed Eastern Shore resort and fishing paradise.

Ah, yes—the captive flying saucer! Well, in reality it's only one of the two aero-cars built as an experimental step in the development of the vertical take-off and landing craft. It was first tested in California in 1960 and flew no higher than four feet. Today, looking more like a huge doughnut than a spacecraft, it is permanently elevated about seven feet above the ground in an outdoor display at Fort Eustis.

For more information write to: Community Services Office, U.S. Army Transportation School and Fort Eustis, Fort Eustis, VA 23604-5000, or call (804) 878-5251.

FORT LEE

If, as Napoleon is supposed to have said, an Army travels on its stomach, and if logistics are the "sinews" of war, then Fort Lee is truly one of our most important military installations.

The U.S. Army Combined Arms Support Command and Fort Lee occupies 5,575 acres three miles east of Petersburg on Virginia 36. The installation has a military population of 3,900 and a civilian complement of 3,300 personnel. The post supports 5,900 family members and an estimated 18,000 retirees living in the area. The CASCOM is responsible for training the personnel who provide logistical support to soldiers and units Armywide.

History. Named in honor of Gen. Robert E. Lee, the installation came to life in July 1917 as Camp Lee and was used as a mobilization and division training center. It

closed after World War I but reopened in 1940, and quartermaster training operations began there in 1941. In 1950, the post was given official recognition and permanent status and designated Fort Lee.

Housing and Schools. There are over 1,400 sets of family quarters on post, the
oldest having been constructed in 1950; guest-house accommodations are also available and reservations are accepted. Dependents of military personnel at Fort Lee
attend the Prince George County Public School System. Military personnel may take
advantage of an extensive adult education program operated at the post. John Tyler
Community College, a state-supported two-year college, offers seven degree programs. Central Texas College, Florida Institute of Technology, Richard Bland
College, Saint Leo College, the Virginia Commonwealth University, and Virginia
State University also offer on-post programs.

Personal Services and Recreation. Fort Lee offers a complete spectrum of support and morale facilities, including a post exchange, a commissary, and complete
medical and dental care facilities at the Kenner Army Community Hospital and two
dental clinics on post.

Recreation facilities include an eighteen-hole golf course, a swimming pool, a
bowling alley, a movie theater, an arts and crafts center, an auto shop, a gymnasium,
and tennis courts. The Traveller Recreation Center assists military personnel and
their families who wish to participate in tours to nearby sites of interest such as
Washington, D.C., Virginia Beach, Williamsburg, Busch Gardens, Kings Dominion,
and Skyline Drive.

The Local Area. The city of Petersburg is located just three miles from Fort
Lee. The Petersburg National Battlefield Monument marks the site of the longest
siege of the Civil War. The Siege Museum in Petersburg depicts the everyday life in
the city both before the war and during the ten months the siege lasted. Richmond,
former capital of the Confederacy and Virginia's leading city today, is only a few
miles to the north of the post off Interstate 95. It was at Richmond's Saint John's
Church that Patrick Henry made his famous "Liberty or Death" speech.

With its relatively mild winters and long summers, Virginia is an ideal place for
camping, fishing, hunting, backpacking, boating, and other outdoor activities. Add
to this the rich historical heritage of the Old Dominion State, and a visit to Fort Lee
can be immensely rewarding professionally and personally.

For more information write to: Army Community Services Office, CASCOM
and Fort Lee, Fort Lee, VA 23801-5000, or call (804) 734-6388.

FORT MONROE

For hundreds of years there has been some kind of fortification on the site of present-
day Fort Monroe. Two of its predecessors were destroyed by hurricanes in 1667 and
again in 1749. Today things are much calmer and safer there.

History. The present structure was begun in 1818 and received its first garrison
in July 1823. Originally named Fortress Monroe, in honor of James Monroe, our fifth

president, it was designated Fort Monroe by the secretary of war in 1832. Today it is the home of the Army's Training and Doctrine Command (TRADOC), whose mission is to develop the doctrine, weapon systems, equipment, organizations, and training needed to win on the battlefields of the twentieth century and beyond.

Housing and Schools. Government quarters are limited to about 190 units at Fort Monroe, and normally there is a waiting list for all grades except general officers. There is some privately owned Wherry housing on the post to which assignments are made; rent for these units is very reasonable. Bachelor and transient quarters are also available. Reservations are accepted for permanent-change-of-station personnel only; others are accepted on a space-available basis.

School-age dependent children attend school at nearby Hampton Roads. The post education center offers a variety of undergraduate and graduate courses as well as educational counseling and testing.

Personal Services and Recreation. A commissary, a post exchange, a medical and dental clinic, and a full range of morale and support facilities required at a major Army headquarters are available. A new child-care facility is also located on post.

Recreational facilities and programs at Fort Monroe include the Casemate Museum, which includes the cell where Jefferson Davis was imprisoned following the War Between the States. Exhibits covering the site's nearly 400-year history are on display. There is also the Historical and Archeological Society, which conducts a variety of projects and features guest speakers at its meetings. Because of its unique location—jutting into the Chesapeake Bay and Hampton Roads—Fort Monroe offers considerable opportunity to participate in sailing, power boating, and water sports in general. There is a marina on post, and fishing and boating equipment is available.

Fort Monroe also offers bowling, tennis, hobby shops, one swimming pool, three racquetball courts, and a movie theater.

The Local Area. A major attraction at Fort Monroe is the rich historical tradition as well as the thriving tourism that makes the area famous. Just across Hampton Roads via bridge and tunnel are Norfolk and Virginia Beach, both renowned vacation spots. Colonial Williamsburg, Jamestown, and Yorktown are situated within easy driving distance to the north of Hampton. Richmond, the capital of Virginia, and even Washington, D.C., are not too far away, easily accessible by a system of well-maintained interstate highways.

For more information write to: Army Community Services, Headquarters, Fort Monroe, Fort Monroe, VA 23651-6130, or call (804) 727-3878.

FORT MYER

The air at Fort Myer is constantly punctuated by martial music, whether the shrill piping of the U.S. Army Fife and Drum Corps playing for a review on Summerall Field or the mournful dirge of a funeral march as a soldier is escorted to his last resting place in nearby Arlington National Cemetery. Fort Myer is truly one of the

Army's finest showplaces, and the primary mission of the major units stationed there—the 3rd U.S. Infantry ("The Old Guard") and the U.S. Army Band ("Pershing's Own")—is ceremonial.

History. Originally established as a bastion in the defenses of Washington during the Civil War, the post was known as Fort Whipple until February 1881 when it was renamed in honor of Brig. Gen. Albert J. Myer, the first chief of the Army Signal Corps. Military aviation was born at Fort Myer with the flight of a Wright flying machine there on 3 September 1908, when the craft managed to stay aloft for one minute and eleven seconds; the first air fatality occurred there when Lt. Thomas Selfridge was killed in the crash of a Wright flying machine, also in 1908.

Housing and Schools. There are only 180 units of family housing at Fort Myer. Key Department of the Army staff officers, including the Chief of Staff of the Army and the Chairman of the Joint Chiefs of Staff, occupy quarters on the post; a small number of brick duplexes are available to certain senior NCOs as well as a modern high-rise for other enlisted ranks, but the waiting list for these quarters is very long.

Troop housing (for 2,400 soldiers) at Fort Myer is plentiful, and much of it is very modern. Most Army personnel on duty in the Washington metropolitan area are assigned to units at Fort Myer, and the post also provides billets and other support to members of the Navy and the Air Force on a limited basis. Other units on the post include the 1101st Signal Brigade, Fort Myer Military Police Company, and D Company, Walter Reed Army Medical Center.

Dependent children of service personnel stationed at Fort Myer attend schools in Arlington. A day-care center is available on post.

Fort Myer is ideally situated for personnel who wish to continue their education. A number of renowned universities and colleges, such as Georgetown and Howard, are located in the area, and most government installations in the area, including Fort Myer, host off-duty college classes for military and civilian personnel.

Personal Services and Recreation. Fort Myer is a small post, but it does have the basic morale and service facilities found on most military installations. A new post exchange/community service center is provided, and Andrew Rader Army Health Clinic (a satellite facility of Walter Reed Army Medical Center) offers outpatient medical care. A large and well-stocked commissary, a bank, and a full-service gasoline station are available.

Recreation facilities include a newly renovated post movie theater, a fitness center, spacious officers and NCO clubs, a twenty-lane bowling alley, a post library, two outdoor swimming pools, tennis and racquetball courts, and a gymnasium.

The Local Area. The Fort Myer area has four distinct seasons, but the general climate is mild and snowfall is usually light. Summers are very warm and humid, but the spring and fall, although generally short, are delightful.

Fort Myer is situated along a high bluff just west of the city of Washington, D.C., directly across the Potomac River and contiguous to the western boundary of Arlington National Cemetery in Arlington County, Virginia. The area is well known for its tourist attractions, not only within the city of Washington itself (the post is within walking distance of the Lincoln Memorial and the Pentagon) but elsewhere in the surrounding area. The Civil War battlefields of Manassas are a short drive from the post. Mount Vernon is a few miles down the Potomac, and the great natural beauty of Virginia and Maryland abound everywhere.

For more information write to: Commander, Headquarters, U.S. Army Garrison, Attention: ANMY-CD, Fort Myer, VA 22211-5050, or call (202) 475-0855/0856.

FORT STORY

Located at historic Cape Henry, three miles north of Virginia Beach, Fort Story looks out into the Atlantic Ocean to the east, the Chesapeake Bay to the north, and Seashore State Park to the west.

History. Fort Story was established in 1914 and is named after Maj. Gen. John Patton Story, a noted artilleryman. The first troops to occupy the area, two Coast Artillery Corps companies, moved in in February 1917.

Known today as "Home of the Amphibians," Fort Story's 343 acres provide space, facilities, and administrative and logistical services for the Army's amphibian operations, logistical-over-the-shore (LOTS) operations, and amphibious test and evaluation activities. The major Army unit at Fort Story is the 11th Transportation Battalion. Fort Story is also home to the 4th Brigade of the 80th Training Division (Army Reserve), the Navy's Explosive Ordnance Disposal Group Two, and the Marine Corps' Landing Force Training Command Atlantic Amphibious Reconnaissance School. The fort also serves as a periodic training site for units stationed at Fort Eustis; Army Reserve and National Guard units; local Navy, Marine, and Air Force active and reserve units; and the ROTC detachments from Old Dominion and Norfolk State Universities.

Altogether approximately 2,000 active-duty personnel, 260 civilian employees, and 1,700 dependents call Fort Story home.

Housing and Services. There are 160 units of family housing at Fort Story and guest accommodations for twenty-three visiting officers and enlisted personnel. The post has a small commissary and exchange. There is also a day-care facility for thirty-five children. There is a medical and dental clinic on post, and definitive medical care is available from local hospitals or Portsmouth Naval Hospital.

Recreation. Of course, there is swimming on the beaches along the Atlantic coast in season, but Fort Story also offers a full range of both indoor and outdoor sports and recreation, including a library, a movie theater, an auto craft shop, a gymnasium, a bowling alley, and an intramural sports program.

Local Attractions. Fort Story is located in one of the most historical regions of the United States. The Cape Henry Memorial Cross on the tip of Cape Henry marks the spot where the Jamestown settlers started Virginia's first real estate boom when they landed there on 26 April 1607. The Battle of the Virginia Capes Monument commemorates the victory of French Admiral Françoise de Grasse over the British fleet sent to relieve Cornwallis's army at Yorktown on 5 September 1781. The first lighthouse authorized by the federal government is also situated at Fort Story: It first cast its beams out to sea in 1792 and remained in operation until 1881.

For more information write to: HQ, Fort Story, Attention: Public Affairs Office, Fort Story, VA 23459-5000, or call (802) 422-7755.

VINT HILL FARMS STATION

The 1993 Base Realignment and Closure Commission recommended closing Vint Hill Farms Station, but as of press time a firm date had not yet been announced.

At one time the Union Jack flew proudly over Vint Hill Farms—not during the days of the American colonies when it had every right to fly there as part of the British Empire, but in 1861 when Andrew Low, the original developer of the estate, decided to claim the area "neutral" in the face of the impending American Civil War. Despite the big battles and maneuvers that occurred in this part of Virginia during the war, there is no record that either side bothered Mr. Low's estate, and it went on to play an important part in establishing northern Virginia as the legendary home for fast horses and beautiful women. Anyway, the officers club was originally Mr. Low's home. The post commander's quarters was built in 1890 for Mr. Low's eldest son and was called "Silvermead." The Low family lived on the property until 1899.

History. The Army came to Vint Hill in 1942, when the government purchased the land for $127,000. Throughout World War II the post served as a signal training and repair station. Today Vint Hill is the home of the U.S. Army Garrison, Vint Hill Farms Station, U.S. Army Electronics Materiel Readiness Activity, and other elements of the Army's communications-electronics community. The station has a population of about 2,200 military and civilian personnel.

Housing and Schools. There are 253 sets of family quarters available for military personnel assigned to Vint Hill, including 9 sets at Independent Hill, twenty miles from the station. The average waiting period for personnel in pay grades E-4 through E-6 is from five to seven months for three-bedroom units. Senior NCOs and officers wait from thirty to ninety days. The installation has 2 self-contained trailers and a guest house consisting of 10 rooms without kitchens. Priority for reservations goes to personnel on permanent-change-of-station orders.

Although there are no schools at Vint Hill for dependent children, preschool, summer camp, school-age latchkey, and family child-care programs are available. The education center offers both credit and noncredit classes from the University of Virginia and Northern Virginia Community College on post.

Personal Services. The U.S. Army Health Clinic at Vint Hill provides primary medical care for military personnel, their dependents, and retirees living in the vicinity of the station. Definitive medical care is available from Walter Reed General Hospital in Washington or DeWitt Army Hospital at Fort Belvoir. The dental clinic is available for dependents for basic care only. Other facilities on post are a bank and credit union, a commissary, a beauty shop, a four-seasons store, and a post exchange.

Recreation. Recreational facilities at the station include officers and NCO clubs, a sportsmen's club, a recreation center, a post library, and a post movie theater. The station also has a six-lane bowling alley; photo, wood, leather, ceramics, and auto craft shops; a gymnasium; two outdoor swimming pools; and a skeet and archery range.

The Local Area. Vint Hill Farms Station is located in the rolling Virginia countryside, about nine miles from Warrenton, population 5,000. Manassas, with about 30,000 people, is fifteen miles away, and the station is about forty-three miles from Washington, D.C. The foothills of the Blue Ridge Mountains are a one- to two-hour drive from the post. Hunting for deer, rabbit, and quail is permitted in the countryside, and the many lakes, ponds, and streams in the area offer good fishing.

Vint Hill is situated in the middle of Civil War country. Manassas Battlefield Park is just to the east along Route 29, but only a few miles away to the south is the rural village of Auburn, which saw fighting and maneuvering during the Bristow Campaign of 1863; Warrenton, just to the northwest, was occupied by both the Confederate and Union armies at different times during the war and many of its beautiful old homes that are still standing today were witnesses to these events. Development has not yet reached this part of Virginia and much of the countryside today is as it was in the 1860s.

For more information write to: Public Affairs Office, VHFS, Warrenton, VA 22186, or call (703) 349-6578.

Marine Corps

QUANTICO MARINE BASE

Quantico has often been called the "Crossroads of the Corps": It is at Quantico that Marine officers undergo their initial training, and they keep returning there to attend other schools, all the way up to the Command and Staff College.

History. First established in 1917, Quantico takes its name from an Indian word meaning "by the large stream." The stream is the Potomac River, which borders the eastern fringes of the reservation. From its beginnings as a training camp in World War I, Quantico is still in the military education business, more so than ever before. Today it is the headquarters for the Marine Corps Development Combat Command, which operates the Officer Candidate School, the basic school for officers, the Amphibious Warfare School, and the Command and Staff College, as well as schools in communications, computer sciences, and management, and a course for staff NCOs.

Housing and Schools. There are more than 1,500 units of family quarters at the base. Waiting times vary, according to rank. Temporary accommodations are offered in the seventy-three-room hostess house, located near the Potomac River. Trailer sites are also available to enlisted personnel who own mobile homes.

Dependent children attend schools on base, but area schools in Stafford and Prince William Counties are highly rated. A day-care center is also located on the base. Several colleges and universities, including Park College and Northern Virginia Community College, provide on-base courses for interested adults.

Personal Services. Medical care is provided by the Naval Regional Medical Clinic, which sees as many as 11,000 patients a month. Serious cases or cases requiring specialized treatment are referred to DeWitt Army Hospital, about thirty miles north of the base at Fort Belvoir. Dental service for dependents is not available at Quantico.

A commissary store and a main exchange with several branches are available on the base, as are a check-cashing facility, a service station, a newsstand, and a cafeteria/snack bar.

Recreation. Recreational facilities are excellent at Quantico and include a sixteen-lane bowling center, a gymnasium, a movie theater, a swimming pool, tennis courts, an eighteen-hole golf course, a riding stable, and a rifle and pistol club. In addition, there are varsity and intramural sports.

Excellent outdoor recreational facilities are located on the base at the Lunga Reservoir Recreational Area. Reservations are required two weeks in advance to use the campers, which are available from April to October. The site offers thirty-six camper spaces (with water and electricity), eighty tent sites, picnic facilities, a playground, a golf course, stables, swimming pools, and boat docks. Motorboats, sailboats, canoes, rowboats, paddleboats, and horses and stables can be rented. The Quantico Marina at the end of Potomac Avenue offers overnight berthing and slip rentals for boats up to forty feet in length.

Hunting and fishing are also allowed on base in an 800-acre tract that has five miles of trout streams. Deer, squirrel, rabbit, quail, and dove can be hunted there. Trout, bass, catfish, bluegill, and pickerel can be caught in the streams.

The Local Area. Quantico is situated about thirty-five miles south of Washington, D.C., along Interstate 95. Because Quantico lies so near the nation's capital, there are many attractions in the area, most of them discussed elsewhere in this book. The immediate area around Quantico is one of small towns and much forestland. Prince William Forest, with hiking and picnic areas, lies only about a mile from the main gate, through the little town of Triangle. The town of Quantico itself lies surrounded on three sides by the base; on the fourth side is the Potomac River. The town of Quantico is a rail stop for the Virginia Rail Express and Amtrak. Fredericksburg is twenty-three miles south of the base.

For further information write to: Public Affairs Office, MCB MCCD, 3098 Range Rd., Quantico, VA 22134-5126, or call (703) 640-2741.

Navy

DAHLGREN DIVISION, NAVAL SURFACE WARFARE CENTER

Located fifty-three miles south of Washington, D.C., on the Potomac River and twenty-eight miles west of historic Fredericksburg, Virginia, the Dahlgren Laboratory is divided into two separate areas: Mainside, which consists of 2,678 acres adjacent to the town of Dahlgren; and Pumpkin Neck, an isolated weapons-testing area occupying 1,641 acres between Machodoc Creek on the north and west and the Potomac on the east.

History. Naval ordnance testing got its start at Dahlgren in April 1918, when Congress voted to buy land in Virginia's Northern Neck area to establish a proving ground. The first piece of ordnance fired there, a seven-inch, forty-five-caliber tractor-mounted cannon, was set off on 16 October 1918. Dahlgren's mission today is to provide research, development, test and evaluation, engineering, and fleet support for surface warfare systems, surface ship combat systems, ordnance, mines, amphibious warfare systems, mine countermeasures, special warfare systems, and strategic systems. To accomplish this mission, Dahlgren maintains an extensive range of facilities, including a twenty-five-mile-long by five-mile-wide downriver test range.

Dahlgren is operated by 810 military personnel and a civilian workforce of 3,536 personnel, in addition to 625 family members.

Housing and Schools. Dahlgren provides 150 units of family housing plus billeting for 35 bachelor officers and 260 unaccompanied enlisted personnel. Dependent children in kindergarten through eighth grade may attend schools on base. A day-care facility at Dahlgren can accommodate up to eighty children.

Personal Services. Dahlgren has a small commissary and Navy exchange. Medical care is provided by branch medical and dental clinics. Long-term and definitive health care are available locally in Fredericksburg or at the National Naval Medical Center in Bethesda.

Recreation. Dahlgren offers a full range of recreational facilities that includes an all-hands club, a gym, a marina, outdoor intramural sports, and arts and crafts shops. But one of the largest recreational attractions at Dahlgren is the outdoors itself. The center is about 50 percent wooded and offers 2,300 acres for hunting, 84 acres of lakes and ponds for fishing, and eight miles of stream and shoreline for fishing.

For more information write to: Public Affairs Office, Code C05, NSWCCDD, Dahlgren, VA 22448-5000, or call (703) 663-8154.

DAM NECK FLEET COMBAT TRAINING CENTER

Established in December 1941 as a live-fire range for the Anti-Aircraft Training and Test Center, the Atlantic Fleet Combat Training Center's 1,171-acre site along the Atlantic coast in Virginia Beach, just south of Oceana Naval Air Station, is home today to the Naval Guided Missile School, Tactical Training Group Atlantic, Navy and Marine Corps Intelligence Training Center, and other commands. The center's complement consists of 5,000 active-duty personnel, 700 civilian employees, and 62 family members.

Housing, Schools, and Personal Services. Dam Neck operates nineteen sets of family quarters, 2,800 bachelor enlisted units, and 200 bachelor-officer quarters. Children attend local schools, but a day-care center at Dam Neck can accommodate forty children. A Navy Campus at the base attends to the educational needs of adults.

Medical and dental services at Dam Neck are provided by small branch clinics with definitive or referral care available at nearby Oceana or local hospitals. There is no commissary at Dam Neck, but there is a small exchange that operates a service station, a shopette, a barber shop, a dry cleaner, and a laundromat. Personnel at Dam Neck can take advantage of the full range of services available at nearby Oceana Naval Air Station.

Recreation. Dam Neck offers a bowling alley, a gym, a recreation center, a fitness center, and an auto shop for indoor recreation. A pool, tennis and racquetball courts, and softball and football fields are available. Fishing and hunting are permitted in the wide variety of highlands, forest, wetlands, coastal beaches, and sand dunes that constitute Dam Neck.

For more information write to: Commander, Fleet Combat Training Center, Atlantic, Attention: Code O1P, 1912 Regulus Ave., Virginia Beach, VA 23461-5200, or call (804) 433-6595.

NORFOLK NAVAL BASE

History. Make no mistake about it, Norfolk is a Navy town. Norfolk is home to 107,000 active-duty naval personnel assigned to shore-based and fleet units. Add to this a total of 41,000 civilian employees, and you have a Navy community larger than most cities. Throughout the entire Norfolk area, the Navy's strength is over 139,000, including retirees and Navy reservists.

Commissioned in July 1917, Norfolk Naval Base is the largest naval installation in the world.

Housing and Schools. There are more than 6,255 government quarters in the Norfolk area. The waiting period for these quarters ranges from two to thirty months, depending on the time of year application is made and family size. Over 17,900 naval personnel rent private housing in the area, and more than 23,900 own their own homes. There is a 90-unit Navy Lodge onboard the base, and another 90 units are available at the Little Creek Naval Amphibious Base.

Public schooling is provided for dependent children, and adult-education programs proliferate throughout the area. The Navy Campus at the naval station coordinates an active program of college-level courses designed to enable active-duty personnel to take advantage of instruction offered by sixteen academic institutions.

Personal Services. Navy exchanges and commissaries are provided in several places in the Norfolk area: at the base, at the naval air station, at the Portsmouth Naval Shipyard, and at the Naval Weapons Station Yorktown. Exchange stores are available at Fort Eustis, Fort Monroe, and Langley Air Force Base. The Naval Regional Medical Center in Portsmouth operates a total of seventeen medical facilities in the area.

Recreation. Three Navy recreational areas are available to personnel stationed at Norfolk: Driver Point at the Naval Radio Transmitter Facility; Stewart Memorial

Campgrounds at the Naval Security Group Activity, Northwest, Chesapeake; and Naval Weapons Station Camp at Yorktown Naval Weapons Station. These areas provide camper spaces and outdoor activities and are generally open during the spring, summer, and fall.

At the naval base itself are six swimming pools, three gymnasiums, two movie theaters of which one is a ten-theater complex, two golf courses, three picnic areas, hobby and craft shops, and three bowling alleys.

The Local Area. The Norfolk–Virginia Beach–Williamsburg–Richmond area is one of the richest in historical points of interest and recreation attractions in the country. The North Carolina coast, Washington, D.C., and the Pennsylvania Dutch country are all within fairly easy driving distance of the Norfolk area. Closer are Colonial Williamsburg, Yorktown, and Revolutionary War and Civil War battle-fields. Fishing, boating, swimming, hunting, and outdoor sports are available in this area year-round. Stables, skeet and trap ranges, swimming pools, and picnic areas and beaches abound. Many of these activities are available at the military installations in the area.

For more information write to: Public Affairs Office, 1530 Gilbert St., Ste. 200, Naval Base, Norfolk, VA 23511-4399, or call (804) 444-1985.

NORFOLK NAVAL SHIPYARD

The Norfolk Naval Shipyard (NNSY) in Portsmouth, Virginia, is one of the largest shipyards in the world, specializing in repairing, overhauling, and modernizing war-ships. NNSY annually does about $650 million in work on U.S. Atlantic Fleet's air-craft carriers, guided missile cruisers, and submarines.

History. Founded in 1767, NNSY is the Navy's oldest shipyard. It was here the Confederate ironclad CSS *Virginia* was built from the frigate USS *Merrimack* during the Civil War. The Navy's first aircraft carrier, USS *Langley*, was built at NNSY. Today NNSY is a 1,200-acre complex with four miles of waterfront, thirty miles of paved streets, and about nineteen miles of railroad track. It has a complement of 166 active-duty personnel as well as some 8,000 shipboard personnel in port on vessels undergoing repair. It has its own police and fire departments, generates electricity and steam by burning trash, and operates about 400 cranes. NNSY employs about 10,000 civilian personnel.

Housing, Schools, and Personal Services. NNSY operates 30 officer and 372 enlisted units of family housing. Children attend schools in Portsmouth, but NNSY operates a day-care center that can accommodate fifty-seven children. College cours-es are available from a number of local institutions including Tidewater Community College, Norfolk State University, Old Dominion University, and C.B.N. University. Medical care is provided by a branch clinic with referral and inpatient care available at Portsmouth Naval Hospital. There is a small Navy exchange at NNSY as well as a medium-size commissary store. The facilities at the Norfolk Naval Base, Oceana Naval Air Station, and Little Creek Naval Amphibious Base are also available to personnel stationed at NNSY.

Recreation. A bowling alley, a gym, a recreation center, a swimming pool, a softball field, and tennis, handball, racquetball, and basketball courts are available onboard the installation.

For more information write to: Public Affairs Office, Code 1160, Norfolk Naval Shipyard, Portsmouth, VA 23709-5000, or call (804) 396-9550.

NORTHWEST NAVAL SECURITY GROUP ACTIVITY

Located just north of the North Carolina–Virginia border and a few miles east of Virginia's Great Dismal Swamp National Wildlife Refuge, the Northwest Naval Security Group Activity (NSGA), Chesapeake, occupies 3,700 acres of wooded farm and swamp lands in one of the most historic regions of Virginia.

NSGA operates facilities and systems necessary to provide cryptologic communications support for the Department of the Navy and the Defense Communications System. Additional missions include direction-finding assistance to navigational aid and air-sea rescue missions. Because of the nature of the highly classified and sensitive work that goes on at NSGA, security is very high there. A personnel identification badge control system is used, and all visitors must be accompanied by an escort.

The NSGA has a complement of 749 personnel, 520 military and 229 civilian employees, not including tenant command personnel. NSGA is host to the NATO Satellite Communications Facility, U.S. Coast Guard Communications Area Master Station Atlantic, Marine Corps Security Force Training Company, and several other activities.

Housing and Schools. NSGA maintains 140 units of family housing as well as quarters for about 140 bachelor enlisted personnel. Transient accommodations are also available. Dependent schooling is available in the local area, as are courses offered by Chesapeake Campus of Tidewater Community College. There is a Navy Family Services Center available on base and home-provided child care.

Personal Services. Medical and dental care are offered at the NSGA branch clinic, and definitive medical care is available at nearby Portsmouth Naval Medical Center and Chesapeake General Hospital. Although there is no commissary at NSGA, the installation has a small Navy exchange that supports a total of 1,800 Navy, Marine, and Coast Guard personnel. A general mess, CPO, petty officers, and enlisted clubs are available on the station. What NSGA does not offer, nearby Norfolk Navy Yard does.

Recreation. The base has excellent recreation facilities for hunting, fishing, boating, and camping enthusiasts, as well as an outdoor swimming pool, ball fields, tennis courts, racquetball courts, a bowling alley, and a fitness center and gym, complete with weight room. There are also auto and woodworking hobby shops

Virginia Beach, Seashore State Park, and Back Bay National Wildlife Refuge, on the Atlantic coast, are only minutes away from NSGA, as are Portsmouth and Norfolk. Newport News, historic Jamestown, and the restored colonial village of Williamsburg are only a bit farther away.

For more information write to: Commanding Officer, Naval Security Group Activity, Attention: Public Affairs, 1320 Northwest Blvd., Ste. 100, Chesapeake, VA 23322-4094, or call (804) 421-8328.

OCEANA NAVAL AIR STATION

Oceana Naval Air Station is a complex of over seven miles of runways with the latest equipment to serve military air traffic on the East Cost, supporting nineteen squadrons of F-14 Tomcat and A-6 Intruder aircraft. This is one of the busiest air stations in the Navy: An aircraft takes off or lands at Oceana approximately every two minutes.

History. What started as 328 acres of swampland fifty years ago has grown to over 5,000 acres today and home to over 15,000 active-duty personnel, civilian employees, and family members. There are 25,000 registered automobiles at Oceana, and the station's annual payroll amounts to $286 million.

Housing and Schools. Oceana has more than 1,100 units of Navy housing, 503 of them apartments at Oceana Apartments on the southeast corner of the station, just outside the main gate. Excellent off-base schooling is available for dependent children, and the station's Navy Campus operates an active series of off-duty educational programs that include courses offered by Tidewater Junior College and Golden Gate, George Washington, Old Dominion, Troy State, Embry-Riddle Aeronautical, Saint Leo State, and Norfolk State Universities.

Personal Services and Recreation. The station also has a complete array of support services, including a Navy exchange mall with specialty shops, a food court, and an adjoining commissary store and gas station, all located off base. A complete officers, CPO, and enlisted club system is located on the station. The station boasts an excellent recreational program that includes both indoor and outdoor activities such as an eighteen-hole golf course, riding stables, a bowling alley, swimming pools, tennis courts, and three large picnic areas. Also available are seven skeet and four trap ranges, a clubhouse, and a retail sporting goods facility.

The Local Area. Oceana is located within the city limits of the world's largest resort city, Virginia Beach. The leading summer attraction is the six miles of sandy beach lined by a boardwalk. With hot summers and cold but usually snowless winters, Oceana offers some kind of activity year-round. The Norfolk–Hampton–Newport News area is just to the north, with its vast complex of naval and military installations, while even Washington, D.C., is within an easy day's drive.

The history buff will find Oceana a pure delight. Nearby Fort Story is where the first permanent settlers from England landed in 1607; almost every spot in the state is near some kind of historic landmark, a Revolutionary or Civil War battlefield, or some place famous in the colonial history of this country.

For more information write to: Public Affairs Officer, Naval Air Station, Oceana, Virginia Beach, VA 23460-5120, or call (804) 433-3131.

YORKTOWN NAVAL WEAPONS STATION

History. The oldest structure onboard the Yorktown Naval Weapons Station is the Lee House, built around 1649, where many generations of the family lived out their lives before the property was acquired by the U.S. government. Long, long before the world ever conceived of such things as the testing and evaluation that now goes on at the weapons station, the infantry of the American Revolution and the Civil War slogged along the Old Williamsburg Road where today it runs through the station.

The site of the weapons station was acquired by the Navy in August 1918 and was at the time the largest naval reservation in the world, with a land area covering about twenty square miles. Over the years, the growth and expansion of the Navy's technical requirements and responsibilities have been reflected by corresponding developments at the station to support the Atlantic Fleet. Based at the station are the Naval Mine Warfare Engineering Activity, the Naval Ophthalmic Support and Training Activity, and the Marine Corps Security Force Company. Today the station is home to about 2,100 civilians and 900 military personnel.

Housing and Schools. There are 470 sets of family quarters on the station, plus sites and facilities for 40 mobile homes. Guest accommodations are not available. The station is not an open facility, and visitors must obtain proper identification and passes.

While there are no dependent schools at the station, a child-care facility is available there; older children attend the public school system in nearby Newport News and York County.

Personal Services and Recreation. A commissary and Navy exchange, a convenience store, a credit union, and an enlisted and officers club system are provided at the station.

The Japanese Gardens camping and picnic area offers space for ten campers as well as showers, toilet facilities, and a laundry facility with washer and dryer. The Wright Circle Picnic Area, also on the station, provides excellent facilities including charcoal grills, sheltered tables, and recreational facilities. Fishing is permitted in various freshwater ponds at the station and off the station's fishing pier.

Other recreational activities include a golf course, a gymnasium, handball/racquetball courts, a hobby shop, two swimming pools, two tennis courts, and a theater. Tours to the Yorktown Battlefield and Colonial Williamsburg and Jamestown are available at discounts through the special services office at the station.

The Local Area. The station is situated along the west bank of the York River, just above Yorktown and off Interstate 64. Yorktown, Williamsburg, Fort Eustis, and Newport News are all within twenty miles of the station. The great naval complex of Norfolk is just to the south, accessible via Interstate 64, and Richmond is somewhat farther to the north, also accessible on the interstate. Washington, D.C., is only several hours' drive to the north on Interstate 95, and a weekend outing from the station could easily take in points as far north as Gettysburg, Pennsylvania.

For more information write to: Public Affairs Office, NWS, Yorktown, VA 23691-0160, or call (804) 887-4444/4521.

WASHINGTON

Air Force

FAIRCHILD AIR FORCE BASE

History. Fairchild Air Force Base occupies over 6,000 acres approximately twelve miles west of Spokane on Highway 2. As is the case with many other sites where military bases are located, the people of Spokane donated the land for Fairchild to the U.S. government. The government accepted, partly because the weather in Spokane is better suited for air operations than in other parts of the state, and partly because the base is located 300 miles from the ocean, with a mountain range intervening. This latter point was very important then because we were at war with Japan.

The base was opened as Spokane Army Air Depot in March 1942. In 1950, it was renamed Fairchild Air Force Base after Gen. Muir S. Fairchild, a native of Bellingham, Washington, and vice chief of staff for air. Today it is home for the 92nd Bombardment Wing (Heavy), the 366th Crew Training Group, and other units.

Housing and Schools. Fairchild offers over 1,500 government housing units, some of them located off the base up to sixteen miles away. Guest housing is available, but reservations are accepted only for personnel on official business; all others are accepted on a first-come, first-served basis only.

Dependent children of military personnel stationed at Fairchild attend local schools, private and public. The base education office operates programs for adults that range from pre-high school level through graduate level. Some of the participating institutions include Eastern Washington University, Gonzaga University, Spokane Falls Community College, Washington Community College District No. 17, and Washington State College District No. 17.

Personal Services. Personal services include the forty-five-bed USAF hospital, a child-care center, a commissary that carries 5,000 line items in stock, and a base exchange that offers a number of concessions.

Recreation. Recreational facilities include a base roller skating rink, a gymnasium, a twenty-five-meter indoor swimming pool, an auto hobby shop, a sixteen-lane bowling center, arts and crafts and wood hobby shops, and a well-equipped recreation center.

Also available is the Clear Lake Resort Area, about twelve miles south of the base. The area contains thirty-five acres and has a beach with swimming, boat docks, cabins, trailer and camper sites, and other facilities.

The Local Area. The climate in eastern Washington has four distinct seasons, but the Spokane area is generally dry and mild in the summer and cold and humid in the winter, with about fifty-three inches of snow and seventeen inches of rain in an average year.

Spokane is a modern, progressive community that is a trade and service center for more than one million people over an 80,000-square-mile area. It was selected as the site for the 1974 World's Fair, and many of the structures built for the occasion are still major attractions. A unique and fascinating aspect of the city is the Skywalk Network, which connects a ten-block area by an intricate system of elevated walkways and malls, all indoors, and offers a large number of shops and restaurants for shoppers and strollers.

This part of Washington is often referred to as "the Inland Empire," and the people living there take outdoor life seriously. There are ten national parks, fifteen national forests, and more than one hundred public and private campgrounds in this area. Hunting and fishing, snow skiing, hiking—almost every sport except surfing is available here.

For more information write to: Public Affairs Office, E. I Bong St., Fairchild AFB, WA 99011-5000, or call (509) 247-5704.

McCHORD AIR FORCE BASE

Majestic, snow-covered Mount Rainier's 14,410-foot peak dominates the southeastern skyline at McChord AFB, as Puget Sound dominates the land to the west of the base. In Washington, appropriately named the "Evergreen State," nature dominates everything.

History. Named in honor of Col. William C. McChord, who died in an aircraft crash near Richmond, Virginia, in 1937, McChord Air Force Base was established in July 1940 as a bomber base. Today it is home for the men and women of the 62nd Military Airlift Wing, the 25th Air Division 446th Military Airlift Wing (Reserve), and various tenant support units.

Housing and Schools. There are over 980 sets of family quarters at McChord.

Waiting lists vary according to the sponsor's grade and the family size: Junior NCOs can expect to wait the longest, from nine to ten months for two-bedroom units. Temporary lodging is available for families permanently changing station but on a space-available basis only.

Excellent educational opportunities are available for children and adults at McChord. For children, the Sunshine Preschool and two elementary schools are located on base, and junior and senior high schools are nearby. The base education center offers 460 undergraduate college courses and 80 graduate courses each year. These are given in cooperation with the University of Puget Sound, Saint Martin's College, Evergreen Community College, Southern Illinois University, Chapman College, Green River Community College, the University of Southern California, and Pacific Lutheran University.

Personal Services. Personal services include the McChord medical and dental clinics and Madigan Army Medical Center, three miles south of McChord. McChord also offers an excellent, newly renovated commissary and base exchange.

Recreation. Recreational activities include a variety of clubs such as aero and officers and NCO wives, as well as a consolidated arts and crafts center; an auto hobby shop; a twenty-lane bowling center; an eighteen-hole, par-seventy-two golf course; a recreation center; a base gymnasium; and swimming pools. Holiday Park is an on-base recreation area that offers eighteen trailer sites, picnic areas, playground facilities, a softball diamond, and horseshoe pits. In addition, there are a lake, a stream, and one pond on base where fishing is permitted.

The Local Area. McChord Air Force Base is sandwiched between the southern outskirts of the city of Tacoma and the vast expanse of Fort Lewis. Tacoma is Washington's third largest city, with a population of over 156,000 people. The Tacoma area has one of the nicest climates to be found anywhere in the Northwest. Summer temperatures seldom exceed the eighties, and winter temperatures average in the forties during the daytime. Snow usually melts before it can accumulate.

The state of Washington offers much in the way of recreation, with 250 miles of Pacific Ocean coastline and over 2,500 miles of saltwater shoreline on Puget Sound and the adjacent waterways. Golf is played year-round on Washington courses; the mountains offer twenty ski areas. Because of the proximity of so much water, fishing and water sports are popular year-round also.

For more information write to: 62nd Airlift Wing Public Affairs Office, 100 Main St., McChord AFB, WA 98438-1109, or call (206) 984-5637.

Army

FORT LEWIS

On a clear day you can see Mount Rainier looming on the horizon to the east of Fort Lewis, towering at over 14,000 feet high above the other noble peaks of the Cascade

Range. From the forestclad mountains to the inland sea waters of Puget Sound, this is a region of great natural beauty, and Fort Lewis is at the heart of it all.

History. Named after Capt. Meriwether Lewis, leader of the historic Lewis and Clark Expedition of 1803, Fort Lewis was founded in 1917. In 1927 it was designated as a permanent Army post, and its name was changed from Camp Lewis to Fort Lewis. Together with Yakima Training Center, east of the Cascades, Fort Lewis's 260,000 acres of training, maneuver, and firing areas make it one of the largest military posts in the United States. Today it is home to the I Corps, 4th ROTC Region, 2nd Battalion, 75th Rangers, 1st Special Forces Group, and Madigan Medical Center.

Housing and Schools. There are over 3,500 sets of family quarters at Fort Lewis, more than 2,700 for enlisted personnel alone. Waiting times vary but as of October 1992, junior NCOs waited two to three months for two-bedroom homes, while company-grade officers waited one to two months for two-bedroom units. Guest accommodations are available for personnel of all ranks, but only those on permanent-change-of-station orders may make reservations; all others are accepted on a space-available basis. These facilities include the Fort Lewis Lodge, with seventy-five guest rooms; the Clark House (for enlisted families), with five suites and three single rooms; and six cabins for officer families.

On-post education facilities include elementary and high schools. Four education centers offer counseling, testing, registration, and instruction for military personnel from remedial training and high school through advanced college degrees.

Personal Services. Madigan Army Medical Center at Fort Lewis offers a complete array of inpatient, outpatient, and specialty care for an active-duty and retired military population of more than 85,000 personnel and their dependents. Post exchange and commissary facilities at Fort Lewis are excellent, and many concessionaires offer a full range of goods and services on the post.

Recreation. Recreation centers offer activities that include parties, stage shows, dances, and tournaments, and the sports branch of the morale, welfare, and recreation office conducts a complete athletic program for both men and women. The Fort Lewis flying, hunting and fishing, and parachute clubs offer exciting outdoor activities for all. The Fort Lewis Travel Camp, located on the installation at the southern end of Puget Sound, and boating from the beach at American Lake, offer further opportunities for outdoor fun and adventure.

The Local Area. Nearby communities include Tacoma, just to the north of the post, a city of about 157,000, and Seattle, forty-five miles northwest. Seattle is the largest city in the Pacific Northwest, with a population of over 500,000. Seattle offers a wide variety of attractions, from Seattle Center on the World's Fair grounds to the Woodland Park Zoological Gardens. The Tacoma area abounds with scenic and natural points of interest, including Wright's Park Botanical Observatory and Point Defiance Park, 640 acres of woodland roads and trails, and a restored outpost of the Hudson Bay Company.

Farther afield are attractions such as Mount Rainier National Park and Lake Chelan, a fifty-mile-long body of water flowing into the Columbia River that has often been compared to the fjords of Norway.

For more information write to: Army Community Services Office, Headquarters, I Corps and Fort Lewis, Attention: AFZH-PO, Fort Lewis, WA 94833-5000, or call (206) 967-7166.

Navy

BANGOR NAVAL SUBMARINE BASE

Occupying 7,000 acres on the east bank of the Hood Canal, just southwest of the town of Poulsbo and thirteen miles north of Bremerton, Bangor Naval Submarine Base is the home port for a squadron of Trident submarines, part of the nation's nuclear deterrent Triad, which also includes land- and air-based systems.

The Trident program can be broken down into three components: the submarine, the missile, and the base. The submarine is the 560-foot Ohio-class sub, which has twenty-four missile tubes and four torpedo tubes, displaces 18,700 tons of water, and costs approximately $1.2 billion. The missile is the thirty-four-foot Trident I, or C-4, which weighs 71,000 pounds, has a range of 4,000 nautical miles (1,500 miles greater than the Polaris), and costs about $17 million.

History. The base began its history in 1942, when it was purchased for use as an ammunition depot. In 1973 it was selected as home port for the Trident subs. In 1977 Bangor Naval Submarine Base was commissioned. In 1981 Commander, Submarine Group 9, and Commander, Submarine Squadron 17, were activated and in 1982 the first Trident sub, USS *Ohio* (SSBN 726) arrived at the base. The base is 155 nautical miles from the Pacific Ocean, with access through the Strait of Juan de Fuca. Approximately 5,500 active-duty personnel are stationed at Bangor.

Housing and Schools. Over 800 units of family housing—modern and very adequate—are available on base, in the southeast and southwest sectors, near the main gate. A Navy Lodge opened in the spring of 1992.

Although there is no dependent schooling on the base, a child-care center is available. The Navy Campus offers programs designed to provide the opportunity for high school completion through master's degree courses from such institutions as Olympic and Chapman Colleges, Central Washington and Southern Illinois Universities, and the Universities of Southern California and Puget Sound.

Personal Services. Medical care is provided at the Bremerton Naval Regional Medical Center, eight miles south of the base. The hospital has 170 beds and offers a full range of services. A large Navy exchange and commissary and a variety of other support facilities are available on base.

Recreation. Recreational facilities include a recreation complex with a gymnasium, saunas, exercise rooms, a swimming pool, indoor handball and squash courts, a bowling alley, hobby and craft shops, tennis courts, a theater, three on-base lakes for fishing, an archery range, and a boat ramp and boat rentals.

The Local Area. Outdoor recreational activities are also important factors in the lives of Navy personnel, as they are for Washingtonians in general: Hunting, trapping, fishing, camping, boating, and snow and water skiing are all available within the Puget Sound region. Just to the west of the base, across Hood Canal, is the Olympic National Forest, open all year. Many of the mountain peaks there exceed 7,000 feet, and visitors may enjoy the pristine beauty of the forests that climb their majestic slopes.

A relatively short distance to the east of the base, across Puget Sound, is Seattle, a major deepwater port and cultural, industrial, and agricultural center of the Northwest. Somewhat farther north, but still easily accessible, are the vast expanses of the Canadian Northwest.

For more information write to: Family Services Center, Naval Submarine Base, Bangor, Bremerton, WA 98315-5000, or call (206) 396-4843.

BREMERTON NAVAL HOSPITAL

Situated on the western side of Puget Sound in a wooded site overlooking Ostrich Bay, Bremerton Naval Hospital is the principal naval health care facility in the Pacific Northwest. It is conveniently located just five miles north of Puget Sound Naval Shipyard, ten miles south of Bangor Naval Submarine Base, and twelve miles south of the Naval Undersea Warfare Center at Keyport.

Along with supporting the personnel stationed at these major facilities, the naval hospital is also the parent command for a branch hospital in Adak, Alaska. Currently operating 109 beds, the naval hospital has a complement of 719 officers and enlisted personnel (including those at outlying facilities) as well as 377 civilian employees. During fiscal year 1992, 373,000 outpatients visited the hospital and 5,253 persons were admitted.

Housing, Schools, and Personal Services. Although there is a small Navy exchange at the hospital itself, all other services are provided by the nearby shipyard, submarine base, or local community.

For more information write to: Commanding Officer, Code OOA3, Naval Hospital, Boone Rd., Bremerton, WA 98312-1898, or call (206) 479-5500.

PUGET SOUND NAVAL SHIPYARD

Puget Sound Naval Shipyard covers more than 680 acres consisting of six dry docks and seven piers and employs more than 12,000 civilian workers. The yard has the capability of overhauling and repairing the most modern vessels in the fleet. In the past its facilities have been used to modernize such mighty warships as the carriers *Nimitz* and *Carl Vinson*. Approximately 9,000 active-duty personnel and their 15,000 family members are assigned to the yard.

Housing and Schools. The base controls more than 1,000 units of family housing. Dependent children attend local public schools; the post has a day-care center that can accommodate up to 140 children. Adult education is available through the Olympic College Extension Office in Bremerton.

Personal Services. The Naval Regional Medical Center, Bremerton, provides the whole range of modern medical care, including surgery, a pharmacy, a lab, and an x-ray clinic.

Other facilities include a Navy exchange; a commissary store; a Navy exchange mini mart; enlisted, CPO, and officers open messes; a beverage store; and a liquor store. The exchange also operates a garage and gas station, a laundry and dry-cleaning shop, and a personalized services facility that includes key-making facilities, an optical service, and a shoe repair store.

Recreation. Recreational facilities include an indoor, heated swimming pool; two athletic fields; a gymnasium; seven tennis courts; an eighteen-lane bowling center; and hobby shops. The Camp McKean Recreation Area, about five miles west of Bremerton, is a summer recreation site consisting of a twenty-acre area where picnicking, organized sports, swimming, and boating may be enjoyed. It is an excellent spot for large bashes and can accommodate parties of up to 300 people.

The Local Area. The city of Tacoma is only thirty-two miles east of Bremerton via the toll-free Tacoma Narrows Bridge. Bremerton itself is a thriving city of more than 35,000 people and has a relatively mild climate year-round. The average summer temperature is only 62° F. with an average winter temperature of 42° F.; about thirty-eight inches of rain fall in the area in an average year.

Skiing in the nearby mountains and water sports in Puget Sound are very popular pastimes in this area. The recreation services office at the yard maintains a ski lodge situated three miles east of North Bend. The lodge is in the form of a trailer that sleeps six.

For more information write to: Morale, Welfare, and Recreation Fund, Bldg. 502, Code 820.5, Puget Sound Naval Shipyard, Bremerton, WA 98314-5000, or call (206) 476-2214/5936.

PUGET SOUND NAVAL STATION

The 1991 Base Realignment and Closure Commission, following the recommendation of the 1988 commission, designated Puget Sound Naval Station to close by October 1995.

Located in Seattle, Puget Sound Naval Station was established as the Naval Air Station, Seattle, in 1925 on land donated by King County. The dirt runways of that era saw the U.S. Army's first around-the-world flight begin and end there. A plaque on a column at the station's entrance commemorates that historic event. Today the station is host to Reserve Readiness Command, Region 22, Mine Group 1, and other activities, and home to about 1,000 military personnel, their 1,000 family members, and a civilian workforce of 100 people. Naval Station Puget Sound is the northwest cornerstone of a logistics network that covers the entire Pacific and Indian Oceans.

Housing and Schools. There are approximately 200 units of family quarters at the station. Temporary lodging is also available.

Children of personnel serving onboard the station attend local schools. Adult education is available on the station through Columbia College, Columbia, Missouri, which offers associate and bachelor degrees in business administration and independent studies.

Personal services. Medical care is provided by a branch medical clinic. All eligible beneficiaries may be seen there and emergency care is available at the Bremerton Naval Hospital. The commissary at the station offers 13,500 square feet of sales space carrying over 7,000 grocery and 200 produce items. The Navy exchange operates a main store, a uniform shop, a laundry and dry cleaner, a country store, a package store, an auto service center, and a gasoline station. Officer and CPO/EM clubs are also available.

Recreation. Recreation facilities available on the station include an eight-lane bowling alley, a gym, a swimming pool, a theater, a marina (with seventeen slip rentals), and outdoor sports facilities including equipment rentals.

The Local Area. Built on seven hills between Puget Sound on the west and Lake Washington (freshwater) to the east, Seattle is a beautiful city with a population of approximately 500,000. Seattle's climate is mild and moist due to the prevailing westerly winds from the Pacific Ocean and the shielding effect of the Cascade Mountains. Extremes of either heat or cold are infrequent in this area and usually do not last very long. The average temperature during the summer is only 64°. During the winters the temperatures seldom drop below freezing. Annual rainfall averages about 36 inches.

For more information write to Family Services Center, Naval Station Puget Sound, Seattle, WA 98115-5001, or call (206) 526-3366.

WHIDBEY ISLAND NAVAL AIR STATION

Whidbey Island sits like a huge stopper in the mouth of Puget Sound, its north end jutting into the Strait of Juan de Fuca and its southern end pointing directly toward Seattle. At sixty-four miles long, Whidbey is the largest island in the continental United States, and Whidbey Naval Air Station is the largest Navy installation in the Northwest.

History. Commissioned in 1942, Whidbey Island NAS is home today for all Navy electronic warfare squadrons flying the EA-6B "Prowler" tactical jamming aircraft, as well as the West Coast training and operations center for the A-6E "Intruder" attack bomber squadrons and Navy and Marine Reserve activities. There are approximately 8,300 active-duty and 2,000 civilian personnel onboard the station today.

Whidbey Island NAS is actually composed of two bases five miles apart: the seaplane base and the naval air station (Ault Field). Located on the western shore of the island, the air station contains most of the military activities. The seaplane base is on the eastern shore, at the edge of the town of Oak Harbor: It houses the family services center, the commissary, the exchange, and some of the family housing units.

Housing and Schools. There are 1,444 sets of family quarters for personnel stationed at Whidbey, although there is no temporary lodging.

While there is no dependent schooling at Whidbey, day-care services are available. The Navy Campus offers college-level courses from Embry-Riddle Aeronautical University, Chapman College, and Skagit Valley College in programs leading to bachelor's and master's degrees.

Personal Services. The Navy exchange operates outlets and concessions at both the station and the seaplane base, while the commissary store provides approximately 12,000 line items for sale. A twenty-five-bed medical-surgical hospital, staffed by approximately 200 personnel, provides medical care for a population of approximately 38,000 eligible active-duty, retired, and dependent personnel.

Recreation. Extensive indoor and outdoor recreation facilities are available to Navy personnel at Whidbey, including two outdoor recreation areas on the base, a thirty-two-lane bowling alley, and an eighteen-hole golf course. Hunting, fishing, camping, hiking, and boating are all offered and avidly pursued by the residents of Washington. Just ten miles north of Oak Harbor is Deception Pass State Park, which is visited each year by more people than any other park in the state. The San Juan Islands, north of Whidbey Island and between the Straits of Georgia, is another very popular outdoor spot. For those who like the big city, Seattle, with a metropolitan population of 1.8 million, and nearby Tacoma are within easy commuting distance.

For more information write to: Public Affairs Office, Naval Air Station, Whidbey Island, Oak Harbor, WA 98278-5000, or call (206) 257-2286.

WISCONSIN

Army

FORT McCOY

The only active U.S. Army installation in the state of Wisconsin, Fort McCoy, named after Maj. Gen. Robert Bruce McCoy, a veteran of the Spanish-American War and World War I, is situated on 60,000 acres between the towns of Sparta and Tomah, 105 miles northwest of the city of Madison and 35 miles east of LaCrosse. The Army has used the area for training troops since 1909. Named in 1910 for General McCoy's father, Civil War veteran and local landowner Bruce E. McCoy, the post was redesignated in honor of the general in 1926.

Today Fort McCoy has a permanent active-duty population of 300 personnel and their 700 family members as well as a civilian workforce of about 1,900. It is a regional training center that annually supports year-round training for approximately 130,000 active-duty and reserve component personnel—143,000 during fiscal year 1992 alone. Among the post's many tenant activities is the Wisconsin State Patrol Academy, which trained over 1,200 personnel during 1993, and the 88th Ordnance Detachment (Explosive Ordnance Disposal), which assists civilian and federal authorities in a six-state, 298,000-square-mile response area.

Housing and Schools. Fort McCoy operates eighty sets of family quarters. For unaccompanied permanent-party personnel there are approximately eighty sets of quarters for officers and enlisted soldiers. Its cantonment areas can accommodate more than 40,000 troops at any time. Schooling for children is conducted by the public school systems in Tomah and Sparta. There is a day-care center at Fort McCoy that can accommodate fifty-eight children.

Personal Services. Medical and dental care are provided by the Fort McCoy Medical Department Activity, which served the needs of 2,800 personnel in 1993. Full commissary and post exchange services are available: The commissary store stocks 3,000 line items in its 9,000 square feet of sales space. A gas station and convenience store are also on post.

Recreation. The recreation scene at Fort McCoy is dominated by the Squaw Lake and Ski Hill recreation areas. Squaw Lake is a 200-acre park with 117 campsites with electric hook-ups, grills, comfort stations, and showers. A variety of outdoor activities are available there, including boating, fishing, swimming, miniature golf, picnicking, and hiking. There is also a snack bar. Ski Hill is open from December through March and serves as both a recreation and a training area. It has both downhill and cross-country courses as well as a tubing slope with rope tow and a chalet where food and beverages are sold. The recreational facilities at both sites are open to the public. The Rumpel Fitness Center on the main post has weight-training rooms, basketball and racquetball courts, saunas, and an indoor, Olympic-size swimming pool. A wide variety of equipment rental is also available just behind the fitness center in the post recreation equipment rental facility. A recreation center and community theater round out the picture.

The Local Area. Tomah and Sparta are thriving little communities, each of about 7,000 people. Tomah was named after a Menominee Indian chief, Thomas Carron ("Tomah" is the French pronunciation of Thomas), because he was so friendly to the early settlers; the citizens of the town named after him have continued that tradition. Sparta is far from Spartan: More than 60,000 people go there every year to use the Sparta State Bike Trail's thirty-two-mile course. The town is also proud of its eighteen-hole municipal golf course, one of the finest in the state.

For more information write to: Headquarters, Fort McCoy, Attention: Public Affairs Office, Sparta, WI 54656-5000, or call (608) 388-2407.

WYOMING

Air Force

F. E. WARREN AIR FORCE BASE

History. If the buildings and grounds at Warren Air Force Base could speak, they would tell a fascinating story, because they have seen everything from the Army's horse cavalry to the Peacekeeper ICBM. There has been some kind of military activity going on at the site of present-day Warren AFB since the winter of 1867–68, when troops of the U.S. Cavalry established Fort D. A. Russell on the site. Troops from the fort participated in the Sioux Campaign of 1876, the same campaign that saw Custer's 7th Cavalry Regiment decimated at the Little Big Horn.

In 1930 the name of the post was changed to Fort Francis E. Warren, in honor of the first governor of Wyoming, a Medal of Honor winner in the Civil War. Then in 1947 the post was ceded to the U.S. Air Force, becoming Francis E. Warren Air Force Base. Today it is home to the 3,500 military personnel and 650 civilians of the 90th Missile Wing. Warren is an Air Force base without a single fixed-wing aircraft and no runway. What it does have, however, are 150 Minuteman III and 50 Peacekeeper missiles.

Housing and Schools. There are 831 units of family housing at Warren, 156 of them brick two-story dwellings that were built between 1885 and 1930. Personnel often wait up to one year for quarters at Warren. Guest housing is available, but reservations may be made only by incoming or outgoing permanently assigned personnel.

There are plenty of educational opportunities at Warren. Courses are offered there by the University of Wyoming, the University of Northern Colorado,

Colorado State University, Chapman College, Southern Illinois University, Lesley College, and Laramie County Community College.

Personal Services. Personal services include a commissary, a base exchange, a service station, and the USAF hospital, a thirty-bed facility that provides for dental and medical care. Cases beyond the capability of the Warren hospital are transferred to Fitzsimons Army Hospital at Denver, Colorado.

Recreation. Recreational facilities at Warren are excellent. The base museum contains many artifacts and memorabilia of the Old West and the Old Army. Also available are a rod and gun club, a roller skating rink, auto and arts and crafts hobby shops, an eighteen-hole golf course, a twelve-lane bowling alley, stables, a gymnasium, a swimming pool, officers and NCO clubs, and a family camp featuring picnicking and camping spaces with hookups for twenty-four campers.

The base itself is a great attraction for most Air Force personnel because it offers a unique opportunity for them to live and work amid reminders of the daily life of a frontier Army garrison: The child-care center building went up in 1885 as an enlisted barracks; the education center was also built in 1885, as enlisted quarters; the indoor track and fitness facility was built as a cavalry drill hall in 1907. In 1975, the base was designated a national historic landmark.

The Local Area. Warren AFB is on the plains at an altitude of over 6,000 feet, which makes breathing difficult for newcomers. The weather changes rapidly there and may go from a minus 25° F. windchill factor to 40° F. very quickly. Winters are

Military history at F. E. Warren AFB extends from 1867, when it was the site of a U.S. Cavalry fort, to its current position as the base for the Minuteman III force. (USAF photo)

cold and the wind blows hard; summers are dry and mild, and it seldom gets hot enough to use air-conditioning.

Warren lies in the northwestern quadrant of the city of Cheyenne, a metropolis that, for its size, has perhaps the cleanest air in the United States. The city boasts four golf courses, three bowling centers, a symphony and choral society, and no traffic jams. To the west and north is Medicine Bow National Forest. Fort Collins, Colorado, is fifty miles south of Cheyenne, and Denver is one hundred miles south. Laramie is fifty miles west.

For more information write to: Public Affairs Division, 5305 Randall Ave., F. E. Warren AFB, WY 82001-2271, or call (307) 775-3381.

PART TWO

Overseas
Installations

AZORES

Air Force

LAJES FIELD

It is said that there are no horizontal spaces at Lajes Field, unless you find them in bed. The people who live in the Azores are as rugged as their country. In 1581 they repelled an invading Spanish army by unleashing a herd of cattle on it, and some believe the Azoreans may even have visited the New World before Columbus.

History. Lajes Field, or Portuguese Air Base No. 4, was activated in 1943 by the British, and the first U.S. military personnel arrived there the same year. In 1953 the 1605th Air Base Wing of the Military Airlift Command, now the 65th Support Wing (AMC), was established there. Today Lajes is home to about 3,000 Americans: military personnel, family members, and civilian employees.

Housing and Schools. There are 489 sets of government quarters at Lajes. One hundred twenty-nine cottages on or immediately adjacent to the base are available for purchase by married personnel under the base-supported leasehold housing program. These dwellings are prorated among eligible personnel with price and disposition strictly prescribed and controlled by base regulations. Prices range from as little as $500 to as much as $16,000, with the local credit union giving signature loans up to $2,500. These cottages are erected on Portuguese land and held on assignable land leases that give full reversionary rights to the landowner upon termination of the land lease. Furnishings are provided by base housing, and utilities are also furnished by the base at established monthly rates. Off-base housing is limited, and the types of units available are small by U.S. standards.

Schooling for dependent children from kindergarten through grade twelve is provided at Lajes Field. A child-development center offers a full range of services for the families stationed at Lajes Field for children from six months to ten years of age. College-level courses from the University of Maryland, Troy State University, and the City Colleges of Chicago are available for adults through the base education center.

Personal Services. Medical care at Lajes is provided by the seven-bed USAF hospital. Dental care is limited, however. Patients requiring special care beyond the local health-care professionals' capabilities are evacuated to Wiesbaden, Germany, or to the United States.

The commissary carries about 4,000 items, and the base exchange, besides operating a main retail store, offers a family shopping center, a toy store, an outdoor-living store, a cafeteria, a service station, and other concessions.

Recreation. One of the premier recreational attractions at Lajes is the eighteen-hole golf course located in a mountain valley approximately ten miles from the base. The course is playable most of the year. Other recreational facilities include ceramics, wood, and auto hobby shops; a skating rink with 4,600 square feet of skating space; a gymnasium; two tennis courts; two swimming pools; a sixteen-lane bowling alley; a base library; a recreation center; and a youth center. Officers and NCO clubs are also available.

The Local Area. The Azores Archipelago consists of nine inhabited islands in the North Atlantic, about 2,300 miles east of Washington, D.C., and 900 miles west of Lisbon, Portugal. They have a total land mass of 888 square miles, and about 250,000 people live on them. Lajes Field is located on the northeast tip of Terceira Island, which measures roughly 10 by 20 miles. The town of Angra do Heroismo, the central district's capital city, is approximately 13 miles from the base and has a population of 20,000. Praia da Vitoria is about 3 miles from the base and has about 7,000 inhabitants. Terceira is almost totally bordered by high cliffs, and many of its roads are narrow, winding, and made of dirt.

The Azores' climate is semitropical. There is little rain in the summer, but the temperatures are ideal, with a daily low of 65° F. and a high of about 75° F. In the winter season (October through May), it can be damp and chilly, and during this period there are frequent rains and high winds while the mountains are generally covered by clouds that often descend into the valleys as thick fog or mist.

Agriculture and fishing are the primary vocations in the Azores. Portuguese is the official language of the islands, although the dialect spoken there is different from that in Brazil or continental Portugal. The people are hardy, independent, and fun-loving.

For more information write to: Public Affairs, 65SW (AMC), APO AE 09720.

BELGIUM

SUPREME HEADQUARTERS ALLIED POWERS EUROPE (SHAPE)

SHAPE is the military headquarters of Allied Command Europe. The Supreme Allied Commander Europe (SACEUR) coordinates the defense of Europe throughout an area that stretches north to south from Norway to the Mediterranean, and west to east from the Atlantic Ocean to the Caucasus Mountains in Turkey—an area of two million square kilometers.

SHAPE is located near Mons, about thirty miles from Brussels, where it moved from Paris after France withdrew from NATO. SHAPE began operations at Mons on 31 March 1967.

The international SHAPE staff is composed of approximately 2,775 personnel: 864 officers, 1,500 enlisted personnel, and 407 civilians. With the addition of locally employed civilians and 7,700 dependents, the SHAPE community consists of over 15,000 personnel. The breakdown of the staff consists of 29 percent American, 20 percent from the United Kingdom, 17 percent German, 12 percent Belgian, 6 percent from the Netherlands, 5 percent Italian, and the remaining 11 percent from other nations.

Housing and Schools. The 498-acre SHAPE complex consists of 198 buildings and 600 apartments and duplexes, 264 for officers and 336 for enlisted personnel. The SHAPE International School provides international and national kindergartens and elementary schools, with an international and an American high school.

Personal Services. Medical and dental care are provided by the SHAPE Medical Center, a thirty-bed hospital with a polyclinic staffed by physicians from the various SHAPE nations.

Recreation. Among the numerous recreational facilities available are fields, pitches, and courts for virtually every type of sport including soccer, football, rugby, cricket, baseball, tennis (indoor and all-weather), squash, racquetball, and basketball. There is also an all-weather athletic track and an indoor swimming pool as well as Nautilus exercise equipment. The arts and crafts center provides woodworking, photography, ceramics, and other hobby facilities as well as a theater that presents six productions a year ranging from musicals to drama.

The Local Area. The city of Mons is over 1,000 years old and today is the capital of the province of Hainaut. It is situated on a ridge between the Trouille and Haine Rivers. Mons has witnessed many major events in European history. In the seventeenth and eighteenth centuries, Mons suffered a series of sieges conducted by French, Spanish, Dutch, and Austrian forces contending for control of the region. On 23 August 1914 it was the site of the Battle of Mons, the first engagement of British and German troops in World War I. This was once the vast coal-mining region. The Borinage coal fields just to the west of Mons were part of an industry that stretched from northern France to the Ruhr in Germany.

For more information write to: Public Information Office B: 7010 SHAPE Belgium, CMR 450, Box 7500, APO AE 09705.

BERMUDA

Navy

BERMUDA NAVAL AIR STATION

Over 1,200 U.S. military personnel and their dependents live on the island of Bermuda. Tenant commands that are supported by Bermuda NAS include branch medical and dental clinics out of Norfolk, Virginia; the Naval Oceanography Command Facility; the Personnel Support Activity Detachment; Navy Resale Activity; Fleet Imaging Facility Atlantic; Defense Reutilization and Marketing Office; Department of Defense Dependents Schools; a Navy Broadcasting Service Detachment; and a Naval Mobile Construction Battalion detachment.

Housing and Schools. There are a limited number of family quarters at the Bermuda Naval Air Station, so some families are required to live on the local economy, at least while awaiting quarters on the station. There is adequate berthing for unaccompanied permanent duty personnel.

Dependent entry approval will not be granted until either a lease has been approved for off-station housing or the sponsor is within two months of obtaining on-station housing. Due to the high cost of living on the local economy, rent plus is available for qualified active-duty personnel.

The Department of Defense operates an elementary school and a high school on the station. Child-care facilities are also provided, and adult education is available through the education center. Courses are offered from City Colleges of Chicago, the University of Maryland, and Webster College.

Personal Services. The station is equipped with a full range of facilities, including a Navy exchange and a commissary. A newly renovated theater, two club facilities, a bowling alley, a gym, racquetball courts, tennis courts, and softball fields are available. The Bermuda NAS Branch Medical Clinic provides primary health-care services, but there is no inpatient capability at NAS Bermuda. People requiring hospitalization or specialized outpatient treatment are referred to Bermuda's King Edward VII Memorial Hospital or evacuated to hospitals in the United States. The station has a dental clinic where routine care is available for family members.

The Local Area. No four-wheel-drive vehicles or vehicles over six months old or more than 64 inches wide or 164 inches long are allowed to be shipped to Bermuda. Written and road tests are required for Bermuda vehicle and moped licenses. A U.S. driver's license is not valid in Bermuda.

Civilian clothing is permitted for wear during liberty hours, but most of the local hotels and restaurants require men to wear coats and ties in the evening. Casual clothing is worn for everyday wear by both men and women. No extremely heavy clothing is required in Bermuda, but sweaters and jackets might come in handy during the winter months. Raincoats are required year-round.

For more information write to: Public Affairs Office, U.S. Navy Air Station, Bermuda, FPO AE 09727, or call (809) 293-5515.

CUBA

Navy

GUANTANAMO BAY NAVAL BASE

Guantanamo Bay Naval Base is the only U.S. military installation located in a Communist country. Situated in the southeast corner of the Republic of Cuba, Guantanamo is the oldest U.S. overseas base, originally leased from the Republic of Cuba in 1903 as a coaling station for Navy ships. In 1934 the original lease agreement was formalized by a treaty signed as part of President Franklin Roosevelt's Good Neighbor policy. Approximately 7,000 military personnel, their dependents, Cuban exiles, and foreign nationals now live on the base.

Housing and Schools. The base has 1,253 housing units. Average wait for housing is four months for officers and five months for enlisted personnel. There are an elementary school and a high school at Guantanamo, along with adult-education programs that offer courses from City Colleges of Chicago and Troy State University.

Personal Services. The base has a Navy commissary/exchange mall, which opened in July 1989. Included in the mall are a laundry, a tailor shop, a bakery, and a Baskin Robbins ice cream parlor. Other facilities include a Marine Corps Exchange, officers and enlisted clubs, and a 100-bed hospital. Recreation facilities include a new gym with modern weight-lifting equipment and boat, bike, and golf and fishing equipment rentals.

The Local Area. Located approximately 525 air miles from Miami, Guantanamo is a closed base with access by air only. Access is strictly controlled, and only official travelers and relatives of naval base personnel are permitted entry, with the approval of the base commander. A ferry crosses the bay to the naval air station located on the leeward, or western, side of the bay. On an average day the ferry transports more than 700 people and 300 vehicles. There is no entry into Communist Cuba from the base except for a small group of Cuban nationals still employed by the U.S. government.

With its tropical climate, outdoor recreation is possible year-round.

For more information write to: Public Affairs Officer, U.S. Naval Station, Box 25, FPO AE 09593-1000.

DIEGO GARCIA

Navy

DIEGO GARCIA U.S. NAVY SUPPORT FACILITY

When they start calling the Navy exchange the "ship's store," you're either far, far from land or you're on land that's far, far from land. Even in the geography of the Indian Ocean, noted for its remote islands, Diego Garcia is far from civilization. The nearest port is Colombo, Sri Lanka, 960 nautical miles (a nautical mile is 1,852 meters) to the north-northeast. Duty on Diego Garcia does not entitle sailors to double sea-duty credit, but the weather there is beautiful.

History. The station was commissioned on 20 March 1973, and following the crises in Yemen in 1979 and Iran-Afghanistan the following year, the strategic importance of the island became apparent, and much money has since been spent there to expand its facilities to meet future operational needs in the Indian Ocean and Middle East.

About 3,500 U.S. personnel live on Diego Garcia, and most of them stand watch on a rotating schedule—six eight-hour watches with thirty-two hours off between—which leaves time for enjoying the sights. Because Diego Garcia is a remote site, two periods of leave, not to exceed thirty days total, are authorized to service personnel during an island tour. Eligibility begins after spending three months on the island. Authorized environmental and morale leave destinations are the United States, the Philippines, Singapore, Japan, Hawaii, Spain, and Italy.

Housing and Schools. Dependents are not authorized on Diego Garcia. Bachelor living facilities are spacious. There are eighteen permanent living facilities available to enlisted personnel on the Indian Ocean side of the island. Officers are accommodated in nine units on the lagoon side of the island just behind the snorkeling reef. Officers and chief petty officers are berthed one to a room; first- and second-class petty officers, two to a room; and all other ranks, three to a room. All quarters are centrally air-conditioned; officer quarters have a small kitchen.

With no social distractions on the island to occupy off-duty hours, education is "in" at Diego Garcia, and the Navy offers everyone plenty of opportunity to pursue educational goals while on duty there. Correspondence courses are available from a variety of colleges and universities, and the University of Maryland and Central Texas College offer courses.

Personal Services. The island dispensary is designed to meet the needs of fleet and island personnel and includes the equipment necessary to respond to most emergencies. The facility includes an operating room, ward space to accommodate eight holding beds, and two treatment areas for sick call. A dental lab, an operatory, and a hygiene room are also located in the dispensary.

The ship's store, the "Island Trading Post," is authorized a two-million-dollar inventory. Health and comfort items plus a limited amount of luxury items such as TV sets, stereo components, and cameras are available. The Army and Air Force Exchange Service Catalog is available to place individual orders for items not carried in the ship's store. The island also has an American Express banking facility and a branch of the Navy Federal Credit Union.

Recreation. One thing Diego Garcia has is places to eat. Besides an officers club that offers a spectacular view of the Indian Ocean and a CPO club that overlooks the island's lagoon, there are the Tiki Lounge and the 61 Club, which cater to the lower enlisted ranks. The Peacekeeper Inn is an all-hands restaurant with an à la carte menu and an order service. Then there are the Diego Burger fast food restaurant; the passenger terminal snack bar; and the Tropical Delight, an ice cream parlor offering hot dogs and assorted bakery products. And to top it all off, there's the new five-million-dollar Galley, with a menu loaded with all sorts of dishes prepared by contract civilians.

In the realm of recreation, Diego Garcia is not to be outdone. There is an Olympic-size swimming pool, a gymnasium, a four-lane bowling alley, a marina with small motorboats, a putt-putt golf course, eight outdoor tennis courts, two outdoor racquetball courts, and lots of swimming and fishing areas. (Watch out for sharks, sea snakes, the sea-wasp jellyfish, and the poisonous stonefish.) Movies are shown nightly (sometimes double features) at the main outdoor theater, the CPO mess, the Tiki Lounge, and the officers club extension. The island also offers a 5,000-volume library.

The Local Area. Diego Garcia is a British territory that was formed in 1965 from territory formerly belonging to Mauritius and the Seychelles. The island is only one of fifty-two in the Chagos Archipelago, which extends over 10,000 square miles of ocean. The island is shaped like a V and consists of a narrow coral atoll with a land area of about 11 square miles nearly enclosing a lagoon. Diego Garcia stretches 37 miles from tip to tip. Shallow reefs surround it on the ocean side as well as within the lagoon. Most of the landfill used in construction there is blasted from the outer reefs and then crushed to the required size. Diego Garcia poses no threat to anyone suffering from acrophobia: It's only four feet above sea level.

The climate on Diego Garcia is tropical, and island plant life is lush. No dangerous wildlife exists there, but there are a few wild horses and some donkeys whose ancestors worked the plantation that once flourished there.

Diego Garcia is on year-round daylight savings time, so from October through April, when it is 6 P.M. there, it's 7 A.M. in Washington, D.C.; 6 A.M. in Gulfport, Mississippi; 5 A.M.. in Denver; and 4 A.M. in San Francisco. From April through October, advance the stateside times one hour.

For more information write to: Commanding Officer, U.S. Navy Support Facility, Diego Garcia, PSC 466, Box 2, FPO AP 96464-0002.

ENGLAND

Air Force

RAF ALCONBURY

Although RAF Alconbury is administered by the U.S. Air Force, it is a Royal Air Force installation—an RAF station commander assigned to Alconbury acts as an advisor to the USAF commander. The U.S. military units operate out of Alconbury and its satellite bases of RAF Upwood and RAF Molesworth. The three bases have a combined military population of about 3,000 personnel.

History. The RAF came to Alconbury village in Cambridgeshire in 1938, followed by thirty-four USAF B-24 Liberators of the 93rd Bombardment Group in September 1942. Today RAF Alconbury is home for the 10th Tactical Fighter Wing, which became a support organization with the departure of its A-10 Thunderbolt IIs in the spring of 1992. The primary mission of the units at Alconbury and its satellite installations is special operations and reconnaissance. Major tenant units include the 352nd Special Operations Group and the 95th Reconnaissance Squadron. RAF Molesworth hosts the Joint Analysis Center, activated in 1992.

The 95th Reconnaissance Squadron flies the U-2 "Dragon Lady," a single-engine, high-altitude surveillance/reconnaissance aircraft, while the 352nd uses the MC-130E Combat Talon, HC-130 Hercules, and MH-53J Pave Low helicopter to execute special operations and combat rescue missions in Europe, Africa, and the Middle East.

Housing and Schools. There are 1,085 family housing units administered by Alconbury, with 211 at Alconbury itself and units in the nearby areas of Upwood,

Molesworth, Chelveston, Wittering, and Wyton. The base also leases 250 units in Huntingdon, Saint Ives, and Yaxley.

Alconbury has an elementary and a high school, Upwood has an elementary school, and some family members attend off-base schools in the British community. A child-development center operates on base. Adult education is conducted on base through the University of Maryland, Embry-Riddle Aeronautical University, Troy State University, and City Colleges of Chicago.

Personal Services and Recreation. Alconbury offers a complete array of service and morale support facilities, including a base exchange, a new (1992) commissary, a base theater, specialty shops, officers and NCO clubs, and exchange-operated dining facilities. RAF Alconbury offers a sixteen-lane bowling center, a fitness center, auto and craft hobby shops, a rod and gun club, a sports bar, and a library.

The Local Area. RAF Alconbury is in Britain's East Anglia region, about sixty miles north of London. Nearby communities include Cambridge (population 104,000), about thirteen miles southeast, home of Cambridge University, founded in 1130; and Peterborough (population 155,000), about twenty miles north. RAF Alconbury is in an ideal location from which to enjoy all of the United Kingdom. The base borders two major motorways, and British rail and coach serve the local town of Huntingdon.

For more information write to: Public Affairs Office, 10th Tactical Fighter Wing, Unit Box 215, APO AE 09470.

An MC-130H Combat Talon II from the 352nd Special Operations Group lifts off at RAF Alconbury. (USAF photo)

RAF BENTWATERS-WOODBRIDGE

RAF Bentwaters-Woodbridge closed in September 1993.

RAF CHICKSANDS

History. RAF Chicksands derives its rather interesting name from an estate that was situated in the area in the year 1086, when the Domesday Survey was conducted. The Royal Air Force came there in 1936, and during World War II the base served as a listening post, intercepting Axis radio traffic. The contingent at Chicksands played an important role in breaking German codes. Today the base is home to the U.S. Air Force's 7274th Air Base Group, with approximately 1,300 military personnel and 150 civilian employees.

Housing and Schools. RAF Chicksands has 413 family housing units on base. Forty of them are four-bedroom units, 245 are three-bedroom units, and 128 are two-bedroom units. Waiting periods vary, depending on the rank of the applicant and the size of the quarters needed. Officers wait from six to eight months; enlisted personnel must wait an average of six months for three-bedroom units to eighteen months for four-bedroom quarters. Housing is available off base. The average rent is $300 a month for two-bedroom homes up to $745 a month for four-bedroom homes. These prices do not include utilities. Temporary accommodations are provided by the Chicksands Inn. Quarters for single enlisted personnel consist of four dormitories.

Dependent children at Chicksands attend an on-base school, kindergarten through junior high. High school students are bused to RAF Alconbury, about thirty-five miles north of Chicksands. Off-duty education is provided through the University of Maryland, Troy State University, City Colleges of Chicago, and Southern Illinois University.

Personal Services and Recreation. The base facilities include a twelve-lane bowling center and a newly renovated gymnasium that has a weight room, a full racquetball court, and saunas. A medium-size exchange and commissary with a beverage store, a dry cleaner, a beauty shop, and banking facilities are conveniently located within the community center complex. The base also has a craft and hobby center, an automotive hobby shop, a recreation center, an open mess, a library, a youth center, and a modern child-care center.

The Local Area. Chicksands occupies about 400 acres of land in Bedfordshire, about forty-five miles north of London, situated between the cities of Bedford (nine miles to the north) and Luton (eleven miles to the south). The weather in the Chicksands area is changeable, cool, and damp with occasional sunny periods. Several small villages and towns surround the base. Hitchin, about eight miles south, is an old market town, and Bedford, the seat of Bedfordshire, offers shopping and entertainment. Each town has a direct railroad service to London.

For more information write to: Public Affairs Office, 7274th Air Base Group (USAFE), APO NY 09193-5000.

RAF FAIRFORD

RAF Fairford closed in December 1990.

RAF GREENHAM COMMON

RAF Greenham Common closed in June 1991.

RAF LAKENHEATH

One of the first things you see upon arriving at Lakenheath is the Statue of Liberty. This is a bronze replica of the famous statue, dedicated 25 November 1981, to commemorate the fortieth anniversary of RAF Lakenheath and the 48th Fighter Wing, "The Statue of Liberty Wing" (after its insignia). With the cooperation of the Bartholdi Museum in Colmar, France, the Lakenheath statue was cast from an original first-step model of the famous Statue of Liberty that French sculptor F. A. Bartholdi created for the American people in 1884.

History. Lakenheath was established in 1940 as a Royal Air Force Base. British fliers conducted nearly 2,250 wartime sorties from the base against targets in Europe. The U.S. Air Force began regular basing of its aircraft there in 1949, and the British government turned over operational control of the base to the USAF in 1951. Today Lakenheath's 1,800-acre expanse is home to two squadrons of F-15E "Strike Eagle" all-weather fighters of the 48th Fighter Wing, a six-time winner of the Air Force Outstanding Unit Award. In 1974 the RAF field at Feltwell came under Lakenheath's control, and today more than 6,000 military and civilian personnel work there, accomplishing the wing's mission as part of the U.S. Air Forces, Europe.

Housing and Schools. Lakenheath controls over 2,000 units of family housing, which it shares with RAF Mildenhall. This includes about 425 leased units. Temporary lodging is available for families in the base visiting officers and visiting airmen's quarters, with up to a sixty-day reservation.

Dependent schools on base include kindergarten through twelfth grade with a middle school at Feltwell. Free transportation is provided for students living within a twenty-five mile radius of the base. A child-care facility is also available. Off-duty adult educational opportunities are plentiful. The base education center offers courses at Lakenheath and Mildenhall from Embry-Riddle Aeronautical University, the University of Maryland, Troy State University, Boston University, and the University of Southern California.

Personal Services. Lakenheath has the largest medical facility in the U.S. Air Force, Europe. While the medical care at Lakenheath is complete, dental care for family members is limited and depends on whether time and space are available. In the fall of 1993, the hospital was undergoing a thirty-five-million-dollar renovation project.

The Lakenheath commissary, which opened in 1986, serves more than 20,000 customers, including personnel from nearby RAF Mildenhall. It carries more than 7,000 line items. The main exchange at Lakenheath carries a full range of department-store items as well as a four-seasons store at RAF Mildenhall, a furniture store at RAF Feltwell, and a service station.

Recreation. Recreational facilities include a gymnasium, a 20,000-volume library, a recreation center, and officers and enlisted clubs. The Lakenheath-Mildenhall Rod and Gun Club offers four skeet ranges and a trap range, and leases a 4,500-acre hunting preserve for the exclusive use of its membership. An Olympic-size, indoor, heated swimming pool, the only indoor pool in USAFE, is open January through November. Lakenheath also has the only USAF golf course in the United Kingdom, a nine-hole course that also has a pro shop and a snack bar. A twenty-four-lane bowling center and hobby shops are also available at the base.

The Local Area. RAF Lakenheath is located in East Anglia, West Suffolk County. East Anglia sticks out into the North Sea and is composed of small market and farming villages. Lakenheath itself is situated in farming and cattle-raising country and boasts a population of around 4,300. The town lies just over the western boundary of the base and consists of only a few shops, a couple of pubs and gasoline stations, and a magnificent old church. The nearest train stop is Lakenheath Halt, five miles to the north. Thetford, about twelve miles northeast of the base, is a thriving metropolis of 15,700 people. It is chiefly notable as the birthplace of Thomas Paine. The town of Bury Saint Edmunds (population 28,000) lies about sixteen miles southeast of the base and is noted for the ancient ruins of the abbey built there to honor the martyred King of the East Angles, Edmund, who was beheaded by the Danes about a thousand years ago.

Newmarket, fifteen miles south of the base, has about 14,500 residents, and the beautiful city of Ely is to the west, in the counties of Cambridgeshire and Ely. Ely was a religious center, founded by Saint Etheldreda in 673 A.D., and in 1973 the town celebrated the thirteen hundredth anniversary of its beautiful cathedral.

For more information write to: 48th FW Public Affairs Office, APO AE 09464-5000.

RAF MILDENHALL

RAF Mildenhall, "Gateway to the United Kingdom," is the aerial port of entry for the majority of U.S. military personnel and their families assigned to the United Kingdom. Each month it processes 8,000 passengers and 2,000 tons of cargo, on the average. RAF Mildenhall is also home to the 100th Air Refueling Wing (USAFE). Flying KC-135 Stratotankers, the 100th provides the aircraft and communications technicians for the Silk Purse Control Group as it supports the U.S. European Commander's airborne command-and-control mission.

History. RAF Mildenhall was established in 1934. Within six hours of the time England declared war on Germany on 3 September 1939, three Wellington bombers left the field to bomb German battleships. Americans first came to the base in July

1950. Today it is home for five major Air Force commands and a U.S. naval flight facility. The base covers about 1,200 acres and has a permanent U.S. military population of about 2,800 personnel. Added to that are 3,500 military dependents, 100 U.S. government employees, and 350 British employees. And at any time there may be as many as 500 military personnel passing through the base on temporary duty.

Housing and Schools. RAF Mildenhall has only 79 family housing units for enlisted members and 40 for officers, but there are an additional 1,828 enlisted and 312 officer family housing units in the local area serving both RAF Mildenhall and RAF Lakenheath. Single enlisted airmen live in the 1,082 on-base dormitory spaces. There are also 40 temporary-lodging facilities for families.

There are no dependents schools at Mildenhall. Dependents schooling is offered at RAF Lakenheath for children in kindergarten through fifth grade and high school, and at RAF Feltwell for grades six through eight. Government transportation is provided for families living within twenty-five miles of the base. The Lakenheath-Mildenhall education center offers a wide selection of courses for adults, from high school completion to postgraduate degrees. Courses are offered from Boston University, City Colleges of Chicago, Embry-Riddle Aeronautical University, the University of Maryland, and Troy State University.

Personal Services. Only active-duty personnel may be treated for routine medical problems at the RAF Mildenhall Medical Clinic. Dependent medical care and specialized medical care for active-duty personnel are available at the RAF Lakenheath hospital, a 105-bed facility, the second largest of its kind in Europe.

Personnel stationed at Mildenhall use the Lakenheath commissary store, which serves a total of 20,000 people in the area. There are a mini commissary and a convenience store at Mildenhall, as well as a package liquor store, a doughnut shop, a four-seasons store, a Stars and Stripes bookstore, and some AAFES concessions such as a service station, a barber and beauty shop, and a laundromat and dry cleaner.

Recreation. Recreation facilities at Mildenhall include officers and NCO clubs, a twelve-lane bowling alley, a base theater, youth and recreation centers, a physical fitness center, a hobby shop complex, and a three-quarter-mile jogging track/par course. At Lakenheath is a nine-hole golf course and a rod and gun club with a 4,500-acre leased preserve for hunting pheasant, partridge, and deer. Lakenheath also offers an Olympic-size indoor swimming pool.

The Local Area. Mildenhall is located in the western part of Suffolk County, which is in the eastern part of England. The town of Mildenhall lies just beyond the southeast corner of the airfield and boasts a population of 8,500. (It's the biggest town within fifteen miles of the base.) Adjacent to the north side of the base is Beck Row, a small village with about 3,000 inhabitants. West Row stretches for about a mile along a winding road southwest of the airfield. Mildenhall is close enough to London for those who want big-city life, but it's far enough out in the country to satisfy the person who wants to get away from the urban sprawl. To the south and east of the base are low, rolling hills with farms growing barley, sugar beets, wheat, and cattle. Across these hills, some forty miles away, is the North Sea.

For more information write to: Public Affairs Office, 100th Air Refueling Wing (USAFE), APO AE 09459-5000.

RAF UPPER HEYFORD

RAF Upper Heyford is now in an inactive status.

Navy

BRAWDY U.S. NAVAL FACILITY, WALES

The Brawdy U.S. Naval Facility is located near Haverfordwest, by the Saint Bride's Bay, in southwest Wales, 265 miles west of London. The command consists of 23 officers and 320 enlisted personnel.

Housing and Schools. Brawdy Naval Facility is adjacent to the Brawdy Royal Air Force Base, which provides support for U.S. personnel, including messing, berthing, and other services. Eighty-five percent of all married personnel occupy RAF married quarters in Haverfordwest, approximately ten miles from the base. As of September 1993 a relocation program was putting the waiting list at four months for enlisted personnel and one month for officers. Servicemembers living on the economy are entitled to all allowances. Rooms for single personnel consist of bachelor enlisted quarters for those in grades E-1 through E-4, and the RAF sergeants mess for all other grades; officers have bachelor officers quarters facilities.

Children attend local Welsh schools. These schools require children aged eleven and up to wear specified uniforms, the cost of which is borne by the parents. Children of high school age attend either the London Central High School (a DoD boarding school in RAF Wycombe) or local schools. School is grouped by term with a two-week break between each term (every six weeks). The longest break begins around 19 July and ends the first week of September. Little or no homework is required.

Personal Services. For active-duty personnel, a medical and dental facility is available on the RAF base. Medical care is provided by a Navy doctor and three corpsmen. Dependent medical care is available through the National Health Service physicians free of charge. There is a community health nurse at Brawdy, who acts as liaison between Navy members and their dependents requiring care from the National Health Service. For specialist services, U.S. personnel are referred to the USAF hospital at Upper Heyford, approximately 200 miles away. Routine dental care for military personnel is provided by a Navy dental officer and two technicians at Brawdy; dependents see local dentists. A local civilian hospital is available for dependents, with full medical care.

A small Navy exchange and commissary store is available at Brawdy six days a week. The commissary has frozen meats, fresh vegetables, and canned foods. All tobacco products and alcoholic beverages are rationed and may be used only by U.S. personnel and their dependents. There are larger USAF commissaries and exchanges at Lakenheath (approximately 400 miles away). The Dragon Stop minimart is located in RAF housing and is open seven days a week from 2:00 to 10:00 P.M.

Recreation. Brawdy has tennis courts, a six-lane bowling center, two squash courts, a softball field, a full gym, and lockers available with camping gear, bikes, golf equipment, and sporting gear. There is also an indoor sports facility that offers racquetball, soccer, a sauna, and Nautilus equipment. An indoor swimming pool is located in Haverfordwest. There are several excellent golf courses in the area, and wind surfing is a popular sport in the summer. Deep sea fishing charters are also available.

The Local Area. The climate in the Brawdy area varies little from season to season. Winters see occasional freezing temperatures, with the norm being daily rain, cold dampness, and strong, frequent winds. Summers are occasionally sunny and pleasant, but remain damp and windy with temperatures only in the sixties and seventies.

As of September 1993, one British pound was equal to $1.55 in U.S. currency. Local gasoline prices average $3.50 per U.S. gallon, and ration coupons are available for travel to and from work at only thirty-five cents per liter.

Interestingly, half the personnel assigned to Brawdy request extensions of their tours.

For more information write to: Commander, U.S. Naval Facility, PSC 808, FPO AE 09420.

GERMANY

Air Force

BITBURG AIR BASE

When "alerts" are called at Bitburg these days, they are announced in advance but last two or three days at a time. Although the airmen on base are only practicing, the citizens of Bitburg know what real air raids are like: By December 1944, 85 percent of the city had been destroyed by Allied bombers in World War II.

History. In 1952 the 36th Tactical Fighter Wing came to Bitburg to start building the base on what had once been farmland. During World War II it was used as a tank staging and supply area by the German Army, in preparation for the Battle of the Bulge. Today it is home to the 36th Fighter Wing and its F-15 Eagles, which stand ready, twenty-four hours a day, to provide air superiority whenever and wherever it is needed. During Operation Desert Storm, the 36th flew nearly 3,000 combat missions, and its pilots shot down seventeen enemy aircraft.

Housing and Schools. On-base housing consists of 50 four-story buildings of 24 apartments each for a total of 600 two-bedroom, 400 three-bedroom, and 184 four-bedroom units. Temporary quarters are limited at Bitburg and consist of two beds per room with a semiprivate bath and some cooking facilities. They are available for a maximum stay of thirty days.

Dependents schooling on base is provided by elementary, middle, and high schools. The base education center also provides a full range of counseling and testing services and access to college courses offered by a number of American universities through their overseas extension programs. There is also a child-development center on the base.

Personal Services. Medical care is provided by the 36th FW Hospital, a thirty-five bed facility located near base housing. Dental services, when available, are scheduled when time and space permit for all family members who require treatment.

The base commissary stocks more than 5,000 line items, including fresh beef from England, Ireland, and Germany as well as fresh dairy products from Holland, Denmark, Germany, and Luxembourg. The exchange, located in the housing area, offers a complete range of merchandise as well as a 1,300-item catalog. The exchange also offers concessions such as two burger bars, a Baskin Robbins ice cream parlor, a snack bar, and a hot dog house. The base filling station offers both leaded and unleaded gasoline.

Recreation. Recreational activities are available in the form of a bowling alley, a field house, a recreation center, and a rod and gun club, which offers its members hunting, fishing, camping, and backpacking equipment and a skeet range for shotgunners. Auto and wood craft shops as well as an audio-photo club are also available.

The Local Area. Bitburg is a fairly young city, a mere 1,500 years of age. It was first mentioned in a document dated 414 A.D. as a fortified city by the name of Bedense. In 1239 Luxembourg acquired Bitburg and kept it for the next 500 years. Bitburg began as a stopover place for Roman legionnaires 2,000 years ago. At Fliessen, only three miles from the base, a partly restored Roman villa with well-preserved mosaics is worth seeing.

Bitburg is only about an hour's drive from Luxembourg City, an international banking center that is also a city of old, narrow streets that run into picturesque old market squares. Gen. George Patton and the soldiers of the 3rd Army are buried in Hamm American Military Cemetery, about three miles outside Luxembourg City.

Many quaint and interesting places are within easy reach of Bitburg, including Echternach, a Benedictine abbey founded in the seventh century, and Liberius Kapelle, a small chapel in the woods overlooking Echternach where you can have a nice picnic with a beautiful view. And about forty-five minutes' drive from Bitburg is Mullerthal, a Switzerland-like place along the River Ernz Moire where you may climb over the interesting limestone formations and have a picnic.

For more information write to: Public Affairs Office, 36th FW, APO AE 09132.

HAHN AIR BASE

Hahn Air Base was closed in September 1993.

HESSISCH OLDENDORF AIR STATION

Hessisch Oldendorf was closed in September 1991.

RHEIN-MAIN AIR BASE

Rhein-Main Air Base is rightfully called the "Gateway to Europe." The base averages 60,000 passengers and moves 10,000 tons of cargo every thirty days. Combining cargo and passenger operations, Rhein-Main runs the largest aerial port in Europe.

History. Named after the Rhein and Main Rivers, which meet just to the west of the city of Frankfurt, the air base is located at Frankfurt International Airport, Germany's busiest passenger airport and the largest cargo port outside the United States. It was the home of the zeppelin airships in the 1930s and the focal point of the Berlin Airlift in 1948–49. American forces came to Rhein-Main in March 1945 when troops of the 10th Infantry Regiment, 5th Division, captured the installation. Today the host organization at Rhein-Main is the 435th Airlift Wing (USAFE), which maintains the 37th Airlift Squadron. The 435th's mission is to provide tactical airlift throughout Europe, Africa, and the Middle East with assigned C-130E aircraft. Fifty-one tenant units from several commands call Rhein-Main home. More than 10,000 people live and work at Rhein-Main.

Housing and Schools. There are a total of 1,106 government-owned or leased family housing units at Rhein-Main, most of them situated in either the Gateway Gardens housing area or the Langen Terrace complex, located two and seven miles respectively from the base. Accommodations are available on the German economy. As of November 1992, apartments were renting from about $900 for one-bedroom units to $1,100 for three bedrooms. These figures do not include utilities.

The Aerial Port Hotel at the base has 275 guest rooms for duty passengers arriving and departing the port. This is the sole temporary facility for families, but it also accommodates other transient personnel. There are 174 guest rooms at the visiting airmen's quarters.

This memorial at Rhein-Main Air Base commemorates the Berlin Airlift. (USAF photo)

Dependent children at Rhein-Main attend school in kindergarten through grade eight at the Gateway Gardens Housing Area, and students in grades nine through twelve go to the Frankfurt American High School. A child-development center is also operated at Rhein-Main. The base education center offers courses from such institutions as Boston University; City Colleges of Chicago; Embry-Riddle Aeronautical, Southern Illinois, and Troy State Universities; the University of Maryland; and the Community College of the Air Force.

Personal Services. Medical services at the base are provided by the Rhein-Main clinic, and specialty clinics and hospitalization are available at the 97th General Hospital in Frankfurt. Dental care for dependents is limited at Rhein-Main.

Exchange services at the base include cafeterias and snack bars, a four-seasons shop, a garage, a parts store, a filling station, and a retail shopping outlet. The commissary opened in 1986. Rhein-Main also has officers and NCO clubs.

Recreation. Recreational facilities include an eighteen-lane bowling center, a gymnasium, hobby shops, a sports center (consisting of a rod and gun club, a pro shop, and a camping shop), two large movie theaters, and picnic areas at four separate locations around the base.

For more information write to: Public Affairs Office, 435th AW (USAFE), Unit 7420, Box 140, APO AE 09057.

SPANGDAHLEM AIR BASE

History. Spangdahlem Air Base is located in the famous Eifel Region of west-central Germany, an area that has seen war since the days of Attila the Hun. The most recent warrior to visit there was none other than Gen. George S. Patton, "Old Blood and Guts" himself. The Germans staged their Battle of the Bulge offensive from there; the region is also famous because it is the birthplace of Karl Marx.

Spangdahlem is home to the 52nd Fighter Wing, USAFE's largest fighter operation, which has the mission of providing fighter support to NATO and U.S. forces. The 23rd, 81st, and 480th Fighter Squadrons fly the F-16 Fighting Falcon, while the 510th Fighter Squadron flies the A-10 Thunderbolt II.

Housing and Schools. There are 964 family quarters at Spangdahlem, including 573 units on the base, 91 in nearby Trier, and 300 units of leased housing. Approximate waiting time for these quarters is from three to thirteen months, depending on the size quarters needed. Transient accommodations for families are available at the temporary-lodging facility in nearby Speicher. Local rents vary from $300 a month for one-bedroom apartments to as much as $700 a month for larger accommodations.

Elementary and middle schools are located on the base, while junior high and high school classes are held at Bitburg, about nine miles away. Government transportation is provided. Two child-care centers are also available. The base education center offers a number of college-level courses for adults under the auspices of the University of Maryland, City Colleges of Chicago, Boston University, Embry-Riddle Aeronautical University, and the Community College of the Air Force.

Personal Services. The base exchange operates a retail store and a number of concessions, including a Burger King. The base commissary, which opened in 1986, carries 5,000 line items. NCO and officers clubs are available.

Recreation. Recreation facilities include a nine-hole golf course, an eighteen-lane bowling center, hobby and craft shops, a recreation center, and several athletic facilities, including a gym. There is also an outdoor recreation facility with a winter ski club.

The Local Area. Spangdahlem is only a thirty-minute drive from Luxembourg, forty-five minutes from Belgium, an hour's drive from the French border, and an hour and a half from Holland. This is the most centrally located of all U.S. bases in Europe.

For more information write to: Public Affairs Office, 52nd Fighter Wing, APO AE 09126-5000.

TEMPELHOF CENTRAL AIRPORT

Tempelhof Central Airport was closed in June 1993.

Army

ARMED FORCES RECREATION CENTERS

Two Armed Forces Recreation Centers (AFRC-E) are located in Germany, Chiemsee and Garmisch, both situated to the south of Munich, in the foothills of the Alps. These are unique, wonderful, and exciting places where military personnel, Department of Defense civilian employees, and their families can enjoy one of the most prized outdoor recreation areas in the world. The Berchtesgaden facility has been closed.

Chiemsee

Chiemsee is the only self-contained AFRC-Europe resort and is located about fifty-six miles southeast of Munich, directly alongside the Munich-Salzburg autobahn and the shores of Germany's largest inland lake. Although Chiemsee is a popular summer destination, the nearby Chiemgauer Alps offer some of the best snow conditions in Germany for downhill and cross-country skiing.

Accommodations include the newly renovated Chiemsee Lake Hotel and the Chiemsee Park Hotel. A year-round AFRC Travel Camp is also located adjacent to the Park Hotel with 100 sites, many equipped with electric hookups, a few hard-side trailers, modern shower facilities, a laundromat, a camp store, a snack-o-mat, and a picnic area. There is also a camp store that is open during the summer months. Authorized campers are allowed access to all other AFRC facilities and recreational programs.

Sports Weeks here include skiing instruction. These are five-day periods of instruction that include theory, training, lift tickets, use of equipment, and transportation. You can also go skiing in nearby Austria. Daily and weekend activities, as well as youth programs and child-care facilities, are also available.

Summer activities include hang gliding, paragliding, scuba diving, sailing, windsurfing, catamaran sailing, canoeing, miniature golf, tennis, swimming, and hiking. Boat rentals are available for paddleboats, rowboats, and a variety of sailing vessels. (Red Cross certification is required.)

Tours are available to Munich, Berchtesgaden, Innsbruck, and Salzburg, Austria; Dachau Concentration Camp; Herrenchiemsee Castle; and several area special events. Special shuttle-bus service is available to and from Munich during the Oktoberfest season.

Garmisch

Located sixty miles south of Munich and set at the foot of Germany's highest mountain, the Zugspitze (9,720 feet), Garmisch is a beautiful alpine village and a magnificent vacation spot. Garmisch is popular as a destination for planned vacations or as a spot for those traveling through southern Bavaria to other vacation areas.

Accommodations include General Patton Hotel, General Von Steuben Hotel, and Haus Flora. Garmisch also has a year-round travel camp that offers more than 100 sites, many equipped with electric hookups; a few hard-side trailers; a bath house with hot water and flush toilets; coin-operated washers, dryers, and ice machines; a picnic area; a playground; and a camp store that is open year-round.

The Sports Weeks summer and winter activities offered at Garmisch are essentially the same as for Berchtesgaden and Chiemsee. Sightseeing tours are offered to Neuschwanstein Castle, Linderhof Castle, Vipiteno and Merano in northern Italy, Venice, Innsbruck, Munich, and the Zugspitze. Special shuttle-bus service is available to and from Munich during the Oktoberfest season.

Reservations. For more information or reservations on AFRC Chiemsee write to: AFRC Chiemsee Reservations, Unit 24604, APO AE 09098, or U.S. Rasthaus am Chiemsee, Felden 25, 8214 Bernau, or call 011-49-8051-803158. AFRC Chiemsee Travel Camp reservations can also be made at the above address.

For AFRC Garmisch contact: AFRC Garmisch Reservations, Unit 24501, APO AE 09053 or Osterfelderstr. 2, 8100 Garmisch-Partenkirchen, or call 011-49-8821-790307/750575 or ETS 440-2575, or fax 011-8821-3942. The AFRC Garmisch Travel Camp may be reached by writing to: AFRC Garmisch Travel Camp, Unit 24501, APO AE 09053, or call 011-49-8821-53554.

ASCHAFFENBURG MILITARY COMMUNITY

Of the eleven sites operated by the U.S. Army in the former Aschaffenburg Military Community, nine have been returned to the Germans, while the training areas and the family housing sites have reduced their operations.

AUGSBURG MILITARY COMMUNITY

Did you know that Augsburg once owned Venezuela? Well, actually, the trading house of the Welser family of Augsburg purchased the area from the Spanish Crown in the year 1526, and it remained in their hands for thirty years. In those days land in the New World was cheap. If the House of Welser had heard of oil in those days, they'd never have let it go.

The Augsburg Military Community (AMC) consists of five kasernes (Sheridan, Quartermaster, Reese, Flak, and Gablingen) and four housing areas (Sullivan Heights, Centerville North and South, Cramerton, and Fryar Circle), plus four leased housing areas. Sheridan Kaserne is the headquarters of the AMC commander and the commander of the 7th Corps Artillery. Altogether (including families), the community supports 15,000 Americans and has a multifaceted mission.

These installations are gathered together across the western branch of the Lech River, with the exception of the Schwaben Center leased housing, which is on the east side of town, and Gablingen Kaserne, which is north of the city, in the suburb of Stettenhofen.

Housing and Schools. Housing in the AMC consists of 2,117 units of government family quarters. Of these, about 125 have been set aside as temporary quarters for incoming families. The American Hotel provides good accommodations for guests and visitors.

Education in the AMC is available through American elementary and high schools. The elementary school is located in the Centerville Housing Area, and the high school is located near Reese Kaserne. Several education centers throughout the community provide adults with excellent educational services. Nursery and preschool facilities are also available.

Personal Services. Medical care is provided by the U.S. Army Hospital, Augsburg, a 105-bed facility located on Flak Kaserne. Two dental clinics, both at Sheridan Kaserne, provide care to military personnel and their dependents.

While small post exchange outlets are located at the hospital annex, Flak annex, and Sheridan Kaserne, the regional main exchange as well as a well-stocked commissary serve the community at the Quartermaster Kaserne. The Augsburg area club system operates a number of clubs on the installations.

Recreation. The AMC contains plenty of recreational facilities, including a twenty-four-lane bowling center. There are also photo, craft, and hobby centers, as well as recreation centers and three gymnasiums. New to the community is a newly designed nine-hole championship golf course, which includes a driving range, a pro shop, and a concession food operation. There is also a family fitness center at Reese Kaserne. The rod and gun club leases a fishing lake in Dillingen, a short distance from Augsburg.

The Local Area. Augsburg lies about thirty-seven miles west of Munich. The Romans founded a city there in 15 B.C. called Augusta Vindelicorum (Munich was not founded until 1158 A.D.). In 955 A.D. the Hungarians assaulted the city. Under the leadership of Bishop Ulrich, the city managed to hold out until the emperor could arrive with an army to win a decisive battle on the Lechfeld. Today the city has a population of over 250,000 people.

For more information write to: ACS, HQ, USMCA, Augsburg, APO AE 09178.

BABENHAUSEN/DARMSTADT MILITARY COMMUNITY

History. The Babenhausen/Darmstadt Military Community (BDMC) is centered on two German communities that bridge the gap between ancient and modern times. Babenhausen was awarded its city charter in 1236. The oldest house still standing in the town is in the Muhlgasse and dates from 1442, which makes it half a century older than the discovery of the New World. Some of the major attractions of the town are the Fachwerk designs on the fronts of the older buildings, which give them a quaint, "gingerbread" appearance.

Darmstadt, the larger of the two communities, is named for one of the men— Mr. Darmunde—who was a gamekeeper for the emperor Charlemagne. From a crossroads along one of the ancient Roman highways, Darmstadt slowly grew to a metropolis of 134,000, home today of many multinational companies. Darmstadt is about twenty-three miles from Babenhausen.

Babenhausen is home to the 41st Field Artillery Brigade, a major subordinate command of the 5th Corps Artillery. The units stationed there are the 1st Battalion, 27th Field Artillery; the 4th Battalion, 77th Field Artillery (203mm); and the 4th Battalion, 18th Field Artillery (203mm). The subcommunity is home to approximately 5,400 military personnel, Department of Defense civilian employees, and dependents. It also includes a substation at Munster, where the 6th Military Police Company and two ordnance companies are stationed.

Darmstadt is the headquarters for the BDMC, which is located on Cambrai Fritsch Kaserne (CFK), about thirty miles south of Frankfurt. The community covers an area of 867 square miles and is home to more than 13,000 military personnel, civilians, and dependents. At Darmstadt itself are the 32nd Army Air Defense Command; Headquarters, 10th Air Defense Artillery Brigade; the 11th Signal Battalion; the 44th Signal Battalion; the 94th Engineer Battalion; the 547th Engineer Battalion; and the 165th Military Intelligence Battalion.

Housing and Schools. There are 1,552 government-owned and -leased quarters in the BDMC. The two main housing areas are at Lincoln and Thomas Jefferson Villages. The average waiting time for quarters in the fall of 1990 was twenty-eight weeks for two-bedroom quarters, nineteen for three-bedroom, and fifteen for four-bedroom units. The waiting period for temporary quarters was running twenty to twenty-four weeks.

American schools are operated in the community. Babenhausen Elementary School offers classes for students in kindergarten through grade six. At Darmstadt there are an elementary and a junior high school at Lincoln Village. Schooling for children in grades ten through twelve is available at the Frankfurt American High School. Child-development centers are located at both Babenhausen and Darmstadt. Army education centers at both Babenhausen and Darmstadt offer soldiers, their dependents, and U.S. government employees a variety of educational programs from high school GED through graduate-level college courses.

Personal Services. Dental and medical clinics are available at Babenhausen and Darmstadt. Specialty and inpatient care are available at the 97th General Hospital at Frankfurt. The commissary-operated Nathan Hale Depot, Darmstadt, carries 5,800 line items, while a branch facility in Babenhausen offers another 2,500 items on its stock list. New improvements at the Darmstadt facility include a deli and pizza stand. A medium-size post exchange is available at CFK, and there is a branch exchange at Babenhausen. A full array of officers, NCO, and enlisted clubs is available throughout the BDMC.

Recreation. Recreational facilities include movie theaters; arts and crafts and auto hobby shops; two bowling centers, an eighteen-lane facility at CFK and another at Babenhausen; five gymnasiums; four racquetball courts; four tennis courts; four recreation centers; two outdoor recreation centers, one at CFK and the other at Babenhausen; and a rod and gun club at CFK.

For more information write to: ACS Office, Babenhausen Subcommunity, APO AE 09455.

BAD KREUZNACH MILITARY COMMUNITY

If you suffer from rheumatism, gout, spinal troubles, circulatory problems, lung trouble, female disorders, or all of the above, Bad Kreuznach might be just the place for you. Since 1817, when a young doctor discovered that the springs in the area had healing properties, the town has been a meeting place for the noble and the rich seeking "the cure" from all of those ailments.

History. The U.S. Army first came to Bad Kreuznach in 1945, when it took over Hindenburg Kaserne from the German Army. In July 1945 the French relieved the Americans and renamed their headquarters Marshal Foch Kaserne. In July 1951 the U.S. 2nd Armored Division took over the kaserne and renamed it Maurice Rose Kaserne, in honor of Maj. Gen. Maurice Rose, a hero of the Second World War. From December 1957 to 17 January 1991 it was the home of the 8th Infantry Division. On that date the 8th ID was inactivated and redesignated the 1st Armored Division, the current occupant of the kaserne.

Today Bad Kreuznach Military Community, 410th Base Support Battalion (BSB), is part of the 53rd Area Support Group. The BSB and the headquarters of the Division Engineer Brigade are at Marshall Kaserne; the headquarters of the 1st Armored Division and the 141st Signal Battalion occupy Rose Kaserne; and the headquarters of the 53rd Area Support Group, the 9th General Hospital, the 766th Dental Detachment, and the high school are located at Hospital Kaserne. The 123rd Support Battalion and the 501st Military Intelligence Battalion are situated at Anderson Barracks, near the small town of Dexheim.

Housing and Schools. There are 1,500 family housing units in the Bad Kreuznach–Dexheim community. Almost all are government-owned. Approximately

200 are in Dexheim. There are 30 rooms available as transient quarters in Bad Kreuznach. The 410th BSB has a high school, an elementary school, and two child-care centers in Bad Kreuznach and an elementary school and a child-care center at Dexheim. A variety of college courses are offered through the education office.

Personal Services. A full range of support facilities is available in the community. Army and Air Force Exchange Service facilities include a post exchange, cafeterias, a convenience store, an auto garage, a gas station, and a laundromat, located near the dependent housing areas at Bad Kreuznach and Dexheim. The commissary at Dexheim opened its doors in March 1990. The nearby communities of Wiesbaden, Kaiserslautern, and Frankfurt offer similar facilities.

Recreation. Recreational activities and programs here are among the best available anywhere in Europe. Two bowling centers are operated in the community, a ten-lane center in Bad Kreuznach and a four-lane center in Dexheim. Dexheim is also home to the Rheinlander Club, open to personnel of all ranks as well as civilians. The Nahe Club, on the edge of Bad Kreuznach near the bachelor officer quarters, is open to officers, enlisted personnel in the senior grades, and civilians; the Century Club, located near Rose Barracks, is open to all enlisted personnel. Dexheim also has its own recreation facilities and a library. An auto hobby shop, a library, and a tour office and travel section are located at Rose Barracks. Dexheim also has its own recreational facilities and a library.

The primary outdoor recreation facility at Bad Kreuznach is the Kuhberg Recreational Complex, almost three miles southeast of Rose Barracks. The complex has twenty-eight paved camping pads, numerous primitive tent sites, large picnic sites with tables and grills, two pavilions, a miniature golf course, an archery range, a skeet range, and a playground. The complex is open year-round.

The Local Area. The climate in this part of Germany is characterized by an early spring and long-lasting fall, with relatively mild winters and cool summers.

The city of Bad Kreuznach dates back to about 839 A.D., when it was first mentioned in old records, although excavations have revealed Roman ruins dating from much earlier. The city is nestled at the foot of the Hunsruck Mountains on the winding Nahe River. Bad Kreuznach has a resident population of 43,000, which swells temporarily during the summer as thousands of tourists and health-seekers come there to visit the springs and baths.

There are a number of excellent restaurants in the city, among them Fausthaus, supposedly the residence of the legendary Dr. Faust, whom the poet Wolfgang von Goethe immortalized in his poem *Faust*. Another attraction is the ruins of Kauzenburg Castle, originally built in 1206 on a hill overlooking the valley. In its dungeon, visitors can enjoy a "knight's meal." Among the city's most famous landmarks are the so-called fifteenth-century bridge houses, built on a 700-year-old bridge that spans the Nahe. The location is also noted for its wine, which can be favorably compared to the more famous vintages from the Rhein and Mosel areas. Every year, on the first full weekend following 15 August, Bad Kreuznach holds its "Jahrmarkt," a five-day festival akin to a state fair.

The Rhein River flows only nine miles from Bad Kreuznach and offers many historic castles, camping sites, and wine fests.

For more information write to: HQ, 410th BSB, Attention: PAO, Unit 23408, APO AE 09252.

BAD TOELZ MILITARY COMMUNITY

All nine sites composing the Bad Toelz Military Community have been returned to German control.

BAMBERG MILITARY COMMUNITY

Bamberg, like Rome, is built on seven hills. The Regnitz River cuts a path through the valley dividing the city into two sections, the Bishop's Town and the Burgher's Town. The civic center of the town is the small islet formed by the two arms of the river. This area is reserved for pedestrians, small shops, and open-air markets; across the river, on the surrounding hills, are the spires of the churches that dominate the high ground in the "ecclesiastical" section of the city. Because the city was not bombed during the war, Bamberg is one place where you can see what Germany really must have looked like before the war, and it is an experience you'll never forget.

The principal installation in the Bamberg Military Community (BMC) is Warner Barracks, named in honor of Pfc. Henry F. Warner, who was killed in action near there in 1945. The principal units are the 3rd Battalion, 1st Field Artillery; 2nd Battalion, 14th Field Artillery; 82nd Engineer Battalion; and numerous support units. Altogether approximately 5,000 military personnel, family members, and Department of the Army civilians live and work in the community.

Housing and Schools. Due to the drawdown of U.S. forces in Germany, there is no waiting list for housing in the BMC. All married military personnel on a three-year tour of duty are guaranteed housing upon arrival. Two school facilities for dependents are operated in the community, one elementary school and one high school. The BMC also has two child-care centers. The education center offers a number of services, including college-level programs.

Personal Services. Medical care is provided by the Bamberg health clinic and dental clinic. Both facilities offer a number of specialty clinics for outpatient treatment. Inpatient services are available in Nurnberg or at the Bamberg city clinic. The BMC has a post exchange that operates several concessions, including a Burger King, a food store, a snack bar, an auto parts store, a beauty shop, and a service station. There are also a commissary, an officers mess, an NCO club, and an enlisted club.

Recreation. Recreational facilities include a bowling alley, a gymnasium, a recreation center, an arts and crafts shop, an entertainment center, a teen center, a movie theater, and a rod and gun club with its own fishing lake. Hunting facilities are available in state-owned forests. Excursion trips are offered to places such as Garmisch and Chiemsee Recreation Areas.

The Local Area. The city of Bamberg today has a population of more than 69,000 people, although the number of inhabitants was presumably much smaller when invading Franks established a castle, the Altenberg, on the site in 531 A.D. In 1007, Emperor Henry II gained control of the city. The center of the town is its magnificent cathedral, built in the late thirteenth century, which contains numerous art treasures of medieval times, including the "Bamberger Rider." An example of virtually every style of architecture since the Romanesque period can be seen in this city.

For more information write to: Public Affairs Office, USMC Bamberg, APO AE 09139.

BREMERHAVEN MILITARY COMMUNITY

All seventeen sites controlled by the U.S. forces in the Bremerhaven Military Community have been returned to German control.

GOPPINGEN MILITARY COMMUNITY

All seven sites operated by the U.S. forces in Goppingen Military Community have been returned to German control.

GRAFENWOEHR TRAINING CENTER

A lot of unpleasant comments have been made about "Graf" over the years, no doubt inspired by the post's isolation (sixty miles east of Nurnberg), its unpredictable weather (the temperature dipped to freezing there one day in August 1987), and the rigors of the military training that goes on there almost year-round. But residents know Graf as one of the cleanest and most picturesque areas in Germany, and while sunbathing days are scarce during the "summer" months, the climate is actually invigorating and a long stay there will endear you to the post and its charming rural environs.

History. Grafenwoehr Training Area's history began in 1907, when it was selected as the training site for the Bavarian III Corps Artillery. Construction began in 1908, and the first artillery round was fired there in 1910.

The training area was expanded in the 1930s to accommodate the growing Wehrmacht, and during World War II thousands of Allied prisoners of war were interned there.

The U.S. Army came to Grafenwoehr in 1945, and in 1958 the 7th Army Training Center was established there. In July 1976 the site was redesignated the 7th Army Training Command. Today Grafenwoehr's 56,615 acres are home to Headquarters, 7th Army Training Command; the 100th Area Support Group; and a number of tenant units, with over 2,500 soldiers and family members and 3,100 German and American civilian employees.

Housing and Schools. Grafenwoehr has 554 units of family housing. Waiting periods vary, depending upon the size and category of unit needed. A limited number of transient billets are reserved for arriving and departing families. Reservations are accepted ninety days in advance.

An elementary school with a student enrollment of over 400 is operated on post. There are intermediate and high schools in Vilseck, about fifteen miles from Grafenwoehr main post. Day-care and preschool facilities are also available.

Personal Services and Recreation. Medical care is provided by a general-health clinic on the main post. Inpatient and specialized outpatient care is available at Nurnberg. The Grafenwoehr dental clinic is a twelve-chair facility staffed with three dental officers and a hygienist.

The post offers a full range of personal services and recreational facilities, including a commissary, a post exchange, clubs, a theater, a golf course, a twenty-four-lane bowling alley, craft shops, a rod and gun club, and a recreation center. A new Burger King and a Chi Chi's restaurant on the main post are sure to tickle the tastebuds of all newcomers. The field house, a newly renovated gym, is one of the best in Germany featuring saunas, cardiovascular and weight machines, Nautilus equipment, racquetball courts, and qualified instructors for a variety of sports.

The Local Area. The Grafenwoehr Training Area is located fifty-five miles north of Nurnberg, in the heart of the "Franconian Alps," a land of rolling, thickly forested hills stretching from the city of Nurnberg to the Czechoslovakian border, which is about thirty miles due east of the main post area. Hunting, fishing, and hiking are the major sporting activities in the area. The major local industry is farming. Traveling along the area's backcountry roads on an early summer's morning is one of the finest and rarest pleasures to be found in Germany, and the food offered in the local Gasthauses (not to mention the German beer!) is delectable.

The climate in this part of Germany is definitely temperate, with many cool, wet days throughout the year. Heavy fog is common in all seasons. Summer temperatures average 75° F. while in the winter they often dip below freezing; during winter heavy snow is rare.

For more information write to: Public Affairs Office, HQ, 7th Army Training Command, Unit 28130, APO AE, 09114-5412.

HEIDELBERG MILITARY COMMUNITY

Heidelberg contains 500,000 years of human history, beginning with the Heidelberg Man whose jawbone was discovered there in 1907, and continuing through the Romans down to the present time. Today Heidelberg is a city of about 150,000, including the student body at Heidelberg University, founded in 1386.

The personnel assigned to the Heidelberg Military Community (HMC) comprise the staff of Headquarters, U.S. Army Europe and 7th Army; Central Army Group (NATO); the 7th Medical Command; the 4th Allied Tactical Air Force; the 1st Personnel Command; and various support groups. The total U.S. population in the HMC, civilian and military, is 24,000.

History. The first U.S. troops entered Heidelberg on Good Friday 1945. The HMC today comprises nineteen separate installations or *kasernes* (German for "barracks"), most originally built between 1890 and 1939. Most of these survived the war intact since Heidelberg was largely spared the devastating air raids of World War II.

On the south side of the city are Campbell Barracks and the family housing area known as Mark Twain Village. Just south of Campbell Barracks in Nachtrichten Kaserne is the 130th Station Hospital and Headquarters, 7th Medical Command. To the northwest of Campbell Barracks is Patton Barracks, headquarters for the HMC and the site of troop barracks. To the west of Campbell, across the autobahn, is Patrick Henry Village, a 250-acre complex built in the 1950s and home to more than 3,500 American troops and their families. Other areas include the Heidelberg Army Airfield, a forty-five-acre complex in the southwest corner of the city, and the Koenigstuhl Relay Station.

The shopping center, across Czernyring from the Heidelberg Mail Railway Station, houses the commissary, main post exchange, and other exchange outlets.

In nearby Schwetzingen are Kilbourne and Tompkins Barracks, where troop housing and the 1st Personnel Command headquarters are located. Stem Kaserne, between Mannheim and Heidelberg, is home to the Criminal Investigation Command's Second Region.

Housing and Schools. More than 2,000 units of government housing are available to eligible soldiers—those serving a thirty-six-month, accompanied tour with command-sponsored families. As of August 1992, waiting periods for these quarters varied from four to six weeks for a two-bedroom unit for field-grade officers to twenty to twenty-four weeks for two-bedroom junior-enlisted quarters. Waiting periods for rental units off post were running sixty to ninety days with rents for one-bedroom unfurnished apartments starting at around $650 per month, not including deposit and utilities.

Dependents schooling is available throughout the HMC: a high school at Mark Twain Village; elementary and middle schools at Patrick Henry Village; and child-care centers at Mark Twain and Patrick Henry Villages and the 130th Station Hospital kaserne. Adult education programs are available through centers located at Campbell, Tompkins, and Patton Barracks and Patrick Henry Village.

Personal Services. Medical and dental services are provided by the 130th Station Hospital. Full commissary and post exchange services are available at the downtown shopping center complex. Also available there are a liquor store, a garage, an auto parts store, a recreation equipment rental service, a bank and credit union, an optical shop, a bookstore, an audio store, a snack bar, and other facilities.

Recreation. The HMC offers a variety of military clubs for entertainment and dining: the Recovery Room at Nachrichten Kaserne; the Pub officers and civilians club at Patrick Henry Village; and the NCO/EM club at Kilbourne and Tompkins Barracks. There are recreation centers at Patton and Tompkins Barracks and an outdoor recreation area at Patrick Henry Village. The Heidelberg Rod and Gun Club offers rifle and pistol and shotgun ranges, archery, a sports equipment store, a picnic area, and a restaurant and bar that serves a variety of German and American food at reasonable prices. Library facilities are available at Patrick Henry Village and Campbell Barracks. Baseball fields, basketball and tennis courts, gymnasiums, two movie theaters, and an eighteen-hole golf course round out the recreational picture.

The Local Area. Heidelberg is nestled on the Neckar River in south-central Germany, between Stuttgart to the south and Frankfurt to the north. Many of the city's ancient buildings, some dating from the twelfth century, are still standing. Visitors can enjoy tours along the Neckar, and the German Grand Prix is held at the Hockenheim Race Track, about twelve kilometers from the city. Heidelberg is only ninety minutes from the Black Forest.

For more information write to: Commander, 26th Area Support Group, Attention: PAO, Unit 29237, APO AE 09102.

HERZOGENAURACH ARTILLERY BASE

Operations at Herzogenaurach Artillery Base have been reduced. See entry for Nurnberg Military Community.

HOHENFELS COMBAT MANEUVER TRAINING CENTER

The Hohenfels Combat Maneuver Training Center is part of the 7th Army Training Command. Located in the state of Bavaria, Hohenfels is the largest maneuver area (as opposed to live-fire area) for the U.S. Army, Europe. Approximately 2,000 soldiers train there each month.

History. The training area takes its name from the rural town of Hohenfels (population 1,500), located one mile east of its boundary. Known history in these parts dates back to about 50 B.C., when Julius Caesar led his army in the conquest of the Celtic and Gallic tribes in that area. In 946, Count Graf von Hohenfels built a castle on a steep rock above the valley. Part of the castle still stands in the center of town.

In 1938, the German army established a training area north of the town. After the collapse of the Third Reich, the camp served as a reception area for displaced persons. In 1951, U.S. forces claimed the area for military training. Today it covers a total area of some 40,000 acres and is home to the 1st Battalion, 4th Infantry Regiment, which acts as the opposing force for all units training at Hohenfels. Other units stationed at Hohenfels include the 282nd Base Support Battalion, and A Company, 94th Engineers, a heavy-construction unit. Altogether, over 5,900 military and civilian personnel call Hohenfels home.

Housing and Schools. There are 539 sets of government-owned and built-to-lease family quarters located both on and off post. More are planned to be constructed in the future but as of fall 1993 there was a shortage of housing at Hohenfels and waiting periods were long. Guest housing is available, but it is also limited.

On-post schooling for dependent children in kindergarten through junior high, as well as preschool and day-care facilities, is available, as are a number of college-level courses.

Personal Services and Recreation. Definitive medical care is provided by the U.S. Army hospital in Nurnberg, about sixty miles from Hohenfels. The 731st General Dispensary and the 561st Medical Detachment provide medical and dental treatment respectively.

Hohenfels has a new commissary, a post exchange, a cafeteria, a shopette, and several clubs. Recreational facilities include a theater, a gym with an annex, a bowling alley, a recreation center, and automotive, photo, ceramics, and leather craft shops. Two swimming pools are available in the town of Parsberg (eight miles away), and there is a golf course in the town of Schmidmuhlen (twelve miles away).

The Local Area. The climate in the Hohenfels area is generally mild, but the weather can be unpredictable. Winter occasionally brings snow, and roads are often covered by freezing rain, particularly in the morning and evening hours. Temperatures in winter dip occasionally into the twenties. Summers are generally cool, with temperatures sometimes rising into the eighties, and sunbathing days are rare. The area is quite picturesque and is among the environmentally cleanest in Germany. The nearest big cities are Nurnberg (sixty miles away) and Regensburg (thirty miles away).

For more information write to: Commander, 282nd BSB, Attention: S-3 (Public Affairs), Unit 28216, APO AE 09173.

KAISERSLAUTERN MILITARY COMMUNITY

Kaiserslautern earned its name because it was once the favorite hunting retreat of the Emperor ("Kaiser") Frederick I, known as Barbarosa ("Red Beard"), who ruled the Holy Roman Empire from 1155 to 1190. When Barbarosa built his castle there between 1152 and 1160, the Lauter River was an important stream that actually formed the center of the town into an island, and today the remains of Barbarosa's castle can still be seen in the front of the city hall (Rathaus). In fact, the shield of the city depicts an open-mouthed carp on it, and it is said that this fish was the emperor's favorite dish, but that may again be nothing more than a fish story.

History. Americans came to Kaiserslautern in March 1945. The Kaiserslautern Military Community (KMC) includes a number of important military installations. Ramstein Air Base, seven miles west of the city, is the largest U.S. air base in Europe. USAFE is headquartered there, and from Ramstein it exercises command and control over all Air Force units in Europe, a command stretching from Great Britain to Turkey.

The 86th Wing is the host unit for Ramstein, and its commander is also the KMC commander. The wing is composed of the 512th and 526th Fighter Squadrons, the 58th Airlift Squadron, and other units. The fighter squadrons fly the F-16C/D aircraft in their attack and clear-weather interception missions.

Army installations in the KMC include the 21st Theater Army Command in Panzer Kaserne and the 29th Area Support Group, at Daenner Kaserne. Opposite Daenner Kaserne is Kleber Kaserne, the headquarters for the 37th Transportation Group and other units.

Kleber Kaserne has been occupied by troops since 1913 when it was called the "Twenty-third Kaserne," after the Twenty-third Bavarian Regiment, which built it. After World War I, it was temporarily occupied by French troops, including Vietnamese motorized support troops. After World War II, the French again occupied the post and renamed it in honor of Gen. Jean Baptist Kleber, a famous general under Napoleon. In the early 1950s, the U.S. Army moved into the post and rebuilt much of it.

On the western side of town are the Vogelweh Complex, the Pulaski Barracks, and the Rhine Ordnance Barracks. The Vogelweh Complex includes the largest family housing area in Europe. The westernmost installation is the Landstuhl Army

Regional Medical Center (LARMC), located on a high and windy hill, the home of the 2nd General Hospital, the largest U.S. forces hospital in Europe; the 10th Medical Laboratory; and the Air Force's 18th Aeromedical Facility.

Housing and Schools. The 60,000 Americans who live and work in the KMC constitute the largest American community outside the United States. The number of family housing units exceeds 5,800. There are family quarters at Vogelweh, Kaiserslautern, Ramstein, Sembach Air Base, and Landstuhl. There are also 600 leased quarters throughout the KMC. Guest accommodations are located at Landstuhl, Ramstein, and Vogelweh.

The KMC's American school system is one of the largest outside the United States, supporting more than 8,000 students. There are two elementary schools in the city of Kaiserslautern and a junior and senior high school. Landstuhl has an elementary school, Ramstein an elementary school and junior and senior highs. Preschool facilities are located in Kaiserslautern, Landstuhl, Ramstein, and Vogelweh. Adult education centers are available in Kaiserslautern, Landstuhl, Miesau Army Depot, and Ramstein, where college courses are conducted from a large number of American universities and colleges, including the University of Maryland and Boston University.

Personal Services. The major medical facility in the area is the 2nd General Hospital, but there are clinics at Kleber Kaserne, Vogelweh, and Ramstein, and dental clinics at Kleber, Vogelweh, Landstuhl, and Ramstein.

The KMC has commissaries at Ramstein and Sembach Air Bases and Vogelweh, and exchanges at Kleber Kaserne, Landstuhl, Ramstein, Rhine Ordnance Barracks, and Vogelweh. The KMC has two NCO clubs, three NCO-enlisted clubs, a combined club, three officers clubs, and one officer-civilian club. The community also offers eighteen snack bars and cafeterias, six libraries, and eight movie theaters. Both Ramstein and Vogelweh have a car wash and car-rental facilities.

Recreation. For recreation, the KMC offers six bowling centers, seven gymnasiums, a golf course at Ramstein, nine arts and crafts shops, five auto hobby shops, six recreation centers, five outdoor recreation equipment rental facilities, a rod and gun club, a roller skating rink, and seven travel and tour offices.

The Local Area. Over 60 percent of Kaiserslautern was destroyed during World War II, but since then it has been totally rebuilt and has a population of 108,000; Ramstein and Landstuhl have more than 10,000 inhabitants each. The weather in this part of Germany is moderate, with lots of rain and occasionally some fog. Measurable rainfall is recorded on an average of 149 days out of the year. Winters are generally not too severe, with morning lows around 15° F. and afternoon highs averaging between 30° F. and 45° F.

For more information write to: 86th Wing Public Affairs Office, Unit 3200, Box 330, APO AE 09094.

KARLSRUHE

Karlsruhe derives its name from the palace of Karl Wilhelm, Prince of Baden Durlach, which he built in the Hardt Forest in 1715 on the site of the camp where he liked to rest while out hunting in the forest. Hence the name, "Karl's rest."

The 291st Base Support Battalion (BSB) provides administrative, logistical facilities, engineering, and housing support to all U.S. forces in South Baden and neighboring areas. This support includes five major bases and numerous small installations with a total population of 11,300 military personnel, local nationals, and U.S. civilian employees. The BSB is home to the 3rd Corps (Forward), the 7th Signal Brigade (302nd, 72nd, and 44th Signal Battalions), the 565th Engineer Battalion, and other units.

Housing and Schools. Approximately 1,000 military-controlled and leased government family quarters are available in the BSB. Family housing is located in the Paul Revere Village. Guest accommodations are available at the award-winning Karlsruhe Lodge. Priority for reservations is given to incoming families.

Dependents schooling facilities include Karlsruhe High School and the Karlsruhe Elementary School. The Army education center provides adult education services that include college programs offered by the University of Maryland, Central Texas College, the City Colleges of Chicago, and Big Bend Community College.

Personal Services. Medical care is offered by the 3rd General Dispensary, and inpatient care is provided through the 130th Station Hospital in Heidelberg, approximately thirty-five miles from Karlsruhe. Emergency care is available at the German Krankenhaus and Kinderklinic.

The main post exchange and commissary are located in the Karlsruhe Shopping Center on Erzberger Strasse, and the Army and Air Force Exchange Service support facilities and a commissary annex are located at the Germersheim installation. The BSB club system consists of the Paul Revere Club, the Gerszweski Club, the Neurat Club, and the Rhineland Club.

Recreation. Recreational facilities include two multipurpose recreation centers, two bowling centers, two arts and crafts centers, a photo lab, two libraries, an auto craft shop, four gyms, a fitness center, and an outdoor swimming pool.

The Local Area. The city of Karlsruhe is located in southwestern Germany on the Rhine River. Karlsruhe began as a city of parks and gardens, and its people devoted to intellectual freedom and humanism. It has kept this reputation to this very day. In 1828 Karlsruhe's college of technology (the oldest in Germany) was founded. The Federal Supreme Court and the Federal Constitutional Court are both located in Karlsruhe, as is the largest atomic research center in Germany.

For more information write to: HQ 291st Base Support Battalion, Karlsruhe, CMR 424, APO AE 09164.

KITZINGEN MILITARY COMMUNITY

Kitzingen is the only town in Germany with its own leaning tower—the Falterturm, which was constructed more than 400 years ago as the tallest of twenty-eight towers on the city wall. Legend has it that the structure was completed during a very hot and dry period of summer weather, and the masons, to save water, mixed the mortar with some local wine. In any event, the tower rises 164 feet above the city, making it three feet shorter than Niagara Falls.

History. The two major installations in the Kitzingen Military Community (KMC) are Harvey and Larson Kasernes. Harvey Kaserne was named in honor of Capt. James R. Harvey, who was killed in Normandy, France, in 1944; Larson was named after Capt. Stanley I. Larson, who was killed at Anzio, Italy, in May 1944. Today the KMC supports the men of the 3rd Infantry (Marne) Division. Larson Kaserne, situated on the southwest side of the city, is home to the 4th Battalion, 3rd Air Defense Artillery; 123rd and 17th Signal Battalions; and other units. Harvey Barracks, on the northeast side of town, houses Headquarters, 3rd Infantry Division Support Command; the 703rd Main Support Battalion; and other units.

Housing and Schools. There is a severe shortage of government housing in the KMC, and there is also a shortage of economy housing. Government quarters may take a year to acquire, and the wait for housing on the German economy is from thirty to ninety days. Limited guest accommodations (twenty beds) are available for all ranks in the Kitzingen Officers Club at Harvey Kaserne.

A preschool and an elementary school are provided within the KMC; junior and senior high classes are available in nearby Wurzburg (thirteen miles away). The Army education center offers study at the college level, including certificates and associate, bachelor's, and advanced degrees.

Personal Services. Medical and dental care are provided by the Kitzingen U.S. Army Health Clinic. Patients requiring specialized medical care or hospitalization are referred to the Wurzburg Army Hospital.

There are post exchanges at both Harvey and Larson Kasernes. Items not sold there may be ordered from the Army and Air Force Exchange Service catalog. Foodland shops are offered at both Harvey and Larson. A commissary and a beverage store are also operated in the community. A shuttle bus runs between Larson and Harvey Kasernes and Wurzburg several times each day, so the post exchange and commissary facilities are accessible to KMC personnel and their families.

Recreation. Recreation facilities consist of officers and NCO-enlisted clubs as well as a golf and ski club that is open to all ranks. A nine-hole golf course and a rod and gun club are also available, as are craft and photo hobby shops, gymnasiums, libraries, recreational centers, a swimming pool, and tennis courts.

The Local Area. In 1951 the city of Kitzingen celebrated its 1,200th anniversary. The city (population 20,000) is on the Main River, a few miles southeast of Wurzburg, in the Steigerwald Forest. The city has recovered completely from its devastation in World War II, when about 35 percent of its homes were destroyed.

For more information write to: Public Affairs Office, U.S. Military Community, Kitzingen, APO AE 09031.

LANDSTUHL ARMY REGIONAL MEDICAL CENTER

Landstuhl Army Regional Medical Center (LARMC) occupies over 470 acres atop Kirchberg Hill overlooking the small town of Landstuhl, which has been inhabited at least since Roman times. Just to the east is the city of Kaiserslautern and a bit farther west is Saarbrucken; Luxembourg and Belgium are also within easy driving distance.

History. The eighteen large stone buildings constituting the Lower Post area of LARMC were originally built by the German Army in 1938 and served first as home for a battalion of infantry, then as a reserve field hospital, and from 1944 to 1945 they were a field hospital for the Waffen SS. The area was captured by U.S. Forces on 19 March 1945. From 1945 through 1947 the French occupied the site; the 320th General Hospital, predecessor to the 2nd General Hospital, arrived there in 1951. Landstuhl Army Regional Medical Center was established in 1952.

The buildings standing today on the higher slopes of Kirchberg Hill are known as Wilson Barracks, in honor of Tech. 5th Grade Alfred Wilson, a medic with the 26th Infantry Division who was awarded the Medal of Honor for action in Europe during World War II. These buildings were originally known as the Hitler School and were built for use by the Hitler Youth Movement.

Today Landstuhl Post comprises 726 acres spread across Kirchberg Hill, predominantly occupied by medical units. The chief units are the 2nd General Hospital, 236th Medical Detachment (Helicopter), 10th Medical Laboratory, the 655th Medical Detachment (EUCOM Blood Bank), the 464th Medical Detachment (Dental Services), and 502nd MASH.

By far the biggest operation at LARMC is the 2nd General Hospital, with a complement of more than 1,700 military and civilian personnel. The hospital has a 180-bed operating capacity and averages 25 admissions each day of the year. It provides primary medical care, hospitalization, and treatment for more than 50,000 personnel within the center's boundaries and specialized care for more than 200,000 personnel as a referral center for Europe.

Housing, Personal Services, and Recreation. Landstuhl controls 290 units of family housing. An elementary school and a day-care center are operated on post. Full post exchange and commissary facilities are available in nearby Kaiserslautern; a post exchange/snack bar facility is located right at Landstuhl. Recreational facilities on post include a gymnasium, a handball and racquetball court, a bowling center, and a community center.

For more information write to: Commander, 2nd General Hospital, Attention: AEMLA-AG, CMR 402, APO AE 09180.

MANNHEIM MILITARY COMMUNITY

The Mannheim Military Community (MMC) consists of seven major installations situated in and around the city of Mannheim that are home to over 30,000 military personnel.

Benjamin Franklin Village, Sullivan Barracks, and Funari Barracks are co-located in the Kafertal suburb on the northwest side of the city. Ben Franklin Village is the largest U.S. forces housing area in Germany, with quarters for over 2,100 families. Sullivan Barracks is home to two battalions of the 3rd Brigade, 1st Armored Division, and is the headquarters for the 51st Maintenance Battalion. Funari Barracks is occupied by Headquarters, Combat Equipment Group, Europe; the 187th Personnel Service Company; the 168th Ordnance Detachment; and the civilian personnel office service center.

Taylor Barracks, just to the west of Ben Franklin Village, is headquarters of the 293rd Base Support Battalion, the 14th Military Police Brigade, the 2nd Signal Brigade, and the 95th Military Police Battalion. Spinelli Barracks, in the Luzenberg section of Mannheim, is home to the 28th Transportation Battalion of the 37th Group, 4th Transportation Command. Just to the east of Spinelli Barracks is Turley Barracks, home of the 181st Transportation Battalion. Coleman Barracks, in the Sandhofen suburb, houses the headquarters of the 3rd Armored Brigade, with the 70th Transportation Battalion, the 97th Signal Battalion, and other units.

Taukkunen Barracks and Thomas Jefferson Village in nearby Worms are also part of the MMC. Taukkunen is home for the 5th Signal Command. Thomas Jefferson Village, less than a mile from Taukkunen Barracks, contains the Worms Elementary School as well as transient accommodations and other personal service facilities.

Housing and Schools. Besides quarters for the 2,100 families that live in Benjamin Franklin Village, the MMC leases quarters for 110 families at nearby Lampertheim and another 600 at Frankenthal. As of spring 1993, waiting periods for two-bedroom units were running eight to twelve weeks for captains; four to eight weeks for senior noncommissioned officers; and four to six months for other enlisted ranks. A two-bedroom unfurnished apartment in Mannheim was renting for $800 a month, not including utilities.

Transient accommodations are available at the Franklin Guest House. Family rates are thirty-six dollars a day plus five dollars for each child.

Dependents schooling for children in elementary through high school is available at Ben Franklin Village. Child-development centers are located at Benjamin Franklin Village and at a leased facility in Vogelstang. Education centers located at Coleman, Spinelli, Sullivan, Taylor, and Turley Barracks offer a variety of college-level courses from Big Bend Community College, Central Texas College, City Colleges of Chicago, the University of Maryland, Boston University, the University of Southern California, the University of Oklahoma, and Troy State University.

Personal Services. Medical and dental care are provided by three clinics located at Ben Franklin Village, Coleman Barracks, and nearby Worms. The largest of these is the 546th General Dispensary, at Ben Franklin Village. Inpatient and specialized medical care are available at the 130th Station Hospital in Heidelberg.

A full-service commissary store is available at Ben Franklin Village, as is a post exchange; there is also a PX at Coleman Barracks. Army and Air Force Exchange Service outlets available throughout the MMC include clothing tailor shops, auto repair shops, barber and beauty shops, a bakery, a liquor store, shopettes, laundromats, four-seasons stores, and video-rental stores.

Recreation. Recreational facilities include outdoor sports fields and playgrounds as well as gymnasiums and fitness centers. The MMC also has a club system that includes the Colonial Manor at Ben Franklin Village, Top Hat NCO/Enlisted Club at Taylor Barracks, and the Coleman Club, at Coleman Barracks. There are also a Burger King at Ben Franklin Village and a pizza parlor at Sullivan Barracks. Bowling is available at Ben Franklin Village, Coleman Barracks. There are six libraries and three movie theaters in the MMC. The recreational picture is rounded out by a variety of arts and crafts facilities as well as an auto craft center.

The Local Area. Mannheim is located fifty miles south of Frankfurt and thirteen miles northwest of Heidelberg, in the Baden-Wurttemburg area, at the confluence of the Neckar and Rhein Rivers. Mannheim and its suburbs have a population of over 300,000.

For more information write to: Commander, 293rd Base Support Battalion, Attention: ACS, Unit 29901, Box 25, APO AE 09086.

NURNBERG

The first images the name Nurnberg causes to jump into most Americans' minds are of the War Crimes Tribunal held there in 1945 and 1946 and the huge Nazi rallies that were once held there. But Nurnberg was famous long before these notorious events as the home of Albrecht Durer, Hans Sachs, and Anton Koberger, who printed the first history book there in the late 1400s. Despite heavy bombing during World War II, many of the city's medieval buildings still stand, and much of the Old City has been restored.

Approximately 10,000 Americans live in the 416th Base Support Battalion (BSB) (formerly the Nurnberg Military Community) situated in a number of installations spread throughout the area. There is William O. Darby Kaserne at Fürth, which houses the headquarters for the 99th Area Support Group, the 416th Base Support Battalion, and the 793rd MP Battalion. Johnson Barracks, also located in Fürth, is home for the 71st Maintenance Battalion. The 317th Maintenance Company is situated at Monteith Barracks, also in Fürth. At Pinder Barracks in nearby Zirndorf is the headquarters for the Army and Air Force Exchange Service. Ferris Barracks, at Erlangen, another suburb of Nurnberg, is home to the 2nd Brigade, the 3rd Infantry Division, and the 16th Engineer Battalion. The 3rd Combat Support Hospital and the 87th Medical Detachment (Dental) are located in the city itself.

Housing and Schools. In the 99th Area Support Group, composed of Ansbach,

Augsburg, Bamberg, and Nurnberg, there are 6,380 housing units. Eight thousand private rental and leased quarters have been returned to the local economy. Temporary lodging is available at the Bavarian American Hotel in Nurnberg, where families on permanent-change-of-station orders have first and second priority with temporary-duty personnel, active-duty personnel on leave, and retired personnel coming third in priority for accommodations.

Dependent children attend American schools in the local area. The 416th BSB has two kindergartens, three elementary schools, one middle school, and one high school. The BSB also offers a child-care center and a quarters-based program for children six weeks through twelve years of age. Two Army education centers serve adults with college courses from Central Texas College, the University of Maryland, and City Colleges of Chicago.

Personal Services. Medical care is provided by a number of dispensaries and clinics located throughout the BSB. The referral medical facility is the 3rd Combat Support Hospital, a sixty-bed facility with an additional forty beds for the USAREUR Alcohol Treatment Facility.

One of the largest shopping centers for U.S. personnel in Europe is located at Fürth and provides everything from a well-stocked department store to U.S. automobile sales points.

Recreation. Two recreation centers as well as three fitness centers and two bowling alleys are located within the 416th BSB. Arts and crafts shops, photo centers, and auto craft shops are also available. The BSB also has two movie theaters, a live stage company, an eighteen-hole golf course, and several clubs offering a wide range of entertainment from live bands to bingo. The rod and gun club, located on William O. Darby Kaserne, sells hunting, fishing, archery, and camping equipment.

The Local Area. Nurnberg is a city of approximately 480,000. It offers visitors and tourists a beautiful combination of a medieval walled city and a thoroughly modern metropolis complete with shops, restaurants, hotels, and an efficient public transportation system.

Fürth, Nurnberg's sister city, boasts 100,000 inhabitants. Fürth was spared the general destruction that was the fate of most German cities during World War II, so today many of its ancient buildings and churches are still standing.

For more information write to: Public Affairs Office, 99th Area Support Group–Nurnberg, Unit 27933, APO AE 09222.

SCHWEINFURT

The city of Schweinfurt, like the legendary phoenix, has twice risen from its own ashes, both times better than it was before. The first occasion was in 1554 and the second was after World War II, when 75 percent of the city was left in ruins by Allied bombing attacks. One of these, in October 1943, was mounted by the U.S. 8th Air Force and involved a force of 228 heavy bombers, 62 of which were lost along with their ten-man crews and 138 others damaged. The removal of the rubble took three years after the war finally ended in 1945.

Schweinfurt is home a number of combat and combat-support units. At Ledward Barracks are the headquarters of the 280th Support Battalion Base (SBB), elements of the 15th Infantry, 10th Field Artillery, and support units. At Conn Barracks are the 3rd Squadron, the 4th Cavalry, as well as elements of the 15th Infantry, the 3rd Support, and the 64th Armor. The 280th SBB has approximately 12,000 military personnel, family members, and Department of the Army civilians.

Housing and Schools. Family housing is situated at York Town Village, a complex consisting of single-family quadruplexes for junior enlisted personnel. A junior high school is adjacent to York Town Village.

Personal Services. Health care for personnel living in the SBB is provided by the 24th Medical Detachment's U.S. Army health clinic. Patients requiring hospitalization or extensive specialist treatment are referred to the U.S. Army hospital in Wurzburg.

The commissary is located at Askren Manor housing area and sells a variety of foods and meat cuts, which can be special-ordered twenty-four hours in advance. The post exchange facility is located at Ledward Barracks.

Recreation. Recreational facilities include three bowling alleys. The Kessler bowling alley, which opened in the spring of 1991, is a twenty-four-lane, fully computerized facility. There is also a theater at both Conn and Ledward Barracks; and automotive, ceramics, and photo craft shops are also available. Gymnasiums are located at Ledward and at Conn Barracks; the new Kessler Fitness Center offers a sauna, a weight room, and racquetball and tennis courts; the officers open mess is located at Conn Barracks. The Community Recreation Division also supports a vigorous sports program open to all who are interested.

The Local Area. Schweinfurt is located in Bavaria, about sixty-six miles east of Frankfurt, on the River Main. The first mention of the city occurs in old records dating from about 714 A.D. when it was little more than a fishing village. Despite the damage done to the city during the war, some of the older buildings are still standing, most of them dating from the sixteenth and seventeenth centuries. The surrounding countryside, which is very scenic, includes the ancient Mainberg, Bad Sennfeld, and Werneck Castles as well as the cliffs of the Steigerwalt, the Hasseberge Hills, and the oak forests in the countryside of the Rhoen and Spessart region.

For more information write to: Army Community Service, 280th SBB, CMR No. 457, APO AE 09033-2012.

STUTTGART MILITARY COMMUNITY

The Stuttgart Military Community (SMC) actually consists of approximately four U.S. Army installations located throughout the city of Stuttgart and in the surrounding countryside. Patch Barracks, site of Headquarters, U.S. European Command, is in the suburb of Vaihingen, on the southwest side of the city, and Kelley Barracks, seat of the European Command Area Support Group and other units, is in the suburb of Moehringen, south of the city. Panzer Kaserne lies on the southwest side of the city, on the west side of Boeblingen, and hosts the 7th Special Operations Support

Command, 1st Battalion, 10th Special Forces Group. The Echterdingen Area Support Team maintains operations at Echterdingen Airfield, south of Kelley Barracks.

The overall U.S. military and family-member population in the area is around 9,000 personnel, down from 33,000 in 1990.

Housing and Schools. There are approximately 1,676 units of government family housing in the SMC, with almost no waiting period for occupancy. Guest accommodations are available at the Hilltop Hotel at the Robinson Barracks Housing Area on the north side of the city.

There are three elementary schools for kindergarten through grade six and a high school for grades seven through twelve. In addition, there are four child-care centers. Adult education is handled through the local Army education centers.

Personal Services. A new medical-dental clinic at Patch Barracks provides health care to personnel in the SMC area. Shuttles carry personnel to the 130th Station Hospital in Heidelberg for referral care. The European Command Demonstration Project provides after-hours and weekend emergency medical care at local German hospitals.

Post exchange facilities are located at Panzer Kaserne and Patch and Kelley Barracks. One large commissary is located at Patch, with two satellite facilities at Panzer and Kelley.

Recreation. The area abounds with recreational facilities: an eighteen-hole golf course; swimming at numerous German pools; three fitness centers; outdoor recreation programs offering equipment rental and trips to local ski areas and the AFRCs; craft centers for textile and fiber arts, silk-screening and ceramic arts, woodworking and frame shops; a post library at Patch Barracks; a theater center at Kelley Barracks; three community clubs, an officers club, and an NCO/enlisted club; three bowling alleys; and two auto craft centers.

The Local Area. Stuttgart is a fascinating place to live and work. Although the city is first mentioned in official records from 1160, there is evidence that the site was occupied by the Romans. Today Stuttgart has a population of over 557,000 and is the headquarters for Mercedes Benz and Porsche—and it has more woods and parks than any other city in West Germany. It is also the gateway to the famous Black Forest area. But its numerous museums, galleries, theaters, castles, and other points of interest are worth staying city-bound to see. Stuttgart also has many fine restaurants, and the wine that is grown locally on the hillsides along the Neckar Valley is worth savoring.

For more information write to: Public Affairs Office, Stuttgart Military Community, CMR 423, APO AE 09107.

VILSECK COMBINED ARMS TRAINING CENTER

The Vilseck Subcommunity is home of the 281st Base Support Battalion; the 3rd Brigade, 3rd Infantry Division; the 94th Engineer Battalion; the 95th Chemical

Company; and the Combined Arms Training Center (CATC). Vilseck is located in a beautiful area of Bavaria known as the Oberpfaelzer Jura, because of the many ridges and hills and steep valleys and gorges that dot the countryside in this part of Germany.

History. U.S. forces first came to Vilseck when a training center was established there in 1947. The post consists of Rose Barracks, named after Maj. Gen. Maurice Rose, commander of the 3rd Armored Division who was killed in action on 30 March 1945. The garrison consists of approximately 5,000 military personnel and 5,000 family members.

Housing and Schools. There are approximately 1,100 sets of family quarters at Vilseck. Waiting times vary according to rank and the size of housing unit needed. As of spring 1993, soldiers were waiting from two to ten months for quarters. Guest housing is available at Vilseck.

On-post dependents schooling, kindergarten through high school, plus preschool and day-care facilities, are provided. The education center at Rose Barracks offers a number of college-level courses, and courses are also available at nearby Grafenwohr.

Personal Services. Definitive medical care is provided by the 12th General Dispensary, which is part of the Nurnberg U.S. Army Hospital, about fifty miles away. Dental care is provided by the 561st Medical Company (DS).

Vilseck has a large commissary and post exchange with a food mall, a cafeteria, a shopette/liquor store, a Stars and Stripes bookstore, a community bank, a federal credit union, a laundromat, a furniture store, a Burger King, and beauty, barber, tailor, and flower shops.

Recreation. Recreation facilities include a newly renovated theater; automotive, photo, ceramics, wood, and leather crafts shops; two gyms; a new twenty-four-lane bowling alley; and new recreation, youth, and outdoor recreation centers. There is also an outdoor swimming pool in the town of Vilseck (about 2.5 miles from post), and a golf course as well as a rod and gun club at Grafenwohr. An indoor pool is scheduled to open in 1995.

The Local Area. The climate in the Vilseck area is generally mild year-round. Winter seldom brings much snow, but it is damp and cold, with the temperatures occasionally dipping into the twenties. The summers are generally cool, with temperatures sometimes rising into the eighties.

Founded about 1000 A.D., Vilseck was granted city status in 1332. Today the town's population is about 5,500. Most of its citizens farm in the fields of the surrounding countryside.

Eating out in Vilseck is affordable, and the local specialties are worth tasting. Try the *Bauernseufzer*, smoke-fired sausage with *Blechtrommel*, "tin drum," and coffee, or *Bratwurstl suss-sauer*, fried sausages in a sweet-and-sour sauce with onions.

For more information write to: Public Affairs Officer, HQ Vilseck Military Community, APO AE 09112-5420.

WIESBADEN-MAINZ COMMUNITY

History. Wiesbaden Air Base, the primary facility in the Wiesbaden geographical area, is known to have been used since at least as early as 1184, not for flying but as a fairgrounds, and it is said that Emperor Friedrich I knighted his sons on the field there. Today Wiesbaden AB is home to the 3rd Command Support (COSCOM).

The Wiesbaden-Mainz Community (WMC) is commanded and serviced by the 221st Base Support Battalion. It consists of over 21,000 people, of whom more than 3,800 belong to the 3rd COSCOM. Other installations in the community include the Mainz facilities and McCully Barracks in Mainz-Wackernheim, and the Mainz-Kastel Storage Station.

Housing and Schools. There are over 3,000 units of family housing in the WMC. Hainerberg in Wiesbaden and Martin Luther King Village in Mainz are the two largest, but seven smaller housing areas are situated within the community.

More than 3,200 school-age dependent children live in the WMC; they attend one of three elementary schools, a middle school, and a high school. Child-development services are available at the Hainerberg Housing Area, MLK Village, and Wiesbaden Air Base. Various education centers about the community offer college courses from Big Bend Community College, Central Texas College, City Colleges of Chicago, the University of Southern California, Boston University, Troy State University, Embry-Riddle Aeronautical University, and the University of Maryland.

Personal Services. Medical services are provided by a troop medical and dental clinic at the air base. The 97th General Hospital, Frankfurt, is used for inpatient services. Local German hospitals provide emergency-room care and other services.

Shopping facilities include a commissary in the Hainerberg Housing Area and an annex in the MLK Village. One of the larger exchanges in Europe is in the Hainerberg section. It includes two theaters and several concessions. There is also a large shopping facility at the Mainz-Kastell Storage Station and a PX shopette in Mainz.

Recreation. Recreation facilities include gymnasiums, the Rheinblick Golf Course, a rod and gun club range, various arts and crafts shops, and a recreation center. An outdoor recreation rental facility provides equipment and services for enjoying the outdoors.

The Local Area. Wiesbaden is the capital of the German state of Hesse, which contains Frankfurt, Darmstadt, Offenbach, Hanau, and a dozen smaller cities that cluster together in a complex of industry, commerce, and culture. Nevertheless, one-quarter of the area is covered in woods and parks. Wiesbaden itself is located between the Taunus Mountains and the Rhine River, in the Rheingau wine-producing area, and is frequently the center of festivals and celebrations. Many Roman archeological sites are situated in and around Wiesbaden, and some of the Rhein's most picturesque castles are nearby, along the Rhine River.

For more information write to: HQ 221st BSB, Public Affairs Office, Unit 29623, APO AE 09096.

WILDFLECKEN COMMUNITY AND TRAINING AREA

In July 1993 the Department of Defense announced that as part of its plan to reduce troop strength in Europe to 100,000 by 30 September 1996, six sites at Wildflecken would be returned to Germany, among them Camp Wildflecken, the family housing area, and the training range.

Wildflecken is a remote community located in the wonderful Rhoen Mountains, a great place for hiking in summer and skiing in winter. The U.S. military community even has its own ski area with ski rental and a ski hut.

History. The Wildflecken camp was established in 1937, when the German government expropriated 15,000 acres to construct a training area. The construction forced the residents of eight villages to abandon their homes. During World War II it served as the third largest training camp for the Wehrmacht. American forces reached Wildflecken in 1945, and in 1951 it became a refugee camp under the direction of the International Refugee Organization and later the United Nations Relief and Rehabilitation Administration. The Polish cemetery behind the middle/elementary school is a sad reminder today of the hardships those people were forced to endure in the immediate post-war years.

In 1951 the U.S. Army took over the post and developed it into a training area for the U.S. forces. Today Wildflecken consists of 17,000 acres in the Rhoen Mountains.

Housing and Schools. Wildflecken has approximately 460 on-post housing units and another 474 situated off post. The community has several child-care facilities, a kindergarten, and an elementary/middle school. The education center offers several college-level courses from various American universities.

Personal Services. The closest hospital is at Wurzburg, fifty miles away. The community itself has a dispensary/dental clinic that was constructed in 1991.

Wildflecken has a commissary, a post exchange, various eating places, a commissary annex, a sight and sound store, Top of the Rock Club, Rhoen View Community Club, and a four-seasons/toy store.

Recreation. Recreation facilities include a gymnasium, a baseball/softball field, a tennis court, a photo lab, a ceramics-leather and woodcraft shop, a library, and a movie theater.

The Local Area. The climate in the Wildflecken region varies sharply with the seasons: Winter months are generally cold with quite a bit of snow and temperatures occasionally dip into the teens. Summers are generally mild, with temperatures sometimes rising into the eighties but usually staying in the lower seventies.

The first attempt to establish a settlement in the Wildflecken area occurred in the year 1000 A.D., when Emperor Otto III presented the southern Rhoen region to the prince-bishop of Wurzburg. Two later attempts to build settlements failed when they were destroyed by fire. Present-day Wildflecken was founded in 1524; the citizens of the newly established village paid their first taxes in 1544.

During the Thirty Years War (1618–48) the Bischofsheim-Gersfeld-Wildflecken area was a strategic location. The Swedish forces withdrew into the Rhoen Mountains in 1634, after their defeat by imperial troops at Nordlingen. Remains of the Swedish fortifications can still be seen all across the area.

In 1866 the former Swedish line of defense was used as a convenient boundary between Bavaria and Prussia (Hesse). Today the town boasts a population of around 5,000, most of whom work for the U.S. Army and various local firms.

For more information write to: Public Affairs Office, USMCA Wildflecken, APO AE 09026-0027.

ZWEIBRUCKEN MILITARY COMMUNITY

Zweibrucken Air Base was closed in September 1991, and in January 1992 the Army announced it was also closing Kreuzberg Kaserne.

GREECE

Air Force

HELLENIKON AIR BASE

After more than twenty years of operation, Hellenikon Air Base was closed in June 1991.

IRAKLION AIR STATION, CRETE

Civilization began in Crete 2,500 years before Christ, at a time when most of the rest of Europe was still in a state of barbarism. Since that time many foreigners have come to Crete. First were the Dorians (early Greeks), then the Romans in 66 B.C., followed in turn by the Byzantines, the Arabs, the Venetians, the Turks, and eventually, in 1941, the Germans, who chose the dangerous but novel method of parachuting onto the island.

History. The U.S. Air Force was a latecomer (but much more welcome than most of the visitors mentioned above) to Crete. Iraklion Air Station was established in October 1954 to provide communications service to Air Force elements throughout the area. Today it is home to the 7276th Air Base Group, which provides administrative and logistical support to the 6931st Electronic Security Squadron, which in turn provides rapid relay and secure communications for the United States and its allies in the Mediterranean area.

Housing and Schools. There are 180 prefabricated (duplex and fourplex) units of family quarters available at Iraklion. Designated key personnel are given priority for these quarters, and all others are assigned according to date of application, rank, and date of rank. The waiting period for housing usually runs six months to one year. Some transient accommodations are available on base for incoming families.

The cost of rent for two- and three-bedroom apartments off base runs from $225 to $450 per month.

On-base schooling for dependent children is conducted in a combined elementary-junior high complex. Students in grades eleven and twelve attend Department of Defense schools elsewhere in Europe. A child-care center and a preschool are also available at the station. College courses are offered on the station through the University of Maryland, City Colleges of Chicago, and Troy State University.

Personal Services. Medical care is provided by the USAF hospital in Iraklion. Dental care is available for dependents on a space-available basis. Medical and dental services that cannot be provided at Iraklion are available at U.S. forces facilities in Germany. Other personal services include a commissary and base exchange store and a number of other retail facilities such as a foodland, a four-seasons store, a Stars and Stripes bookstore, a liquor store, and a Baskin Robbins ice cream parlor.

Recreation. Iraklion has plenty to offer in the way of recreation, including the Dag Hammarskjold Theater; a consolidated open mess; a ten-lane bowling center; an amateur theater; a recreation center; wood, auto, and ceramics hobby shops; and a 14,000-volume library. Outdoor recreation includes a marina equipped with docking facilities, a sand beach with space for ten camp sites located within only a five-minute walk of the base, and intramural sports and athletics.

The Local Area. The climate on Crete is hot and dry in the summer and mild but wet in the winter. Crete is 160 miles long and varies in width from 7 to 35 miles. The terrain is rugged and mountainous with deep snow in the higher elevations. The highest peak is Mount Ida, which stands over 8,000 feet.

The station is located ten miles east of the seaport of Iraklion (population about 100,000), on the north, or Aegean Sea, coast of the island. The base shuttle makes ten round trips to Iraklion every day. The trips take about thirty minutes, over very narrow and winding roads.

Although Crete is small, nobody can see all of it in one day. But since most travel distances are short, mopeds are a popular method of getting about on the island and are available for purchase through the base exchange. As hunting is restricted to rabbit and fowl during designated seasons, and as only shotguns and smooth-bore muskets are allowed on the island, military personnel are discouraged from bringing their own weapons with them. Besides, hunting licenses are very expensive.

Iraklion is an ancient city with miles of picturesque streets ideal for wandering about and photographing. The city has a fine archeological museum, and to the south lie the ruins of the Minoan palace of Phaestos and the ancient Roman city of Gortys. West of Iraklion is the medieval city of Rethimnon and the port of Souda.

For more information write to: Public Affairs Office, 7276 Air Base Group, APO AE 09846.

Navy

NEA MAKRI NAVAL COMMUNICATIONS STATION

The Nea Makri Naval Communications Station has been returned to the Greek government.

GUAM

Air Force

ANDERSEN AIR FORCE BASE

At the site of the old 8th Air Force headquarters building at Andersen Air Force Base is the final resting place for "Old 100," one of the last B-52 aircraft to bomb North Vietnam and a machine that flew over 5,000 hours in the air war over Southeast Asia. The bomber gets its nickname from its tail number, 55-0100. Old 100 is part of the Arc Light Memorial at Andersen, dedicated to the seventy-five men who lost their lives flying B-52 missions against the Communist forces in Vietnam.

History. Named in honor of Brig. Gen. James Roy Andersen, who was lost at sea in a flight that originated on Guam in February 1945, the base today is home to the 633rd Air Base Wing of the Pacific Air Forces, which is responsible for host support of all assigned and tenant units, including the 13th Air Force, the 605th Airlift Support Squadron (AMC), and the U.S. Navy's Fleet Logistics Support (VRC-50) Squadron.

Housing and Schools. There are 1,452 family quarters at Andersen in the Fleming Heights, Capehart, Roberts Terrace, and Wilson Homes housing areas. There are also 300 units at the Andersen South area.

Dependents education is handled through the government of Guam's department of education. The Andersen child-development center offers day-care and preschool services for children at reasonable rates. Adult on-base education is offered by the Universities of Guam, Oklahoma, Maryland, and Southern California and through Central Texas College. Off-base education is available at the University of Guam and Guam Community College.

Personal Services. The USAF clinic at Andersen provides outpatient care along with a variety of medical services. Specialty and inpatient services are available at the U.S. Naval Regional Medical Center, Agana, about forty-five minutes south of Andersen.

The base exchange at Andersen offers a number of facilities including a camera shop, a furniture mart, an audio center, a china shop, a four-seasons shop, a toy store, and a garage. A number of exchange food services are operated on base, including the Latte Stone Burger Bar and the Hafa Adai Inn, which is open twenty-four hours a day in the passenger terminal. Andersen also has a newly renovated and expanded commissary.

Recreation. Recreational facilities include an auto hobby shop, a theater, a twelve-lane bowling center, a youth center, a base gymnasium, a library, arts and crafts shops, and a Baskin Robbins ice cream parlor in the plaza shopping mall.

Outdoor recreation facilities include the Palm Tree Golf Course, an eighteen-hole, 13,800-yard course; two swimming pools; and four beaches—Tarague, Scuba, C.E., and Pati Point. At Tarague Beach a natural cave has been set aside for use by picnickers, and the other beaches have acres for picnicking and leisure time activities, which include camping, hiking, shell gathering, fishing, swimming, snorkeling, and scuba diving.

Andersen is located at the north end of the island of Guam.

For more information write to: Public Affairs Office, 633rd Air Base Wing, Unit 14003, Box 25, APO AP 96543-5000.

Navy

U.S. NAVAL FORCES

Guam is 205 square miles of lush and rugged hills, colorful reefs, luxuriant waterfalls, warm blue waters, and sandy beaches inhabited by some of the most beautiful and friendly people on earth. It is also sometimes referred to as being in the middle of nowhere, 6,000 miles west of San Francisco, 3,340 miles beyond Honolulu, and 1,500 miles east of Manila, in the northwest corner of three million square miles of ocean expanse dotted with the islands of Micronesia.

History. The U.S. Navy first came to Guam in 1898, when Capt. Henry Glass captured the island by firing a volley over the rooftops of Agana from the USS *Charleston.* For many years thereafter the island was administered by the U.S. Navy until 1950, when it became an organized unincorporated territory of the United States. Today the citizens of the territory elect their own governor and send a delegate to the U.S. Congress.

More than 7,300 naval personnel are stationed on Guam, assigned to a number of commands. West of Agana, the capital city, overlooking Apra Harbor, is Commander, U.S. Naval Forces Marianas, who provides support to the operating forces of the U.S. Navy and shore facilities on Guam, Australia, and New Zealand. Co-located with Guam International Airport, in the middle of the island, is the U.S. naval air station. The Naval Computer and Telecommunications Area Master Station Western Pacific (NCTAMS) occupies about 4,800 acres of land on the northwest side of the island and is home for 1,200 naval personnel. In the south-central part of the island, isolated from populated areas, is the U.S. Naval Magazine Guam (NAVMAG), sitting upon 8,800 acres. Other commands include the naval regional medical center, the naval station, the Marine barracks, the naval supply depot, and a ship repair facility.

Housing and Schools. U.S. government housing is available to Navy personnel in sixteen areas throughout the island. The quarters are built in a number of styles. The housing referral office also maintains a listing of approved off-base apartments available for rent.

Dependents education is carried out in the Guamanian public school system. Location of schools attended is determined by the housing area in which the children live. Child-care and nursery facilities are available at NAS, NCTAMS, and the naval hospital. Adult education is carried on through the Navy Campus, and college classes off base may be attended at either the University of Guam or Guam Community College, both of which are located on the eastern coast of the island in the village of Mangilao.

Personal Services. Medical care is provided by the naval hospital in Agana Heights. The hospital operates four dispensaries around the island.

Navy exchange and commissary facilities on the island are modern and well stocked. All stations have a retail store and concessions, which range from a Baskin Robbins to watch-repair shops. The NAVSTA commissary is well stocked and carries almost 3,800 line items. Meat items from the United States, Australia, and New Zealand are available for purchase there.

Recreation. The recreational facilities for service personnel on Guam are among the best offered anywhere. The Nimitz Golf Course, located at the naval air station, is an eighteen-hole championship course. Four bowling centers, seven swimming pools, six beaches and picnic areas, twenty-eight tennis courts, three hobby centers, and gymnasiums are available to military personnel on the island.

The Local Area. Guam has a tropical climate with annual temperatures averaging between 75° F. and 85° F. About eighty-five inches of rain fall on the island in a year. March is the driest month, with about two and one-half inches of precipitation. Typhoons sometimes come ashore on Guam. The worst in recent times was Karen, in 1962. Karen carried maximum winds of 150 knots, but Pamela, in 1976, reached winds of 120 knots. The island is about thirty miles long. At its narrowest point it is about four miles across. At its widest, it is about twelve miles.

The highest point of Guam is Mount Lamlam in the south, which soars to an elevation of 1,334 feet. The northern part of the island reaches an elevation of 600 feet at Ritidian Point, which is a limestone plateau about eight miles across. Today approximately 120,000 people live on Guam.

Europeans first came to Guam in 1531, when explorer Ferdinand Magellan claimed the island for Spain, although Spanish colonists did not actually take possession until 1668. The Spanish conquered the island by killing off most of the native Chamorros men and marrying their women. Today the local population shows a strong mixture of Filipino and Mexican-Spanish intermarriage.

For more information write to: Public Affairs Office, Commander, U.S. Naval Forces Marianas, PSC 489 Box 10, FPO AP 56536-0051.

ICELAND

Navy

KEFLAVIK NAVAL AIR STATION

Iceland is known as the "Land of Fire and Ice." Mount Hekla, the largest of Iceland's volcanoes, was once believed to be the mouth of Hell; its last eruption occurred on 17 August 1980. In contrast to this, 13 percent of Iceland is still covered by glacial ice, including Vatnajokull, larger than all of Europe's glaciers combined.

History. American forces first came to Iceland during World War II, but after the war they departed, and an arrangement was made with the Icelandic government so that U.S. planes could be refueled at Keflavik Airport. The U.S. military role expanded in Iceland during the fifties, and in 1961 the Navy assumed host command status from the Air Force. Today Keflavik Naval Air Station (NAS) provides services and materiel in support of the 3,200 military personnel and 2,500 family members of the Navy and other services in Iceland.

There are over 900 family housing units on the station. A well-furnished Navy Lodge is also available, with 31 rooms that can be reserved for up to fourteen days, but because the Icelandic government requires all personnel to live on base, space there is very tight.

Dependents schooling, kindergarten through high school, is provided on the base. Adult education courses, through the Navy campus, include instruction from the University of Maryland, City Colleges of Chicago, and Webster University.

Personal Services. Medical and dental care are provided by a station hospital and a dental clinic. Medical and dental treatment are also available in Reykjavik and

Keflavik, and personnel requiring specialty care and hospitalization are sometimes evacuated to hospitals in the United States.

A Navy exchange, a commissary, a mini mart, a service station, and a cafeteria are available at the station.

Recreation. Recreation facilities include a 500-seat movie theater, a gymnasium, a pool, an eighteen-lane bowling alley, a community center, and various hobby and craft shops. The Hvitarbakki Lodge, a recreation facility leased by the Navy in the Borgarfjordur Valley, about 100 miles northeast of Keflavik, provides camping, lodging, swimming, horseback riding, hunting, and fishing.

The Local Area. Although its northern tip nearly touches the Arctic Circle, Iceland's climate is moderated by a current of the Gulf Stream. But Keflavik's exposed position, surrounded by ocean on three sides, results in rainy, windy, cloudy winters and cool, windy, cloudy summers. Temperatures average 32° F. in January and only 52° F. in August! Prolonged snow rarely occurs at Keflavik. During the months from May to July the sun never sets, which permits extensive outdoor activities during that time.

Civilian clothing is required off base.

Eighty percent of Iceland is uninhabited, and of the island's 260,000 people, fully 90 percent of them live in towns and cities. Icelanders, with a per capita income of $15,000, enjoy one of the highest standards of living in Europe, so buying things off base can be expensive. Reykjavik, the capital of the Republic of Iceland, is its cultural and population center, with a total of 100,000 inhabitants. Icelanders are very independent and well-educated people. In fact, more books are published per capita in Iceland than in any other country in the world. Iceland has the oldest existing parliament in the world, the Althing, which was established in 930 A.D. Norse influence is strong in Iceland, and schoolchildren today can read ancient Norse sagas as they were originally written, because their language has changed very little in the past 1,000 years.

For more information write to: Commander, Iceland Defense Force, PSC 1003, Box 1, FPO AE 09728-0301.

ITALY

Air Force

AVIANO AIR BASE

Aviano Air Base is located in the extreme northeast corner of Italy, at the foot of the Pre-Alps. It is in a beautiful setting with excellent recreation and travel opportunities.

History. Aeroporto Pagliana e Gori was established in 1911 as Aviano Airfield. During World War II the Germans used the base, and the USAF came there in 1954. Today it is the home of the 40th Tactical Group (USAFE), which has 2,000 military personnel, 3,000 dependents, and more than 600 civilian employees. In addition, the 40th Group controls the activities at Rimini, where there are about 100 USAF personnel, and at Ghedi Air Base in the Po Valley. They also control an ammunition supply squadron at Camp Darby.

Housing and Schools. There is no on-base family housing at Aviano. All single and unaccompanied officers also live off the base. Generally, newly arrived personnel find housing within forty-five days of their arrival, and most live within fifteen miles of the flight line.

Dependents schooling is conducted in two American elementary schools and the Aviano High School. A child-care center is also available at the base. The Aviano education center offers college courses from the City Colleges of Chicago and the University of Maryland.

Medical services are provided by the USAF Clinic Aviano, where only routine medical and dental treatment are available. Patients with serious conditions are referred to hospitals at Vicenza, nearby Pordenone, or Germany.

In 1979, a base exchange opened with 13,000 square feet of display space. The commissary, with 6,500 square feet of space and more than 2,800 line items for sale, is adequate for the population served. In January 1980 a foodland was opened, which includes four-seasons and toy stores. There is also a consolidated open mess that serves both officers and enlisted personnel, and the base has a liquor store as well.

Recreation. Recreational facilities include a base gymnasium; a nine-hole golf course; an outdoor, Olympic-size swimming pool; a twelve-lane bowling center; a sports center where a wide variety of sporting, camping, backpacking, and ski equipment can be rented; and a fully equipped recreation center. There are also a wood and an auto hobby shop.

The Local Area. The weather in this part of Italy is generally cold, foggy, and wet in winter and moderate the rest of the year, with four distinct seasons.

Aviano is an agricultural town with a population of over 8,000. The base areas nestle at the foot of the Alps, and Mount Cavallo, the highest peak, looms 7,000 feet above the village. Southward the terrain flattens out. The city of Pordenone, provincial capital, is eight miles south of the flight-line area and inhabited by about 50,000 people. The closest major city, Udine, is thirty miles east. Udine is an alpine city, and the Germanic influence is very strong there. Venice, on the Adriatic Sea, is only fifty miles to the southwest. While most Americans can only dream of spending a weekend in Venice, airmen at Aviano can spend every weekend of their tour there, dreaming about being back home in Indiana.

For more information write to: Public Affairs Office, 40th TACG (USAFE), APO AE 09601.

SAN VITO DEI NORMANNI AIR STATION

San Vito Dei Normanni Air Station was closed in September 1993.

Navy

LA MADDALENA NAVAL BASE

La Maddalena is a small island that sits just off the north coast of the island of Sardinia (or *Sardegna*, in Italian). La Maddalena is actually the largest island in an archipelago of seven islands and some fourteen islets. The island is a tourist resort with a permanent population of 14,000 (of which 2,300 are Navy personnel, DoD employees, and their dependents). During the tourist season, La Maddalena's population swells to as many as 40,000 people. But Navy personnel get the benefits of living in a tourist attraction year-round, absolutely free.

On the southern side of La Maddalena is the rocky and uncultivated island of Santo Stefano, where there is a NATO facility that is the home port of the U.S. Navy submarine tender USS *Simon Lake*, aboard which Commander Submarine

Squadron 22 is embarked. The U.S. Navy Support Office is also located on the island of La Maddalena.

Housing and Schools. Government housing is very tight at La Maddalena, with 164 units available, most of which are allotted to enlisted personnel. Cost of local rental housing varies between $600 and $1,200 a month. Bachelor housing consists of two BEQs, one in La Maddalena and the other on Santo Stefano. There are no transient accommodations.

Dependents schools at La Maddalena operate classes for kindergarten through eighth grade. High school students attend an American school in England. Limited nursery and day-care facilities are available at La Maddalena. Limited off-duty adult education is provided by the University of Maryland.

Personal Services. Medical and dental facilities are limited. The clinic is staffed by two family practice medical officers, two nurses, a dental officer, three dental technicians, one clinical social worker, and ten hospital corpsmen. More extensive care is available at the Naval Regional Medical Center in Naples. La Maddalena is considered an isolated station, and personnel with medical conditions cannot be sent there.

A combination commissary and Navy exchange facility is housed on the island of La Maddalena.

Recreation. Navy facilities are located primarily on the island of Santo Stefano and La Maddalena, with a recreation center in the town of Palau, the nearest city to the base on the northern Sardinian mainland. On La Maddalena there are limited athletic facilities and a recreation center, a hobby and craft shop, a marina, and a movie theater.

The Local Area. The local area is an ideal location for most water sports, including swimming, sailing, boating, wind surfing, diving, and fishing. There are many beautiful beaches with crystal-clear water in the La Maddalena and northern Sardinia area. La Maddalena may be reached from the port city of Palau by a twenty-minute ferry ride.

The climate on Sardinia offers hot and dry summers and cool winters. The island itself, the second largest in the Mediterranean, averages more than 2,000 hours of sunshine per year, but winds are strong and constant there. There are the northwesterly wind known as the *maestrale*, the *tramontana* from the north, the *scirocco* from the southeast, and the *ponente* from the west. The *maestrale* is violent in the winter and actually bends trees toward the southeast. The *scirocco* is a warm, humid wind that sometimes brings dust from North Africa.

La Maddalena as an inhabited island has a history stretching back only to 1767, but Sardinia, an autonomous province of Italy, has been inhabited for thousands of years. An ancient people who lived on the island built a number of tombs and other structures that are still standing. The Phoenicians began colonizing the island in 900 to 800 B.C., and since then the area has seen the Carthaginians, the Romans, the Pisans, the Genovese, the Aragonese, and the French.

For more information write to: Public Affairs, Naval Support Office, PSC 816, FPO AE 09612.

SIGONELLA NAVAL AIR STATION

Sicily is the largest island in the Mediterranean, with nearly five million inhabitants and more than 9,900 square miles of land, which makes it about the size of the state of Maryland. A large number of Sicilians make their living farming and observe the customs and traditions of their forefathers, and although many Americans have their roots in Sicily, it's still a very different country.

History. Sigonella bills itself as the "Fastest Growing Naval Air Station in the World." Sigonella and its many tenant commands have a population of over 6,200 military personnel, civilian employees, and their dependents. Over 350 personnel deploy to Sigonella with patrol squadrons that come to the base on six-month rotations. In addition, VRC-40, a cargo squadron that supports a deployed carrier battle group, rotates almost 100 personnel to Sigonella with each battle group. Sigonella's airfield and port liaison operations have greatly increased over the past years, and the station is now an important staging and resupply point for the U.S. military and NATO forces in the Mediterranean.

There are two main parts to the station: NAS I, the support base, and NAS II, the airfield, eight miles away. Sigonella itself is located about ten miles southwest of Catania, Sicily.

Housing and Schools. On-station housing consists of about 120 units for military families plus 205 units that are leased near NAS I, and another 104 leased at Costanzo, just north of the city of Catania.

An elementary school/junior-senior high and an education center are located in the NAS I area.

Personal Services. Medical and dental care are provided by a new, full-service hospital.

The Navy exchange offers a limited range of services and merchandise, which includes a retail store, a food-service department with two cafeterias, a beverage store, and some personal services such as barber and beauty shops. The commissary supplies about 2,300 items. About 16,000 pounds of frozen meats are purchased there each month, most of which are shipped in from Iceland.

Recreation. Recreation facilities include tennis courts, a gymnasium, a swimming pool, a ten-lane bowling alley, a movie theater, and a library at NAS I. At NAS II are an auto hobby shop, a gymnasium, athletic fields, four tennis courts, a weight-lifting room, and an Olympic-size swimming pool and diving pool.

The Local Area. During the winter and early spring, skiing can be enjoyed on the slopes of nearby Mount Etna.

The climate in the Sigonella region is similar to that of the Gulf Coast but without the high humidity. The temperatures during the coldest month, January, average between 40° F. and 50° F. During the warmest months the temperatures sometimes exceed 100° F. when the hot *scirocco* winds blow in from the African desert. The summer months are dry and dusty, and rain occurs seasonally from October through February.

This beautiful coastal area offers sun, azure seas, and white, sandy beaches.

For more information write to: Public Affairs Office, U.S. NAS Sigonella, PSC 812, FPO AE 09627.

U.S. NAVAL SUPPORT ACTIVITY, NAPLES

The Naval Support Activity (NSA), Naples, provides administrative and logistic support to U.S. personnel of NATO commands in the Naples area and to the forces of the 6th Fleet. The U.S. community in Naples consists of approximately 10,000 people, including 2,000 Navy personnel and their dependents at the coastal town of Gaeta, about sixty miles north of Naples; 6th Fleet activities encompass 40 ships, 175 aircraft, and 21,000 other personnel. Altogether, NSA is responsible for more than 96 activities that range from support of the U.S. Embassy in Rome to Monte Vergine, a radio relay site seventy miles north of NSA, high in the mountains.

Housing and Schools. There is little family housing for officers in Naples, and about one-half the enlisted personnel live in government-leased apartments, so most Americans assigned there rent apartments or villas on the local economy. Enlisted housing is located at Coppola Pinetamare, about sixteen miles north of NSA, on the beach. A Navy Lodge opened there in 1990. Temporary-lodging allowance is available while looking for permanent accommodations. A housing referral office is available to help.

The Department of Defense operates three American schools in the area. One elementary school is in Pinetamare, and the junior high/high school is next to the NSA, at the Agnano Compound; another elementary school is operated at Gaeta. High school students living in Gaeta attend classes at Naples, where they are bused daily. Child-development centers are also available at Naples and Gaeta. The tri-service education center at the Allied Forces Southern Europe (AFSOUTH) compound, in Bagnoli (a short distance from the NSA) offers undergraduate and graduate courses.

Personal Services. Medical care at Naples is provided by the naval hospital located two blocks from the NSA compound. Personnel having complex problems or in need of prolonged hospitalization are evacuated to medical facilities in Germany or the United States. Dental care for dependents is available at the U.S. naval dental clinic, located on the top deck of the hospital building. Priority for treatment is given to members of the visiting operating forces and shore-based active-duty military personnel. Further dependent dental care is available at the Pinetamare Dental Clinic, and a smaller dental clinic is located at the high school.

The main Navy exchange is located at the NSA compound and offers a wide selection of concessions, including a Wendy's, a Baskin Robbins, a snack bar, and a family-style restaurant. A commissary store is situated next to the exchange. The AFSOUTH compound also offers a variety of shopping outlets for military personnel.

Recreation. Recreation facilities in the area are excellent. The ninety-six-acre Admiral Carney Recreation Park, on the outskirts of Naples, just five miles from the NSA, is a sports complex offering baseball/softball diamonds, tennis courts, football/soccer fields, volleyball and basketball courts, an Olympic-size swimming pool, a fitness trail, a miniature golf course, picnic and camping areas, a snack bar, and a convenience store. A nine-hole golf course is available at Carney Park.

NSA also operates a recreation center at Capodichino, and there are recreational facilities at the NSA compound itself, including an indoor-outdoor sports complex, a theater, and an enlisted club. Located at AFSOUTH are a gymnasium with locker space for 200 persons, a theater, a bowling alley, officers and enlisted clubs, and an Olympic-size swimming pool. The AFSOUTH beach, at Licola, just to the south of the enlisted housing area, has 150 cabañas, a cafeteria-style restaurant, and a 300-yard swimming beach on the Mediterranean Sea.

The Local Area. The climate in the Naples area is Mediterranean—mild but with wet winters and warm and dry summers. The average rainfall in Naples between October and January is about 4.5 inches, with the driest month being July.

The equable climate promotes outdoor activities and tourism in the south of Italy. Naples sits on the Gulf of Naples, and just to the south of the city are Mount Vesuvius and the excavated ruins of the Roman cities of Herculaneum and Pompeii, which were buried by the volcano when it erupted in 79 A.D. Farther south are Sorrento and the Isle of Capri, which are reached by a coastal roadway that offers one of the most breathtaking drives in Europe. The NSA special services office conducts frequent short tours to local spots, and American Express offers extended tours to places like Spain, Greece, the Holy Land, Rome, the north of Italy, Austria, and Switzerland. Even Germany is accessible by automobile from Naples.

For more information write to: Public Affairs Office, PSC 810, Box 40, FPO AE 09619-1000.

JAPAN

Air Force

MISAWA AIR BASE

What do the cities of Misawa, Japan, and Wenatchee, Washington, have in common? Almost nothing, but there is a link. The first nonstop flight across the Pacific originated at Misawa in October 1931 when American pilots Clyde Pangborn and Hugh Nerndon flew from Misawa to Wenatchee in forty-one hours and ten minutes. The Misawans are proud of this accomplishment, and today a memorial to the American fliers stands at Sabishiro Beach, near the spot where the aircraft, *Miss Veedol*, took off on its historic flight.

History. Built in 1942 as an air facility for the Japanese Naval Air Force, Misawa first saw Americans on 15 September 1945. Today the base is home to the 432nd Fighter Wing, which supports a base population of more than 15,000. There are also 2,000 members of the Japan Air Self-Defense Force at the base. The 432nd provides tactical airpower in both air-to-air and air-to-ground missions in support of U.S. forces and our allies throughout the Pacific theater. It performs these roles with two squadrons of F-16 C/D aircraft and MH60G helicopters for day- and night-rescue operations.

Housing and Schools. On-base family housing consists of over 2,000 four- and three-bedroom units and commodity credit housing built by the Japanese government in the mid-1950s and consisting of twenty-six apartment buildings with eight living units per building. There are sixteen temporary family quarters and 100 transient quarters on the base.

Misawa has both an elementary school and a high school, which enroll an average of 1,900 students. Preschool facilities are also available. Adult education is provided through the base education center and consists of college courses offered by the University of Maryland, Central Texas College, and the University of Oklahoma.

Personal Services. Misawa has a state-of-the-art hospital scheduled for completion in 1994. The current facility provides both inpatient and outpatient services. Dental service is available to all members of the military community, including dependents.

The base offers an excellent exchange and commissary store. The exchange also operates a number of concessions, including a service station and a personal services arcade as well as several fast-food restaurants.

Recreation. Recreation facilities include an eighteen-hole golf course; a twenty-six-lane bowling center; a base gymnasium; a base beach on Lake Ogawara; and a ski lodge with a slope and tow, located near Lake Ogawara. There are also arts and crafts centers, a rod and gun club, a recreation supply office that offers equipment for checkout, and a truck and car rental service.

The Local Area. Misawa is located on the north tip of Honshu Island (the main island of Japan), along the Pacific coast, not far from the city of Aomori. Although archeological evidence points to human inhabitation of the area more than 8,000 years ago, Misawa Hamlet was founded under the jurisdiction of Momoishi Village in 1872 and became an independent village in 1879. The area is noted for its horse breeding: In 1371, the Nambu Clan established nine horse farms in the area, and eventually between 8,000 and 10,000 animals were being bred there each year between the months of April and October.

Since the 1940s, the population of Misawa has grown from about 1,200 to more than 40,000.

This part of Japan has four distinct seasons and in this it is similar to the midwestern region of the United States. The major difference is that the area averages 121 inches of snow a year. The winters there are cold, with the temperatures averaging between 20° F. and 30° F.

For more information write to: Public Affairs Office, HQ, 432nd FW, APO AP 96319-5000.

YOKOTA AIR BASE

To virtually everyone in the western world, Mount Fuji *is* Japan. Indeed, at more than 12,000 feet, Mount Fuji dominates the horizon from Yokota and is only a two-hour drive from the base. Downtown Tokyo is only twenty-four miles from Yokota. With an 11,000-foot runway, the base serves as a layover point for Air Mobility Command flights originating throughout the Far East. The aerial view of Tokyo and Mount Fuji has proven unforgettable for thousands of U.S. servicemembers and their families over the years.

History. Yokota Air Base was originally known as Tama Army Air Field, a

Japanese base that opened in 1939. The Occupation Forces changed the name to Yokota after a small village located at the northeast corner of the base in August 1945. Today Yokota is home for the 5th Air Force, whose tactical fighter and reconnaissance squadrons support our defense treaties with Japan. The base is also headquarters for a number of other units, including the host wing, the 374th Airlift Wing, the 316th Airlift Support Group, and Headquarters, U.S. Forces, Japan. Yokota has a U.S. military population of 4,500 and their 5,300 family members plus more than 7,000 civilian employees.

Housing and Schools. There are about 2,200 units of family housing at Yokota. The average wait for on-base housing is from 90 to 180 days. Temporary lodging is also available for about 296 family members. Off-base rentals are extremely expensive in Japan. A two-bedroom apartment will cost $1,000 a month not including utilities, which average $300 per month.

Yokota has two elementary schools (Yokota East and Yokota West) and a high school. There are also a variety of child-development services available at the base. On-base college courses are available from the University of Maryland, Central Texas College, the University of Oklahoma, Troy State University, and Chapman College.

Personal Services. Among the personal support facilities available at Yokota is an Air Force hospital, a modern medical facility operated by the 374th Medical Group. The commissary store offers shoppers more than 6,000 line items displayed in over 20,000 square feet of shopping space. The JAAX (Japan Area Exchange) also offers Yokota shoppers an excellent facility with well-stocked shelves and many bargains. Concessions available at Yokota include an audio-photo center, a furniture mart, a four-seasons store, a Mexican restaurant, an ice cream parlor, a Burger King, a cookie shop, two cafeterias, three snack bars, a full-service garage, and many other facilities.

Recreation. Yokota boasts some of the best recreational facilities in the Far East. There are the Tomodachi Lanes, a thirty-two-lane bowling center; a nine-hole, par-three golf complex; officers and enlisted clubs; craft and hobby centers; and a gymnasium. Added to all of this is the unique Tama Hills Recreation Area, a picnic and camping ground about fifteen miles southeast of Yokota. Another delightful aspect of duty at Yokota is that as a major aerial port, flights are available there for trips to many other places in the Far East.

The Local Area. Yokota is bordered by small cities that make up part of the suburban environment of Tokyo in an area known as the Kanto Plain. The city of Fussa, considered the Yokota Air Base City, has enjoyed an excellent relationship with the base down through the years. Tokyo, with all the sights and excitement of one of the largest and most modern cities in the world, is only a two-hour trip from the base. There are many other attractions as well, such as the Imperial Palace and famous shrines.

For more information write to: Public Affairs Office, HQ 374th Airlift Wing (PACAF), APO AP 96328-0000.

Army

CAMP ZAMA

In both 1992 and 1993 Camp Zama was named the Army Communities of Excellence (Overseas) runner-up. The installation earned this honor because its commanders are dedicated to the military personnel who live there, their families, and the base's civilian workforce.

History. U.S. troops first came to what is now Camp Zama on 5 September 1945, when one battalion of the 1st Cavalry Division entered Sobudai, the Japanese equivalent of West Point, which had been moved there in 1937. In 1950 Headquarters, U.S. Army, Japan, moved to the site and has remained there ever since. The Commander, USARJ, commands all assigned U.S. Army forces in Japan and is responsible for logistical support to Army and U.S. government agencies in Japan, as well as the maintenance of war reserves and stocks for contingencies. About 1,900 Army personnel are assigned to duty in Japan, about 1,100 at Camp Zama and 800 on Okinawa.

Housing and Schools. Approximately 1,124 sets of family quarters are available to people assigned to Camp Zama, including a high-rise apartment building and 64 town houses that were completed in 1991. These quarters are situated in three areas: Sagamihara Housing Area, Sagami General Depot, and Camp Zama itself. All three are within a short commute from the headquarters. The waiting time for occupancy varies from no wait to as much as eight months. Zama has 90 units for temporary lodging.

Dependents education is conducted at two Department of Defense schools: Zama American High School and Arnn Elementary School. Total enrollment as of spring 1993 was over 1,180 children. The Army academic training division offers resident credit from the University of Maryland, the University of Oklahoma, and Central Texas College.

Personal Services. Adequate medical and dental facilities are provided at the Camp Zama clinic. Specialized medical and surgical care are offered at nearby military facilities. The post exchange offers a broad selection of clothing and electronic equipment. Concessions include a Burger King, a Baskin Robbins ice cream shop, and an Anthony's Pizza.

Recreation. A full range of recreational activities, including an active Army sports program, is offered to personnel living at Zama. In addition, the Far East Network of the Armed Forces Radio and Television Services broadcasts U.S. radio programs and closed-circuit English TV programs. The outdoor recreation program operates a rental center that features camping, hiking, skin diving, and fishing gear and supplies. Tours to Tokyo Disneyland and numerous other Japanese attractions are offered on a regular basis through the base tours office. A new 43,000-square-foot community club offers a formal dining room, three lounges, and a ballroom for the enjoyment of its patrons.

The Local Area. The weather in the Tokyo area is often compared to that of Washington, D.C., with warm, humid summers and rather mild winters. This is not typical of all of Japan, however. In the mountainous areas of Honshu, winters are severe, and on the western slopes of these mountains there is frequently enough snow for long skiing seasons. This part of Japan has a feature that is reminiscent of the American West Coast—in the Tokyo area mild earthquake tremors often can be felt.

Camp Zama is only 40 miles from Tokyo, the world's most populous city. Within its 796 square miles live more than eleven million people. The city is a blend of the East and the West. Within walking distance of the Imperial Palace is the Ginza, one of the best-known shopping centers of the city. Tokyo's modern architecture and public transportation system are the envy of many more-modern American cities.

For more information write to: Chief, Public Affairs Office, HQ USARJ, Unit 45005, APO AP 96343-0054.

Marine Corps

IWAKUNI MARINE CORPS AIR STATION

If you can imagine a Baskin Robbins ice cream parlor coexisting with the graceful and ancient shrines of Japan, nestled among groves of bamboo and pine, you can imagine Iwakuni, Japan, where the very new and the very old manage to get along quite peacefully.

History. The air station at Iwakuni began originally as a Japanese airfield in 1940 and then passed to the U.S. Air Force after passing through the hands of the British, Australian, and New Zealand forces. The Marines came here in 1962, and today Iwakuni is the only Marine Corps base on the mainland of Japan. Iwakuni MCAS is home for Marine Aircraft Group 12's F/A-18 Hornets, A/V8-B Harriers, and support units.

Housing and Schools. There are a variety of government family quarters at Iwakuni, but even so, some families must rent private dwellings on the Japanese economy. There are 300 approved private rentals within a two-mile radius of the station. Rents are from $290 to $700 a month, with utilities ranging from $90 to $264 per month, depending on the size of the house and family. A 48-room temporary lodging facility is available at the station.

The Matthew C. Perry School has an enrollment of approximately 600 dependent children in kindergarten through grade twelve. The station also has a child-care center and preschool facilities. Off-duty education is available through the Joint Education Center and includes college courses from the University of Maryland, Central Texas College, and Troy State University.

Personal Services. Medical care at Iwakuni is provided by a branch medical clinic. Patients requiring extensive hospitalization or specialized care are flown to the naval regional medical center at Yokosuka. General dental treatment, as well as most specialty services, is available for military personnel at Iwakuni, but dependent care is limited.

The station has both an exchange and a commissary store with 10,000 square feet of sales space and over 5,000 brand name items, as well as fresh fruits and vegetables and bread and bakery products. The Marine Corps exchange, besides retail sales, offers a number of concessions, including a cookie shop and an ice cream parlor. An officers club, a staff NCO club, and two enlisted clubs are also available on the station.

Recreation. Recreation facilities include a gymnasium with basketball courts, handball courts, a sauna, and a number of tennis courts. There are also a hobby shop, a tape room, a theater, a nine-hole golf course, a fourteen-lane and a six-lane bowling center, a swimming pool, and a roller rink. In addition, a special services travel bureau offers an easy and quick way for the military or family traveler to arrange travel plans.

The Local Area. Iwakuni lies at the southeasternmost end of the Yamaguchi Prefecture, facing the Inland Sea on the southeast and adjoining Otake City in Hiroshima Prefecture on the north; the Ozu River flows in between. The city is backed by the mountains and its front borders the Inland Sea. The Nishiki River runs through the city of Iwakuni from east to west.

The climate in this part of Japan is wet with plenty of fog in the spring and autumn.

Iwakuni has a population of over 100,000. It is noted for the beautiful cherry trees (over 2,000 of them) that bloom in April.

For more information write to: Public Affairs Office, MCAS Iwakuni, Japan, Unit 35408, FPO AP 96310-5408.

Navy

ATSUGI NAVAL AIR FACILITY

Atsugi personnel rarely venture off base without being heavily armed—with cameras, that is, because the area abounds with so many contrasting views of Japanese culture, traditional and modern, that even the most camera-shy sailor will turn into a shutterbug after a while.

History. The U.S. Navy first came to Atsugi in October 1950, when a team of a dozen Seabees arrived there to renovate the installation after it had been abandoned by the U.S. Army. Atsugi Naval Air Facility was officially commissioned on 1 December 1950. Today it is used jointly by the U.S. Navy and the Japan Maritime Self-Defense Force. The base provides various aviation support functions for tenant and transient commands—for instance, Marine Corps helicopter units that support operations at nearby Camp Fuji. When the USS *Independence* uses nearby Yokusuka as its home port, Atsugi has been host to the embarked air wing, which flies there as the carrier nears its home port.

Housing and Schools. There are 493 sets of family quarters at Atsugi. While there are no guest facilities, the Yokosuka Navy Lodge offers accommodations on a space-available basis.

Children living at Atsugi attend the Shirley Lanham Elementary School at the air facility or Zama American Middle and High School at nearby Camp Zama. A preschool program is also available at the air facility. The Navy Campus provides educational guidance and counseling to active-duty military personnel and their dependents, and courses at the college level are offered on base by the University of Maryland, the University of Oklahoma, and Central Texas College.

Personal Services. Most medical and dental services are available on base through the naval regional medical center branch clinic. Supportive dependent dental care is of the maintenance type only, but a percentage of time is usually available for these services.

The Atsugi Navy exchange offers a broad range of outlets where articles and services may be obtained. These include a main retail store; a mini mart; a furniture mart; a pro golf shop; snack bars; and a personal services arcade, which houses a flower shop, a portrait painter, and other concessions. The exchange also operates a garage that can repair most automobiles. Atsugi's commissary store offers a wide variety of goods such as fresh fruits and vegetables, as well as many stateside products such as frozen, canned, and packaged goods.

There is also a Japanese-American exchange that includes three dining facilities. This exchange, commonly known as the Kosei Center, offers items sold on the Japanese economy at a discount.

Recreation. Recreation facilities at Atsugi include the Gateway enlisted club, the CPO club, and the officers club. The facility's eighteen-hole golf course is used by service personnel from stations throughout the area. The rod and gun club organizes shooting, hunting, fishing, and other outdoor sports and maintains a skeet and trap range for the use of its members.

The Local Area. Atsugi is in nearly the same latitude as Washington, D.C., and has a similar climate. The four seasons are distinct, with warm and humid summers and chilly winters, but snow is rare. Rain is frequent and sometimes very heavy. Atsugi is not in an area of Japan often touched by typhoons, but its closeness to the sea often exposes it to heavy winds that sometimes brew rainstorms that can be quite violent.

For more information write to: Atsugi Family Services Center, PSC 477, Box 32, FPO AP 69306-1232.

FLEET ACTIVITIES, SASEBO

Sasebo has been a naval city since the time in 1888 when, as a lowly lieutenant commander, the famous Admiral Heihachiro Togo—victor over the Russian fleet at the Battle of Tsushima in 1905—visited there.

History. The land parcels around Sasebo Harbor were developed as an Imperial

Japanese Navy Base in 1889, and during World War II ships like the battleship *Musashi* operated from its facilities. U.S. forces first came to Sasebo in September 1945, and Fleet Activities was established there on 30 June 1946. The old Imperial Japanese Navy dockyard is occupied today by SSK, a commercial company and the largest employer in Sasebo.

Today Sasebo supports U.S. naval forces in four principal areas: fuel storage, ordnance storage, ship repair, and fleet liberty. The city of Sasebo with a population of 250,000 is an ideal liberty port, from the Navy's standpoint, with a clean downtown area virtually free of crime and drugs, and many tourist attractions. During 1991, seventy-five ships visited Sasebo to take advantage of its facilities, which can service conventional aircraft carriers as well as nuclear submarines. Sasebo is home to approximately 2,200 active-duty military personnel.

Housing and Schools. There are 546 housing units available at Sasebo, 154 at Main Base and 392 at the Hario Village, about a thirty- to forty-five-minute drive away. Nearly 400 families live at Hario. The Navy runs free bus service between Main Base and the Hario Village complex. A new Navy Lodge opened in 1992.

School facilities for dependent children in kindergarten through twelfth grade are available on base. Approximately 300 children are enrolled in the DoD schools at Sasebo.

Personal Services and Recreation. Medical care is provided by the U.S. naval regional medical center at Yokosuka, which maintains a branch clinic at Sasebo. Hario Village has a gym, a softball field, a golf driving range, a swimming pool, a Navy exchange and commissary, an all-hands club, a post office, a dispensary, a library, a community center, hobby and woodworking shops, and a gas station.

The Local Area. Sasebo is located on the western shore of Kyushu Island and is the second largest city in Nagasaki Prefecture. It is about 800 miles from Tokyo, 120 miles from the Korean peninsula, and 40 miles from Nagasaki. Within a few miles of the base is the Saikai National Sea Park, a marine preserve of more than 1,500 small islands that offers excellent fishing and boating. Other sightseeing havens include the cities of Nagasaki and Fukuoka, and historic Hirado Island, the area in which the novel *Shogun* was based.

The average temperature in Sasebo seldom dips below 42° F., with the hottest months being July and August.

For more information write to: Public Affairs Office, Fleet Activities, Sasebo, PSC 476 Box 1, FPO AP 96322-1100.

FLEET ACTIVITIES, YOKOSUKA

Yokosuka is a city of many faces. For example, only a five-minute walk from the bustling metropolis surrounding Chuo train station is a tranquil seaside park built around the old Imperial battleship *Mikasa*. There are also many small Japanese restaurants where you may buy a beer to go with your dinner, which might include sushi (strips of uncooked fish atop cakes of cold cooked rice), kake soba (plain noodles served in broth), or shabu-shabu (thinly sliced meat served in boiling water).

History. Yokosuka (pronounced "yo-ko-ska") Naval Base laid the keel of its first ship in 1866, and the largest Japanese ship, the *Shinano*, a 68,000-ton aircraft carrier, was launched there in October 1944. It was sunk by a U.S. sub while in trials in Sagami Bay in November 1944, never having launched a plane or fired a shot. The base surrendered on 30 August 1945. Today Yokosuka is the largest U.S. naval shore facility in the Far East, covering approximately 500 acres. The Commander, Fleet Activities, Yokosuka (COMFLEACT), maintains and operates the base for logistic servicing of U.S. naval forces assigned to the western Pacific.

Housing and Schools. Yokosuka has housing facilities for 1,286 families at the station itself. Additional housing is available for 405 families in the Negishi Housing Area, Yokohama, seventeen miles north of the base. About 1,900 families live off base in private rental units. The Navy Lodge has 127 rooms available for transients and guests.

There are two elementary schools, Sullivan's Elementary at Yokosuka and Byrd at Negishi. Nile C. Kinnick High School at Yokosuka draws students from Yokosuka and Negishi. The fleet Navy Campus provides college courses from Central Texas College, the University of Maryland, and Chapman College.

Personal Services. Medical care is provided by Yokosuka U.S. Naval Hospital, a five-story, 110-bed facility. The Yokosuka U.S. Naval Dental Clinic provides routine dental care on a space-available basis for command-sponsored dependents.

The Navy Resale Activity has an exchange and commissary in Yokosuka and a smaller Navy exchange/commissary facility in Negishi. The exchanges offer a department-store selection, and the commissaries stock what you would expect in a medium-size stateside grocery store. Other major exchange services include a contract taxi service, several fast-food emporiums (including a Pizza Inn and a McDonald's), a variety of restaurants, home appliance and car rentals, a gas station, an auto hobby shop, barber/beauty shops, an optical shop (no contact lenses available, however), and a popular video-rental shop. The fleet exchange carries popular electronic equipment at reasonable prices for military personnel.

Recreation. Recreation facilities include four military clubs and athletic facilities. The new enlisted club, Club Alliance, is the largest military club in the world and offers three floors of discos, bars, and dining areas. Yokosuka's other three clubs are the officers club, the CPO club, and an all-hands club, which is conveniently located adjacent to the Navy Lodge. A wide range of athletic and recreational facilities are available in Yokosuka. Two large gyms offer saunas, Nautilus equipment, extensive outdoor athletic fields and tennis courts, a racquetball court complex, a pro shop, and gear issues. Negishi's gym offers a new aerobics center, a pro shop, saunas, weight room, gear issue, and tennis, basketball, and volleyball courts.

Also available are four swimming pools (one fully enclosed), a thirty-two-lane bowling center, a roller skating rink, a sailing facility that offers free lessons, two movie theaters, and a tour office that gives Navy people and their families a chance to partake in a wide variety of shopping, special events, entertainment, and sightseeing tours to such places as Mount Fuji, Tokyo, Kyoto, Hong Kong, and even Thailand.

Yokosuka's climate has often been compared to that of Washington, D.C. Summers are hot and humid with temperatures in the eighties and nineties; the winters are cold, with temperatures in the twenties and thirties but little snow accumulation.

Not more than half an hour from the base is historic Kamakura, which is accessible by rail. (It's the fifth stop from Yokosuka, known as Kita-Kamakura.) Here is the world-famous Daibutsu, the Great Buddha, cast in bronze in the year 1252. At forty-four feet high, it is the largest uncovered buddha in Japan. Among the many attractions here is the Enkakuji Temple, founded in 1282; one of its features is an immense bronze bell cast in 1301.

For more information write to: COMFLEACT Family Service Center, Code 200, PSC 473, Box 1, FPO AP 96349-1100.

KOREA

Air Force

KUNSAN AIR BASE

Kunsan Air Base, home of the 8th Fighter Wing, "Wolf Pack," lies seven miles from Kunsan City on the west coast of the Korean peninsula, near the Kum River estuary.

History. Originally built by the Japanese as a fighter-interceptor base in 1938, the base became home for the U.S. Military Assistance Advisory Group following World War II. In August 1950, Kunsan was captured by the North Koreans; in September of that year U.S. forces recaptured the city and the base. The 8th FW, Kunsan's current occupant, flies the F-16 Fighting Falcon aircraft.

Housing and Schools. There are no family housing or child-care facilities at Kunsan. A few personnel do have their families there, but they are required to live on the local economy. For the most part, economy housing is substandard, and strict safety and hygiene rules must be met before American personnel are authorized to occupy off-base housing. There are no schools on base or in Kunsan City to serve American dependents.

Personal Services. Medical care is provided by the USAF Hospital, Kunsan. Patients requiring care beyond the capabilities of the hospital are sent to the 121st Evacuation Hospital at Yongsan, in Seoul.

The Local Area. Kunsan City is a deepwater port that can accommodate large ocean-going vessels. With a population of almost 200,000, the city lists fishing as a major industry along with plywood and shoemaking. The city has many interesting places to see such as parks and temples, and there are plenty of markets in which to shop. Commercial airline service to Kunsan began in December 1992.

For more information write to: Public Affairs Office, Unit 2090, 8th FW (PACAF), APO AP 96264-5000.

OSAN AIR BASE

The country around Osan Air Base has seen some of the most desperate fighting in the annals of American military history.

At a spot only a few miles north of the base on the road to Suwon, 408 men of Task Force Smith lost their lives in the initial action between U.S. and Communist forces in the Korean War on 5 July 1950. The task force held its positions for seven hours that day against an entire North Korean division with thirty-seven tanks supporting it. The survivors fought on for another sixteen days, delaying the North Koreans until the 24th Infantry Division could land at the port of Pusan and secure a defensive perimeter around the city.

On 7 February 1951, along the slopes of Hill 180, which today dominates Osan Air Base, Capt. Lewis L. Millett led his men in a bayonet charge against Communist Chinese forces. That action was the first company-size bayonet charge made by the U.S. Army since World War I, and for his heroic action that day Captain Millett was awarded the Medal of Honor.

History. Prior to the outbreak of the Korean War, the area now designed Osan Air Base consisted of four villages and a number of rice paddies where the runway now lies. Originally designated K-55, the base was not renamed until late 1956. Today the base covers 1,565 acres and boasts a 9,000-foot runway. It is home to the 7th Air Force Headquarters, the 51st Wing, and the air arm of the U.S. Forces, Korea, Air Combat Command. The pilots of the 36th Fighter Squadron of the 51st Wing fly F-16 C/D model aircraft, while those of the wing's 19th Tactical Air Support Squadron fly OA-10 Thunderbolt IIs. Osan is home to 5,200 U.S. military personnel, their 2,100 family members, and 300 DoD civilian employees.

Housing and Schools. There are 285 units of family housing available for authorized military personnel on base at Osan's Mustang Village. Housing is also available off base but must meet required health and safety inspections. The housing referral office at Osan keeps track of acceptable housing in the area.

Single military personnel live in 5,200 dormitory rooms on base and 90 units in Air Force Village. Dorms on base include carpeting, refrigerators, and semiprivate baths. Officers and senior NCOs have private rooms, and many have cooking facilities.

Osan American School for elementary and junior high students is located next to the commissary. High school students attend classes at Seoul American School located at Yongsan Army Garrison; bus transportation is provided. A child-care facility and a preschool are also available at Osan. The base education office offers college-level courses from Central Texas College, the University of Maryland, the University of Southern California, and the University of Oklahoma. Osan's base library offers 50,000 volumes for the reader and researcher.

Personal Services. Medical and dental care at Osan is provided by the 51st Medical Group in a thirty-bed, 92,000-square-foot hospital facility. Specialized care is available at the 121st Evacuation Hospital in Seoul or from hospitals in Japan and Hawaii.

Osan has a well-stocked commissary, an exchange, a barber shop, a beauty shop, a food court, a launderette, a dry cleaner, a gas station, and a movie theater. An arcade also offers everything from custom tailoring to Korean-made furniture and sporting goods.

Recreation. For the bowler, there is a twenty-two-lane alley at Osan; golfers will enjoy the newly expanded eighteen-hole course there. Officers and NCO clubs, as well as an aero club, arts and crafts facilities, a twenty-four-hour recreation facility, and a base gymnasium round out the recreational facilities at Osan.

The Local Area. The village of Osan lies thirty-five miles south of Seoul and six miles from Osan-Ni, its namesake village. The climate in Korea is temperate, with generally humid weather; the hottest months are July and August and the coldest, December and January. The mean temperature at Osan is in the eighties in the summer and in the mid- to upper thirties in the winter.

For more information write to: 51st Wing Public Affairs Office, Unit 2067, APO AP 96278.

An honor guard of both U.S. and ROK soldiers stands at attention at Osan Air Base. (USAF photo)

SUWON AIR BASE

Suwon AB is now a co-located operating base under the 51st Wing (see the entry for Osan) and is no longer a fully operational facility.

TAEGU AIR BASE

Taegu AB is now a co-located operating base under the 51st Wing (see the entry for Osan) and is no longer a fully operational facility.

Army

CAMP AMES

Camp Ames has been returned to the control of the ROK Army.

CAMP CARROLL

Sometimes called "Wigwam," after the nearby town of Waegwan, population 30,000, Camp Carroll lies near the Naktong River, nestled among rolling, tree-covered hills and terraced rice fields only a three-hour drive from Seoul.

History. Named in honor of SFC Charles R. Carroll, who was killed in action near Waegwan, what is today called Camp Carroll was part of the famous Pusan Perimeter established in the early days of the Korean War to halt the Communist North Korean armies sweeping down on the United Nations forces from the north. It was from this contracted, defensive posture in September 1950 that the UN forces burst out upon the invading armies, in conjunction with General MacArthur's landing at Inchon, to pinch off the North Korean assault.

Today Camp Carroll is home to the U.S. Army Materiel Support Center-Korea (USAMSC-K), a subordinate element of the 19th Support Command. In addition, the 307th Signal Battalion, 69th Transportation Battalion, and approximately twenty other units and activities are stationed there.

Housing and Schools. Currently, all government family quarters and schools are located in Taegu, about fifteen miles southeast of Waegwan. School, work, and other shuttle buses run from 6:30 A.M. to as late as midnight on weekends to provide access to the Taegu military community. The education center provides complete vocational and technical programs in automotive, electrical, welding, and computer science disciplines. College courses available on post are given under the auspices of the University of Maryland and Central Texas College. There are also a language lab and a post library.

Personal Services. Medical and dental care are available on post, although the major medical facility for soldiers and their dependents is the 121st Evacuation Hospital, in Seoul. A post exchange, a commissary, and a clothing sales store are also located on the installation.

Recreation. Camp Carroll boasts a complete range of recreational facilities. The all-ranks club, opened in 1986 at a cost of two million dollars, is available to military personnel and their families; a gymnasium with fully equipped weight room and racquetball courts opened in 1982; a music/theater entertainment center was completed in 1987; and the arts and crafts center was totally refurbished in 1986. In addition, there are a movie theater, a swimming pool, a bowling alley, a recreation center, and three snack bars.

On the weekends there are a number of inexpensive day-long tours offered to a large number of attractions, including the Joint Security Area in Panmunjom, shopping trips to the markets of Seoul, and visits to the grounds of ancient Buddhist temples.

For more information write to: Army Community Service, USAMSC-K & CC, APO AP 96260.

CAMP CASEY

Camp Casey is located only twelve miles from the 38th Parallel, which has divided the Republic of Korea from the "Workers' Paradise" of North Korea since 1953. Named after Maj. Hugh B. Casey, who died on a hill overlooking Camp Casey in January 1952, today the installation covers over twelve square miles and is home to the majority of the 2nd Infantry Division's 13,000 soldiers. The units stationed there consist of the 1st and 2nd Brigades, the Division Support Command, and several separate battalion- and company-size units. The division headquarters is located at Camp Red Cloud, just outside scenic Uijongbu, nine miles south of Camp Casey.

Personal Services. Because duty at Camp Casey is considered a hardship tour, family members do not live there. Since on-post transient quarters are limited, visitors must find accommodations in nearby Tongduchon. The cost of living there is expensive by American standards.

Camp Casey has an efficient bus service that can take you across post for forty cents. On-post taxi services are also available. Both bus and taxi service end at midnight daily.

Recreation. Camp Casey boasts several modern athletic and recreation facilities. There are two theaters, three recreation centers, two libraries, four gymnasiums, two bowling alleys, two swimming pools, and several tennis and racquetball courts. There are also officers and NCO clubs. A commissary and post exchange complex provide a wide variety of food and merchandise. Camp Casey's commercial vendors include a Burger King, a Popeye's chicken restaurant, and a Baskin Robbins ice cream parlor. Banking and credit union facilities are also available.

The Local Area. Camp Casey is located twenty-five miles north of Seoul, the capital city of the Republic of Korea. Just outside the gate is the town of

Tongduchon, which occupies over fifty square miles of land and has a population of 70,000. Tongduchon is renowned for its shopping and entertainment districts.

Railroad and bus services are available for transportation to and from Seoul, but most soldiers take the Myung Jin Shuttle Bus, which cost $3.10 as of spring 1993. A taxi cost around $40.00 at that time. The trip to Seoul takes approximately one and a half hours by road.

An area of interest is Soyo Mountain, where there are beautiful Buddhist temples and waterfalls.

For more information write to: Public Affairs Officer, 2nd Infantry Division, Unit 15041, APO AP 96258-0289.

CAMP HIALEAH

At first glance there appears to be nothing in common between Camp Hialeah, the Pusan Military Command's major installation, and the famous racetrack in Florida after which it is named. But the main area of Camp Hialeah was once owned by the Morning Calm Horse Racing Association. The road circling the Hialeah Heaven Club and Headquarters, 20th Area Support Group, was the track and the entrance to the Pusan officers open mess was the ticket office. So hence the name—Camp Hialeah—which in the circumstances seems quite natural.

History. During World War II the area now known as Camp Hialeah was used by the Japanese Imperial Army for training and maneuvers. U.S. troops occupied the site in 1945. In those days, Hialeah was in the suburbs of Pusan City, but today it is in the middle of a bustling neighborhood and home to the Army, Navy, Air Force, and Marine Corps in the southern part of Korea. Approximately 400 military personnel, 200 U.S. civilian employees, and 400 dependents live and work within the 137-acre confines of Camp Hialeah.

Housing. There are 180 units of government family housing available at Camp Hialeah. Housing rental costs on the local economy range from about $450 a month for a two-bedroom duplex to as much as $1,000 a month for a four-bedroom apartment; utilities can range from $150 to as much as $250 a month, depending on the size of the unit.

Personal Services. Camp Hialeah is a small, self-contained city that offers its residents the services available to any comparable community in the United States. The housing area contains schools, a dispensary and dental clinic, retail sales outlets in the post exchange, and various concessions including a garage, a snack bar, and a commissary.

Recreation. Sedentary entertainment is available through the community club system and a post theater. The more athletically inclined may take advantage of a bowling alley, a gymnasium, a tennis court, a swimming pool, and a lighted athletic field. The recreation center provides various craft shops, weekly tours, and many organized seasonal sporting events.

The Local Area. Pusan, the largest port city in the Republic of Korea, boasts a population of four million. The metropolis sprawls eighteen miles east to west and thirteen miles north to south; the port alone measures fourteen miles in circumference.

The climate in this part of Korea is generally comfortable year-round. In July and August the temperatures sometimes reach as high as 95° F., and rainfall during those months averages six to twelve inches. In December and January, the coldest months, the thermometer may dip to as low as 20° F., but there are only traces of snow in winter. The temperature in Pusan is generally about ten degrees warmer in the winter and cooler in the summer than it is in Seoul, about 200 miles to the north.

Pusan is a city of vivid contrasts, combining the hustle and bustle of a major deepwater port city with the splendid parks, museums, and ancient temples for which most Korean cities are famous. First opened to international trade in 1876, Pusan now receives approximately 60 percent of South Korea's export items and 95 percent of its container transport. Bomo Temple, about fifteen miles north of Camp Hialeah, has been a center of Buddhist ritual for more than 1,300 years. The UN cemetery in Pusan, the only one of its kind, is the final resting place for over 2,000 soldiers from sixteen nations who died fighting in the Korean War.

For more information write to: Public Affairs Office, 20th Area Support Group, Pusan, APO AP 96259-0270.

CAMP HOWZE

Camp Howze is a small installation located just eight miles from the 38th Parallel and Communist North Korea. Roads in the vicinity have checkpoints to restrict travel of unauthorized people and vehicles.

History. Named in honor of Maj. Gen. Robert Lee Howze, winner of the Medal of Honor in 1891 and the first commanding general of the 1st Cavalry Division, Camp Howze is home for the 3rd Brigade, 2nd Infantry Division. The brigade has the mission of maintaining operational control of all U.S. Army elements in the Western Corridor of the Republic of Korea, including the American sector of the Demilitarized Zone.

Personal Services and Recreation. A post exchange, a theater, a snack bar, a recreation center, a library, and a banking facility are available at Camp Howze, as is an arts and crafts center with a variety of equipment and activities. Sports facilities include a swimming pool, tennis courts, and a softball field. There are also a six-lane bowling center, officers and enlisted clubs, and a large gymnasium.

The Local Area. Seoul, just twenty-five miles south of Camp Howze, is a big off-duty attraction for soldiers stationed there. Regularly scheduled bus service is provided seven days a week between Yongsan (Seoul) and Camp Howze as well as to other points in the 2nd Division area. Another is Panmunjom, within the Demilitarized Zone where, in July 1953, the armistice ending the Korean War was signed. The small village just outside Camp Howze offers an entertainment district consisting of restaurants and variety stores.

For more information write to: Headquarters, 3rd Brigade, Attention: EAIDTB-SO, APO SF 96251-0384.

CAMP HUMPHREYS

Located about fifty miles south of Seoul, Camp Humphreys is home to the 3,200 personnel of the 19th Support Command, the 23rd Support Group, and other units. The 19th Support Command's mission is to administer all support activities vital to the 8th U.S. Army.

History. Camp Humphreys was established on the site of an airfield built by the Japanese when they occupied what is now the Republic of Korea. After World War II the U.S. Air Force renovated the field to accommodate Marine and USAF aircraft. During the Korean War the site was called Pyongtaek Airfield, after the nearby city of Pyongtaek. In 1961 it was renamed Camp Humphreys, in honor of CWO Benjamin K. Humphreys of the 4th Transportation Company, who died in a helicopter accident near there.

Housing and Schools. Government housing for family personnel is limited to only those who are command sponsored—assigned to duty that specifically authorizes them to bring their families to the Republic of Korea. Rental housing is available in the nearby village of An Jung Ri, but it is considered generally substandard for U.S. personnel. As of August 1993, rent for a one-bedroom unfurnished apartment was running as high as $350 a month and utility bills were as much as $250 a month.

Department of Defense Dependents Schools are available for children of command-sponsored familes at Osan Air Base, about eighteen miles from Camp Humphreys, and in Seoul: There are a middle and high school at Yongsan Garrison, Seoul, and an elementary school at Osan. Other children are taken on a space-available basis. Adults may obtain credits toward associate and bachelor's degrees from Central Texas College, the University of Maryland, and the University of Maryland at Osan.

Personal Services. Medical care is available from the 43rd Mobile Army Surgical Hospital and the 543rd General Dispensary. Specialty and long-term inpatient medical care are provided by the 121st Evacuation Hospital in Seoul.

A post exchange and a commissary are available at Camp Humphreys, as are a shopette and a post exchange food cluster offering a Baskin Robbins ice cream shop, an Anthony's Pizza, and a Burger King. Snack bars are also provided. For those who wish a more refined atmosphere, Camp Humphreys offers the Gateway, Freedom Inn, and Night Watch clubs. A large community activities center, comparable to a stateside mini mall, is scheduled for completion sometime during fiscal year 1996. Until then, bus and taxi services are available on post. Also available are barber and beauty shops, a gas station, banking services, custom tailoring, and a custom shoe shop.

Recreation. Recreational facilities include an arts and crafts center, an automotive crafts center, a twelve-lane bowling center, a library, a post theater, a gym, a thirteen-hole miniature golf course at the Jordan Recreation Center, and an outdoor swimming pool in operation from Memorial Day through Labor Day. Major outdoor sports such as tennis and basketball are also available.

The Local Area. The village of An Jung Ri offers some shopping and recreational activities such as the Boo Hung Restaurant; the UN, Paradise, Maxim, and Peacock clubs; and the Italy Pizza phone and delivery service. For travel farther afield, the Myung Jin Transportation Company offers bus service daily to Osan and Seoul. The city of Pyongtaek, only eight miles from Camp Humphreys, offers somewhat more of the same. The Koreans are noted for their brass ware, antiques, jewelry, handicrafts, and tailoring. The nightlife in these places can also be interesting for the young and fancy free.

For more information write to: HQ, 23rd Area Support Group, Attention: EANC-HG-PAO, APO AP 96271-0164.

TAEGU MILITARY COMMUNITY

The Taegu area sits in a "bowl," surrounded on all sides by a wall of steep hills. It is known as both the hottest and the coldest city in the Republic of Korea.

The Taegu Military Community (TMC) consists of four military installations— Camp Henry, Camp Walker, Camp George, and the Taegu Storage Area. The major U.S. military command in the community is the 19th Support Command, which plans and directs the provision of direct combat service support throughout Korea.

Housing and Schools. There are 96 units of family housing at Camp Walker and 200 at Camp George. Waiting times vary from fewer than sixty days for quarters at Camp Walker to sixty to ninety days at Camp George.

The Taegu American School serves students in all grades, from kindergarten through high school. Adult education is available from the University of Maryland, Chapman College, the University of Southern California, and the Central Texas College.

Personal Services. Medical care is provided by a local health clinic, but the major medical facility for U.S. forces personnel throughout Korea is the 121st Evacuation Hospital in Seoul, with a 300-bed inpatient and an extensive outpatient clinic facility.

Recreation. Located at Camp Walker, about a twenty-minute walk from Camp Henry, are a post exchange, an arcade, a commissary, a snack bar, a Burger King, a recreation center, a gymnasium, bowling lanes, a library, a chapel, officer and enlisted clubs, a nine-hole golf course, a swimming pool, and most of the troop billets. The movie theater, an NCO club, a snack bar, and some bachelor enlisted rooms are at Camp Henry.

The Local Area. Taegu is known as the "Apple Capital of Korea" and is one of the Republic's larger cities, with a population of 2.5 million. It lies 170 miles southeast of Seoul and 86 miles northwest of Pusan, in the Nakdong River Valley, bounded on the north and south by the Palgong Mountains.

Taegu first appears in the historic record in 366 A.D. In 757 A.D., the city was granted its present name, which means "great hill," perhaps a reference to the mudwall fortress that once formed the center of the ancient city.

For more information write to: Public Affairs Office, 19th Support Command, APO AP 96218-0171.

U.S. ARMY GARRISON, SEOUL

At one time duty in Korea was considered the "best-kept secret" in the Army. Considered a hardship tour even today (most soldiers cannot bring their families), the fact is that a tour of duty in Korea can be one of the most pleasant and educational interludes in a soldier's enlistment or career. This is due in part to the fact that since the end of the Korean War, U.S. forces have acted as a bulwark against incursions from North Korea (Seoul is less than forty miles from the Demilitarized Zone). But more importantly, the Koreans have used the years of peace since 1954 to build for themselves one of the most modern and progressive societies in all Asia.

History. The primary U.S. Army headquarters in Korea is 8th U.S. Army. The 2nd Infantry Division, the principal ground defense component of 8th Army, currently occupies blocking positions north of Seoul, along the traditional invasion routes from the north. In July 1957, the Headquarters, United Nations Command, moved from Tokyo to Seoul; concurrently, Headquarters, U.S. Forces, Korea, was formed to serve as a control and planning headquarters for all U.S. ground, air, and naval elements assigned to the Republic of Korea. Yongsan is also home to the UN Command, Combined Forces Command (the Republic of Korea and United States), and U.S. Forces Korea. Yongsan compound houses the headquarters and military community support facilities.

Housing and Schools. There are 2,500 sets of family housing in the Seoul area, consisting of two-, three-, and four-bedroom duplex and apartment units. Priority for occupancy goes to key personnel whose positions are considered essential to the command and who are in Korea on a two-year tour; other command-sponsored military personnel are placed on a waiting list.

Seven Department of Defense schools are located throughout Korea. Families assigned to the Seoul area may send their children to the Seoul American Elementary School or the Seoul American High School. A child-care center is available at Yongsan South Post and Hannam Village, a housing area near the Han River. The Yongsan education center offers adult education in the form of college programs from several well-respected, fully accredited U.S. colleges and universities.

Personal Services and Recreation. On-post facilities in the Seoul area are excellent. The Yongsan Library, for instance, is the largest Army library in Korea, with 140,000 volumes. Also located on Yongsan are a modern NCO club, a modern thirty-two-lane bowling center, a community club, a youth activities center, a music theater, two gymnasiums, three swimming pools (including one year-round pool on the main post), and tennis courts. The Moyer Community Activities Center includes a recreation center, an arts and crafts center, and Yongsan Tour and Travel, which runs an extensive domestic and out-of-country tour program. AAFES operates a movie theater on Yongsan, with another located at nearby Camp Coiner. The 8th Army Golf Club, a championship eighteen-hole course that serves an important role in both the U.S. and Korean communities, has been relocated to Sungnam, a suburb of Seoul about forty-five minutes from the Yongsan compound. Bus transportation is provided to players and guests.

Situated in the middle of Yongsan Compound is the Dragon Hill Lodge (DHL), a 277-room military hotel for the use of all classes of DoD-affiliated personnel. Rates for military personnel on leave start at thirty-five dollars per night, depending on rank. All rooms are equipped with TV, VCR, refrigerator, microwave oven, double bed, and sleeper sofa. The DHL also has four restaurants, two lounges, and a shopping arcade offering everything from Asian gift items to designer suits. There are also a banking facility, a hair care center, and a tailor shop. Reservations may be made by writing to Dragon Hill Lodge, Reservations Dept., Unit No. 15355, APO AP 96205-0427.

One of the most spectacular tourist attractions in this part of Asia is Cheju Island, an hour's flight from Seoul, about halfway between Japan and Korea. Fresh- and saltwater fishing are available in the many lakes, ponds, streams, and off-shore waters.

The Local Area. Seoul, the capital city of Korea, was founded in 1392. Although it was almost totally destroyed during the war (Seoul was captured twice by the Communists and recaptured by the UN forces), today Seoul is an ultramodern metropolis with a population of over ten million. It was chosen as the site of the 1988 Summer Olympics.

Korea is a peninsula that extends 525 miles from the Asian mainland, varying in width from 100 to 130 miles. While Korea's mountains are not spectacularly high, the country is extremely rugged, with only 20 percent of its land flat enough to be cultivated. Roughly equal in size to the state of Virginia, the Republic of Korea has a population of about forty-three million. The literacy rate among its people is 97 percent, and the per capita income is $6,400 per year. The climate is rarely extreme. Winters are mildly cold and dry with little snow accumulation outside the mountainous areas. Summers are sultry with a distinct rainy season, not unlike those of Washington, D.C.

For more information write to: Army Community Service, Attention: Family Services Program (Relocation), HQ, 34th Support Group (EANC-SA-ACS), Unit No. 15333, APO AP 96205-0177.

THE NETHERLANDS

Air Force

SOESTERBERG AIR BASE

Soesterberg Air Base (SAB) is located in a beautifully wooded but very heavily populated area of the Netherlands, about forty miles from Amsterdam. The 32nd Fighter Group is the only American unit at Soesterberg Air Base, a major Royal Netherlands Air Force facility. The 32nd Fighter Day Squadron originally deployed there on 16 November 1954.

Housing and Schools. About 330 leased units of family housing available to personnel at SAB are located in the nearby community of Soesterberg. Housing is also available on the Dutch economy. The average waiting period for these quarters is about three months. Although temporary-lodging allowance is paid to those living in temporary accommodations, establishing a household on the economy requires a minimum of $2,000. Single airmen live in nine dormitory buildings that can accommodate a total of 383 personnel. The facilities are located about four blocks from the SAB main gate.

Soesterberg American School (kindergarten through grade twelve) is located just inside the SAB main gate and has an average enrollment of 560 students. A child-care center, also located near the main gate, has a capacity of 62 children. The education services office offers a number of college programs from such institutions as the University of Maryland, City Colleges of Chicago, Troy State University, and Embry-Riddle Aeronautical University.

Personal Services. Medical care is provided by the USAF clinic, which has a staff of six military physicians and six dentists. The SAB commissary offers 3,800 line items, including fresh meat, fruits, vegetables, and dairy products. The base exchange offers convenience and necessary items for shoppers as well as a number of concessions such as a barber shop, a foodland, a launderette, and a base theater.

Recreation. Recreational facilities include an audio-photo club, an auto hobby shop, an eight-lane bowling alley, officers and enlisted clubs, and an active intramural sports program.

The Local Area. The climate throughout the Netherlands is moderate, with an average temperature of 50° F. and rainfall averaging about twenty-nine inches per year. The waters of the North Sea make for cool, damp, extremely changeable weather. The country is low and flat and about one-fourth of its land is actually below sea level.

Holland (another name for the Netherlands) itself is about the size of New Jersey with a population of fourteen million. This makes it one of the most densely populated areas in the world. But its location makes the Netherlands an ideal spot from which to launch visits to other places in Western Europe; Germany is directly to the east; Belgium, to the south; and England, directly across the channel to the west. Because the distances are so short, one can reach southern Germany or France in one day's easy driving. Spain, Austria, Switzerland, and Italy are only a little farther. The Scandinavian countries (Denmark, Norway, Sweden, and Finland) are easily accessible to the northeast.

For more information write to: 32 FG/PA, Unit 6760, Box 195, APO AE 09719.

OKINAWA

Air Force

KADENA AIR BASE

Okinawa is primarily a Marine Corps station, but Kadena Air Base is home to 5,800 Air Force personnel, their family members, and more than 300 Department of the Air Force civilian employees, for a total base population of 25,000.

History. Kadena was originally built by the Japanese, who surrendered it on 7 September 1945 following the Battle of Okinawa. The fighting resulted in the deaths of more than 12,500 Americans, 100,000 Japanese soldiers, and about 100,000 Okinawan civilians. The surrender site memorial is located in what is now the Stearley Heights housing area. Today its 14,000 acres are home to the 18th Wing's twenty-one squadrons, consisting of over 100 aircraft, including F-15C/D fighters, KC-135R tankers, E-3B AWACs, HH-3 rescue helicopters, and C-12F airlifters.

Housing and Schools. There are more than 3,500 units of family housing at Kadena, situated among eleven different housing areas; total housing assets on the island are over 7,000 units, all of which, even those on Marine Corps, Army, and Navy installations, are managed by the Air Force. Guest facilities are available through the base billeting office.

All American children on Okinawa attend Department of Defense schools. The schools have an enrollment of approximately 8,500 students. Kadena has both primary and intermediate schools as well as child-development and child-care centers. Adult education is offered through the base education office and includes college courses from Michigan State University, the University of Oklahoma, and the University of Maryland.

Personal Services. Health services are offered through the Wing Medical Group and dental clinics. A medical staff of about 440 doctors, dentists, nurses, and technicians attends to the many needs of Kadena's Air Force population, seeing an average of 850 patients each day. Further care is available at the U.S. Naval Regional Medical Center at Camp Lester, a first-class medical facility with a staff of 3,500 personnel.

The Air Force commissary operates three branches on the island, while diverse shopping needs are met by the Army and Air Force Exchange Service outlets, which annually boast the largest sales volume in the AAFES worldwide system.

Eating establishments abound on Kadena and Okinawa. Mexican, Italian, barbecue, and sandwich fare plus a number of other concessions tempt the taste buds. In addition, a Burger King and three clubs—officers, NCO, and airmen's—round out the opportunities for indoor dining. Outdoor meals can be enjoyed at the Kadena Marina Seaside Inn, which features dining on the waterfront with an open-air atmosphere that only the South Pacific can offer.

Recreation. Recreational facilities include the Kadena Marina, just outside Gate Four, where a charter fishing boat may be reserved; an eighteen-hole golf course; a miniature golf course; a 44,000-volume base library; a forty-six-lane bowling center; arts and crafts centers; several swimming pools; one of the Air Force's finest athletic facilities, the $7.2 million Risner Athletic Complex; dozens of tennis courts and ball fields; and a community activities center.

The Air Force operates the Okuma Recreation Center, an island vacation site fifty-one miles north of the base, which offers seven year-round air-conditioned cabañas with sixty-four rooms and two large camp sites. Facilities include a surfside restaurant, a bar and lounge, an indoor and outdoor theater, a nine-hole golf course, tennis courts, and a pool. Swimming, fishing, and boating can also be enjoyed in the area.

For more information write to: Public Affairs Office, HQ, 18th Wing, Unit 5141, Box 10, APO AP 96368-5141.

Marine Corps

U.S. MARINE CORPS INSTALLATIONS, OKINAWA

History. The battle for Okinawa, which commenced on 1 April 1945, was one of the longest and most bitterly fought campaigns of the war in the Pacific. But with time even the most bitter memories fade, and in 1972 the Ryukyu Islands (there are about 140 islands in the chain, of which Okinawa is the largest) were returned to Japan after being under American administration since 1945.

Of the approximately 34,000 U.S. personnel currently based on Okinawa, fully 20,000 of them are Marines, and the U.S. Marine Corps installations occupy about

10 percent of the island's total land area. The Marine installations on Okinawa stretch from one tip of the island to the other and fall under the corporate title of Camp S. D. Butler.

Going from the southwest to the northeast is Camp Kinser on the north, or East China Sea, side of the island, home for the 3rd Force Service Support Group; and the Marine Corps Air Station at Futenma, home of the helicopter and transport aircraft of the 1st Marine Air Wing. Farther north, at Camp Foster, are the headquarters of the Commander, Marine Corps Bases Japan; Commanding General, 1st Marine Aircraft Wing; and the Commanding General, Marine Corps Base, Camp S. D. Butler. The naval regional medical center (NRMC) is at Camp Lester and borders Kadena Air Base. On the Pacific side of the island are Camp McTureous, consisting mainly of military family housing units, and Camp Courtney, site of the command elements of the 3rd Marine Expeditionary Force, 3rd Marine Division, and 31st Marine Expeditionary Unit, overlooking Kin Bay. On the other side of the bay is Camp Hansen, home for the 9th Marine Regiment, and a bit farther north is Camp Schwab, headquarters for the 4th Marine Regiment. In addition to all this real estate, large areas in the central and northern regions of the island are used as training areas.

Housing and Schools. More than 7,400 sets of family quarters are available for Marine and Navy personnel on Okinawa. The waiting period for these quarters varies from none to one year. The Kuwae Lodge at Camp Lester offers 70 single rooms and 40 adjoining rooms for incoming families. Other transients may be accommodated there on a space-available basis. There are also lodges at Camp Courtney and Camp Hansen.

Dependent children attend one of ten Department of Defense schools on Okinawa. These include seven elementary, one junior high, and two high schools. There are also three preschools on the island. A number of education centers on Okinawa offer college courses at both the graduate and undergraduate levels. These include the University of Maryland, the University of Oklahoma, the University of Southern California, and Central Texas Community College.

Personal Services. The primary medical care facility for Marine and Navy personnel on Okinawa is the U.S. naval hospital at Camp Lester. There are branch clinics at Camp Kinser, MCAS, Futenma, Camp Foster, and Camp Courtney.

Commissaries are located at Camp Foster, Kadena Air Base, Camp Courtney, and Camp Kinser. Exchanges are located at Kadena, Camp Foster, Futenma, Camp Kinser, Camp Courtney, Camp Hansen, Camp Schwab, and Camp Lester. Foodlands and laundromats are conveniently located at facilities throughout the island. There are seven service stations and ten snack bars, as well as more than thirty different kinds of exchange repair outlets offering services from air-conditioning repair to watch repair.

Recreation. Recreational activities and facilities are plentiful on Okinawa. There are ten bowling centers available to the military community, ranging in size from the forty-six-lane center at Kadena Air Base to the four-lane center at White Beach. Three military golf courses are also provided, as are two driving ranges. There are two skeet/trap ranges located at Camp Courtney and Camp Hansen. Swimmers have their choice of numerous sandy, tropical island beaches or sixteen pools. There are seven gymnasiums on the island and even a roller skating rink at Kadena AB.

Outdoor recreation is even better. The Okuma Rest and Recreation Center, fifty-one miles north of Kadena and just outside the town of Hentona, is a 120-acre complex operated by the Air Force for all the military personnel on the island. Located on the East China Sea side of the island, the complex offers seven air-conditioned cabañas with a total of sixty-four rooms. There are also a base exchange and a laundromat, a surfside restaurant, a bar and lounge, and a recreation center. Camping is permitted in specified areas. Swimming, fishing, sailing, water skiing, wind surfing, a nine-hole golf course, and many other facilities are available there. Another beach is Oura-Wan, at Camp Schwab; this 300-foot beach has beach house facilities. Marek and Schilling Parks, Kadena AB, and Camp Lester have picnic facilities for parties ranging in size from 75 to 200 persons.

The Local Area. Okinawa is sixty-seven miles long and from two to sixteen miles wide. To the east is the Pacific Ocean, and to the west is the East China Sea. The island lies about halfway between Japan and Taiwan. Over a million Okinawans (Japanese citizens) live there. Temperatures range from the low fifties during the winter to the nineties during the summer, so outdoor activities are possible year-round. Rainfall averages about eighty-three inches per year. The total land area of the island is 454 square miles. Northern Okinawa is heavily forested and has some rather high mountains and a few short rivers. At the southern end of the island is a plateau with steep cliffs. The southern portion of the island is densely populated. The city of Naha (population 310,000) is the principal metropolis of the island.

The original people of Okinawa were most probably a mixture of several ethnic strains. Chinese culture made an impact on the islanders when trade began with them in 1372, but the islands were conquered by a band of Japanese warriors from southern Japan in 1609 and have remained under Japanese influence since then. Today the islands are a prefecture of the Japanese home islands.

For more information write to: Community Relations Officer, Marine Corps Base, Camp Smedley D. Butler, Unit 35001, FPO AP 96373-5001.

PANAMA

Air Force

HOWARD AND ALBROOK AIR FORCE BASES

In 1513, the Spanish explorer Vasco Nunez de Balboa climbed a hill near here, saw the Pacific Ocean, and claimed it for Spain. By doing so he missed the once-in-a-life-time chance to have the world's greatest body of water named after himself. (It was named a few years later by Ferdinand Magellan, who, impressed by its calmness, named it El Mar Pacifico.)

History. Albrook Field, built on top of material dredged from the Panama Canal (and known at first as the Balboa Fill Landing Field), was named in honor of Lt. Frank P. Albrook in 1924. It became a full-fledged Air Force base in 1948 and was redesignated an Air Force station in 1975. Its sister field, Howard Field, was named in honor of Maj. Charles H. Howard in 1939 and became Howard Air Force Base in 1948. Both bases are operated by the 24th Wing. The 24th, located at Howard, uses both bases in its mission of providing tactical air support for the Army in defense of the Panama Canal. Closed in 1950, Howard was reopened and renovated in the 1960s and now has an 8,500-foot runway.

Howard AFB is on the southwest bank of the canal, and Albrook AFS is on the southeast side, approximately eight miles away. Albrook borders Fort Clayton, while Howard is near the Panama Canal U.S. Naval Station.

Housing and Schools. There are 706 family housing units at Howard and 468 at Albrook. These units are some of the finest in the Air Force, although waiting times for some of them can be up to one year, depending on the size of the unit required, the sponsor's grade, and month of arrival in the command. Rental housing is available in Panama City, which is about fifteen miles from Albrook and twenty-five miles from Howard.

Dependent schooling is conducted by the Department of Defense Dependent School System, Panama Region, which operates a complete system from kindergarten through high school. Preschool and child-care facilities are also available. Adult education is available through the Panama Canal College, Florida State University, the University of Oklahoma, and Nova University.

Personal Services. Medical care is provided through the 24th Medical Group at Howard AFB and Albrook AFS. Patients requiring hospitalization are referred to Gorgas Hospital. Dental care is available for all active-duty personnel at the dental clinic.

The main Army and Air Force exchange is located near Albrook, in the Corozal area, while smaller stores are available at Howard AFB, the naval station, and the Marine barracks. Commissaries are located at Corozal and Howard. Officers and enlisted clubs are operated at Howard and an all-ranks club at Albrook. There are other clubs located at other military installations throughout the area.

Recreation. Recreational facilities include an eighteen-hole golf course, youth centers, a gym, bowling centers, swimming pools, hobby and craft shops, riding stables, and picnic areas. Panama offers some of the finest fishing in the world, and rental boats are available through the recreation activities office.

The Local Area. Located some 650 miles north of the equator, Panama has a tropical climate. The rainfall on the Pacific side of the isthmus averages about sixty-five inches per year.

The estimated population of the Republic of Panama was 2.1 million in 1984. The country is about 385 miles long and varies from 32 to 113 miles in width. The total land area of the Republic is 3,993 square miles. The canal itself does not run east to west, as most people who have never been there imagine it does, but in a northwest-to-southeast direction with the Atlantic terminal port of Cristobal to the northwest of the Pacific port of Balboa, so that the sun rises over the Pacific Ocean, as seen from Howard AFB.

The Panama Canal is run by the Panama Canal Commission, the U.S. government agency that replaced the Canal Zone Government in 1979. In keeping with the treaty signed between the government of Panama and the United States in 1977, the commission will continue to operate the canal until noon on 31 December 1999, when it will turn the canal over entirely to the Republic of Panama. As of December 1992, 87 percent of the commission employees, or 7,500, were Panamanians. During fiscal year 1992, more than 12,000 vessels transited the canal, carrying a total of more than 159 million tons of cargo for which tolls of more than $368 million were collected.

The canal was opened to commerce on 15 August 1914. It is 85 feet above sea level and more than fifty-one statute miles in length from deep water in the Caribbean to deep water in the Pacific. The channel ranges in bottom width from

500 to 1,000 feet. Normally, the average time of a vessel in canal waters is about twenty-four hours, eight to twelve of them in the canal itself.

For more information write to: 24th Wing Public Affairs Office, Unit 0506, APO AA 34001-5000.

Army

FORT CLAYTON

A component of the U.S. Southern Command, U.S. Army South at Fort Clayton deploys its soldiers from Guatemala to the tip of South America in support of our nation's strategic interests throughout an area comprising nineteen nations covering nearly 22 percent of the earth's surface. These troops are also responsible for protecting and defending the Panama Canal as well as supporting security assistance and counterdrug missions in the region.

History. The U.S. Army first came to Panama on 4 October 1911, when the 10th Infantry was assigned to defend the Panama Canal. U.S. Army South was activated on 4 December 1986 with the 193rd Infantry Brigade (Light) as its major subordinate command. Today Fort Clayton is home to the approximately 2,000 military personnel of the command.

Housing and Schools. More than 3,000 sets of family quarters are available to personnel assigned to the Canal Zone. Waiting periods as of January 1993 varied from two to twelve months, depending on category and bedroom size. Off-post rentals were running from $800 for a one-bedroom furnished apartment to $1,300 for a three-bedroom furnished house. Electric bills for these rentals were averaging $250 a month at that time. Guest housing is available at Clayton House, which offers thirty-five rooms and five suites available at rates from $22 to $44 per night.

On-post schooling is available for children, as are preschool and day-care facilities. Adult education is provided by such institutions of higher learning as Panama Canal College, Florida State University, and the University of Oklahoma.

Personal Services. Both commissary and post exchange facilities are available, but items such as beer, tobacco, and liquor are rationed, as are some household and food items and appliances.

Medical care is available from Gorgas Army Hospital. Dental service is provided by a clinic at Fort Clayton and Gorgas Hospital.

Recreation. A full range of recreational facilities is available at Fort Clayton and nearby installations. Included are officers and enlisted club systems, hobby and craft shops, sports facilities, a golf course, a gym, riding and rod and gun clubs, a swimming pool, theaters, and a library.

The Local Area. While Panama City offers many attractions such as dining and shopping and sightseeing, it has some high-crime areas, particularly El Chorrilo, a district just north of Balboa that is not considered safe at night. Transiting this area should prove no problem if one exercises the same commonsense precautions as required in any major U.S. metropolitan area. In fact, Panama City might actually be safer than some U.S. cities.

For more information write to: Public Affairs Office, Headquarters, U.S. Army South, APO AA 34004-5000.

Navy

U.S. NAVAL STATION PANAMA CANAL

"A man, a plan, a canal—Panama," as the palindrome has it (it can be read the same way backward as forward), does not mean that you won't know if you're coming or going at the U.S. Naval Station, Panama Canal (USNAVSTAPANCANAL). Chances are, once you've been there, you'll want to go back.

U.S. Naval Station Panama Canal's mission is to exercise command and area coordination of forces of the Navy and other activities.

Housing and Schools. The station administers 285 housing units in the canal area for use by locally assigned Navy and Marine Corps personnel and their families. Housing is available at the Farfan housing area, Fort Amador, and Rodman annexes.

The Department of Defense operates fourteen grammar schools, a junior-senior high, a junior high, and a senior high school. Also available are courses from the Panama Canal College, Florida State University, the University of Oklahoma, and Nova University.

Personal Services. Medical care is available at the USAF clinic at Howard AFB (west bank), or Gorgas Army Hospital. Gorgas Army Hospital provides the only inpatient treatment in the Canal Zone for active-duty personnel and their dependents. Medical and dental care for Navy personnel and their dependents are available at the station clinic.

A number of exchanges and commissaries are located on military installations throughout the Canal Zone. There is a Marine Corps exchange on the Pacific side at the USNAVSTA. Exchange concessionaires provide shoe, radio-TV, and watch repair shops; dry-cleaning facilities; and tailoring and laundering services. Beauty and barber shop facilities are also available. The commissaries stock a variety of foods, most of which are shipped in from the United States. Fresh milk and baked goods are acquired locally from commercial sources, and the Army bakery also produces fresh bread and rolls.

Recreation. Recreation facilities available to USNAVSTA personnel and their families include two swimming pools; a bowling alley; a gym; a gun club; officers, CPO, and enlisted clubs; and a sailing club at the marina.

The Local Area. The Republic of Panama is only 600 miles north of the equator, so the climate in the area is tropical with high humidity and high temperatures

(98° F. was the highest temperature ever recorded there, and the lowest was 59° F.). Temperatures vary little, ranging from 73° F. to 87° F. on the Pacific side and 73° F. to 85° F. on the Atlantic side. The average rainfall on the Atlantic side is 130 inches per year, while it is only 68 inches on the Pacific side.

Panama is the kind of place where there's something to do year-round, and out-door activities are the rule. Fishing, boating, yachting, and all kinds of water sports, available from a variety of magnificent beaches, may be pursued without regard to season.

The first Europeans came to Panama in 1501, and Columbus visited there on his fourth voyage in 1502; Balboa discovered the Pacific Ocean by crossing the Isthmus in 1513, and the first city was founded on the Caribbean coast in 1519. For nearly 400 years the Isthmus served as a short land bridge between the Atlantic and Pacific Oceans and invited all sorts of characters, from pirates and privateers to the Forty-niners and engineers with plans to build a canal there. In 1670 the English buccaneer Henry Morgan sacked and destroyed Panama City. The ruins of the old city may still be seen a few miles from the present-day Panama City, on the Pacific Coast.

For more information write to: Commanding Officer, USNAVSTA Panama Canal, Box B, FPO Miami 34061.

THE PHILIPPINES

Air Force

CLARK AIR FORCE BASE

Clark Air Force Base has been turned over to the Republic of the Philippines.

Navy

U.S. NAVAL FACILITIES, SUBIC BAY

On 30 September 1992, all U.S. facilities at Subic Bay were returned to the Republic of the Philippines, ending a U.S. presence that had lasted there for ninety-five years.

PUERTO RICO

Army

FORT BUCHANAN

Fort Buchanan is the Army's only active post in Puerto Rico and the Antilles. Today it is a Forces Command installation providing administrative and logistical support to all active-duty Army and reserve elements on the island, including one of the largest Reserve Officer Training Corps programs in the nation.

History. Fort Buchanan was named after Brig. Gen. James A. Buchanan, first commander of the Puerto Rican Regiment, U.S. Volunteers, which was formed in 1900. The post was established on a 300-acre tract along the south shore of San Juan Bay in 1923, and served as a target range and maneuver area for Army and National Guard troops. Today it is one of the fifteen lead mobilization stations in the United States.

Housing and Schools. There are 362 sets of government quarters at Fort Buchanan: 32 for field-grade officers, 232 for company-grade and warrant officers and senior NCOs, and 98 for enlisted personnel. The Su Casa Guest House offers 29 air-conditioned rooms for military personnel on permanent-change-of-station orders and for visiting military and civilian personnel. The rate is twenty-seven dollars per night, with special rates for additional guests and children. Information or reservations may be obtained by calling (809) 273-3821.

The Antilles Consolidated School System operates four schools at Fort Buchanan: an elementary school, an intermediate school, a middle school, and a high school. In addition, there is a child-care center that can accommodate children from six months to ten years of age. This facility also offers two preschool programs. The post education center offers a full range of educational assistance.

Personal Services. Medical care is provided by the U.S. Army Health Clinic, a satellite of the Eisenhower Medical Center of Fort Gordon, Georgia. The clinic provides general ambulatory care, including two family practice physicians, one internal medicine officer, and one general medicine officer. Dental services for active-duty military personnel and their dependents are available on a space-available basis.

The Fort Buchanan post exchange offers a wide range of services, including a main store, a convenience store, a toy store, a new car sales outlet, a beer and soda store, a service station, barber and beauty shops, optical and watch shops, a dry cleaner, a flower shop, a TV rental and repair shop, and a cafeteria. There is also a full-service commissary on post.

Persons being stationed at Fort Buchanan should be aware that a valid Puerto Rico driver's license must be obtained within 120 days of arrival. Also, an excise tax may be imposed on motor vehicles brought into Puerto Rico if they are purchased and shipped after the date of military orders assigning an individual to Fort Buchanan. The minimum tax payable is $250.

Recreation. The Morale Support Activities (MSA) program at Fort Buchanan offers six core programs: arts and crafts, sports, youth activities, library, tours and travel, and outdoor recreation/supply. The sports program provides a fitness center complete with swimming pool, sauna, and various courts, as well as an excellent scuba program. An eighteen-lane bowling center was opened in August 1992.

The outdoor recreation/supply program makes available boats and camping and picnic equipment at no charge for active-duty personnel and for a minimal fee to other authorized users.

MSA also operates a nine-hole golf course and various picnic areas throughout the post. A fitness/nature trail has recently been constructed at Fort Buchanan for those who enjoy walking and getting in touch with nature.

The Fort Buchanan Community Club features a large common ballroom and separate lounges as well as dining and private activity rooms offering a menu of select cuisine and varied entertainment. Opened in 1982, it is one of the most modern club facilities in the Army.

The Local Area. Puerto Rico was discovered by Christopher Columbus on 19 November 1493, during his second voyage to the New World. He named the island San Juan Bautista. Spanish settlement began in 1508, and the city of San Juan, the second oldest in the New World, was founded in 1521. Since 1917 the people of Puerto Rico have been U.S. citizens.

Nowhere else will you find scenery so varied in such a small place as you will in Puerto Rico. The island boasts glistening, palm-fringed beaches and green mountains. The sun shines steadily there throughout the year. San Juan is a city surrounded by ancient walls and fortresses that contrast with modern buildings and hotels.

There are a number of state forests in the Commonwealth of Puerto Rico as well as Luquillo National Forest, on the slopes of El Yunque, the only tropical rain forest in the U.S. National Park System. Along its coasts and in its mountains, Puerto Rico offers a number of beautiful resorts easily accessible by paved roads. Puerto Ricans are avid sports fans, and fishing, skindiving, sailing, and surfing are among their favorite pastimes. The island has one of the world's largest underground cave systems and the world's largest radio telescope, both open to the public.

For more information write to: Public Affairs Officer, HQ, Fort Buchanan, PR 00934, or call (809) 273-3999.

Navy

ROOSEVELT ROADS NAVAL STATION

The name Roosevelt Roads is the heritage of both the station's wartime mission and the man who first conceived it, Franklin D. Roosevelt. The roadstead as envisioned by the president was never completed, but the name was carried over when the base was named after him.

History. Located on the eastern tip of Puerto Rico, the U.S. Naval Operation Base, Roosevelt Roads, was commissioned in 1943. The station's airfield stretches for 11,000 feet. "Roosey" is the largest naval station in the world, with 9,000 acres on the island of Puerto Rico and another 23,000 on nearby Vieques Island. Today the Commander, Naval Forces, Caribbean, and a number of tenant activities are based there. About 3,000 military personnel and their dependents, as well as 2,500 civilians, live and work there.

Housing and Schools. The station has 962 family housing units consisting of Capehart housing, built in 1959, which are single-level, single-family quarters, and Turnkey housing, built in 1974, which are two-story, multifamily units. These homes are situated in four housing areas. The waiting period can exceed six months. There are accommodations for 1,300 temporary-duty personnel; there are also 12 temporary housing units for families waiting for a housing opening, but they are booked far in advance. There is also a Navy Lodge at the station.

There are an elementary school, a middle school, and a high school at Roosey and adult education programs that offer courses from Central Texas University and New Hampshire College.

Personal Services. Medical care is provided by a Navy hospital. The station has an exchange and a commissary and numerous concessions including a furniture store, a deli and pizza shop, snack bars, a mini mart, a package store, an auto service center, and a gas station.

Recreation. Roosey offers a nine-hole golf course; a marina; stables; a movie theater that offers two or three movies daily; clubs for dining, dancing, and special functions; a fitness center; outdoor equipment rentals; a flying club; and two guarded beaches for swimming and other water fun.

The Local Area. The coldest temperature ever recorded in Puerto Rico was 40° F. in Aibonito in 1911; otherwise, the averages range from 70° F. in winter to 73° F. in July.

The nearest towns to Roosey are Ceiba, a small village, and Farjardo, a medium-size town, both right outside the base. Luquillo, famous for its beaches, and Humacao are within a thirty-minute drive, while San Juan, the largest city on the island, is only about an hour away from Roosey, on the Atlantic side of the island. There is no government transportation between Roosey and San Juan. A taxi ride will cost about fifty dollars.

Puerto Rico is 100 miles long by 30 miles wide at its widest point. The interior is quite mountainous, with Cerro de Punta reaching an elevation of 4,389 feet. The island has a population of 3.4 million people. Discovered by Columbus in 1493 and settled by Ponce de Leon in 1508, Puerto Rico was part of the Spanish empire until 1898. Since 1917, Puerto Ricans have been U.S. citizens. San Juan has been the capital city of Puerto Rico since 1521. With its tropical climate, water sports are available year-round, and every year tourists flock to the island to enjoy its many beaches. Naval personnel and their families assigned duty at Roosey get it all free.

For more information write to: Family Service Center, U.S. Naval Station, Roosevelt Roads, PSC 1008, Box 3591, FPO AA 34051.

SCOTLAND

Navy

THURSO NAVAL COMMUNICATIONS STATION

Operations at Thurso Station have been drastically reduced and of the ten sites once located there, nine have been returned to the control of the British government.

SPAIN

Air Force

TORREJON AIR BASE

Torrejon Air Base was closed in May 1992.

ZARAGOZA AIR BASE

Zaragoza Air Base was closed in September 1992.

Navy

ROTA U.S. NAVAL STATION

Rota is located on the Atlantic coast of Spain, across the bay from the city of Cadiz in Cadiz Province, in the region of Spain known as Andalusia. The vineyards of Jerez de la Frontera, eighteen miles inland from the base, are known for the excellent sherry produced there.

History. The U.S. Navy first came to Rota in September 1953. A Spanish naval base (Base Naval de Rota) covering more than 6,000 acres just outside the city walls of Rota, the naval station is also home to approximately 9,000 U.S. military personnel. The U.S. Navy controls approximately 5,200 acres at Rota. The mission of the station is to service the 6th Fleet with fuel, ammunition, and spare parts and to coordinate all U.S. naval activities in Spain, Portugal, and Gibraltar.

Housing and Schools. There are more than 800 units of government housing at Rota. The older sets were built between 1957 and 1959, while the newer ones were built in 1965. Two-bedroom units for enlisted families are usually available in eighteen months, while two-bedroom units for officers have a waiting list of nine to twelve months. The Navy Lodge offers 22 guest units suitable for families of up to 5 people.

Education for dependent children is provided by Department of Defense schools located on the base. The Navy Campus provides college courses from the City Colleges of Chicago, Embry-Riddle Aeronautical University, Rota Community College (short-term, self-improvement, noncredit courses), and the University of Maryland.

Personal Services. Medical services are provided by the U.S. naval hospital, a facility opened in 1989 that offers family-practice care as well as inpatient and outpatient care, dental facilities, and a number of specialty clinics. Extensive hospitalization or conditions beyond the capability of the local medical staff are handled by evacuating the patients either to other U.S. hospitals in Europe or to the United States.

The Navy exchange at Rota is one of the largest in the Mediterranean, offering many retail and service outlets including furniture, appliances, hardware, small-appliance repair, a video rental shop, a service station, and a computer store. The commissary store at Rota offers shoppers more than 3,400 line items. Eggs, fruits, and vegetables are available year-round from Spain and Germany; fresh meat is available from Germany and England.

Recreation. Recreation facilities include a sixteen-lane bowling center, two swimming pools, fourteen tennis courts, and five handball/racquetball courts. The base also has a Nautilus center; a fitness center with steam rooms, saunas, and retail pro shop; a marina; a 360-seat movie theater; and a drive-in theater. A woodworking shop, an auto hobby shop, an arts and crafts center, and a photo lab are also available. The station golf course is situated on a 200-acre site and is an eighteen-hole, par-seventy-two course.

The Local Area. The climate in this part of Spain is sunny and warm and the temperatures range from 75° F. to 90° F. in summer and from 40° F. to 70° F. in winter. Don't let the comparative mildness of the winters fool you: They can be very damp, so you will find sweaters and coats handy. The summers are very dry.

Spain is a land of oranges, olives, horses, and sherry. It has been populated continuously for over 2,000 years.

The nearby town of Puerto da Santa Maria, only fifteen minutes away, offers rows of sidewalk cafes with fresh seafood and shellfish ready to eat. This is a country where you can windsurf, sail, fish, and skindive along the Atlantic in the morning, and ski and mountain climb in the Sierra Nevada in the afternoon. Within only a few hours' drive from Rota are the cities of Seville, Cordoba, and Grenada. The region offers entertainment ranging from flamenco dancing and city fairs to bull-fights and religious festivals.

For more information write to: Navy Family Service Center, Box 57, FPO AE 09645.

TURKEY

Air Force

INCIRLIK AIR BASE

Hos geldiniz, as the Turks say: "Welcome" to Incirlik Air Base, the only U.S. tactical air operation between Italy and the Far East. Turkey occupies a strategic position within the NATO Alliance, sharing, as it does, borders with Bulgaria, Syria, Iran, Iraq, and Greece. Turkey contributes more manpower to NATO than any other member nation, including the United States.

History. *Incirlik* (pronounced "in-jur-lick") in the Turkish language means "fig orchard," which is what the land was used for before 1951, when construction on the air base began. The first U.S. unit arrived there on 10 May 1954, when the 7216th Air Base Squadron at Wheelus Field, Libya, began transferring personnel and equipment to the installation, known in those days as Adana Air Base. It was from Incirlik, on 1 May 1960, that Francis Gary Powers began his ill-fated reconnaissance flight over the Soviet Union, where his shootdown caused international embarrassment to the United States.

Today Incirlik is home to the 39th Tactical Group, which is responsible for preparing and conducting air support and training operations as directed by the U.S. Air Forces, Europe. One of these missions is to provide a support base for training rotational fighter aircraft. Personnel of the 628th Airlift Support Squadron provide airlift service for the Mediterranean region, supporting C-5 Galaxy, C-141 Starlifter, and C-9 Nightingale aircraft, moving an average of 3,400 personnel and 1,800 tons of cargo each month aboard 100 regularly scheduled flights through Incirlik. The

American population at Incirlik, which is a joint-user air base (shared with the Turks) is 6,237—approximately 4,000 military (including members deployed to support the Combined Task Force) and 2,200 civilians (U.S. government employees and family members).

Housing and Schools. There are 950 units of family housing at Incirlik, 800 new homes and 150 older, single-family dwellings that are undergoing renovation. Transient housing is available at the Hodja Inn, a forty-nine-unit temporary-living facility available to accompanied personnel on a reserved basis. (Other guests are accommodated on a space-available basis.)

Off-base housing is available in Adana, about eight miles from Incirlik. Apartment rentals range up to $275 a month, plus another $80 to $120 a month for utilities. Local power is wired at 220 volts, 50 cycles. (Power on base is 110 volts, 50 cycles; housing off base may also be found wired for 110 volts.)

Incirlik has an elementary school, a middle school, and a high school for dependent children, as well as a child-care center/preschool activity. Adult education is available through the base education office and includes college courses from the University of Maryland and City Colleges of Chicago.

Personal Services. Medical care at Incirlik is provided by the base hospital and dental clinic. A wide range of services are available, including internal medicine, optometry, general surgery, radiology, obstetrics, and veterinary services.

The base exchange at Incirlik is open seven days a week and includes retail shopping needs, and a catalog service. The exchange also operates a number of concessions, including a furniture store, an optical shop, a car sales outlet, a video rental club, and a foodland. The food mall complex, opened in the summer of 1986, provides a variety of fast-food fare upon which Americans subsist, including a Baskin Robbins ice cream shop, a submarine sandwich stand, and a pizza restaurant. The exchange also operates the Oasis Theater, featuring popular stateside movies seven days a week (two showings every day except Monday, when there is only one movie).

The commissary at Incirlik is comparable to any stateside grocery store. The produce section features a combination of U.S. and locally purchased fresh produce; meat from the States and England is available in a variety of popular cuts.

Recreation. A wide variety of recreation facilities are available at Incirlik, including an Olympic-size swimming pool; a nine-hole golf course; an eighteen-lane bowling center; arts, craft, and auto hobby shops; a gymnasium; a rod, gun, and scuba club; a library with 20,000 books; and a complete officers and enlisted club system.

The Local Area. Incirlik is located in the southern part of Turkey, about eight miles east of Adana, Turkey's fourth largest city (population one million), and twenty-five miles from the Mediterranean Sea. The seasons in this part of Turkey are distinct and correspond to those we are used to in the States; the winters are cool and damp and the late summer months (July, August, September) are hot and dusty. The climate farther east is more severe, particularly in winter.

Turkey is a bridge between Europe and Asia. It consists of more than 300,000 square miles and is separated from European Thrace by the Bosphorus, the Sea of Marmara, and the Dardenelles. Recorded history began in Turkey with the Hittite Empire, more than 4,000 years ago. Today Turkey is an agricultural/industrial nation,

whose four major cities (Adana, Izmir, Istanbul, and Ankara) have populations ranging up to eight million. In latitude, Turkey is on a line shared by Philadelphia,
Indianapolis, and Denver.

Turkey abounds in historic sites. Only twenty-four miles from Adana is Tarsus,
birthplace of Saint Paul and rendezvous of Antony and Cleopatra; within easy
driving distance is Antakya-Antioch, where Saint Peter founded the first Christian
community; sixty-six miles southeast of Adana is the Plain of Issos, where Alexander
the Great defeated Darius in 333 B.C.

The Turks are a very proud and conservative people who consider casual man-
ners and clothing inappropriate. While Turkish men do not consider it "odd" to hold
hands in public, they view shorts as unacceptable masculine wearing apparel. As a
general rule, it is not wise for a man to strike up a conversation with a Turkish
woman unless he has been formally introduced to her. Insulting the Turkish flag,
armed forces, or Mustafa Kemal Ataturk, the founder of the Republic of Turkey, can
land you in jail. Trafficking in narcotics *will* land an American in jail—for a *long*
time, a *minimum* of thirty years for manufacturing, exporting, or importing drugs; the
penalties for possession of illegal drugs are three to five years in prison and fines ranging into the millions of Turkish lira. (There are about 9,500 lira to the dollar.)

The American who can observe these cultural sensitivities will find the Turks
an interesting and hospitable people, staunch allies of the United States who fought
with extraordinary valor alongside our forces during the Korean War. For the
American so privileged, traveling and living in Turkey can be an exceptionally
rewarding experience.

For more information write to: Public Affairs Office, 39th Tactical Group
(USAFE), APO NY 09824-5000.

IZMIR AIR STATION

Izmir Air Station (IAS) is located in the port city of Izmir, the third largest city in
Turkey. Approximately 800 U.S. military personnel and 105 civilians are assigned to
the station's various units. The host unit at Izmir is the 7241st Air Base Group,
which has the mission of supporting all U.S. and NATO units in the Izmir vicinity.
Additionally, the group manages U.S. support to a nearby Turkish air base.

The 7241st ABG is headquartered in an eight-story office building three blocks
from Izmir Bay. Other group functions are housed in approximately thirty leased
buildings located throughout the city.

Located just fifteen minutes from downtown Izmir is Sirinyer Garrison, home of
the Sixth Allied Tactical Air Force. SIXATAF's mission is to ensure full-time air
defense of Turkey, and the combat readiness of all assigned forces. Overlooking Izmir
Bay is Allied Land Forces Southeastern Europe headquarters, a NATO command
responsible for deterring all forms of aggression along the Turkish Straits, eastern
Thrace, and Turkey's southern border and eastern frontier.

Personal Services. The Izmir Community Center features a child-development
activity, a family support center, a fitness center, a recreation center, a library, a

bookstore, an audiovisual sales store, a thrift shop, and the American Youth Activities Center. The nearby exchange mini mall houses a base exchange, a snack bar, an ice cream shop, beauty and barber shops, a dry cleaner, a tailor shop, and various specialty shops.

The Local Area. The metropolitan city of Izmir is located on a bay of the Aegean Sea on Turkey's west coast. The people of Izmir earn their living in tourism, industry, the import/export business, and agriculture. Major businesses are found in food, heavy steel, automotive, and import/export. Izmir is divided into four boroughs, each with its own mayor and subgovernor, who report to the Izmir governor.

Local water and electricity services may cause infrequent hardships on the American residents in Izmir. Tap water is generally considered nonpotable, but bottled water is readily available. Home telephone service is available but expensive. As Izmir is located in a cove, winter coal-burning (for heating purposes) and the massive number of diesel-burning vehicles are causing an increasingly hazardous air pollution problem in the city. Public transportation is very convenient and cheap. A sixty-kilometer bus ride to tour the city costs only about the equivalent of fifty cents. Taxi rates are correspondingly affordable.

The Local Area. With a recorded history going back as far as 3000 B.C., there are many historical sites to visit in the area. Smyrna, Ephesus, and Pergamum are just a few. An ancient castle, built by Alexander the Great, still stands today, overlooking Izmir from Kadifekale Hill. The area is well known for its gold, copper, brass, carpets, and embroidered goods. August in Izmir presents the opportunity to visit the city's international fair, famous throughout Europe.

For more information write to: Public Affairs Division, 7241st Air Base Group (USAFE), Unit 6870 Box 120, APO AE 09821.

WEST INDIES

Navy

ANTIGUA U.S. NAVAL SUPPORT FACILITY

The Antigua U.S. Naval Support Facility supports joint service special operations forces training and exercises, joint service survival, evasion, resistance, and escape training, and a regional program of security assistance training for and combined exercises with eastern Caribbean security personnel.

The U.S. military community consists of approximately 120 personnel and their families. The support facility is located along Antigua's northern coastline, six miles from the capital city of Saint John. It is situated about one mile from the Antigua Air Station, a subordinate command of the Eastern Space and Missile Center.

Housing and Schools. Navy family housing consists of twenty-eight duplex units (four with four bedrooms). The bachelor officer quarters can accommodate five permanent-party personnel in two-room suites. Enlisted personnel live in a facility offering twenty-four furnished rooms. A wide variety of housing is available locally.

There are no DoD schools on Antigua. Local schools are certified by the Director, DoD Dependents Schools, Panama Region, prior to enrollment. Schools on Antigua follow the British educational system. Courses in U.S. history and geography are not taught in these schools, but tutoring in those subjects is available. Children in ninth through twelfth grades are required to live in London during the school year while attending London Central High School, a DoD Dependents Schools boarding school.

Personal Services. The base dispensary is a branch clinic of the Naval hospital, Roosevelt Roads, Puerto Rico, with one family physician and two corpsmen. Care is limited to routine medical problems and minor injuries. Pharmacy and lab service are very limited. X rays are not available on base. Dental care is available only once a quarter, when a team from Roosevelt Roads comes to Antigua to screen personnel and perform minor procedures.

The Resale Activity Roosevelt Roads Detachment in Antigua operates a combined Navy exchange/commissary, a snack bar, an all-hands bar, a barber shop, and a coin-operated laundromat. Perishables are transported weekly in military aircraft and other merchandise is shipped by boat every two weeks.

Recreation. Antigua is a sportsman's paradise. There are endless beaches and magnificent coral reefs. The base special services office rents two boats for use by fishermen and boating enthusiasts. Windsurfing and many other maritime activities are available locally, as are tennis, softball, basketball, handball, racquetball, and golf. On base are ceramics, woodworking, and auto hobby shops.

The Local Area. The climate in Antigua is consistently superb. Temperatures range from the mid-sixtiess to the low nineties. Cooling tradewinds help to make it comfortable even in the hottest months of August and September. Tourism is the mainstay of the local economy. The local people are friendly and helpful to all visitors. Travel to neighboring islands is economical and very convenient.

For more information write to: Public Affairs Office, NAVSUPPFAC Antigua, PSC 1010, FPO AA 34054-1010.

PART THREE

Maps

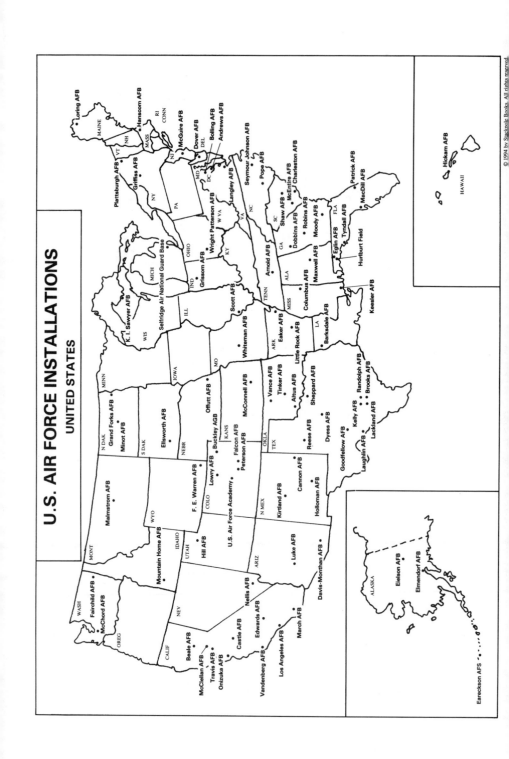

U.S. AIR FORCE INSTALLATIONS
UNITED STATES

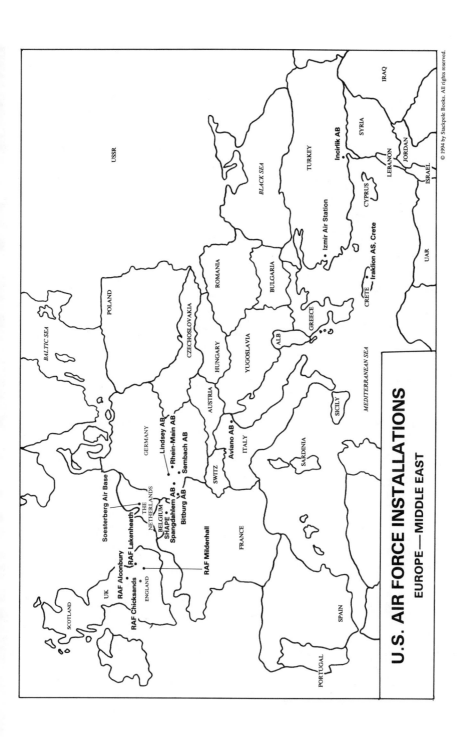

U.S. AIR FORCE INSTALLATIONS
EUROPE—MIDDLE EAST

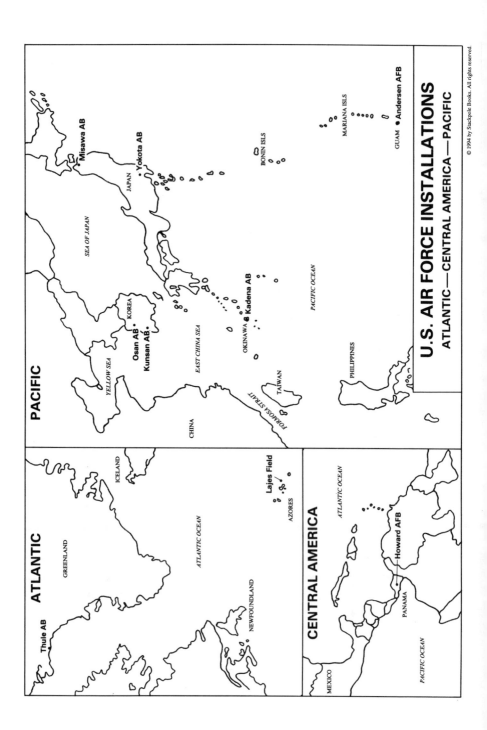

U.S. AIR FORCE INSTALLATIONS
ATLANTIC—CENTRAL AMERICA—PACIFIC

PACIFIC

Misawa AB
Yokota AB
JAPAN
SEA OF JAPAN
KOREA
Osan AB
Kunsan AB
YELLOW SEA
EAST CHINA SEA
OKINAWA & Kadena AB
CHINA
TAIWAN
FORMOSA STRAIT
PHILIPPINES
PACIFIC OCEAN
BONIN ISLS
MARIANA ISLS
GUAM • Andersen AFB

ATLANTIC

Thule AB
GREENLAND
ICELAND
NEWFOUNDLAND
ATLANTIC OCEAN
Lajes Field
AZORES

CENTRAL AMERICA

ATLANTIC OCEAN
Howard AFB
PANAMA
MEXICO
PACIFIC OCEAN

U.S. ARMY INSTALLATIONS
UNITED STATES

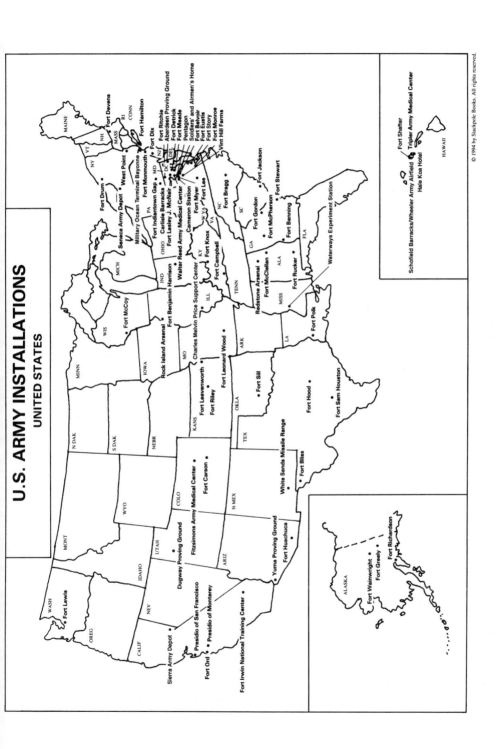

Fort Lewis
Sierra Army Depot
Presidio of San Francisco
Presidio of Monterey
Fort Ord
Fort Irwin National Training Center
Dugway Proving Ground
Fitzsimons Army Medical Center
Fort Carson
Yuma Proving Ground
Fort Huachuca
White Sands Missile Range
Fort Bliss
Fort Hood
Fort Sam Houston
Fort Sill
Fort Leonard Wood
Fort Riley
Fort Leavenworth
Rock Island Arsenal
Charles Melvin Price Support Center
Fort Benjamin Harrison
Fort McCoy
Seneca Army Depot
Fort Drum
West Point
Fort Devens
Military Ocean Terminal Bayonne
Fort Hamilton
Fort Monmouth
Fort Dix
Fort Indiantown Gap
Carlisle Barracks
Fort Lesley J. McNair
Walter Reed Army Medical Center
Cameron Station
Fort Myer
Fort Lee
Fort Knox
Fort Campbell
Redstone Arsenal
Fort McClellan
Fort Rucker
Fort Polk
Fort Benning
Fort McPherson
Fort Gordon
Fort Jackson
Fort Stewart
Fort Bragg
Waterways Experiment Station
Fort Ritchie
Aberdeen Proving Ground
Fort Detrick
Fort Meade
Pentagon
Soldiers' and Airmen's Home
Fort Belvoir
Fort Eustis
Fort Story
Fort Monroe
Vint Hill Farms

Fort Wainwright
Fort Greely
Fort Richardson
ALASKA

Fort Shafter
Triple Army Medical Center
Schofield Barracks/Wheeler Army Airfield
Hale Koa Hotel
HAWAII

U.S. ARMY INSTALLATIONS
CENTRAL EUROPE

BALTIC SEA

THE
NETHERLANDS

GERMANY

POLAND

Wildflecken Community and Training Area

BELGIUM

SHAPE

CZECHOSLOVAKIA

Weisbaden-Mainz MC

Schweinfurt MC

Bad Kreuznach MC

Kitzingen MC

Bamberg MC

Vilseck Combined Arms Training Center

Babenhausen/Darmstadt MC

Grafenwoehr Training Area

Landstuhl Army Medical Center

Mannheim MC

Heidelberg MC

Ansbach MC

Nurnberg MC

Kaiserslautern MC

Stuttgart MC

Augsburg MC

Hohenfels Training Area

Karlsruhe MC

Chiemsee Armed Forces Recreation Center

Garmisch Armed Forces Recreation Center

HUNGARY

SWITZ

AUSTRIA

FRANCE

ITALY

YUGOSLAVIA

ALB

SARDINIA

MEDITERRANEAN SEA

SICILY

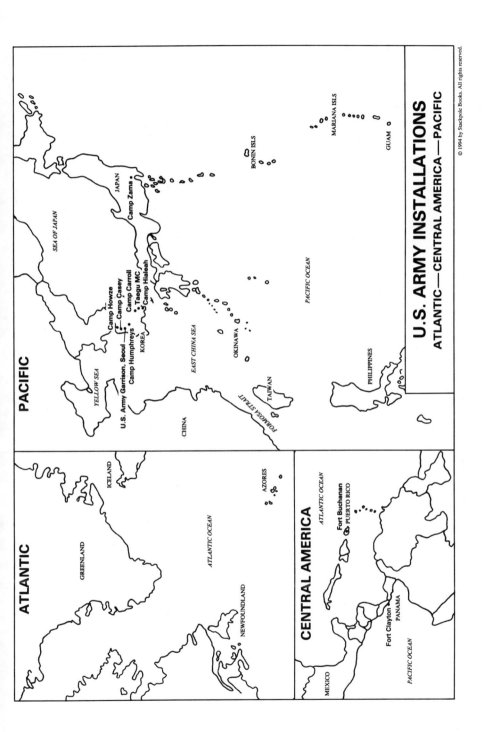

U.S. ARMY INSTALLATIONS
ATLANTIC — CENTRAL AMERICA — PACIFIC

COAST GUARD INSTALLATIONS
UNITED STATES

Cape Cod Coast Guard Air Station

U.S. Coast Guard Academy

Governors Island Coast Guard Support Center

Cape May Coast Guard Training Center

Miami Coast Guard Air Station

Mobile Coast Guard Aviation Training Center

Petaluma Coast Guard Training Center

Alameda Coast Guard Support Center

MAINE

VT

NH

MASS

RI

CONN

NY

NJ

DEL

DC

MD

PA

W VA

VA

NC

SC

OHIO

KY

GA

FLA

MICH

IND

ALA

ILL

TENN

MISS

WIS

ARK

LA

IOWA

MO

MINN

KANS

OKLA

TEX

N DAK

S DAK

NEBR

COLO

N MEX

WYO

MONT

IDAHO

UTAH

ARIZ

WASH

OREG

NEV

CALIF

U.S. NAVY AND MARINE CORPS INSTALLATIONS
UNITED STATES—BERMUDA

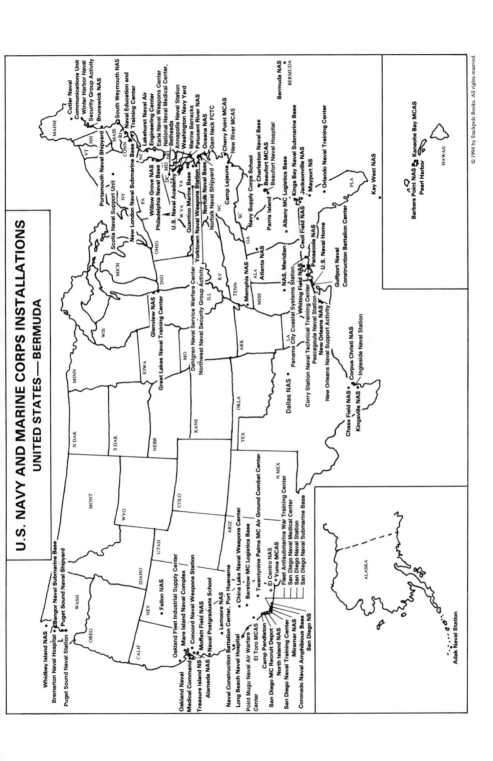

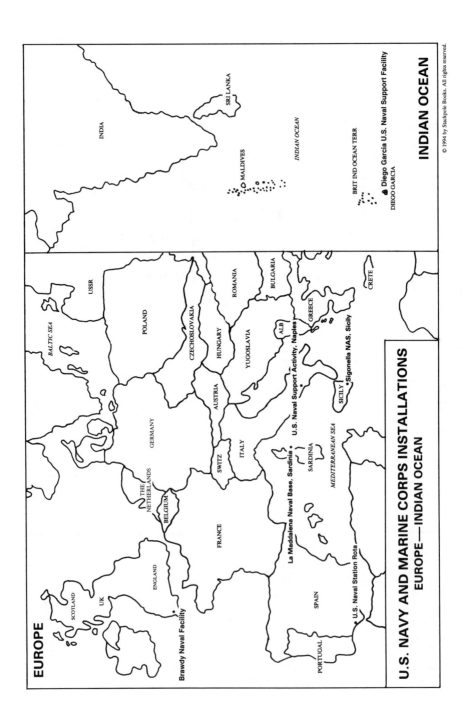

EUROPE

INDIAN OCEAN

U.S. NAVY AND MARINE CORPS INSTALLATIONS
EUROPE—INDIAN OCEAN

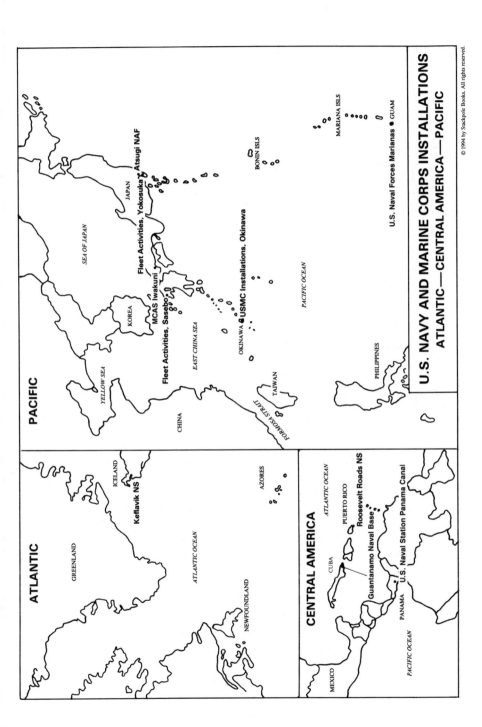

U.S. NAVY AND MARINE CORPS INSTALLATIONS
ATLANTIC—CENTRAL AMERICA—PACIFIC

APPENDIX

Additional Installations

The author and publisher strive to make this guide as complete as possible by contacting all U.S. military installations and inviting them to submit current information for the guide. As a service to our readers, addresses of installations for which insufficient information had been received as of press time are included here.

Adak Naval Security Group: Commander, Attention: Public Affairs Office, Anchorage, AK 96505-5000, phone (907) 592-6000.

Ansbach MC, Germany: Ansbach Military Community, APO AE 09177.

Augsberg MC, Germany: Public Affairs Office, Augsberg Military Community, APO AE 09178.

Aviano AB, Italy: Public Affairs Office, Aviano Air Base, APO AE 09601-0054.

Babenhausen MC, Germany: Public Affairs Office, APO AE 09089.

Baumholder MC, Germany: Public Affairs Office, APO AE 09034.

Bremerton Naval Hospital: Public Affairs Office, Bremerton, WA 98312-1898, phone (206) 479-6600.

Buckley Air National Guard Base: Commander, 200th Airlift Squadron, Attention: Public Affairs Office, Aurora, CO 800011-9599, phone (303) 366-5363.

Camp Darby, Livorno, Italy: Public Affairs Office, Livorno Military Community, APO AE 09613.

Camp Red Cloud, Korea: Public Affairs Office, HQ 2nd Infantry Division, APO AP 96258-2089.

Caserma Ederle, Vincenza, Italy: Public Affairs Office, Vincenza Military Community, APO AE 09630.

Clearwater Coast Guard Air Station: Commander, Attention: Public Affairs Office, Tampa, FL 34662-2990, phone (813) 535-1437.

Eastern Pacific Naval Computer and Telecommunications Area Master Station: Commander, Attention: Public Affairs Office, Wahiawa, HI 96786-3050, phone (808) 653-5385.

Elizabeth City Coast Guard Support Center: Public Affairs Office, Elizabeth City, NC 27909-5004.

Fort Gillem: Commander, Second U.S. Army, Attention: Public Affairs, Fort Gillem, GA 30330-5000, phone (404) 363-5000.

Fort Hunter Liggett: Public Affairs Office, Army Test and Experimentation Command, Fort Hunter Liggett, CA 93928-5000, phone (408) 385-2528.

Giessen MC, Germany: Public Affairs Office, Giessen Military Community, APO AE 09169.

Henderson Hall: Commander, HQ, USMC, Attention: Public Affairs Office, Henderson Hall, Arlington, VA 22214-5000, phone (703) 614-2013.

Idaho Falls Naval Nuclear Power Training Unit: Commander, Attention: Public Affairs Office, Idaho Falls, ID 83403-2751, phone (208) 533-5334.

Kodiak Coast Guard Support Center: Public Affairs Office, Kodiak Island, AK 99619-5000, phone (907) 487-5525.

Little Creek Naval Amphibious Base: Public Affairs Office, Norfolk, VA 23451-5000, phone (804) 464-7000.

Miesau Army Depot, Germany: Public Affairs Office, Miesau Army Depot, APO AE 09059.

Naval Security Station, District of Columbia: Public Affairs Office, Washington, DC 20393-5230, phone (202) 282-0211.

Pacific Fleet Combat Training Center: Commander, Attention: Public Affairs Office, San Diego, CA 92147-5081, phone (619) 553-8300.

Pensacola Naval Hospital: Commander, Pensacola Naval Hospital, Attention: Public Affairs, Pensacola, FL 32512-0003, phone (904) 452-6601.

Portsmouth Naval Hospital: Portsmouth Naval Hospital, Portsmouth, VA 23708-5100, phone (804) 399-1100.

Seattle Coast Guard Support Center: Public Affairs Office, Seattle, WA 98134-1192, phone (206) 286-9650.

Sembach Air Base, Germany: Public Affairs Office, APO AE 09130.

Yorktown Coast Guard Reserve Training Center: Public Affairs Office, Yorktown, VA 23690-5000, phone (804) 898-3500.

INDEX

447